TORONTO
422

NORTH
EAST
12-189

WEST
LAKES
330-445

332

CHICAGO

98 NEW
YORK

PHILADELPHIA 154

St. Louis 384

204 ★

WASHINGTON D.C.

250 ATLANTA

SOUTH
EAST
190-329

Houston
538

276 NEW
Orleans

MIAMI
222

The New York Times

36

HOURS

EDITED BY BARBARA IRELAND

The New York Times

36
HOURS
USA & CANADA

3RD EDITION · 150 DESTINATIONS

TASCHEN

Contents

NORTHEAST

SOUTHEAST

MIDWEST & GREAT LAKES

NORTHEAST

SOUTHEAST

MIDWEST

SOUTHWEST

WEST COAST

SOUTHWEST & ROCKY MOUNTAINS

WEST COAST

Foreword

The 36 Hours *feature made its first appearance on the pages of* The New York Times *in 2002, became an immediate hit with readers, and has been inspiring trips and wish lists ever since. Created as a guide to that staple of crammed 21st-century schedules, the weekend getaway, it takes readers each week on a carefully researched, uniquely designed two-night excursion to an embraceable place. With a well-plotted itinerary, it offers up an experience that both identifies the high points of the destination and teases out its particular character.*

The 36 Hours *book series, published by* The Times *and TASCHEN since 2011, collects* 36 Hours *stories and photographs from the newspaper's deep travel journalism archive and offers them in book form for readers who dream of seeing faraway places and love to make those dreams real. The series now includes volumes from around the world. This book, the third edition of* The New York Times 36 Hours USA & Canada, *incorporates 33 new stories: 8 brand-new destinations and 25 new versions of cities that were also featured in the second edition. All of the remaining 118 itineraries are newly fact-checked and updated to remain current.*

Together, these 150 choices reflect the richness of the vast territory of the United States and Canada, from glittering cities and eccentric small towns to heart-stopping mountains and seacoasts. Some destinations are obvious for any traveler's list: the marquee metropolises like New York, Montreal, and Los Angeles; the world-famous natural wonders at Niagara Falls and the Grand Canyon; the national icons of Washington, D.C., and Quebec City. Others are larger regions to explore: the Connecticut coast, with its tidal marshes and old Yankee towns; the Laurel Highlands of Pennsylvania, where Frank

Lloyd Wright's masterpiece, Fallingwater, is hidden away in the woods; the majestic Big Sur coast of California. There are plenty of surprises. Nashville has its own Parthenon. Seattle dresses up a statue of Lenin for Gay Pride Week. So-called "secondary" Rust Belt cities like Buffalo and Detroit turn out to be rich repositories of spirit and culture, now enjoying resurgence as new generations take to urban living.

Each 36 Hours *story gives a well-informed inside view of the place it covers, a selective summary that lets the traveler get to the heart of things in minimal time. Well known* Times *writers are among your many guides on these journeys. In New York City alone, William Grimes escorts you through Manhattan; Sam Sifton through Brooklyn; and John Eligon through Harlem. Robert Draper takes you to favorite haunts of Washington insiders. Stephanie Rosenbloom accompanies you in the Hamptons; Penelope Green in Newport, Rhode Island; the late David Carr in his home city of Minneapolis.*

As one of the dozens of editors who have worked on 36 Hours *over the years, along with hundreds of writers, photographers, graphic artists, and designers, I've become convinced that the column's popularity is based on its special feeling of accessibility. The framework is the weekend, when everyone longs for a break, and the pathway from Friday to Sunday invites the reader to participate. The audience is broad; with a little adapting, these itineraries are meant to work for both the backpacker and the jet-setter. And the destination might be anyplace where there is fun to be had and a quirk or two to discover.*

Travelers who have more than two days to spend may want to use a 36 Hours *as a kind of nugget, supplementing it with their own discoveries for a longer stay. Or, since the book is organized regionally, two or three of these itineraries can be strung together to make up a longer trip. There are no rules. Whatever the journey or the wanderer's choice, the star of this book is North America itself, shining out page after page in all of its amazing variety, energy, and grandeur.*

— BARBARA IRELAND, EDITOR

PAGE 2 The Statue of Liberty, icon and inspiration since 1886, lifts her famous torch in New York Harbor.

PAGE 7 Delicate Arch at sunset in Arches National Park outside Moab, Utah.

OPPOSITE Manhattan at night, in a bird's-eye view looking east toward the skyscrapers of Midtown.

Tips for Using This Book

Plotting the Course: The United States and Canada offer travelers miles and miles of possibility, from Anchorage to Miami and from Hawaii to Quebec. To help in trip planning, this book is organized into five sections, each based on a region — Northeast, Southeast, Midwest & Great Lakes, Southwest & Rocky Mountains, and West Coast — and introduced with a regional map. Within the regions, destinations are organized alphabetically for easy reference.

On the Ground: Every *36 Hours* story follows a workable numbered itinerary, which is both outlined in the text and shown with corresponding numbers on a detailed destination map. The itinerary is practical: it really is possible to get from one place to the next easily and in the allotted time, although of course many travelers will prefer to take things at their own pace and perhaps make some of their own detours. Astute readers will notice that the "36" in *36 Hours* is elastic, and the traveler's agenda probably will be, too. Some travel knowledge is assumed: most travelers already know, for example, that it's always wise to make a reservation at a restaurant, and that businesses in beach destinations or ski towns may be closed in the off-season.

The Not So Obvious: The itineraries do not all follow the same pattern. A Saturday breakfast choice may or may not be recommended; after-dinner night life may or may not be included. The destination dictates, and so, to some extent, does the personality of the author who researched and wrote the article. For some of the largest cities, this book offers multiple itineraries.

Travel Documents: A passport is now required for travel between the United States and Canada, and where a visa is required, travelers should be prepared to show that, as well, at the international border. Goods and luggage may be inspected by customs agents.

Finding Your Way: Street and website addresses are provided wherever possible. Some telephone numbers are also listed. However, businesses are changing with the times. Some shops now rely more on social media than on websites. Most restaurants prefer that reservations be made online. Travelers need less guidance, as well. They use smartphones to help them stay oriented, and they know about services not specifically covered in this book, like vacation rentals and ride sharing.

Updates: While all the stories in this volume were updated and fact-checked for 2019 publication, it is inevitable that some of the featured businesses and destinations will change in time. If you spot any errors in your travels, please feel free to send corrections or updates via email to 36hours@taschen.com. Please include the book title and the page number in the subject line of your email to assure that it gets to the right person for future updates.

OPPOSITE The Lincoln Memorial in Washington, an inspiring monument to freedom, is lighted dramatically after dark.

THE BASICS

A brief informational box for the destination, called "The Basics," appears with each *36 Hours* article in this book. The box provides some orientation on transportation or other factual information that is helpful for first-time visitors. "The Basics" also recommends two or three reliable hotels.

PRICES

Since hotel and restaurant prices change quickly, this book uses a system of symbols, based on 2019 United States dollars.

Hotel room, standard double:
Budget, under $125 per night: $
Moderate, $125 to $250: $$
Expensive, $251 to $375: $$$
Luxury, $376 and above: $$$$

Restaurants, dinner entree:
Budget, under $15: $
Moderate, $15 to $29: $$
Expensive, $30 to $44: $$$
Very Expensive, $45 and up: $$$$

Restaurants, full breakfast, or lunch entree:
Budget, under $10: $
Moderate, $10 to $20: $$
Expensive, $21 to $29: $$$
Very Expensive, $30 and up: $$$$

NORTH EAST

172

Quebec City

142

Ottawa

166

Montreal

186

Burlington

92 Lake Placid

the Hudson Valley

86

th

New Haven

18

NEW YORK CITY

98

130 Queen

GETTYSBURG

150

PHILADELPHIA

154

76 Princeton

108

the Brandywine Valley

146

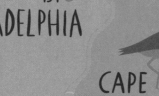

CAPE MAY 70

Brooklyn

Prince
Edward
Island 160

Bar
Harbor
22

Midcoast
Maine 28

the Bay
of fundy 66

Halifax
138

34

PORTLAND

BOSTON
42

Berkshires
38

48

Cambridge

PROVINCETOWN
60

the
Connecticut
Coast

PROVIDENCE 182

Newport
178

14

Shelter Island
134

APOLLO

Harlem 120

MARTHA'S
VINEYARD
52

82

East
Hampton

NANTUCKET
56

114

Central Park

104

Broadway

Lower
Manhattan
126

The Connecticut Coast

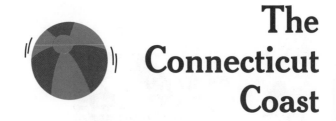

A summertime drive up Connecticut's coast on Long Island Sound, from the New York City suburbs at its western end to the quiet old town of Stonington about 150 miles to the east, passes bustling marinas, peaceful green fields, and tidal marshes with nesting osprey. It's no secret that this shore is pretty. With a tutored eye and a carefully planned route of discovery, it can be enchanting. The magic is in the sights, smells, and tastes waiting for the traveler. Keep a leisurely pace and stop to spend time with the 21st-century Connecticut Yankees and the ocean waves.
— BY AMY M. THOMAS

FRIDAY

1 *The Gold Route* 1 p.m.

The initial impression of Connecticut can be deceiving. In Greenwich, just over the state line from New York, four-figure baby strollers, six-figure cars, and seven-figure yachts parade along the waterfront. The Gold Coast ambience stretches east to Fairfield, through towns like Westport, where Tiffany sells its gems not far from restaurants with elegant menus and upscale prices. See a different kind of display at the **Bruce Museum of Arts and Sciences** (1 Museum Drive, Greenwich; 203-869-0376; brucemuseum.org), where natural science exhibits draw from the local sea and shore while rotating shows have featured the work of artists from Rembrandt to Chuck Close.

2 *Marsh and Sea* 3 p.m.

Soon the formality fades. The moneyed enclaves turn into relaxed seaside towns. Mansions give way to clam shacks. See open shoreline, barrier beach, and a remnant of the natural coastal marsh at the **Connecticut Audubon Society Coastal Center at Milford Point** (1 Milford Point Road; 203-878-7440; ctaudubon.org/coastal-center), at the mouth of the Housatonic River. The center, with its interpretive displays, closes at 4 p.m., but you can stay later and experience more of the natural shoreland at the adjoining wildlife refuge, which remains open until dark. Heading east from here, you'll pass New Haven, famed as the home of Yale University. Skip it for now and return when you have more time. It's worth a weekend of its own.

3 *Roadside Cookout* 7 p.m.

Two towns over, in Guilford, is another restaurant with a cult following. **The Place** (901 Boston Post Road, Guilford; 203-453-9276; theplaceguilford.com; $-$$) occupies a roadside expanse that is partly covered by a tattered red-and-white striped tarp. Come in warm weather for classic cookout fare in a casual outdoor setting. (If you want alcohol, bring your own.) The restaurant was founded in 1971 by Gary and Vaughn Knowles, brothers looking to supplement their teachers' salaries. Today, it is a raucous backyard party, with disco and doo-wop, and tree stumps for seats. Everything from catfish to chicken to corn on the cob is cooked on the 24-foot grill, and on any summer night, you will see Yale students, families, and tourists feasting on the clams roasted in butter and cocktail sauce.

SATURDAY

4 *Book Center* 9 a.m.

Have an egg white omelet or some buttermilk pancakes at the **Wharf** restaurant in the seafront **Madison Beach Hotel** (94 West Wharf Road, Madison; 203-350-0014; curiocollection3.hilton.com/en/index.html; $$), and then explore **Madison**'s town center. The don't-miss shop here is the beloved and capacious independent bookstore **R. J. Julia** (768 Boston Post Road; 203-245-3959; rjjulia.com), which stocks

OPPOSITE Stonington's First Congregational Church.

BELOW The A.C. Petersen Drive-In in Old Lyme.

thousands of carefully chosen books and regularly brings in well-known authors for readings and events.

5 *Salt in the Air* 11 a.m.

All along the stretch of Route 1 from Guilford to Old Saybrook, you can roll down the car window for a whiff of salty air and feel your tires rippling over steel drawbridges that cross inlets and marshlands. Canoes flit along tributaries, and cruisers and sailboats decorate the Sound. The roadside scenery is a mix of antique and bric-a-brac stores, 17th-century homes and cemeteries, bait-and-tackle shops, and farm stands selling strawberries and squash. To soak up some sun and dip a toe in the Sound, hit the state's largest public beach at **Hammonasset State Park** (1288 Boston Post Road, Madison; 203-245-2785). Then push on a few more miles to Old Lyme for a break at **A.C. Petersen Drive-In** (113 Shore Road, Old Lyme; 860-598-9680), formerly the Hallmark Drive-In, which carries on a long tradition of serving homemade ice cream.

6 *Favorable Impressions* 1 p.m.

A century ago, **Old Lyme**, with its reedy riverbanks, tidal estuaries, and bohemian air, was known as an inspiring setting for painters. The **Florence Griswold Museum** (96 Lyme Street, Old Lyme; 860-434-5542; florencegriswoldmuseum.org), set on a sloping lawn overlooking the Lieutenant River, shows the work of American Impressionists who were part of the Old Lyme art colony of that era, including Henry Ward Ranger, William Chadwick, and Childe Hassam.

7 *Among the Reeds* 3 p.m.

For a close encounter with the water, rent a kayak from **Black Hall Outfitters** (132 Shore Road; 860-434-9680; blackhalloutfitters.com), which is on the Connecticut River Estuary Canoe and Kayak Trail. In the quiet inlets, you'll paddle past regal herons and fishermen looking to land striped bass. When you're ready to get back on the road, stay close

to the shore on Route 156, and then head north and pick up Route 1 again in New London.

8 *Succulent and Sculptured* 6 p.m.

Find your way to the sleepy town of Noank and join the parade of cars flocking to **Abbott's Lobster in the Rough** (117 Pearl Street, Noank; 860-536-7719; abbottslobster.com; $$). A Connecticut classic, it's a seasonal restaurant with picnic tables perched overlooking the water. You can't go to Connecticut and not have a lobster roll, and as all the tourists documenting their meals with digital cameras attest, the quarter-pound of succulent, buttered lobster meat at Abbott's, sculptured into a perfect round puck and served on a seeded hamburger roll, fits the bill.

9 *A Drink With the Captain* 8 p.m.

You'll be rolling into **Mystic** with just enough time left in the evening for a look at the compact downtown, with its cluster of little clothing and knickknack shops, galleries, and restaurants. Drop in for a drink at the **Captain Daniel Packer Inne** (32 Water Street; 860-536-3555; danielpacker.com), which was built in 1756. Packer, the original owner, was a former square-rigger skipper who operated a rope ferry across the Mystic River. The inn's impressive stone foundation gives way to a cozy dark wood downstairs bar.

SUNDAY

10 *Mystic Morning* 10 a.m.

Mystic Seaport (75 Greenmanville Avenue; 860-572-0711; mysticseaport.org), a 17-acre complex

on the banks of the Mystic River, simulates a 19th-century New England coastal village. Some of the buildings are authentic and have been moved to the seaport; others are reproductions of buildings that were once there or in other coastal towns. Stroll around to see maritime life recreated in buildings like the Mallory sail loft, constructed in the early 19th century and named for Charles Mallory, who made ships' sails. Museum workers use the loft to maintain sails used by the exhibition vessels that are at docks alongside the village.

11 *Last Port of Call* 1 p.m.

Stonington, the last town before Rhode Island, lives up to its name with old stone walls (built by sheep farmers a couple of centuries ago) lacing its green fields. The small borough, or village, at the waterfront is a former whaling port with plain fishermen's cottages wedged next to each other and pillared homes facing Fishers Island Sound. Out on a peninsula, a lonely stone lighthouse, which dates to 1840 and has survived Category 3 hurricanes, stands across from a wee public beach. Here, as you feel the sun, solitude, and sea air and see water in every direction, you'll know you have seen the authentic Connecticut coast.

OPPOSITE ABOVE The Seashore at Hammonasset State Park.

OPPOSITE BELOW A lobster roll at Abbott's Lobster in the Rough.

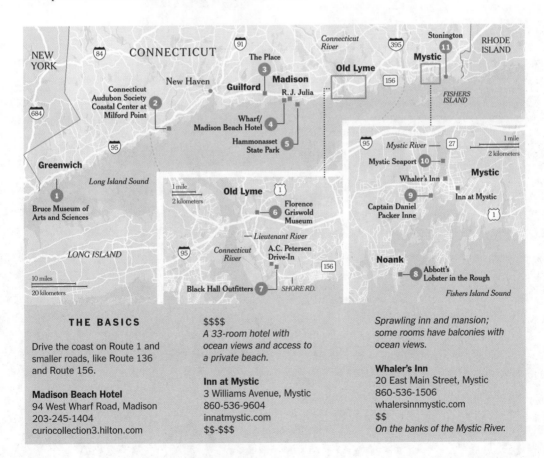

THE BASICS

Drive the coast on Route 1 and smaller roads, like Route 136 and Route 156.

Madison Beach Hotel
94 West Wharf Road, Madison
203-245-1404
curiocollection3.hilton.com

$$$$
A 33-room hotel with ocean views and access to a private beach.

Inn at Mystic
3 Williams Avenue, Mystic
860-536-9604
innatmystic.com
$$-$$$

Sprawling inn and mansion; some rooms have balconies with ocean views.

Whaler's Inn
20 East Main Street, Mystic
860-536-1506
whalersinnmystic.com
$$
On the banks of the Mystic River.

New Haven

It wasn't long ago that New Haven was a poster child for the troubled college town, a place where the graduates of prep schools rubbed shoulders with victims of the mid-'80s and early-'90s crack epidemic. While New Haven's hard-luck reputation lingers, it is no longer fully deserved. The city's historic center, which fans out around twin lawns planted with towering elms, maintains an older New England character, with neo-Gothic towers and working-class neighborhoods of faded but elegant Victorian houses. While town and gown have worked to attract brand-name businesses to downtown (among them an Apple Store and a Shake Shack), New Haven remains complex and layered — a city of taco trucks and barbecue shacks as well as high-end clothiers and stylish cocktail lounges. — BY FREDA MOON

FRIDAY

1 *Get Coastal* 5 p.m.

Take a walk along Long Island Sound, from **Sandy Point Bird Sanctuary** (Beach Street, West Haven; 203-937-3712), where birders glimpse red-billed oystercatchers and green-winged monk parakeets, to **Bradley Point Beach** (Captain Thomas Boulevard, West Haven), near the site of the British invasion of July 5, 1779. Between the two, a paved 1.7-mile promenade keeps the sand from your toes. At sunset, stop into the scuba-themed **Dive Bar & Restaurant** (24 Ocean Avenue, West Haven; 203-933-3483; divebarandrestaurant.com) for a cocktail — a margarita, Key lime martini, or spicy mojito — or a flight of five pours from the rotating tap of 10 craft beers.

2 *Apizza Aplenty* 7 p.m.

In the perennial debate over which local joint serves the superior New Haven-style pie, **Zuppardi's Apizza** (179 Union Avenue, West Haven; 203-934-1949; zuppardisapizza.com; $$), which has been around since 1934, is too often overlooked. On an otherwise residential street, behind a red, green, and white awning, Zuppardi's serves Napolitano "apizza" (pronounced "ah-BEETZ") to families crowded into orange vinyl booths. Order the fresh clam, a thin, bubbling, slightly blackened crust brushed with olive oil, garlic, and parsley and loaded with just-shucked littleneck clams.

3 *Way Off Broadway* 8:30 p.m.

New Haven is a theater town, with three well-respected playhouses, each with its own creative niche. Check schedules and find a play that interests you. Near the industrial waterfront at the foot of the city's food terminal is **Long Wharf Theatre** (222 Sargent Drive; 203-787-4282; longwharf.org), founded in 1965, where performers have included Hollywood powerhouses like Al Pacino and Kevin Spacey as well as up-and-coming Broadway talent. The **Yale Repertory Theatre** (1120 Chapel Street; 203-432-1234; yalerep.org) produces new plays and bold interpretations of classics on three stages. Lighter fare, like musicals and comedy, often predominates at the **Shubert Theater** (247 College Street; 203-562-5666; shubert.com), which has been in operation since 1914.

4 *Porter and Punk* 11 p.m.

On a two-block stretch best known for thumping multistory clubs, the **Cask Republic** (179 Crown Street; 475-238-8335) is a comparably more studious place devoted to the less-than-quiet contemplation of fine ales, lagers, stouts, and porters — some 60 or so on draft alone, including rare and cask-conditioned beers. For live jazz or punk rock, Scottish folk or Texas blues, settle in at the **Cafe Nine** (250 State Street; 203-789-8281; cafenine.com), beloved by locals and dubbed the "musician's living room" for its intimate scale. Along Crown Street, notice the Walk of

OPPOSITE Harkness Tower, a symbol of Yale.

BELOW At the Owl Shop. Smoking a cigar is not required.

Fame-style stars embedded in the sidewalk, the work of the artist Sheila Levrant de Bretteville, designed to celebrate the grocers, cigar makers, and ship captains of New Haven's past.

SATURDAY

5 *Olmsted on the River* 9 a.m.

In the quiet Westville neighborhood, **Bella's Café** (896 Whalley Avenue; 203-387-7107; bellascafect.com; $$) invites brunch crowds with a menu that includes selections like crab and shrimp omelet or grilled peach shortcake. Eat your fill and then take a walk along the banks of the West River in the 120-acre **Edgewood Park** (Edgewood Avenue; cityofnewhaven.com/parks), which was designed by Frederick Law Olmsted Jr.

6 *Art for Free* Noon

The **Yale University Art Gallery** (1111 Chapel Street; 203-432-0600; artgallery.yale.edu), which underwent a 14-year renovation that was completed in late 2012, offers expanded (and free) access to its 200,000-piece collection. Across the street, the equally impressive (also free) **Yale Center for British Art** (1080 Chapel Street; 203-432-2800; britishart.yale. edu) holds the largest collection of British art outside Britain, including dramatic George Stubbs lion-and-horse oil paintings, Surrealist triptychs by Francis Bacon, and Pop Art from the 1960s.

7 *Say Cheese* 1 p.m.

Its crowded shelves of imported artisanal pasta and olive oils are reason enough to make the trek to **Liuzzi Cheese** (322 State Street, North Haven; 203-248-4356; liuzzicheese.com). But the shop also sells sandwiches made with cured meats, like Parma prosciutto and sopressata, and house-made cheeses, like burrata. **Olmo** (93 Whitney Avenue; 203-624-3373; olmokitchen. com; $$), previously Caseus Fromagerie Bistro, is another option, a perfect spot for savoring new American comfort food like a Puerto Rican-inspired pork sub with mojo, vegetables cooked in coals with honey and house-made ricotta, and house-made pastas. There's also a weekend brunch menu (pancakes, omelets, a brunch burger) and a takeout bagel/sandwich shop. Next door, **Fashionista Vintage & Variety** (93 Whitney Avenue; 203-777-4434; fashionista-vintage-variety. com) sells costumes (harem outfits, animal heads); men's clothing; and vintage wear for women.

8 *The Outlook's Fine* 5 p.m.

Time your visit to the season for a drive to the top of the 426-acre **East Rock Park** (cityofnewhaven. com/parks), where a 350-foot basalt cliff offers a magnificent vantage for catching the sunset over Elm City and Long Island Sound. The park closes at dusk.

9 *Old-World New England* 8 p.m.

A French restaurant in the high Yankee style, **Union League Cafe** (1032 Chapel Street; 203-562-4299; unionleaguecafe.com; $$$) has an inscription above the fireplace marking a 1789 visit by George Washington. This mix of history and Beaux-Arts grandeur is one reason for visiting; the other reasons are service that's formal without being finicky and food that tastes decadent—foie gras, caviar, and truffles—without being overly rich.

10 *Retro Bar Crawl* 10 p.m.

If only for the atmosphere, stop by the **Owl Shop** (268 College Street; 203-624-3250; owlshopcigars.com), a vintage cigar lounge, draped in leather and wood, where bourbon flows and tobacco is blended. Next door, the **Anchor Spa** (272 College Street; 203-821-7065; anchorspa.com) has tin ceilings, blue leather booths, and a long history, dating back to 1939. **Rudy's** (1227 Chapel Street; 203-865-1242) is no longer the charmingly grimy dive bar it was in a former location, but the back room still pays homage to Yale football, and the frites are still hand-cut, twice-cooked, and Samurai sauce-ready.

SUNDAY

11 *Coffee on the Lawn* 9 a.m.

In the shadow of the Corinthian portico and steeple of St. Michael's Catholic Church, designed in 1855 and

among Connecticut's first Italian-American churches, **Wooster Square** is awash in church bells and bordered by cherry trees. Stop at **Lucibello's Italian Pastry Shop** (935 Grand Avenue; 203-562-4083; lucibellospastry.com) for marzipan-flavored, pine nut-topped pignoli, clam-shaped sfogliatelle, and crispy cannolis; then pick up an espresso-to-go at **Wooster Square Coffee** (516 Chapel Street). Pass the rest of the morning wandering the Yale campus. On a peaceful Sunday, the architecture (yale.edu/architectureofyale), from the 1752 Connecticut Hall to the turtle-shaped shell of the 1958 Eero Saarinen ice skating rink, takes center stage.

OPPOSITE New Haven from East Rock Park.

THE BASICS

New Haven, about 80 miles northeast of New York, is easily reached by car or Metro-North train.

The Study at Yale
1157 Chapel Street
203-503-3900
thestudyatyale.com
$$$
Plays on its university connection with lobby décor of bookshelves, leather armchairs, and modern art.

Omni New Haven Hotel at Yale
155 Temple Street
203-772-6664
omnihotels.com
$$$
On the upper floors of one of downtown's taller buildings. Ask for a room with a view of the Yale campus or Long Island Sound.

New Haven Hotel
229 George Street
203-498-3100
newhavenhotel.com
$$$
Renovated downtown hotel.

Map of New Haven, Connecticut showing locations including: Liuzzi Cheese (7), Bella's Café (5), East Rock Park (8), Edgewood Park, Zuppardi's Apizza (2), Sandy Point Bird Sanctuary (1), Long Wharf Theatre (3), New Haven Harbor, Bradley Point Beach, Dive Bar & Restaurant, Fashionista Vintage & Variety, Olmo, Yale University Art Gallery, Rudy's (6), Yale Center for British Art, Lucibello's Italian Pastry Shop, The Study at Yale, Yale Repertory Theatre, Anchor Spa, Union League Cafe (9), Owl Shop (10), Shubert Theater, Omni New Haven Hotel at Yale, Wooster Square (11), New Haven Hotel, Cask Republic (4), Cafe Nine, Wooster Square Coffee.

21

Bar Harbor

There are summer resorts that get busier and more chic over the years. And then there are the ones, like Bar Harbor, Maine, that feel deliciously frozen in time. Bar Harbor is the largest town on Mount Desert Island, and nearby Acadia National Park encompasses some 50 square miles. The rest of Mount Desert belongs to residents and a tony array of summer tenants: Brooke Astor summered here, as did myriad Rockefellers; and once upon a time, the town of Northeast Harbor had so many well-to-do Philadelphia families that it was dubbed "Philadelphia on the rocks." They all came lured by the striking setting of mountains, woodlands, lakes, and ocean waves crashing against granite cliffs. Then and now, Mount Desert has served as a glorious nature camp for biking, hiking, and boating. At day's end, a visitor can cozy up with a blueberry beer and lobster. Evening strollers can watch sailboats drop anchor and the mist slip down over the hundreds of islands that dot the water. — BY GERALDINE FABRIKANT

FRIDAY

1 *Toast the Sunset* 6 p.m.

Take the two-hour cruise on the *Margaret Todd*, a four-masted schooner that sails through Frenchman Bay and the Porcupine Islands (207-288-4585; downeastwindjammer.com). You'll pass Ironbound Island, still owned by descendants of the painter Dwight Blaney, who with his contemporary John Singer Sargent and others painted the remarkable vistas of the bay and Acadia. A guitarist may serenade you, but if you want to toast the sunset, bring your own wine.

2 *Seafood Extravaganza* 8:30 p.m.

It may be called the **Reading Room** (7 Newport Drive; 207-288-3351; barharborinn.com/dining.html; $$), but dining in a rotunda that overlooks the harbor feels more like eating on a ship than in a library. On weekends, a pianist usually plays old favorites. Lobster lovers can opt for the lobster pie, but the broiled fish like local haddock with butter crumb crust is also a treat. For a more exotic setting, dine at the red-walled **Havana** (318 Main Street; 207-288-2822; havanamaine.com; $$), which was the Obamas' choice when they visited one year.

The paella with lobster, mussels, clams, and chorizo is worth the stop.

3 *Blueberry Beer* 10 p.m.

Hang with the locals at **Geddy's** (19 Main Street; 207-288-5077; geddys.com), a fun, funky pub filled with old photographs and local signage. Blueberries thrive in the local terrain, and aficionados can try the Sea Dog blueberry draft beer or a blueberry margarita.

SATURDAY

4 *Book Lover's Breakfast* 8:30 a.m.

By 8 o'clock the line is already forming at the cheerful **Cafe This Way** (14½ Mount Desert Street; 207-288-4483; cafethisway.com; $) on a tiny back street off the town square. Inside, tables sit near bookshelves filled with classics and poetry. Mainers don't stint on breakfast, nor should you; fill up on French toast with real maple syrup or a McThisWay

OPPOSITE Main Street in Bar Harbor, a resort town on Mount Desert Island with a history as a summer place dating back to the 19th century.

BELOW The four-masted schooner *Margaret Todd* at rest in Bar Harbor's morning fog.

sandwich of fried eggs, tomatoes, Cheddar cheese, and bacon. Those who want some oomph can try a mimosa or a Bloody Mary.

5 *Bike Acadia* 10 a.m.

There are numerous entrances to Acadia National Park (207-288-3338; nps.gov/acad). Take a drive around the 27-mile Park Loop Road and head to the top of **Cadillac Mountain**, the highest point on the Eastern Seaboard. It was named after the French explorer who called himself Sieur de la Mothe Cadillac. He went on to help found Detroit, where the car was named after him. You cannot rent bikes or canoes within the park, but in Bar Harbor, **Acadia Bike** (48 Cottage Street; 207-288-9605;

acadiabike.com) fills the need. If you are not inclined to bike the steep 2.5 miles into the park, pack your bike on the free Island Explorer Shuttle (207-667-5796; exploreacadia.com; daily service in summer from 9:15 a.m. at the Village Green to the Eagle Lake Carriage Road entrance). In the park, 45 miles of biking paths wind through forests, along beaver dams, and around lakes. Take a map — even the road signs can get tricky.

6 *Popovers in the Park* 1 p.m.

Lunch at the **Jordan Pond House** (207-276-3316; acadiajordanpondhouse.com; $$) comes with views across the park's Jordan Pond to the Bubble Mountains. Popovers as rounded as the mountain-tops are a specialty and can accompany your lunch entree, which might be lobster Niçoise or chicken salad. If you have brought your kayak or canoe, you can use it on the pond.

7 *Maine Merchandise* 4 p.m.

Back in town, do some Maine-appropriate shopping. **Window Panes** (166 Main Street; 207-288-9550; windowpanesmdi.com) carries

LEFT During a two-hour sailing cruise on Frenchman Bay off Bar Harbor, passengers take part in hoisting the sails onboard the *Margaret Todd*.

gifts including coasters made from local granite. **Cool as a Moose** (118 Main Street; 207-288-3904; coolasamoose.com) is a place to grab a sweatshirt for a chilly night. You can immerse yourself in Maine lore at **Sherman's Book and Stationery Store** (56 Main Street; 207-288-3161; shermans.com), where you might want to pick up a copy of *Time and Tide in Acadia* by Christopher Camuto or *The Maine Wild Blueberry Cookbook*. For the Lilly Pulitzer look of hot pink, orange, and blue tops or straw hats and summer bags, check the racks at the **Romantic Room** (132 Main Street, Northeast Harbor; 207-276-4005; theromanticroom.com).

8 *It's All About Lobster* 7 p.m.

Any stay in Maine is partly about lobster. Nowhere is that fact driven home more bluntly than at **Thurston's** (9 Thurston Road, Bernard; 207-244-7600; thurstonslobster.com; $$), in a half-plastic, half-canvas tent on a working harbor, surrounded by stacks of lobster pots. You choose your live lobster,

OPPOSITE ABOVE The rocky coast that defines the rugged beauty of Acadia National Park. Offshore, lobstermen haul a catch into their boat.

ABOVE The Reading Room, a dining rotunda with a sea view at the Bar Harbor Inn, and the yellow umbrellas of the outdoor tables on a terrace just below.

they cook it, and you pick it up on a plastic tray. The result: high turnover and surprisingly low prices. For variety try the lobster stew. If you prefer a cottage setting, try **Abel's Lobster Pound** (13 Abels Lane off Route 198, south of Junction 233; 207-276-5827; abelslobsterpound.com; $$$), a lively family-owned restaurant set in a spruce grove on a fjord. Eat at picnic tables illuminated by tiki torches and overlooking the yacht basin, or indoors in the knotty pine dining room.

SUNDAY

9 *Garden Spots* 9:30 a.m.

At the **Asticou Azalea Garden** (Peabody Drive and Sound Drive; 207-276-3727; gardenpreserve.org; free) in Northeast Harbor, pines, hemlocks, Korean firs, Japanese maples, azaleas, and blueberries are set around a pond. The garden's hybrid of styles includes a small Japanese karesansui garden composed of Maine granite island stones in a sea of raked white sands; lanterns and stepping-stones add to the Japanese look. Nearby, on Peabody Drive, is the **Thuya Garden** (207-276-5130; gardenpreserve.org; free), named after the house built by the landscape architect Henry Curtis, who summered there. The lodge is now a horticultural library, and the setting features a broad array of trees and shrubs and an English-style garden with everything from wood

lilies to Beverly Sills irises. One can drive or climb to the garden; but the climb, which affords broad views of Northeast Harbor, is well worth the effort.

10 *Truly Local* 11 a.m.

Take the mail boat to **Little Cranberry Island** from Northeast Harbor, and you may find yourself helping locals unload their groceries on the dock (207-244-3575; cranberryisles.com/ferries.html). Stop at the free **Islesford Historical Museum**, with its

collection of ship models, tools, and dolls (207-244-9224; acadianationalpark.com/bar_harbor_maine_attractions), and then have brunch or a drink at the **Islesford Dock Restaurant** (Marina, Islesford; 207-244-7494; islesforddock.com). The harbor setting and views capture the Maine atmosphere, and the place has been mentioned in Martha Stewart's blog (she is a Seal Harbor summer resident). Try the Maine lobster fritter and grits.

ABOVE Sunrise viewing at the top of Cadillac Mountain in Acadia National Park.

OPPOSITE Cycling up Cadillac Mountain. Rent a bicycle in Bar Harbor and take a free shuttle into the park.

THE BASICS

Drive to Bar Harbor on Routes 1A and 3 from Bangor, which is on Interstate 95 and has an airport.

Asticou Inn
15 Peabody Drive
207-276-3344
asticou.com
$$$
Overlooks the water in Northeast Harbor and has the feel of a roomy old Maine home, but one with a tennis court and heated swimming pool.

Ullikana
16 The Field
207-288-9552
ullikana.com
$$$
Two cheerful cottages near the water, with each room decorated in a panoply of colors and fabrics.

Bar Harbor Inn
1 Newport Drive
207-288-3351
barharborinn.com
$$$-$$$$
Stay in the main building for the grand-old-hotel experience.

CANADA
MAINE
Augusta
Area of detail
Portland
Atlantic Ocean

2 miles
4 kilometers

3
BURNT PORCUPINE ISLAND
SHEEP PORCUPINE ISLAND
LONG PORCUPINE ISLAND
EDEN ST.
Bar Harbor
IRONBOUND ISLAND
Area of detail
BALD PORCUPINE ISLAND

Eagle Lake
MT. DESERT ISLAND
Acadia National Park
PARK LOOP ROAD
Frenchman Bay

Abel's Lobster Pound
SOUND DR.
Bubble Mountains
Cadillac Mountain
5
3

Somes Sound
198
Jordan Pond
Margaret Todd **1**
Reading Room **2**
Geddy's **3**

102
Jordan Pond House **6**
Asticou Azalea Garden **9**
Asticou Inn
Romantic Room
Thuya Garden
Southwest Harbor
Northeast Harbor

Sherman's Book and Stationery Store
Bar Harbor Inn
Ullikana

Acadia Bike
Cool as a Moose

Manset
LITTLE CRANBERRY ISLAND
VILLAGE GREEN

MOUNT DESERT ST.
Window Panes **7**

Islesford Historical Museum/ Islesford Dock Restaurant **10**

Bernard
102A
GREAT CRANBERRY ISLAND

4
Cafe This Way

MAIN ST.

8 Thurston's

Atlantic Ocean
Bar Harbor
Havana

Midcoast Maine

Wedged between the indie urbanity of Portland and the great outdoors of Acadia National Park, Maine's midcoast region has long enthralled summertime travelers with its quaint towns and pastoral, pine-lined roads. The tranquil harbors and craggy beaches along U.S. Route 1 offer settings as quintessentially Maine as can be. (Lobster roll with a lighthouse view, anyone?) But lately, as Portland's arty influence creeps northward, the midcoast is flush with chic new inns, art galleries, and a modern, hyper-local food scene. For visitors, that means the best of both Maines: a cool, innovative spirit that lures city dwellers from Portland and beyond, blended with the laid-back Down East spirit that has long been a point of local pride.
— BY BRENDAN SPIEGEL

FRIDAY

1 *Modern-Day Mills* 3 p.m.

Brunswick, a former mill town that serves as the gateway to the midcoast, these days is known less for lumber and textiles than for craft beer and art. The Fort Andross Mill, a large, 19th-century brick structure where textiles were once produced, is now occupied by an antique store, a yoga studio, and **Frontier**, a restaurant and bar, theater and cafe, and event venue (14 Maine Street, Brunswick; 207-725-5222; explorefrontier.com). Stop at Frontier's bar for a cappuccino made with locally wood-roasted beans or a locally brewed beer and head into the small theater for a documentary screening or a set from a local songwriter. Or visit the **Peary-MacMillan Arctic Museum** (9 South Campus Drive; 207-725-3416; bowdoin.edu/arctic-museum) at Bowdoin College, the polar explorer Robert E. Peary's alma mater, and view expedition gear, early photographs, and Inuit art. Wind up by driving or walking across the truss bridge to **Sea Dog Brewing Company** (1 Bowdoin Mill Island, Topsham; 207-725-0162; seadogbrewing.com), a former pulp mill where wheat ales accented by blueberries and apricots pair nicely with a view over the Androscoggin River.

2 *Scenic Detours* 5 p.m.

As Route 1 winds eastward, the region's major towns lie close together, but opportunities for rewarding detours are endless. Just beyond Brunswick, the area commonly called **Harpswell Peninsula**, made up of an oblong peninsula, islands, and connecting bridges, provides plenty of options for waterfront wandering. Farther east is **Reid State Park** (375 Seguinland Road, Georgetown; 207-371-2303), a pine-filled preserve with a picnic area that has views of a rocky shore and one of the area's few stretches of sand beach. Towering green pines overlook a sea of swimmers and sunset surfers.

3 *Backyard-to-Table* 7 p.m.

A good spot for farm-to-table dining on the midcoast is **Primo** (2 Main Street, Rockland; 207-596-0770; primorestaurant.com; $$$$), set in a century-old house on a hill just south of downtown Rockland. Stroll past the backyard organic gardens, greenhouses, chicken coops, and pig pens; then taste the fruits of all that husbandry in dishes like honey wine-braised moulard duck over roasted beets, farro, baby leeks, hazelnut, and rhubarb chutney. Choose the formal setting downstairs; a more modern, barnyard-chic ambience upstairs; or the bar, for snacks like house-made wild boar salami.

4 *Produce at the Bar* 9:30 p.m.

Just north of Rockland in the tiny harbor community of Rockport, a wood-walled former general store

OPPOSITE A walk on the breakwater in Rockland, one of the harbor towns that make this section of coast a stretch of quintessential Maine.

BELOW Rockland's revitalized downtown. Galleries among the shops show and sell the work of Maine artists.

has been remade into a restaurant called **18 Central Oyster Bar & Grill** (18 Central Street, Rockport; 18central.com) with a long bar. Try one of its fruit cocktails infused with herbs, like the Lighthouse, with vermouth, rosemary, peach bitters, and prosecco, or a local draft beer.

SATURDAY

5 *Walk on Water* 10 a.m.

There is no shortage of ways to get out on the water around here, but one of the most spectacular is the 4,346-foot walk along the breakwater jutting into **Rockland Harbor** (end of Samoset Road, Rockland; rocklandharborlights.org). The narrow

granite structure took 18 years to build in the late 19th century, and it stretches nearly a mile out into the harbor. In morning light the red brick lighthouse and accompanying wood-frame keeper's house set at the breakwater's end form a dramatic sight as they seem to float in the middle of the harbor.

6 *Art Crawl* 11 a.m.

The hub of the midcoast's lively art scene is Rockland's revitalized Main Street. The **Farnsworth Art Museum** (16 Museum Street, off Main Street; 207-596-6457; farnsworthmuseum.org) holds one of the largest collections of works by Andrew, Jamie, and N.C. Wyeth. **Asymmetrick Arts** (405 Main Street; 207-594-2020; asymmetrickarts.com) focuses on emerging Maine artists. And a block from the Farnsworth,

ABOVE The Sea Dog Brewing Company in Topsham.

BELOW The blue sweep of Camden Harbor.

the new building of the **Center for Maine Contemporary Art** (21 Winter Street; 207-701-5005; cmcanow.org), designed by Toshiko Mori and featuring a glass-enclosed courtyard, presents the work of both emerging and established artists with ties to Maine.

7 *Boat Town* 1 p.m.

Camden Harbor is one of Maine's preeminent sailing spots. Visitors can explore it from the deck of a windjammer fishing yacht like the old schooner *Surprise* (Public Landing, Camden; 207-236-4687; schoonersurprise.com). Or get even closer with a sea kayak tour from **Maine Sport Outfitters** (24 Main Street, Camden; 207-230-1284; mainesport.com). Guides teach kayaking basics before taking paddlers across the harbor and circling tree-lined Curtis Island. Kayakers may spot harbor seals and porpoises; and if they dare, they can pop in for a dip in the sub-60-degree water.

8 *Camden Thai* 7 p.m.

Camden, which looks like quintessential Maine, is not the first place you might expect to find superior Thai cuisine. Yet here it is, at **Long Grain** (20 Washington Street, Camden; 207-236-9001; $$), a 30-seat restaurant with simple décor and food made with ingredients sourced from the Maine coast but reflecting flavors of Bangkok. Try the chewy, slightly charred broad noodles, pad kee mao, which are made

in-house, or the Thai beef salad. The place is justly popular; don't try coming without a reservation.

9 *Bonfire Bocce* 10 p.m.

At the working wharf a few miles north in Belfast, you'll find **Three Tides** (40 Marshall Wharf, Belfast; 207-338-1707; 3tides.com), perhaps the

ABOVE The Atlantic Climbing School shepherds rock climbers in Camden Hills State Park. The reward at the top of the cliffs is wide-angle views of Penobscot Bay, Megunticook Lake, and the forested hills.

BELOW An upstairs room at Primo, one of the best local restaurants for farm-to-table dining.

closest thing midcoast Maine has to a hipster bar scene. The nautical-themed bar (a pile of shucked oyster shells serves as décor) includes a bocce court and a bay-view bonfire pit, and the drinks include two dozen house-brewed beers.

SUNDAY

10 *Mountain Bound* 8 a.m.

Camden may be known for sailing, but for landlubber adventure-seekers it's also fast emerging as a rock climbing destination. With fewer people on the rocks than up north in Acadia, it's an excellent place to learn the basics. **Atlantic Climbing School** (207-288-2521; climbacadia.com) runs half-day courses for beginners in Camden Hills State Park, where the climb is rewarded with views of Penobscot

Bay and Megunticook Lake. The school serves experienced climbers, too.

11 *Greens to Go* 12:30 p.m.

The vegetarian restaurant **Chase's Daily** (96 Main Street, Belfast; 207-338-0555; $$) not only sources most of the menu from a family farm in Freedom, 20 miles inland, but also devotes space to an art gallery and a farmers' market. Order a pizza baked in a bread oven and topped with four local cheeses and fresh marjoram, and then grab some beet greens or Maine products like Swan's raw, unfiltered wildflower honey to take home.

OPPOSITE The old schooner *Surprise*, a windjammer fishing yacht, sails out of Camden Harbor.

THE BASICS

Drive up U.S. 1, and be ready to make frequent stops.

Camden Harbour Inn
83 Bayview Street, Camden
207-236-4200
camdenharbourinn.com
$$
A design-conscious boutique hotel in a formerly dilapidated Victorian building dating to 1874. Sweeping bay views.

Belfast Bay Inn
72 Main Street, Belfast
207-338-5600
belfastbayinn.com
$$
In two Main Street row houses, with an airy garden courtyard.

Hawthorn Inn
9 High Street, Camden
207-236-8842
camdenhawthorn.com
$$
Ten rooms, including suites with garden views.

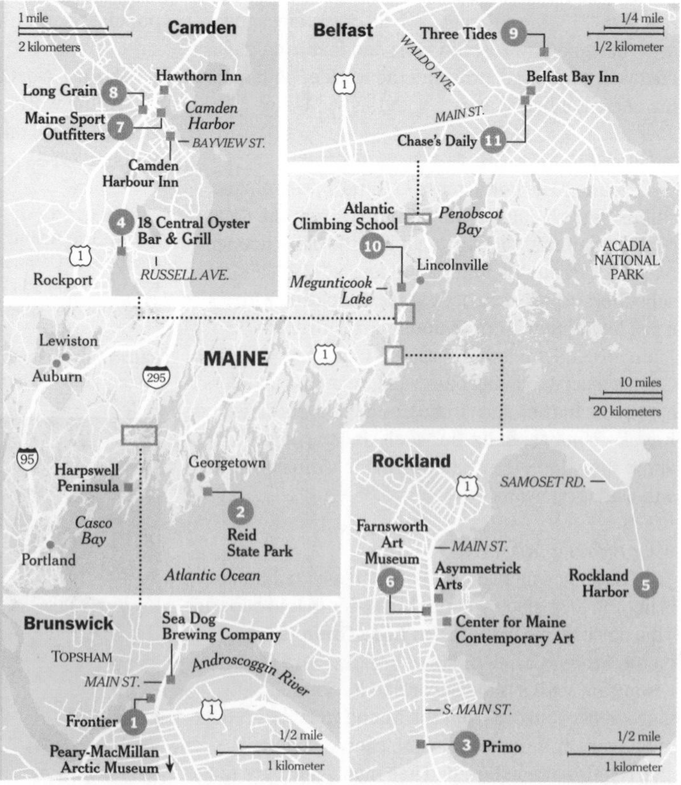

Portland

With its cobblestone lanes and photogenic harbor, Portland's Old Port district has long been a draw for travelers seeking a quick dose of urban New England charm before moving on to Maine's more bucolic pleasures. These days visitors are dropping in for longer spells as Portland's allure spreads to the Congress Street arts district and indie-spirited neighborhoods like East Bayside and Munjoy Hill. Much of that allure has to do with food. Portland's reputation as a great dining town is well-deserved, with an abundance of good choices. Visitors are also discovering what residents have long loved most about their town: local art and music, gracious parks, a stunning array of 19th-century architecture, and the city's layered history. — BY SUZANNE MACNEILLE

FRIDAY

1 *360-Degree View* 1 p.m.

You can't miss the red octagonal **Portland Observatory** (138 Congress Street; portlandlandmarks.org) rising above the wooden and brick houses and small businesses on Munjoy Hill. Climb the 104 creaking steps of this former maritime signaling tower, built by the enterprising Capt. Lemuel Moody who, some 200 years ago, wasn't above augmenting his business with a little income from view-seekers like you. Now, as then, one's gaze turns to the east, to the silver waters and green islands of Casco Bay. The loquacious guides take their time pointing out lighthouses and landmarks, as appreciative of the view as you are. Back on the ground, look for Capt. Moody's burial site among the tombs and tilting gravestones in nearby Eastern Cemetery, which is threaded with paths and beloved by grave tourists.

2 *A Brush With the Past* 5 p.m.

Below a row of rambling, mostly turn-of-the-last-century houses, the **Eastern Promenade** is one of two parks that curve around either side of old Portland. Above the bayside trail, Fort Allen Park, with its gazebo and sloping lawn, offers a serene glimpse of the bay. Several blocks away is the wood-and-brick **Abyssinian Meeting House** (75 Newbury Street), once a hub on Portland's Underground Railroad and one of more than a dozen sites on the city's **Freedom Trail** (mainehistory.org/PDF/walkingtourmap.pdf). Portland had a robust antislavery movement, and the freedom trail is indispensable for a thorough understanding of the city's past.

3 *Harborside* 7 p.m.

Commercial Street is the touristic heart of Portland, but don't be deterred by the prospects of kitschiness. This harborside stretch is as inviting a tourist boulevard as you'll find anywhere. Get off the main drag to explore wharves and docks where seaweed dries on racks and gulls poke around nets and lobster pots. Stop for a drink on the deck of **Portland Lobster Co.** (180 Commercial Street; portlandlobstercompany.com), where a local band might be playing blues or rock covers, or find a seat at the long bar at **Liquid Riot Bottling Co.** (250 Commercial Street), which, besides being a restaurant and bar, is also a distillery and brewing establishment churning out an impressive list of libations. For dinner, walk to **Scales** (68 Commercial Street; scalesrestaurant.com; $$-$$$), a big, light-filled restaurant on Maine Wharf with a shiny open kitchen and views of the docks. The coastal New England menu emphasizes dishes like Maine clam chowder and pan-roasted halibut.

SATURDAY

4 *Breakfast at Sea* 8 a.m.

The extraordinarily moist doughnuts at the **Holy Donut** (7 Exchange Street; theholydonut.com),

OPPOSITE Casco Bay from the Portland Observatory.

BELOW Lines form in the morning at the Holy Donut.

in flavors like blueberry and maple bacon, draw morning lines at the Exchange Street location. Pick up a few and have breakfast at sea. With a busy day ahead, save the Casco Bay Lines' multi-island mailboat route for another visit, and opt for the ferry to **Peaks Island** (cascobaylines.com/schedules). The roughly 40-minute round trip offers a bracing view of busy Casco Bay and Portland's harbor. The island itself is worth a visit when you have more time.

5 *East End Exploration* 11 a.m.

Rent a bike at **CycleMania** (65 Cove Street; cyclemania1.com) in East Bayside, and hit the trails. One choice for an hourlong ride is the Back Cove trail, which curves 3.6 miles around a circular cove. Then refresh yourself with kombucha at **Urban Farm Fermentory** (200 Anderson Street; fermentory.com). In a town where distilling and fermenting are apparently native skills, Urban Farm, in a warehouse-type space, is evidence of Portland's entrepreneurial zeal. In addition to fermented tea — recent flavors included mint, nettle and turmeric — it makes mead, hard ciders, and gruit (beer with herbal flavoring).

6 *Asian Lunch, Maine Style* 1 p.m.

The seating is communal, the dishes are mismatched and the menu is irresistible at the **Honey Paw** (78 Middle Street; thehoneypaw.com; $$). Its East-meets-New England approach is evident in dishes like smoked lamb khao soi with housemade noodles and lobster won tons with confit mushrooms. Or sample the eclectic small plates

at **Central Provisions** (414 Fore Street; centralprovisions.com; $$), known for both its food and its exquisite sleek-rustic interior.

7 *Homer to Nevelson* 2 p.m.

Winslow Homer was born in Massachusetts, but Maine, where he eventually moved, is the state the artist is often associated with. With its impressive Homer collection, and the weekly tours it offers to the artist's home and studio, the **Portland Museum of Art** (7 Congress Square; portlandmuseum.org) is the place to go for your Homer fix. But there's much more beyond the brick facade on Congress Square: some 18,000 works by artists like N. C. and Andrew Wyeth, Alex Katz, Louise Nevelson, Monet, Matisse and Kandinsky, among others.

8 *A Visit to Henry* 4 p.m.

Stroll along Congress Street, with its many galleries, and stop by the **Wadsworth-Longfellow House** (489 Congress Street; mainehistory.org), dating from the late 18th century. Even if you don't tour the house, where Henry Wadsworth Longfellow grew up, you can take a breather in its peaceful ornamental garden.

9 *On the Town* 8:30 p.m.

At the intimate Greek restaurant **Emilitsa** (547 Congress Street; emilitsa.com; $$$), the plush seating and attentive service encourage diners to linger. Start with the potent house cocktail and scan the menu. It changes often, but past entrees have included a salad of local roasted red and golden beets in olive oil and muscatato vinegar, and a delicious, incredibly rich version of moussaka topped with Greek yogurt béchamel. Then sample Portland's

ABOVE Portland remains a busy port for oceangoing cargo ships, but small boats and recreational craft share the waterfront, and tourists linger at the Old Port.

music scene at places like **One Longfellow Square** (1 Longfellow Square; box office at 181 State Street; onelongfellowsquare.com) and **Blue** (650A Congress Street; portcityblue.com). Both feature a variety of styles, including jazz, folk, rock and blues (often by such Maine artists as Samuel James).

SUNDAY

10 *Eggs Becky* 9 a.m.

There's usually a breakfast crowd at **Becky's Diner** (390 Commercial Street; beckysdiner.com; $), where locals and tourists sit at Formica tables beneath a press-tinned ceiling and fill up on buttermilk pancakes, eggs done any way you want, and

huge sides of home fries. Expect a modest check and the satisfaction that you've experienced a Portland classic.

11 *Another View* 1:30 p.m.

You've been to the Eastern Promenade, now visit its western counterpart, by way of Danforth Street, for a glimpse of **Victoria Mansion** (109 Danforth Street; victoriamansion.org), an Italianate mansion with a grand flying staircase and lavish interiors by Gustave Herter. Continue past shady Western Cemetery to the Western Promenade. Invariably, there are artists on the grassy slopes, fixated on the distant White Mountains — yet another view, and another side of Portland.

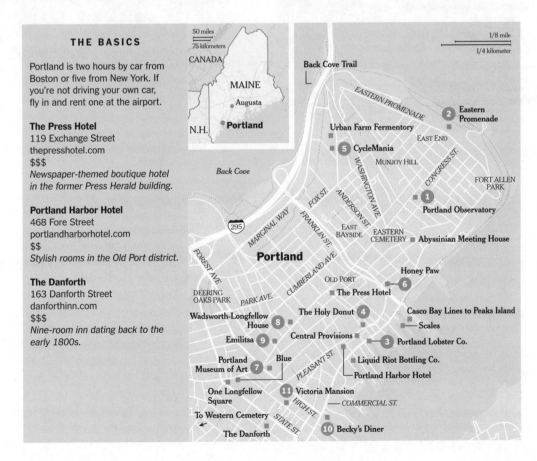

THE BASICS

Portland is two hours by car from Boston or five from New York. If you're not driving your own car, fly in and rent one at the airport.

The Press Hotel
119 Exchange Street
thepresshotel.com
$$$
Newspaper-themed boutique hotel in the former Press Herald building.

Portland Harbor Hotel
468 Fore Street
portlandharborhotel.com
$$
Stylish rooms in the Old Port district.

The Danforth
163 Danforth Street
danforthinn.com
$$$
Nine-room inn dating back to the early 1800s.

The Berkshires

The Berkshire countryside is crisscrossed by lines of music and literature, by crumbling stone walls running like half-forgotten stories through farms and woodlands, by ellipses of deep green hills fading to blue. You can't go far here without encountering a remnant of the Gilded Age, when this region first became a summer destination. But you won't go far, either, without finding some alluring new mark on the cultural, culinary, or pleasure-seeking landscape. The decisions you'll face every Berkshire morning — old or new? art or the outdoors? — are getting harder than ever to make. — BY MARK VANHOENACKER

FRIDAY

1 *Nature as You Like It* 2 p.m.

To start the weekend in the peace of a natural cathedral, take a walk in the **Hopper** (1136 Hopper Road, Williamstown; wrlf.org/the-hopper-trails), a glacial cirque that makes up the bowl-shaped end of a valley below Mount Greylock. Lovely trails branch off to follow streams or the lines of the mountain, but you can find transcendence even in the first few hundred yards. If you'd rather get going with an adrenalin rush, choose **Ramblewild** (110 Brodie Mountain Road, Lanesborough; ramblewild.com), a ravine-straddling rope adventure course built across a sustainable forestry site. Suspended on safety lines between the earth and the forest canopy, you'll scramble — terrified and exhilarated — along eight aerial "trails" in a tree-to-tree adventure.

2 *So Euro* 6 p.m.

You've earned a meal at **Brava** (27 Housatonic Street, Lenox; bravalenox.com; $$$), a wine and tapas bar on a quiet village street. Before you wade through the meticulously curated wine list (the beer pages are a treat, too), get in a few orders for the melt-in-your-mouth lamb chops, which often run out.

3 *Dancers and Drinkers* 8 p.m.

More choices. For a first-rate cultural performance, spend an evening at **Jacob's Pillow** (358 George Carter Road, Becket; jacobspillow.org), where major national and international ballet companies perform, along with dance innovators, in a renowned annual summer festival. Or to indulge a

different kind of connoisseurship, travel to the town of Lee for some drink sampling at **Moe's Tavern** (10 Railroad Street, Lee; nocoorslight.com), whose owner, Josh Cohen, has quietly built a near-cultish following among both craft beer and American whiskey lovers.

SATURDAY

4 *Berry's Bears* 9 a.m.

While it's still early, drive to **Pittsfield State Forest** (1041 Cascade Street, Pittsfield; 413-442-8992), where Shaker cemeteries, home sites, and holy areas once set aside for dancing and music still dot the deep woods. A one-way loop drive takes you up to the sky-high Berry Pond (named for William Berry, a Revolutionary War veteran), where mist-shrouded waters, azaleas, and mountain laurel, the occasional blueberry-nibbling black bear, and the distilled simplicity of a Berkshire morning await.

5 *Brunch to Grow On* 10:30 a.m.

Back in Pittsfield, stop for brunch at **Otto's Kitchen** (95 East Street; ottoskitchen.com; $), a locally owned and community-minded breakfast place that has earned a big following in this small city's resurgent downtown. Expect the usual hearty eggs and pancakes, but also a few surprises, like shrimp and grits or a ham and chèvre omelet.

OPPOSITE The bucolic beauty of summer in the Berkshires.

BELOW Treetop adventure at Ramblewild.

6 *"I and My Chimney"* Noon

Herman Melville lived at **Arrowhead** (780 Holmes Road, Pittsfield; mobydick.org), his 18th-century home, from 1850 to 1863, shocking the neighbors with a porch on the chilly north side (to better see Mount Greylock). Inspired by the wintry mountain, he completed *Moby-Dick* here on a "sleigh load" of paper purchased in nearby Dalton, home of the Crane mills that still supply paper for American currency. Wander the nature trail or ponder the community farm, focusing on crops Melville grew here (eggplant, peas, brassicas). Then take the guided tour. Replicas of the harpoon in Melville's study, sadly, aren't for sale. Console yourself with a "Call Me Ishmael" T-shirt.

7 *Golden Ponds* 2 p.m.

Get back to the outdoors at **Savoy Mountain State Forest** (260 Central Shaft Road, Florida; mass.gov/locations/savoy-mountain-state-forest). There are plenty of hiking trails here, but for a memorable change of pace, take a swim in one of the crystalline ponds.

8 *Basket Cases* 4 p.m.

Assembling a picnic is a rewarding task in Berkshire County, which has a proud history of both agricultural fairs and community-supported agriculture. Start at **Berkshire Organics** (813 Dalton Division Road, Dalton; berkshireorganics.com) for fresh produce and groceries. Next, head to **Spirited** (444 Pittsfield Road, Lenox; spirited-wines.com), which offers fine salumi, local cheeses, and Berkshire booze. Your last stop may be the most important: don't miss the cider doughnuts at **Bartlett's Orchard** (575 Swamp Road, Richmond; bartlettsorchard.com).

9 *The Hills Are Alive* 6 p.m.

In 1853, thousands of New Yorkers streamed north to watch an illegal Berkshire boxing bout between James Sullivan and John Morrissey, nicknamed Old Smoke when an opponent pinned him in the burning coals of an overturned stove. Sullivan, recently arrived from Australia, ended up in a Lenox jail; Morrissey, the winner, became a congressman. For more genteel entertainment, cart your provisions to **Tanglewood** (297 West Street, Lenox; tanglewood.org), summer home of the Boston Symphony Orchestra, for a picnic on the lawn and a starlit night of world-class music.

SUNDAY

10 *W. E. B. Du Bois Country* 9 a.m.

Join the **Upper Housatonic Valley African American Heritage Trail** (africanamericantrail.org) at the Du Bois River Garden Park in Great Barrington to learn about the environmental activism of this civil rights icon ("I was born by a golden river," Du Bois wrote), and then drive to his boyhood home. Or follow the life of an earlier hero, starting at the Col. John Ashley House. The 1773 Sheffield Declaration—a precursor to the Declaration of Independence—was probably drafted here, and one of Colonel Ashley's house slaves, Elizabeth Freeman, known then as Mum Bett, surely heard both discussed. Her successful 1781 lawsuit helped bring slavery in Massachusetts to an end. Freeman chose her own name, eventually bought her own farm, and is buried in the Stockbridge Cemetery.

11 *For Art's Sake* 11 a.m.

Relax over brunch at the **Prairie Whale** (178 Main Street, Great Barrington; facebook.com/prairiewhale; $$) while you plan your next move. The Clark Art Institute in Williamstown? The Norman Rockwell Museum or Chesterwood, home of the Lincoln sculptor Daniel Chester French, both in Stockbridge? The sprawl of contemporary art at MASS MoCA in North Adams? If you're an art lover, you can't quite head home yet.

OPPOSITE Mount Greylock rises above a quiet lake. Herman Melville supposedly saw a whale shape in its contours.

THE BASICS

Plan for a lot of driving. The pleasures of the Berkshires are scattered in villages and along country roads.

Guest House at Field Farm
554 Sloan Road, Williamstown
thetrustees.org/field-farm
$$$
A B&B set in what is essentially a museum of well-preserved midcentury modernism, amid hundreds of acres of meadows, beaver ponds, and forests.

Old Inn on the Green
134 Hartsville-New Marlborough Road,
New Marlborough
oldinn.com
$$$-$$$$
Candlelit meals, friendly service, and a front porch that just won't quit.

Kemble Inn
2 Kemble Street, Lenox
kembleinn.com
$$$-$$$$
B&B near Tanglewood.

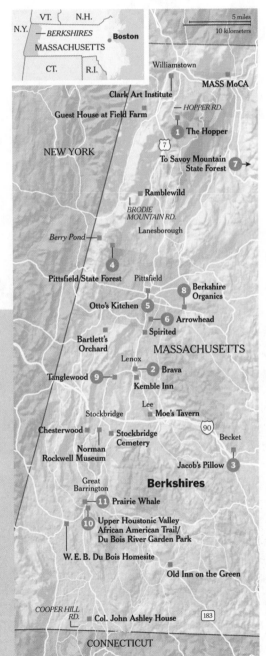

Boston

Thanks to the 50-some colleges in it and around it, Boston has a reputation for hitting the books first, goofing off second. Venerable institutions like Symphony Hall, the Museum of Fine Arts, and Faneuil Hall still anchor the city's hold on music, art, and history. But in recent years, this little big town has emerged from its brainy, introverted shell to offer a livelier mix of cultural offerings, plus an exploding food scene. The Rose Fitzgerald Kennedy Greenway parkland extends from the North End to Chinatown, connecting a new frontier of glass and steel construction known as the Seaport District to downtown. Of course, this is also a sports- and craft beer-obsessed city, meaning you're never far from a Celtics, Bruins, Patriots, or Red Sox fan hoisting a pint for the home team in one of the Hub's zillion pubs. Go Boston.

— BY ETHAN GILSDORF

FRIDAY

1 *Uncommonly Local* 2 p.m.

The classic tour begins at the 50-acre **Boston Common** (visitor center at 139 Tremont Street; bostonusa.com), the United States' oldest public park and the endpoint of Frederick Law Olmsted's green-space network known as the Emerald Necklace. From here, if history's your thing, walk the 2.5-mile Freedom Trail, which wends its way through 16 Revolutionary War-era sites. Just follow the red brick (or painted) trail as far as your legs can take you. The adjacent Public Garden's *Make Way for Ducklings* sculpture is a tribute to Robert McCloskey's picture book, and the bench featured in the film *Good Will Hunting* is now an unofficial memorial to the late Robin Williams.

2 *Back Bay Watch* 4:30 p.m.

From the Public Garden, stroll down Newbury Street into the heart of Back Bay. Designer shops are closest to the Public Garden, while you'll find increasingly funkier boutiques as you walk west toward Massachusetts Avenue. Homegrown **Newbury Comics** (332 Newbury Street; newburycomics.com)

is a mecca to music and pop culture. Drop into **Rick Walker's** (306 Newbury Street; rickwalkers.com) for leather jackets, cowboy hats, and vintage boots. The whimsical **Fairy Shop** (272 Newbury Street; 617-262-2520) features knickknacks devoted to unicorns, Alice in Wonderland, and Tim Burton. Heading back east via Boylston Street, stop by Copley Square and pop in at the **Boston Public Library** (700 Boylston Street; bpl.org). In its 1895 wing, the McKim Building, gaze at the sumptuous Edwin Austin Abbey floor-to-ceiling painting series *The Quest and Achievement of the Holy Grail* and John Singer Sargent's spectacular ceiling mural cycle *Triumph of Religion*. Outside the library, on Boylston between Exeter and Dartmouth streets, pause to reflect at the Boston Marathon finish line.

3 *Southern Comfort* 7:30 p.m.

Home to the nation's largest Victorian brick rowhouse district, the South End is also a place to go for fresh, bold dining spots. One such down-home, artisanal-spirited place is the **Gallows** (1395 Washington Street; thegallowsboston.com; $$). Try one of the "boards," little bites arranged on a wooden slab. Main dishes on one menu here included steak frites with summer succotash.

4 *Choose Your Music* 10 p.m.

Got room for music? The **Paradise Rock Club** (967 Commonwealth Avenue; paradiserock.club), on

OPPOSITE A swan boat on the pond of the Public Garden.

RIGHT A tour guide leads the way on the Freedom Trail.

Commonwealth Avenue nestled next to Boston University, features performances by alternative and indie bands. If you're in a mellower mood, check out **Wally's Café Jazz Club** (427 Massachusetts Avenue; wallyscafe.com). Billie Holiday, Charlie Parker, and Art Blakey once played at this legendary nightspot; these days, it's mostly Berklee College of Music students and local jazz masters on stage, but this snug venue still swings.

SATURDAY

5 *Breakfast Beacon* 10 a.m.

Beacon Hill is famous for its brick and stone Federal, Greek Revival, and Gothic-style buildings, and its myriad shops and cafes lining Charles Street. Begin your day at the **Paramount** (44 Charles Street; paramountboston.com; $$), whose beloved breakfast menu incudes omelets, toast with hearty toppings, and waffles.

6 *Two if by Land, One if by Sea* Noon

Here are three unconventional ways to get the lay of the land and the sea. Head down to Long Wharf and jump a ferry to the **Boston Harbor Islands** (bostonharborislands.org), a park encompassing 34 islands and peninsulas. One highlight is Georges Island, site of the Civil War-era Fort Warren, where a vintage baseball game or a concert may be on the schedule. **Boston Duck Tours** (1 Central Wharf; neaq.org) ply the city and the Charles River in World War II-style amphibious landing vehicles. A third alternative is the **Blue Bikes** bicycle-sharing system (bluebikes.com), with locations throughout the city.

7 *Seaport and Swing Sets* 4 p.m.

At the rapidly developing Fort Point and the Seaport District, wander the Boston Harborwalk and make a late afternoon refueling stop at the **Flour**

BELOW Venetian inspiration at the Gardner Museum.

Bakery (12 Farnsworth Street; flourbakery.com), or get a Vietnamese iced coffee at **Bon Me** (313 Congress Street; bonmetruck.com), a brick-and-mortar outpost of a fixture in Boston's food truck scene. Outdoor spaces are being reinvented at **Lawn on D** (420 D Street; lawnond.com), an innovative park with swing sets for adults, a beer tent, more food trucks, free games like bocce and cornhole, and live performances; in winter, events have included fire art performers and an ice maze.

8 *Seafood by the Sea* 7:30 p.m.

Pendant lights and fresh tile accent the cavernous brick-and-rafter space of **Row 34** (383 Congress Street; row34.com; $$). Here, at one of the city's best raw bars, begin with local oysters and choose from two dozen beers on tap. Main dishes may include crispy oysters, a creamy lobster roll, or pan-roasted bluefish.

9 *Down Cellar* 11 p.m.

Two basement hangouts show the range of bar life along the waterfront. There's the quasi-French Bastille Kitchen's underground **Chalet** (49 Melcher

ABOVE Sailors take full advantage of the Charles River.

RIGHT A bounce and a splash in the Rose Kennedy Greenway.

Street; bastillekitchen.net), where low seating, candles, a fireplace, and a deer-antler chandelier attract a trendy crowd. Here, you can tuck into a late-night snack and a glass of wine or a cocktail. **Lucky's Lounge** (355 Congress Street; luckyslounge.com), decorated with photos of the Rat Pack set, is part dive bar, part throwback to your parents' wood-paneled rec room. Live music here pays homage to Frank Sinatra.

SUNDAY

10 *Books and Brunch* 11 a.m.

For eclectic reads and eats, stop by Back Bay's multilevel **Trident Booksellers and Café**

(338 Newbury Street; tridentbookscafe.com; $$). Its brunch menu ventures far beyond the usual standbys, and you'll also find vegetable juice, beer, wine, and mimosas. Afterward, browse the books and one of the best magazine racks in town.

11 *Baseball and Botticelli* 1 p.m.

Two of Boston's most beloved shrines are accessible by the quirky Green Line MBTA trolley (mbta. com/schedules/Green). At the **Isabella Stewart Gardner Museum** (25 Evans Way; gardnermuseum. org), the works range from ancient statuary to 19th-century masters to the landscaped courtyard of the original building, a faux Venetian palace. The glassy modern addition was designed by Renzo Piano. More than just Red Sox fans will appreciate the behind-the-scenes tour at **Fenway Park** (4 Yawkey Way; mlb.com/redsox/ballpark/tours). Sit atop the famous Green Monster, and then see the inside of the press box and the visiting team's clubhouse (not as luxurious as you'd think).

OPPOSITE A 21st-century open-space design complements the Custom House Tower, built in 1915.

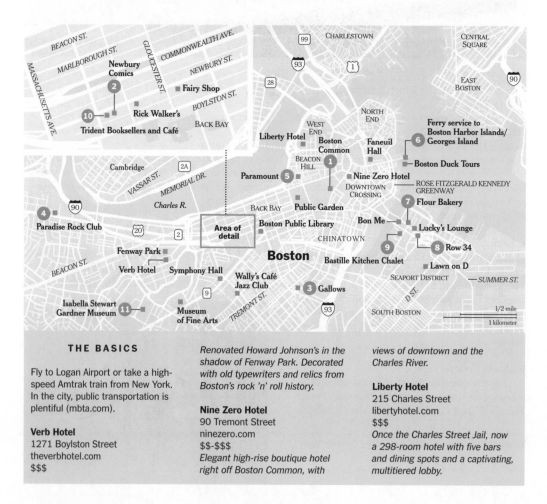

THE BASICS

Fly to Logan Airport or take a high-speed Amtrak train from New York. In the city, public transportation is plentiful (mbta.com).

Verb Hotel
1271 Boylston Street
theverbhotel.com
$$$

Renovated Howard Johnson's in the shadow of Fenway Park. Decorated with old typewriters and relics from Boston's rock 'n' roll history.

Nine Zero Hotel
90 Tremont Street
ninezero.com
$$-$$$
Elegant high-rise boutique hotel right off Boston Common, with

views of downtown and the Charles River.

Liberty Hotel
215 Charles Street
libertyhotel.com
$$$
Once the Charles Street Jail, now a 298-room hotel with five bars and dining spots and a captivating, multitiered lobby.

Cambridge

Anchored to the banks of the Charles River by both Harvard University and the Massachusetts Institute of Technology, Cambridge blends its storied past and erudite character with a rich serving of arts and culture. Today, the stamp of gentrification on Harvard Square and the gleaming biotech development flanking M.I.T., a.k.a. "Genetown," make it harder to tune into Cambridge's legendary countercultural vibe of used bookstores and punk rockers. Still, the outward-looking citizens, known as Cantabrigians, keep finding ways to express their funky, geeky flair, be it via political protests, copious bike lanes, or science-driven cuisine and mixology. — BY ETHAN GILSDORF

FRIDAY

1 *Bookish Beat* 3 p.m.

What better way to taste the brainy shock waves of Harvard Square, Cambridge's commercial and spiritual epicenter, than to sample its indie bookstores? Stroll the streets near the square, and you'll find the **Grolier Poetry Book Shop**, said to be the country's oldest continuous poetry-only store (6 Plympton Street; grolierpoetrybookshop.org); the **Curious George Store**, for children (1 J.F.K. Street; thecuriousgeorgestore.com); **Raven Used Books** (23 Church Street; ravencambridge.com); the **Million Year Picnic**, with indie and alternative comics (99 Mount Auburn Street, No. 2; themillionyearpicnic. com); and **Harvard Book Store** (1256 Massachusetts Avenue; harvard.com). Browse and enjoy.

2 *Square Meal* 7 p.m.

For a lowbrow Harvard Square institution, dine at **Mr. Bartley's** (1246 Massachusetts Avenue; mrbartley.com; $), whose walls, festooned with Ted Kennedy portraits and Red Sox ephemera, resemble those of a dorm room. The burgers are named for famous folk and political issues, like the Liz Warren or Trump Tower. For fancier fare, try the **Parsnip Restaurant & Lounge** (91 Winthrop Street; parsniprestaurant.com; $$$), where menus have featured citrus scallop crudo, roasted duck breast with bacon and date purée, and lime crémeux. For

OPPOSITE Harvard Square, home of shops and bookstores that serve the city's multitude of students.

an after-dinner drink, move upstairs to the Parsnip Lounge, overlooking Winthrop Square.

3 *Night Moves* 9:30 p.m.

Take in a late show at the **Brattle Theater** (40 Brattle Street; brattlefilm.org), a legendary arthouse and repertory cinema where offerings range from film noir to quirky fare like a Bugs Bunny Film Festival. At **ImprovBoston** (40 Prospect Street; improvboston.com), a spirited troupe of performers stage-manage chaos in an audience-involving mix of improv, stand-up, and topical sketches. For live music, Harvard Square has the **Sinclair** (52 Church Street; sinclaircambridge.com), with a bar, restaurant, rooftop patio, and 500-seat performance space.

SATURDAY

4 *Canoe With a View* 9:30 a.m.

Your morning can begin with a waterborne tour if you rent a kayak, canoe, or stand-up paddleboard from **Charles River Canoe & Kayak** (15 Broad Canal Way; paddleboston.com). Pilot your watercraft to the Charles River, then under the Longfellow Bridge and upstream to Harvard and beyond, with views of Boston landmarks like the Museum of Science and the Esplanade.

5 *Fast Vegetarian* Noon

Jump into lunch mode at **Clover Food Lab** (5 Cambridge Center; cloverfoodlab.com; $$), run by Ayr Muir, an M.I.T. materials scientist and Harvard M.B.A. grad; his super-fresh vegetarian fast-food joint has more than a dozen Boston-area locations, including four in Cambridge. Look for items like a chickpea fritter, egg and eggplant sandwich, or killer French fries with deep-fried rosemary sprigs. A nearby option where meat is on the menu is **Commonwealth Cambridge** (11 Broad Canal Way: commonwealthcambridge.com; $$), on the patio by the Broad Canal and kayak dock.

6 *Academic Modern* 1 p.m.

You have probably already strolled in Harvard Yard. Now how about a tour of **M.I.T.**? Download a map (institute-events.mit.edu/visit) or campus public art map (listart.mit.edu/public-art-map), and then

wander the campus, where buildings are referred to by number. Highlights include the Frank Gehry-designed Ray and Maria Stata Center (Building 32), which pays tribute to famous M.I.T. hacks, or pranks, such as turning the campus's Great Dome into R2-D2. There's also the List Visual Arts Center (E15), and buildings designed by I. M. Pei (class of '40), Alvar Aalto, and Eduardo Catalano. Outdoor art includes pieces by Picasso and Henry Moore.

7 *Robots and Holograms* 3 p.m.

To study Cambridge's innovative, D.I.Y. spirit, look no further than the **MIT Museum** (265 Massachusetts Avenue; web.mit.edu/museum). You'll find an exhibit documenting the history of artificial intelligence research and robots at M.I.T., an extensive holography collection, and Arthur Ganson's surreal kinetic sculptures — one depicts a tiny chair doing cartwheels over a cat.

8 *Eating Experiments* 7:30 p.m.

Another less-traveled Cambridge neighborhood is Inman Square, near Central. **The Druid** (1357 Cambridge Street; druidpub.com; $), an Irish pub, is perfect for a pint and a tremendous fish sandwich and Irish music. **BISq** (1071 Cambridge Street; bisqcambridge.com; $$$) pursues higher culinary aims with outstanding small plates like roasted chicken ceviche and cornbread blood sausage, plus a board of pastries and sweets called the "dessert charcuterie." For a dining trip that feels like eating a science

experiment, head back to Kendall Square for **Café ArtScience** (650 East Kendall Street; cafeartscience.com; $$$). The ambience is lablike, and the food is wonderfully fussy. Menus here have included smoked duck salad with foie gras "snow," bison tartare, and strawberry lemongrass creamsicle. The bartender's "Le Whaf" cocktails turn liquids into breathable vapor. The devices that hatch them, invented by a Harvard engineering professor, are also on sale.

9 *Massachusetts Night Life* 9:30 p.m.

A bar hop based in grittier Central Square might begin at **Brick & Mortar** (567 Massachusetts Avenue; brickmortarltd.com), a cocktail nook that feels secretive but whose drinks are city-known. Or you might brave the cramped Irish pub and restaurant **Plough and Stars** (912 Massachusetts Avenue; ploughandstars.com), where patrons transition from food to live music. Then there's the celebrated **Middle East and Zuzu** complex (472-480 Massachusetts Avenue; mideastoffers.com), whose four stages host national indie rock acts and D.J. nights.

ABOVE Clover Food Lab specializes in vegetarian fast food and has several locations around town.

RIGHT A colorful pileup at Charles River Canoe & Kayak.

SUNDAY

10 *A Brunch Runs Through It* 10 a.m.

At **Harvest** (44 Brattle Street; harvestcambridge.com; $$$), a Harvard Square classic, one Sunday's three-course prix fixe brunch menu featured dried fruit fritters, the Tom Waits Nighthawks at the Diner Breakfast (eggs and sausage with toast and hash browns) and Taza Chocolate Pâté. After your brunch there, take a peaceful walk along the banks of the Charles River (in the warmer months, Memorial Drive is closed to traffic on Sundays).

11 *Frames and Flora* 12:30 p.m.

After a $350 million rehab by Renzo Piano, Harvard's Fogg, Busch-Reisinger, and Arthur M. Sackler museums, collectively known as the **Harvard Art Museums** (32 Quincy Street; harvardartmuseums.

org), are under one roof; the spectacular collection includes works from nearly every period of art history. Another top draw is the **Harvard Museum of Natural History** (26 Oxford Street; hmnh.harvard.edu), known for its Glass Flowers, intricately made botanical models. The adjacent **Peabody Museum of Archaeology and Ethnology** (11 Divinity Avenue; peabody.harvard.edu) is packed with giant totem poles, casts of Maya stelas, and Penobscot birch bark canoes.

ABOVE The Stata Center, a Frank Gehry-designed contribution to the architecture of the M.I.T. campus.

THE BASICS

Avoid Cambridge's parking-starved streets. Instead of driving, take the MBTA's squeaky Red Line subway, which bisects the city north to south and stops in both Harvard Square and Kendall Square, home to M.I.T.

The Charles Hotel
1 Bennett Street
charleshotel.com
$$$
A known haunt of Bill Clinton and Bill Gates when they come to Harvard.

Mary Prentiss Inn
6 Prentiss Street
maryprentissinn.com
$$$
Gorgeously adapted Greek Revival home in a quiet neighborhood. Near the Red Line.

Hotel Veritas
1 Remington Street
thehotelveritas.com
$$$
Intentionally old-looking 31-room hotel just east of Harvard Square.

Mary Prentiss Inn
Harvard Museum of Natural History
SOMERVILLE AVE.
WASHINGTON ST.
Peabody Museum of Archaeology and Ethnology
WEBSTER AVE.
INNER BELT RD.
28
11 Harvard Art Museums   The Druid
8
MCGRATH HWY.
Area of detail
Harvard Book Store
CAMBRIDGE ST.
2 Mr. Bartley's
BISq
THIRD ST.
BROADWAY
PROSPECT ST.
HAMPSHIRE ST.
SIXTH ST.
1 Hotel Veritas
Cambridge
Grolier Poetry Book Shop
MASSACHUSETTS AVE.
Plough and Stars
ImprovBoston
Café ArtScience
Cambridge
HARVARD YARD —
9 Brick & Mortar
Commonwealth Cambridge
CHURCH ST.
Raven Used Books
Middle East and Zuzu
MAIN ST.
Harvest **10**
The Sinclair
MIT Museum **7**
5
Clover Food Lab
4
3 Brattle Theater
SIDNEY ST.
Charles River Canoe & Kayak
The Million Year Picnic —
Curious George Store
ALBANY ST.
VASSAR ST.
6 Massachusetts Institute of Technology (M.I.T.)
MT. AUBURN ST.
Parsnip Restaurant & Lounge
MEMORIAL DR.
Charles River
The Charles Hotel
WINTHROP ST.
BACK BAY
SOUTH ST.
FENWAY/ KENMORE
1/2 mile
— JOHN F. KENNEDY ST.
1 kilometer

Martha's Vineyard

What is it about presidents (at least Democratic ones) and Martha's Vineyard? The Kennedys have been coming since there were actual vineyards. The Clintons turned up nearly every summer of their White House years, and the Obamas followed. Wealthy A-listers usually hover nearby, hoping for invitations to the same parties where the First Families show up. But part of the Vineyard's appeal is its easy way of shrugging off snobbery. Despite its popularity among the presidential set, this island, off Cape Cod in Massachusetts, is still a laid-back place with a lot of mopeds, fish shacks, and nice beaches. Folks here will tell you that the Vineyard is really just an old fishing community — that is, if you don't get stuck behind a motorcade. — DANIELLE PERGAMENT AND MARY SUH

FRIDAY

1 *Lobster Worship* 5 p.m.

Lobsters are practically a religion on the island, so it's fitting that some of the freshest are served in a church. On summer Fridays from 4:30 to 7:30 p.m., **Grace Church** in the tree-lined town of Vineyard Haven (Woodlawn Avenue and William Street; 508-693-0332) sets up picnic tables and sells lobster rolls — fresh, meaty cuts tossed lightly with mayonnaise and served on soft hot dog buns. Judging by the long lines, the church-supper prices ($20 for lobster roll, chips, and a drink) might be the best deal in town. Sit with fellow worshipers, or take your meal down by the docks for a view of the harbor.

2 *Your Inner Oak Bluffs* 6:30 p.m.

The Vineyard is an island of small towns, and Oak Bluffs is the slightly disheveled member of the family, the one that has a hard time getting dressed for dinner. So, it's a fun place to just stroll. Start by heading for the famed **Trinity Park Tabernacle** (80 Trinity Park; mvcma.org) and its campgrounds. Once a retreat for Methodists, who pitched tents there,

OPPOSITE The Allen Sheep Farm & Wool Company, where even the livestock has an ocean view.

RIGHT By the sea in Oak Bluffs, a town of beaches, boats, and Victorian gingerbread houses.

the area has an open-air auditorium and frequent concerts. Surrounding the park are Lilliputian gingerbread cottages, many dating from the mid-1800s. Once you've seen them, it's not hard to understand why their architectural style is called Carpenter Gothic. Continue your stroll past the marina to the Flying Horses Carousel (15 Oak Bluffs Avenue), the country's oldest operating platform merry-go-round, dating to 1876. Yes, it even has brass rings. Grab one and get a free ride. Then head toward Ocean Park (Seaview Avenue), which is ringed by beautiful old houses. Watch people fly kites, ride bikes, and just hang out.

3 *Secret Sweets* 9 p.m.

On summer nights, in a dark parking lot in Oak Bluffs, a small crowd lines up at the screen door of the **Martha's Vineyard Gourmet Cafe and Bakery** (5 Post Office Square; 508-693-3688), waiting for warm doughnuts right out of the oven. This open secret is known as Back Door Donuts. The doughnuts are soft, sticky, and delicious, though some veterans will tell you the apple fritters are superior.

SATURDAY

4 *Egg Rolls and Wool* 9 a.m.

Get to the **West Tisbury Farmers' Market** (1067 State Road; 508-693-9561; wtfmarket.org) when it opens at 9 so you can watch the stalls being set up — and shop before the best produce is picked over. Take your camera along on this expedition:

you'll find a colorful scene of wildflowers, organic fruits and vegetables, alpaca-yarn clothing, home-made jams, and, somewhat curiously, a stall selling egg rolls.

5 *Say Baaah* 10:30 a.m.

Martha's Vineyard is like a miniature Ireland —roads wind among bright green pastures where sheep, horses, and cattle graze. Many of the farms welcome visitors. The **Allen Farm Sheep & Wool Company** in the bucolic town of Chilmark (421 South Road; 508-645-9064; allenfarm.com) has been run by the same family since 1762. Take in the views of rolling fields. Buy lamb chops or try on a handmade wool sweater in the gift shop. Those things grazing out front? They're lambs, and they're very friendly.

6 *Shore Lunch* 1 p.m.

An up-island summer begs for a walk-up seafood shack, and you'll find it in the old fishing village of Menemsha. **Larsen's Seafood Market** (56 Basin Road; 508-645-2680; larsensfishmarket.com; $$), family-owned and -operated since 1969, serves what many regard as the island's best steamers, quahogs, or clams on the half-shell. Or try the "Lazy Man's Lobster"—pre-cracked for you. Sit at a lobster-trap table on the deck with a view of the busy harbor. Or take your catch to the local beach, footsteps away.

7 *Time in the Sand* 2 p.m.

The nicest beaches on Martha's Vineyard are private; you need a key to get in. But one that's open to the public is **Menemsha Beach**, a lovely stretch of sand just outside of town (ask for directions at Larsen's; you're close). It is popular with families, and in the evening, it's a favorite place to watch the sunset. Swim a little, walk a little, or just hang out.

8 *Take a Hike* 4 p.m.

Yes, the Vineyard looks great from the water. But for a less-photographed view of the island's

natural beauty, drive inland to **Waskosim's Rock Reservation** (mvlandbank.com/13waskosims_rock), a nature reserve with 185 acres of open fields, wooded trails, and marshes. A modest, mile-long hike takes you to Waskosim's Rock, the boulder that divided the island between the English and the native Wampanoag people 350 years ago. Tempting though it may be, resist climbing the rock — Vineyarders want to make sure it's around for another 350.

9 *State Dinner* 8 p.m.

They may not be as famous as the vegetable garden on Pennsylvania Avenue, but the herb and vegetable patches that supply the **State Road** restaurant (688 State Road; 508-693-8582; stateroadmv.com; $$) have their admirers. State Road features American cuisine using local ingredients: lobster, fresh fish, locally raised chicken and lamb, and a bounty of produce from farms on the Vineyard and nearby. The dining room is simple and sleek, with hardwood floors, high ceilings, and Edison bulb chandeliers.

10 *Night at the Ritz* 11 p.m.

The Vineyard isn't known for night life, but your best bet for a nightcap is in the handful of lively bars along Circuit Avenue in Oak Bluffs. Stop by the **Ritz Café** (4 Circuit Avenue; 508-693-9851; theritzmv.com),

which attracts locals and has live music. Don't be fooled by the name; this is more of a draft beer than an appletini kind of joint.

SUNDAY

11 *Stores by the Seashore* 10 a.m.

There's a lot of good shopping between all those seagull paintings and dancing-lobster napkins. In Vineyard Haven, drop by the island's beloved **Bunch of Grapes Bookstore** (23 Main Street, 508-693-2291; bunchofgrapes.com) for a wide selection of nonfiction and fiction, with a number of books on Martha's Vineyard. Up the street is **Nochi** (29 Main Street; 508-693-9074; nochimv.com), which sells robes, blankets, and all things cozy. And down the street

is **LeRoux at Home** (62 Main Street; 508-693-0030; lerouxkitchen.com), a housewares store with a great selection of kitchen supplies, linens, cookbooks, and tableware.

OPPOSITE ABOVE The Menemsha Inn.

OPPOSITE BELOW A view out to sea on a calm day.

ABOVE The twice-a-week West Tisbury Farmers' Market attracts farmers and shoppers from all over the island.

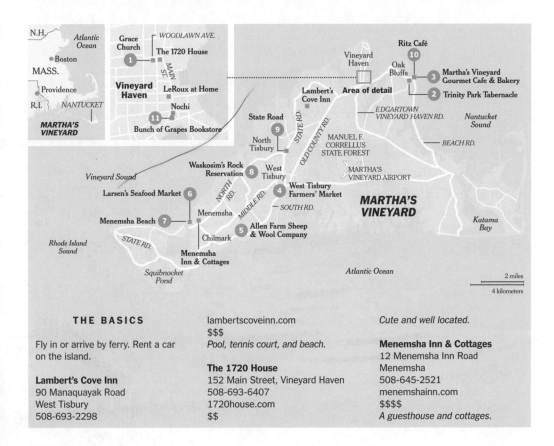

THE BASICS

Fly in or arrive by ferry. Rent a car on the island.

Lambert's Cove Inn
90 Manaquayak Road
West Tisbury
508-693-2298

lambertscoveinn.com
$$$
Pool, tennis court, and beach.

The 1720 House
152 Main Street, Vineyard Haven
508-693-6407
1720house.com
$$

Cute and well located.

Menemsha Inn & Cottages
12 Menemsha Inn Road
Menemsha
508-645-2521
menemshainn.com
$$$$
A guesthouse and cottages.

Nantucket

Near the beginning of Moby-Dick, *Ishmael explains why he decided to set sail from Nantucket: "There was a fine, boisterous something about everything connected with that famous old island." Today, more than a century and a half after it was written, that characterization still rings true. Though its downtown cobblestone streets and windswept fringes are now filled with expensive restaurants and elegant cocktail bars, the island still has a swagger. To see it in full swing, linger over pints at one of the many harborside pubs, especially at sundown when sailors and fishing boats return to port.* — BY SARAH GOLD

FRIDAY

1 *Historic Bearings* 3 p.m.

Main Street is lined with 19th-century storefronts and buckled brick sidewalks that seem to require deck shoes. To bone up on island history, visit **Mitchell's Book Corner** (54 Main Street; 508-228-1080; mitchellsbookcorner.com), a bookstore that first opened in 1968. The beloved Nantucket Room holds hundreds of titles about island lore. The store also hosts weekly readings by such local authors as Elin Hilderbrand and the National Book Award winner Nathaniel Philbrick. A few blocks away, a sister store, **Nantucket Bookworks** (25 Broad Street; 508-228-4000; nantucketbookpartners.com), offers readers more shelves to browse.

2 *Preppy It Up* 5 p.m.

You can still find a bona fide pair of the pinkish chinos called Nantucket Reds at **Murray's Toggery Shop** (62 Main Street; 508-228-0437; nantucketreds.com), and buy sunscreen or fancy bath products at **Nantucket Pharmacy** (45 Main Street; 508-228-0180), another classic of Nantucket shopping. But there are plenty of much newer boutiques to explore. **Jack Wills** (11 South Water Street; 508-332-1601; jackwills.com), the first stateside outpost of the British university outfitter, carries jaunty polos, cable-knit sweaters, and canvas totes in signal-flag colors.

OPPOSITE Yachts rule in Nantucket Harbor, once the refuge of whaling ships.

RIGHT Brant Point Lighthouse in the harbor.

Milly & Grace (2 Washington Street; 508-901-5051; millyandgrace.com) sells youthful summer dresses and tops, jewelry, and home accessories.

3 *Fish of the Moment* 8 p.m.

Dune (20 Broad Street; 508-228-5550; dunenantucket.com; $$$) serves local seafood and produce in a warmly illuminated space. There are three dining rooms as well as a patio, but you'll need to book ahead. Changing menus have included dishes like sautéed local cod with Parmesan broth, wax beans, tomatoes, pea greens, and dill spaetzle. Stop by the petite quartzite bar on your way out.

4 *Beach Martinis* 10 p.m.

A young, tanned crowd fills the back room of **Galley Beach** (54 Jefferson Avenue; 508-228-9641; galleybeach.net; $$$). A cherished beachside restaurant, it has also become a late-night gathering spot, serving wines by the glass and drinks like pear sage martinis. The party also spills outside, where sofas and candlelit tables line the sand.

SATURDAY

5 *Island Market* 10 a.m.

The **Nantucket Farmers & Artisans Market** (Cambridge and North Union Streets; 508-228-3399;

sustainablenantucket.org) offers the wares of dozens of island farmers and artisans throughout the season and hosts workshops to encourage other would-be island growers and craftsmen. Keep an eye out for handmade quilts, freshly picked blueberries and raspberries, and fresh baked goods.

6 *Surf and Seals* Noon

If you're looking for a day of sand and saltwater and don't mind company, decamp to one of the favorite public swimming beaches, like Cisco Beach in the island's southwest, where strong waves draw surfers. But to see a wilder and more natural Nantucket, drive out to the far west end, where the island tapers to the twin forks of **Eel Point** and **Smith's Point**. You'll need to rent a four-by-four — make sure it has a beach-driving permit; if not, you'll have to buy one for $100 to $200 at the Nantucket Police Station. You'll also need to reduce the tire pressure to maximize traction and minimize environmental damage. But after bumping along hillocky dune trails, you'll enter onto wide open, mostly empty shores. There are no amenities to speak of, so bring all the supplies you'll need, including food and water. Oh, and a camera. You might spot gray seals.

7 *Brew with a View* 5 p.m.

An afternoon of salty, sandy fun can leave you pretty thirsty. So it's convenient that you're close to **Millie's** (326 Madaket Road; 508-228-8435; milliesnantucket.com), a fabled west-end watering hole. Millie's takes full advantage of the sunset location. A glassed-in second-floor bar lets you drink in panoramic vistas along with your Grey Lady or Whale's Tale Pale Ale, both from the Cisco Brewery a few miles down the road.

8 *Well-Traveled Palate* 8 p.m.

Nantucket mariners once sailed the world, and that globe-spanning spirit lives on at **Proprietors Bar & Table** (9 India Street; 508-228-7477; proprietorsnantucket.com; $$$). Dishes, many of which are designed to be shared, on one menu ranged from tater cubes topped with joppiesaus, a creamy yellow Dutch sauce; to local monkfish with seafood kibbe; to sliders made from a kimchi biscuit stuffed with pork and barbecue sauce. Wind up with some house-made soft-serve ice cream, then stroll down to the wharves and savor the evening breeze.

SUNDAY

9 *Sea Saviors* 10 a.m.

More than 700 shipwrecks litter the treacherous shoals and surrounding waters around Nantucket. For a fascinating glimpse into the island's underwater heritage, visit the **Nantucket Shipwreck & Lifesaving Museum** (158 Polpis Road; 508-228-1885; nantucketshipwreck.org), which has vintage surfboats once used to save wreck survivors, child-friendly exhibits on Coast Guard sea dogs, and — most chillingly — grainy black-and-white 1956 film footage of one of the most infamous wrecks, the Italian ship *Andrea Doria*, shown slowly listing into the sea after its collision with a Swedish ocean liner.

ABOVE Sunbathing in the Nantucket summer.

BELOW Traditional weathered wooden shingles are everywhere, even on this luxury hotel, the White Elephant.

10 *Beachside Brunch* Noon

The **Summer House Restaurant** in Siasconset village (17 Ocean Avenue; 508-257-9976; thesummerhouse.com; $$$$) is the island's most civilized spot for lunch, especially at its umbrella-shaded Beachside Bistro. Look for jazzed-up summertime classics like crab cake with corn salsa and tarragon aioli or a warm poached lobster salad with green beans and beurre blanc.

11 *Not Quite Open House* 1 p.m.

The **Bluff Walk** in Siasconset village was once the south shore's most fiercely guarded secret. But though you will probably share the unmarked path with other visitors these days, a stroll here is still breathtaking. Pick up the trail in the village center (take a right and then a quick left at the end of Front Street) and walk along the high, Atlantic-skirting bluffs, past some of the island's stateliest gray-shingled private houses. Erosion has left its mark (the last third of a mile, which used to extend all the way to Sankaty Head lighthouse, is now closed). But just stay on the path, keep your voice down, and wear long pants — some residents, whether intentionally or not, let their sections become overgrown.

ABOVE Surfers young and old, beginning and experienced, find waves to fit their skills at Nantucket's beaches.

THE BASICS

Fly into the Nantucket airport or take a ferry from Hyannis, Massachusetts, on Cape Cod. Buses of the Nantucket Regional Transit Authority (nrtawave.com) run all over the island.

The Cottages & Lofts at the Boat Basin
24 Old South Wharf
508-325-1499
thecottagesnantucket.com
$$$$
Shipshape cottages at the harbor.

The White Elephant
50 Easton Street
508-228-2500
whiteelephanthotel.com
$$$$
Harborside patio, spa, and 64 rooms, suites, and cottages.

The Union Street Inn
7 Union Street
508-228-9222
unioninn.com
$$$
In a 1770 house.

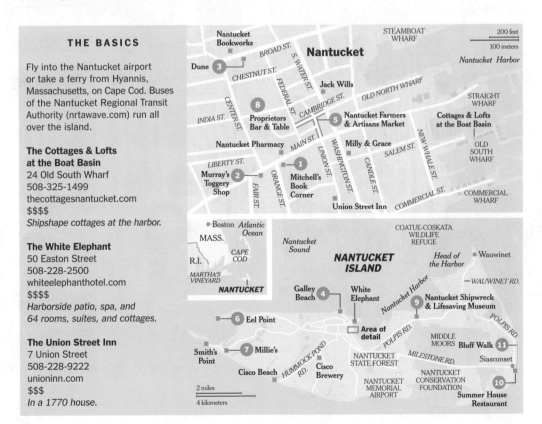

Provincetown

Park yourself anywhere on Commercial Street, the bustling main artery of Provincetown, and you will see celebrities, some real (John Waters, Paula Poundstone), some fake (that wasn't Cher). But mostly you will see ordinary people — lesbian, gay, bisexual, transgendered, and none of the above. Of the first 100 obvious couples to walk past Wired Puppy, a coffee-and-Wi-Fi joint, one typical summer night, 28 were female-female, 31 male-male, and 41 male-female. Four hundred years after the Pilgrims arrived here on the Mayflower, *water is still Provincetown's raison d'être; it provides the gorgeous scenery and the cod, sole, haddock, clams, lobsters, and oysters that make this a food lover's paradise. The trick, as in any resort town, is to eat at odd hours, which makes it possible to avoid crowds even on weekends. And then exercise. With great places to walk, bike, and swim, Provincetown makes burning calories as much fun as consuming them.* — BY FRED A. BERNSTEIN

FRIDAY

1 *On Two Wheels* 4 p.m.

Try to arrive in Provincetown by plane or boat. A car is useless in Provincetown, and besides, you can't really appreciate the place unless you see it as the Pilgrims saw it — on the ground, with the ocean out the front door and a vast bay out the back. Have the taxi driver take you straight to **Ptown Bikes** (42 Bradford Street; 508-487-8735; ptownbikes.com) for a reasonably priced bicycle rental. Then beat the evening crowd with an early trip to **Fanizzi's by the Sea** (539 Commercial Street; 508-487-1964; fanizzisrestaurant.com; $$), where you can find cold beer and the classic fish and chips, lightly battered fried clams, or a local fishermen's platter.

2 *Dune Buggin'* 5:30 p.m.

Time to burn off some of what you just ate. Ride your bike southwest to the end of Commercial Street, turn right at the traffic circle, and pedal till you see the Herring Cove Beach parking lot. At the end of the lot, a small opening in the fence leads to the bike trail into the **Province Lands** (nps.gov/caco). It's a five-foot-wide strip of asphalt that swoops up and down the dunes like a glorious doodle. It's about four miles to **Race Point**

Beach — perhaps the town's most breathtaking stretch of sand. Fill up at the water fountain and return to town in time for sunset.

3 *Night Galleries* 7:30 p.m.

Park your bike at the **Provincetown Art Association and Museum** (460 Commercial Street; 508-487-1750; paam.org). The town's premier art space, it grew with a smart addition by Machado and Silvetti (the architects of the Getty Villa restoration in Los Angeles). It's open till 10 p.m. (and free) on Friday nights. There are dozens of other galleries in Provincetown, and they, too, are open late on Fridays. Walk through the commercial district and drop in on a few.

4 *Love the Night Life* 10 p.m.

The **Crown & Anchor** (247 Commercial Street; 508-487-1430; onlyatthecrown.com) offers one-stop shopping for gay entertainment. Arrayed around its courtyard are a disco with laser lights and throbbing speakers, a leather bar with hirsute habitués, a piano

OPPOSITE Leave the car at home. Provincetown's main drag, Commercial Street, is best navigated on foot or by bicycle.

BELOW A trail ride down the Beech Forest Trail in the Province Lands area.

bar where everyone knows the lyrics, and more. When the bars close at 1 a.m., follow the crowd to **Spiritus Pizza** (190 Commercial Street; 508-487-2808; spirituspizza.com; $). Some call it the "sidewalk sale"—the last chance for a hookup—but really it's a giant block party. The pizza, with thin crust and more marinara than cheese, is super.

SATURDAY

5 *Window Seat* 10 a.m.

If your hotel doesn't have breakfast, head to **Cafe Heaven** (199 Commercial Street; 508-487-9639; cafeheavenptown.com; $$) for delicious omelets, house-made granola, and banana pancakes. From

behind its big windows, you can peruse the local papers for concert and theater listings.

6 *Stairway After Heaven* 11:30 a.m.

You loved those pancakes. Now work them off at the **Pilgrim Monument**, a gray stone crenellated tower that has looked out over the town and out to sea since 1910 (pilgrim-monument.org). Buy a bottle of water from the machine outside and then start climbing; a mix of stairs and ramps will take you to the top of the 252-foot tower. On a clear day, you can see the tops of Boston's tallest buildings.

7 *The End of Cape Cod* 1 p.m.

Stop at **Angel Foods** in the East End (467 Commercial Street; 508-487-6666; angelfoods.com) for takeout—ask for the delicious lobster cakes and a savory curry chicken salad. With lunch in your backpack, ride to the traffic circle at the end of Commercial Street and lock your bike to the split-rail fence. Walk out onto the breakwater, a 1.2-mile-long line of rocks the size of automobiles. After a spectacular 25-minute trek, you'll find yourself on a deserted beach.

ABOVE The West End, at Provincetown Harbor.

LEFT Provincetown is on the East Coast, but its location at the end of curving Cape Cod makes it a good place for watching sunsets, like this one at Herring Cove Beach.

8 *Retail Corridor* 4 p.m.

Time to shop. **Loveland** (120 Commercial Street; 508-413-9500; lovelandprovincetown.com) is a bohemian marine boutique that stocks little treasures like Artiga totes or pottery and woodblock prints from the local artist Gail Browne. Inspired by '70s graphics, Tim Convery, owner of the clothing shop **Tim-Scapes** (208 Commercial Street; 917-626-4052; tim-scapes.com), uses duct tape to create Provincetown-inspired designs. At **Alice Brock Studio** (69 Commercial Street; 508-487-2127; alicebrock.com), you may meet the proprietor, who sells her artwork here. It's not her first commercial venture — she is the Alice immortalized by Arlo Guthrie in the song *Alice's Restaurant*.

9 *Inn Fare* 8:30 p.m.

You've planned ahead and made a reservation weeks in advance, so claim your spot at the **Red Inn**

ABOVE AND BELOW Walkers on the breakwater and the view inland from Cape Cod Bay.

(15 Commercial Street; 508-487-7334; theredinn.com; $$-$$$), a 200-plus-year-old house that has been beautifully maintained and updated. The food is not adventurous (pan-roasted cod, Long Island duck, lamb chops with a Dijon crust), but it is well prepared, and the place is gorgeous, with tongue-and-groove paneling over a bay window in the back room, fireplaces, a great barroom, and a deck right on the water.

SUNDAY

10 *Portuguese Breakfast* 10 a.m.

This time, have breakfast at **Chach** (73 Shank Painter Road; 508-487-1530; chachprovincetown.com; $$), an update on the diner theme with a retro checkered floor and vinyl booths. There are plenty

of typical breakfast choices, and this is a good place for Portuguese sweet bread, a nod to the Portuguese fishermen who once dominated this town. The abundant cod that sustained them are largely fished out, but Provincetown celebrates Portuguese traditions with an annual summer festival.

11 *The Windblown Shore* 1 p.m.
    Take a guided trip by S.U.V. through the **Cape Cod National Seashore** with **Art's Dune Tours** (4 Standish

Street; 508-487-1950; artsdunetours.com). The tour ventures out into the sand dunes on protected lands at the tip of Cape Cod, and will take you past dune shacks where such writers and artists as Eugene O'Neill, Jack Kerouac, Tennessee Williams, and Jackson Pollock once spent summers working in near total isolation. The dunes are a magical experience, and the guides are happy to share their knowledge about the people who once lived here and the hardy plants and wildlife that find sustenance in this remote and windy spot.

ABOVE A view along Commercial Street.

OPPOSITE Although Provincetown today is anything but austere, the Pilgrim Monument celebrates its Puritan roots.

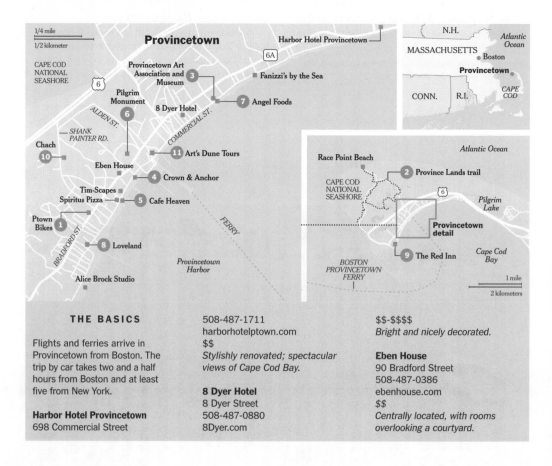

THE BASICS

Flights and ferries arrive in Provincetown from Boston. The trip by car takes two and a half hours from Boston and at least five from New York.

Harbor Hotel Provincetown
698 Commercial Street

508-487-1711
harborhotelptown.com
$$
Stylishly renovated; spectacular views of Cape Cod Bay.

8 Dyer Hotel
8 Dyer Street
508-487-0880
8Dyer.com

$$-$$$$
Bright and nicely decorated.

Eben House
90 Bradford Street
508-487-0386
ebenhouse.com
$$
Centrally located, with rooms overlooking a courtyard.

The Bay of Fundy

At Fundy National Park in New Brunswick, the salty ocean air is laced with the scent of pine. The park's smooth lakes and quiet forests would be enough alone to make it one of Canada's favorites. But the real wonder here is a strange natural phenomenon: the sweeping tides of the Bay of Fundy. Residents around the bay say its tides are the highest in the world, and only a bay in far northern Quebec challenges the claim; the Canadian government diplomatically calls it a tie. Highest or not, the Fundy tides are extreme and dramatic, rising at their largest surge by 33 feet and leaving, when they recede, vast tidal flats ready for exploring. Tourists who drive north through New Brunswick on their way to Fundy will be struck by the forests stretching to the horizon and by the comfortable mix of French and English influences that has cashiers and waitresses calling out "Hello bonjour!"
— BY KAREN HOUPPERT

FRIDAY

1 *Park Central* 3 p.m.

The main attraction is **Fundy National Park** (506-887-6000; pc.gc.ca/eng/pn-np/nb/fundy/index.aspx), which covers about 50,000 acres and is laced with trails and sprinkled with campsites that make it a paradise for backpackers. Away from the hub of activity around the park headquarters (and not counting the surprising presence of a nine-hole golf course), there are few tourist services. Get your bearings at the **Visitor Reception Centre**, close to the southeastern park entrance near the gateway town of Alma. Pick up maps, find out about the interpretive programs for the weekend, and most important, check the tide tables.

2 *Fundy Fare* 6 p.m.

Drive into Alma for dinner (there's no dining in the park itself). You'll find lobster with a view at the **Tides Restaurant**, located in the **Parkland Village Inn** (8601 Main Street, Alma; 506-887-2313;

OPPOSITE AND RIGHT Fundy National Park's 68 miles of well-tended trails wind into forests and meadows, past waterfalls and beaver dams. Although spectacular tides, rising 33 feet, are the area's major attraction, the park is also prized for its inland natural beauty.

parklandvillageinn.com; $$), where the dining room overlooks the bay. The choices run to the traditional and hearty, including steaks and various kinds of Atlantic seafood, good for packing it in at the start of an active weekend. Tables at the Tides can fill up fast, so take care to reserve in advance.

3 *Brushwork* 7 p.m.

Fundy's vast, muddy stretches of beach make for poor swimming, even at high tide. The water remains shallow for a quarter mile out to sea. The park does its best to compensate, offering visitors a swim in its heated salt-water pool overlooking the bay. But if the Bay of Fundy is not great for swimming, it is a sensuous delight. As evening approaches, stroll along the coastal paths to take it in. At dusk, as the fog rolls in, the hills and cliffs beyond the shore shimmer with the deep green of thousands of pines. The silky-smooth red clay of the tidal flat provides a rich saturation of complementary color. It's like stepping into a Van Gogh.

SATURDAY

4 *Sticky Fingers* 9 a.m.

You could go for the fresh home-baked bread or doughnuts, or come back at lunch for sandwiches and chili, but the star of the show at **Kelly's Bake Shop**

(8587 Main Street, Alma; 506-887-2460) is the sticky bun. Locally renowned and alluring for tourists, the buns keep customers lined up at Kelly's, which sells as many as 3,000 of them on a busy day. They're sweet, flavorful, and enormous. Don't expect to eat more than one.

5 *Reset the Clock* 9:30 a.m.

Venture to one of Alma's two small general stores to pick up provisions for later. Then consult your new clock, the lunar version that announces itself in the Fundy tides. It's important to be at the beach when the mud flats are exposed — that's the experience that draws people here. So plan your day accordingly — not by the numbers on your watch or cellphone, but by the water's flow.

6 *Out to Sea* Low Tide

At low tide the vast intertidal zone is other-worldly: endless red muddy flats, shallow pools, and sporadic, massive barnacle-covered boulders that appear to have been randomly dropped into the muddy flatness from an alien spaceship. Beachcombers can walk along the exposed ocean floor, hunting for shells and bits of sea-smoothed glass, for more than half a mile before they reach the water's edge. The impulse to scoop up the clay underfoot and squeeze it through your fingers is hard to suppress. While grown-up travelers seem to enjoy the delightful respite the wet clay of the bare ocean floor provides to tired feet after a hard day of hiking, kids have been known to do full body rolls in the squishy muck. The spot where you're standing will probably be under water again before long, but there's no need to fear. The tide's return is gradual, progressive, and orderly — very Canadian — and nicely nudges you back shoreward with small, gentle, very cold waves.

7 *Into the Woods* High Tide

When the water claims the beach, go hiking. The park's 68 miles of well-tended trails wind deep into forests and flower-strewn meadows, past waterfalls and beaver dams, and even to a covered bridge. By the standards of many busier parks, it is blissfully quiet. Even in August, the prime season, it is possible for hikers to trek the 2.8-mile **Matthews Head** trail along the park's rocky southern shore and not pass a single person. The path offers teasing ocean views from atop red-clay cliffs that drop to the sea. Amid the solitude is a silence so pervasive that even children grow pensive at the wonder of these headlands, which feel like the end of the earth.

8 *Shell and Claw* 7 p.m.

Do as the locals do and find a table at the **Harbour View Market & Restaurant** (8598 Main Street, Alma; 506-887-2450; $). You can get your daily ration of shell-fish — in the seafood chowder or a lobster roll — and perhaps pick up some local gossip at the same time.

9 *Nature Theater* 8 p.m.

Don't look for rangers at Fundy National Park — here they are interpreters. The staff is serious about the job of making Fundy accessible, and in summer there is a program almost every night at the **Outdoor Theatre**. You may learn about the wildlife, from moose and bears to flying squirrels. You may hear about the rivers that wash kayakers upstream when the tide comes in, the whales and migratory

birds that thrive offshore, or the area's history—this is Acadia, where French and English cultures clashed and mingled. Expect a multimedia experience, with video, music, comedy, or even drama.

SUNDAY

10 *Water Power* 10 a.m.

For an appropriate last stop, drive about 25 miles north of Alma to Hopewell Cape, where the bay shore is littered with eroded sea stacks known as the **Flowerpot Rocks**. See them from a clifftop trail, and if it's low tide inspect them close up, at the **Hopewell Rocks Ocean Tidal Exploration Site** (Highway 114; 877-734-3429; thehopewellrocks.ca). Resembling pillars or top-heavy mushrooms, some with trees growing on their tops, the rocks are part of a rugged shoreline of caves, tunnels, and misshapen crags, all

of it a testament to the relentless force of the water constantly tugged back and forth against the shore by the Fundy tides.

OPPOSITE ABOVE The world's highest tides (officially tied with those in a more remote Quebec bay) flow out to leave vast flats for exploring.

OPPOSITE BELOW Matthews Head, a high rocky headland on the Fundy coast.

ABOVE A sunrise over Owl's Head, seen from Alma Beach in Fundy National Park.

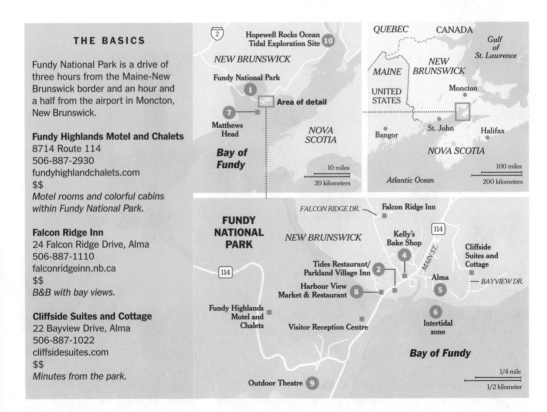

THE BASICS

Fundy National Park is a drive of three hours from the Maine-New Brunswick border and an hour and a half from the airport in Moncton, New Brunswick.

Fundy Highlands Motel and Chalets
8714 Route 114
506-887-2930
fundyhighlandchalets.com
$$
Motel rooms and colorful cabins within Fundy National Park.

Falcon Ridge Inn
24 Falcon Ridge Drive, Alma
506-887-1110
falconridgeinn.nb.ca
$$
B&B with bay views.

Cliffside Suites and Cottage
22 Bayview Drive, Alma
506-887-1022
cliffsidesuites.com
$$
Minutes from the park.

Hopewell Rocks Ocean Tidal Exploration Site 10

NEW BRUNSWICK

Fundy National Park 1

Area of detail

Matthews Head 7

Bay of Fundy

10 miles
20 kilometers

QUEBEC   CANADA
Gulf of St. Lawrence

MAINE   NEW BRUNSWICK

UNITED STATES   Moncton

Bangor   St. John   Halifax

NOVA SCOTIA

Atlantic Ocean

100 miles
200 kilometers

NOVA SCOTIA

FUNDY NATIONAL PARK

FALCON RIDGE DR.   Falcon Ridge Inn

NEW BRUNSWICK   Kelly's Bake Shop   114

Cliffside Suites and Cottage

Tides Restaurant/ Parkland Village Inn 2   MAIN ST.   Alma 5   BAYVIEW DR.

114   Harbour View Market & Restaurant 8   4

Fundy Highlands Motel and Chalets   Visitor Reception Centre   Intertidal zone 6

Bay of Fundy

Outdoor Theatre 9

1/4 mile
1/2 kilometer

Cape May

One of the oldest seaside resorts in the nation, Cape May, the southernmost town on the New Jersey coast, has welcomed vacationers for more than 200 years. The entire city is a National Historic Landmark, with hundreds of sturdily built Victorian houses — and fortunately, Hurricane Sandy, which ravaged much of the Jersey Shore, spared the 3.5-square-mile island on which this town is built. Yet despite its antique look, Cape May knows how to embrace a more modern persona as well. Several of its once-faded grande dame hotels and low-slung motels have been updated and transformed into chic escapes for stylish beachgoers. Located on the Atlantic Flyway, Cape May is also an internationally renowned birding hot spot, especially busy with the bird-watching crowd during the avian migration seasons in spring and fall.
— BY MICHELLE HIGGINS AND LOUISE TUTELIAN

FRIDAY

1 *Catch of the Day* 4:30 p.m.

Crowds gather early at the **Lobster House** on Fisherman's Wharf (906 Schellengers Landing Road; 609-884-8296; thelobsterhouse.com; $$), which serves up traditional surf 'n' turf dishes, with the catch often hauled in by its own fleet of commercial fishing boats. Because the restaurant doesn't take reservations, securing a spot in one of its traditional dining rooms often involves a wait of at least an hour. To avoid the bedlam, head to the dockside Raw Bar and order a lobster platter and a beer. Then stake out a shaded table alongside the ships in Cape May Harbor. Another option: hop aboard the *Schooner American*, a 130-foot-long sailing vessel turned cocktail lounge that's moored alongside the restaurant, for appetizers. Have kids? Call in your order to the Lobster House's Take-Out shop (609-884-3064), which offers a kids' menu online, so it's ready when you arrive.

OPPOSITE The Cape May Lighthouse, a favorite symbol of this traditional summer beach town. The entire city is a National Historic Landmark.

RIGHT It's 199 steps to the top (and 199 back down), but the panoramic view of New Jersey and Delaware from the top of the lighthouse is worth the climb.

2 *Shop and Stroll* 7 p.m.

Burn off your meal with a stroll along the **Washington Street Mall** (washingtonstreetmall.com), a three-block pedestrian concourse between Perry and Ocean Streets that is lined with clothing boutiques, kitschy souvenir shops, toy stores, and candy and ice cream shops. Many stay open until 9 p.m. on summer weekends. Then make your way to Cape May's so-called boardwalk, a paved promenade just a few blocks away that runs parallel to the beach for nearly two miles. Stop in at the **Family Fun Arcade** (Beach Avenue and Howard Street; 609-884-7020) for Skee-Ball, photo booth shots, and games.

3 *Bar Below* 9 p.m.

Duck into the cavelike Boiler Room in the basement of the **Congress Hall hotel** (Beach Avenue and Congress Street, with an entrance on Congress Place; 609-884-8421; caperesorts.com/hotels/capemay/congresshall) for drinks, dancing, and live music. Exposed brick walls, low red lighting, and fixtures from days when this really was a boiler room all lend the bar a cool industrial feel.

SATURDAY

4 *On the Wing* 7:30 a.m.

Cape May is on the Atlantic Flyway, one of the planet's busiest bird migratory corridors, navigated

by hundreds of species in spring and fall. Because of its location amid barrier islands and wetlands, fresh water and ocean, birds come to rest, eat, and nest. Things are calmer in summer, but there are still plenty of birds to be seen, especially with the help of a good guide. The **Cape May Bird Observatory** (701 East Lake Drive, Cape May Point; 609-884-2736; birdcapemay.org) sponsors naturalist-led walks early on many Saturdays and also offers free maps for self-guided walks. Not a birder? Start your day with a flowing yoga class offered on either the beach or amid the scent of hydrangeas on the expansive lawn in front of the Congress Hall hotel, depending on the heat and humidity. Sign up and grab a mat at the check-in desk in the hotel lobby. Afterward, load up on carbs with a pancake platter at **Uncle Bill's Pancake House** (261 Beach Avenue; 609-884-7199; unclebillspancakehouse.com).

ABOVE Quiet, smoothly paved streets and a bicycle-friendly attitude make cycling one of the best ways to get around in Cape May. Rentals are easy to find, and some inns provide bikes for their guests.

OPPOSITE ABOVE Hundreds of substantial and well preserved Victorian houses and inns give Cape May its distinctive architectural look. Many have multi-level porches facing the water and cooled by the ocean breeze.

5 *Hit the Beach* 11 a.m.

You can pick up your beach tags (required on summer days) at any beach entrance. Need chairs? **Steger Beach Service** (609-884-3058; stegerbeachservice.com), which rents umbrellas, chairs, and other beach gear from 12 locations along Cape May's wide stretch of beach, will stake out your spot in the sand.

6 *Family Affair* 2 p.m.

Beachgoers line up for American fare with a Greek twist and a seat at one of the cozy booths at **George's Place** (301 Beach Avenue; 609-884-6088; $$), originally opened by George Tsiartsionis, the father-in-law of the current owner, John Karapanagiotis, in 1968. Family portraits line the walls. The lemon chicken Greek salad is a good bet after the beach, but if you need a reminder that you are close to Philadelphia, order the substantial cheese steak. Another option: just down the block, the **Y.B.** (314 Beach Avenue; 609-898-2009), run by George's brother, Peter, who has cooked under the chef Georges Perrier at Le Bec-Fin in Philadelphia, offers a range of salads and sandwiches in a small but inviting space decorated in black and white. Both restaurants are cash-only.

7 *Just a Summer Cottage* 3:30 p.m.

Now that you've crisscrossed the streets amid Cape May's majestic Victorian houses, satisfy

your curiosity about what lies behind the ginger-bread with a tour of the **Emlen Physick Estate** (1048 Washington Street; 609-884-5404; capemaymac. org), a mansion constructed for a Philadelphia physician in the Stick style of the late 1800s. Fifteen of the rooms have been restored with historical accuracy, and the lavish interiors shed some light on how the privileged social leaders of Cape May's affluent summer colony vacationed in their 19th-century heyday.

8 *Beach Shack Update* 6:30 p.m.

Order a beer and a bucket of peel-and-eat shrimp at the bustling **Rusty Nail** (205 Beach Avenue; 609-884-0017; beachshack.com/rusty-nail. php; $), an updated twist on a surfer bar that occupied the same spot in the '70s. It's equal parts hip, family-friendly, and laid-back, depending on the spot you snag. Families congregate around the fire pit and picnic tables, a young crowd lines the bar inside, and heavily tanned locals gather around the outdoor tap, singing to the Grateful Dead and Melissa Etheridge covered by local musicians.

RIGHT When the summer crowd has departed, the birders take over, drawn in spring and fall by migrators stopping off on their seasonal journeys. Cape May is well known as a prime spot for seeing birds in variety and abundance.

SUNDAY

9 *The Pig Is Blue* 8:30 a.m.

Fuel up for a morning bike ride at Congress Hall's **Blue Pig Tavern** (251 Beach Avenue; 609-884-8422; caperesorts.com/restaurants/capemay/bluepigtavern; $$), which serves fresh and simple American fare and offers crayons for the kids. Ask for a seat in the outdoor courtyard next to the trickling fountain and order a side of turkey sausage for sustenance.

10 *On Two Wheels* 9 a.m.

Rent some wheels at nearby **Shields Bike Rental** (11 Gurney Street; 609-898-1818; shieldsbikerental.

com). Flat roads, wide shoulders, and slow-moving traffic make Cape May perfect for the casual bike rider. If you want to make the beachfront promenade part of your ride, do so before 10 a.m.; later than that, bikes are not allowed.

11 *One Last Look* 11 a.m.

If you have the energy to keep pedaling, take Broadway to Sunset Boulevard to visit the **Cape May Lighthouse** (609-884-5404; capemaymac.org),

built in 1859 and in continuous operation ever since. It's in Cape May Point State Park. Climb the spiraling 199-step staircase, and at the top you'll be rewarded with a panoramic vista of the Cape May Peninsula, with a sweeping view of the coast from Wildwood to the north to—on a clear day—Cape Henlopen, Delaware, to the west.

ABOVE The wildlife refuge at Cape May Point is a rest stop on the migratory path along the Atlantic Seaboard for millions of birds. This guest is a cedar waxwing.

OPPOSITE Elaborate gingerbread exteriors, a hallmark of lavishly decorated Victorian houses, survive in style in Cape May. This building is the Virginia Hotel.

THE BASICS

Drive 160 miles from New York City or 95 miles from Philadelphia. A bicycle is handy to use around town.

Virginia Hotel
25 Jackson Street
609-884-5700
virginiahotel.com
$$-$$$$
Boutique hotel that looks the part, with sophisticated design and plush amenities, half a block from the beach.

Congress Hall
251 Beach Avenue
609-884-8421
congresshall.com
$$-$$$$
Steps from the beach in the center of town, with pool and spa.

Queen Victoria Bed & Breakfast
102 Ocean Street
609-884-8702
queenvictoria.com
$$$-$$$$
Choose from among 32 rooms and suites in four luxuriously renovated Victorian buildings.

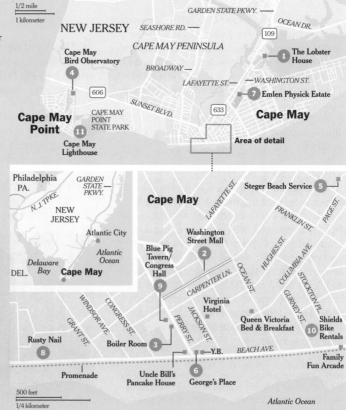

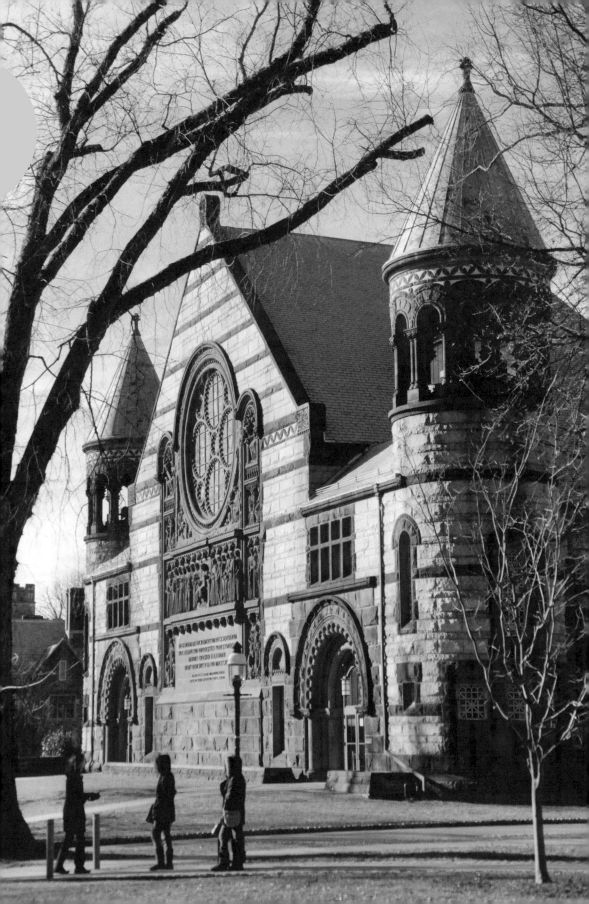

Princeton

"I think of Princeton as being lazy and good-looking and aristocratic — you know, like a spring day," F. Scott Fitzgerald *wrote in* This Side of Paradise. *More than 90 years later, the appraisal still fits. From the century-old wrought-iron FitzRandolph Gate of Princeton University to the sleek rowing shells on sparkling Lake Carnegie, this small New Jersey town retains an air of easygoing noblesse. It is studded with landmarks, from a Revolutionary War battlefield to Albert Einstein's workplace, but nevertheless lives firmly in the present — traditional but not stuffy, charming but not quaint. In the tree-shaded downtown, Colonial-era buildings and high-end spots coexist with jeans-and-corduroy vegetarian hangouts and ice cream shops. And the campus is its own luxurious green city, in the words of Raymond Rhinehart, author of a guide to campus architecture, "a marketplace of ideas, set in a garden."* — BY LOUISE TUTELIAN

FRIDAY

1 *Catch of the Day* 6 p.m.

There's great fishing at the **Blue Point Grill** (258 Nassau Street; 609-921-1211; bluepointgrill.com; $$-$$$). The menu typically lists more than 20 fish specials, from Barnegat sea scallops to Brazilian swordfish. It's B.Y.O., but not to worry: **Nassau Liquors Grape & Grain** (264 Nassau Street; 609-924-0031) is a handy half-block away.

2 *The Flavor of the Place* 8 p.m.

Get out onto Nassau Street, Princeton's main street, to window-shop the bookstores and boutiques, check out vintage buildings, and peek down side streets at beautifully kept Victorian houses. The red-brick **Bainbridge House** (158 Nassau Street), dating to 1766, houses the **Historical Society of Princeton**. The Tudor Revival building at 92 Nassau Street, built in 1896, was once a Princeton dormitory.

SATURDAY

3 *Stack 'em Up* 8 a.m.

Get up and go early to **PJ's Pancake House** (154 Nassau Street; 609-924-1353; pancakes.com; $$), Princeton's breakfast nook since 1962, with the initial-carved wooden tables to prove it. Students,

young families, and gray-haired couples rub elbows while plunging their forks into the tender pancakes — buttermilk, blueberry, buckwheat, and more — served with eggs and bacon. After breakfast, stroll down to the **Princeton University Store** (114 Nassau Street; 609-921-8500; pustore.com) and pick up a map of the university campus. (Online maps are at princeton.edu.)

4 *Take a Tiger by the Tail* 9 a.m.

The bronze tigers flanking the entrance to **Nassau Hall** are a fitting invitation to the architecturally rich Princeton University campus, though their dignity is compromised by the generations of children who have clambered over them. Built in 1756, Nassau Hall survived bombardment in the Revolution and now holds the office of the university president. Alexander Hall has echoed with the words of speakers from William Jennings Bryan to Art Buchwald; Prospect House, deeper into the campus, was Woodrow Wilson's home when he was president of the university. Don't be surprised if a wedding is under way at University Chapel, a Gothic-style landmark. The Frank Gehry-designed **Peter B. Lewis Science Library**, opened in 2008, adds swooping stainless-steel curves to Princeton. The 87,000-square-foot building includes a second-floor "tree house" with 34-foot-high ceilings and clerestory

OPPOSITE Alexander Hall has echoed with the words of speakers from William Jennings Bryan to Art Buchwald.

BELOW The 18th-century Nassau Inn.

windows framing the trees outside. All over campus, look for unusual spires and whimsical gargoyles of cackling monkeys, dinosaurs, and dragons.

5 *Art in the Heart of Campus* 10:30 a.m.

Besides giving Princeton one of the richest endowments of any university in the world, wealthy benefactors have provided it with a wealth of outstanding art from many eras at the **Princeton University Art Museum** (609-258-3788; artmuseum. princeton.edu). Don't rush it — there are more than 60,000 works, and the galleries are spacious, peaceful, blessedly uncrowded — and free. The pre-Columbian and Asian collections are notable, but you can also see Monet's *Water Lilies and Japanese Bridge* and Warhol's *Blue Marilyn*. If you remember reading the 2004 best-selling novel *The Rule of Four*, set on the Princeton campus, picture the student heroes sneaking around these premises in the dark.

6 *Follow the Icons* 12:30 p.m.

Pick up a sandwich on excellent fresh bread at the **Terra Momo Bread Company** (74 Witherspoon Street; 609-688-0188; terramomo.com; $) and set out to trace the footsteps of giants. "It's a fine fox hunt, boys!" George Washington is said to have cried to his troops as the British fled from them on Jan. 3, 1777, at **Princeton Battlefield** (500 Mercer Road in neighboring Princeton Township; 609-921-0074; state.nj.us/dep/

parksandforests/parks/princeton.html). The victory helped restore faith in the American cause at a critical time in the war. Check out the small museum and picture the troops clashing where students now sunbathe. Back toward town on Mercer Road, turn right onto Olden Lane to reach the **Institute for Advanced Study** (1 Einstein Drive; 609-734-8000; ias.edu). Einstein used to walk to work there from his house at 112 Mercer Street — sometimes, legend has it, after forgetting to put on his socks. The buildings, still a rarefied haven for distinguished scholars, are closed to the public, but the 500-acre Institute Woods, where violets bloom along the banks of the Stony Brook, is open to the public year-round.

7 *Relativity and Retail* 3 p.m.

Only in Princeton will you find a store that combines an Einstein mini-museum with great deals on woolens. Walk directly to the rear of **Landau of Princeton** (102 Nassau Street; 609-924-3494; landauprinceton.com) to see the Einstein photos, letters, and sketches. Then check out the pop-top mittens made of Alpaca yarn, perfect for texting.

ABOVE Lewis Science Library, designed by Frank Gehry.

OPPOSITE ABOVE The tap room at the Nassau Inn.

OPPOSITE BELOW Bronze tigers guard Nassau Hall.

Steps away in Palmer Square, dozens of shops sell well-designed and indulgent goods from eye kohls to stemware and sandals. Revive at the **Bent Spoon** ice cream shop (35 Palmer Square West; 609-924-2368; thebentspoon.net), whose owners pledge to use local, organic, and hormone-free ingredients whenever possible in the treats they make fresh every day. Who knew nectarine sorbet could taste so good?

8 *For the Record* 5 p.m.

Since 1980, the **Princeton Record Exchange** (20 South Tulane Street; 609-921-0881; prex.com) has been dispensing used vinyl, CDs, and DVDs at irresistible prices. The store, which is open to 9 p.m., crams 150,000 items onto its floor at any one time.

9 *Sustainable Dining* 8 p.m.

One relaxing choice for dinner is **Mediterra** (29 Hulfish Street; 609-252-9680; terramomo.com; $$$), where wines from 10 countries line the walls; look for paella or locally raised chicken. Locally sourced and sustainable food is the focus at **elements** (66 Witherspoon Street; 609-924-0078; elementsprinceton.com; $$$). Monkfish and other seafood are from area waters.

10 *Brews and Blues* 10 p.m.

You may hear anything from pop to blues to classic rock 'n' roll for a modest cover at **Triumph Brewing Company** (138 Nassau Street; 609-924-7855; triumphbrewing.com), where the crowd is student-heavy but not raucous. A busy bar dispenses handcrafted beers, and physics graduate students rub elbows with 40-somethings escaping their teenage children.

SUNDAY

11 *The Tow Path* 11 a.m.

Rent a mountain bike at **Jay's Cycles** (249 Nassau Street; 609-924-7233; jayscycles.com) and cruise southeast on Alexander Street for about a mile and a half until you see Turning Basin Park on the right. You'll be next to the Delaware-Raritan Canal tow path, a level dirt trail that is a delightful place to walk, bike, or jog. If you'd rather be

on the water, you can stow the bike at **Princeton Canoe & Kayak Rental** (483 Alexander Street; 609-452-2403; canoenj.com) and rent a watercraft. Make your way a half-mile up to the Washington Road Bridge and look for impossibly fit young Princetonians sculling under a bright blue spring sky on Lake Carnegie.

ABOVE Regulars can browse the 150,000 or so titles at the Princeton Record Exchange, open since 1980. The store is known for its selection of vinyl.

OPPOSITE Students walk the Princeton University campus, which in the words of Raymond Rhinehart is "a marketplace of ideas, set in a garden."

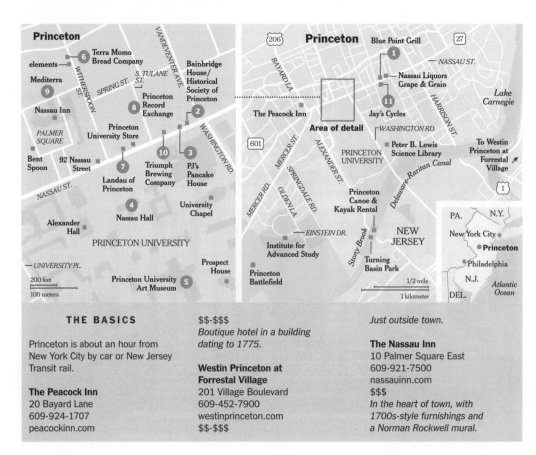

THE BASICS

Princeton is about an hour from New York City by car or New Jersey Transit rail.

The Peacock Inn
20 Bayard Lane
609-924-1707
peacockinn.com

$$-$$$
Boutique hotel in a building dating to 1775.

Westin Princeton at Forrestal Village
201 Village Boulevard
609-452-7900
westinprinceton.com
$$-$$$

Just outside town.

The Nassau Inn
10 Palmer Square East
609-921-7500
nassauinn.com
$$$
In the heart of town, with 1700s-style furnishings and a Norman Rockwell mural.

East Hampton

On the east end of Long Island, New York, the Atlantic Ocean crashes onto the shores of the lavish string of villages known as the Hamptons. When New York City's movers and shakers migrate here in the summer for sunning, surfing, fishing, and flirting, the center of the social swirl is historic East Hampton. Lately a raft of luxurious boutiques and restaurants have opened in town. Beloved old hotels and barrooms have been renovated. And celebrities — including Madonna and Scarlett Johansson — keep snapping up property in the area. — BY STEPHANIE ROSENBLOOM

FRIDAY

1 *Social Calendar* 4 p.m.

Want to plunge into the Hamptons social scene? Then your first order of business is to grab the free newspapers and glossy magazines — *Social Life, Hampton Life, Hamptons, Hampton Sheet, Dan's Papers, The East Hampton Star* — and scan them for the weekend's fete, charity event, or oceanfront screening of *Jaws.* You'll find them near the door of many boutiques in East Hampton, but perhaps the most indulgent place to get them is **Scoop du Jour** (35 Newtown Lane; 631-329-4883), the ice cream parlor where waffle cones are stacked with cavity-friendly flavors like cake batter and cotton candy. This is also where you can buy Dreesen's doughnuts, a Hamptons staple since the 1950s. Need a gift for a party host (or yourself)? Shops have sprouted along Main Street, including **Tory Burch** (No. 47) and **Roller Rabbit** (No. 21).

2 *Pizza Patio* 7 p.m.

It's not just socialites who flee New York for the Hamptons in summer. Manhattan restaurateurs migrate here, too. One establishment is the Italian standby **Serafina** (104 North Main Street; 631-267-3500; hamptons.serafinarestaurant.com; $$$).

OPPOSITE At the Pollock-Krasner House and Study Center visitors don slippers to walk on the paint-splattered floor of Jackson Pollock's studio.

RIGHT A converted storage barn, which Jackson Pollock and Lee Krasner used as their studio, is open to tours at the Pollock-Krasner House and Study Center.

Yellow umbrellas poke up like daffodils from its sidewalk patio and vine-covered pergola. Fresh pastas and seafood are on the menu, though the brick oven pizzas — in more than two dozen varieties, including pesto — are among the most popular picks. On a typical night, couples canoodle at the bar while well-manicured families stream into the dining room. If your taste leans toward fried seafood, homemade chowder, and frosty drinks, however, head to **Bostwick's Chowder House** (277 Pantigo Road; 631-324-1111; bostwickschowderhouse.com; $$), which has indoor-outdoor dining.

3 *Dock of the Bay* 9 p.m.

Watching boats glide along the horizon is perhaps the simplest and most peaceful of Hamptons pleasures. Happily, a favorite haunt, the **Bay Kitchen Bar** (39 Gann Road; 631-329-3663; baykitchenbar.com), occupies a secluded spot overlooking Three Mile Harbor. The open-air decks of this gleaming, popular restaurant are an idyllic perch from which to watch the long summer sunset. Or have a drink at the indoor-outdoor bar or on the long, cushy banquettes of the main lounge.

SATURDAY

4 *Farm Fresh* 10 a.m.

Before men in golf shirts roamed the Hamptons, it was the purview of farmers. Fortunately, there are still some left. Pick up fresh eggs, local produce, and home-baked muffins and scones for breakfast at **Round Swamp Farm** (184 Three Mile Harbor Road;

631-324-4438; roundswampfarm.com). Be sure to buy enough for lunch so you can skip the interminable snack bar line at the beach.

5 *Where to Tan* 11 a.m.

Choosing a favorite Hamptons beach is not unlike choosing a favorite child. Still, there are distinctions. In 2013, Stephen P. Leatherman, director of the Laboratory for Coastal Research at Florida International University, named **Main Beach** (in East Hampton) America's best beach, beating out beaches in Hawaii and Florida, by ranking it No. 1 in his annual Top 10 Beaches rankings (drbeach.org). In 2010, **Coopers Beach** (in Southampton) captured the No. 1 spot. Both are wide and clean and — very important — sell food. Many beaches require seasonal parking permits, though visitors can park at Coopers Beach for $50 a day. Parking at Main Beach is $30 a day, but weekdays only; on weekends visitors must walk or ride bikes. (For details, go to the Long Island Convention & Visitors Bureau's Web site, discoverlongisland.com.)

6 *East End Expressionism* 3:30 p.m.

The wetlands and dunes that draw pleasure-seekers today also inspired some of the greatest abstract and landscape artists of our time. Go see why at **LongHouse Reserve** (133 Hands Creek Road; 631-329-3568; longhouse.org), a sprawling but less-visited garden and sculpture park with works by Buckminster Fuller, Dale Chihuly, Willem de Kooning, and Yoko Ono. Founded by the textile designer Jack Lenor Larsen, the 16-acre reserve is open to the public Wednesdays through Saturdays during the summer. Nearby is the **Pollock-Krasner House and Study Center** (830 Springs-Fireplace Road; 631-324-4929; pkhouse.org), which Jackson Pollock and Lee Krasner bought for $5,000 in 1946 and turned into their home and studio. Visitors must don booties to enter the barn because the floor is splattered with paint that Pollock dripped and flung for his masterpieces. In fact, some of his paint cans are still there.

7 *For All Seasons* 8 p.m.

Summers are easy, but winters make or break Hamptons restaurants, and a local following is indispensable. A locals' choice with a big-city pedigree (from the same ownership group as New York City's Loring Place and Shuko), the open, airy **Highway Restaurant and Bar** (290 Montauk Highway; 631-527-5372; highwayrestaurant.com; $$$$) serves indoors or out on a backyard patio. A menu standout: an Instagram-ready spit-roasted organic chicken with Swiss chard and cippolini onions. The cocktail list features a phenomenal house margarita made with ginger and Saint Germain (an elderflower liquor), and a tap beer selection with an emphasis on local breweries.

8 *No Velvet Rope* 10 p.m.

The Hamptons nightclub scene has quieted in recent years as action shifts to the tip of Long Island at Montauk, where shabby motels and quaint restaurants are being remade into boho-chic establishments. But there are still plenty of pleasures to be had in East Hampton after sunset. One good option is to head to the **Restaurant at the Maidstone** (207 Main Street; 631-324-5006; themaidstone.com). The Maidstone Hotel's restaurant and lounge lure a lively, attractive crowd until closing time, sometime before midnight.

SUNDAY

9 *Morning Runway* 11:30 a.m.

Catch a tennis match or baseball game on flat screens while enjoying panini or frittatas at **CittaNuova** (29 Newtown Lane; 631-324-6300; cittanuova.com; $$$), a Milan-inspired cafe with a facade that peels back to provide indoor-outdoor seating along the village's prime shopping strip. A backyard patio has more tables. The pretty space can be jammed during events like the World Cup. Should there be no games to hold your attention, people-watching (O.K., fashion-policing) from the outdoor tables will.

10 *Artful Afternoon* 1 p.m.

Many of the artists who settled in the Hamptons exhibited at **Guild Hall** (158 Main Street; 631-324-0806;

guildhall.org), the region's celebrated arts center, and current artists still do. Performances are held all summer long.

11 *Behind the Hedges* 2:30 p.m.
    Real estate is a blood sport here. And one of the most coveted addresses is Lily Pond Lane. Take a leisurely drive along the wide road where beyond the hedges you can glimpse houses that belong to the likes of Martha Stewart. Grey Gardens, once the decayed home of Edith Ewing Bouvier Beale and her daughter, can be found where Lily Pond meets West End Road. Along the way you're likely to spot many material girls, but if you are desperately seeking the original, head over to Bridgehampton, where Madonna owns a horse farm on Mitchell Lane.

OPPOSITE Tanning at Main Beach, one of the East Hampton beaches frequently rated among the best places in the United States to sun and swim.

ABOVE Home furnishings in an East Hampton shop.

THE BASICS

The hundred-mile drive from Manhattan can be frustrating in summer traffic. Alternatives are the Long Island Railroad and buses run by Hampton Jitney (hamptonjitney.com) and Hampton Luxury Liner (hamptonluxuryliner. com). In town, ride a bike.

The Maidstone Hotel
207 Main Street
631-324-5006
themaidstone.com
$$$$
19 modish rooms, vintage Scandinavian bicycles, beach parking permits, and yoga classes.

The 1770 House Restaurant & Inn
143 Main Street
631-324-1770
1770house.com
$$$$
Feels like the home it once was.

The Huntting Inn
94 Main Street
631-324-0410
thepalm.com/Huntting-Inn
$$$-$$$$
A pretty inn that is also home to the popular Palm restaurant.

4 miles
8 kilometers

Gardiners Bay   *Block Island Sound*

SHELTER I.

Bay Kitchen Bar **3**
                    Pollock-Krasner
                    House and Study Center
                                        Montauk

SPRINGS —   *Napeague*
FIREPLACE RD.   *Bay*

Little
Peconic
Bay   **East**
                      Hampton

SUFFOLK   *OSBORNE LN.* **East**   **2**
                                                     Hampton *Serafina*

    Bridgehampton   *LONG ISLAND R.R.*   *N. MAIN ST.*

                      Atlantic   CittaNuova
    Southampton   *Ocean*
                                        NEWTOWN LN. **9**
    ■ Coopers Beach   ┌ Roller Rabbit
                                        1
                                        Scoop   Tory ■
                                        du Jour   Burch
                      — OLD   — MAIN ST.
                    NORTHWEST RD.
    HANDS CREEK RD. —
                              4 Round Swamp Farm   *LONG ISLAND R.R.*
    SUFFOLK   **6**   — THREE MILE HARBOR RD.
                  LongHouse
                  Reserve   **27** Amagansett
    [114]
         East Hampton Train Station   **Area of** *L PANTIGO RD.*
                                         detail ■ Bostwick's Chowder House
         1770 House Restaurant & Inn ■   *East*
                                     ■ Huntting Inn *Hampton*
                 7 Highway Restaurant
                     and Bar   **10** ■ Guild Hall
    MONTAUK HWY. [27]   **8** ■ Restaurant at the Maidstone/
                                         The Maidstone Hotel   *Atlantic Ocean*
       LILY POND LN. ─┐
                                    5 ■ Main Beach   *1 mile*
    Grey Gardens **11**   *2 kilometers*
              — *WEST END RD.*

The Hudson Valley

The Hudson Valley is miles of sandstone and granite cliffs, cattail-lined riverbanks, former factory towns, orchards, farmland, and forests. The constant is the wide and beautiful Hudson River, pushing south toward its mouth at New York City. It's a one-hour train trip from Manhattan to Peekskill, at the doorstep of the mid-Hudson Valley, but the region can be fully explored only on a road trip—skirting one side of the river and winding down the other; hopscotching between historic estates, reawakened old villages, and sizable arts institutions; and detouring for farm stands, roadside diners, and seductive swimming holes.

— BY FREDA MOON

FRIDAY

1 *Peek Into Peekskill* 4 p.m.

Escape the city early and arrive in Peekskill in time for "hoppy hour" at **Peekskill Brewery** (47-53 South Water Street; 914-734-2337; peekskillbrewery.com), a 7,000-square-foot space. Or you might choose the **Birdsall House** (970 Main Street; 914-930-1880; birdsallhouse.net), where there's an antique cash register, live music on weekends, and a good craft beer list. While you're in town, drop into **Bruised Apple Books and Music** (923 Central Avenue; 914-734-7000; bruisedapplebooks.com), which has a section devoted to the Hudson Valley's past and present, a pulp-mystery reading room, and a vinyl-record listening station.

2 *Merci Beaucoup* 6 p.m.

Drive north to Hyde Park for dinner at the **Bocuse Restaurant** (Hyde Park; 845-451-1012; bocuserestaurant.com; $$) of the Culinary Institute of America, the prestigious cooking school housed in a former seminary. The restaurant's name is a homage to the Lyonnaise chef Paul Bocuse, and the menu may include some of his creations. Entrees like roasted meats and seared fish arrive with pleasing accompaniments. (Don't linger if you're going next to the Midnight Ramble.)

OPPOSITE Olana, the painter Frederic Church's home high above the river in Hudson, New York.

RIGHT Paddling in the Hudson near Cold Spring.

3 *Folkies and Newbies* 8 p.m.

Levon Helm, former drummer of The Band, has died, but his **Midnight Ramble** endures at the Levon Helm Studio (160 Plochmann Street, Woodstock; 845-679-2744; levonhelm.com). Buy tickets in advance to catch one of the big-name music acts that appear there, sometimes accompanied by musicians who played with Helm. Another option is to backtrack to Beacon for drinks and music at **Dogwood** (47 East Main Street, Beacon; 845-202-7500; dogwoodbar.com) or **Max's on Main** (246 Main Street; 845-838-6297; maxsonmain.com).

SATURDAY

4 *Active Outdoors* 9 a.m.

Dip south to Cold Spring for biscuits with sausage gravy or raspberry cornmeal pancakes at **Hudson Hil's Cafe & Market** (129-131 Main Street; 845-265-9471; hudsonhils.com; $$) and then walk to **Hudson River Expeditions** (14 Market Street; 845-809-5935; hudsonriverexpeditions.com) for advice on local hikes, like the not-for-novices Breakneck Ridge Trail (nynjtc.org/hike/breakneck-ridge-trail), or kayak rentals. Take your pick for an active morning. Afterward, you'll be ready to tackle the Texas-style dry-rubbed, hickory-smoked barbecued brisket, sausage, or ribs at **Round Up Texas BBQ**

& Tumbleweed Saloon (2741 Route 9; 845-809-5557; rounduptxbbq.com; $$). It is housed in a former gas station with picnic tables outside, and also serves Lone Star beer and classic sides like Frito pie and jalapeño mac 'n' cheese.

5 *Tasting Trails* 2 p.m.

In 2007, the **Tuthilltown Distillery** (14 Grist Mill Lane, Gardiner; 845-419-2964; tuthilltown.com) became New York State's first post-Prohibition whiskey distillery, operating in an old grist mill and selling its four-grain bourbon, Manhattan rye, and single-malt whiskey under the Hudson Whiskey label. Tours include a tasting. If wine's your thing, the Shawangunk Wine Trail (shawangunkwinetrail. com) winds to 14 wineries, including **Benmarl Winery** (156 Highland Avenue, Marlboro; 845-236-4265; benmarl.com), which claims to be the oldest commercial vineyard in the country. And the Web site hvciderguide.com offers yet another beverage-themed option, a directory of more than two dozen apple cider makers in the area.

6 *Walking on Water* 4 p.m.

Cross the Hudson on foot on the **Walkway Over the Hudson** (walkway.org), a 1.28-mile former railroad bridge transformed into a park. Then take a drive through New Paltz and out on Mountain Rest Road, past the 144-year-old Mohonk Mountain House lake resort, to the Mohonk Preserve (mohonkpreserve. org). Continue through the hamlets of High Falls and Stone Ridge, and over the Ashokan Reservoir, one of New York City's pristine water sources. Along the way, stop in at the **Last Bite** (103 Main Street, High Falls; 845-687-7779) for a cup of Catskill Mountain Coffee or at the kitschy, 1970s-era **Egg's Nest** (1300 State Route 213, High Falls; 845-687-7255; theeggsnest.com) for a Sicilian egg cream.

7 *Old World Redux* 6 p.m.

Take two-lane back roads to **Gunk Haus Restaurant** (387 South Street, Highland; 845-883-0866; gunkhaus.com; $$). Sit on the biergarten deck and look out over apple orchards and "the Gunks" — the Shawangunk Mountains, one of the country's best-known rock-climbing ridges. The menu lives up to the Teutonic promise of the name with dishes like pork loin jäger schnitzel served with wild mushroom ragout and spaetzle, and the addictive obatzda, a Bavarian cheese dip that's a potent mix of cheeses, beer, and spices and is served with a chewy house-made pretzel.

8 *Nighttime in Kingston* 10 p.m.

Relax with drinks and music in Kingston, a small city that served as the capital of New York State in the 18th century. **Stockade Tavern** (313 Fair Street, Kingston; 845-514-2649; stockadetavern. com) sells sophisticated cocktails in a one-time

Singer sewing machine factory in the 17th-century Stockade District. **BSP Lounge** (323 Wall Street, Kingston; 845-481-5158; bsplounge.com) hosts local and touring bands in a former vaudeville theater. If you get into town while the sun is still up, have a drink at a cafe in the **Rondout Historic Waterfront District** (thekingstonwaterfront.com) to get a feel for Kingston's shipyard-and-seafaring past.

SUNDAY

9 *Hike in the Hills* 9 a.m.

Drive into the hills beyond Woodstock to the 900-acre **Overlook Mountain Wild Forest** (dec.ny. gov/lands/73982.html). Look for the parking lot of the Overlook Mountain Fire Tower trail across Meads Mountain Road from the Tibetan Buddhist monastery strung with prayer flags. The hike follows a wooded former carriage road to the eerie ruins of a 19th-century Catskills resort and onto the 60-foot fire tower;

climb the steel structure for views that extend from the Berkshires to the Catskills.

10 *Hudson on the Hudson* 11 a.m.

With its dozens of showrooms selling midcentury furniture with five-figure price tags, the old river port city of Hudson feels incongruously cosmopolitan. For brunch, sit in the backyard patio at **Cafe Le Perche** (230 Warren Street, Hudson; 518-822-1850; leperchehudson.com; $$) and choose from dishes like spiced brioche French toast with poached pear or a roasted four-mushroom tartine with melted Brie, baguette, micro greens, and truffle oil. Then

OPPOSITE A rocky shore at Cold Spring, with a view of the hilltops across the Hudson River.

BELOW Inside Olana, the Persian-inspired home overlooking the Hudson River that Frederic Church designed for himself and his family.

spend some time coveting antiques on Warren Street. The Hudson Antiques Dealers Association (hudsonantiques.net) has a guide to the 40-plus artfully curated shops.

11 *Far From the Old School* 2 p.m.
Drive out of town to the **Olana State Historic Site** (5720 Route 9G, Hudson; 518-828-0135; olana.org), the 250-acre estate of the 19th-century painter Frederic Edwin Church. Crisscrossed with trails and planted

with Church's "designed landscape," the property is crowned by the painter's elaborate Persian-style home that now holds a collection of works by Hudson River School painters. If you have time to see more on your way back to the big city, stop in Beacon at the sprawling contemporary museum **DIA Beacon** (3 Beekman Street, Beacon; 845-440-0100; diaart.org) for art that's equal parts intriguing, bewildering, and bizarre.

ABOVE A meal of rainbow trout at the Gunk Haus.

OPPOSITE A perfect Hudson Valley weekend mixes indulgences like shopping and upscale dining with hiking and outdoor sports. This trailhead is near Cold Spring.

THE BASICS

Drive north from New York City on the expressways, and then exit for village main streets and country roads.

Buttermilk Falls Inn + Spa
220 North Road, Milton
845-795-1310
buttermilkfallsinn.com
$$$
On 75 acres along the river, with 17 rooms and suites, a farm-to-table restaurant, and a spa with an indoor pool.

Roundhouse at Beacon Falls
2 East Main Street, Beacon
845-765-8369
roundhousebeacon.com
$$$$
In an old mill in Beacon; rooms overlook a waterfall.

The Rhinecliff
4 Grinnell Street, Rhinecliff
845-876-0590
therhinecliff.com
$$$
Queen Anne-style inn built in the 1850s and revived in the 21st century as a riverside hotel.

HUDSON VALLEY (map)

10 miles
20 kilometers

Cafe Le Perche **10** — Hudson
11 Olana State Historic Site
Overlook Mountain Wild Forest **9**
NEW YORK STATE THRWY.
Hudson River
Tibetan Buddhist Monastery
3 Midnight Ramble
TACONIC STATE PKWY.
Woodstock
MASS.
Ashokan Reservoir
BSP Lounge
8 Stockade Tavern
NEW YORK
Kingston
Rondout Historic Waterfront District
The Rhinecliff
Stone Ridge
Last Bite — The Egg's Nest
High Falls
2 Bocuse Restaurant
Mohonk Preserve
Hyde Park
Tuthilltown Distillery **5**
Highland
6 Walkway Over the Hudson
Gardiner
Poughkeepsie
Gunk Haus Restaurant **7**
Buttermilk Falls Inn + Spa
Marlboro
CONN.
Benmarl Winery
CANADA
Max's on Main
Beacon
ADIRONDACK PARK VT.
DIA Beacon
Roundhouse at Beacon Falls
Dogwood
Roundup Texas BBQ & Tumbleweed Saloon
NEW YORK
Breakneck Ridge Trail
Albany
Hudson Hil's Cafe & Market **4**
Cold Spring
Area of detail
MASS.
Hudson River Expeditions
Peekskill Brewery **1**
Birdsall House
PA.
CONN.
Peekskill
N. J.
New York City
Bruised Apple Books and Music

Lake Placid

In any trip to Lake Placid, there will be a moment when you catch yourself thinking: Do you believe this little place was the host of two Olympic Games? Not because something so symbolic and global does not fit in a tiny upstate New York village of 3,000, but, more striking, because it will dawn on you that it is the perfect place. While the Olympics have become outsized, intimate Lake Placid retains ties to simpler times, whether 1932, when the Winter Games first came to visit, or 1980, a time remembered fondly by Americans for the "Miracle on Ice" United States hockey team. Still, a visit is less about the Olympics as they were than about life as it was. Lake Placid has the rhythm of a small town, albeit one with the sophistication to have played host to the world, and its pace is spiked by active people who embrace the mountain-and-lake setting that has attracted visitors for centuries. In the end, at least occasionally, you have to buy into the Olympic motto — Swifter, Higher, Stronger — and just go with it. Oh, and hold on for dear life. — BY BILL PENNINGTON AND LIONEL BEEHNER

FRIDAY

1 *Scream or Skate* 7 p.m.

Park your car in the center of the village, get out, and follow the screaming. It will lead you to a metal and wood three-story ramp next to Mirror Lake — the **Lake Placid Toboggan Chute** (Parkside Drive; 518-523-2591; northelba.org/government/park-district/toboggan-chute.html). The chute is actually a converted ski jump. Thrill-seekers buy a ticket to rent a four-person toboggan, climb to the top, and place the toboggan on the solid-ice runway. After a few harrowing seconds at 40 miles an hour, you are flung out across the frozen lake. (Because the lake freezes at different times every year, the official opening day varies.) The toboggan often does 360-degree turns before it stops. For something that entails less screaming, head south a few hundred feet, strap on

your blades, and follow the skating path cleared on Mirror Lake by the local parks district. There's nothing like skating on a frozen lake, surrounded by the High Peaks.

2 *Toast Your Triumph* 8 p.m.

Now that you have been baptized in the ways of the Olympic village, your bravery will be rewarded at the **Lake Placid Pub and Brewery** (813 Mirror Lake Drive; 518-523-3813; ubuale.com), a few steps from the toboggan chute. Its signature Ubu Ale, a dark, smooth brew, is a fitting laurel.

3 *Window or Hearth?* 9 p.m.

A short trip up the hill on Olympic Drive offers a wonderful overlook of the village of Lake Placid, even at night. That frozen patch where you skated or your toboggan flew, Mirror Lake, is the dominant feature of the village. (Lake Placid itself is to the north.) Savor the views of the lake and mountains from the **Great Room Bar** in the Crowne Plaza (1 Olympic Drive; 518-523-2556; crowneplaza.com; $$$), where you can warm up at a table by the fire (or around the outdoor fireplace).

SATURDAY

4 *Sourdough Breakfast* 8 a.m.

At **Saranac Sourdough** (2126 Saranac Avenue; 518-523-4897; lakeplacidmenus.com; $), Eileen and John Black have been serving up yeasty sourdough breads and tangy sourdough pancakes in this converted log cabin since 1998. The dining room is encased in

OPPOSITE Olympic trails and rinks, Adirondack views, and some of the best skiing in the East keep the winter weekenders coming to Lake Placid.

RIGHT Snow-season downtime in one of the cozy common rooms at the Mirror Lake Inn.

swirling twigs and Impressionist paintings of the Adirondacks. Try the Mountain Man Combo, a mighty stack of pancakes, eggs, meats, and sourdough toast.

5 *Into Thin Air* 9 a.m.

Although *Ski Magazine* has called **Whiteface Mountain** (518-946-2223; whiteface.com), seven miles from Lake Placid, the best ski area in the Eastern United States, somehow the place remains the most underrated snow sports destination in North America.

People used to say it was too hard and too cold. It is true Whiteface's black diamond runs include the trails used for the Olympic races, but the mountain has expanded its terrain to soften the harsh edges.

6 *Wine, Cheese, Venison* Noon

The **J. Lohr Vineyards and Wines Café** ($$), at the Whiteface Main Base Lodge, serves up tasty platters of French cheeses as well as chef's salads, panini, and a selection of elk, rabbit, and venison sausages. They all go well with a Belgian hot chocolate or hot mulled wine.

7 *Hockey and More* 2 p.m.

Smack in the middle of town is Lake Placid's main attraction: the **Olympic Center** (2634 Main Street; 518-523-1655; whiteface.com/facilities/lake-placid-olympic-center). It is a draw for not just hockey dads but also winter sports buffs. The museum displays an impressive collection of miscellany, like coach Herb Brooks's natty suit (or at least the one worn by Kurt Russell, who played him in *Miracle on Ice*), monogrammed ice skates, and Olympic torches that look

ABOVE The Olympic speed skating oval, where Eric Heiden won five gold medals in the 1980 Winter Games, is open to the public for skating.

LEFT Whiteface Mountain, where Olympic skiers raced.

like medieval weapons. A motion theater simulates the feeling of soaring off a ski jump or barreling down a bobsled run. The main attraction remains the hockey rink—a smallish arena whose rafters are festooned with American flags.

8 *Tasty Inventions* 7 p.m.

Don't be fooled by the dive-bar facade and no-frills interior of **Liquids and Solids** (6115 Sentinel Road; 518-837-5012; liquidsandsolids.com; $$). It's a gastropub with an inventive, changing menu of dishes like pork rillette or grilled monkfish. The list of draft beers, ales, and lagers is extensive.

9 *Consider the Atmosphere* 9 p.m.

Lake Placid's Main Street retains its party atmosphere all winter, luring tourists and townies alike to commingle over pints of local lager. **Zig Zags Pub** (134 Main Street; 518-523-8221), named for the deadliest pair of turns on the old bobsled course, is a lively bar that doubles as a shrine to bobsled paraphernalia, yellowed world maps, and vintage signs. By 10 p.m., the place fills up with rugged-looking locals in floppy dog-eared hats and flannel shirts,

ABOVE Dogsledding on frozen Mirror Lake.

RIGHT The view from the top of the Lake Placid bobsled run, which was used in the 1932 and 1980 Olympics.

as a live band belts out oldies. For something less crowded, you could head to the **Cottage** (77 Mirror Lake Drive; 518-523-2544; mirrorlakeinn.com), a rustic spot that offers a late-night happy hour.

SUNDAY

10 *Mush Much?* 10 a.m.

Greet the morning with the sounds of eight Alaskan huskies barking and pulling a sled across

a glistening Mirror Lake. Just off Main Street, **Thunder Mountain Dog Sled Tours** (across from the High Peaks Resort; 518-891-6239) provides the sled, the dogs, and the musher. Watch out for flying toboggans.

11 *Devil's Highway* Noon

Take the bobsled ride at the **Olympic Sports Complex**, if you dare (220 Bobsled Run Lane; 518-523-4436; whiteface.com/activities/bobsled-experience). As you speed down the track, a

squiggly chute of steel, concrete, and ice, you'll share the sled with a pair of pros who look like Navy Seals. To go it alone, choose the skeleton, a face-first solo thrill ride aboard what feels like a cafeteria tray affixed to steel runners. For something tamer (and cheaper), go instead to the **Olympic Jumping Complex** (5486 Cascade Road; 518-523-8830) and take the glass-enclosed elevator up 394 feet to the top for spectacular views of the Adirondacks' majestic peaks.

ABOVE Professional sledders swoosh paying thrill-seekers down the Olympic bobsled run.

OPPOSITE Mirror Lake in Lake Placid on a fall day, before the Adirondack snowfalls and the winter rush.

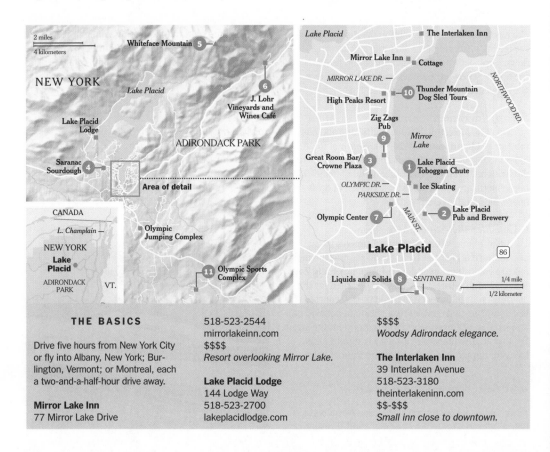

THE BASICS

Drive five hours from New York City or fly into Albany, New York; Burlington, Vermont; or Montreal, each a two-and-a-half-hour drive away.

Mirror Lake Inn
77 Mirror Lake Drive

518-523-2544
mirrorlakeinn.com
$$$$
Resort overlooking Mirror Lake.

Lake Placid Lodge
144 Lodge Way
518-523-2700
lakeplacidlodge.com

$$$$
Woodsy Adirondack elegance.

The Interlaken Inn
39 Interlaken Avenue
518-523-3180
theinterlakeninn.com
$$-$$$
Small inn close to downtown.

New York City

The English writer Michael Pye came up with a clever title for his book on New York: Maximum City. *That says it all in two words. The place is just too much. It's an all-out assault on the five senses, exhilarating but unnerving, that even hardy New Yorkers struggle to contain. Visitors, all too often, are simply crushed, but there are ways around the problem. The most effective is to divide and conquer. When it's split up into bits and pieces, neighborhood by neighborhood, or even block by block, the city shows a more human scale and a softer side. Quirks come to the surface, odd corners reveal themselves, and unexpected pleasures turn up, not all of them wallet-draining experiences. New York can be tamed.* — BY WILLIAM GRIMES

FRIDAY

1 *Art Crawl* 1 p.m.

For gallery hopping, Chelsea is the place, with hundreds of art galleries clustered in the far west of streets numbered in the teens and 20s. While high rents have driven smaller operators to the Lower East Side and Brooklyn, big names like Gagosian, Pace, and David Zwirner have expanded, creating megagalleries that can accommodate huge installation shows. The smaller fry still carry on at buildings like 547 West 27th Street, a warren of small exhibition spaces like the artist-run **Painting Center** (212-343-1060; thepaintingcenter.org). For guidance, pick up a free *Gallery Guide*, found at most galleries.

2 *Rail, River, and Post-Modernism* 3:30 p.m.

Stroll the hugely popular **High Line** (thehighline.org), an abandoned elevated rail line transformed into a garden walkway that meanders from West 34th down to Gansevoort Street. At its south end stands the new home of the **Whitney Museum of American Art** (99 Gansevoort Street; 212-570-3600; whitney.org), a Renzo Piano-designed agglomeration of glass and terraces overlooking the Hudson River. Join the crowds viewing the permanent collection

of paintings, sculpture, photography, film, and new media, and exhibitions celebrating the work of artists like Frank Stella, Jeff Koons, and Laura Poitras. On Fridays and Saturdays it's open until 10 p.m., so feel free to linger.

3 *Sole on Ice* 7 p.m.

The **Ace Hotel** (20 West 29th Street) is one of the landmarks in a district of hip hotels and restaurants north of Madison Square that has acquired, inevitably, a nickname: NoMad. The **John Dory Oyster Bar** (1196 Broadway; 212-792-9000; thejohndory.com; $$$), in the hotel, is a tiled, clamorous brasserie with multilevel seafood plateaus served with the restaurant's Parker House rolls and small plates like chorizo-stuffed squid with smoked tomato. This is your chance to indulge in a lobster roll.

SATURDAY

4 *Lone Star Eats* 9:30 a.m.

The neighborhood around the **Flatiron Building** (23rd Street, Broadway, and Fifth Avenue), on Madison Square, enjoyed its heyday in the late 19th and early 20th centuries, when the square was ringed with fashionable restaurants, theaters, and, of course, the grand entertainment venue named after it: Madison Square Garden (now in its latest incarnation

OPPOSITE Manhattan at dusk.

RIGHT Madison Square Park, a welcoming green space with changing displays of public art, attracts lawn loungers, strolling art lovers, and canine athletes.

on 34th Street). Today, the square and its splendidly renovated park anchor a neighborhood known for unusual specialty shops and terrific restaurants at all price points. To kick off the day, it is hard to beat breakfast at **Hill Country Chicken** (1123 Broadway, at 25th Street; 212-257-6446; hillcountrychicken.com; $). The décor is 1940s diner, the menu robust: egg and cheese or chicken biscuits with sausage or bacon, breakfast tacos, and flaky two-cherry turnovers made on site.

5 *Pop Quiz* 10:30 a.m.

The **National Museum of Mathematics** (11 East 26th Street; 212-542-0566; momath.org) offers a change of pace from the Museum of Sex a block to the north. Pull the oversize "pi" door handles, and a hands-on wonderland awaits, a mathematical fun house that lets children and their parents explore Platonic solids, fractals, and other heroes of the mathematical universe. Visitors can ride tricycles with square wheels around a series of arcs radiating from the center of a circular track. The ride is smooth because the length of each side of the square is equal to the length of the arc in each bump. Those who struggled with high school geometry, and you know who you are, can amuse themselves at the miniature roller coaster, arranging dips and climbs to achieve maximum speed for the little car that runs along its rails.

6 *Asia on a Plate* Noon

It's a short walk to **Num Pang** (1129 Broadway; 212-647-8889; numpangnyc.com), an Asian sandwich shop just a few doors north of Hill Country Chicken. The specialties include a five-spice-glazed pork belly sandwich, a Khmer sausage sandwich with Asian slaw, and a grilled ear of corn swabbed with chili mayonnaise and coconut flakes.

7 *Dogging It in the Park* 12:30 p.m.

Walk off lunch in **Madison Square Park**, whose expansive lawns, sinuous paths, and comfortable benches make it one of the city's most welcoming green spaces. The dog run is a treat, with top-quality canine athletes eager to show off their skills. On the lawn, an ever-changing program of public art catches the eye. In one commissioned work, *Ideas of Stone*, the Italian artist Giuseppe Penone balanced large boulders in three bronze trees.

8 *Blood, Sweat, and Sweets* 1:30 p.m.

The shopping is eclectic in these parts. Well-known chains line Fifth Avenue, but interesting hold-outs still populate the side streets. **New York Cake** (118 West 22nd Street; 212-675-2253; nycake.com) contains thousands of baking pans, cookie cutters, and decorative doodads. That includes margarita-shaped birthday candles, and molds that turn out insect-shaped cookies. This shop can also show you

how to decorate a styrofoam wedding cake so that it looks like the real (and much more expensive) thing. **Bxl Zoute** (50 West 22nd Street; 646-692-9282; bxlrestaurants.com) is good for a break, with a stellar lineup of Belgian beers on tap as well as a house specialty, Cuvee Bxl, an amber beer brewed with orange peel, curacao, coriander, and grains of paradise. **Abracadabra** (19 West 21st Street; 212-627-5194; abracadabrasuperstore.com) is your headquarters for zombie blood and vampire teeth. There's a magic department, a deli counter with body parts and brains, and a nice selection of classic gag items like joy buzzers and red-hot chewing gum. Dressed dummies, available for rental, lurk in every corner. Step up to the wretch bent over a drum of toxic waste near the front door and press the button. You'll get a big surprise.

9 *Destination Italy* 7 p.m.

Eataly (200 Fifth Avenue, near 24th Street; 212-229-2560; eataly.com), a mammoth Italian food market, has a life of its own from its opening at 9 a.m., when a human tide rolls in, drawn by the

OPPOSITE The High Line rises above Chelsea along a former elevated train track.

ABOVE At Columbus Circle, the Museum of Arts and Design stands out in silvery tones below the skyscrapers.

superabundance of cheeses, salumi, pastas, vegetables, breads — anything and everything Italian and food-related. At dinner time, choose from its six restaurants. Manzo, linked to the meat counter, is one of three that take reservations. At La Piazza, an enoteca with standing marble tables, the accent is on cheeses, salumi, and Italian wines by the glass. You can also order inventively garnished slices of raw fish in olive oil from the crudo bar, Eataly's answer to Japanese sashimi. On the way out, pick up a take-home gift from the fresh-pasta department. Say, pumpkin-filled ravioli or spaghetti alla chitara.

SUNDAY

10 *East Riv Vu* 10 a.m.

Uptown, across from East End Avenue, a street so discreet that most city residents have never heard of it, **Carl Schurz Park** (carlschurzparknyc.org) overlooks the East River from 84th Street to 90th Street. It has two priceless features. The first is a raised riverside esplanade that offers views of Ward's Island and the once-dangerous tidal strait known as Hell Gate. The second is Gracie Mansion, the stately official residence of New York City's mayor.

11 *Art With Umlauts* 11:30 a.m.

A ride on the 86th Street bus leads directly to the **Neue Galerie** (1048 Fifth Avenue, at 86th Street;

212-994-9493; neuegalerie.org), a small museum created by the philanthropist Ronald S. Lauder to honor the dealer Serge Sabarsky and to showcase both men's collections of German and Austrian modernist art. The museum specializes in small-scale, focused exhibitions of artists like Ernst Ludwig Kirchner and Wassily Kandinsky, or movements like the Blaue Reiter. The sweet conclusion awaiting every visitor is **Café Sabarsky** (212-288-0665; kg-ny.com) on the ground floor, which replicates a

traditional Viennese cafe right down to the Meinl coffee. The menu includes wursts, sandwiches, and salads, but these are mere distractions from the stunning parade of Viennese and Hungarian pastries.

ABOVE A view of New York Harbor.

OPPOSITE New York's iconic Flatiron Building, at the confluence of Fifth Avenue and Broadway.

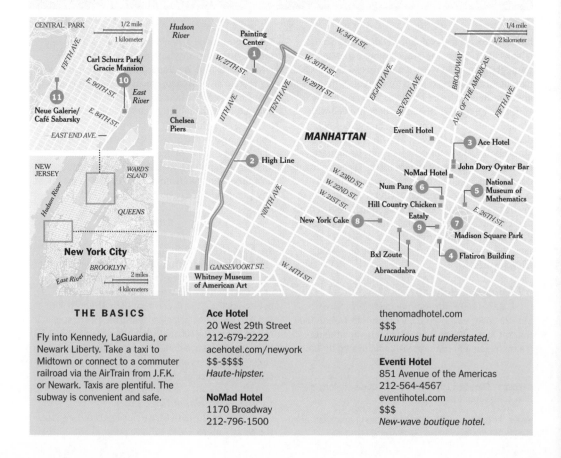

THE BASICS

Fly into Kennedy, LaGuardia, or Newark Liberty. Take a taxi to Midtown or connect to a commuter railroad via the AirTrain from J.F.K. or Newark. Taxis are plentiful. The subway is convenient and safe.

Ace Hotel
20 West 29th Street
212-679-2222
acehotel.com/newyork
$$-$$$$
Haute-hipster.

NoMad Hotel
1170 Broadway
212-796-1500

thenomadhotel.com
$$$
Luxurious but understated.

Eventi Hotel
851 Avenue of the Americas
212-564-4567
eventihotel.com
$$$
New-wave boutique hotel.

Broadway

NEW YORK CITY

Four plays in one weekend? Why not? On Broadway, the best of American theatrical talent comes together in 40 theaters within a tight cluster of walkable New York City blocks. The schedules are right, the marquees are bright, and the variety of the productions gives you plenty to choose from. Between shows, follow celebrity footsteps into some hangouts of the theater people and learn some Broadway history. This district has been home of the best (and worst) of what the New York stage has to offer for more than a century.
— BY MERVYN ROTHSTEIN

FRIDAY

1 *Ticket Strategy* 2 p.m.

Lengthy treatises have been written about how to get Broadway tickets. One option is to join the line at the discount **TKTS** booth at the north end of Times Square at 47th Street (tdf.org/tkts), sponsored by the nonprofit Theater Development Fund. The latest hits aren't likely to show up here, but good productions well into their runs may, at savings of up to 50 percent. Lines form well before the booth opens at 3 p.m. Whether you buy at TKTS, pay full price at a theater box office, or book weeks ahead through Telecharge (telecharge.com) or Ticketmaster (ticketmaster.com), study the reviews and listings first. Plan to see a mix of shows — light and serious, traditional and daring.

2 *Evening Joe* 6:15 p.m.

Join pre-theater crowds at **Joe Allen's** (326 West 46th Street; 212-581-6464; joeallenrestaurant.com; $$), a very busy, very New York place. While eating your meatloaf or pan-roasted cod, check out the posters for the biggest flops in Broadway history. You no doubt know the book, and the movie, of *Breakfast at Tiffany's*. But did you know there was also a 1966 musical version? It starred Mary Tyler Moore and Richard Chamberlain. The world may have forgotten, but the memory is alive here.

OPPOSITE Times Square is at the heart of Broadway and home to the TKTS booth for discounted theater tickets.

RIGHT A scene in *Hamilton*, a marriage of history, hip-hop, and Broadway success.

3 *Song and Dance* 7:45 p.m.

Get your theater weekend off to a high-energy start with a musical. Broadway is most famous for its musicals, and the top 16 longest-running shows in Broadway history are creatures of song and dance (No. 1 is *The Phantom of the Opera*). A tip: musicals that have been playing for years can sometimes be tired, with sets shopworn and stars long gone. Choose one that's still fresh, and arrive early. Latecomers are despised almost as much as people who forget to turn off their cellphones.

4 *Life Is a Cabaret* 11 p.m.

Broadway also means cabaret, so head to **Feinstein's/54 Below** (254 West 54th Street; 646-476-3551; 54below.com), the comfortably luxe nightspot nicknamed "Broadway's living room." Housed in the basement of the old Studio 54 and curated by the Great American Songbook performer and impresario Michael Feinstein, the club hosts nightly shows featuring stars like Lorna Luft and Ben Vereen, or something quirkier, like songs from the films of Quentin Tarantino. There's a cover and minimum; advance tickets are a must for early shows. Late shows start at 11:30, so you can cap your night at the musical with more music.

SATURDAY

5 *Walls of Fame* Noon

The legendary **Sardi's** (234 West 44th Street; 212-221-8440; sardis.com; $$-$$$) is to Broadway as the Hall of Fame in Cooperstown is to baseball: a true

fan will want to see its gallery of immortals — in the case of Sardi's, more than 1,200 caricatures of theater luminaries and "friends of the house." (Bob Hope! James Earl Jones! Helen Mirren!) The well-worn but still lovely restaurant opened in 1927 and reached its zenith in the days of Walter Winchell and Arlene Francis, but it has never stopped being relevant. Actors, producers, and playwrights gather after opening nights, reporters interview stars over lunch, and the downstairs and upstairs bars remain famous for martinis served by bartenders in burgundy Sardi's jackets. But it's still early, so maybe you just go with the appetizer-size portion of the distinctive cannelloni au gratin.

6 *Get Serious* 1:45 p.m.

You want to see at least one meaty serious play, the kind with a chance of showing up someday on college reading lists. Schedule it for today's matinee, to leave yourself time afterward to contemplate and discuss. While waiting for the show to begin, scan the "At This Theater" feature in your *Playbill* to see what giants of yesteryear appeared on the stage you'll be viewing. Humphrey Bogart became a star at the Broadhurst in 1935 in *The Petrified Forest*. Marlon Brando made his Broadway debut in 1944 in *I Remember Mama* at the Music Box (which was built by Irving Berlin) and astonished audiences as Stanley Kowalski in *A Streetcar Named Desire* in 1947 at the Ethel Barrymore.

7 *Dinner Break* 6:15 p.m.

Refortify with a French-inspired dinner at **Chez Josephine** (414 West 42nd Street; 212-594-1925; chezjosephine.com; $$$). Founded as a tribute to the chanteuse Josephine Baker by her adopted son Jean-Claude Baker, who died in 2015, it remains vibrant and welcoming. A pianist accompanies the meal — and whoever's playing that evening counts among his predecessors Harry Connick Jr. For Japanese, try **Kodama Sushi** (301 West 45th Street; 212-582-8065; kodamasushi.net;

$$), a home away from home for supporting casts, stage managers, and other theatrical types. Stephen Sondheim and William Finn have been spotted at the sushi bar, and the autographed posters on the wall from recent hits (and misses) add to the ambience. It's a neighborhood place, but the neighborhood is Broadway.

8 *Seeing Stars* 7:45 p.m.

For the biggest night of the week, find a show with top-tier leads. Then file in with the rest of what's likely to be a full audience, and share the night with the other star watchers. Seeking autographs? Head for the stage door right after the curtain drops, and don't be dismayed if you're part of a crowd. Celebrity actors are usually willing to pause before entering their limos and sign all of the *Playbill* copies thrust at them. Before the show, check out the theater itself: many Broadway houses are stars in their own right. Notice the ornate decoration, and remember the history. **The Lyceum** on West 45th Street, for example, dates to 1903 and was put up by a producer named David Frohman. The story has it that he built an apartment high up

ABOVE A cluster of theater marquees along West 45th Street between Eighth Avenue and Broadway.

BELOW Chez Josephine, a restaurant that pays tribute to the legendary Josephine Baker.

OPPOSITE Queuing for theater tickets at the TKTS booth in Times Square.

inside with a small door for observing the stage—and that he would wave a white handkerchief to warn his actress wife, Margaret Illington, that she was overacting.

9 *And More Stars* 11 p.m.

The post-performance star gazing is usually good at **Bar Centrale** (324 West 46th Street; 212-581-3130; barcentralenyc.com), where actors often retire for a cocktail after two or three hours of performing. It's run by Joe Allen, above his eponymous restaurant. Don't seek autographs here, though—the performers expect post-play privacy.

SUNDAY

10 *Brunch, Anyone?* 12:30 p.m.

If the weather's good, the idyllic garden of **Barbetta** (321 West 46th Street; 212-246-9171;

barbettarestaurant.com; $$$) is an enchanting space for a light pasta and a lighter wine, giving you a feel of northern Italy.

11 *Grand Finale* 2:45 p.m.

Make your last play memorable. Broadway and its audiences have fallen under the spell of Hollywood-style special effects, and if you want something splashy, you can probably find it. In theater, you're seeing the pyrotechnics live (despite all the publicity, accidents are rare), and producers can't rely as much on computer-generated sleight of hand. Sit back and enjoy the spectacle.

THE BASICS

Taxis, trains, buses, and subways all converge on Times Square. Everyplace in the theater district is walkable from anyplace else in the theater district.

Marriott Marquis
1535 Broadway
212-398-1900
marriott.com
$$$-$$$$
In the heart of Broadway, with a theater inside.

W Times Square
1567 Broadway
212-930-7400
wnewyorktimessquare.com
$$$-$$$$
Stylish and luxurious.

Hilton Times Square
234 West 42nd Street
212-840-8222
hilton.com
$$$-$$$$
Spacious rooms, many amenities.

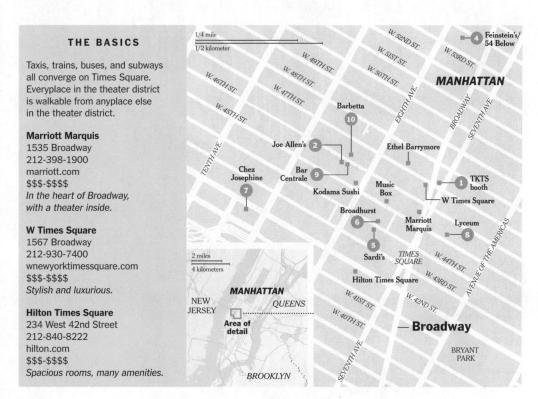

Brooklyn
NEW YORK CITY

The Brooklyn Cruise Terminal on the Buttermilk Channel has picturesque views even when the Queen Mary 2, *which docks there regularly, is at sea. There is verdant Governor's Island across the water and, behind it, the heaving, jagged rise of Manhattan. To the north are the great bridges of the East River. To the west, the Statue of Liberty. And to the east, beyond chain link and forbidding streets, there is Brooklyn itself, New York City's most populous borough, a destination in its own right.* — BY SAM SIFTON

FRIDAY

1 *Waterfront Stroll* 4 p.m.

The cobblestone streets beneath the looming Manhattan and Brooklyn Bridges are home to small shops and shiny new condominiums, and to **St. Ann's Warehouse** (45 Water Street; 718-254-8779; stannswarehouse.org), a theater group that has been a mainstay of the Brooklyn arts scene for more than three decades. Housed since 2015 in a Civil War-era tobacco warehouse adjacent to Fulton Ferry State Park, it is an excellent destination after a walk along the **Promenade** in Brooklyn Heights (parallel to Columbia Heights, a grand old street of towering brownstones, running from Remsen to Orange Streets). Check ahead, then amble to the box office to pick up your tickets.

2 *Into the Borough* 5 p.m.

Alternatively, head inland, toward the leafy precincts of Fort Greene, for a show at the **Brooklyn Academy of Music** (bam.org) or the **Mark Morris Dance Group** (markmorrisdancegroup.org). Atlantic Avenue, which runs deep into the borough, will lead you most of the way, through a stretch of antiques shops and restaurants.

3 *Pre-theater Dinner* 6:30 p.m.

Once you get strolling, it is easy to drift into other pretty residential neighborhoods: Cobble Hill

OPPOSITE Brownstone-lined streets invite long strolls in Park Slope and Prospect Heights.

RIGHT The Brooklyn Academy of Music, a home for music, theater, dance, film, and literary events.

and Carroll Gardens nearby and, slightly farther afield, Park Slope and Prospect Heights. There is excellent eating along the way. At the bottom of Court Street in Carroll Gardens: **Prime Meats** (465 Court Street at Luquer Street; 718-254-0327; frankspm.com; $$), a chic Germanish steak and salad restaurant. A block or so farther south, on the corner of Huntington Street: **Buttermilk Channel** (524 Court Street; 718-852-8490; buttermilkchannelnyc.com; $$), where you can get local cheeses and pastas and a superlative duck meatloaf. Ten minutes before the end of your meal, use your ride-share app or have the host call for a car, and go to the performance you've chosen.

4 *Drink After the Curtain* 10 p.m.

Fort Greene abounds in bars suitable for a late-evening drink. A cocktail at the minimalist and homey **No. 7** is no-risk (7 Greene Avenue at Fulton Street; 718-522-6370; no7restaurant.com). Those seeking rougher charms can venture to the **Alibi** (242 DeKalb Avenue between Clermont Avenue and Vanderbilt Avenue), where there are cheap drinks, a pool table, and a crowd that runs equal parts artist and laborer.

SATURDAY

5 *Breakfast Paradise* 9 a.m.

Tom's Restaurant in Prospect Heights (782 Washington Avenue at Sterling Place; 718-636-9738; $) has been a crowded, friendly mainstay of this neighborhood for decades, and is a winning place to begin a day in Kings County (that's Brooklyn, to you

outsiders; each of New York City's five boroughs is a separate county). Eat pancakes and waffles in a room filled with tchotchkes and good cheer, and watch the marvelous parade.

6 *Parks and Arts* 10 a.m.

A Tom's breakfast provides a strong foundation for a visit to the exhibitions of the nearby **Brooklyn Museum** (200 Eastern Parkway at Washington Avenue; 718-638-5000; brooklynmuseum.org). It is also useful in advance of a walk through the **Brooklyn Botanic Garden** (990 Washington Avenue; 718-623-7200; bbg.org), a 19th-century ash dump that is now home to some of the best horticultural displays in

the world. And of course there is **Prospect Park** (prospectpark.org), Frederick Law Olmsted and Calvert Vaux's triumphant 1867 follow-up to Central Park in Manhattan. Those with children may wish to visit the zoo (450 Flatbush Avenue near Empire Boulevard; 718-399-7339; prospectparkzoo.com), where the daily feedings of the sea lions are a popular attraction.

7 *A Visit to Hipchester* 2 p.m.

Boutiques, coffee bars, and restaurants continue to flourish in Williamsburg and Greenpoint, north Brooklyn's youth-culture Marrakesh. Amid these, **Artists and Fleas** is a weekend market where artists, designers, collectors, and craftspeople show their work (70 North Seventh Street between Wythe Avenue and Kent Avenue; 917-488-4203; artistsandfleas. com). **Spoonbill and Sugartown, Booksellers** offers an eclectic mix of art and design books and academic

ABOVE A storefront on Eighth Avenue in Brooklyn's Chinatown, in Sunset Park.

LEFT Prime Meats, a stylish dining spot for people who like their cuisine on the hearty side.

OPPOSITE The much loved and well used Prospect Park, designed by Frederick Law Olmsted and Calvert Vaux after they completed Central Park in Manhattan.

tracts (218 Bedford Avenue at North Fifth Street; 718-387-7322; spoonbillbooks.com). And **Bird** (203 Grand Street near Driggs Avenue; 718-388-1655; shopbird.com) offers the "Brooklyn Look" in women's clothing, minus the kale chips and bike helmets. For a pick-me-up or a new coffee machine for home, try **Blue Bottle Coffee** (76 North Fourth Street; bluebottlecoffee.com/cafes/williamsburg), an impossibly nerdy outpost of the original Oakland coffee bar. Siphon? French press? Cold drip? All available, plus all the crazy coffee talk you like. Get your geek on.

8 *Dinner for Kings* 7:30 p.m.

Those enamored of the Williamsburg scene can stay in the neighborhood for a smoky dinner at **Fette Sau**, an awesome barbecue joint set in a renovated garage and narrow alleyway (354 Metropolitan Avenue near Havemeyer Street; 718-963-3404; fettesaubbq.com; $$). In Greenpoint, there is the excellent and slightly more adult-themed **Anella**, where the chef works marvels with vegetables and duck (222 Franklin Street at Green Street; 718-389-8100; anellabrooklyn.com; $$). Parents with children might try the pizzas at **Motorino** (139 Broadway; 718-599-8899; motorinopizza.com; $$) or scoot back to Park Slope, where the brothers Bromberg offer a welcoming family atmosphere with food to match at their **Blue Ribbon Brooklyn**

(280 Fifth Avenue, near First Street; 718-840-0404; blueribbonrestaurants.com).

9 *Pazz and Jop* 10 p.m.

Brooklyn's music scene keeps growing. Two places to hear bands are **Union Pool** in Williamsburg (484 Union Avenue at Meeker Avenue; 718-609-0484; union-pool.com) and **Brooklyn Bowl**, also there (61 Wythe Avenue near North 12th Street; 718-963-3369; brooklynbowl.com). **The Bell House** in Gowanus (149 Seventh Street near Second Avenue; 718-643-6510; thebellhouseny.com) hosts a great mix of music, storytelling, and radio shows. Jazz heads should get to **Barbès** in Park Slope (376 Ninth Street at Sixth Avenue; 347-422-0248; barbesbrooklyn.com), where a rich calendar of readings and concerts can take a visitor from early Saturday evening well into Sunday morning.

SUNDAY

10 *Dim Sum à Go-Go* 10 a.m.

Brooklyn's first and biggest Chinatown, along Eighth Avenue in the Sunset Park neighborhood, has grown as populous as Manhattan's and offers great pleasures. Arrive early at **Pacificana** (813 55th Street at Eighth Avenue; 718-871-2880; pacificanabrooklyn.com; $$) for a dim sum meal and watch as the dining room fills into an approximation of a rush-hour

subway car. Then stop in at **Ba Xuyen** (4222 Eighth Avenue, between 42nd and 43rd Streets; 718-633-6601; $) for a banh mi brunch sandwich and a Vietnamese coffee, or at **Yun Nan Flavour Garden** (5121 Eighth Avenue; 718-633-3090; $) for a rare, elaborate, and delicious soup called Crossing-the-Bridge Noodles.

11 *History in the Ground* 1 p.m.
Walk off all the food with a tour of **Green-Wood Cemetery** (Fifth Avenue and 25th Street; 718-768-

7300; green-wood.com), the hilly and beautiful parkland where generations of New Yorkers have moved after death. Admission is free, as are the maps available at the entrance. Look for Boss Tweed, for Jean-Michel Basquiat, for Leonard Bernstein, and for other once-boldfaced names, as parrots (really!) fly about and the wind ruffles the trees and that view of Manhattan opens up in the distance once more. It appears smaller from this vantage, as if placed in perspective.

ABOVE The view of Manhattan from the Battle Hill Monument at Green-Wood Cemetery, which was a popular tourist attraction in the 19th century.

OPPOSITE The pedestrian path on the Brooklyn Bridge.

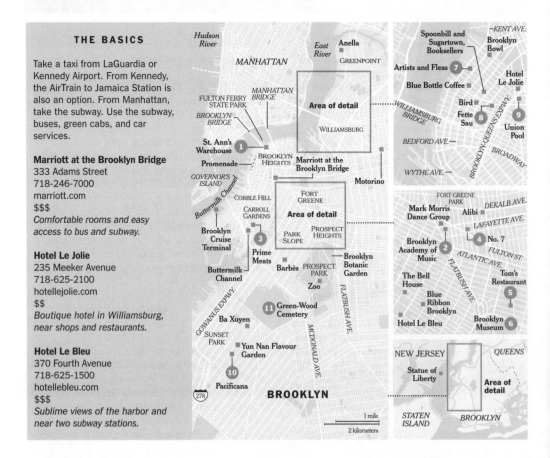

THE BASICS

Take a taxi from LaGuardia or Kennedy Airport. From Kennedy, the AirTrain to Jamaica Station is also an option. From Manhattan, take the subway. Use the subway, buses, green cabs, and car services.

Marriott at the Brooklyn Bridge
333 Adams Street
718-246-7000
marriott.com
$$$
Comfortable rooms and easy access to bus and subway.

Hotel Le Jolie
235 Meeker Avenue
718-625-2100
hotellejolie.com
$$
Boutique hotel in Williamsburg, near shops and restaurants.

Hotel Le Bleu
370 Fourth Avenue
718-625-1500
hotellebleu.com
$$$
Sublime views of the harbor and near two subway stations.

Central Park
NEW YORK CITY

Designed by Frederick Law Olmsted and Calvert Vaux in the 1850s, Manhattan's Central Park today is 840 verdant and flourishing acres of hills and meadows dappled with lakes, sculptures, fountains, and monuments to heroes real and imaginary: Columbus, Beethoven, Duke Ellington, John Lennon, Alice in Wonderland. The park has tennis and handball courts, baseball fields, croquet greens, a carousel, a castle, a marionette theater, a zoo, and more than a dozen playgrounds. It is crisscrossed by horse-drawn carriages and ringed by astronomically priced apartments and luxury hotels. Yet in its quiet trails and hidden nooks, and in the museums and bars within and around it, one can find a more tranquil, timeless Manhattan. — BY STEPHANIE ROSENBLOOM

FRIDAY

1 Celebrity Guides 2 p.m.

It's easy to get lost in Central Park, and even easier to miss interesting spots you would like to see. So download the free Central Park app (centralparknyc.org/tours/self-guided/mobile-app.html) to your smartphone. Its map allows you to pinpoint where you are, and celebrities guide your tour in its audio clips. Jerry Seinfeld welcomes you to the Mall and Literary Walk; Whoopi Goldberg discusses Wollman Rink, where she learned to ice skate. Take your first step into the park through iron gates near 105th Street and Fifth Avenue, and enter the formal, six-acre **Conservatory Garden**. In its Italian garden, climb the stairs to the tall wisteria pergola. Sit on a shaded bench and observe the 12-foot-tall jet fountain below. Now is a good time to press play on the app and listen to Candice Bergen discussing what is around you.

2 Museum Mile 3:30 p.m.

Exit the gardens onto Fifth Avenue through the soaring wrought-iron Vanderbilt Gate, made in Paris in 1894 and once part of Cornelius Vanderbilt II's mansion at 58th Street. Walk south. You're on the aptly named Museum Mile. Already been to

heavyweights like the Guggenheim? Stop by less-trafficked spots. At the **Museum of the City of New York** (1220 Fifth Avenue; 212-534-1672; mcny.org), you'll find vestiges of the city's younger days, including handwritten manuscripts by Eugene O'Neill. The **Cooper Hewitt, Smithsonian Design Museum** (2 East 91st Street; 212-849-8400; cooperhewitt.org) is a shrine to design, honoring everything from Modernist teapots to Victorian advertising to medieval tapestries to Braille wallpaper, all displayed inside the former 64-room Georgian mansion of Andrew Carnegie. As the sun sets, have a snack at the Roof Garden Café and Martini Bar (open May through late fall) of the **Metropolitan Museum of Art** (1000 Fifth Avenue; metmuseum.org/visit). The museum itself is open until 9 p.m. on Fridays.

3 A Southern Crawl 7:30 p.m.

Begin at the **Plaza** (Fifth Avenue at Central Park South; 212-759-3000; theplazany.com), the famous luxury hotel across the street from the park's southeast corner. Skip the buzzy Champagne Bar in the lobby and climb the stairs to the more intimate Rose Club, where plush chairs are ideal for tête-à-têtes. The drink prices are high, but, hey, you can almost make a meal of free nuts and popcorn. (Also take note of the Plaza Food Hall, a great place to

OPPOSITE Central Park, the green heart of Manhattan.

RIGHT Dancing at the Bethesda Fountain.

pick up pastries and other treats to eat in the park.) Then walk west along Central Park South. When you reach the Museum of Arts and Design, go to the ninth floor, where you'll find **Robert** (2 Columbus Circle; 212-229-7730; robertnyc.com; $$$), a restaurant and lounge with live piano music and views of Columbus Circle. Across the street at the Time Warner Center (10 Columbus Circle; theshopsatcolumbuscircle. com), there are several drinks stops, including the lovely Center Bar, which also has live piano music, and Landmarc, which serves casual bistro fare.

SATURDAY

4 *Early Birds* 7:30 a.m.

Bird lovers know that daybreak is magical. In the **Ramble**, a more-than-30-acre maze of boulders and trees, the birds are up, singing, and ready to be spotted. It's easy to forget that this section of the park is almost entirely man-made: The running water in the stream can be turned on and off as if it were coming from a kitchen faucet.

5 *Lawns and Woods* 10 a.m.

On sunny days, Central Park's vast lawns are littered with people. If you want a little peace — and a hint of the Adirondacks — head to the **North Woods**. Be cautious, though, as this is a dense, somewhat

isolated area. That said, the 90 acres of wildflowers, trees, a ravine, and a waterfall will transport you to the country. These woodlands (another bird-watching hot spot) were designed to block out the skyline and drown out the noise of the city with babbling water. Look, too, for the nearby **Pool**, where ducks nestle on the banks beneath weeping willows. Farther north, at the **Harlem Meer**, you can try catch-and-release fishing.

6 *Tasting Menu* 1 p.m.

When you're in the mood for lunch, walk over to Trump Hotel Central Park and into **Nougatine** (1 Central Park West; 212-299-3900; jean-georges. com; $$$$), the elegant yet "casual sister" of another much-praised restaurant in the hotel, Jean-Georges. At Nougatine, Jean-Georges Vongerichten's prix fixe lunch menu changes with the seasons but includes an appetizer, a main course — past examples are seared salmon with corn pudding and organic chicken with ricotta gnocchi — and dessert.

7 *Star Gazing* 3 p.m.

Across from the park is the **American Museum of Natural History** (Central Park West at 79th Street; 212-769-5100; amnh.org). Its main building is crammed with scientifically oriented exhibits,

and an adjacent giant orb in a glass box holds its Rose Center for Earth and Space. There are few better ways to spend a rainy day than gazing at star clusters and galaxies, watching an Imax nature film, or marveling at dinosaur fossils. For the best view of the 94-foot-long, 21,000-pound fiberglass model of a blue whale, suspended from the ceiling, it's acceptable to lie down.

8 *All That Jazz* 7:30 p.m.

In the warmer months you can catch a concert or play in Central Park or at nearby Lincoln

Center, but any time of year is right for listening to jazz while eating finger-licking fare like a catfish po'boy or bourbon-glazed barbecued baby back ribs at **Dizzy's Club Coca-Cola** (10 Columbus Circle; 212-258-9595; jazz.org/dizzys; $$). Part of Jazz at Lincoln Center, this intimate club has table and bar seating, all facing a vertiginous wall of windows behind the performers — almost close enough to touch — that lets in Central Park and the twinkling city lights.

9 *Nightcap in the Park* 10 p.m.

The rustic (think hunting lodge) **Tavern on the Green** (67th Street and Central Park West; 212-877-8684; tavernonthegreen.com) has an oval indoor bar and fireplace to take the chill out of fall nights. For something more romantic, visit the outdoor bar and sip a drink beneath glowing lanterns.

OPPOSITE The Sheep Meadow, an expansive green space that serves New Yorkers as a picnic ground, sunbathing lawn, concert venue, and communal backyard.

ABOVE Not in the park but at its edge, the Rose Center for Earth and Space takes earthlings to the stars.

LEFT The "Imagine" mosaic in Strawberry Fields, a memorial to John Lennon on the park's west side.

10 *Waffles and Rowboats* 9:30 a.m.

Yes, it's rife with tourists. But do visit the **Loeb Boathouse** (enter at East 72nd Street and Fifth Avenue; 212-517-2233; thecentralparkboathouse. com; $$-$$$), which opened in 1954. How often can one tuck into breakfast waffles and watch rowboats glide by on a lake—in the middle of Manhattan? After brunch, rent a boat yourself and go for a row.

11 *On the Wild Side* 11:30 a.m.

Tigers, red pandas, and an emerald tree boa are a few of the creatures you may encounter at the **Central Park Zoo** (between East 63rd and 66th Streets; 212-439-6500). There are penguin and sea lion feedings, a children's zoo with a nature trail, and a 4-D theater. The zoo is tiny compared with New York's impressive Bronx Zoo, but it is a delightful way to end a weekend in an urban jungle.

OPPOSITE Music still reverberates out into the park from free summer concerts played in one of its oldest structures, the Naumburg Bandshell. It was built in 1862.

THE BASICS

Central Park, a long rectangle in the heart of Manhattan, runs north from 59th Street (Central Park South) to 110th Street (Central Park North) and west from Fifth Avenue to Central Park West.

The Mark
25 East 77th Street
212-744-4300
themarkhotel.com
$$$$
In a 1920s landmark building, with one of the slickest lobbies around, featuring a bold black-and-white-stripe floor and modern art.

Excelsior Hotel
45 West 81st Street
212-362-9200
excelsiorhotelny.com
$$-$$$
Steps from the park, in the midst of the action; yet still feels like a low-key apartment building.

Harlem

In Harlem, the first years of the 21st century may best be remembered for a seismic demographic shift: an influx of whites and a drop in the black population that put it below 50 percent for the first time in decades. This shifting landscape has brought with it a new cultural scene with a distinct cosmopolitan vibe. But even with the arrival of new doorman buildings, luxurious brownstone renovations, and chichi boutiques and restaurants, this swath of Upper Manhattan still brims with the cultural landmarks that made it the capital of black America.
— BY JOHN ELIGON

FRIDAY

1 *The Collector* 4 p.m.

Stop in at the **Schomburg Center for Research in Black Culture** (515 Malcolm X Boulevard; 917-275-6975; nypl.org/locations/schomburg), a trove of manuscripts, rare books, photos, videos, and recordings. Its exhibitions have included photos of early 20th-century Harlem life and private papers of Maya Angelou. It is named for Arturo A. Schomburg, a visionary Puerto Rican-born black private collector who amassed a significant portion of this material before his death in 1938. In late 2015 the center began a $22 million, multiyear facelift, so check the schedule for films, lectures, discussions, and musical performances.

2 *Strivers' Row* 6 p.m.

The timing may not have been great when a group of elegant townhouses went up in Central Harlem in the 1890s — it was shortly before an economic panic. But the development, on 138th and 139th Streets between Adam Clayton Powell Jr. and Frederick Douglass Boulevards, survived. Today it is one of New York's most graceful and integrated examples of period architecture. Stroll past Italian-palazzo and neo-Georgian former homes of high achievers like Scott Joplin and Bill (Bojangles)

OPPOSITE Italianate and neo-Georgian townhouses line Harlem's Strivers' Row, once home of Scott Joplin.

RIGHT Named for one of New York's first black-owned bars, 67 Orange Street is on Frederick Douglass Boulevard.

Robinson, who gave this section its nickname, **Strivers' Row**. Don't miss a nod to the past, painted on some of the entrances to the rear courtyard: "Private Road; Walk Your Horses."

3 *Culinary Eclectic* 8 p.m.

Marcus Samuelsson, true to his heritage as Ethiopian born and Swedish raised, has done with his restaurant, **Red Rooster Harlem** (310 Lenox Avenue; 212-792-9001; redroosterharlem.com; $$), what few can: attract a clientele diverse in both color and age. The menu pulls from all cultural corners (blackened catfish, lemon chicken with couscous, steak frites with truffle Béarnaise). Stick around after dinner for a drink at the horseshoe-shaped bar or in the basement lounge.

4 *Old-World Charm* 11 p.m.

After eating at Red Rooster, head downstairs to another Samuelsson creation, **Ginny's Supper Club**. Although both are housed in the same building, Ginny's has a different menu of creative small plates and cocktails and its own unique speakeasy vibe, with live performances (tickets required) or a D.J. spinning tunes. You could, in theory, dance off your dinner.

SATURDAY

5 *The Main Drag* 10 a.m.

The 125th Street corridor stands at the convergence of old and new. On the sidewalks, vendors sell fragrant oils and bootleg DVDs. Indoors, you can find shops like **Atmos** (203 West 125th Street;

212-666-2242; atmosnyc.blogspot.com), with cool sneakers and streetwear, and **Carol's Daughter** (24 West 125th Street; 212-828-6757; carolsdaughter.com), the flagship store of a successful local maker of cosmetics and lotions. In the midst of it all is the **Apollo Theater** (253 West 125th Street; 212-531-5300; apollotheater.org), where black entertainers have gotten their start for generations. Group tours are available by appointment; if you're not traveling with a pack, you may be able to tag along with one. (Call to check availability.) To catch the famed Amateur Night, return on a Wednesday.

6 *El Barrio* Noon

Harlem's east side is El Barrio, a repository for Spanish culture. Have an authentic Dominican meal amid murals depicting rustic tropical scenes at **Lechonera el Barrio** (172 East 103rd Street; 212-722-1344; $$); you can't go wrong with the pernil (roast pork) or a morir soñando (literally, "to die dreaming"), a soft drink made of milk and orange juice. Walk off lunch with a tour of the murals on nearby buildings. A mosaic at 106th Street and Lexington Avenue honors the Puerto Rican poet Julia de Burgos. The four-story-tall *Spirit of East Harlem*, on Lexington at 104th Street, includes men playing dominoes, a woman holding a baby, and the Puerto Rican flag. Uptown, stop at **Almacén y Botanica Ochun II** (1630 Park Avenue; 212-831-9228),

a store, named for a spirit in Caribbean folk religion, filled with African and Native American carvings, prayer cards, candles, and beads. For a history of Spanish Harlem, visit **El Museo del Barrio** (1230 Fifth Avenue; 212-831-7272; elmuseo.org).

7 *The New Renaissance* 3 p.m.

The true Harlem Renaissance was centered on art, and now new art spaces are popping up again. **Casa Frela Gallery** (47 West 119th Street; 212-722-8577; casafrela.com), in a Stanford White brownstone, exhibits small collections and screens films, and the **Dwyer Cultural Center** (258 St. Nicholas Avenue; 212-222-3060; dwyercc.org) celebrates black culture through art. **The Studio Museum** (144 West 125th Street; 212-864-4500; studiomuseum.org) shows fine art, photography, and film. Its collection includes several works by the artist Romare Bearden and the photographer James VanDerZee, who chronicled Harlem life for more than half a century.

8 *The Scene* 6 p.m.

Hard to believe, but the stretch of Frederick Douglass Boulevard where the 1970s drug lord Frank Lucas boasted he made $1 million a day selling heroin is now Harlem's Restaurant Row, a stretch of inviting bistros and lounges. If the weather's nice, enjoy a drink in the neighborhood's best outdoor space at **Harlem Tavern** (No. 2153; 212-866-4500;

harlemtavern.com). Find an ode to multiculturalism at **Bier international** (No. 2099; 212-280-0944; bierinternational.com), a twist on the German beer garden. Check out **Moca Restaurant & Lounge** (No. 2210; 212-665-8081; facebook.com/mocalounge) for the latest in hip-hop tracks. At No. 2082 and named for the address of one of New York's first black-owned bars, **67 Orange Street** (212-662-2030; 67orangestreet.com) offers exotic cocktails in a cozy space.

9 *Soul Food* 8 p.m.

Those who know genuine soul food know that it is best when it has been prepared in the kitchen at home. So it should come as no surprise that good soul food restaurants are difficult to find even in

Harlem. **Sylvia's** (328 Lenox Avenue; 212-996-0660; sylviassoulfood.com) gets the most buzz, but it's more about the restaurant's history than the food. Better options are **Amy Ruth's** (113 West 116th Street; 212-280-8779; amyruths.com; $), where dishes are named for famous African-Americans, or **Miss Mamie's Spoonbread Too** (366 West 110th Street; 212-865-6744; spoonbreadinc.com; $-$$), where the banana pudding is one of the specialties.

10 *A World of Music* 11 p.m.

For a great combination of live music and dance space, take a seat at **Shrine** (2271 Adam Clayton Powell Jr. Boulevard; 212-690-7807; shrinenyc.com), a no-frills restaurant and bar where everyone feels like a local. This is a true melting pot of music. Jazz, reggae, hip-hop, pop, and more might be played by the live bands on a single night. And with lots of floor space to maneuver in, you'll be dancing until your feet are sore.

OPPOSITE Manuel Vega's mosaic tribute to the poet Julia de Burgos at East 106th Street and Lexington Avenue.

ABOVE The Abyssinian Baptist Church, where the Sunday morning service is as theatrical as a Broadway production.

LEFT Generations of black entertainers have performed in the Apollo Theater on busy 125th Street.

SUNDAY

11 *Gospel and Brunch* 11 a.m.

Gospel churches are a staple of Harlem visits. A tourist favorite is **Abyssinian Baptist Church** (132 Odell Clark Place; 212-862-7474; abyssinian.org), a megachurch with a Broadway-like music production. For something more serene, yet still inspiring, attend a service at **Mount Olivet Baptist Church** (201 Lenox Avenue; 212-864-1155; mountolivetbaptistchurch.org).

Afterward, join the crowd having Sunday brunch at **Kitchenette Uptown** (1272 Amsterdam Avenue; 212-531-7600; kitchenetterestaurant.com; $$). The restaurant is designed like a rural porch, providing a homestyle feel with hearty dishes to match. Try the baked crème brulée French toast, turkey sausage, or one of the thick omelets.

ABOVE A Rafael Ferrer exhibit at El Museo del Barrio in Spanish Harlem. The museum tells the neighborhood's story with a focus on its artistic landscape.

OPPOSITE The interior of Mount Olivet Baptist Church on Lenox Avenue, one of the Harlem churches that welcome Sunday morning visitors.

THE BASICS

Harlem spans a section of northern Manhattan roughly from 110th Street to 155th Street. Get around on the subway, or hail taxicabs.

Aloft Harlem
2296 Frederick Douglass Boulevard
212-749-4000
aloftharlem.com
$$
A stylish boutique hotel to represent Harlem's changing face. High design in contemporary style.

The Harlem Flophouse
242 West 123rd Street
347-632-1960
harlemflophouse.com
$$
Charming four-room bed and breakfast in an 1890s brownstone.

255West Guesthouse
255 West 132nd Street
646-838-3687
255west.com
$$
Four spacious rooms in a 130-year-old brownstone on a quiet street.

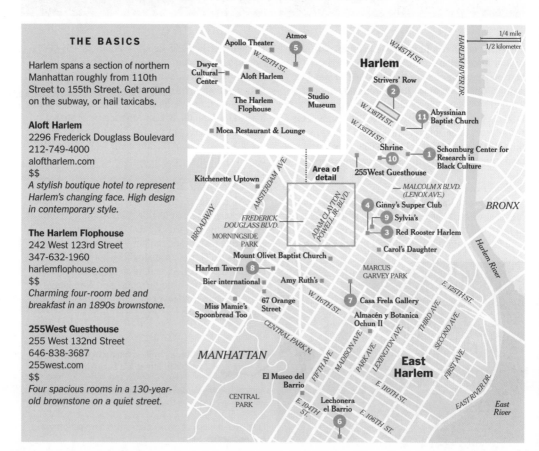

Lower Manhattan

One World Trade Center, the new tallest building in New York, has risen where the Twin Towers once dominated, at the tip of Manhattan Island. The 9/11 Memorial is there, too, drawing hushed and respectful visitors from around the world. No one will ever forget the terrorist attacks, but the neighborhoods nearby long ago recovered from both the physical devastation and the economic jolt several years later. The financial district is bustling, Chinatown is as quirky and enticing as ever, and TriBeCa is bursting with new restaurants, bars, and hotels. With the exception of those seeking a night of relentless club-hopping, travelers hardly need venture north of Canal Street for a complete New York weekend. — BY SETH KUGEL

FRIDAY

1 Cruising the Harbor 2 p.m.

Been there (the Statue of Liberty) and done that (taken the free Staten Island Ferry)? There are other options for harbor cruises, and what better way to get an overview of Lower Manhattan? One possibility is a 90-minute sail on the *Clipper City* tall ship, a replica of a 19th-century lumber-hauling schooner (Manhattan by Sail; 212-619-6900; manhattanbysail.com), which departs from the South Street Seaport. Another is a one-hour harbor cruise with **Statue Cruises** (201-604-2800; statuecruises.com). The company has even launched a Hornblower Hybrid, which relies on several power sources, including hydrogen fuel cells, solar panels, and wind turbines.

2 Sugar and Shopping 4 p.m.

Venture to TriBeCa for a lemon tart or a "magic cupcake" at **Duane Park Patisserie** (179 Duane Street; 212-274-8447; duaneparkpatisserie.com) on the shaded pocket park it is named after. Then browse the nearby shops, which range from the cute to the serious, sometimes in the same store. **Torly Kid** (51 Hudson Street; 212-406-7440; torlykid.com) has funky, functional clothes for babies to tweens. **Patron of the New** (151 Franklin Street; 212-966-7144; patronofthenew.us) sells aggressively fashion-forward clothes and shoes. Salute the Motor City at **Shinola**

OPPOSITE One World Trade Center, America's tallest building, overlooks the site once occupied by the Twin Towers.

(177 Franklin Street; 917-728-3000; shinola.com), which specializes in bicycles, watches, and leather goods, many of which are made in Detroit or at least assembled there.

3 Bankers' Happy Hour 6:30 p.m.

If you resent investment bankers' salaries and bonuses, then here's something else to be envious of: the cobblestone stretch of Stone Street. What might be New York's greatest outdoor drinking spot happens to be right next to Goldman Sachs's former headquarters. When it's warm, this quaint block, lined with 19th-century Greek Revival buildings, is practically blocked by tables occupied by financial types, a few sundry locals, and knowledgeable tourists. Choose a table outside **Adrienne's Pizzabar** (54 Stone Street; 212-248-3838; adriennespizzabarnyc.com; $$) and order a bottle of wine and a meatball and broccoli rabe pizza, enough for three people.

4 TriBeCa Nights 10 p.m.

The night-life impresario Paul Sevigny runs the intimate, eponymous **Paul's Cocktail Lounge** (2 Avenue of the Americas; paulscocktaillounge.com), in the Roxy Hotel, where staffers wear retro Palm Beach garb designed by his sister, the actress and fashion icon Chloë Sevigny. D.J.'s shuffle New Wave, soul, and oldies — that is, if you're lucky enough to get past the velvet rope.

SATURDAY

5 In Memoriam 9 a.m.

Buy your passes online in advance to avoid long lines at the **National September 11 Memorial and Museum** (180 Greenwich Street; 212-312-8800; 911memorial.org). The memorial is a pair of one-acre reflecting pools in the footprints of the fallen towers, names of victims inscribed in bronze panels, and rustling swamp white oak trees overhead. The museum lies in the bedrock below, taking visitors on a gradual descent from light to darkness, past the "Survivors' Stairs," a crushed fire truck, and gigantic, twisted remnants of the original World Trade Center, down to the foundations themselves. Most moving are the personal artifacts of those who died that day, and the reminiscences of their loved ones.

6 *Manahatta* Noon

Most people don't put the Smithsonian on their New York must-do list. But the **National Museum of the American Indian** (1 Bowling Green; 212-514-3700; nmai.si.edu), in the Beaux Arts splendor of the old Customs House near Battery Park, is a reminder that Manhattan and the rest of the Western Hemisphere has a long and vibrant cultural history. The Infinity of Nations exhibition has everything from a macaw and heron feather headdress from Brazil to a hunting hat with ivory carvings from the Arctic. To get an up-close view of a wampum belt and corn pounder used by the Lenape Indians, who called the island Manahatta, head to the museum's resource center and ask. The museum is free — not far from the price for which the Lenapes sold Manhattan to the Dutch.

7 *Doctoral Downtown* 2 p.m.

Continue your historical education with a **Big Onion tour**. Downtown is a complicated place, with layers upon layers of history: Dutch, African-American, Revolutionary, and financial, among others. It takes a doctoral candidate to decode it, and that is who will probably lead you on a two-hour tour that might include "Historic TriBeCa," "Revolutionary New York," or "The Financial District." Times vary; see bigonion.com.

8 *Wine by the T-Shirt* 7 p.m.

At the wine bar **Terroir Tribeca** (24 Harrison Street; 212-625-9463; wineisterroir.com), the young servers in wine-themed T-shirts don't look as if they could know what they are talking about, but don't get them started. (Actually, do get them started.) A glass of wine can be had at many prices, and the menu is full of nonstandard temptations to go with it: fried balls of risotto, wine, and oxtail, for example, are a fine way to spend your allotment of deep-fried calories.

9 *Salvage and Bruschetta* 9 p.m.

Who knows how many diners have walked out of Robert De Niro and company's Locanda Verde, the big northern Italian spot, and wondered what was going on in the tiny, bustling restaurant across the street? Decked out with salvaged materials that evoke an old factory or warehouse, **Smith and Mills** (71 North Moore Street; 212-226-2515; smithandmills. com; $$) seats 22 at tables shoehorned between the standing, drinking crowds. The menu includes items like tomato bruschetta, oysters with horseradish, burgers, and brioche bread pudding. One must-see: a restroom in a turn-of-the-century iron elevator.

10 *Drinks on Doyers* 11 p.m.

Head east to Chinatown, where **Apotheke** (9 Doyers Street; 212-406-0400; apothekenyc.com)

is a non-Chinese intruder sitting on the elbow of L-shaped Doyers Street, the spot known as the Bloody Angle for the gang-related killings there in the early 20th century. Here you'll find one of the city's top cocktail bars, with old-time décor and dim lighting. Try a drink like the Deal Closer, made with cucumber, vodka, mint, lime, vanilla, and "Chinatown aphrodisiacs."

SUNDAY

11 *Brooklyn Bridge Crossing* 9 a.m.

In a hot New York summer, you have to get up pretty early to walk across the **Brooklyn Bridge** in comfort. As romantic as ever, a walk along the elevated pedestrian walkway provides a photo opportunity a minute. On your way back, stop by **City Hall Park**, and then head west across Chambers Street to pick up bagels and smoked salmon from **Zucker's** (146 Chambers Street; 212-608-5844; zuckersbagels.com).

OPPOSITE A view of Lower Manhattan and the East River from below the Brooklyn Bridge.

ABOVE A sightseeing cruise heads up the East River between Manhattan and Brooklyn.

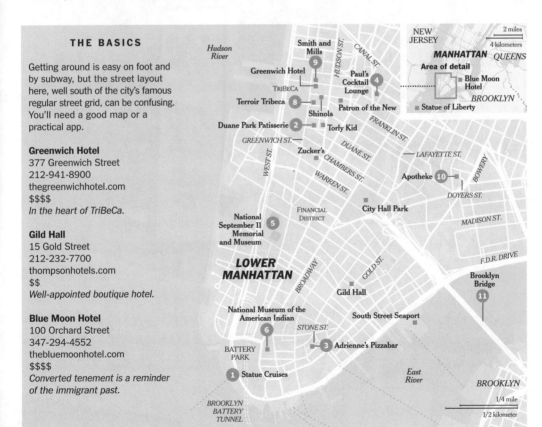

THE BASICS

Getting around is easy on foot and by subway, but the street layout here, well south of the city's famous regular street grid, can be confusing. You'll need a good map or a practical app.

Greenwich Hotel
377 Greenwich Street
212-941-8900
thegreenwichhotel.com
$$$$
In the heart of TriBeCa.

Gild Hall
15 Gold Street
212-232-7700
thompsonhotels.com
$$
Well-appointed boutique hotel.

Blue Moon Hotel
100 Orchard Street
347-294-4552
thebluemoonhotel.com
$$$$
Converted tenement is a reminder of the immigrant past.

Queens
NEW YORK CITY

Remember old New York, where immigrants strived, cultures collided, grit outshone glamour, and ethnic restaurants were filled with ethnic crowds rather than Instagramming foodies? That city lives on in Queens, where the forces of gentrification have barely nipped at the edges. Queens is the city's most expansive borough, home to 2.3 million people from (it seems) 2.3 million backgrounds. It is full of sights and sounds unlike anything you'll find a short subway ride away, and across the East River, in Manhattan.
— BY SETH KUGEL

FRIDAY

1 *Tinseltown, Astoria* 5 p.m.

Hollywood gets all the publicity, but Astoria, one of Queens's most energetic neighborhoods, is home to Kaufman Astoria Studios, where the Marx Brothers shot *Animal Crackers* in 1930 and where Big Bird still resides. One building is now the **Museum of the Moving Image** (36-01 35th Avenue; 718-777-6888; movingimage.us), which is free on Fridays from 4 to 8 p.m. The displays cover not just television (J. R. Ewing's cowboy hat and Mork from Ork's spacesuit) and film (telegrams sent by Orson Welles, Winona Ryder's prosthetic legs from *Black Swan*), but also digital entertainment, including functioning Donkey Kong, Space Invaders, and Ms. Pac-Man machines, as well as special exhibitions.

2 *Little Egypt* 8 p.m.

Long known as a Greek neighborhood, Astoria is now wildly diverse, with Colombians, Brazilians, and Slavs, and, at the end of Steinway Street, a big Middle Eastern commercial district known as Little Egypt. You are unlikely to find better, more simply prepared fish than at **Sabry's Seafood** (24-25 Steinway Street; 718-721-9010; $$), an informal, popular spot where whole snapper, branzino, and tilapia are grilled, fried, or barbecued Egypt style. Start with the grilled calamari, and try an Egyptian lemonade. (No alcohol is served.)

OPPOSITE An agglomeration of street signs proclaim the vibrancy of the Chinatown in Flushing, Queens.

RIGHT A belly dancer at Layali Dubai, a night spot that draws a mostly Muslim crowd.

3 *Hookahs and Tea* 10 p.m.

Little Egypt is filled with the informal hookah lounges called shisha bars. For a lavish version, head up the stairs from Sabry's to **Layali Dubai** (24-17 Steinway Street; 718-728-1492; facebook.com/layalidubainy). The dress code for the mostly Muslim crowd is shocking in its range, from conservative to the near scandalous. Groups of men and women (often separated) smoke hookahs, sip mint tea and fruit juice (no alcohol is served), and take in live music and belly-dancing until late.

4 *Choose Your Party* Midnight

Drink like a hipster at **Dutch Kills** (27-24 Jackson Avenue; 718-383-2724; dutchkillsbar.com), a fashionable cocktail hideaway in the Queens neighborhood of Long Island City, for a Rum Buck, Bloody Knuckle, or — why not? — a Manhattan. (The specialty drinks are likely to be several dollars cheaper than those you'd find at similar Manhattan joints.)

SATURDAY

5 *Eat, Drink, Shop* 10:30 a.m.

Walk out of the subway at the Roosevelt Avenue-Jackson Heights stop, and you have entered a land of diversity you previously assumed was metaphorical. How else to explain Jackson Heights, a place where

Panorama of the City of New York, an astonishing scale model of the five boroughs with 895,000 houses and buildings. (There are even planes taking off from La Guardia Airport.)

a pharmacy sign reads "Bangladesh Farmacia" (to appeal to both South Asian and South American constituencies) and where a Guatemalan shop closes and is fast replaced by a Russian deli? Head north up 74th Street, stopping in **Patel Brothers** supermarket (No. 37-27; 718-898-3445) to ogle exotic produce, **India Sari Palace** (No. 37-07; 718-426-2700) to shop for saris, and **Al Naimat** (No. 37-03; 718-476-1100) to buy South Asian sweets. Take a right on 37th Avenue, Jackson Heights's main thoroughfare. Pick up a Colombian salpicón, halfway between fruit salad and juice, at **La Paisa Bakery** (37-03 82nd Street; 718-779-2784) to tide you over until you reach **La Gran Uruguaya** (85-02 37th Avenue; 718-505-0404) for coffee and buttery soft Uruguayan and Colombian pastries.

6 *Chez Satchmo* 1 p.m.

At the **Louis Armstrong House Museum** (34-56 107th Street; 718-478-8274; louisarmstronghouse.org), the décor was more or less frozen in time when Armstrong, the jazz giant, died in his sleep (in the bed you'll see) in 1971. His wife, Lucille, lived on in the house until 1982 but left most things untouched, down to the reel-to-reel tape recorders in Satchmo's office-studio, a bottle of his cologne, and the gilded bathroom fixtures. Why did a celebrity like Armstrong choose to live the last three decades of his life in a modest house in the working-class Corona neighborhood of Queens? That question is explored on the guided tour.

7 *Panoramic View* 3 p.m.

Take the No. 7 train two stops down from the Armstrong house to **Flushing Meadows-Corona Park**. The borough's biggest park, it hosts sporting events ranging from the annual United States Open tennis championships to hardscrabble immigrant cricket games. Walk toward the 12-story-high Unisphere sculpture, built for the 1964 World's Fair, and seek out the etched granite work nearby in which the artist Matt Mullican recounts the history of the park. Then head into the **Queens Museum of Art** (718-592-9700; queensmuseum.org), home to the

8 *Eat Uzbek* 8 p.m.

Of course Queens has a restaurant specializing in Bukharan Jewish cuisine from Uzbekistan — need you even ask? **Cheburechnaya** (92-09 63rd Drive; 718-897-9080; $) is a diner-like restaurant in the Rego Park neighborhood with food not like that of any diner you've ever seen. This area's so-called "Russian" Jewish community is largely from Central Asia, and foods from that region are the specialties here. The namesake chebureki may look like the stuffed fried pockets of countless other cultures, but the Central Asian spice blend makes it clear these are no empanadas. Even better are the samcy — flaky savory pastries filled with pumpkin or ribs.

9 *Taste of Home* 10 p.m.

Despite its international flair, Queens is situated (did you forget?) in the United States. Two subway stops farther down Queens Boulevard is **Forest Hills**, a suburban-feeling neighborhood where a buzzing

ABOVE Reel-to-reel tape recorders at the Louis Armstrong House Museum, where many things remain as they were when Armstrong died in 1971.

BELOW Well stocked with memorabilia, the Museum of the Moving Image is a must-see for television and movie fans, especially if they have long memories.

night-life spot is, surprisingly, an American bakery that gets as packed on late evenings as it does for weekend brunch. **Martha's Country Bakery** (70-28 Austin Street; 718-544-0088; marthascountrybakery.com) serves cappuccino and tantalizing desserts like red velvet cheesecake and absurdly scrumptious sour cream apple pie.

SUNDAY

10 *Korean Resort* 8 a.m.

It's worth getting up early and taking a cab to the **Spa Castle** (131-10 11th Avenue; 718-939-6300; ny.spacastleusa.com), an immaculate, Korean-owned palace of relaxation in College Point that attracts a cross section of Queens. For just twice the price of a standard storefront massage, you can spend all day enjoying the wondrous variety of saunas (including

one lined with plates of gold), elaborate hot tubs with acupressure jets (both indoors and out), and rooms for meditation and sleeping — plus, for an extra charge, massages and treatments. There's even sushi, Korean, and other fare.

11 *Upstairs, Downstairs* 11:30 a.m.

Flushing, Queens, is New York's most vibrant Chinatown, exemplified by the boisterous scene at **Grand Restaurant** (40-21 Main Street; 718-321-8258; $$), a mind-bogglingly huge dim sum palace on the third floor of the New World Mall. Choose from delicate shrimp dumplings, sticky rice with chicken wrapped in lotus leaves, and tofu rolls stuffed with pork and mushroom. For more variety and even lower prices, visit the food court downstairs and choose from a continent's worth of noodles, soups, and dumplings — from China, Hong Kong, Taiwan, Korea, and beyond.

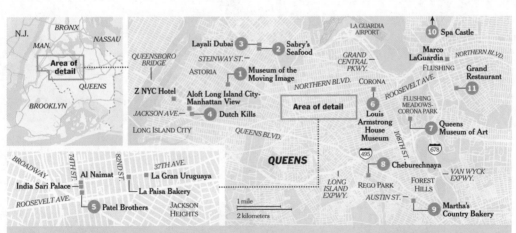

THE BASICS

Queens is served by several New York City subway lines and is a short ride from Manhattan.

Z NYC Hotel
11-01 43rd Avenue
212-319-7000
zhotelny.com
$$
Manhattan-style chic decidedly out

of place in Long Island City. Rooms have floor-to-ceiling windows with views of the skyline across the East River.

Aloft Long Island City - Manhattan View
27-45 Jackson Avenue
718-433-9305
$$$
Colorful, contemporary hotel with Manhattan views in Long Island City.

Marco LaGuardia
137-07 Northern Boulevard
718-445-3300
marcolaguardiahotel.com
$$
Billed as an airport hotel, it's actually just a few blocks from the No. 7 train in central Flushing.

Shelter Island

Shelter Island—about 12.5 square miles of wetlands, forests, beaches, golf courses, marinas, and homes from humble to grand—lies snugly between the North and South Forks of Long Island, protected from wind and rough seas. Reachable only by ferries, it has about 2,400 year-round residents, but the population grows to about 12,000 in the summer. Still, with one-third of the island set aside as a nature preserve, it remains a bucolic place, beloved by long-timers and newcomers alike. — BY JANE BLACKBURN BORNEMEIER

FRIDAY

1 *Island Immersion* 2 p.m.

From the North Ferry landing (that's the ferry from Greenport on the North Fork), head up the hill to **Stars Café** (17 Grand Avenue; starscafeshelterisland. com) for a snack. Then immerse yourself in history with a stroll through Shelter Island Heights, the most charming nook on the island. Originally named Prospect by the landowner Frederick Chase in the early 19th century, the area later became the site of camp meetings for the Methodist Episcopal Church. Its current design dates to about 1872 and was conceived by, among others, Frederick Law Olmsted and the landscape architect Robert Morris Copeland. The centerpiece of the Heights, the Union Chapel, was built in 1875.

2 *Find Your Perch* 5 p.m.

You'll find yourself discovering scenic views all weekend, and taking note of vantage points. One spot is the porch of the **Shelter Island Country Club** (26 Sunnyside Avenue; shelterislandcountryclub.com), looking toward the Peconic River and Dering Harbor from one of the island's highest points. The country club, also known as Goat Hill, is a public nine-hole golf course established in 1901, and its restaurant, the Flying Goat, and bar are favorite gathering places for locals. Order a drink and soak in the view. Another lookout point nearby is at the historic **Chequit** hotel, pronounced CHEE-quit (23 Grand Avenue; thechequit. com), facing the water and the North Fork.

3 *Island Pasta* 7 p.m.

Have a relaxed dinner at **Caci Shelter Island** ($$$), a branch of a popular North Fork Italian restaurant. You'll find it at the Shelter Island House (11 Stearns Point Road; shelterislandhouse.com), a hotel with a long history and resort touches like bocce courts and Adirondack chairs. Reserve well in advance for an outdoor table, and order from a menu featuring house-made pastas and sauces made with locally sourced ingredients.

SATURDAY

4 *Harbor Cycle* 10 a.m.

Rent a bicycle at **Piccozzi's Bike Shop** (177 North Ferry Road; jwpiccozzi.com) and take a ride through the tiny village of Dering Harbor and its surroundings. On Winthrop Road, pass Dering Harbor Inn, another of the island's resort hotels. This one has tennis courts and a fitness center that offers yoga, spinning, and Zumba classes. Cross a fishing bridge between the harbor and Gardiner's Creek, and explore small streets and country roads. The harbor is full of grand sailboats in summer, while the stately homes along the way are among the island's most elegant.

5 *Beach Selection* 1 p.m.

For some, the lovely, protected beaches (shelter-islandchamber.org/beaches) are the real reason to come here. Pick up sandwiches at the **Marie Eiffel Market** (184 North Ferry Road; marieeiffelmarket. com; $$) across from Piccozzi's Bike Shop and head

OPPOSITE Out for a hike at Mashomack Preserve.

BELOW Pick up sandwiches at the Marie Eiffel Market.

to Wades Beach on the south side of the island. **Shelter Island Kayak** (80 Burns Road; kayaksi.com) offers two-hour kayak tours from Coecles Harbor through nearby waterways and will also transport kayaks and paddleboards to the beach of your choice with a little advance notice. Wades, with picnic tables, lifeguards, and a restroom, is a family favorite. The adjoining Dickerson Creek is a treasured spot for clamming at low tide and watching the tiny fiddler crabs burrow into the sand. (If you want to dig for edible clams, you'll need a shellfish permit from the town hall.) Across the way is a hook of land known as Shell Beach, accessible by water or by the narrow, sandy Oak Tree Lane.

6 *No-Bathing Beauty* 4 p.m.

It would be wrong to miss what some people think is the loveliest beach of them all: **Hay Beach** on Menhaden Lane. It has no services, and a sign declares it is not a bathing beach. It does have nesting areas for piping plovers and mesmerizing views of Gardiner's Bay, the lighthouse known as Bug Light, and the meandering coastline leading to Orient Point on the North Fork.

7 *Prep at the Pridwin* 6 p.m.

Head back toward the North Ferry and prepare yourself for the only real nighttime scene on the island, along Shore Road and Crescent Beach. Start with dinner at the 1920s-era **Pridwin Hotel** (81 Shore Road; pridwin.com; $$). Entrees like lobster roll,

ABOVE Coecles Harbor and Bay, the launching point for tours given by Shelter Island Kayak.

RIGHT Stars Café in Shelter Island Heights.

slow-cooked salmon, and local striped bass are a good bet here. Of course, you'll want a view, and the upstairs balcony facing Greenport has one of the best for diners on the island.

8 *Teens With Strings* 7:30 p.m.

Take in a concert at the **Perlman Music Program** (73 Shore Road; perlmanmusicprogram.org). If the name sounds familiar, it should. The center—on land that was once Dr. Pettit's Camps and then the Peconic Lodge—was created in 1994 by Toby Perlman, the wife of the violinist Itzhak Perlman. It provides a summer of intensive musical training for talented young string musicians, and its evening performances of classical music are popular among locals and visitors alike. Perlman himself makes occasional appearances.

9 *The Party* 9 p.m.

For many visitors, the two-story party scene at **Sunset Beach** (35 Shore Road; sunsetbeachli.com), a hotel and restaurant, is not to be missed. Some arrive

by boat — or more accurately, by yacht — from the Hamptons, anchoring off the beach for late-night mingling over food and drinks. There's a daytime scene here, too, with guests ordering drinks, playing beach volleyball, or having massages on the beach.

SUNDAY

10 *Well Preserved* 9 a.m.

Take a hike at **Mashomack Preserve** (shelter-island.org/mashomack.html), which is protected from development by the Nature Conservancy. The preserve has more than 2,000 acres of forests and wetlands, threaded with trails that range in length from 1.5 miles to nearly 11. A renovated manor house is the scene of social events in the summer.

11 *Brunch on a Promontory* 11:30 a.m.

Ram's Head Inn (108 Ram Island Drive; theramsheadinn.com), on the island's picturesque eastern end, sits on a promontory overlooking Coecles Harbor on one side and Gardiner's Bay on the other. Narrow causeways connect two islands — Little Ram Island and Ram Island (also known as Big Ram) — to the rest of Shelter Island. Brunch ($$) features entrees like shrimp and grits and duck confit hash with poached eggs and hollandaise. After consuming your choice, stroll down the luxurious lawn and sit in an Adirondack chair or make your way to the little private beach. Sit back and plan your next trip to Shelter Island.

ABOVE The Chequit, an inn dating from 1872, offers genteel relaxation and views of the water.

THE BASICS

Check the locations and schedules of the Shelter Island ferries at their websites, northferry.com and south-ferry.com. Either ferry will transport your car, which you are likely to want with you on the island. Taxi service is available.

The Chequit
23 Grand Avenue
thechequit.com
$$$
Inn dating from 1872 and with a history of celebrity guests. Imposing hilltop location in easy walking distance of the North Ferry.

Seven
7 Stearns Point Road
sevenonshelter.com
$$$-$$$$
B&B just uphill from Crescent Beach. Once a farmhouse, built in 1902, it features kinetic sculptures and a contemporary art collection.

CONNECTICUT

SHELTER ISLAND

NEW YORK

Atlantic Ocean

North Ferry Landing
Dering Harbor

— CLINTON AVE.

Union Chapel
The Chequit
5 Marie Eiffel Market

SHELTER ISLAND HEIGHTS
Dering Harbor Inn

Stars Café
1
4
Piccozzi's Bike Shop
WINTHROP RD.
Gardiner's Creek

— PROSPECT AVE.

Crescent Beach
SHELTER ISLAND
114

2 Shelter Island Country Club

Peconic River
SUNNYSIDE AVE. —

Sunset Beach
9

1 mile
2 kilometers
Long Island Sound
25
Orient Point

Seven
Peconic River
Gardiner's Bay

Pridwin Hotel
42
SHORE RD.
STEARNS POINT RD.
7
8
3
Caci Shelter Island/ Shelter Island House
Greenport
Bug Light
6 Hay Beach

Perlman Music Program
Area of detail
Coecles Harbor
Ram's Head Inn
11
— RAM ISLAND

W. NECK RD.
SUFFOLK

Shelter Island Kayak

1/4 mile
1/2 kilometer
Shell Beach
114
10 — Mashomack Preserve
Wades Beach

Halifax

Halifax is a harbor city steeped in maritime history. Founded in 1749 as a British naval and military base, it served originally as a strategic counter to French bases elsewhere in Atlantic Canada, and many years later as an assembly point for shipping convoys during World Wars I and II. Today, Halifax is better known for its lobster, which you can fill up on from morning (lobster eggs Benedict anyone?) till night while still having enough cash left for a sail around the harbor on a tall ship. A vibrant student population—the city has six universities—gives Halifax a youthful, bohemian feel, too. As a result, it's often compared with that other hilly town on the ocean, San Francisco, but you'll find that Halifax's blend of fair-trade coffee bars, wharfside lobster shacks, and public gardens has a character all its own.
— BY TATIANA BONCOMPAGNI

FRIDAY

1 *A Pint and a Pirate Joke* 5 p.m.

Start the weekend right at **Alexander Keith's Nova Scotia Brewery** (1496 Lower Water Street; 902-455-1474; alexanderkeithsbrewery.com). Take the 55-minute tour led by local actors in 19th-century garb, and you'll get not only a primer on the history of Halifax's oldest working brewery—it dates back to the 1820s—but a pint of its finest as well. Find a comfy bench in the brewery's Stag's Head Tavern, where barkeepers have been known to regale the crowd with old pirate jokes and barmaids have burst into song.

2 *Bard of Nova Scotia* 7 p.m.

Shakespeare is so much better in the grass, methinks. Grab a blanket and some cushions and head to **Point Pleasant Park** (Queen Victoria leased it to Halifax around the mid-19th century for one shilling a year, which the city still pays), where the **Shakespeare by the Sea Theater Society** (902-422-0295; shakespearebythesea.ca) stages the Bard's plays. The park overlooks the entrance to Halifax

OPPOSITE The *Bluenose II*, a replica of the schooner on the back of the Canadian dime, docked on the waterfront.

RIGHT Firing the noon-day gun at Halifax Citadel.

Harbor, so enjoy the sublime views, then arrive for the performance 10 minutes before show time and stake your claim on the grass. A donation is encouraged.

3 *Dinner at the Shoe Shop* 10 p.m.

For a late meal, a sophisticated spot is the **Economy Shoe Shop** (1663 Argyle Street; 902-423-8845; economyshoeshop.ca; $-$$), a cafe and bar that takes its name from a salvaged neon sign hanging from the side of its building. Honor Haligonian tradition by ordering seafood chowder.

SATURDAY

4 *Breakfast on the Commons* 9 a.m.

In the 18th century, town authorities set aside more than 200 acres for community cattle grazing and military use. The part that remains, called the Commons, is a municipal complex of sports fields and playgrounds—a great place for a morning jog. And for those who would rather stroll a bit and then slip into the day more gently, there's brunch nearby at the **Coastal** (2731 Robie Street; 902-405-4022; thecoastal.ca; $$), where just reading the menu can keep you entertained. Selections include Breakfast of Champignons (eggs with asparagus, mushrooms, tapenade, and other fixings) and the Elvis (a waffle sandwich with peanut butter, bananas, and bacon).

5 *Antiquing on Agricola* 10:30 a.m.

If you're in the market for well-priced antiques or reproductions, make sure you hit Agricola Street.

ABOVE The view down to the harbor from Citadel Hill.

At **McLellan Antiques & Restoration** (2738 Agricola Street; 902-455-4545; mclellanantiques.com), you'll find furniture including bureaus and cupboards, early pine pieces, and 1920s mahogany. **Finer Things Antiques** (2797 Agricola Street; 902-456-1412; finerthingsantiques.com) is the place to go for nautical antiques like old ship's wheels and compasses. For more eclectic shopping (and to pick up a snack for an on-the-go lunch), hike down to the harbor to the **Halifax Seaport Farmers' Market** (1209 Marginal Road; 902-492-4043; halifaxfarmersmarket.com), established in 1750 and now operating in a 56,000-square-foot market hall that opened in 2010.

6 *Sail On* 1 p.m.

You haven't really seen Halifax until you tour its harbor — considered the second-largest natural harbor anywhere, after Sydney's — in one of the tall ships that dock at the wharves along Lower Water Street. Sail aboard the *Silva* (902-420-1015; ambassatours.com) and dress warmly; it can get cold on deck. You may have another option: the *Bluenose II* (902-640-3177; bluenose.novascotia.ca) sometimes sails here. It's a replica of the schooner engraved on the Canadian dime, an honor it earned by collecting racing trophies in the 1920s and '30s. Its home port is Lunenburg, about 60 miles away,

but it travels the New England and Maritime Provinces coasts.

7 *Remembrance* 4 p.m.

Halifax's role as a busy port city, sometimes complicated by the North Atlantic's infamous fog, has cursed it with a legacy of shipwrecks and catastrophe. The **Maritime Museum of the Atlantic** (1675 Lower Water Street; 902-424-7490; maritimemuseum.novascotia.ca) has moving displays of artifacts from voyages gone wrong. One commemorates the disaster most horrific for Halifax. It happened in 1917, when a French ship loaded with explosives collided in the harbor with a Belgian relief ship, resulting in a blast that killed nearly 2,000 people, injured thousands more, and obliterated the north end of the city. The museum also displays an incredibly well-preserved deck chair from the *Titanic*, which sank off the Grand Banks (the famous fishing grounds northeast of here) in 1912. Of the 328 bodies recovered from the *Titanic*, 150 are buried in Halifax.

8 *Menu Study* 8 p.m.

Make your way to the neighborhood of Dalhousie University's downtown Sexton campus for dinner at **Chives Canadian Bistro** (1537 Barrington Street; 902-420-9626; chives.ca; $$$). Its imaginative dishes are made with local and seasonal ingredients, so selections change. Scan the menu for entrees like lamb Mykonos or caramelized sea scallops with pork

belly, spinach-and-ricotta ravioli, and mustard crème fraîche. If you're out late, stop almost anywhere for another Haligonian tradition: a donair — a messy, tasty beef kebab or gyro sandwich, meant to be eaten outside after a night at the pub.

SUNDAY

9 *The Citadel* 11 a.m.

The best views in the city can be had from the **Halifax Citadel** (5425 Sackville Street; 902-426-5080; pc.gc.ca/lhn-nhs/ns/halifax/index.aspx), a star-shaped fort built on its highest hill. The British built four forts atop the summit, the last of which was

ABOVE Homage to the original brewmaster at Alexander Keith's Nova Scotia Brewery.

completed in 1856, when the United States posed the greatest threat to the harbor and city. Be sure to get there in time for the "noon-day gun" firing of the cannon. Afterward watch pipers and drummers perform in the enormous gravel courtyard.

10 *Last Call for Lobster* 1 p.m.

It wouldn't be right to leave without a taste of sweet Nova Scotia lobster. Snag an umbrella-shaded outdoor table at **Salty's** (1877 Upper Water Street; 902-423-6818; saltys.ca; $$-$$$). Go for a steamed one-and-a-half-pounder and a side of hot sweet-potato fries, and you won't be hungry on the plane going home.

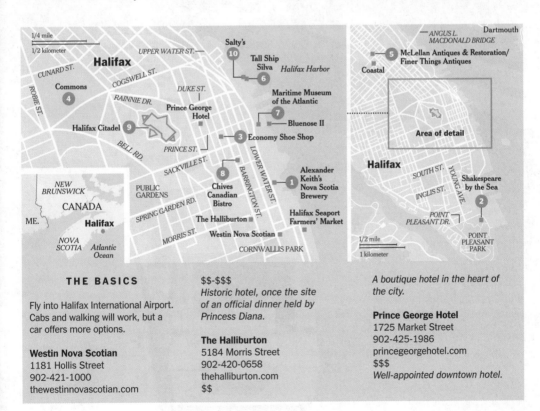

THE BASICS

Fly into Halifax International Airport. Cabs and walking will work, but a car offers more options.

Westin Nova Scotian
1181 Hollis Street
902-421-1000
thewestinnovascotian.com

$$-$$$
Historic hotel, once the site of an official dinner held by Princess Diana.

The Halliburton
5184 Morris Street
902-420-0658
thehalliburton.com
$$

A boutique hotel in the heart of the city.

Prince George Hotel
1725 Market Street
902-425-1986
princegeorgehotel.com
$$$
Well-appointed downtown hotel.

Ottawa

Ottawa has always had image problems. Back in 1857, when it beat out its rivals Toronto and Montreal in a bid to become Canada's national capital, the governor general bemoaned Parliament's move to what seemed a frontier outpost on the Ottawa River as an "exile to wilderness." Since then, it has often been written off as a staid hub of government. But beneath Ottawa's buttoned-up, civil-servant demeanor lies a vibrant community, with enough green space, trails, and water within city limits to satisfy the most hyperactive of travelers. — BY KATIE ARNOLD AND REMY SCALZA

FRIDAY

1 *Homage to the Hill* 2 p.m.

With a metropolitan-area population of about 1.2 million, Ottawa is smaller than many national capitals, but it holds the machinery of government, the requisite share of pomp and circumstance, and more than 125 embassies. You're too late today for the British-style changing of the guard on **Parliament Hill** (111 Wellington Street; 613-992-4793; visit.parl. ca), but you can view the stolid granite buildings with their formal neo-Gothic turrets. Just steps from downtown, across an emerald lawn, the nexus of Canada's government is accessible. Tours are available, but because of a decade-long renovation of the main building, the Centre Block, they are now of the West Block, new home of the House of Commons, and the Government Conference Center, where the Senate sits.

2 *Over the River* 4 p.m.

It's an easy walk through **Major's Hill Park**, a grassy headland with unobstructed views of Parliament Hill, to the footpath across Alexandra Bridge. Beneath you is the imposing Ottawa River, once frequented by fur traders and loggers. At this spot it forms the border between two huge provinces, Ontario and Quebec. Just across the river in Gatineau, Quebec, the **Canadian Museum of History** (100 Laurier Street; 819-776-7000; historymuseum.ca)

tells Canada's story from its fur-trading frontier days and before. The First Peoples Hall displays relics from Canada's 53 cultural groups, some dating as far back as 20,000 years.

3 *Breaking for Mussels* 6 p.m.

Come quitting time, government workers and others in the know descend on **Métropolitain Brasserie** (700 Sussex Drive; 613-562-1160; metropolitainbrasserie.com), with its ruby-leather banquettes and hammered zinc bar. During Hill Hour (weeknights from 3 till 7), it dishes up plates of steaming Prince Edward Island mussels, fresh Malpeque oysters, and jumbo shrimp from the raw bar.

4 *Fare of the Country* 8 p.m.

Just a block east of Sussex, **ByWard Market** is a bustling, three-by-five-block warren of hip boutiques, wine bars, and restaurants — an unexpected microplex of cool in the middle of the city. For food from one of the city's highly regarded kitchens, dine at **Restaurant 18** (18 York Street; 613-244-1188; restaurant18.com; $$$-$$$$). The cuisine is French; the décor is sophisticated. Expect fresh produce, interesting flavors, and sturdy main dishes like Quebec wild boar or Nova Scotia swordfish.

SATURDAY

5 *Run the Canal* 9 a.m.

The fastest way to wake up in Ottawa is with a sprint along the city's beloved **Rideau Canal**, part of a

OPPOSITE The Rideau Canal, a playground year-round.

RIGHT Berries in season at the ByWard Market.

125-mile-long waterway that links the Ottawa River to Lake Ontario. It first opened in 1832. Start at the hydraulic locks below Sussex Street, and head south along the paved paths that are used by joggers, bicyclists, and inline skaters. In winter, the canal turns into a perfect linear rink, with skaters (including commuters headed to work) and ice sleighs crowding the glassy-smooth surface. The city's Winterlude festival, which draws hundreds of thousands of people annually, grew up around the canal. In warmer weather, you may see canoeists and kayakers on the canal's placid waters and also nearby on the much wider Ottawa River. Downstream, the river funnels into the Champlain Rapids and white-water kayakers surf a Class III standing wave.

6 *The Baguettes Are Dynamite* 11 a.m.

Lines out the door attest to the popularity of the French-trained pastry chef Kevin Mathieson's **Art-Is-In Boulangerie** (250 City Centre Avenue; 613-695-1226, extension 801; artisinbakery.com; $), a bakery and cafe. Weekend mornings, the bright, unfinished space is crammed with patrons who come for white sourdough loaves and Dynamite Baguettes (blistered crust over an explosion of air pockets), or for croissants, brioche, scones, and more. Order a breakfast sandwich from the cafe, and try to resist the pastries.

7 *Neighborhood Rising* Noon

A once shady stretch of dilapidated houses and storefronts, Wellington West has morphed into an "it" neighborhood. Inside **Maker House Co.** (987 Wellington Street West; 613-422-6253: makerhouse.com), find quirky objets d'art, furniture, and housewares, most locally made. Farther on, the ceramicist Ginger McCoy's **Hintonburg Pottery** (1242 1/2 Wellington Street West; 613-725-6909; hintonburgpottery.

ABOVE Taking in the scenery at Gatineau Park.

RIGHT Native art in the First Peoples Hall at the Canadian Museum of History.

ca) showcases her turquoise-hued vessels. Stop into the tasting room at **Tooth and Nail** (3 Irving Avenue; 613-695-4677; toothandnailbeer.com) for great small-batch beers.

8 *Time for Tea* 3 p.m.

Traditional afternoon tea is serious business at **Zoe's** ($$$) in the Fairmont Château Laurier (1 Rideau Street; 613-241-1414; fairmont.com/laurier-ottawa), a grand railway hotel choicely located between Parliament and the Rideau Canal, but the experience is anything but stuffy. Come as you are, and when the tea wagon rolls around, take a sniff of several loose-leaf black teas. Your choice is brewed in a pot at your table and served with a meal's worth of tidbits like Nova Scotia lox and tiny bagels, Canadian white Cheddar, and just-baked scones with Devonshire cream. You'll be relaxed when you re-emerge onto the street. But if you haven't had your fill of shopping, go from here back to ByWard Market, which by day is an amateur shopper's dream: just enough unexpected finds to keep you scouting and not too many to overwhelm the brain or the bank account.

9 *Diplomatic Dining* 7 p.m.

Just opposite the United States Embassy, **Play Food & Wine** (1 York Street; 613-667-9207; playfood.ca; $$) is Stephen Beckta's and Michael Moffatt's

casual, small-plates restaurant, spread over two floors. Their Beckta restaurant has long been synonymous with Ottawa fine dining. Here the fare runs to items like cauliflower and apple soup followed by hanger steak and frites.

10 *Sip High or Low* 10 p.m.

On the 16th floor of the Andaz hotel, **Copper Spirits and Sights** (325 Dalhousie Street; 613-321-1234; ottawa.andaz.hyatt.com) is a pleasurably conspiratorial rooftop lounge. Lights are low, the better to admire views of the twinkling city while sipping a martini made with local Top Shelf vodka. On ground level, head to the 1849 **Château Lafayette** (42 York Street; 613-241-4747; thelaff.ca), fittingly nicknamed

the Laff, said to be Ottawa's oldest tavern, complete with quart bottles of Labatt 50 and rowdy live music.

SUNDAY

11 *Hike and Look Back* 10 a.m.

Across the river in Quebec, **Gatineau Park** (819-827-2020; ncc-ccn.gc.ca/places-to-visit/gatineau-park) shelters 140 square miles of wooded backcountry. The park's western boundary, the Eardley Escarpment, marks the edge of the Canadian Shield, a slab of granite bedrock that sprawls northward to the Arctic. Hike the three-mile Skyline trail, where you will get a taste of wilderness and some great views back toward Ottawa.

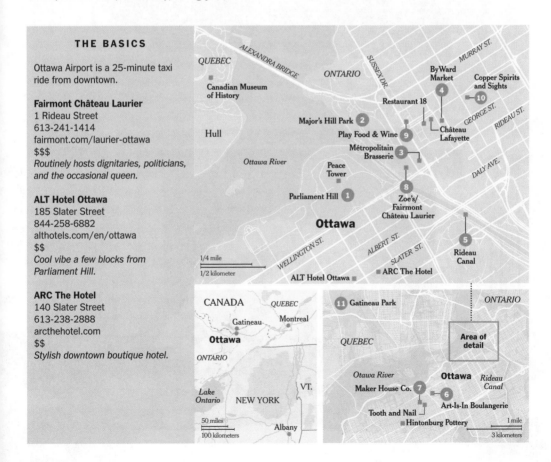

THE BASICS

Ottawa Airport is a 25-minute taxi ride from downtown.

Fairmont Château Laurier
1 Rideau Street
613-241-1414
fairmont.com/laurier-ottawa
$$$
Routinely hosts dignitaries, politicians, and the occasional queen.

ALT Hotel Ottawa
185 Slater Street
844-258-6882
althotels.com/en/ottawa
$$
Cool vibe a few blocks from Parliament Hill.

ARC The Hotel
140 Slater Street
613-238-2888
arcthehotel.com
$$
Stylish downtown boutique hotel.

The Brandywine Valley

In the Brandywine Valley, spanning Pennsylvania and Delaware, one can canoe past riverbanks where George Washington placed his troops and visit the house in which he prepared for battle. Minutes away, perfectly maintained, are estates and gardens of the kind that became symbols of young America's rise to global power, all of them connected with the du Pont family of industrialists. The Wyeth clan of artists, too, left its mark, living and painting here. Preservationists have assured that there are still untrammeled vistas in the valley today, giving it the allure of landscapes that have been spared suburban sprawl. — BY GERALDINE FABRIKANT

FRIDAY

1 *A Watershed Battle* 2 p.m.

As he prepared to stop General William Howe and his British troops at Chadds Ford, George Washington took over the simple two-story stone house of Benjamin Ring, a local farmer and mill owner who was the town's most prominent businessman. Now it is part of the 52-acre **Brandywine Battlefield Park** (1491 Baltimore Pike, Chadds Ford; 610-459-3342; brandywinebattlefield.org). You can stand in the room where Washington strategized, and the park also has a 20-minute movie about the battle as well as cannons, guns, and maps. The battle, on Sept. 11, 1777, was a stinging defeat for the Americans.

2 *On the Brandywine* 3 p.m.

Whether you choose a canoe, kayak, or tube, don't miss a trip down the Brandywine from the **Northbrook Canoe Co.** (1810 Beagle Road, West Chester; 610-793-2279; northbrookcanoe.com) or **Wilderness Canoe Trips** (2111 Concord Pike/Route 202, Wilmington; 302-654-2227; wildernesscanoetrips.com). You may pass the site of Trimble's Ford, where British and Hessian forces crossed the Brandywine to flank Washington. You are also likely to see turtles, birds, and deer as you glide by walnut, oak, and sycamore trees.

3 *Jaguar on Your Plate* 7:30 p.m.

The menu is imaginative, and so is the décor, at **Krazy Kat's** (528 Montchanin Road, Montchanin; 302-888-4200; krazykatsrestaurant.com; $$$), with its washed peach walls, tapestry-upholstered side chairs, colorful dinner plates with jaguars racing across them, and portraits of cats and dogs in military uniform. Choose from dishes like corn duck with sourdough spaetzle or swordfish with fennel.

SATURDAY

4 *Breakfast With Hank* 8 a.m.

No restaurant in town is probably busier for an early breakfast than **Hank's Place** (1625 Creek Road, Chadds Ford; 610-388-7061; hanks-place.net; $) in Chadds Ford. This lively diner, with its baskets of petunias and impatiens hanging along the outdoor terrace, was a favorite of Andrew Wyeth's. Lines can be long, but the reward is corned beef hash and eggs or Italian-style scrambled eggs with mild Italian sausage.

5 *Wyeth Country* 9:30 a.m.

The Brandywine area has been home to three generations of Wyeths, and about 40 years ago the Brandywine Conservancy bought a grist mill that was set to be demolished. It created the **Brandywine River Museum of Art** (1 Hoffman's Mill Road, Chadds Ford; 610-388-2700; brandywine.org/museum) at a

OPPOSITE A Gilbert Stuart portrait of George Washington decorates the dining room of Winterthur, Henry Francis du Pont's country estate.

BELOW The Benjamin Ring House, George Washington's headquarters, at the Brandywine Battlefield State Park.

location along the meandering river where the views are as enchanting as the works by the three Wyeths — N.C., Andrew, and Jamie — that you will find inside.

6 *Bring On the Books* 11 a.m.

Kennett Square may be small, but it is big on books. **Thomas Macaluso Used and Rare Books** (130 South Union Street, Kennett Square; 610-444-1063) is a labyrinth of a store where readers can find historical maps and books, like a first edition of *Official Letters to the American Congress by His Excellency George Washington Commander-in-Chief of the Continental Forces*, published in 1795. Or drive out from Kennett Square along open country roads to **Baldwin's Book Barn** (865 Lenape Road, West Chester; 610-696-0816; bookbarn.com), a five-story extravaganza of a bookstore in a converted dairy farm. An estimated 300,000 books fill the place, with specialties in rare books and books on local history.

7 *A Place of Her Own* 1 p.m.

"You might like the garden, but it is a bit over-grown," said Susan Teiser as she welcomed a guest to her casual **Centreville Café** (5800 Kennett Pike, Centreville; 302-777-4911; centrevillecafe.com; $$). She makes just about everything on the premises; two good choices were tomato soup and a hearts of palm salad with a mix of pecans, cheese, and apples.

8 *How Henry Kept Busy* 2 p.m.

Henry Francis du Pont's wife, Ruth, called it "Henry's Hobby," and the estate he named **Winterthur** (5105 Kennett Pike, Winterthur; 302-888-4600; winterthur.org) was certainly an expensive du Pont indulgence. While visiting Electra Havemeyer Webb's Vermont home in 1923, Henry du Pont experienced a coup de foudre for American furniture and decorative arts, and he soon began a shopping spree that resulted in a house filled with American antiques. Among the discoveries in

Winterthur's 175 rooms are 69 of the 302 pieces of a dinner service that belonged to George and Martha Washington. The nearly 1,000-acre property includes 60 acres of gardens that are as naturalistic as the nearby Longwood Gardens, created by Henry's cousin Pierre S. du Pont, are manicured. So enamored of his trees was this du Pont that he instructed his staff that in case of a fire, they were to save the trees before the house. Along with an azalea woods, there is a charming children's garden complete with a tulip tree house and a fairy cottage.

9 *Great Style, Great Food* 7 p.m.

Don't let the mall location fool you. **Sovana Bistro** (696 Unionville Road, Kennett Square; 610-444-5600; sovanabistro.com; $$$) in Kennett Square, with its high ceilings and elaborate wood chandeliers that give off a warm glow, is one of the trendiest restaurants in the valley. Mushrooms, the pride of this area, appear in dishes like grilled mushroom tart and pan-roasted chicken with

ABOVE Andrew Wyeth's studio at the Brandywine River Museum of Art. The area has been home to three generations of painters from the Wyeth family.

BELOW The conservatory at Longwood Gardens, one of the du Pont family estates in the area that are open to the public for tours.

mushrooms and wilted spinach (but not in the liquid-center butterscotch cake).

10 *Where the Locals Loll* 9 p.m.
Have an evening drink at the **Gables at Chadds Ford** (423 Baltimore Pike, Chadds Ford; 610-388-7700; thegablesatchaddsford.com), a converted dairy barn with red-leather-upholstered metal stools and high-backed banquettes lining the walls. A piano player entertains on weekends.

SUNDAY

11 *Pierre the Gardener* 10 a.m.
Gardens were the passion of Pierre S. du Pont, who purchased the original 202 acres of what is now **Longwood Gardens** (1001 Longwood Road, Kennett Square; 610-388-1000; longwoodgardens.org), then

known as Peirce's Park, in 1906 to preserve its wealth of trees. His obsession went beyond flowers and plants to fruits and vegetables, and there is still a small house there where he grew bananas and plantains for employees and friends. As you explore the 1,077 acres, which include an outdoor topiary garden and a silver garden of succulents and cactuses in the conservatory, be sure to check out the water lily pond in a courtyard outside the hothouses. Some lily pads grow as wide as eight feet.

ABOVE Sampling the merchandise at Baldwin's Book Barn.

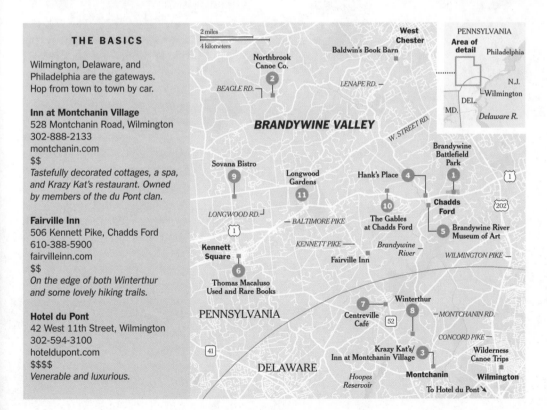

THE BASICS

Wilmington, Delaware, and Philadelphia are the gateways. Hop from town to town by car.

Inn at Montchanin Village
528 Montchanin Road, Wilmington
302-888-2133
montchanin.com
$$
Tastefully decorated cottages, a spa, and Krazy Kat's restaurant. Owned by members of the du Pont clan.

Fairville Inn
506 Kennett Pike, Chadds Ford
610-388-5900
fairvilleinn.com
$$
On the edge of both Winterthur and some lovely hiking trails.

Hotel du Pont
42 West 11th Street, Wilmington
302-594-3100
hoteldupont.com
$$$$
Venerable and luxurious.

Gettysburg

On July 1, 1863, Confederate and Union troops descended on the grassy hills of Gettysburg, thrusting the sleepy town of 2,400 into the Civil War. The three-day Battle of Gettysburg ended the Confederate invasion of the North and resulted in staggering losses for both sides — an estimated 51,000 casualties in all for the campaign. Each year, about 1.2 million visitors journey to the Gettysburg National Military Park to see the battlefield and imagine the struggle unfolding in this peaceful setting. Gettysburg itself — still a small town, with a population of only 7,700 — has a lot to offer beyond its compelling history. The town's compact but lively center, lined with Federal-style buildings, is filled with mom-and-pop shops and restaurants, and serves as a great base for exploring the region's vineyards and winding country roads. — BY EMILY BRENNAN

FRIDAY

1 *Students' Union* 3 p.m.

Founded in 1832, **Gettysburg College** (300 North Washington Street; gettysburg.edu) sits on 200 bucolic acres north of the town's center. Walk among the mostly brick Georgian and Victorian buildings and stop at the stately white Pennsylvania Hall, an administrative building that was a signal corps station and field hospital for Union and Confederate troops during the battle. Sit in the Adirondack chairs on its expansive lawn, and then step into the Musselman Library to see if there's an exhibition on view.

2 *Homegrown and Homemade* 5 p.m.

Walk down North Washington Street to the **Ragged Edge Coffee House** (110 Chambersburg Street; 717-334-4464) for a snack in a bright, cheerful space decorated with original local art and with books and plants lining the window sills. There is an outdoor terrace and a children's corner. Menu options include smoothies, small plates and pastries. The **Wells Family Baking Company** (100 Chambersburg Street; 717-337-2900) nearby is also a good place for coffee and biscotti (try the lemon anise or cranberry pecan). For shopping, stop in at **A & A Village Treasures** (53 Chambersburg Street; 717-398-2555; aavillagetreasures.com) for jewelry, scarves, and goat-

milk soaps or at **Gallery 30** (26 York Street; 717-334-0335; gallery30.com), which sells pottery and hand-painted gourds by local artisans, as well as blankets, pillows, and tablecloths woven in Pennsylvania.

3 *Meal With a View* 8 p.m.

You used to have to drive about 30 minutes to the chef Neil Annis's restaurant Sidney in East Berlin, Pa., for his locally sourced, seasonal American menu. Now you'll find an outpost, **Sidney Willoughby Run** (730 Chambersburg Road; 717-334-3774; restaurantsidney.com/willoughby-run; $$$$), overlooking the battlefield. Menus vary; one included fall-off-your-fork-tender braised beef short ribs and a salsify purée so creamy it was like a sauce to the broccoli rabe and wild mushrooms.

SATURDAY

4 *Cup of Joe with Abe* 8:30 a.m.

Grab a quick breakfast of coffee, Amish baked goods, and fresh berries at the **Gettysburg Farmers' Market** (gettysburgfarmmarket.com) in Lincoln Square, which is marked by a bronze life-size sculpture (by J. Seward Johnson Jr.) of Abraham Lincoln greeting a modern man with a wave of his stovepipe hat. For a souvenir, pick up a bottle from Torchbearer Sauces; its recipes include Pennsylvania-grown peppers, and the sauces come in tongue-in-cheek flavors like Zombie Apocalypse (ghost and habanero peppers) or Oh My Garlic.

5 *Origin Story* 9 a.m.

Arrive at the **Gettysburg National Park Service Museum and Visitor Center** (1195 Baltimore Pike; 717-334-1124; nps.gov/gett) before the crowds descend at midmorning. The most popular way to navigate the park's 26 miles of roads is by car. CDs of self-guided tours are sold in the bookstore. For a tour with a licensed battlefield guide, reserve a two-hour bus tour or take a two-hour private tour with a guide in your own car. Reservations can also be made online at tickets.gettysburgfoundation.org up to three

OPPOSITE The battlefield, still a focus of reverence and curiosity a century and a half after the Civil War.

days in advance or by phone at 877-874-2478 within three days of your visit. The museum offers a primer on the Civil War through short videos, photographs, and artifacts like Robert E. Lee's battlefield cot and desk. The short film *A New Birth of Freedom* covers the origins of the war; the debate over slavery's expansion to new territories; and the battle's legacy, immortalized by Lincoln's Gettysburg Address, as a defense of democratic ideals. The *Gettysburg Cyclorama*, a monumental 1884 painting by the French artist Paul Philippoteaux that depicts Pickett's Charge, is worth a look.

6 *Battle and Burial* 10 a.m.

Gettysburg National Military Park spans 5,989 acres of woodlands, farmlands, craggy ridges, and sloping valleys, with more than 1,300 monuments erected by the battle's veterans and state governments. Start at McPherson Ridge, where, early in the morning of July 1, 1863, fighting broke out between Union cavalry and Confederate infantry. Then drive south to Little Round Top, the craggy hill that Union soldiers, in a downhill bayonet charge, defended against Confederate troops. At the High Water Mark, look out on the open field that some 12,000 Confederate infantrymen crossed in a mile-long front known as Pickett's Charge. After their decisive defeat, Confederate troops retreated to Virginia, ending Lee's campaign into Pennsylvania. Cross the road to Soldiers' National Cemetery, where about

ABOVE The Cyclorama, a wraparound depiction of the great battle at Gettysburg.

OPPOSITE The national cemetery dedicated by Abraham Lincoln in his Gettysburg Address.

3,500 Union soldiers lie buried. When the cemetery was dedicated on November 19, 1863, Lincoln took two minutes to deliver "a few appropriate remarks" — his Gettysburg Address.

7 *Sushi Fix* 1:30 p.m.

For lunch, **Ping's** (34 Baltimore Street; 717-334-2234; gettysburgpings.com; $) is a friendly Asian restaurant offering Japanese, Chinese and Thai cuisine. Choose from the extensive menu that includes everything from sushi to hot pots, crab rangoon to sweet and sour chicken. You can pick up dessert nearby at **Mr. G's Ice Cream** (404 Baltimore Street; 717-334-7600).

8 *Civilian Side* 3 p.m.

A number of historic houses and foundations line Gettysburg's streets. Skip most of them and go to the **Shriver House** (309 Baltimore Street; 717-337-2800; shriverhouse.org), which gives a glimpse of the battle's effect on civilians. A guide in 19th-century costume takes you through the meticulously refurbished home of the Shrivers, a family who, having fled the battle, returned to find their house repurposed to treat wounded soldiers. At Lincoln Square, drop into the **David Wills House** (8 Lincoln Square; 717-334-2499; gettysburgfoundation.org/david-wills-house), a lawyer's Federal brick home where President Lincoln stayed the night before he delivered the Gettysburg Address. A bedroom, with its original mahogany Rococo bed, is said to be where Lincoln added finishing touches to his speech.

9 *Stout Spot* 8 p.m.

You could go to the darkly lighted, laid-back **Garryowen Irish Pub** (126 Chambersburg Street;

717-337-2719; garryowenirishpub.net; $$) just for a pint of stout, but it would be a shame to miss out on its rib-sticking Irish food, like shepherd's pie or an Irish onion soup made with Guinness instead of wine. Live music ranges from Irish to alt-country.

SUNDAY

10 *Wine Way* Noon

Apple orchards and farms still blanket Adams County, and some have reinvented themselves as vineyards. Take Lincoln Highway to the **Adams County Winery** (251 Peach Tree Road, Orrtanna; 717-334-4631; adamscountywinery.com), an 1860s red barn in Orrtanna where you can taste up to six wines for free. **The Historic Round Barn and Farm Market** (298 Cashtown Road, Biglerville; 717-334-1984; roundbarngettysburg.com), in a 1914 white barn in

Biglerville, sells fresh produce and its own pickled vegetables and jams. Pick up some cheeses and snacks for a picnic across the road at the **Hauser Estate Winery** (410 Cashtown Road, Biglerville; 717-334-4888; hauserestate.com). After sampling some wines here, order a glass of your favorite and set up your picnic on the patio overlooking the valley.

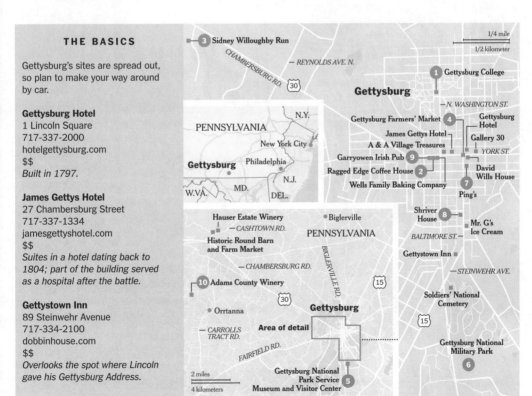

THE BASICS

Gettysburg's sites are spread out, so plan to make your way around by car.

Gettysburg Hotel
1 Lincoln Square
717-337-2000
hotelgettysburg.com
$$
Built in 1797.

James Gettys Hotel
27 Chambersburg Street
717-337-1334
jamesgettyshotel.com
$$
Suites in a hotel dating back to 1804; part of the building served as a hospital after the battle.

Gettystown Inn
89 Steinwehr Avenue
717-334-2100
dobbinhouse.com
$$
Overlooks the spot where Lincoln gave his Gettysburg Address.

Philadelphia

The 18th-century city tucked inside Philadelphia, where the United States was born at Independence Hall, swarms all year with curious tourists, history buffs, and children on school trips. Sprawling out from it is the other Philadelphia, firmly rooted in the 21st century and bustling with the activity of a rapidly evolving destination city. Adventurous restaurants reinforce the city's growing culinary reputation, though an obligatory cheese steak still hits the spot. Neighborhoods in transition provide hot spots for shopping and night life, while other areas keep dishing out some old-school Philly "attytood." And traditional leisure-time stops like the Schuylkill riverbanks and the venerable Franklin Institute keep right on drawing them in. — BY JEFF SCHLEGEL AND FREDA MOON

FRIDAY

1 *Another Go-to Building* 2 p.m.

Independence Hall belongs to the ages; **City Hall** (Broad and Market Streets; 215-686-2840; visitphilly.com/history/philadelphia/city-hall) belongs to Philadelphia. This 548-foot-tall 19th-century building is more than just a big hunk of granite interrupting traffic in the heart of the city — it is topped by a 27-ton bronze statue of William Penn, one of 250 statues by Alexander Milne Calder ornamenting the building inside and out. Take the elevator to the top for 35-mile views from the observation deck. For another kind of overview, take in the displays at the **Philadelphia History Museum** (15 South Seventh Street; 215-685-4830; philadelphiahistory.org), which spans 330 years of local history with objects including a belt given to William Penn by the Lenape people, Schmidt's beer cans, and a collection dedicated to the African-American experience.

2 *Sichuan Style* 5 p.m.

Across the Schuylkill River, the University City location of the locally beloved **Han Dynasty** (3711 Market Street; 215-222-3711; handynasty.net; $$) has a

wide-open dining room with modern lines, rough-hewn wood, and a kitschy cocktail list including bucket-size drinks like the Scorpion Bowl and Singapore Sling. But the food is the real attraction. Plates come one after the other in family-style portions — dan dan noodles, double-cooked fish, and spicy, crispy cucumbers, each rated 1 to 10 on Han's hot-or-not index.

3 *World-Class Collection* 8 p.m.

For most of its 90-year history, the **Barnes Foundation Museum** (2025 Benjamin Franklin Parkway; 215-278-7000; barnesfoundation.org) was seven miles away in suburban Merion. But in 2012 it relocated in the city, bringing one of the world's great collections of works by Picasso, Renoir, Matisse, and Modigliani (and many others) to Philadelphia's Museum Row. On Friday nights, the museum stays open until 10 p.m. and enlivens its atmosphere with music and wine. Day or night, reserve museum tickets well in advance.

SATURDAY

4 *Slice of Local Color* 10 a.m.

Enticing aromas of homemade sausages, cheeses, and pastries infuse the air along the **Ninth Street Italian Market** (Ninth Street, between Wharton and

OPPOSITE AND RIGHT Philadelphia's massive City Hall is topped by a bronze statue of William Penn that weighs 27 tons. The artist Alexander Milne Calder was responsible for the structure's 250-plus statues, including this likeness of Benjamin Franklin.

Fitzwater Streets; phillyitalianmarket.com). Produce vendors ply their wares under green-and-red awnings in front of shops selling Italian specialties and assorted merchandise at this century-old South Philadelphia outdoor market. Hungry? **Lorenzo's Pizza** (Ninth and Christian Streets; 215-922-2540; lorenzospizza.net; $) is an unpretentious corner shop serving one of the city's best pizza slices. The secret: no skimping on spices.

5 *Ben's Place* 1 p.m.

Noted for its giant two-story model of a human heart and interactive displays that make it seem more like a theme park than a science museum, the **Franklin Institute** (222 North 20th Street; 215-448-1200; fi.edu) is aptly named for Benjamin Franklin, the city's favorite polymath. Flight simulators, giant locomotives parked indoors, a virtual trip to astronaut world — it's tough to know where to look. The place to start, though, may be on the Web, where you can buy tickets in advance and skip the long lines waiting at the door.

6 *Shop Your Way* 2 p.m.

Shop your way along 13th Street, visiting interesting shops like **Verde** (108 South 13th Street; 215-546-8700; verdephiladelphia.com), which sells an eclectic mix of charm bracelets, women's clothing by international designers, patent leather bags, and handcrafted Marcie Blaine chocolates. For a midafternoon sugar

fix, try a scoop of Thai coconut, pistachio, or decadent dark chocolate at **Capogiro Gelato Artisans** (119 South 13th Street; 215-351-0900; capogirogelato.com).

7 *Books in the Square* 5 p.m.

Built during the booming 1850s, the **Rittenhouse Square** neighborhood was home to the city's Victorian aristocracy. The park has a reflecting pool; diagonal walkways crisscrossing beneath oak, maple, and locust trees; and bronze sculptures, like the 1832 allegory of the French Revolution, *Lion Crushing a Serpent*, by Antoine-Louis Barye. Stop in at **Joseph Fox Bookshop** (1724 Sansom Street; 215-563-4184; foxbookshop.com), a Philadelphia institution since 1951. Its crowded shelves are stocked with everything from art and architecture to fiction and poetry, and its events bring in big-name writers like David Sedaris.

8 *Israeli and More* 8 p.m.

Decked out in the dun colors of Jerusalem stone, **Zahav** (237 St. James Place; 215-625-8800;

ABOVE A jogger strikes a *Rocky*-esque pose atop the stairs of the Philadelphia Museum of Art.

OPPOSITE ABOVE The Philadelphia skyline.

OPPOSITE BELOW Rowers make their way down the placid Schuylkill River.

zahavrestaurant.com; $$$) features Israeli recipes and a healthy dose of North African and Middle Eastern fare, too. The ta'yim tasting menu has made this Society Hill fixture one of the nation's most acclaimed Middle Eastern restaurants. First up is a collection of six daily vegetable salads (like twice-cooked eggplant or cabbage), followed by a bowl of creamy hummus and a large round of house-baked, earthy flatbread. Then come two small plates and perhaps a Syrian lamb kebab grilled over coals, and finally, dessert. Reservations strongly suggested.

9 *Down in Fishtown* 10:30 p.m.

For live music and locally brewed beer, go to **Johnny Brenda's** (1201 North Frankford Avenue; 215-739-9684; johnnybrendas.com) in Fishtown, where the small stage attracts some surprisingly big indie music acts, like Grizzly Bear and Vampire Weekend. Across the street, **Frankford Hall** (1210 Frankford Avenue; 215-634-3338; frankfordhall.com) is less aggressively

stylish and more family friendly, with Ping-Pong and picnic tables, an affinity for wood block games, and an excellent beer list. Around the corner, the inventive taco joint **Sancho Pistola's** (19 West Girard Avenue; 267-324-3530; sanchopistolas.com) serves food, cocktails, and tequilas until 2 in the morning.

SUNDAY

10 *Morning Constitutional* 8:30 a.m.

The best time to hit **Independence National Historical Park** (nps.gov/inde) is first thing in the morning, ahead of the crowds. Pick up your free tickets (the Visitor Center at 6th and Market Streets opens early) and start with the main attraction,

Independence Hall, where lines will soon be longest. Take a quick look at the Liberty Bell through the glass at its dedicated building, and then poke around the restored buildings and inviting lawns.

11 *Riverside* 11 a.m.

Head over to the **Philadelphia Museum of Art** (26th Street and Benjamin Franklin Parkway; 215-763-8100; philamuseum.org), take your picture with the Rocky statue out front, and then walk in to

enjoy the collection. From there, walk behind the museum to the **Breakaway Bikes** shed (215-568-6002; breakawaybikes.com) to rent a bike and ride along the path paralleling the Schuylkill River in Fairmount Park. Look for elegant Victorian-era boathouses built in the heyday of the city's rowing clubs. One of the city's Olympic-level rowers was Grace Kelly's father. Watch today's rowers in their shells as they glide along the river.

ABOVE Trying out a model telescope in a Galileo exhibition at the Franklin Institute.

OPPOSITE A view from the City Hall observation deck of the grand Benjamin Franklin Parkway.

THE BASICS

Philadelphia is about an hour and 10 minutes from New York on Amtrak's fast Acela train. For information on transportation within the city, check visitphilly.com/getting-around or inquire at your hotel.

The Independent
1234 Locust Street
215-772-1440
theindependenthotel.com
$$
Boutique hotel in a restored building.

The Alexander Inn
301 South 12th Street
215-923-3535
alexanderinn.com
$$
Art Deco-inspired touches in designer rooms.

Hotel Palomar
117 South 17th Street
215-563-5006
hotelpalomar-philadelphia.com
$$
Stylish hotel near City Hall.

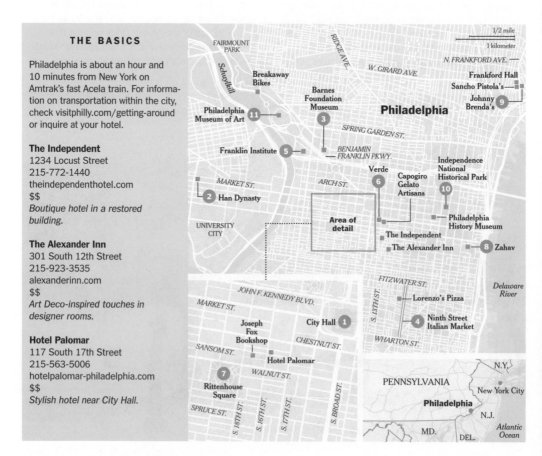

Prince Edward Island

Prince Edward Island, Canada's smallest province, is a puffy green comforter of an island embroidered with flowers and farms and ribboned with empty roads, some of them still red clay. Nestled just above Nova Scotia in the Gulf of St. Lawrence, it is blessed with river flows and sandbars that warm its waters to 70 degrees and higher in July, a quirk of geography that makes its beaches more swimmable than most of New England's. For shellfish, this is paradise. Lobsters love it here, at least until they take a wrong turn on the ocean floor and end up in one of the countless traps you see at the ends of piers, by the sides of the roads, even on stoops. Clams and scallops flourish as well. But the biggest stars are the oysters, which go by designations or labels like Malpeque, Raspberry Point, and Colville Bay. A P.E.I. mussel is a brand with real clout in the world of gourmet cooks and restaurateurs.
— BY FRANK BRUNI AND JAMES LEDBETTER

FRIDAY

1 *Pick a Route* 1 p.m.

The eight-mile-long **Confederation Bridge**, the island's first link to the mainland, was not completed until 1997, and there are still only about 140,000 residents here, scattered over a clump of land 140 miles long. The quiet roads invite a drive. (Pick up maps at the tourist information center at the bridge, or find routes at tourismpei.com/pei-scenic-heritage-roads.) On the northern shore, just an hour's drive from the capital, Charlottetown, you stare out at what looks like infinity from a series of low-lying, red-soil cliffs with a peculiar, desolate beauty. Elsewhere there are dune-skirted beaches or forests of evergreens sloping to the water's edge.

2 *Follow the Piper* 3:30 p.m.

If you arrive before 3:30 p.m. in Summerside, west of Charlottetown, you can catch a summer mini-concert at a standout island academic institution, the **College of Piping and Celtic Performing Arts** (619 Water Street East, Summerside; 902-436-5377; collegeofpiping.com). Affiliated with the College of Piping in Glasgow, Scotland, the school turns out specialists in Highland bagpiping, drumming, and step dancing, all much-loved arts on this island. (As you watch this performance-in-plaid, you'll have

no trouble guessing the ancestry of many Prince Edward Islanders.)

3 *Harbor Shopping* 5 p.m.

Stroll around **Old Charlottetown**, near the harbor. On Queen Street, exquisitely quaint shops inhabit many of the classic Victorian brick buildings. **Northern Watters Knitwear**, around a corner at 150 Richmond Street (902-566-5850; nwknitwear.com) makes and sells knitted clothing of fine British wool; this is the place to order a bespoke cardigan or a classic fisherman's sweater. **Moonsnail Soapworks** (85 Water Street; 902-892-7627; moonsnailsoapworks.com) has fine homemade soaps, some of which contain a bit of the famous red island clay. **Peakes Quay** (peakesquay.com) is the place for waterfront restaurants and bars (some of which have live Celtic music into the evening), boat tours, and shops including the self-explanatory **Flip Flop Shop** (902-566-9898) and **Cow's** (Great George Street; 902-566-4886), a popular ice cream chain headquartered on the island.

4 *At the Source* 8 p.m.

Local seafood is a specialty at the **Claddagh Oyster House** (131 Sydney Street, Charlottetown;

OPPOSITE "Bucolic" is still the right word for Prince Edward Island, even though its beaches, warm ocean waters, and seafood bring savvy summer tourists.

BELOW Red-soil cliffs give the island's coastline a singular desolate beauty.

902-892-9661; claddaghoysterhouse.com; $$-$$$). Try the Oysters Rockefeller, with oysters from Malpeque Bay, or an Irish-inspired dish (this place and many others celebrate the Irish side of the island's heritage), like the prawns and scallops bathed in a mix of ingredients including Irish Mist.

SATURDAY

5 *Walking With the Foxes* 8 a.m.

Take a morning walk among the splendid, well-preserved dunes of **Prince Edward Island National**

BELOW Hauling in some of P.E.I.'s renowned oysters from Colville Bay.

OPPOSITE ABOVE A red fox at the national park.

OPPOSITE BELOW Countryside reminiscent of *Anne of Green Gables*, the classic children's book set on P.E.I.

Park (902-672-6350; pc.gc.ca), a half-hour drive from Charlottetown on the northern coast. Watch for the signature blue heron, and try not to trip over the stealthy red foxes that will dart across your path. To test the island's reputation for warm water, wade in at **Brackley Beach**.

6 *Lake View by the Sea* Noon

Without leaving the park, have a leisurely lunch at **Dalvay by the Sea** (Route 6, 16 Cottage Crescent; 902-672-2048; dalvaybythesea.com; $$), a gorgeous, stately Victorian house that is now a resort hotel. Built in 1896, it was the summer home of Alexander McDonald, a former president of Standard Oil of Kentucky. You can sit outdoors on oversize wooden chairs overlooking one of the island's few freshwater lakes—don't worry about false advertising; the sea is close by, too. One lunch possibility is the restaurant's refined take on chowder, with caramelized scallops, shrimp, chorizo, corn and red potato.

7 *You Must Meet Anne* 2 p.m.

Prince Edward Island's reigning celebrity is fictional. She's Anne of Green Gables, the heroine of a series of children's books by Lucy Maud Montgomery, who made her home and set her stories here. Anne is to Prince Edward Island what Francis is to Assisi, or maybe what Mickey is to Orlando. Actually, she's a deeply revered, exhaustively merchandised combination of both. Souvenir shops hawk Anne bric-a-brac. An island theatrical production based on Anne's life story lays claim to being the longest-running musical in Canada. And a specially designated **Green Gables House** (8619 Route 6, Cavendish; 902-963-7874; pc.gc.ca/en/lhn-nhs/pe/greengables) is the island's most heavily promoted tourist destination, beloved in particular by travelers from Japan. Japanese couples have civil wedding ceremonies there, and Japanese girls have been known to show up with their hair dyed red and in pigtails, just like Anne's.

8 *Eat Your Lobster* 8 p.m.

Seafood is practically a religion on Prince Edward Island, and because the supply is fresh and essentially uniform, you can choose a restaurant by its view. **Lobster on the Wharf** (2 Prince Street, Charlottetown; 902-368-2888; lobsteronthewharf.com; $$) offers open-air tables facing the cozy harbor. The fish and chips are good, but it's hard to beat the specialty of the house.

SUNDAY

9 *Links and Bikes* 9 a.m.

A surprisingly high proportion of Prince Edward Island is taken up by golf courses, thanks to arable

soil and relatively flat topography. For a genuine challenge, try the **Links at Crowbush Cove** (Route 350, Lakeside; 800-235-8909; peisfinestgolf.com), widely considered one of the best courses in North America. The oceanside fairways make a breathtaking setting, but the winds off the Gulf of St. Lawrence have been known to add strokes on many of the holes. Not a golfer? Rent a bike and ride as much as you can of the **Confederation Trail** (tourismpei.com/pei-confederation-trail), which follows old railroad

lines and will take you past enough rolling fields (most grow potatoes), hardwood forests, rivers, and charming villages to let you feel you've really gotten to know this island.

ABOVE Farms remain, but vacation homes with sea views are increasingly a part of the landscape.

OPPOSITE The dining room at the Johnson Shore Inn on the northern coast.

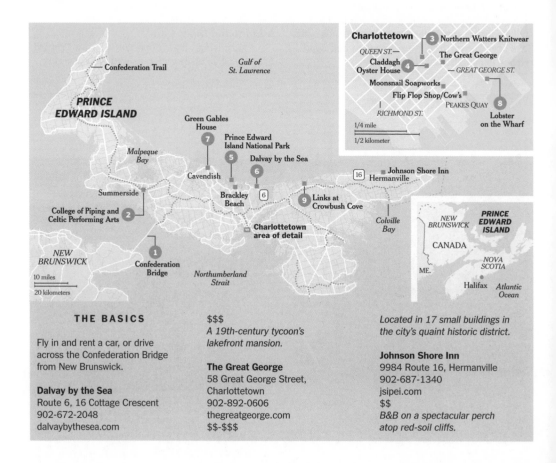

THE BASICS

Fly in and rent a car, or drive across the Confederation Bridge from New Brunswick.

Dalvay by the Sea
Route 6, 16 Cottage Crescent
902-672-2048
dalvaybythesea.com

$$$
A 19th-century tycoon's lakefront mansion.

The Great George
58 Great George Street,
Charlottetown
902-892-0606
thegreatgeorge.com
$$-$$$

Located in 17 small buildings in the city's quaint historic district.

Johnson Shore Inn
9984 Route 16, Hermanville
902-687-1340
jsipei.com
$$
B&B on a spectacular perch atop red-soil cliffs.

Montreal

French or English? One of the beautiful things about Montreal is that you never know in what language you will be greeted. Which brings up a second thing: Maybe it's the good food, the open skies, or the free-spirited students who call this city their campus, but the folks of Montreal are friendly. Ask someone for directions in the Métro, part of the vast Underground City that stays toasty during the winter, and you may end up making drinks plans later. That's not a bad thing, bien sûr. With the city's music-charged night life, chic restaurants, and postindustrial revival, it helps to have a guide.
— BY DENNY LEE AND SETH SHERWOOD

FRIDAY

1 *Get Wheels* 3 p.m.

For bicycle touring, Montreal delivers, with 310-plus miles of bike lanes that crisscross the city, about half of which are physically separated from cars. Visitors can use the public **Bixi** bike program (montreal.bixi.com; stations all over town) for one-way, 24-hour, or 72-hour rentals. Or rent a bike the more conventional way at **Montreal on Wheels** (27, rue de la Commune Est; 514-866-0633; caroulemontreal.com), where you can also pick up a map and get advice on routes.

2 *Downtown Roll* 3:30 p.m.

Pedal toward the river, and you may get a view of the **Montreal Biosphère**, a geodesic dome left from Expo 67, the 1967 world's fair that is still a symbol of the city. But to see more of why Montreal was designated a Unesco City of Design, point your handlebars toward the Lachine Canal, a former industrial waterfront that has been transformed into a lush green belt. The path is dotted with architectural treasures like the delightful **Habitat 67** (2600, avenue Pierre-Dupuy; cac.mcgill.ca/safdie/habitat/), a Brutalist-style experiment in modular housing designed by Moshe Safdie in the heady days of Expo.

3 *Québécois Plates* 8 p.m.

Normand Laprise, who pioneered the use of fresh Québécois ingredients at the pricey Toqué!, often praised by critics as the city's best restaurant, opened a midpriced sister restaurant, **Brasserie T!**

(1425, rue Jeanne-Mance; 514-282-0808; brasserie-t.com; $$$). Situated at the foot of the Contemporary Art Museum, the brasserie looks like a sleek cargo container. Inside, a contemporary French menu showcases unfussy dishes like grilled flank steak and cod brandade.

4 *Musical Mile* 10 p.m.

It's impossible to talk about the Mile End district without name-dropping bands like Arcade Fire and the gritty stages that gave them their start. Upstart bands are still jamming at **Divan Orange** (4234, boulevard Saint-Laurent; 514-840-9090; divanorange.org). An alternative, with a bigger stage and sound, is **Bar Le Ritz P.D.B.** (179, rue Jean-Talon Ouest; 514-274-7676; barleritzpdb.com).

SATURDAY

5 *History With Noodles* 10 a.m.

For shopping and a selection of cafes, head to Old Montreal, where historic cobblestones and high foot traffic ensure the survival of indie stores. You'll find designer boutiques, finely crafted ceramics and housewares, and contemporary galleries,

OPPOSITE The Biosphère, designed by Buckminster Fuller, lives on as a Montreal landmark. It was built for the 1967 world's fair called Expo 67.

BELOW The shopping is good in Old Montreal, where busy tourist traffic on the historic cobblestones provides a healthy environment for indie boutiques.

along with an imposing clock tower and a Ferris wheel. While you're there, take time to ogle the pastries at **Maison Christian Faure** (355, place Royale; maisonchristianfaure.ca). A few blocks away in Chinatown, lunch comes with a spectacle at **Nouilles de Lan Zhou** (1006, boulevard Saint-Laurent; Facebook,

ABOVE From the Lachine Canal bicycle path, cyclists can get a glimpse of this experiment in modular housing, Moshe Safdie's Habitat 67.

BELOW A charcuterie spread paired with a glass of red wine at Brasserie T!, where the sleek, ultra-modern architecture complements contemporary French fare.

search Nouilles de Lan Zhou; $). While customers watch, a cook twirls, stretches, spins, and cuts hand-pulled noodles.

6 *The Old and the New* 2 p.m.

Modern design gets its due in an expansive setting at the **Musée des Beaux-Arts de Montreal** (1379-80, rue Sherbrooke Ouest; 514-285-2000; mmfa. qc.ca). All sorts of European and Canadian art are on display in this outstanding museum, but head to the multilevel design pavilion. There you'll find a kaleidoscopic array of iconic objects, from Arne Jacobsen "Egg" chairs to space-age 1970s red televisions to a sleek yellow Ski-Doo snowmobile from 1961 that begs to be borrowed for a joy ride.

7 *French Bites* 8 p.m.

A neighborhood wine bar that happens to serve terrific food is one of those pleasures that make Paris, well, Paris. That's the vibe at **Buvette Chez Simone** (4869, avenue du Parc; 514-750-6577; buvettechezsimone.com; $$$), a bar in Mile End with sly design touches. The comfy brasserie menu features dishes like a roast chicken served on a carving board with roasted potatoes. If you're hankering for more inventive fare, bike over to **Pullman** (3424, avenue du Parc; 514-288-7779; pullman-mtl.com; $$$), a high-end tapas bar that serves clever plates like venison tartare, foie gras cookies, and olives with

candied lemon. The crowd at both restaurants skews young, fashionable, and chatty.

8 *Canadian Libations* 10 p.m.

Choose from the staggering whisky menu at the **Burgundy Lion** (2496 rue Notre Dame Ouest; 514-934-0888; burgundylion.com), a lively British-style pub with dark wood surfaces and frosted glass. The more exotic specimens hail from Taiwan, Sweden, France, and Switzerland, while Canadian representatives include Wiser's Red Letter, a mellow elixir with

ABOVE On the dance floor at the Velvet Speakeasy, one of a variety of music and dance clubs that make up Montreal's active night-life scene.

BELOW The path along the Lachine Canal is part of a 310-mile system of bicycle routes and lanes that make Montreal an exceptionally bicycle-friendly city.

a hint of toasted nut. For dancing, head to **Velvet Speakeasy** (426, rue Saint-Gabriel; velvetspeakeasy.ca), a posh basement club amid the cobblestones of the Old Port district.

SUNDAY

9 *Eggs to Go* 9:30 a.m.

For a delightful morning meal served in an old town house with communal tables, have brunch at **Le Cartet** (106, rue McGill; 514-871-8887; facebook.com/Lecartetresto; $$). Part cafe, part grocery store, Le Cartet draws young families and professionals with hearty platters of eggs that come with figs,

cheese, and salad greens, and soft, flaky croissants to swoon for. On your way out, feel free to stock up on crusty baguettes, French mustards, and picnic cheeses.

10 *Canal or Rapids* 11 a.m.

Join the city at play back at the **Lachine Canal**, nine miles of smooth water originally built as a bypass around the Lachine Rapids, which roil and churn in the St. Lawrence River right inside the city. Now the canal is filled in summer with sailboats, canoes, and other small craft. Secure a kayak or pedal boat from **H2O Adventures** (2727 B, rue Saint-Patrick; 514-842-1306; h2oadventures.ca) or one of the other boat rental businesses along the canal, and join in. Or skip the tame canal and go jet-boating through the rapids themselves with **Rafting Montréal** (8912, boulevard LaSalle; 514-767-2230; raftingmontreal.com).

11 *Where the Bugs Are* 3 p.m.

The 190 acres of the **Montreal Botanical Garden** (4101, rue Sherbrooke Est; 514-868-3000; espacepourlavie.ca) contain greenhouses and gardens replicating alpine, aquatic, and desert flora, First Nations horticulture, and much more. Don't miss the **Insectarium** (4581, rue Sherbrooke Est), a vast, lively, and very popular bug museum. Another popular feature of this complex is the **Biodôme** (4777, avenue Pierre-De Coubertin), a glass-roofed nature preserve containing multiple ecosystems and some 4,500 animals from 250 different species, like sloths (in the Tropical Rainforest sector), auks (in the Labrador Coast sector), and penguins (in the Sub-Antarctic sector).

OPPOSITE The elegant front of Le Petit Hôtel in Old Montreal.

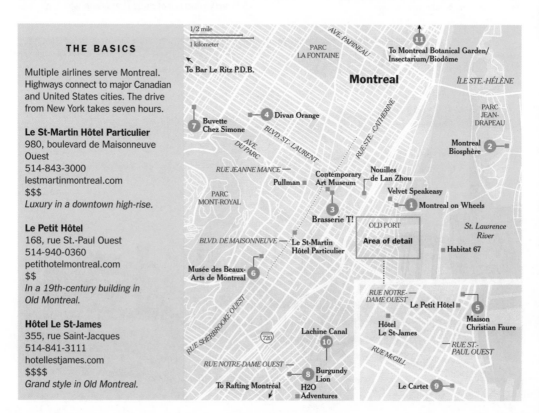

THE BASICS

Multiple airlines serve Montreal. Highways connect to major Canadian and United States cities. The drive from New York takes seven hours.

Le St-Martin Hôtel Particulier
980, boulevard de Maisonneuve Ouest
514-843-3000
lestmartinmontreal.com
$$$
Luxury in a downtown high-rise.

Le Petit Hôtel
168, rue St.-Paul Ouest
514-940-0360
petithotelmontreal.com
$$
In a 19th-century building in Old Montreal.

Hôtel Le St-James
355, rue Saint-Jacques
514-841-3111
hotellestjames.com
$$$$
Grand style in Old Montreal.

Quebec City

Quebec can give provincialism a good name. Orphaned by mother France, dominated by Britain (after what Québécois still call the Conquest) and then for years by majority-Anglophone Canada, the people of Quebec have followed Voltaire's advice to tend to their own garden. This is especially true of Quebec City, the provincial capital. Proudly dated, lovingly maintained, Quebec City has charm to spare, particularly within the city walls of the Old Town and in the Lower Town tucked between those walls and the St. Lawrence River. The city's French heart is always on its sleeve, and a stroll over the cobblestones leads to patisseries, sidewalk cafes, and a profusion of art galleries. Yet a vast wilderness is the next stop due north, putting game on restaurant menus and a kind of backwoods vigor in the city's spirit. To a Yankee it all seems European. But there is no place like this in Europe; there is nothing else like it in North America, either. And that's reason enough to celebrate. — BY SCOTT L. MALCOMSON

FRIDAY

1 *A Drink at the Château* 5 p.m.

It's too late in the day for kayaking on the St. Lawrence River, so go instead to the first-floor **Le Sam Bistro Bar & Atrium** at the **Fairmont Le Château Frontenac** (1, rue des Carrières; 418-692-3861; fairmont.com/frontenac) for cocktails. You're atop the city's cliffs, and this room has wonderful views of the St. Lawrence. A drink in the château, as it is called (it's that enormous castle-like building, built as a grand hotel for the Canadian Pacific Railway) is always pricey, but luxury can be like that. Even the bar food is classy, running to snacks like Atlantic salmon tartare. This huge grand hotel is a spectacle itself, dominating the city skyline and rich in history (Franklin Roosevelt and Winston Churchill met here on one memorable occasion during World War II). Take this opportunity to explore the opulent lobby and find the cliffside boardwalk called the **Dufferin Terrace**.

2 *Lower Town Update* 8 p.m.

Fast-forward a few decades by finding your way down to St.-Roch in the Lower Town, an epicenter of high-tech businesses, artists' studios, galleries, shops, and cafes. At **L'Affaire est Ketchup** (46, rue St.-Joseph Est; 418-529-9020; facebook.com/laffaireest.ketchup;

$$$), a tiny, always crowded storefront bistro, young chefs conjure up magnificent dishes of octopus, bison, or scallops on a vintage electric stove as French-language rock and pop fills the air. Call ahead to reserve a table, and it's all good, which is what the phrase "l'affaire est ketchup" means in English.

3 *Back to the Future* 10 p.m.

Stay in St.-Roch for an '80s flashback at the **Macfly Bar Arcade** (422, rue Caron; 418-528-7000; macflybararcade.com), a two-room bar with an electrifying orange color scheme, craft beers, and vintage arcade games like Ms. Pac-Man that are all free to play. Later, sidle up to the bar at the microbrewery **La Korrigane** (380, rue Dorchester; 418-614-0932; korrigane.ca) for an only-in-Quebec nightcap: a pint of Croquemitaine, a pale ale made with maple syrup.

SATURDAY

4 *On the Plains* 10 a.m.

Jog or amble the **Plains of Abraham**, an extensive, undulating rectangle on the heights above the St. Lawrence just west of the Frontenac. This is where, in 1759, British invaders led by James Wolfe defeated Louis-Joseph de Montcalm in the battle that set in motion the decline of French power in North America. Today it is an urban park (ccbn-nbc.

OPPOSITE The guards at Quebec's Citadel may look English, but their regiment's official language is French.

BELOW For tourists, walking is the way to get around.

gc.ca) where children race around the open spaces, actors stroll by in 18th-century garb, and Paul McCartney gave a free concert in 2008 before 200,000 fans to mark Quebec City's 400th birthday. For a concrete example of Quebec's mixed historical legacy, stop off at the **Citadel** (1, côte de la Citadelle; 418-694-2815; lacitadelle.qc.ca), where an officially French-speaking regiment performs an English-style changing of the guard, complete with black bearskin hats, every summer morning at 10.

5 *National Dish* 2 p.m.

At least once this weekend you have to eat poutine, the concoction of French fries, cheese curd, and gravy that is close to the French Canadian soul, if not particularly friendly to its heart. Find it

at **Buffet de l'Antiquaire** (95, rue St.-Paul; 418-692-2661; lebuffetdelantiquaire.com; $), a Lower Town institution with sidewalk tables in summer. It is a very good, very local diner that serves all kinds of Canadian comfort food and is always worth a visit at breakfast, too.

6 *That Perfect Find* 3 p.m.

Walk out into the **rue St.-Paul**, a street lined with easygoing antiques shops and art galleries, to poke through Victoriana, country furniture, Art Deco relics, and assorted gewgaws. If you still can't find the right present to take home, take the first left up into the Old Town and head for **Artisans du Bas-Canada** (30, côte de la Fabrique; 418-692-2109; artisanscanada.com), which has jewelry made from Canadian diamonds and amber as well as an abundance of Québécois tchotchkes.

7 *Take to the Ramparts* 6 p.m.

Stroll along the ramparts of the Old Town for a stirring view of the St. Lawrence. Quebec City was strategic because of its commanding position on the

ABOVE The Lower Town along the St. Lawrence River.

LEFT J. A. Moisan, a gourmet grocery store.

OPPOSITE The Château Frontenac towers over Quebec.

river just at the point where it begins to widen and expand into the Gulf of St. Lawrence. Then proceed downhill for a drink at the friendly and cozy **Tavern Belley** (249, rue St.-Paul; 418-692-1694; facebook.com/tavernebelley). Or, farther downhill in the Lower Town, try **L'Oncle Antoine** (29, rue St.-Pierre; 418-694-9176; facebook.com/oncleantoine), a pub in the stone cellar of a 1754 house where you can sip a Quebec microbrew or maple whiskey.

8 *Haute Cuisine* 8 p.m.

Many Québécois speak English, but French, even bad French, goes over well. So use yours to ask for directions to the luxury hotel called **Auberge Saint-Antoine** (8, rue St.-Antoine). Its restaurant, **Chez Muffy** (418-692-1022; saint-antoine.com/en/dining; $$$$), is a point of reference for Quebec City's farm-to-fork haute cuisine. Start off with Champagne cocktails,

then move on at a leisurely pace to an amuse-bouche and an appetizer, perhaps foie gras, through seafood and meats that sometimes include Canadian game, and finally to dessert, all with suitable wines chosen from among 700 labels and 14 countries of origin. It is easy to drag this out — in a space that is like a rustic loft with upholstered chairs — for three hours or more. After dinner, walk the narrow streets to admire the restored buildings of the Place-Royal.

9 *Québécois Cabaret* 11 p.m.

For a late night out that will connect you with the artistic types in St.-Roch, hit **Deux 22** (222, rue St.-Joseph Est; 418-742-5222; deux22.com), a chic boutique in the daytime that's also a Mexican resto-bar. The lively crowd that congregates here in the evening for food and drink keeps the covered terrace (which is heated in the winter) hopping well into the wee hours.

SUNDAY

10 *Riverside* 11 a.m.

You've gazed at the St. Lawrence from the heights; now it's time to get close. Join the locals catching the breeze on the **Promenade Samuel de Champlain**, a riverfront strip park on land between the boulevard Champlain and the river — for many years a degraded industrial area. The first 1.5-mile-long section of the promenade (named, of course, for the French explorer who founded New France

here in 1608) became quickly popular; it was such a hit that the city soon set to work extending it to a length that will eventually reach for six more miles.

11 *One Last Chance* Noon

If you're still in the market for something to take home, check out **J. A. Moisan** (699, rue St.-Jean; 418-522-0685; jamoisan.com), which claims to be the oldest gourmet grocery store in North America. Should the cheeses, chocolates, pasta, and other fare fail to charm, you'll find a selection of other high-end shops on rue St.-Jean.

ABOVE AND OPPOSITE Quebec City's Old Town caters to tourists with shopping, restaurants and bars, and its well preserved native charm.

THE BASICS

On the Old Town's narrow streets, plan to walk. To go from Lower to Upper Town, take the funicular or the Breakneck Staircase.

Fairmont Le Château Frontenac
1, rue des Carrières
418-692-3861
fairmont.com/frontenac
$$$
A classic grand hotel with 618 rooms and river views. Quebec's gold standard.

Auberge Saint-Antoine
8, rue St.-Antoine
418-692-2211
saint-antoine.com
$$
Built around a cannon fortification; displays artifacts like coins and cannonballs.

Hotel Le Germain
126, rue St.-Pierre
418-692-2224
legermainhotels.com/en/quebec
$$
An airy and modern break from fleurs-de-lis and polished wood.

CANADA

JEAN-LESAGE INTERNATIONAL AIRPORT

Area of detail

QUEBEC

4 miles
8 kilometers

St. Lawrence River

Estuaire de la Rivière Saint-Charles

Taverne Belley **7**

Buffet de l'Antiquaire **5**

ST.-ROCH

RUE ST.-JOSEPH EST

LOWER TOWN

RUE DU PARVIS

Rue St.-Paul **6**

RUE SAINT-PIERRE

Hotel Le Germain

Auberge Saint-Antoine/ Chez Muffy **8**

Deux22

La Korrigane **9**

Artisans du Bas-Canada

OLD TOWN

L'Oncle Antoine

3

BOULEVARD CHAREST EST

Macfly Bar Arcade UPPER TOWN

Le Sam Bistro & Atrium/ Fairmont Le Château Frontenac **1**

LOWER TOWN

2

L'Affaire est Ketchup

RUE SAINT-JEAN

11

J. A. Moisan

— Old Town Wall

Citadel

Dufferin Terrace

Quebec City

GRANDE-ALLÉE EST

4 Plains of Abraham

St. Lawrence River

To Promenade Samuel de Champlain **10**

1/4 mile
1/2 kilometer

Newport

Each summer, two million tourists head to Narragansett Bay to shuffle their way through the Gilded Age trophy homes of Newport, Rhode Island — the lumbering white elephants (or are they overdressed maiden aunts?) perched hip to hip on the city's glittering rocky coastline. You too can explore America's insatiable appetite for...darn nearly everything here, and ponder the freakishness of the wealthy. Glut your senses by driving down Newport's main drag, otherwise known as Bellevue Avenue, a weird bazaar of architectural expression that includes more Versailles references than is probably healthy. If you continue along Ocean Drive, you will note attempts by contemporary architects to be this century's Stanford White (and that is not necessarily a good thing). But keep your eyes on the rugged coast, green parks, and yacht-filled harbor, all cooled on hot summer days by the ocean breeze, and you will remember how all of this got here.

— BY PENELOPE GREEN

FRIDAY

1 *The Cliff Walk* 3 p.m.

Get a jump on the weekend crowd with a Friday afternoon trip to the Fifth Avenue of nature walks. Newport's famous **Cliff Walk** (cliffwalk.com) runs for three and a half miles along shoreline that makes everyone love an ocean view. It can be jam-packed on the weekends with tourists ogling the backyards of the Bellevue Avenue estates, many of which it slices into. Here is a strategy: Park at Easton's Beach on Memorial Boulevard, just below the Chanler at Cliff Walk hotel. You will find the path entrance right there. Follow the path to the end at Ledge Road (only if you are strong; this will take more than an hour) or to the stone staircase called the 40 Steps (about 20 minutes). Walk up Ledge Road to Bellevue Avenue, make a left, and you will see a bus stop for Newport's trolleys

(if you make it only to the 40 Steps, there is a stop at Narragansett and Ochre Point). Take a trolley back into town, get off at the Newport Casino, and walk down Memorial Boulevard to your car.

2 *Find Salvation* 7 p.m.

Have drinks and dinner at the **Salvation Restaurant and Bar** (140 Broadway; 401-847-2620; salvationcafe.com; $$), the way the locals do. The tattooed waiters and vaguely Asian-hippie menu remind you that Newport is only 40 miles from the Rhode Island School of Design. Dinner can jump from a Hoisin Sticky Ribs appetizer to an entree of vegan risotto. Stick around for dessert.

SATURDAY

3 *Eggs at the Dock* 9 a.m.

Take an outdoor table for breakfast at **Belle's Cafe**, at the Newport Shipyard (1 Washington Street; 401-619-5964; newportshipyard.com; $$). The eggy burritos are good, and the yacht-people watching is, too.

4 *A Heart-Shaped World* 10 a.m.

One of Stanford White's prettiest and silliest houses is **Rosecliff** (548 Bellevue Avenue), built for the heiress Tessie Oelrichs in 1902. You can read all about it in *The Architect of Desire*, a hypnotic family memoir about the tragic and emotional legacy of the Gilded Age's favorite architect, written by his great-granddaughter, Suzannah Lessard. (Tessie died alone at Rosecliff in 1926, Lessard wrote, talking to

OPPOSITE The Breakers, one of the trophy mansions that typified Newport's golden age. Several of the most lavish and eye-popping are now open for tour.

RIGHT The 3.5-mile Cliff Walk, where the public now enjoys the same ocean views that were treasured by the mansion builders of the Gilded Age.

imaginary guests.) With its heart-shaped double staircase and baby-blue trompe-l'oeil ballroom ceiling, Rosecliff is sweeter and lighter than many of Newport's lavish hulks from the same period. Allow an hour for a tour of the house and a little more time to wander Rosecliff's green lawns, which swoop down to the cliffs. The house is one of 11 properties and landscapes owned by the Preservation Society of Newport County, which runs this and other mansion tours (401-847-1000; newportmansions.org).

5 *Rare Books* Noon

If the crowds haven't gotten to you yet, they soon will. Find an oasis at the **Redwood Library & Athenaeum** (50 Bellevue Avenue; 401-847-0292; redwoodlibrary.org), the oldest lending library in the United States. There's a collection of furniture, sculpture, and paintings, including six portraits signed by Gilbert Stuart. But even more charming is the Original Collection of 750 titles, purchased from England in 1748 by a group of Newport citizens. You may not always be able to just drop in to read them, but a look at the titles is an interesting window on the wide interests of the library's founders—from theology to bloodletting techniques to how to build a privy.

6 *Make Mine Gothic* 1 p.m.

Bannister's and Bowen's wharves, smack in the middle of Newport Harbor, make up ground zero for Newport's seafaring past. They are very scenic and wharfy. But you knew that. What you might not know is that many of the exteriors in a marvelous camp classic, the gothic soap opera *Dark Shadows*, were shot in Newport. Have a salad at the **Black Pearl** (Bannister's Wharf; 401-846-5264; blackpearlnewport.com; $$), which was known as the Blue Whale in *Dark Shadows*.

7 *Teak and Brass* 2 p.m.

Newport, sometimes called the "sailing capital of the world" (it hosted the America's Cup from 1930 to 1983), is an appropriate home for the **International Yacht Restoration School** (449 Thames Street; 401-848-5777; iyrs.edu/our-boats). There are heartbreakingly beautiful boats everywhere, in all stages of restoration. Make sure you wander through the 19th-century factory building and out to the water, where you will find the school's most ambitious project, a 133-foot schooner, built in 1885, called *Coronet*. To see more, take a water taxi (newportharborshuttle.com) to **Fort Adams State Park** (401-841-0707; fortadams.org), on an island at the mouth of Newport Harbor. There you can get instruction in sailing or windsurfing. Rental boats include some specially equipped for the physically challenged.

8 *Back to the Wharf* 7 p.m.

Have dinner (make a reservation) at the reliably posh and lively **Clark Cooke House** (26 Bannister's Wharf; 401-849-2900; clarkecooke.com; $$$$). Book a table at the Sky Bar, and you can watch the harbor below from the third floor of this lovely, rambling 18th-century house and wait for the dancing to start around 11. Or go down a floor and a half to the somewhat more casual but still highly atmospheric Candy Store. Either upstairs or down, native lobster sautéed out of the shell requires no disassembly.

SUNDAY

9 *Around the Dunes* 9 a.m.

You will need a salty wind to ruffle your hair today, something brisk and fresh to blow away all that dust and glitter. Head a few miles north out of town to the **Sachuest Wildlife Refuge** (769 Sachuest Point Road, Middletown; 401-619-2680; fws.gov/refuge/sachuest_point). 242 acres of salt and fresh-

ABOVE Fog over the Newport-Pell Bridge. Originally a seafaring settlement, Newport is still a boatman's town, especially if that boat is a yacht.

OPPOSITE Harborside dining at Bannister's Wharf in the old Narragansett Bay port area.

water marshes, rocky coastline, sea grass, bayberry, and bittersweet are host to all manner of wildlife, including seals, nesting terns, and harlequin ducks. Take the three-mile perimeter trail so you can be constantly on the water.

10 *In the Bay* 11 a.m.

For another perspective on Narragansett Bay, drive out onto the two-mile-long Claiborne Pell Bridge, which soars some 215 feet above the bay, and take the first exit, at Jamestown. This much smaller town is overshadowed by Newport, but its waterfront is worth a visit, with its own galleries, restaurants, and shops. Pick up some provisions, find the dock for the **Jamestown-Newport Ferry**

(Conanicut Marina, One East Ferry Wharf; jamestownnewportferry.com), and park your car. Then ride the ferry to its first stop, Rose Island, and eat your lunch at the **Rose Island Lighthouse** (401-847-4242; roseisland.org), which is owned and maintained by a nonprofit group and has an associated museum and wildlife refuge. You'll find yourself in the middle of the bay, with gorgeous views of boats, harbors, and the sparkling water in every direction.

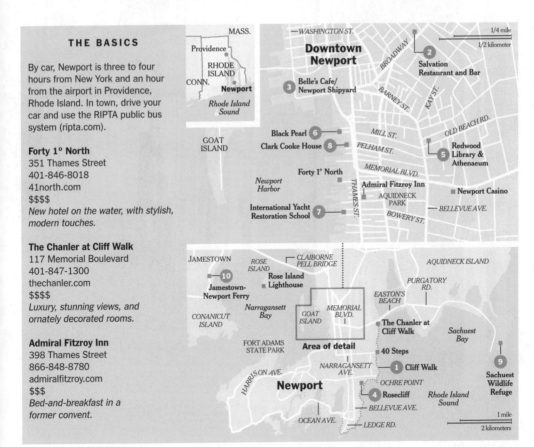

THE BASICS

By car, Newport is three to four hours from New York and an hour from the airport in Providence, Rhode Island. In town, drive your car and use the RIPTA public bus system (ripta.com).

Forty 1° North
351 Thames Street
401-846-8018
41north.com
$$$$
New hotel on the water, with stylish, modern touches.

The Chanler at Cliff Walk
117 Memorial Boulevard
401-847-1300
thechanler.com
$$$$
Luxury, stunning views, and ornately decorated rooms.

Admiral Fitzroy Inn
398 Thames Street
866-848-8780
admiralfitzroy.com
$$$
Bed-and-breakfast in a former convent.

Providence

Overshadowed by Boston 50 miles up the East Coast and the mammoth New York City megalopolis a couple of hours' drive in the other direction, Providence, the smallish capital of the country's smallest state, is easy to underestimate. But spend a weekend there, and you'll discover a city many times more creative and cosmopolitan than its relative obscurity and modest population of 180,000 might suggest. Home to an Ivy League college, one of the best design schools in the United States, and a major culinary institute, Providence has exceptional food, compelling art and architecture, a thriving gay scene, and an inordinate number of very smart people. Yet it remains unpretentious and affordable.

— BY FREDA MOON AND KAREN DEUTSCH

FRIDAY

1 *Art Through the Ages* 3 p.m.

With 84,000 objects housed in its six stories, the Rhode Island School of Design's **RISD Museum** (224 Benefit Street; 401-454-6500; risdmuseum.org) could easily consume an entire day. The collection ranges from ancient Roman, Egyptian, and Greek artifacts to midcentury modern Eames furniture and Frank Lloyd Wright stained-glass windows.

2 *Hidden Beauty* 5 p.m.

Cross into downtown via one of the elegant bridges over the Woonasquatucket and Moshassuck Rivers. Both rivers were covered by concrete and rail lines until the mid-1990s, when a considerable effort was undertaken to unearth the city's waterways. Knock on the door at **Big Nazo Lab** (63 Washington Street; 401-831-9652; bignazo.com), where gleeful monsters and alien creatures — colorful wearable sculptures made of latex — peer from storefronts. Founded by Erminio Pinque, an instructor at Rhode Island School of Design, the studio has a gracious open-door policy: "Visitors of all shapes and sizes are welcome," Pinque said.

OPPOSITE A street in the College Hill neighborhood, home to Brown University and the Rhode Island School of Design. College Hill recalls the city's colonial past.

RIGHT Gondola tours are a good fit in a city with three rivers and its own Little Italy.

3 *Bank on It* 8 p.m.

In a lesser food town, the **Dorrance** (60 Dorrance Street; 401-521-6000; thedorrance.com; $$) could rest on the laurels of its architectural splendor — stained-glass windows; gilded candelabra; and elaborate, cake-frosting molding. But it wouldn't have to. Dorrance serves food as ornate as its surroundings, the opulent lobby of the former Union Trust building. Diners at one visit had mild Peruvian ceviche with tomatillo, fried sweet potato chips, and herbs, followed by Rhode Island blackfish crusted in quinoa, with quahogs, asparagus, and sunchokes, drowned in grass-green ramp dashi.

4 *Dim the Lights* 10 p.m.

Two of Providence's most enticing bars are hidden on a residential Federal Hill side street. Signless and easy to miss, the **Avery** (18 Luongo Memorial Square; 401-286-0237; averyprovidence.com) has dim lights, woodcuts of Art Nouveau vixens, and the varnished woodwork of a luxury yacht. Just down the block, **E&O Tap** (289 Knight Street; 401-454-4827; eandotap.com) is a raucous dive bar with a changing list of tap beers and a kitschy black velvet painting of Elvis.

SATURDAY

5 *Eggs From the Reds* 9 a.m.

Appropriately enough, the Rhode Island Red, the state bird — a chicken renowned for its eggs — figures in the sign for **Ellie's Bakery** (61 Washington Street; 401-228-8118; elliesbakery.com; $), whose Parisian-style confections depend on eggs, locally sourced, of

course. Seating is limited in this tiny shop/cafe, but an inventive menu has locals lining up. Try the signature breakfast sandwich, with egg, Cheddar cheese, and tomato jam on a house-made English muffin. Then pick up some croissants or macarons to power the rest of the morning.

6 *Going Downtown* 11 p.m.

Troll the shops of Westminster Street, an eclectic retail enclave. The historical center is the **Westminster Arcade** (130 Westminster Street; arcadeprovidence. com), the nation's first enclosed shopping mall, built in 1828; pop in for a look at the shops on the first floor. Nearby are more stores worth a visit, like the fashion-conscious **Queen of Hearts** (222 Westminster Street; 401-421-1471; queenofheartsri.com) and **Craftland** (212 Westminster Street; 401-272-4285; craftlandshop. com), an emporium devoted to locally made ceramics, art prints, soaps, T-shirts, and more. On Saturdays, there's traditional Irish music on fiddles and flutes, guitars, and concertinas at **AS220 FOO(d)** (115 Empire Street; 401-831-3663; facebook.com/AS220. FOOd), a restaurant run by the non-profit AS220 (as220.org), which has transformed the downtown neighborhood with its music, gallery, and art studios. Grab a sandwich there for lunch.

7 *Walk Back in Time* 4 p.m.

Take a long look at some of the architecture that gives Providence its powerful sense of place. On Benefit Street, a quaint strip that sits on College Hill, find the **Old State House** (150 Benefit Street;

ABOVE *WaterFire*, a river installation by the sculptor Barnaby Evans that comes to shimmering life downtown on some Saturday nights from May to November.

401-222-3103) where, in 1776, Rhode Islanders declared independence two months before the rest of the American colonies. Nearby are the **Providence Athenaeum** (251 Benefit Street; 401-421-6970; providenceathenaeum.org) and the **John Brown House** (52 Power Street; 401-273-7507), completed in 1788 and home to one of the founders of Brown University. Turn in at the picturesque Brown campus (brown.edu), which looks just the way a venerable Ivy League university should.

8 *A French Accent* 7 p.m.

Chez Pascal (960 Hope Street; 401-421-4422; chez-pascal.com; $$$) is a French restaurant with white tablecloths, leopard print furniture, and the open arms of a neighborhood brasserie. The menu emphasizes Rhode Island ingredients, but the food is traditional and exquisite: a selection of house-made pâtés and charcuterie, escargots à la Bourguignon, and slow-roasted duck with a seared root vegetable cake and golden raisin and red wine sauce. Across the street is the much-hyped **Cook & Brown Public House** (959 Hope Street; 401-273-7275; cookandbrown.com), one of several options for excellent craft cocktails in this cocktail-happy city.

9 *Watermark* 9 p.m.

In 1994, a Brown alumnus and artist named Barnaby Evans created a sculpture of 100 mini-bonfires that marked the convergence of the Providence, Moshassuck, and Woonasquatucket Rivers in the heart of downtown. The work, *WaterFire* (waterfire. org), has a mesmerizing quality and continues today, drawing crowds on about a dozen Saturday evenings between May and November. If you're not here when *WaterFire* is lighted, catch a show at **Cable Car**

Cinema and Cafe (204 South Main Street; 401-272-3970; cablecarcinema.com), where you can sip a glass of wine while watching a little-known feature film straight from the festival circuit.

SUNDAY

10 *Hair of the Dog* 8:55 a.m.

Get to **Julians** (318 Broadway; 401-861-1770; juliansprovidence.com; $$) before it opens, or plan on waiting in line. The brunch includes a selection of vegetarian dishes, like the Paesano tofu scramble with Roma tomatoes, crimini mushrooms, mozzarella, and fresh basil. Alongside are carnivore-pleasing concoctions like a flavorful hash made with house-

made chorizo, kale, jalapeño, and Cheddar. Julians is a popular hangover spot; many a customer here has been seen gripping a tall, spicy Bloody Mary in one hand and a coffee cup in the other.

11 *Noodle Picnic* 11 a.m.

Take a lazy stroll along the **Blackstone Boulevard Walking Path** (blackstoneparksconservancy.org), which begins at Blackstone Park at Angell Street and River Road and cuts through one of Providence's most beautiful and historic neighborhoods. Then head down to Fox Point and pick up an unusual picnic: Asian takeout at **Noodles 102** (102 Ives Street; 401-383-5004; noodles102.com), and sit by the water in **India Point Park** (friendsofindiapointpark.org).

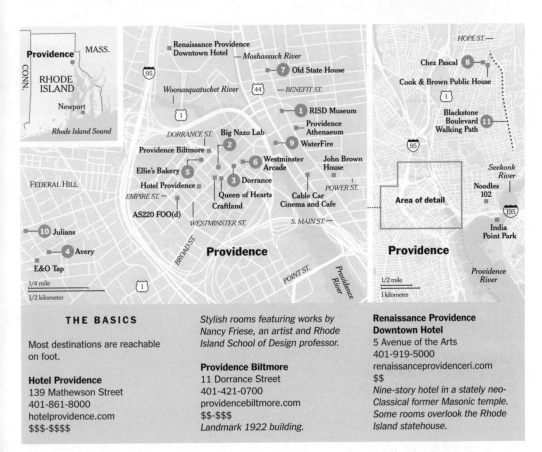

THE BASICS

Most destinations are reachable on foot.

Hotel Providence
139 Mathewson Street
401-861-8000
hotelprovidence.com
$$$-$$$$

Stylish rooms featuring works by Nancy Friese, an artist and Rhode Island School of Design professor.

Providence Biltmore
11 Dorrance Street
401-421-0700
providencebiltmore.com
$$-$$$
Landmark 1922 building.

Renaissance Providence Downtown Hotel
5 Avenue of the Arts
401-919-5000
renaissanceprovidenceri.com
$$
Nine-story hotel in a stately neo-Classical former Masonic temple. Some rooms overlook the Rhode Island statehouse.

Burlington

It is no surprise that Burlington, Vermont, a city whose best known exports include the jam band Phish, Ben & Jerry's ice cream, and Bernie Sanders, has a hip, socially conscious vibe. But in counterpoint to its worldliness and political awareness — even when Vermont's best-known senator isn't running for president — Burlington turns a discerning eye to the local. The Lake Champlain shoreline has undergone a renaissance, with hotels, bike and sailboat rental shops, and parks with sweeping views of the Adirondack Mountains. In the city's restaurants, local means urbane menus filled with heirloom tomatoes and grass-fed beef from (where else?) Vermont. And you're practically required to sample a local microbrew. — BY KATIE ZEZIMA

FRIDAY

1 *Stroll, Shop, Snack* 4:30 p.m.

With its lively mix of students, activists, artists, families, and professors (the University of Vermont is based here), Burlington offers some interesting people-watching. Take in the sights at the **Church Street Marketplace** (2 Church Street; churchstmarketplace.com), a wide, four-block concourse that is the city's social center and home to more than 100 shops and restaurants. The pace is slow, leisurely, and crowded, so be sure to leave plenty of time to explore. Pop into **Sweet Lady Jane** (40 Church Street; 802-862-5051; sweetladyjane.biz) for funky women's clothes and accessories; **Frog Hollow** (85 Church Street; 802-863-6458; froghollow.org) to check out treasures created by Vermont artists; and **Lake Champlain Chocolates** (65 Church Street; 802-862-5185; lakechamplainchocolates.com), where a hot chocolate doubles as a meal and you'll be hard put to eat just one truffle.

2 *Chic Tables* 7:30 p.m.

Long known as a town where the menus ran to gravy fries, pizza, and other collegiate staples, Burlington now has a complement of upscale restaurants. One place where Vermont pride meets gastronomic inspiration is **Hen of the Wood** (55 Cherry Street; 802-540-0534; henofthewood.com; $$). This casually refined restaurant features local meat (rabbit leg with parsnips, for example) and

vegetable (grilled cauliflower) entrees. The menu changes, but one constant is the mushroom toast, with house-cured bacon and a poached farm egg.

3 *Music and Lamplight* 10 p.m.

If there are three things that Burlington does well, they are live music, beer, and coffee. **Radio Bean** (8 North Winooski Avenue; 802-660-9346; radiobean.com) has all three. Catching a performance here is like hearing a band at a friend's party, if your friend lives in a ridiculously cool loft. For a different vibe, turn to the Light Club Lamp Shop, a sister venue in the same complex. It's lighted by dozens of vintage lamps, some of which are for sale, and the music is likely to be a jazz combo.

SATURDAY

4 *View from a Bicycle* 9 a.m.

Playing outside, whether on ski slopes, hiking trails, or lakes, is a way of life in Burlington, so it's no surprise that biking is a popular way to get around. Rent a bike at one of the many local shops. For those who want to see the city, marked bike lanes make it look easy, but beware of steep hills. Head out along Lake Champlain, and the terrain is mostly

OPPOSITE Sunset kayaking in Burlington Harbor on Lake Champlain. The city has reclaimed its once-dingy waterfront for recreation and outdoor sports.

BELOW The Frog Hollow Gift Shop, an arts center and gallery of Vermont-made arts and crafts.

flat. The city has several parks on the lakeshore, including **Waterfront Park**, built on industrial land reclaimed in the 1980s during Sanders' tenure as mayor. Vermont's trails join up to some 1,100 miles of trails in New York and Canada. Maps are available at champlainbikeways.org.

5 *Weightless Suds* 1 p.m.

Chances are when you get to **American Flatbread Burlington Hearth** (115 St. Paul Street; 802-861-2999; americanflatbread.com; $) it will be packed with a crowd that ranges from kids to beer geeks. But don't panic; just order one of the Zero Gravity house beers — this place believes bread-making and beermaking go together. The crispy flatbreads are essentially thin-crust pizzas with toppings like kalamata olives, sweet red peppers, goat cheese, rosemary, and red onions.

6 *Wrecks and Monsters* 3 p.m.

Lake Champlain isn't just what makes Burlington so picturesque. It's also a huge ecosystem that is the home of one of the world's oldest coral reefs (now fossilized) and hundreds of species of fish and plants. **ECHO, Leahy Center for Lake Champlain** (1 College Street; 802-864-1848; echovermont.org) explores the scientific, ecological, cultural, and historical importance of the lake with hands-on exhibitions, including the remnants of an old shipwreck and an installation that gives visitors new respect for frogs. The center even explores Lake Champlain's biggest mystery: Is Champ a mythical lake monster or real? Try to spot him from the second-floor deck.

7 *No Page Unturned* 5 p.m.

Reading and recycling are cultivated arts in Burlington, and no place combines both better than the **Crow Bookshop** (14 Church Street; 802-862-0848; crowbooks.com). Stroll on the creaky wooden floor and browse a trove of used and rare books as well as publisher's overstocks, ranging from gardening guides to gently used copies of Shakespeare. Let

the children explore their part of the store while you hang out on one of the couches and thumb through a stranger's old textbook.

8 *Paris in Vermont* 8 p.m.

In a city where style is inspired more by Birkenstocks than Birkin bags, **Leunig's Bistro** (115 Church Street; 802-863-3759; leunigsbistro.com; $$) offers a welcome dash of French flair. With its cherub lamps, cozy booths, and alfresco dining, it remains a social center. Go for a traditional beef Bourguignon or look for something with a local touch, perhaps maple-and-cardamom-marinated pork loin.

9 *On the Town* 10:30 p.m.

Follow the thumping bass to **Red Square** (136 Church Street; 802-859-8909; facebook.com/redsquarevt), a friendly spot that draws club kids and music lovers. If the weather is warm, you might find a band playing on the patio. Indoors, Red Square hosts both bands and D.J.'s who spin hip-hop, rock, and reggae for college students in halter tops and T-shirts. For something on the mellower side, head to **Nectar's** (188 Main Street; 802-658-4771; liveatnectars.com), the club where Phish got its start.

SUNDAY

10 *Green Eggs or Tofu* 11 a.m.

Prefer tofu in your breakfast scramble? Try the **Magnolia Bistro** (1 Lawson Lane; 802-846-7446; magnoliabistro.com; $), where eggs are always

interchangeable for tofu, and homemade granola is on the menu. For meat eaters, there are choices like a meat lover's omelet with maple sausage, bacon, and Cheddar, as well as sandwich selections like open-face steak and barbecued pork. Magnolia also claims to be one of Burlington's most environmentally friendly restaurants, which means it must be really, really green. Indeed, everything is recycled, and it's certified by the Green Restaurant Association.

11 *Could This Be Stonehenge?* 1 p.m.
Not sure of the time? Find out at the **Burlington Earth Clock**, a 43-foot-wide sundial at Oakledge Park and Beach (end of Flynn Street) made of slabs of granite from local quarries. Stand in the middle and look toward the mountains; the stones in front of you represent where the sun sets during equinoxes

and solstices. On the other end of the park is a studio apartment-size treehouse reachable even for kids in wheelchairs. It's an inclusive childhood fantasy come true.

OPPOSITE ABOVE On the popular Burlington Bike Path.

OPPOSITE BELOW The Earth Clock, a 43-foot sundial, shares Oakledge Park with a beach and recreation spaces.

ABOVE Church Street Marketplace, the place for shopping, people watching, and decadent hot chocolate.

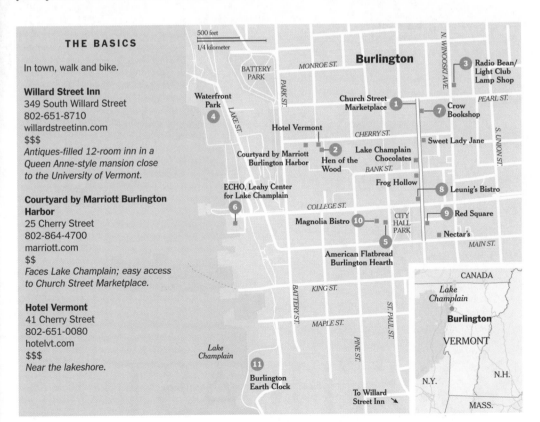

THE BASICS

In town, walk and bike.

Willard Street Inn
349 South Willard Street
802-651-8710
willardstreetinn.com
$$$
Antiques-filled 12-room inn in a Queen Anne-style mansion close to the University of Vermont.

Courtyard by Marriott Burlington Harbor
25 Cherry Street
802-864-4700
marriott.com
$$
Faces Lake Champlain; easy access to Church Street Marketplace.

Hotel Vermont
41 Cherry Street
802-651-0080
hotelvt.com
$$$
Near the lakeshore.

500 feet
1/4 kilometer

Burlington

BATTERY PARK
MONROE ST.
PARK ST.
N. WINOOSKI AVE.

3 Radio Bean/ Light Club Lamp Shop

Waterfront Park **4**
LAKE ST.

Church Street Marketplace **1**
PEARL ST.
7 Crow Bookshop

Hotel Vermont
CHERRY ST.
Sweet Lady Jane
S. UNION ST.

Courtyard by Marriott Burlington Harbor
2 Hen of the Wood
Lake Champlain Chocolates
BANK ST.

ECHO, Leahy Center for Lake Champlain
Frog Hollow
8 Leunig's Bistro

6
COLLEGE ST.
CITY HALL PARK
9 Red Square

Magnolia Bistro **10**
5
Nectar's
MAIN ST.

American Flatbread Burlington Hearth

BATTERY ST.
KING ST.
ST. PAUL ST.

MAPLE ST.
PINE ST.

Lake Champlain

11
Burlington Earth Clock

To Willard Street Inn ↘

CANADA
Lake Champlain
Burlington
VERMONT
N.Y.
N.H.
MASS.

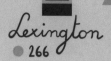

Louisville 272

Lexington
266

NASHVILLE
314

308 MEMPHIS

ASHEVILL

290

302
Chattanooga

192 Birmingham

JACKSON
286

198
Montgomery

276

NEW
Orleans

SOUTHEAST

arlottesville
320

204
WASHINGTON D.C.

BALTIMORE
282

324
Richmond

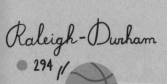
Raleigh-Durham
294

LANTA

charleston
298

260
SAVANNAH

St. Simons
Island
256

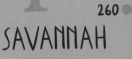

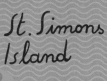

ORLANDO
232

214
fort
Lauderdale
South
Beach
226

St. Pete
Beach
242

Sarasota
246

Palm Beach 238

222
MIAMI

218
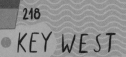
KEY WEST

210

the Everglades

Birmingham

Founded in 1871 at the junction of railroad lines, Alabama's largest city is used to moving forward. Part stone-ground grits and part steely grit, Birmingham flourished so quickly that it earned the name Magic City during the heyday of its iron trade. But this melting pot has also been a pressure cooker of racial tensions, overshadowed by a violent history of segregation and brutality against African-Americans. Today, as you retrace the steps of demonstrators who changed the course of American history on the Civil Rights Heritage Trail, you'll find a city experiencing an electrifying revival. Creative entrepreneurs are returning home, airy lofts breathe new life into downtown, and Southern cooking gets global makeovers. The bike-share program was the first in the nation to incorporate electric pedal-assisted bikes. — BY CHANEY KWAK

FRIDAY

1 *Artsy Souvenir* 4 p.m.

A cluster of eclectic merchants enlivens Forest Park, a stately neighborhood of early 20th-century homes. The vibrant gift shop **Naked Art** (3831 Clairmont Avenue; nakedartusa.com) champions local artisans by stocking objects like hand-thrown pottery and delicate watercolors of local landmarks. The gallery also features prints by the owner, Véronique Vanblaere, who was so enchanted by the city during her high school exchange year that she relocated from Belgium in 1996. On the third Friday of each month, the shop teams up with nearby businesses like the consignment store **Zoe's** (3900 Clairmont Avenue South; facebook.com/zoeshopbham) in Forest Park and the bistro **Little Savannah** (3811 Clairmont Avenue South; littlesavannah.com) for the offbeat Tour de Loo, which invites guests to visit bathrooms transformed by artists into installations that often stay up for a month.

2 *Grub Street* 6:30 p.m.

Avondale, which used to be an unremarkable district of automotive parts shops and service stations,

is now a walkable enclave chockablock with well-regarded restaurants concentrated around 41st Street. Returning home after stints at Per Se and Momofuku Ssäm Bar, John Hall runs the wood-fired pizzeria **Post Office Pies** (209 41st Street South; postofficepies. com; $$). For a more local flavor, try the excellent fried chicken that is brined in sweet tea and cooked to a succulent and crunchy perfection at **Saw's Soul Kitchen** (215 41st Street South; sawsbbq.com; $). For night life, check the website of **WorkPlay** (500 23rd Street South; workplay.com) for live music.

SATURDAY

3 *Market Options* 9 a.m.

Over a hundred farm stands, food stalls, and craft sellers sprout each Saturday morning at the popular **Market at Pepper Place** (2829 Second Avenue South; pepperplacemarket.com; $), in the parking lot of a handsome brick complex that used to house a Dr Pepper factory. Graze for blackberries, buttery pound cake (made with a recipe by a matriarch named Big Mama), and sheep's milk dulce de leche.

4 *Pig Iron in the Past* 11 a.m.

Check out a green Zyp bicycle (zypbikeshare. com) from a bike-share kiosk next to Pepper Place. Then explore the expansive grounds of **Sloss Furnaces** (20 32nd Street North; slossfurnaces.com), which manufactured pig iron from 1882 for nearly a century. Now a National Historic Landmark building with a ruddy patina, this interpretive museum is not only a site for concerts and metal-forging classes, but also

OPPOSITE Vulcan, cast in iron, stands atop Red Mountain. The iron and steel industry built Birmingham.

RIGHT The Negro Southern League Museum tells a story of African-Americans and baseball.

a symbol of the city's industrial foundation and green evolution.

5 *Rail to Trail* 11:45 a.m.

A pleasant 1.5-mile ride, which includes zipping down an abandoned railroad reborn in 2016 as the **Rotary Trail** (facebook.com/rotarytrail), will lead you to **Railroad Park** (railroadpark.org). This 19-acre green lung, molded largely with materials reclaimed from the site where warehouses once occupied the heart of the city, has become a communal garden with ponds, streams, hills, and a skate park. To admire the skyline, dock your bike and join the joggers and stroller-pushers on the three-quarter-mile loop path.

6 *Out of the Park* 12:30 p.m.

The intimate **Negro Southern League Museum** (120 16th Street South; birminghamnslm.org) views baseball through a distinctively local lens. As you browse the memorabilia, interactive displays, and uniforms of players like the pitcher Satchel Paige, you'll learn about not only how the sport has evolved, but also how the United States changed in the 20th century, causing the league to rise and fall.

7 *Global Aspirations* 1:30 p.m.

Once deserted after business hours, downtown has made a dazzling comeback in the last decade, with lofts occupying historic buildings along First and Second Avenues North. Catering to the young professionals who flock here, the **Pizitz Food Hall** (1821 Second Avenue North; thepizitz.com) includes globally minded dining spots like Eli's Jerusalem Grill, which pairs a shawarma pocket with sweet tea, and Lichita's, which scoops out Mexican-style (eggless) ice cream made with local fruits, all centered on a bar serving milkshakes and cocktails.

ABOVE A drinking fountain display, with separate fountains for white and black, part of the chronicle of racial injustice at the Birmingham Civil Rights Institute.

LEFT Sloss Furnaces, a relic of Birmingham's industrial foundation and a symbol of its green evolution.

8 *"Yearning for Freedom"* 3 p.m.

Designated a national monument by President Barack Obama during his last days in office, the Birmingham Civil Rights District consists of sites like the A. G. Gaston Motel, where the Rev. Dr. Martin Luther King Jr. met with activists, and the 16th Street Baptist Church, where a 1963 bombing killed four girls and injured many other congregants. Today the Romanesque church remains a thriving place of worship that testifies to the community's resilience. Tour the adjacent **Birmingham Civil Rights Institute** (520 16th Street North; bcri.org), which chronicles African-Americans' continuing struggles through photographs, multimedia, and objects like the bars of the cell where Dr. King wrote the "Letter From Birmingham Jail." At the eerily quiet Kelly Ingram Park across the street are a number of sculptures, including a police dog lunging at a boy and three pastors kneeling in prayer.

9 *Points Well Taken* 7 p.m.

Spend your Saturday evening in Five Points South, where the idyllic neighborhood of Highland Park collides with the University of Alabama at Birmingham. This dynamic area is home to convivial gastropubs as well as James Beard winners like Frank Stitt, who runs two French-accented restaurants, **Highlands Bar & Grill** (2011 11th Avenue South;

ABOVE Naked Art, a gallery in the Forest Park neighborhood, sells the work of local artisans.

BELOW Shoppers find plenty of browsing at the Market at Pepper Place, where more than 100 vendors set up on Saturday mornings to sell produce, snacks, and crafts.

highlandsbarandgrill.com; $$$) and **Chez Fonfon** next door (fonfonbham.com; $$), and Chris and Idie Hastings, whose **Hot and Hot Fish Club** (2180 11th Court South; hotandhotfishclub.com; $$$) serves plates like rabbit roulade with okra, corn, and field peas. After dinner, sip a dessertlike martini at the intimate **Blue Monkey Lounge** (1318 Cobb Lane) or rock out to live music at **Marty's PM** (1813 10th Court South).

SUNDAY

10 *Treks With Tales* 10 a.m.

Red Mountain, a ridge named for its rust-colored hematite ores, was once the force behind Birmingham's prosperity. Until the 1,500-acre grounds opened as the nonprofit **Red Mountain Park** (2011 Frankfurt Drive; redmountainpark.org) in 2011, the ridge lay untouched after mining ceased in 1962. Today you can explore a 15-mile trail system that threads together

panoramic views, tree houses, and former mines. To enrich your hike, download the free TravelStorysGPS app to listen to former miners, park rangers, and others share stories about life in Alabama's Appalachia region. When you reach the trail's northeastern terminus at Grace's Gap Overlook, the Magic City's silhouette will rise in the distance like an illusion.

11 *Next Act* 1 p.m.

Get a preview of what's to come in Birmingham with a stop in the resurgent Woodlawn neighborhood. At **Woodlawn Cycle Cafe** (5530 First Avenue South; woodlawncyclecafe.com; $), have a macchiato and a light brunch (granola, bagels, and grits are typically all on the menu).

OPPOSITE The 16th Street Baptist Church, now a national monument, came by its fame tragically. It was the site of a bombing in 1963 that killed four young girls and became a symbol of violent repression against African-Americans.

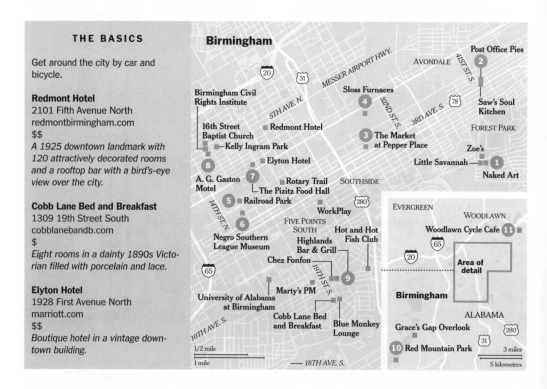

THE BASICS

Get around the city by car and bicycle.

Redmont Hotel
2101 Fifth Avenue North
redmontbirmingham.com
$$
A 1925 downtown landmark with 120 attractively decorated rooms and a rooftop bar with a bird's-eye view over the city.

Cobb Lane Bed and Breakfast
1309 19th Street South
cobblanebandb.com
$
Eight rooms in a dainty 1890s Victorian filled with porcelain and lace.

Elyton Hotel
1928 First Avenue North
marriott.com
$$
Boutique hotel in a vintage downtown building.

Birmingham

Post Office Pies 2
AVONDALE
41ST ST. S.
MESSER AIRPORT HWY.
20
31
Birmingham Civil Rights Institute
Sloss Furnaces
5TH AVE. N.
32ND ST. S.
3RD AVE. S.
78
Saw's Soul Kitchen
16th Street Baptist Church
Redmont Hotel
The Market at Pepper Place 3
FOREST PARK
Kelly Ingram Park
Elyton Hotel
Little Savannah
Zoe's
8
A. G. Gaston Motel 7
Rotary Trail
SOUTHSIDE
Naked Art 1
The Pizitz Food Hall
5
Railroad Park
280
EVERGREEN
WOODLAWN
14TH ST. N.
WorkPlay
Woodlawn Cycle Cafe 11
6
FIVE POINTS SOUTH
Hot and Hot Fish Club
65
Negro Southern League Museum
Highlands Bar & Grill
20
Area of detail
Chez Fonfon
19TH ST. S.
65
9
Birmingham
Marty's PM
University of Alabama at Birmingham
ALABAMA
Cobb Lane Bed and Breakfast
Blue Monkey Lounge
Grace's Gap Overlook
280
10TH AVE. S.
31
10 Red Mountain Park
3 miles
1/2 mile
1 mile
18TH AVE. S.
5 kilometers

Montgomery

A souvenir button sold at the Civil Rights Memorial Center in Montgomery reads, "The March Continues." It refers to the Civil Rights March of 1965 from Selma to Montgomery, a galvanizing event that led to the Voting Rights Act protecting African-Americans' right to the ballot box. New projects, including the nation's first monument to the victims of lynching, combine with landmarks of the civil rights movement and Civil War-era sites to make Montgomery a vital stop on any history tour of the United States. — BY ELAINE GLUSAC

FRIDAY

1 *Reckoning With Race* 2 p.m.

According to the nonprofit legal center Equal Justice Initiative, more than 4,400 African-Americans were murdered by white mobs between 1877 and 1950. The E.J.I.'s deeply moving **National Memorial for Peace and Justice** (417 Caroline Street; museumandmemorial.eji.org), the nation's first to recognize those atrocities, forces viewers to a grim reckoning with a horrific past. Visitors to the hilltop site will initially see columns representing the 800 counties throughout the United States where lynchings occurred. Perception shifts inside the plaza, revealing the steel monuments as suspended, like hanging figures. The companion **Legacy Museum** downtown (115 Coosa Street) traces the evolution of inequality from slavery and racial terror to police violence and mass incarceration.

2 *Savoring the South* 7 p.m.

You know you're in the South when bacon is deep fried and served like French fries. That dish, called fett sow fries, came with an addictive peach chutney one night at **Central** (129 Coosa Street; central129coosa.com; $$), which occupies a rustic 1890s warehouse with exposed brick walls and a bustling open kitchen. The menu marries regional classics to ethnic influences in dishes like hot chicken in steamed Asian buns.

3 *Bunker Bars* 9:30 p.m.

The downtown entertainment district spans a few blocks of renovated warehouses close to the river, home to interesting bars where you're likely to rub elbows with local residents. **Aviator Bar** (166

Commerce Street; facebook.com/Aviatorbar) attracts servicemen and women from nearby Maxwell Air Force Base with its military theme: sandbag-ringed nooks with World War II vintage photos and model airplanes hanging from the ceiling. A block away, the subterranean jazz club **Sous La Terre** (82 Commerce Street; facebook.com/TheBlueRoomSLT) entertains night owls after midnight with live music from the keyboardist Henry Pugh. If you arrive earlier, join the crowd around the U-shaped bar in the affiliated La Salle Bleu Piano Bar upstairs.

SATURDAY

4 *Civil Rights Roots* 9 a.m.

The civil rights movement was already underway when Rosa Parks, a seamstress riding home from her job at a downtown department store in 1955, refused to cede her seat on a crowded bus to a white passenger, leading to her arrest, the Montgomery bus boycott, and the explosion of the campaign to end segregation. Run by Troy University, the **Rosa Parks Museum** (252 Montgomery Street; troy.edu/rosaparks) tells the story in multimedia displays. Artifacts include a bus from the 1955 fleet.

5 *Depth and Delight* 10:30 a.m.

More Than Tours (39 Dexter Avenue; 334-296-3024; facebook.com/MORE-THAN-TOURS-1690389210988363) offers 90 minutes of entertainment

OPPOSITE Martin Luther King's church on Dexter Avenue.

BELOW The Goat Haus Biergarten in elegant Cottage Hill.

covering the past, present, and future of civil rights struggles. Michelle Browder, the impassioned owner and guide, might break into a Freedom Rider song or recite a Martin Luther King speech near the steps of the Alabama State Capitol. "To get rid of your preconceived ideas about Montgomery, you need a fresh pair of eyes," she said on a recent tour, doling out red cat-eye sunglasses, her signature look.

6 *To the Pulpit* Noon

Martin Luther King Jr. was only 24 when he came to Montgomery to accept his first appointment as a pastor, at the handsome red-brick church now named **Dexter Avenue King Memorial Baptist Church** (454 Dexter Avenue; dexterkingmemorial.

org). In a memorable juxtaposition, the church lies just a block from the state Capitol, which is still presided over by a statue of Jefferson Davis, the Confederate president. Take the tour of the church to learn about its role in the campaign that made King a national leader.

7 *A Life Story* 1 p.m.

The modest clapboard house where the King family lived between 1954 and 1960 has been preserved as the **Dexter Parsonage Museum** (309 South Jackson Street; dexterkingmemorial.org). Visits begin at the Interpretive Center next door and proceed to the 1912-vintage house, which is furnished much as it was when the Kings lived in it. A plaque embedded in the front porch identifies a nearby crater marking the spot where the house was bombed by segregationists in 1956. Behind the buildings, the King-Johns Garden for Reflection invites visitors to spend a few quiet moments.

8 *Arty Happy Hour* 3 p.m.

If any neighborhood is poised for a comeback, it's nearby Cottage Hill, home to elegant 19th-century

ABOVE The Fitzgerald Museum. Montgomery was the city where the romance of F. Scott and Zelda Fitzgerald began.

LEFT The King family kitchen at Dexter Parsonage Museum.

houses. **Goat Haus Biergarten** (532 Clay Street; goat-haus-biergarten.business.site) operates in one of them, a restored Victorian on a bluff. Grab a lager from Ghost Train Brewing in Birmingham and sit at a picnic table on the lawn overlooking the Alabama River. Next door **21 Dreams: Arts & Culture Collective** (facebook.com/21DreamsMGM) includes a small gallery.

9 *Shakespeare and Friends* 7 p.m.

The **Alabama Shakespeare Festival** (1 Festival Drive; asf.net) presents musicals, dramas, original productions, and, of course, Shakespeare on two stages in Blount Cultural Park, which is also home to the Montgomery Museum of Fine Art. Much more than a summer festival, ASF is an ambitious professional regional theater operating year-round. Besides mounting productions of classics and tried-and-true musicals, it also sponsors the Southern Writers' Project to commission and produce new plays. Topics have ranged from the quiltmakers of Gee's Bend, Alabama, to the famous University of Alabama football coach Paul (Bear) Bryant.

TOP The theater of the Alabama Shakespeare Festival, which presents a variety of plays and musicals.

ABOVE The Rosa Parks Museum. Parks's defiance of racial segregation on city buses made her a civil rights icon.

10 *Nightcap and Nosh* 10 p.m.

Pinched between an alley and a parking lot, **Leroy Lounge** (2752 Boultier Avenue; leroylounge. com) offers some 18 craft beers on tap and mixes craft spirits in cocktails. Sample and relax, and should hunger strike, walk down the alley to the bar's sibling hipster **El Rey Burrito Lounge** (burritolounge. com; $).

SUNDAY

11 *Scott and Zelda* 9 a.m.

At the bustling **Cahawba House** (31 South Court Street; cahawbahouse.com; $), breakfast is all about the buttery biscuits. Add bacon, cheese, and other fixings to build your own sustaining 'Bama breakfast. Then head to the gracious neighborhood of Cloverdale to visit the **Fitzgerald Museum** (919 Felder Avenue; thefitzgeraldmuseum.org), the last home of F. Scott and Zelda Fitzgerald. The pair met in 1918 in Montgomery, her hometown, when he was stationed at a nearby army camp. They moved into this 1910-era house with their daughter, Scottie, in 1931, and stayed for about six months before Zelda

was hospitalized for mental illness. Galleries feature exhibits devoted to the couple's courtship, Zelda's paintings, Scottie's memories, and Fitzgerald's literature and decline.

OPPOSITE The fountain at the Civil Rights Memorial Center is a reminder of both the American civil rights struggle and Martin Luther King's eloquent expression of its meaning.

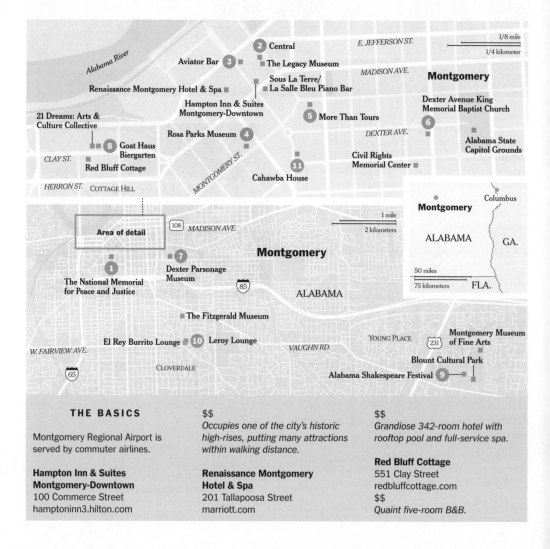

THE BASICS

Montgomery Regional Airport is served by commuter airlines.

Hampton Inn & Suites Montgomery-Downtown
100 Commerce Street
hamptoninn3.hilton.com

$$
Occupies one of the city's historic high-rises, putting many attractions within walking distance.

Renaissance Montgomery Hotel & Spa
201 Tallapoosa Street
marriott.com

$$
Grandiose 342-room hotel with rooftop pool and full-service spa.

Red Bluff Cottage
551 Clay Street
redbluffcottage.com
$$
Quaint five-room B&B.

Washington D.C.

No longer does the nation's capital have the starchy, insular appearance of a white male fiefdom. Over-looking (if one can) the federal government's mal-adroitness, Washington today possesses a dynamism that, along with its fabled history, qualifies it as a great American city. It's now entirely possible to spend a couple of memorable days here without once eating a New York strip steak or darkening a marble corridor. You checked those boxes on your first visit, so now come back for This Town's revelations.
— BY ROBERT DRAPER

FRIDAY

1 *African-American Journey* 3 p.m.

Since its opening in September 2016, the city's hottest draw has been the Smithsonian National **Museum of African American History & Culture** (1400 Constitution Avenue Northwest; nmaahc.si.edu) on the National Mall. The museum's immense collection is well worth the long lines. The artifacts — including Nat Turner's Bible, Louis Armstrong's trumpet, and the first edition of Booker T. Washington's 1907 book *The Negro in Business* — are themselves impressive. But the three-tiered layout lends the feeling of a journey, by turns painful and triumphant. The path ends with a moving video collection of contemporary African Americans reflecting on their life experiences.

2 *Japanese Inflection* 6:30 p.m.

The galloping culinary scene in Washington coincides with a regrettable trend of no-reservations restaurant policies. **Himitsu** (828 Upshur Street Northwest; himitsudc.com; $$$), one of the city's most creative dining spots, minimizes the ordeal by taking your name and cell number, freeing you to amble down the street to one of the many Petworth neighborhood waystations (such as Ruta del Vino and Hank's Cocktail Bar), until a text informs you that your table awaits. Once seated, choose from an ever-rotating, Japanese-inflected menu that includes

OPPOSITE Inside the Capitol Hill Visitor Center, where guests can see the Capitol Dome peering through a large glass ceiling.

shareable and uniformly delectable plates of raw seafood, roasted soy chicken, and Asian-spiced vegetables. In suitable weather, the streetside tables maximize Himitsu's chill, not-your-grandfather's-Washington vibe.

3 *Nightcap With the Demimonde* 10 p.m.

The "No Clowns" sign on the door hints at the stodge-free ethos of **Showtime Lounge** (113 Rhode Island Avenue Northwest; facebook.com/showtimebardc), a miniature and easily overlooked cash-only pub in the unprepossessing neighborhood of Bloomingdale. Step inside and you're under the city's floorboards: framed images of Humphrey Bogart and spaghetti Western stars on the walls, foreign-language songs from the speakers, and a beguiling cast of locals not likely to be found on a CNN panel. Beers on tap, Utz potato chips for food.

SATURDAY

4 *Upmarket Morning* 9 a.m.

It took a few years, but now **Union Market** (1309 Fifth Street Northeast; unionmarketdc.com) in the city's northeastern quadrant has become Washington's swankiest and most-trafficked indoor market. Though the 22,000-square-foot space hosts several restaurants, some excellent specialty vendors, and a seasonal farmers' market, it achieves peak appeal during weekend breakfast hours. That's when mostly young and affluent locals gather at tables over freshly prepared goods like empanadas, fresh pastry, and espresso. After becoming properly caffeinated, stretch your legs and search for take-home items like imported spices and high-end cutlery.

5 *Where Are the Women Artists?* 11 a.m.

The sumptuous and expansive **National Museum of Women in the Arts** (1250 New York Avenue Northwest; nmwa.org) opened in 1987 but has never received the touristic attention it deserves. Special exhibits have included abstract works by female African-American artists and a Mexico City-based artist's use of a clothesline to depict instances of violence against women. The permanent collection features work from around the globe, as well as from revered American artists like the celebrity

photographer Annie Leibovitz and the impressionist painter Ellen Day Hale. On the mezzanine level, a quiet and lovely cafe is one of the city's best refuges.

6 *Capital Winery* 1 p.m.

One of the fastest-growing neighborhoods is the 42-acre stretch along the Anacostia River known as the Yards. Though it teems with barhopping millennials, it also offers a sophisticated lunch stop. **District Winery** (385 Water Street Southeast; districtwinery. com) makes more than a dozen uniformly excellent wines on-site, using grapes harvested from Virginia, California, and New York. You can tour the winery, try selections at the tasting bar, and buy bottles to take home. Best of all, enjoy exquisite pairings of the wines with New American cuisine at the casually elegant in-house restaurant Ana ($$$), overlooking the river.

7 *Forgotten Warriors* 4 p.m.

A trip to the nation's capital wouldn't feel complete without at least a glancing view of its many war monuments. One that has been too often overlooked is the **Korean War Veterans Memorial** (nps.gov/ KWVM), on the western flank of the National Mall, in the shadows of the much-visited Lincoln Memorial. Dedicated in 1995, its evocative centerpiece consists of 19 stainless-steel statues of American soldiers trudging through heavy brush with grim and hyper-alert expressions. In subtle acknowledgment of that war's vague objectives and not-altogether-satisfying outcome, the etched tribute notes that the soldiers

ABOVE Union Market in Northeast Washington.

BELOW Presidential artwork at Ana, a restaurant in a winery.

"answered the call to defend a country they never knew and a people they never met."

8 *Rooftop Refreshment* 5:30 p.m.

Though the botched burglary in 1972 that metastasized into the toppling of the Nixon presidency began in what the **Watergate Hotel** (2650 Virginia Avenue Northwest; thewatergatehotel.com) now bills as "Scandal Room 214," today there's an additional reason to visit the Watergate: the **Top of the Gate** outdoor bar, which offers the best 360-degree, cocktail-laden views of the city. There is even a small ice-skating rink (with artificial ice) nestled beside the bar. If the weather turns foul, repair to the amply stocked whiskey bar on the lobby level.

9 *Riverside Seafood* 7:30 p.m.

The Spanish and seafood-centric **Del Mar de Fabio Trabocchi** (791 Wharf Street Southwest; delmardc.com; $$$$), is the brainchild of Fabio Trabocchi, who also owns the celebrity magnet Italian restaurant Fiola Mare in Georgetown. In studied contrast to hip newcomers like Himitsu, Del Mar's cavernous and fish-sculpture-bedecked interior is

designed to dazzle the eyes. But the food still counts most here, and it is one of Washington's best culinary experiences. From mango-colored gazpacho to velvety Iberian ham to a selection of standout paellas, Del Mar shines.

10 *Cozy Coda* 10 p.m.

Another fast-developing Washington neighborhood is Brookland, dominated by Catholic University and the majestic Basilica of the National Shrine of

ABOVE The National Museum of African American History & Culture, a recent addition to the Smithsonian.

RIGHT The Lincoln Memorial at night.

the Immaculate Conception. Journey there for a nightcap at **Primrose** (3000 12th Street Northeast; primrosedc.com), a gorgeously appointed yet casual French bistro. Sit at the bar and order one of the wines by the glass perfectly selected to accompany stout cheeses and rillettes de lapin.

SUNDAY

11 *District Dim Sum* 10:30 a.m.

Among northwest Washington's many high-activity neighborhoods—Logan Circle, Columbia

Heights, Adams Morgan—the Shaw district is the latest to be lit up with clever dining spots. One of the best is **Tiger Fork** (922 (rear) N Street Northwest; tigerforkdc.com; $$), a temple of Hong Kong cuisine situated in an alleyway. The eclectically red-and-bamboo Chinese interior is smile-eliciting, as is the weekend "Dim Sum and Then Some" menu. Look for items like Hong Kong-style French toast, Chinese bacon, and creamed tofu, best teamed with a fruity and bubbly cocktail.

ABOVE Outside a fence at the White House. The familiar monuments will always draw the curious, but there's more to Washington than its power centers.

OPPOSITE A dusting of snow whitens one of the sculpted soldiers at the Korean War Veterans Memorial.

THE BASICS

Washington's two airports are well served by an array of airlines. The subway, usually called the Metro, has many convenient stops.

Ritz-Carlton, Georgetown
3100 South Street Northwest
ritzcarlton.com
$$$
Chic 86-room hotel, very small for a Ritz-Carlton, feels more like an elite Alpine nook than a hub of ever-bustling Georgetown.

Watergate Hotel
2650 Virginia Avenue Northwest
thewatergatehotel.com
$$$
The iconic site of the break-in that set off a scandal leading to a president's resignation; updated in a sweeping 2017 makeover.

Liaison Capitol Hill
415 New Jersey Avenue Northwest
jdvhotels.com
$$$
Conveniently located. Seasonal rooftop deck and pool.

The Everglades

Not quite the brackish swamp that many imagine it to be, the vast south Florida wetland known as the Everglades is actually a clear, wide, shallow river that flows like molasses. And living within its million-plus acres are 200 types of fish, 350 species of birds, and 120 different kinds of trees, just for starters, all less than an hour south of Miami. Of course, to see the iridescent-winged purple gallinule, breaching bottlenose dolphins, and still alligators soaking in the sun, you have to be willing to stop and slow down, moving as languidly as the River of Grass itself. Luckily, the availability of ranger programs and self-guided tours means you needn't be an expert hiker or kayaker to get below the surface of this beautiful, tangled landscape. — BY BETH GREENFIELD

FRIDAY

1 *Under the Boardwalk* 2 p.m.

To hang with more creatures than you can count, head into the **Everglades National Park**'s main **Ernest F. Coe** entrance (305-242-7700; nps.gov/ever/planyourvisit/visitorcenters.htm), near Homestead. You'll find winding boardwalks like the Anhinga Trail, named for the majestic water bird that stands with wings stretched wide to dry its black and white feathers in the sun. A stroll is likely to reveal several anhingas, plus green and tri-colored herons, red-bellied turtles, double-crested cormorants, and many alligators. Don't miss the striking Pahayokee Overlook, a short and steep walkway that juts out over a dreamily endless field of billowing, wheat-colored sawgrass.

2 *Pleasure Cruise* 4:45 p.m.

Pick up maps at the Coe entrance and then head deeper west in the park to the **Flamingo Visitor Center** (239-695-2945; nps.gov/ever/planyourvisit/flamdirections.htm), where a small, quiet tour boat whisks passengers from the close wetlands of the park out into the glimmering, airy expanse of Florida Bay. In just under two hours, you'll get a narrated tour, glimpses of elegant water birds (perhaps the great white heron or roseate spoonbill), and a glorious, multicolored sunset over the water.

3 *Search for Tamale* 7:30 p.m.

There's nothing much going on in Homestead, the scruffy town that borders the park's eastern entrance, but a small collection of Mexican restaurants serving tasty fare on North Krome Avenue ensures that you'll at least be well fed. **Casita Tejas** (27 North Krome Avenue, Homestead; 305-248-8224; casitatejas.com; $) offers authentic dishes like beef gorditas, chicken tamales, and chile rellenos in a homey, festive atmosphere.

SATURDAY

4 *Fruit Basket* 8 a.m.

Start your morning off with a thick, fresh-fruit milkshake at **Robert Is Here** (19200 Southwest 344th Street, Homestead; 305-246-1592; robertishere.com), a family-run farm stand offering papayas, star fruits, kumquats, guavas, sapodillas, mameys, and other tropical treats among heaps of fresh oranges and grapefruits.

5 *In the Loop* 10 a.m.

Along the northern rim of the national park you will find the **Shark Valley** entrance (Route 41, Tamiami Trail; 305-221-8455), where a paved loop is traversable by foot, bicycle, or guided tram ride and is often host

OPPOSITE Big Cypress National Preserve.

RIGHT Boardwalks in the swamps of Everglades National Park are vantage points for seeing alligators, turtles, and a multicolored profusion of water-loving birds.

to sleepy crocs or gators. (The Everglades is the only place in the world where alligators, which live in fresh water, and saltwater crocodiles live side by side.) The two-hour tram ride, led by a naturalist, is the best option for coping with the heat and the mosquitoes, which peak here between June and October. It will pause halfway through to let you climb to the top of a 45-foot-high observation deck affording 20-mile wilderness views in all directions.

6 *Swamp Things* 1 p.m.

Just north of the Everglades National Park is the **Big Cypress National Preserve** (nps.gov/bicy) — a tract that narrowly escaped being developed as Miami's international airport in the 1970s. And within its borders lies a novel opportunity for those who prefer to explore this region on foot: ranger-led swamp hikes that set off from the **Oasis Visitor Center** (52105 Tamiami Trail East, Ochopee). "From the highway, all you see is brown and green," a ranger, Corinne Fenner, said as she led people into the thigh-deep waters of cypress-tree stands. "It's nice to get out into the prairie and notice all the colors." And the hues you'll see are certainly

BELOW Take a ranger-led hike in water that looks surprisingly clean and feels deliciously cool on a hot day.

magical: the butter yellow of the Everglades daisy, bright violet of nettle-leaf velvetberry flowers, electric lime of freshwater sponges, and deep scarlet of a red-bellied woodpecker. The water itself — which collects in a sandy peat and limestone basin, helping silvery bald cypress trees thrive — looks shockingly clear and feels deliciously cool soaking through jeans and sneakers.

7 *Drive-Thru Wilderness* 3:30 p.m.

A Big Cypress driving tour, north of the Gulf Coast canoe launch on the gravel Turner River Road, offers various close-up encounters with wildlife. Along the scenic 17-mile route, you're sure to rub elbows with creeping turtles, nesting ospreys, and clusters of the alligators that like to float lazily in the narrow creeks here, leaving nothing but steely eyes and snouts above water.

8 *Stuffed Animals, Stuffed Belly* 6 p.m.

Not for the faint of heart when it comes to pushing carnivorous limits, the **Rod and Gun Club**, in the small fishing village of Everglades City (200 West Broadway; 239-695-2101; facebook.com/everglades.rgc; $$), is a handsome, historic riverside inn where you can unwind from your full day of touring with a hearty dinner. Swamp and Turf (steak and frogs' legs) and gator nuggets are among the menu items. Afterward, have a cocktail in the cozy lounge, where you can shoot pool under the eerie double gaze of a gator skin and deer head, both mounted on the wall.

SUNDAY

9 *Paddle Your Own Canoe* 10 a.m.

The southwest edge of the park sits at the precipice of glistening Chokoloskee Bay and the Ten Thousand Islands area — a pristine region of mangroves and sandy keys mostly reachable only by boat via the 99-mile Wilderness Waterway canoe and kayak trail. While experienced paddlers can plunge right into a days-long journey, camping on raised "chickee" platforms or sand spits along the way, beginners are best off joining one of the many shorter, organized trips on more navigable creeks, like the one led weekly by national park naturalists, leaving from the park's **Gulf Coast Visitor Center** (815 Oyster Bar Lane, Everglades

City). "I never get tired of this area," a naturalist, Brian Ettling, said during one such four-hour journey, leading canoeists single file beneath a cathedral of arching mangrove branches. He excitedly pointed out blue herons, jumping mullet fish, and skittish tree crabs. He gave lessons on the hunting habits of swooping turkey vultures, which have a sense of smell rivaling a bloodhound's, and on the hip attributes of screechy red-shouldered hawks: "They're like the local punk rockers. They eat lizards and scream."

10 *Caught on Film* 3 p.m.

On your way back east along the Tamiami Trail, be sure to stop and visit the **Big Cypress Gallery** (52388 Tamiami Trail, Ochopee; 239-695-2428;

clydebutcher.com). Here the photographer Clyde Butcher's large-format, black-and-white landscapes perfectly capture the romantic essence of this swampland and put your own fresh experiences into striking artistic perspective. Butcher also provides naturalist-led swamp walks on his 13 acres within the Big Cypress National Preserve.

ABOVE Wild beauty at sunset in the Big Cypress National Preserve.

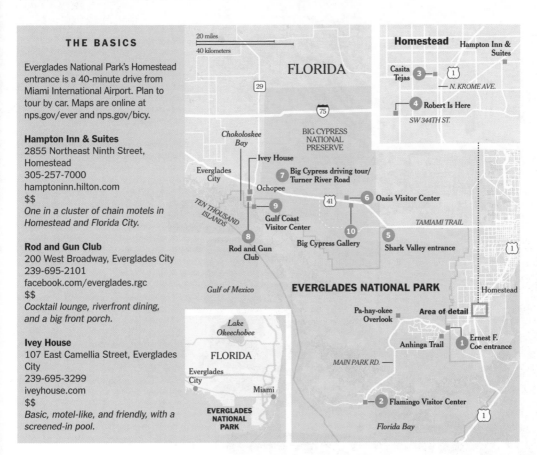

THE BASICS

Everglades National Park's Homestead entrance is a 40-minute drive from Miami International Airport. Plan to tour by car. Maps are online at nps.gov/ever and nps.gov/bicy.

Hampton Inn & Suites
2855 Northeast Ninth Street,
Homestead
305-257-7000
hamptoninn.hilton.com
$$
One in a cluster of chain motels in Homestead and Florida City.

Rod and Gun Club
200 West Broadway, Everglades City
239-695-2101
facebook.com/everglades.rgc
$$
Cocktail lounge, riverfront dining, and a big front porch.

Ivey House
107 East Camellia Street, Everglades City
239-695-3299
iveyhouse.com
$$
Basic, motel-like, and friendly, with a screened-in pool.

Fort Lauderdale

Fort Lauderdale continues to mature beyond its spring-break days, with posh resorts now rising along the beach. Meanwhile, Las Olas Boulevard, the lively commercial strip that links the beach to downtown, has welcomed an array of new boutiques and restaurants. There is still some youthful partying—a smattering of raucous bars still dot the beach, and rowdy clubgoers flock to Himmarshee Village downtown. But at the end of a sunny, water-logged day, this Florida resort town offers a sophisticated evening that doesn't involve neon bikinis and syrupy daiquiris. — BY GERALDINE FABRIKANT

FRIDAY

1 *Seaside Dusk* 5 p.m.

There are a plenty of beachfront restaurants and bars in Fort Lauderdale where you can have a drink, watch the clouds roll over the ocean, soak up the sea air, and catch the parade of sun-soaked tourists in beachwear and residents going home in suits and ties. One of the more welcoming spots is the relatively quiet **H2O Café** (101 South Fort Lauderdale Beach Boulevard; 954-414-1024; facebook.com/h2ocafefl), which occupies part of an Art Deco building dating to 1937.

2 *Waterfront Wahoo* 7 p.m.

Fort Lauderdale's dining scene is alive and well inland as well as on the water. **Boatyard** (1555 Southeast 17th Street; 954-525-7400; boatyard. restaurant/about-us; $$) evokes a New England-style boathouse with its crisp blue and white décor, enormous cathedral ceiling, gleaming oak floors, and portal-style windows. An outdoor bar facing a marina brings in a nautical mix of young and old who dine on fresh seafood like wood-grilled wahoo and yellowtail snapper.

3 *Nice and Cool* 9 p.m.

For a cool nightcap, slide over to **Blue Jean Blues** (3320 Northeast 33rd Street; 954-306-6330;

OPPOSITE Fort Lauderdale's sun-kissed beach.

RIGHT The International Swimming Hall of Fame. Among the curious facts to learn inside: Leonardo da Vinci and Benjamin Franklin both experimented with swim fins.

bjblive.com), where you can sit at the bar and listen to live jazz and blues bands. The club has a tiny stage and a dance floor, and the music can go from jazz to rock depending on the evening.

SATURDAY

4 *Dawn Patrol* 8 a.m.

Take an early morning stroll along the wide, white beach. It is open to joggers, walkers, and swimmers and is surprisingly clean. For a leafier, more secluded adventure that is a favorite with resident runners and walkers, try the two-mile loop through the woods in the **Hugh Taylor Birch State Park** (954-564-4521; floridastateparks.org/park/hugh-taylor-birch). Its entrance is only steps from the beach at the intersection of A1A and Sunrise Boulevard. If you're not a jogger, take a drive through the park.

5 *Sunny Nosh* 10 a.m.

Finish off the jog at the beachside **Ritz-Carlton** (1 North Fort Lauderdale Beach Boulevard; 954-465-2300; ritzcarlton.com/fortlauderdale) with a relaxed breakfast at **Burlock Coast** ($$$), the hotel's waterfront restaurant. The menu offers traditional morning fare like omelets, bacon and eggs, and a breakfast sandwich on brioche. If you'd rather recharge with something lighter, choose one of the interesting combinations at the juice bar.

6 *Super Swimmers* 12:30 p.m.

Water sports enthusiasts should stop in at the **International Swimming Hall of Fame** (One Hall of

Fame Drive; 954-462-6536; ishof.org), a repository of history and curious facts about swimming and aquatic celebrities. Did you know that both Leonardo da Vinci and Benjamin Franklin experimented with swim fins? Or that Polynesian swimmers used palm leaves tied to their feet? Those and other nuggets of swimming trivia are lovingly conveyed at this sleek white building on the Intracoastal Waterway.

7 *Cruising the Pier* 3:30 p.m.

If you want to go a bit off the beaten track, drive up Route A1A to Commercial Boulevard and hang out on **Anglins Fishing Pier** (954-491-9403; facebook.com/AnglinsFishingPier). There's a little shopping area for swim gear, and you can rent a fishing pole. Or just sit and have a coffee.

8 *Crabs or Pizza* 7 p.m.

One trendy restaurant is **Truluck's**, at the Galleria Mall (2584A East Sunrise Boulevard; 954-396-5656; trulucks.com; $$$$). An elegant room with dark woods and red leather upholstery, it adds a bit of glamour to the popular mall and has a busy bar with low-key live music every night. It has a surf-and-turf menu but is perhaps best known for stone crabs. For a casual dinner, try **Luigi's Coal Oven Pizza** (1415 East Las Olas Boulevard; 954-522-8888; luigiscoalovenpizza.com; $$), a small, cozy place with pizza, pastas, salads, and a wide selection of wines.

9 *Mall Party* 9 p.m.

It may not be spring break, but you would never know, looking at the huge crowds at the **Blue Martini**, at the Galleria Mall (2432 East Sunrise Boulevard; 954-653-2583; fortlauderdale.bluemartinilounge.com). But the patrons are decidedly more upscale. By 8 p.m. when the band is playing, the bar is busy with snowbirds and young professionals, schmoozing and dancing. The cocktails come in many varieties, with emphasis on the martinis. There are many fruity flavors; the Blue Martini is made with blue Curaçao.

SUNDAY

10 *Southern Comfort* 11:30 a.m.

The **Pelican Grand Beach Resort** (2000 North Ocean Boulevard; 954-568-9431; pelicanbeach.com; $$$$) offers a Sunday brunch with omelets, salads, seafood, pasta, blintzes, and all manner of other foods, plus Bloody Marys, mimosas, and desserts. You will pay for the experience, but it's a light-hearted way to start the day, and you may not have to eat again until tomorrow. The plantation-style restaurant overlooks the beach, with a big veranda with white wicker tables and rocking chairs that catch the sea breezes.

11 *Eccentric Estate* 1 p.m.

Bonnet House (900 North Birch Road; 954-563-5393; bonnethouse.org) was the vacation home of the artists and art patrons Frederic Bartlett and his wife, Evelyn. They created an eccentric, brightly painted

ABOVE The Bonnet House museum was the vacation home of the artists Frederic and Evelyn Bartlett in the days when panthers roamed the nearby swamps.

BELOW Morning exercise on the sand. Fort Lauderdale's expansive beach has plenty of room for joggers, early-bird swimmers, and martial artists.

retreat, now a museum—more Caribbean mansion than Florida estate—near a swamp where alligators thrived. Window bars protected the house from the panthers that once roamed the estate and the monkeys that still live there.

12 *Las Olas Stroll* 2 p.m.

In an era when shopping in new cities can remind you of every mall back home, Fort Lauderdale has kept its streak of independence: nothing fancy but fun. Walk off brunch with a stroll and shopping on East Las Olas Boulevard. A rash of one-off stores and galleries there invite lazy browsing. If you want to take edible gifts home or you can't resist them yourself, drop in at **Kilwin's**,

an ice cream, chocolate, and fudge shop (No. 809; 954-523-8338; kilwins.com/stores/all). Its motto is "Life is uncertain. Eat dessert first." Ponder that over a bag of caramel corn as you explore the rest of the shops.

ABOVE The elegant dining room at Truluck's, a glamorous local dinner spot known for steaks and seafood, especially its stone crab.

THE BASICS

The Fort Lauderdale International Airport is served by multiple airlines. You will need a car if you plan to spend any time away from the beach.

Pelican Grand Beach Resort
2000 North Ocean Boulevard
954-568-9431
pelicanbeach.com
$$-$$$
156 rooms, directly on the beach.

Ritz-Carlton
1 North Fort Lauderdale Beach Boulevard
954-465-2300
ritzcarlton.com/fortlauderdale
$$$-$$$$
192 rooms, full-service spa and wine room with more than 5,000 bottles.

W Fort Lauderdale
401 North Fort Lauderdale Beach Boulevard
954-414-8200
wfortlauderdalehotel.com
$$$-$$$$
Sleekly modern, with spa and two pools.

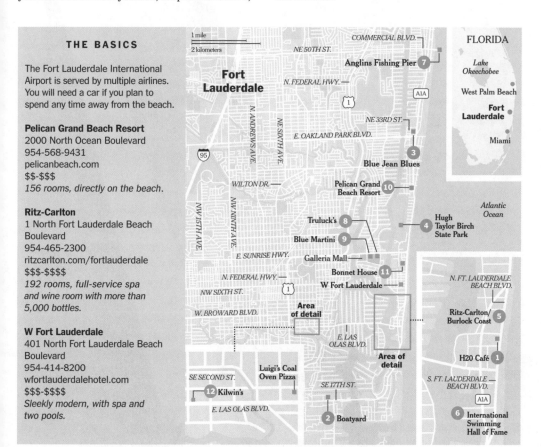

Key West

Key West, haven to artists and writers, chefs and hippies, is somehow more Caribbean than Floridian. The independent-spirited transplants who inhabit it work hard to keep it that way. One-speed bicycles weave their way through colorful village streets crammed with almost as many chickens as cars. Happy hour blends into dinner. And everything is shaped by the ocean, from the fish on market-driven menus and the nautical-inspired art to the dawn gatherings of sunrise worshipers and the tipplers' goodbye waves at sunset. Be careful or you might just catch what islanders call "Keys disease" — a sudden desire to cut ties with home and move there.

— BY SARAH WILDMAN

FRIDAY

1 *Two Wheels Are Enough* 4 p.m.

As any self-respecting bohemian local knows, the best way to get around Key West is on a bicycle. Bike rental businesses offer drop-off service to many hotels. Two reliable companies are **Eaton Bikes** (830 Eaton Street; 305-294-8188; eatonbikes.com) and **We-Cycle** (5160 Overseas Highway; 305-292-3336; wecyclekw. com). Orient yourself by cycling over to the **Truman Annex**, a palm-lined oasis of calm that surrounds the **Little White House** (111 Front Street; 305-294-9911; trumanlittlewhitehouse.com), where Harry Truman spent working vacations.

2 *Cleanse the Palate* 8 p.m.

Key West chefs pride themselves on a culinary philosophy of simple cooking and fresh ingredients. A perfect example is the **Flaming Buoy Filet Co.** (1100 Packer Street; 305-295-7970; theflamingbuoy.com; $$), a nouveau seafood restaurant owned and run by two Cincinnati transplants, Fred Isch and his partner, Richard Scot Forste. The 10 rustic wood tables are hand-painted in orange and yellow; the lights are low and the crowd amiable. This is home-cooking, island style, with dishes like black bean soup swirled with Cheddar cheese, sour cream, and cilantro or the

fresh catch of the day served with a broccoli cake and tasty mashed potatoes.

3 *Observe the Customs* 10 p.m.

Contrary to popular belief, people in Key West are not drunk all the time. But let's just say it's late, and you have some catching up to do. **Capt. Tony's Saloon** (428 Greene Street; 305-294-1838; capttonyssaloon. com) is the original location of Sloppy Joe's, an old Ernest Hemingway hangout; decades of dollar bills and other memorabilia (bras, license plates, photos) festoon the walls and ceiling. After that, perhaps a visit to the Garden of Eden, the clothing-optional bar on the rooftop of the **Bull and Whistle** (224 Duval Street; 305-296-4545; bullkeywest.com). If you're looking to hit a drag show — and the ever-popular **Aqua** (711 Duval Street; 305-294-0555; aquakeywest.com) is packed — check out the lively and less crowded cabaret at **801 Bourbon Bar** (801 Duval Street; 305-294-4737; 801bourbon.com).

SATURDAY

4 *Salute the Sun* 8:15 a.m.

Every morning, a dozen spiritual seekers — an eclectic mix including tattooed artists and elementary-school teachers — assemble at Fort Zachary Taylor State Park for **Yoga on the Beach** (305-296-7352;

OPPOSITE The Seven Mile Bridge on the highway to Key West.

RIGHT Some of the finds at Bésame Mucho, one of multiple shopping options around town.

yogaonbeach.com). Nancy Curran and Don Bartolone, yogis from Massachusetts, teach energetic vinyasa-style yoga in a clearing of pines facing the sea. The drop-in fee includes state park entrance, muslin drop cloths, and yoga mats.

5 *Imports at Breakfast* 11 a.m.

An island of transplants offers plenty to sample from the world over. Craving France? Stop at **La Crêperie Key West** (300 Petronia Street; 305-517-6799; lacreperiekeywest.com; $$), founded by Yolande Findlay and Sylvie Le Nouail, both Brittany-born. Start with a savory crepe from the open kitchen like ratatouille and then move on to something sweet like red velvet with dark Belgian chocolate, strawberries, and English custard. If you feel more like New York, try **Sarabeth's** (530 Simonton Street; 305-293-8181; sarabethskeywest.com; $), a branch of a popular Manhattan brunch spot.

6 *Island Style* 1 p.m.

Islanders pride themselves on being casual yet looking great. **Bésame Mucho** (315 Petronia Street; 305-294-1928; besamemucho.net) is an Old World general store packed with everything from Belgian linen to Dr. Hauschka skin care, to delicate baubles like tiny beaded pyrite necklaces. Across the street is **Wanderlust kw** (310 Petronia Street; 305-509-7065; wanderlustkw.com), stocked with well-priced dresses and whimsical watercolors of Key West houses by local artists. Browse nearby blocks for other entertaining shops as well.

7 *Drinks at Sunset* 5 p.m.

Skip the hustle of Mallory Square and work your way through the white-tablecloth dining room to

Louie's Backyard Afterdeck Bar (700 Waddell Avenue; 305-294-1061; louiesbackyard.com), where a large wood-planked patio faces the ocean and the setting sun. A gregarious crowd of artists and New England snowbirds gathers daily. It's like an outdoor *Cheers*.

8 *Dining on the Duval* 7 p.m.

Since opening in 2002, the restaurant **Nine One Five** (915 Duval Street; 305-296-0669; 915duval.com; $$$) has gotten high marks for its Asian-inspired seafood and ambience — a large white porch that's great for people-watching. Later the owner, Stuart Kemp, turned the second floor into the Point5 lounge, serving drinks and smaller bites like grilled snapper tacos and stick-to-your-ribs mac and cheese to a younger crowd.

9 *Mix It Up* 9 p.m.

While Key West night life has long been synonymous with boozy karaoke and mediocre margaritas, watering holes like the tiny **Orchid Bar** (1004 Duval Street; 305-296-9915; orchidkeyinn.com)

are quietly moving in a more sophisticated direction. Bartenders there take mixology seriously. Try the St.-Germain 75, with Hendrick's Gin, St.-Germain, fresh lemon juice, and Champagne. This Deco-cool sliver of a space overlooks an illuminated pool and draws a mellow crew.

SUNDAY

10 *Seaworthy Pursuits* Noon

With all the shopping and eating, it is easy to forget why you're really here: to get off the street and onto the water. **Lazy Dog** (5114 Overseas Highway; 305-295-9898; lazydog.com) offers two- and four-hour kayaking or two-hour paddleboard

tours through crystal-clear coastal waters and into the deep green waterways of the gnarled mangrove forests. Or if you're just looking to dip a toe in the sea, bike over to Clarence S. Higgs Memorial Beach, a strip of sand by the genial beach bar restaurant **Salute!** (1000 Atlantic Boulevard; 305-292-1117; saluteonthebeach.com), rent a beach chair, and kick back.

OPPOSITE ABOVE A Key West sunset. Many of the growing population of islanders moved in after succumbing to what they call "Keys disease," a visitor's sudden desire to stay for good.

OPPOSITE BELOW Touring the city streets by bicycle.

THE BASICS

Fly into Key West airport, take a fast ferry from Miami, or drive Overseas Highway (U.S. Route 1) through the Florida Keys. In town, rent a bicycle.

Gardens Hotel
526 Angela Street
305-294-2661
gardenshotel.com
$$-$$$$
Seventeen suites spread across an acre of tropical gardens, steps from everything but as quiet as a country inn.

Alexander's Guest House
1118 Fleming Street
305-294-9919
alexanderskeywest.com
$$-$$$
Stylish bed-and-breakfast that attracts a primarily gay and lesbian crowd.

Casa Marina
1500 Reynolds Street
305-296-3535
casamarinaresort.com
$$$-$$$$
A Waldorf-Astoria property.

1/4 mile
1/2 kilometer

Key West

Key West Bight

Capt. Tony's Saloon

Alexander's Guest House

Greene St.

Caroline St.

Grinnell St.

Frances St.

3

The Bull and Whistle

Truman Annex

Front St.

Eaton St.

Duval St.

1 Eaton Bikes

Little White House

Sarabeth's

— SIMONTON ST.

Olivia St.

Truman Ave.

United St.

Whitehead St. —

Angela St.

Gardens Hotel

— PACKER ST.

Bésame Mucho **6**

801 Bourbon Bar

Aqua

2 Flaming Buoy Filet Co.

Petronia St.

8 Nine One Five

White St.

La Crêperie Key West **5**

Wanderlust kw

Louie's Backyard Afterdeck Bar

Fort Zachary Taylor State Park

4 Yoga on the Beach

9 Orchid Bar

7

Casa Marina

Atlantic Blvd.

Salute!

Atlantic Ocean

Gulf of Mexico

Lazy Dog **10**

N. Roosevelt Blvd.

Flagler Ave.

S. Roosevelt Blvd.

Area of detail

We-Cycle

Atlantic Ocean

1 mile
2 kilometers

FLORIDA

Miami

Gulf of Mexico

Everglades Nat'l Park

Key West

Florida Bay

Overseas Hwy.

Straits of Florida

Florida Keys

50 miles
100 kilometers

Miami

Every few years, the Miami area seems to reinvent itself. Its latest renewal, led by a blooming of new condos, hotels, and architectural showpieces, has re-energized midtown, downtown, and the Miami River. Forget the old one-dimensional image of sun worshiping and unbridled partying. You can still find that sort of revelry, but now there is also a thriving cultural scene, stylish new restaurants, and all the other accoutrements of a multifaceted destination with global appeal. — BY PAOLA SINGER

FRIDAY

1 *Backwater View* 3 p.m.

Downtown's River District, a formerly desolate area of boatyards, loading docks, and seafood grills on the banks of the Miami River, is being repopulated with luxury residential towers, shopping arcades, and riverside promenades. Get a sneak peek of this renaissance and take in the waterfront-and-city views at **Seaspice** (422 Northwest North River Drive; seaspicemiami.com), a former warehouse converted into a sleek, airy brasserie. Pick your spot in the outdoor lounge and order a snack and something cool to drink. Then watch the passing parade, which may include a celebrity sighting.

2 *Eye Candy* 4 p.m.

The Miami Design District features an eye-catching collection of flagship stores for brands like Hermès, Dior, Loewe, and Tom Ford. The Dior boutique, for example, was conceived by Barbarito Bancel Architectes, a French studio that draped the three-story building in white panels emulating the pleats of a skirt. Nearby are whimsical public sculptures and the **Institute of Contemporary Art** (61 Northeast 41st Street; icamiami.org; online reservations encouraged), dedicated to experimental works.

3 *Eclectic Sounds* 8 p.m.

Go to a show at the **Adrienne Arsht Center for the Performing Arts** (1300 Biscayne Boulevard; arshtcenter.org), a modern, multitheater venue

OPPOSITE The Pérez Art Museum Miami has hanging gardens, sea views, and nearly 2,000 works by Latino artists.

with performances by the Miami City Ballet and the Miami Symphony Orchestra. Designed by César Pelli, it is South Florida's leading arts center. For a more informal musical experience, head to **Ball & Chain** in Little Havana (1513 Southwest Eighth Street; ballandchainmiami.com), where the entertainment runs to jazz vocalists, salsa bands, and indie acts. The bar, a contemporary take on 1940s Cuban lounges, is packed with a mix of millennials and oldtimers ordering guayaba daiquiris.

4 *Pan-Latin Palate* 10 p.m.

Since the 1950s, when Cubans began to arrive in large numbers, there has been a steady influx of immigrants from across the Hispanic world, particularly the Caribbean and South America, and their influence extends to the restaurant scene. Locals flock to the leafy outdoor patio of **Sugarcane** (3252 Northeast First Avenue; sugarcanerawbargrill.com; $$$), a Midtown mainstay where flavors from Argentina, Peru, and Mexico make up a menu of international greatest hits. At the homey **Cardón y El Tirano** (3411 Southwest Eighth Street; cardonyeltirano.com; $$), in a strip mall in Little Havana, dine on Latin fusion dishes like tostones with charred queso and seared picanha, a Brazilian beef cut.

SATURDAY

5 *Cool Sweat* 9:30 a.m.

Walking through the exuberantly landscaped gardens of the **Standard Spa** (40 Island Avenue; standard-hotels.com/miami/spa), on an islet just off Miami Beach, can transport you to faraway lands, priming you for relaxation. Continue to loosen up at the spa's Turkish-style hammam. This softly lit oasis has a 90-degree main room clad in tiered marble berths and features a cedar sauna, aromatherapy steam room, hydrotherapy stations, and soaking tubs. Then fuel up at the hotel's chic waterfront restaurant, the **Lido Bayside Grill** ($$), with coffee and an omelet or a smoothie.

6 *Pedals and Paintings* 11:30 a.m.

Grab a bike at a Citi Bike station (there is one outside the Standard Spa) and pedal west along the Venetian Causeway, which crosses 11 man-made

islands linked by bridges. You'll see mansions surrounded by azure waters, as well as views of the downtown skyline. Park outside the **Pérez Art Museum Miami** (1103 Biscayne Boulevard; pamm. org). Named for Jorge Pérez, a long-time trustee and benefactor, and designed by the Pritzker Prize-winning architects Herzog & de Meuron, the gallery has sweeping views of Biscayne Bay and is surrounded by hanging gardens by the French botanist Patrick Blanc. The museum has a collection of nearly 2,000 works by American and Latin American artists.

7 *Caribbean Enclave* 1:30 p.m.

Little Haiti began to take its current shape in the late 1970s with the arrival of thousands of Haitian refugees. Start your tour at the **Little Haiti Cultural Complex** (212-260 Northeast 59th Terrace; littlehaiticulturalcenter.com), which hosts Afro-Caribbean exhibitions and concerts. The center hosts a Caribbean Marketplace, with a focus on arts and crafts. The area has attracted a handful of young entrepreneurs who have established shops like **Sweat Records** (5505 Northeast Second Avenue; sweatrecordsmiami.com), a vinyl emporium that draws music geeks. Stop for lunch at

ABOVE For jazz, salsa, or indie music in an easygoing atmosphere, stop by the Ball & Chain, a modern version of the Cuban bars of the 1940s.

the **Buena Vista Deli** (4590 Northeast Second Avenue; buenavistadeli.com; $$), a corner bistro and bakery known for its renditions of French classics like quiche Lorraine and salade Niçoise.

8 *Graffiti Scene* 4 p.m.

Thanks in part to the efforts of the late Tony Goldman, an arts patron and businessman, a no man's land scattered with abandoned warehouses became an open-air museum for street art in the Wynwood neighborhood. The center of the action is **Wynwood Walls** (2520 Northwest Second Avenue; thewynwoodwalls.com), a park enclosed by murals by some of the world's best graffiti artists. All around are restaurants, art galleries, and boutiques.

9 *Top Chef* 8 p.m.

The chef Brad Kilgore is elevating Miami's culinary standards at **Alter** (223 Northwest 23rd Street; altermiami.com; $$$-$$$$). Menus change regularly, but expect creativity—for example, a cassoulet made with slow-cooked mahi mahi served alongside a smoked white bean mousse.

SUNDAY

10 *Sandy Morning* 10 a.m.

Take a cue from locals and head to SoFi (South of Fifth Street), an uncrowded part of Miami Beach whose unofficial name, **Brazilian Beach**, points to

the near absence of beachwear. Don't worry, board shorts and one-pieces are welcome.

11 *Fire and Gold* Noon

Alan Faena, the Argentine real estate developer who rebuilt a swath of Buenos Aires's waterfront, descended on Miami with even more ambitious plans. His Faena District spans six blocks along Collins Avenue and includes residential towers, a cultural center called the Faena Forum, and hotels. Behind the gold columns and allegoric murals of the **Faena**

ABOVE Collectors forage for vinyl treasures at Sweat Records, an indie shop in Little Haiti.

Hotel (3201 Collins Avenue; faena.com/miami-beach), you'll find **Los Fuegos by Francis Mallman** ($$$$), which on Sundays offers a traditional asado, or barbecue, on communal tables on a shady patio.

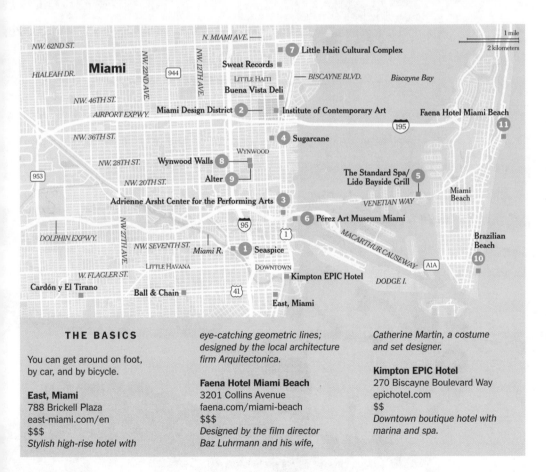

THE BASICS

You can get around on foot, by car, and by bicycle.

East, Miami
788 Brickell Plaza
east-miami.com/en
$$$
Stylish high-rise hotel with

eye-catching geometric lines; designed by the local architecture firm Arquitectonica.

Faena Hotel Miami Beach
3201 Collins Avenue
faena.com/miami-beach
$$$
Designed by the film director Baz Luhrmann and his wife,

Catherine Martin, a costume and set designer.

Kimpton EPIC Hotel
270 Biscayne Boulevard Way
epichotel.com
$$
Downtown boutique hotel with marina and spa.

South Beach Miami

A weekend in South Beach ought to begin not with "What to pack?" but rather with "What to pursue?" Do you long for the South Beach of painted-on dresses, frozen margaritas, and electric neon? The South Beach of slick new hotels and restaurants? Or the South Beach of yesteryear, of pastel Art Deco buildings, museums, and monuments? Perhaps you simply crave the beach? Miami can be whatever you want it to be—laid back, decked out, gay, straight, a family vacation, a singles' playground—which is precisely what makes it such an effortless getaway. In this dreamland at the southern tip of Miami Beach, you get to choose your own adventure. All you need is sunscreen. — BY STEPHANIE ROSENBLOOM

FRIDAY

1 *Fill the Spare Suitcase* 4 p.m.

South Beach is a breeze to tour by foot or on a bicycle (rentals at DecoBike.com), and one of the easiest places to begin is **Lincoln Road**. Retailers high and low line this wide outdoor pedestrian shopping and eating zone between Alton Road and Washington Avenue. You can pick up South Beach essentials like crystal-embellished Havaianas flip-flops and sarongs in tropical hues. You'll also find coffee shops, ice cream parlors, art galleries, bars, clubs, and retail chains like Anthropologie, Madewell, and Kiehl's. Designer brand names dot the surrounding streets. In other words: pack light.

2 *Spectator Sport* 7 p.m.

For some, nothing beats the absurdity of drinking a frozen margarita the size of a noodle bowl stuffed with two upside-down bottles of Corona beer (yes, people do this) at one of the outdoor tables lining the sidewalk on Ocean Drive. This touristy beachside stretch of restaurants doesn't offer the finest cuisine, though what the area lacks in culinary flavor it makes up for with flavor of a different sort — an endless parade of creatively dressed (or undressed)

OPPOSITE A cruise ship glides past South Pointe, the southern tip of South Beach.

RIGHT The view of South Beach, with the ocean in the background, from Juvia, an indoor-outdoor restaurant and bar.

revelers enjoying the breeze coming off the ocean. More refined restaurants are on Lincoln Road. For some of the best outdoor gawking there, head over to **SushiSamba** (600 Lincoln Road; 305-673-5337; sushisamba.com; $$-$$$) and take in the unofficial fashion show with an irresistible plate of rock shrimp tempura and specialty rolls like the Ezo (salmon, asparagus, onion, chives, sesame, tempura flakes, and wasabi mayonnaise).

3 *Symphony on the Wall* 8 p.m.

South Beach has many soundtracks, but few musical institutions here are as beloved as the **New World Symphony** (500 17th Street; 305-673-3330; nws.edu), an orchestral academy founded by the conductor Michael Tilson Thomas. You won't find it hard to locate the symphony's home — it was designed by Frank Gehry. Some concerts are even free to the public and shown via "live Wallcast" on a 7,000-square-foot projection wall adjacent to the New World Center. For other sorts of music and theatrical productions, there's also the Art Deco-style Colony Theatre (1040 Lincoln Road).

4 *Hotel Crawl* 10 p.m.

After dark, when the sun-kissed passersby are but shadows, it's time for another walk on Ocean Drive, this time to check out the Art Deco hotels, like the Colony, Boulevard, and Starlite, illuminated in neon blue, pink, and red. Stop by **Hotel Victor** (1144 Ocean Drive; 305-779-8700; hotelvictorsouthbeach.com), next to the mansion once owned by the designer Gianni

Versace. Sit at a sidewalk table with a glass of wine and enjoy live music on the hotel's porch. For a little flash and glamour, stroll to Collins Avenue to tour the lobbies and bars of classic Miami hotels like the Delano, the Stork Club, and the Fontainebleau.

SATURDAY

5 *Art Deco Town* 10 a.m.

Miami's sizable Art Deco district has hundreds of buildings from the 1920s through the 1940s, many of them prime examples of the era's favorite architectural style. Think pastel hues and architecture evocative of ships. The **Art Deco Welcome Center** (1001 Ocean Drive; 305-672-2014; mdpl.org) offers guided 10:30 a.m.

tours that include stops at hotels, restaurants, and other commercial buildings. If you'd prefer to go on your own, rent an audio tour at the center. Either way, make a reservation in advance.

6 *Pop Over for Brunch* Noon

Extend your trip back in time with brunch at the **Betsy Hotel** (1440 Ocean Drive; 305-531-6100; thebetsyhotel.com), a renovated structure that captures an old-fashioned charm that flappers could appreciate. Head to the hotel's **LT Steak & Seafood** (305-673-0044; $$$). As you consume a popover Benedict (a twist on eggs Benedict) or multigrain pancakes with rum-caramel banana flambé and almond butter, scan the crowd, an interesting mix of the wealthy and established with the young and scantily dressed.

7 *Sun, Surf, Sand* 1 p.m.

The afternoon is for relaxing amid miles of white sand. The free public sands generally defined as South Beach stretch from Ocean Drive and Fifth

ABOVE Palms and atmosphere at the Betsy Hotel, a good place for brunch. The Betsy has been renovated, but with a charm that flappers could appreciate.

LEFT The fountain in front of the Colony Theatre, one of the favorites in South Beach's cherished collection of preserved Art Deco buildings.

Street to 21st Street and Collins Avenue. **Lummus Park** (Ocean Drive between Fifth and 15th Streets) has beach volleyball courts and a playground, while **South Pointe Park** (1 Washington Avenue) has interactive water features and an observation deck. Bring a deli picnic or, if you want a scene (music, money, pretty young things), seek a restaurant in one of the newer hotels, like **SLS South Beach** (1701 Collins Avenue; 305-674-1701; slshotels.com), where **Bar Centro** ($$$) has outdoor seating and serves salads, burgers, and tuna ceviche.

8 *Indoor Art* 4 p.m.

South Beach is home to the **Bass Museum of Art** (2100 Collins Avenue; 305-673-7530; thebass.org), with paintings and sculpture spanning 500 years of European art history. Among the artists represented are Rubens, Rembrandt, Botticelli, and Domenico Ghirlandaio. Art lovers who have time to venture beyond South Beach will also want to explore the dozens of galleries, bars, and antiques stores in the **Wynwood Arts District** of Miami; it's a short cab ride away.

9 *Moon View* 9 p.m.

Venture away from kitschy Ocean Drive for a different view of the city from the penthouse of **Juvia** (1111 Lincoln Road; 305-763-8272; juviamiami.com; $$$$), a 10,000-square-foot indoor-outdoor restaurant and bar. The restaurant serves Japanese, French, and Peruvian food as varied as salmon nashi and roasted chicken vadouvan, but the view is the real showstopper. Juvia won a James Beard award for restaurant design and graphics. From its roof, the moon over Miami can seem almost close enough to touch.

BELOW Early morning beach yoga. A vacation here can work for everyone from fitness addicts to big spenders.

SUNDAY

10 *Oceanfront Workout* 10 a.m.

There are few places in South Beach better designed for a workout than the 17th Street Beachwalk, where runners and people on a variety of wheels — in-line skates, bicycles, Segways — swish by (seriously, be careful). Should you wish to join them, you'll have no problem spotting one of the beachside rental companies. For a quieter, more leisurely workout, take a walk through the **Miami Beach Botanical Garden** (2000 Convention Center Drive; 305-673-7256; mbgarden.org), which is stocked with tropical and subtropical plants:

orchids, bromeliads, flowering trees, and, of course, palms.

11 *Taste of the Mediterranean* 12:30 p.m.

Don't leave South Beach without wandering over to **Española Way**, a short stretch north of 14th Street between Washington and Pennsylvania Avenues with Spanish colonial architecture as reinterpreted in 1925. Swing by for a casual meal, a savory snack (margaritas and chips hit the spot), or some ice cream. The streets, inspired by Mediterranean villages in Spain and France and once a destination for gamblers like Al Capone, are a cleaner, sleepier, more inter-national version of New York's Little Italy — minus the karaoke and cannoli.

ABOVE The newly refurbished South Pointe Park.

OPPOSITE SoundScape park, near the New World Symphony.

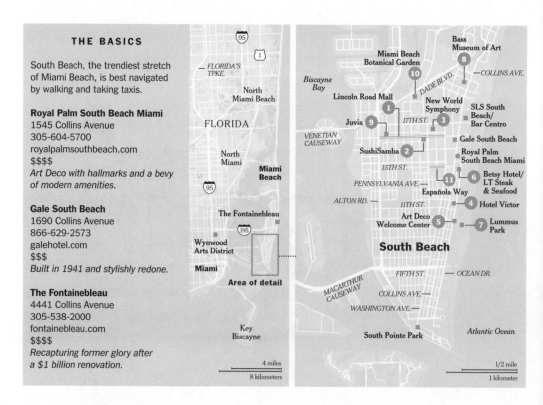

THE BASICS

South Beach, the trendiest stretch of Miami Beach, is best navigated by walking and taking taxis.

Royal Palm South Beach Miami
1545 Collins Avenue
305-604-5700
royalpalmsouthbeach.com
$$$$
Art Deco with hallmarks and a bevy of modern amenities.

Gale South Beach
1690 Collins Avenue
866-629-2573
galehotel.com
$$$
Built in 1941 and stylishly redone.

The Fontainebleau
4441 Collins Avenue
305-538-2000
fontainebleau.com
$$$$
Recapturing former glory after a $1 billion renovation.

Orlando

People who live in the Orlando area will tell you that there is life here beyond the theme parks, gator farms, and citrus groves. You can't go far without stumbling upon a picturesque lake, and the area abounds with small regional museums like the Zora Neale Hurston National Museum of Fine Arts in nearby Eatonville. Downtown, the Amway Center, home of the Orlando Magic, has given a boost to the night-life district on Church Street. And Orlando's many neighborhoods are home to retro lounges, vintage fast-food joints, and brick-paved streets.
— BY SHAILA DEWAN

FRIDAY

1 *Plunge In* 1 p.m.

Wakeboarding is to water skiing what snowboarding is to downhill skiing—in other words, the punk version of the sport—and Orlando likes to call itself the "wakeboarding capital of the world." At the **Orlando Watersports Complex** (8615 Florida Rock Road; 407-251-3100; orlandowatersports.com), a beginner's cable tow, anchored to poles in the lake, pulls you and your wakeboard around at 17 miles per hour. The patient instructor will give you pointers, and you can watch some of the sport's best-known hot-doggers navigate the ramps and slides.

2 *High Design* 3 p.m.

Just a few miles from downtown Orlando, Winter Park, part of the greater Orlando area, is famous for the brick-paved streets of chichi chocolatiers and its boutiques along Park Avenue. But across the railroad tracks near Hannibal Square, there's a bent toward high design. Amid the newer shops and restaurants, you can find **Rifle Paper Co.** (558 West New England Avenue, Suite 150; 407-622-7679; riflepaperco.com), the fashionable Orlando-based stationer, and the studio where **Makr** churns out its minimalist leather bags, billfolds, and device cases (520 Clay Street; 407-745-0958; makr.com). For a taste of local history, visit the **Hannibal Square Heritage Center** (642 West New England Avenue; 407-539-2680; hannibalsquareheritagecenter.org), where photographs and oral histories document the area's early role as a Reconstruction-era community for freed slaves.

3 *Gastropub in Demand* 7 p.m.

The **Ravenous Pig** (565 West Fairbanks Avenue, Winter Park; 407-628-2333; theravenouspig.com; $$$) has served farm-to-table sustainable, seasonal cuisine since 2007. And with attention to detail like an Old Fashioned made with bacon-infused bourbon at the bar and much-in-demand cheese biscuits, James and Julie Petrakis have made this one of Orlando's most popular gathering spots. The menu toggles between gastropub fare like shrimp and grits with green tomato chutney and more dignified entrees like pork porterhouse with heirloom tomato pie and salsa verde. Reserve a table or hover in the bar.

4 *Rumpus Room* 10 p.m.

Sure it's a gimmick, but "retro cocktail den" is a good gimmick. There's no sign outside **Park Social** (358 Park Avenue North, Winter Park; 407-636-7020; parksocialwinterpark.com). But after you've given the password at the door (you get it by calling ahead) and climb the narrow stairs, you enter a ring-a-ding space that feels like a swinger's rec room in the early Steely Dan era: plush couches and wingback chairs from the '60s and '70s, a D.J. spinning ABBA and Ricky Martin, and a sophisticated crowd that dresses the part while sipping cocktails with names like the Serpico.

OPPOSITE Wakeboarding on the advanced cable tow at the Orlando Watersports Complex.

RIGHT The Ravenous Pig in Winter Park is one of the area's most popular gathering spots.

5 *Tiffany Extravaganza* 10 a.m.

Louis Comfort Tiffany's masterpiece was Laurelton Hall, his estate on Long Island, which featured a wisteria blossom window over 30 feet long and a terrace whose columns were crowned in glass daffodils. When the house burned in 1957, Jeannette and Hugh McKean, from Winter Park, rescued those pieces and many more, adding them to what would become the most comprehensive collection of Tiffany glass, jewelry, and ceramics in the world. The collection, including a chapel with a stunning peacock mosaic that was made for the Chicago World's Fair in 1893, is housed in the **Morse Museum of American Art** (445 North Park Avenue, Winter Park; 407-645-5311; morsemuseum.org), now expanded to allow the largest Laurelton Hall pieces, including the daffodil terrace, to be on permanent display.

6 *A Fast-Food Original* Noon

Devotees of American fast food in all its glory will not want to miss the roast beef sandwiches and cherry milkshakes at **Beefy King**, a lunchtime standby for more than four decades (424 North Bumby Avenue; 407-894-2241; beefyking.com; $). Perch on the old-fashioned swivel chairs and admire the vintage logo of a snorting steer, also available on hot pink T-shirts.

7 *Pontoon Tour* 3 p.m.

Orlando is not quite an American Venice, but it does have about 100 lakes, many connected by narrow canals. Despite the alligators, the lakes are prime real estate, and at **Lake Osceola**, you can board a pontoon boat and take an hourlong cruise (**Scenic Boat Tour**; 312 East Morse Boulevard; 407-644-4056; scenicboattours.com) that will provide glimpses of Spanish colonial-style mansions, azalea gardens, stately Rollins College, and moss-laden cypresses. The ride is billed as Florida's longest continuously running tourist attraction, though you are likely to find plenty of locals aboard. The guide will entertain you with celebrity anecdotes, a smattering of history, and a reasonably small number of cheesy jokes. Tours leave on the hour.

8 *Cultural Fusion* 6 p.m.

The city of theme parks does have a studious side, as evidenced in a blossoming neighborhood called College Park, where the streets have names like Harvard and Vassar and where Jack Kerouac wrote *Dharma Bums*. The main commercial drag, Edgewater Drive, is chockablock with local favorites like **K Restaurant** (1710 Edgewater Drive; 407-872-2332; krestaurant.net; $$), where the servers'

ABOVE The Morse Museum of American Art.

habit of asking for and using your name makes you feel like a regular. The menu could be called haute hearty, with appetizers like baked oysters, bone marrow tartar, and foie gras custard with brandy-glazed mushrooms. At **Infusion Tea** (1600 Edgewater Drive; 407-999-5255; infusionorlando.com; $), choose from dozens of loose teas like Organic Monkey-Picked Oolong to go along with a fresh-baked cookie or gelato. Or you can choose among the scarves, vintage aprons, and jewelry at the attached artists' collective.

9 *Crafty Brews* 9 p.m.

Craft beers have proliferated in Orlando. The lively **Cask & Larder Brewery** (565 West Fairbanks Avenue, Winter Park; 407-628-2333), which shares space with the Ravenous Pig restaurant (the two venues have the same owners) has a menu of small-batch craft beers as well as a rotating selection of limited-edition seasonal beers, all brewed in a glassed-in room so customers can watch the process. **Orlando Brewing** (1301 Atlanta Avenue,

Orlando; 407-872-1117; orlandobrewing.com), which bills itself as a U.S.D.A.-certified organic brewery, operates in a 7,000-square-foot space where bands play and drum circles gather on weekends.

SUNDAY

10 *Sweet Potato Hash* 11 a.m.

You never know what will turn up on the improvised brunch menu—a slip of notebook paper with a ballpoint scrawl—at **Stardust Video and Coffee** (1842 East Winter Park Road; 407-623-3393;

ABOVE A display at the Hannibal Square Heritage Center.

BELOW A Winter Park canal, part of the Orlando area's abundant supply of lakes and connecting waterways.

stardustvideoandcoffee.wordpress.com; $), a hub for Orlando's artistic types. Zucchini pancakes, maybe, or vegan sweet potato hash with eggs and (real) bacon. You're also likely to find art installations, an old-fashioned photo booth, and a slew of obscure videos and DVDs on the shelves at the far end of this sunny, airy space. There is a full bar for the performances, screenings, and lectures that unfold here in the later hours.

11 *Fool's Gold, Real Finds* Noon

Flea markets can offer too many tube socks and T-shirts, while antiques markets can be entirely too stuffy. **Renningers Twin Markets** in Mount Dora (20651 Highway 441; 352-383-3141; renningers.net), about a 30-minute drive from downtown, puts the thrill back in the hunt. Just past the main entrance, you can turn right and head to a vast antiques barn crammed with treasures like meticulously constructed wooden model ships and 19th-century quilts. Or you can turn left for the flea and farmers' market, where home-grown orchids and leather motorcycle chaps compete for attention. Behind that, there is a field where curio dealers set up tables with all manner of bona fide junk, fool's gold, and the occasional real find that make it clear why so many thrift aficionados make road trips to Florida.

OPPOSITE The Morse Museum of American Art displays an extensive collection of works by Louis Comfort Tiffany.

THE BASICS

Orlando's busy airport is served by many major airlines. You will need a car in Florida's Sunbelt sprawl.

Eō Inn
227 North Eola Drive
407-481-8485
eoinn.com
$$
Boutique on swan-infested Lake Eola. Good base for exploring Orlando beyond the theme parks.

Hyatt Regency Orlando
9801 International Drive
407-284-1234
orlando.regency.hyatt.com
$$-$$$
Formerly the Peabody. Luxury accommodations and a spa.

Grand Bohemian Hotel
325 South Orange Avenue
407-313-9000
grandbohemianhotel.com
$$$
Swankiest hotel downtown.

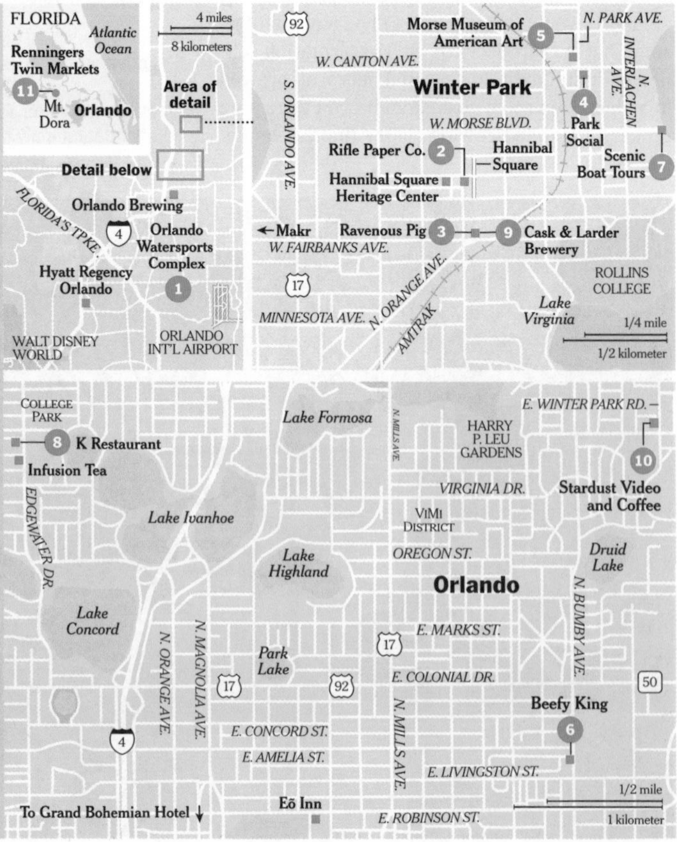

[Map: Orlando and Winter Park area showing FLORIDA inset with Atlantic Ocean, Renningers Twin Markets, Mt. Dora, Orlando, Walt Disney World, Orlando Int'l Airport; detailed map with Morse Museum of American Art (5), Winter Park, N. Park Ave., Interlachen Ave., W. Canton Ave., S. Orlando Ave., W. Morse Blvd., Rifle Paper Co. (2), Park (4), Social, Scenic Boat Tours (7), Hannibal Square, Hannibal Square Heritage Center, Makr, Ravenous Pig (3), Cask & Larder Brewery (9), W. Fairbanks Ave., Rollins College, Lake Virginia, Minnesota Ave., N. Orange Ave., Amtrak; College Park, Lake Formosa, Harry P. Leu Gardens, E. Winter Park Rd., Stardust Video and Coffee (10), K Restaurant (8), Infusion Tea, Edgewater Dr., Lake Ivanhoe, Virginia Dr., ViMi District, Oregon St., Druid Lake, Lake Highland, Orlando, Lake Concord, N. Orange Ave., N. Magnolia Ave., Park Lake, E. Marks St., E. Colonial Dr., N. Mills Ave., N. Bumby Ave., Beefy King (6), E. Concord St., E. Amelia St., E. Livingston St., To Grand Bohemian Hotel, Eō Inn, E. Robinson St.]

Palm Beach

The tiny island of Palm Beach, now best known as the location of President Donald Trump's Mar-a-Lago private club and unofficial second White House, has long been the favorite Florida hangout for the Rolls Royce-and-diamonds set. On some of its dreamy estates, generally well hidden from easy public view, the staff lives better than many Americans. But if you can't afford a mansion (and aren't looking for a job at one), Palm Beach is still a gorgeous sand-and-sun island for a weekend getaway, with inviting places to walk the beach, swim, shop, and hang out. To get here, cross the bridge from the humbler sister town of West Palm Beach. — BY GERALDINE FABRIKANT

FRIDAY

1 *The Big Gape* 4 p.m.

First things first. If you're hoping to see the Trumps' 114-room mansion, come prepared to pay $200,000 for a club membership, or at least multiple thousands at a charity event. If you're accepted at either one, that is. What you can do instead is get a look at the neighborhood, home of millionaires and billionaires. Drive south along South Ocean Boulevard, starting at Barton Avenue, for about six miles, catching glimpses of the oceanfront mansions where the gates and hedges are low enough. If the road is blocked near Mar-a-Lago, take a detour.

2 *Grande Dame* 6:30 p.m.

For a sunset cocktail, glide into the **Breakers Hotel** (1 South County Road; 561-655-6611; thebreakers.com), originally built in 1896. So central is its location that the hotel has been rebuilt twice after fires destroyed it. The Seafood Bar has delightful views of the sea. If you prefer upholstered opulence, head for the lavish HMF bar, where the younger crowd goes to see and be seen.

3 *Diner's Club* 8:30 p.m.

Palm Beach dining runs from supremely pretentious to casually simple. Many restaurants survive over decades, and because Palm Beach is a small town, where the same cast shows up frequently, they have the feel of private clubs. The **Palm Beach Grill** (340 Royal Poinciana Way No. 336; 561-835-1077; palmbeachgrill.com; $$$) is a social fixture that is a favorite of James Patterson, the hyperprolific crime novelist, and almost everyone else. If the mobbed dining room is for the island's old guard, the bar seems to attract newcomers: snowbirds deciding whether to move south, city types longing for a slower, more glamorous life, and locals who want to have fun. Don't miss American classics like spare ribs and ice cream sundaes. Book before you fly.

SATURDAY

4 *Early Snowbirds* 9 a.m.

This may be a party town, but it wakes up early. A clutch of restaurants along Royal Poinciana Way are busy by 8:30 a.m., with diners sitting outside and savoring the sunshine and breakfast. **Sant Ambroeus** (340 Royal Poinciana Way No. 304; 561-285-7990; santambroeus.com; $$$), is a luxurious outpost of the Milan and New York restaurants, serving crostini, citrus ricotta pancakes, and the like. Nearby is **Green's Pharmacy** (151 North County Road; 561-832-4443; $$), which offers breakfast at an old-fashioned luncheonette counter. After your meal, pick up candy buttons and other long-forgotten stuff.

5 *History Class* 10 a.m.

For an authentic sense of Palm Beach in its early days, drop by the **Flagler Museum** (1 Whitehall

OPPOSITE The lobby at the Breakers, the iconic Palm Beach hotel where the wealthy have long come to be pampered.

BELOW For drive-by glimpses of the waterfront mansions, head out along South Ocean Boulevard.

Way; 561-655-2833; flaglermuseum.us). It was once the home of Henry Morrison Flagler, one of the founders of Standard Oil and the man who brought the railroad to southern Florida. He spent millions in 1902 to build the 75-room Beaux Arts "cottage" that became a hotel and finally a museum. The decoration is lavish: gilded furniture and ceilings, marble pillars and fireplaces, golden bed curtains. One of the items on display is Flagler's private railway car.

6 *Retail Strut* Noon

On **Worth Avenue**, where every brand that you've seen in *Vogue* has a storefront, the real fun is the crowd: women in green cashmere sweaters walking dogs in matching outfits; elderly gents with bow ties and blazers. Amid the big-name stores, search for the smaller, lesser-known shops that survive by wit and originality, or concentrate on the designer resale shops clustered around the corner of North County and Sunset. Get lost in the meandering "vias" off the avenue, savoring the music of gurgling fountains, and study the excellent Palm Beach Preservation Foundation map you've downloaded (palmbeachpreservation.org) to better explore the neighborhood's architecture and small parks, especially **Pan's Garden** (386 Hibiscus Avenue).

7 *The Beach* 3 p.m.

The beaches here are flat, wide, and clean. Grab a snack and head for one. The **Amici Market** (155 North County Road; myamicimarket.com)

ABOVE Palm Beach feels exclusive, but the beach is public. Walk it in the early morning, when few people are out.

sells everything from chicken Marsala and panini to caviar and Champagne. Take your goodies and go to South Ocean Boulevard, where beach entrances run between Royal Palm Way and Hammon Avenue.

8 *Mediterranean Flavor* 8 p.m.

For a casual (but still elegant) dinner in the heart of town, head to **Cucina Palm Beach** (257 Royal Poinciana Way; 561-655-0770; cucinapalmbeach.com; $$$), which serves locally sourced Italian-inspired fare in a lively setting. Try the vegan "impossible burger"; it consistently delights vegans and non-vegans alike). You can eat outdoors and watch the crowds go by. Or come late, when it becomes a full-on dance club.

9 *Party Time* 10:30 p.m.

There are plenty of multi-carat jewels in Palm Beach, but they are generally worn at private parties. The night life for visitors is casual. For dancing, you may want to stay at Cucina Palm Beach, which has a busy late-night bar scene. Or stop in for a drink and cabaret-style music at the very pretty **Brazilian Court Hotel** (301 Australian Avenue; 561-655-7740; thebraziliancourt.com). Another choice is back across the bridge at **Blue Martini** (CityPlace, 550 South Rosemary Avenue, West Palm Beach; 561-835-8601; bluemartinilounge.com) in a trendy shopping mall.

SUNDAY

10 *Hit the Trail* 10 a.m.

A flat and easy bike trail hugs the Intracoastal Waterway, which skirts the west side of Palm Beach, and offers fantastic views of the Marina in West

Palm Beach. Rent a bike at **Palm Beach Bicycle Trail Shop** (50 Cocoanut Row, Suite 117; 561-659-4583; palmbeachbicycle.com), which has multispeed bikes. Cross Bradley Place to enter the six-mile-long Lake Trail, and then ride north, the waterway on your left and the mansions on your right, past the Sailfish Club where the path ends. Continue on North Lake Way to the Inlet, where cruise and container ships come and go from the Port of Palm Beach. As you ride back toward town, notice the ficus hedges, artfully sculpted or forming towering walls, and watch for pelicans and parrots overhead.

11 *Lunch With a Breeze* Noon

Perched atop the two-story, Key West-style clubhouse at the Palm Beach Par 3 Golf Course, the **Al Fresco** restaurant (2345 South Ocean Boulevard; 561-273-4130; alfrescopb.com; $$$) is one of the most beautiful outdoor dining spots in the area. You can enjoy the breeze on the covered deck overlooking the ocean and sample an Italian specialty like the ravioli with burrata cheese, arugula, sun-dried tomatoes, and shallot sauce.

ABOVE The Blue Martini in West Palm Beach, the humbler sister town across the Intracoastal Waterway.

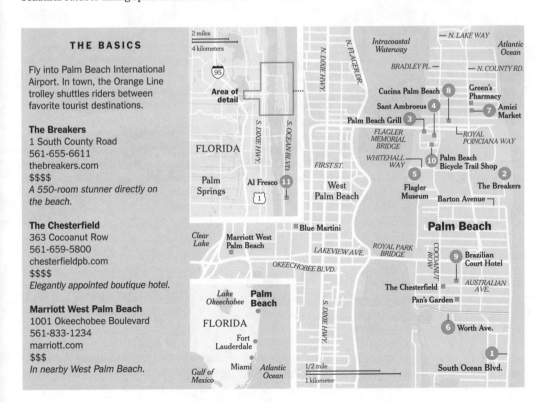

THE BASICS

Fly into Palm Beach International Airport. In town, the Orange Line trolley shuttles riders between favorite tourist destinations.

The Breakers
1 South County Road
561-655-6611
thebreakers.com
$$$$
A 550-room stunner directly on the beach.

The Chesterfield
363 Cocoanut Row
561-659-5800
chesterfieldpb.com
$$$$
Elegantly appointed boutique hotel.

Marriott West Palm Beach
1001 Okeechobee Boulevard
561-833-1234
marriott.com
$$$
In nearby West Palm Beach.

St. Pete Beach

Not far from downtown St. Petersburg, Florida, lies a string of barrier islands edged with a perfect seam of white sugar-sand beaches on the Gulf of Mexico. The main town of what is often referred to as the "Gulf beaches" is bustling St. Pete Beach; neighboring communities like Indian Shores, Madeira Beach, and Treasure Island are studded with midcentury gems like the Bon-Aire Resort Motel, the Algiers Beach Motel, and the Postcard Inn. Early morning walks along the water at these beaches can be blessedly solitary, but the nights are hopping. Each community has its own tiki and beach bars, often within a stroll of one another along the sand. The area is also known for its "Gulf to grill" restaurants; it's not uncommon to see sunburned customers wander into even the best restaurants with their fresh fish catch to be prepared in the kitchen. — BY COLLEEN CREAMER

FRIDAY

1 *Cocktails in the Air* 7 p.m.

Watch the sun go down in spectacular fashion at **Level 11 Rooftop Artisan Bistro Bar** (5250 Gulf Boulevard; grandplazaflorida.com). This circular bar offers views not only of the Gulf but also of Boca Ciega Bay and glittering St. Petersburg. The crowd is diverse and friendly, as is the staff. A "light fare" menu won't wipe out your appetite for dinner, and the craft cocktails include light and fruity options. Patrons wander about, awaiting a perfect view of the sun as it bids adieu, often drawing applause.

2 *Pink Palace Repast* 8:30 p.m.

Head a few blocks south to the **Don CeSar** (3400 Gulf Boulevard; doncesar.com) for dinner Gatsby-style. This enormous "pink palace" opened in 1928, its architecture a blend of Mediterranean and Moorish. It immediately pulled in some of the era's most celebrated figures; both F. Scott Fitzgerald and Al

Capone stayed here. Have a casual dinner at the **Sea Porch Café** ($$-$$$). Starters might include fried calamari with key lime rémoulade or goat cheese fritters with açaí poached pear salsa. Entrees include burgers and a catch of the day. Key lime pie here was a tangy mousse surrounded by pillows of whipped cream. Upstairs at the hotel's plush Lobby Bar, there's live jazz and creative mixologists.

SATURDAY

3 *Morning Brew and Bite* 8 a.m.

Sweet Brewnette in nearby Madeira Beach (13999 Gulf Boulevard; sweetbrewnettecafe.com; $) is a retro coffee shop/restaurant that serves nitro cold-brewed coffee. Its eclectic cafe (chandeliers and local art coexist nicely) offers smoothies, waffles, and veggie scrambles for breakfast lovers.

4 *A Bit of Everything* 10 a.m.

Set your GPS to nearby **John's Pass Village and Boardwalk** (12901 Gulf Boulevard, Madeira Beach; johnspass.com), a Rubik's Cube of restaurants, bars, confectioneries, and trinket merchants. In between the T-shirt/flip-flop shops are real gems like the Spice and Tea Exchange and Treehouse Puppets & Treasures. Book a trip to watch dolphins or throw out a line to fish. For lunch, grab some fresh-as-it-gets seafood at **Walt'z Fish Shak** (waltzfishshak.com; $$$).

5 *Time Travel* 1:30 p.m.

The **Gulf Beaches Historical Museum** (115 10th Avenue, St. Pete Beach; gulfbeachesmuseum.com), in the heart of the community known as Pass-a-Grille,

OPPOSITE Sun, sand, and breezes off a warm sea are still the heart of the St. Pete Beach allure, as in this scene at Madeira beach. But other diversions are plentiful.

RIGHT A great egret savors its fresh catch while nearby anglers concentrate on hooking their own at this fishing pier at Fort De Soto Park.

at the very tip of the main barrier island, is one of those finds that thrill history buffs. Here, in what was the first church in this small coastal hamlet, are exhibits highlighting life in the early development of the area's beach communities. Read about Silas Dent, the hermit of Cabbage Key; or examine old postcards, World War II exhibits, and photos from the early 1900s. The museum's store offers books on local lore as well as a collection of sea-themed children's books and jewelry. Pick up a free brochure including instructions for a walking tour of the area.

6 *Walking Tour* 4 p.m.

The community of Pass-a-Grille is recognized as a National Register Historic District and is thought to be named for the 18th-century "grilleurs" who dried fish on the beach. The self-guided walking tour includes some of the town's earliest buildings, many still functioning in this community, including a home once used for U.S.O. dances during World War II. If biking is more your style, head over to nearby **Merry Pier** (801 Pass-a-Grille Way; merrypier.com) to rent bikes. Be sure to cruise Eighth Avenue, believed to be one of the tiniest Main Streets in America and seriously charming. Or stay and fish: The pier rents fishing tackle.

7 *Eat Like a Local* 6 p.m.

Sea Critters Cafe (2007 Pass-a-Grille Way; seacritterscafe.com; $$) is a rustic, relaxed, fun-but-no-nonsense seafood restaurant on the water that local residents love, not only because the food is fantastic but also because those who can prove they live here pay less. Follow your cocktail (say, a tiramisù martini) with a seafood platter.

8 *Boogie Nights* 9 p.m.

Consistently topping the area's list of "best beach bars" is **Jimmy B's Beach Bar** at the Beachcomber Beach Resort Hotel in St. Pete Beach (6200 Gulf Boulevard; beachcomberflorida.com). Overlooking the Gulf, it's a sprawling outdoor space with scattered bars and a dance floor. Make no mistake, this is a party bar — but one with style, and not just of the thatched-roof kind. Music is bouncy enough to get the crowd on its feet without causing tinnitus. To lengthen the evening, strike out on the sand for a pub crawl to neighboring spots like the Sandbar Beach Bar or the Toasted Monkey. But as you go, take note of the long boardwalk jutting out from Jimmy B's. It will be a much-needed landmark heading back.

SUNDAY

9 *Fortified and Fun* 9 a.m.

Head to Tierra Verde to visit **Fort De Soto Park** (3500 Pinellas Bayway South; pinellascounty.org), more than 1,000 acres over five interconnected isles. Named for the Spanish explorer Hernando De Soto, the fort was used as a stronghold by the Union Army during the Civil War and was further constructed as a defense in the Spanish-American War. The park is a rest stop for more than 300 species of birds and has something for everyone: history, self-guided interpretive trails, fishing, or simply lazing on a pristine beach. You can kayak to two island preserves, Shell Key and Egmont Key, or walk to the end of the Fort De Soto fishing pier for a wide view of the Gulf or to cast your line.

10 *Last Resort* Noon

If you've snagged something edible, take it to the **Island Grille and Raw Bar** (210 Madonna Boulevard, Tierra Verde; islandrawbar.com; $$) — the chef knows what to do. If you didn't catch anything, don't despair. This pretty, sprawling restaurant and bar has something for everyone: seafood, oysters, or pork and chicken dishes. The lobster bisque is heavenly, and if you're ready for early happy hour, the Grille has a full bar.

OPPOSITE The pink peaks of Don CeSar stare out over the beach. Built in 1928, it still draws luxury lovers with its guest rooms, restaurants, and bars. In its heyday, luminaries from F. Scott Fitzgerald to Al Capone dropped by.

THE BASICS

If you yearn for a break from the beach, go inland to St. Petersburg. It has seven arts districts; the Salvador Dalí Museum; and Haslam's Book Store, a mecca for book lovers and writers.

Kimpton Hotel Zamora
3701 Gulf Boulevard
thehotelzamora.com
$$$
Boutique hotel with architecture inspired by its namesake Spanish province. Balconies overlook both the Intracoastal Waterway and the Gulf of Mexico.

Don CeSar
3400 Gulf Boulevard
doncesar.com
$$$$
Landmark historic hotel with over 277 rooms and suites, four restaurants, two bars, and retail shops.

Beachcomber Beach Resort and Hotel
6200 Gulf Boulevard
beachcomberflorida.com
$$
Beachfront hotel with landscaped gardens.

Sweet Brewnette
3 Walt'z Fish Shak
FLORIDA
275
Boca Ciega Bay
MADEIRA BEACH
St. Petersburg
4
ISLE OF PALMS
John's Pass Village and Boardwalk
CENTRAL AVE. NORTH
Haslam's Book Store
TREASURE ISLAND
699
PASADENA AVE. SOUTH
19
Salvador Dalí Museum
Jimmy B's Beach Bar/
Beachcomber Beach Resort and Hotel
SUNSET BEACH
8
GULFPORT
Toasted Monkey Beach Bar
Sandbar Beach Bar
1 Level 11 Rooftop Artisan Bistro Bar
GULF BLVD.
Kimpton Hotel Zamora
Don CeSar/
2 Sea Porch Café
St. Pete Beach
7 Sea Critters Cafe
PASS-A-GRILLE
10 Island Grille and Raw Bar
Gulf Beaches Historical Museum 5
TIERRA VERDE
SHELL KEY 6
Merry Pier
Gulf of Mexico
Tampa Bay
PINELLAS BAYWAY S.
Fort De Soto Park 9
275
679
MULLET KEY
2 miles
3 kilometers
EGMONT KEY

Sarasota

Where else can one spend the morning reveling in the beauty of works by Peter Paul Rubens, Frans Hals, and Botticelli and the afternoon lolling on a powdery white sand beach? That is the lure of Sarasota, the city perched on the Gulf of Mexico where John and Mable Ringling, the circus impresario and his wife, set the stage for a vibrant cultural life after buying land in 1911. Not only did John Ringling create the John and Mable Ringling Museum of Art, but he brought the Ringling Brothers and Barnum & Bailey Circus to winter in Sarasota. His elephants even hauled timber for the John Ringling Causeway, which links the mainland to Lido Key. Nature, which initially attracted the Ringlings and other wealthy Midwesterners, provides its own set of pleasures beyond the beaches: whether it's fishing, watching manatees and sea turtles, or strolling past orchids and mangroves in an expansive botanical garden. For more civilized diversions, there is an abundance of restaurants and shops, and even an opera and an orchestra. — BY GERALDINE FABRIKANT

FRIDAY

1 *First Look* 4 p.m.

Sarasotans are serious about happy hour, when drink prices often drop to half-price Monday through Friday. Enjoy the vista and the good value at **Marina Jack** (2 Marina Plaza; 941-365-4232; marinajacks.com) on the marina between downtown Sarasota and St. Armands Circle. Take in the expansive view of Bird Key as you sip a Southern Peach Tea, made with vodka, lemonade, and iced tea. Music lovers will enjoy the live band that plays every afternoon. On the quieter outdoor deck, you can admire the yachts in the harbor.

2 *Fried Green Tomatoes* 8 p.m.

Whether you have dinner in one of the series of rooms with dark parquet wood floors, a profusion of plants, and smoky emerald green walls covered with art, or eat upstairs in the more casual dining room and bar, don't pass up appetizers like the fried green tomato fusion (panko- and cornmeal-crusted green tomatoes pan-fried with sweet chili sauce) at **Euphemia Haye** (5540 Gulf of Mexico Drive; 941-383-3633; euphemiahaye.com; $$$). Then splurge on roast duckling filled with breadcrumb stuffing

and topped with a tangy fruit sauce. The lush dessert menu includes Key lime pie.

SATURDAY

3 *A Taste of France* 8:30 a.m.

Arrive early for chocolate croissants or cheese-and-ham crepes at **C'est la Vie** (1553 Main Street; 941-906-9575; cestlaviesarasota.com; $); locals often line up for breakfast at this Provence-style cafe. Then beat the crowd to Sarasota's loveliest beach, **Siesta Beach** on Siesta Key (948 Beach Road; simplysiestakey.com/beaches.htm); later in the day, its wide expanse of soft-as-cotton sand gets clogged with families and a parade of beachgoers, both old and young. In 2011 Siesta Beach was designated America's best beach by Stephen Leatherman, a professor and director of the Laboratory for Coastal Research at Florida International University; its sand is 99 percent quartz crystal and stays white in part because it does not need replenishment from darker sands dredged from the seabed.

4 *Waterside Lunch* 12:30 p.m.

For buckets of peel-and-eat shrimp, or blackened grouper sandwiches with a chipotle tortilla, locals love the **Old Salty Dog** (1601 Ken Thompson Parkway;

OPPOSITE A painting by Peter Paul Rubens on view at the John and Mable Ringling Museum of Art.

BELOW The koi pond is an extra at the Marie Selby Botanical Gardens. The main attraction is exotic plants.

941-388-4311; theoldsaltydog.com; $$) on Sarasota Bay. You can smell the sea and watch the Longboat Key Pass Bridge open periodically for boats heading out into the Gulf of Mexico. The original owners were English and wanted to create a publike atmosphere; today, you can still order fish 'n' chips.

5 *Manatees and More* 2 p.m.

Hugh and Buffett, two placid manatees each weighing well over 1,000 pounds, were raised in captivity at the **Mote Marine Laboratory and Aquarium** (1600 Ken Thompson Parkway; 941-388-4441; mote.org). Watch them smush their noses against the glass or consume a few of the approximately 75 heads of romaine lettuce that the pair devour each day. Or gape at Shelley and Montego (two loggerhead sea turtles), sharks, toadfish, convict cichlid fish, and hundreds of other kinds of marine life. You're sure to pick up some stray facts — for instance, did you know that dolphins get arthritis?

6 *Seashells and Cover-Ups* 4:30 p.m.

Don't miss St. Armands Circle, where you'll find coffee shops, formal restaurants, and a wide range of shops. If you need protection from the sun, **Island Pursuit** (355-357 St. Armands Circle; 941-388-4004; islandpursuit.com) has casual wear for men and Scala cotton hats and multicolored bathing suit cover-ups for women; **FantaSea** (378 St. Armands Circle; 941-388-3031; shopfantasea.com) stocks seashell night lights and towels decorated with mermaids.

7 *Martini Time* 5 p.m.

Head downtown and sit under the umbrellas at **Mattison's City Grille** (1 North Lemon Avenue; 941-330-0440; mattisons.com) in time for happy hour. The cocktail hour is cooler and plusher indoors at the **Bar at Hyde Park Prime Steakhouse** (35 South Lemon Avenue; 941-366-7788; hydeparkrestaurants. com) where you can drop into a deep velveteen sofa or sit at the bar and order a martini.

8 *Mediterranean Medley* 7 p.m.

The chef Dylan Elhajoui came to the United States from Morocco more than two decades ago, and at his colorful 24-table restaurant **Mozaic** (1377 Main Street; 941-951-6272; mozaicsarasota.com; $$) in downtown Sarasota, he combines Moroccan and Southern European cuisine. Choose an appetizer like fricassee of escargot and shiitake mushrooms with white wine; for a main course you might try a tangy tagine of chicken breast and artichoke with couscous. After dinner, check out the **Jack Dusty** bar at the Ritz-Carlton (1111 Ritz-Carlton Drive; 941-309-2266; ritzcarlton.com); its heavy wood paneling and upholstered sofas don't intimidate the casual crowd that shows up for drinks like the toasted almond martini, with amaretto, Kahlúa, half-and-half, and a cherry garnish.

SUNDAY

9 *Hash and Hot Sauce* 9:30 a.m.

With its brightly painted walls and paisley-print booths, the **Blue Dolphin** (470 John Ringling Boulevard; 941-388-3566; bluedolphincafe.com; $$) is the funky Florida version of a coffee shop. The corned beef hash topped with two eggs is popular, as are the six versions of hot sauce on each table. "Some people even put it on pancakes and some just pour a spoonful and eat it straight," one waitress said.

10 *The Ringling Legacy* 11 a.m.

The **John and Mable Ringling Museum of Art** (5401 Bay Shore Road; 941-359-5700; ringling.org) reflects John Ringling's dual passions: Baroque art

and the circus. His collection, which includes five paintings by Rubens, as well as works by Botticelli and Hals, is housed in a mansion resembling an Italian villa and overlooking Sarasota Bay. The **Circus Museum**, also on the property, has its own share of wonders, including a car from the Pullman train in which John and Mable traveled. There is also a version of the circus in miniature, with figurines of more than 900 animals.

11 *Opulent Orchids* 1 p.m.
    Situated on Sarasota Bay, the **Marie Selby Botanical Gardens** (811 South Palm Avenue; 941-366-5731; selby.org) has a profusion of orchids and other plants. Here you might learn that twigs from the neem tree were used to fight tooth decay and

that its extracts helped cure athlete's foot, and that leaves from the seagrape, a plant native to Florida and Central and South America, may have been used for writing paper by early Spaniards in Mexico.

OPPOSITE ABOVE The Old Salty Dog serves buckets of peel-and-eat shrimp along with its close-up view of Sarasota Bay.

OPPOSITE BELOW Seagulls and friend at Siesta Beach.

ABOVE Cafe dining downtown at C'est la Vie.

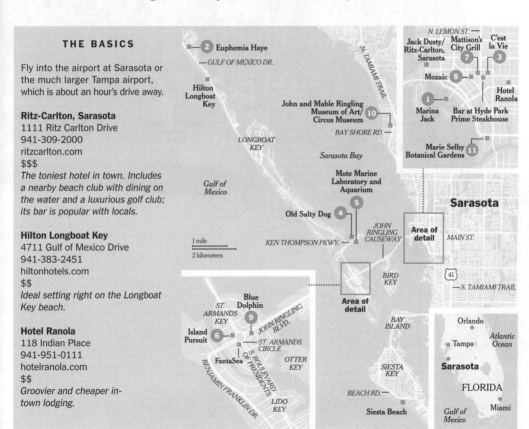

THE BASICS

Fly into the airport at Sarasota or the much larger Tampa airport, which is about an hour's drive away.

Ritz-Carlton, Sarasota
1111 Ritz Carlton Drive
941-309-2000
ritzcarlton.com
$$$
The toniest hotel in town. Includes a nearby beach club with dining on the water and a luxurious golf club; its bar is popular with locals.

Hilton Longboat Key
4711 Gulf of Mexico Drive
941-383-2451
hiltonhotels.com
$$
Ideal setting right on the Longboat Key beach.

Hotel Ranola
118 Indian Place
941-951-0111
hotelranola.com
$$
Groovier and cheaper in-town lodging.

Map labels:
Euphemia Haye
GULF OF MEXICO DR.
Hilton Longboat Key
LONGBOAT KEY
Gulf of Mexico
John and Mable Ringling Museum of Art/ Circus Museum
BAY SHORE RD.
Sarasota Bay
Mote Marine Laboratory and Aquarium
Old Salty Dog
JOHN RINGLING CAUSEWAY
KEN THOMPSON PKWY.
1 mile
2 kilometers
Area of detail
BIRD KEY
Blue Dolphin
ST. ARMANDS KEY
JOHN RINGLING BLVD.
Island Pursuit
ST. ARMANDS CIRCLE
FantaSea
S. BOULEVARD OF PRESIDENTS
OTTER KEY
BENJAMIN FRANKLIN DR.
LIDO KEY
Area of detail
BAY ISLAND
SIESTA KEY
BEACH RD.
Siesta Beach
N. LEMON ST.
Jack Dusty/ Ritz-Carlton, Sarasota
Mattison's City Grill
C'est la Vie
Mozaic
Hotel Ranola
Marina Jack
Bar at Hyde Park Prime Steakhouse
Marie Selby Botanical Gardens
Sarasota
MAIN ST.
S. TAMIAMI TRAIL
N. TAMIAMI TRAIL
Orlando
Tampa
Atlantic Ocean
Sarasota
FLORIDA
Miami
Gulf of Mexico

Atlanta

Corporate stronghold, Olympic host, hip-hop epi-center, Southern belle, a capital of black America: Atlanta is many things. Major civic additions, like a grand $290 million aquarium financed by private donors, a significant expansion of the High Museum of Art by the architect Renzo Piano, and a new center for human rights that displays the municipally purchased papers of the Rev. Dr. Martin Luther King Jr., add up to a high tide of enthusiasm — even in a city where optimism is liberally indulged.

— BY SHAILA DEWAN

FRIDAY

1 *Necklace of Green* 4 p.m.

When railroads ruled American transportation and commerce, Atlanta was the rail hub of the South. Part of that legacy is the network of old tracks and lines being transformed into an ambitious necklace of green ringing the city, the Atlanta BeltLine (beltline. org). By 2020, the city plans to have added 1,300 acres of parks and 33 miles of trails along the BeltLine, increasing its green spaces by nearly 40 percent, along with 22 miles of light rail, 5,600 affordable housing units, and lots of public art. The **Eastside Trail**, a two-mile corridor bustling with joggers, cyclists, and strollers, ambles past pine and sassafras trees. Like all the BeltLine's trails, leafy or urban, it is lined with sculptures and murals, an art show al fresco.

2 *Tastes of the Town* 7 p.m.

Few places can be said to be definitively Atlantan, but the **Colonnade** (1879 Cheshire Bridge Road NE; 404-874-5642; colonnadeatlanta.com; $$) is one: a meat-and-three restaurant with a full bar (rare), a sizable gay clientele (more rare), and a sizable clientele of elderly ladies (rare in this particular context). The resulting gay-and-gray mix is spectacular: Sansabelt trousers, black fingernails, sensible shoes, birthday tiaras, canes and walkers, all in a buzzing carpeted dining room. When it comes to ordering, stick to the

OPPOSITE A young visitor at the Martin Luther King birth-place, part of a national historic site devoted to King.

RIGHT The railroads have largely gone, but their old tracks and lines are being converted into urban trails.

classics: a Bloody Mary to start, fried chicken with yeasty dinner rolls straight from the school cafeteria, and the day's pie.

3 *Where Heads Spin* 9 p.m.

The **Sun Dial**, the revolving bar atop the 73-story Westin hotel (210 Peachtree Street; 404-589-7506; sundialrestaurant.com), is where Atlantans go for throwback cool. Sip an Atlanta Hurricane (it's in the colada-daiquiri family and arrives in a souvenir glass) or a chocolate martini as you orient yourself with a glittery panoramic view of downtown, the Georgia Dome, CNN's headquarters, the Center for Civil and Human Rights, and the Georgia Aquarium.

4 *On a Roll* 11:30 p.m.

Roller-skating is an integral part of hip-hop culture in Atlanta, which is home to OutKast, Usher, and Childish Gambino, among other stars. Beyoncé had her 21st birthday party at the Cascade roller rink here, and the film *The ATL* paid homage to the flawless moves of the city's skate dancers. On Friday nights, the virtuosos descend on **Golden Glide** (2750 Wesley Chapel Road in Decatur, tucked behind a shopping strip; 404-288-7773; atlantafamilyfuncenters.com) for adult skate, where posses practice their smooth moves until

the wee hours. If you haven't been practicing, skate inside the green line for your own safety. Or just stay on the sideline and gawk.

SATURDAY

5 *Robust Start* 11:30 a.m.

You had a late night, so take your time getting to brunch at **Superica** (99 Krog Street; 404-791-1310; superica.com/krog-street; $$), a bustling Tex-Mex spot whose hubcap-scale pancakes come with a delectable dulce de leche syrup. It's in the Krog Street Market, so if you can't snag a table, there are plenty of other tempting choices just down the hall.

6 *A Little Shopping* 1:30 p.m.

In the affluent **Buckhead** area, hotels and sky-scrapers have edged out some mansions and period commercial buildings, but if you look, you can still get a glimpse of old Atlanta. There are plenty of malls here, like **Lenox Square** (3393 Peachtree Road Northeast; lenox-square.com) and **Phipps Plaza** (3500 Peachtree Road Northeast; phippsplaza.com). At the **Peachtree Battle Shopping Center** (2385 Peach-tree Road Northeast), the locally owned stores include **Richards Variety Store** (richardsvarietystore. com), a throwback to the five-and-dime that invites extended browsing.

7 *War on Canvas* 3:30 p.m.

When Gen. John A. Logan was considering a run for vice president in the 1880s, he commissioned a political ad in the form of a giant painting of the Battle of Atlanta, in which he had for a time com-manded the Army of the Tennessee for the Union. The 30-foot-high, 358-foot-long work was wrapped around the walls of a circular room in a Grant Park building called the Atlanta Cyclorama from 1921 to 2015. Now reassembled at the new **Cyclorama Building** on the Buckhead campus of the **Atlanta History Center** (130 West Paces Ferry Road NW; 404-814-4000; atlantahistorycenter.com) it is restored to its original length, height, and hourglass shape— adding another 3,268 square feet to the already vast panorama. In its new home, projected images give it a virtual reality twist and thoughtful exhibits provide context.

8 *Country Captain* 6 p.m.

A city where a treasured chef's departure can be front-page news, Atlanta has more than its share of fine restaurants, lately on the Westside, an

ABOVE AND OPPOSITE The Martin Luther King Jr. National Historic Site includes King's tomb and exhibits recalling his leadership in the struggle to end racial segregation in the South. Other stops are his boyhood home and the Old Ebenezer Baptist Church where he served as pastor.

old industrial area now dotted with farm-to-table cafes. There, **Miller Union** (999 Brady Avenue NW; 678-733-8550; millerunion.com; $$$), gives Southern fare a fresh makeover in dishes like smoked rabbit mousse over grilled bread or Country Captain chicken — a form of chicken curry — served with Carolina gold rice, scallion, peanut, coconut, and chutney.

9 *Culture and Cars* 8 p.m.

If you like theater, opera, ballet, or Broadway shows, check the schedules at the **Woodruff Arts Center** (1280 Peachtree Street NE; 404-733-4200; woodruffcenter.org) and the **Fox Theatre** (660 Peachtree Street NE; 404-881-2100; foxtheatre.org). For something more downmarket, drive out to the **Starlight Six Drive-In** (2000 Moreland Avenue SE; 404-627-5786; starlightdrivein.com) for Southern-culture-on-the-skids charm, retro with a hint of

rockabilly. Sometimes used for campy evenings of B-movies and bands, the rest of the time this is just a straight-up, steamy-windowed cinematic experience in a hummocky parking lot.

SUNDAY

10 *Pancakes and Quiet Neighbors* 10 a.m.

The gruff proprietor of **Ria's Bluebird** (421 Memorial Drive SE; 404-521-3737; riasbluebird.com; $) had the word "hate" tattooed on her neck, but local residents gave her nothing but love. She died in 2013, but still they line up, pleasantly sleep-tousled, on weekend mornings for what some customers say are the world's best pancakes. The light-filled storefront is just right if you feel the need to keep your sunglasses on in the morning. The restaurant is across the street from Atlanta's oldest and loveliest cemetery, **Oakland**

Cemetery (248 Oakland Avenue SE; 404-688-2107; oaklandcemetery.com), where Margaret Mitchell, author of *Gone with the Wind*; 25 mayors; and thousands of unidentified Confederate soldiers are buried. In warm weather, guided tours are available on Sunday afternoons.

11 *The King Legacy* 11 a.m.

At the **Martin Luther King Jr. National Historic Site** (450 Auburn Avenue NE; 404-331-5190; nps. gov/malu), you can take a tour of the house where King was born (501 Auburn Avenue NE; reserve in advance) and, at the visitor center, see his life retraced in photos, print, film, video, and art. If you get an earlier start, you might want to stop

by the new Ebenezer Baptist Church, adjacent to the visitor center, for a service. The historic **Old Ebenezer Baptist Church**, where King, his father, and his grandfather preached, is across the street (407 Auburn Avenue NE), no longer used for services, but open to view. Inside, in the quiet sanctuary where King's inspiring words once echoed, visitors may find their emotions running high.

OPPOSITE An elaborate mausoleum at Oakland Cemetery. A burial ground for generations of Atlantans, the cemetery holds the graves of Confederate soldiers, 25 Atlanta mayors, and Margaret Mitchell, the author of *Gone With the Wind*.

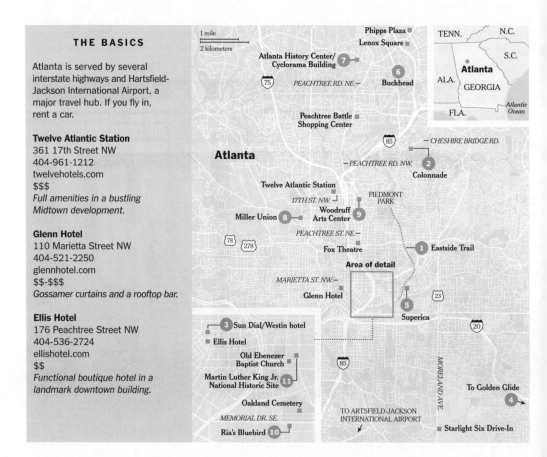

THE BASICS

Atlanta is served by several interstate highways and Hartsfield-Jackson International Airport, a major travel hub. If you fly in, rent a car.

Twelve Atlantic Station
361 17th Street NW
404-961-1212
twelvehotels.com
$$$
Full amenities in a bustling Midtown development.

Glenn Hotel
110 Marietta Street NW
404-521-2250
glennhotel.com
$$-$$$
Gossamer curtains and a rooftop bar.

Ellis Hotel
176 Peachtree Street NW
404-536-2724
ellishotel.com
$$
Functional boutique hotel in a landmark downtown building.

St. Simons Island

The Golden Isles, the barrier islands of Georgia's coast, meld two worlds: the sunny beaches and lollygag pace of island life and the stately Spanish moss-draped grace of the South with antebellum graveyards and ruined plantations. St. Simons, about equidistant between Jacksonville and Savannah, in particular is a literary haunt, home of writers' conferences and a favorite location of authors including Tina McElroy Ansa, whose popular black heroine, Lena McPherson, can see ghosts. Hidden amid the island's resorts and golf courses are remnants of the time when the only residents were Gullah-Geechee people, rice-tenders descended from slaves who speak their own blend of African languages and English. St. Simons, where oak trees turn avenues into tunnels of green, is the hub of the barrier islands, with about 13,000 residents and a bustling strip of restaurants and shops called the Village. — BY SHAILA DEWAN

FRIDAY

1 *On the Pier* 3 p.m.

Start at the **St. Simons Bait & Tackle** shop (121 Mallery Street; 912-634-1888), where you can try for a greeting from the African gray parrot, Mr. Byrd (who has his own Facebook page), and rent fishing poles. Walk outside to the pier to try for anything from sheepshead to flounder, or just dangle the line in the water and daydream. A short stroll takes you to the **St. Simons Island Lighthouse** (912-638-4666; saintsimonslighthouse.org; arrive before 4:30 if you want to climb the tower), built in 1872 after Confederates destroyed the original. It is a quaint white structure with a 360-degree observation deck overlooking St. Simons Sound and the mainland. And it gives you some exercise before you embark on a series of buttery, greasy, delicious Southern meals.

2 *Crab Stew and a Beer* 5:30 p.m.

Head north on scenic Highway 17 to experience a true Georgia tradition, the seafood shack. **Hunter's Cafe** (1093 River Road; $) is on a dirt road amid the marinas — or, as they are called here, fish camps — of

Shellman Bluff, a quaint village of screened cottages among the live oak hung with Spanish moss about a 30-minute drive toward Savannah. The diners at the next table are likely to be fishermen just returned from a day in the salt marshes. To the basic shack formula of bright lighting and linoleum floors, Hunter's has added a full bar and a screened porch overlooking the Broro River, but it maintains the customary disdain for any decoration not furnished by a taxidermist. Have the crab stew and fluffy oniony hushpuppies.

3 *Tree Spirits* 9 p.m.

Back on St. Simons, in the commercial district known as the Village, look for the green and yellow awning of **Murphy's Tavern** (415 Mallery Street; 912-638-8966), a favorite haunt of shrimpers, summer residents, and townies. Order a beer, pick someone out, and suggest a game of pool. Outside, look for the face of a "tree spirit" carved into a huge old oak tree. A handful of these spirits, sculptures by Keith Jennings, are on public sites scattered around St. Simons; more are hidden away on private property.

SATURDAY

4 *The Breakfast Rush* 9 a.m.

Busy day ahead, a good excuse to feast on breakfast at **Palmer's Village Cafe** (223 Mallery Street;

OPPOSITE The Avenue of Oaks at Sea Island resort.

RIGHT A "tree spirit" sculpture by Keith Jennings.

912-634-5515; palmersvillagecafe.com; $). Try the Surf Squared: crab cakes over a smoked Gouda grit cake, topped with poached eggs, hollandaise, and seared tomatoes. You're early, so you should beat the rush of retirees, young couples, families, tourists, and regulars who descend like gulls in the morning.

5 *The Little Island* 10:30 a.m.

If you doze off when you hear the phrase "bird-watcher's paradise," just forget about the bird part and catch the boat to **Little St. Simons Island**, a private retreat where you can spend the day lying on the beach and touring the near-pristine live oak and magnolia forest. Two of the resort's main buildings are an old hunting lodge and a stunning cottage made of tabby, a stuccolike material of lime and oyster shells. Family owned, the resort is also family style, which means help yourself to towels, sunscreen, bug spray, and the beer set out in coolers on the porch. Most of the island has been left virtually untouched, and it is possible in one day to observe river otter, dolphins, the endangered greenfly orchid, and bald eagles, as well as roseate spoonbills and a host of other birds. The beach is littered with sand dollars and conch. A day trip is about $100 a person and includes lunch, transportation to and from the island, a naturalist-guided tour, and time at the beach. You'll leave from the Hampton River Marina (1000 Hampton River Club Marina Drive on St. Simons) at 10:30 and will be back by 4:30. Reservations are required (the Lodge on Little St. Simons Island; 912-638-7472; littlessi.com).

6 *Alligator Hazard* 5:30 p.m.

Back on the big island, there's still time for nine holes of golf at the **King and Prince Golf Course** (100

ABOVE Christ Church, built by a lumber magnate mourning the death of his wife on their honeymoon.

RIGHT The King and Prince Golf Course, where you might see an alligator eyeing the golfers.

Tabbystone; 912-634-0255; hamptonclub.com), a course that makes full use of the starkly beautiful marsh landscape. Ask to play 10 through 18; four of these holes are on little marsh islands connected by bridges. You'll putt surrounded by a sea of golden grasses that even non-golfers will appreciate. One hole is near an island with a resident alligator.

7 *Upscale Seafood* 8 p.m.

Settle in for drinks and a leisurely dinner at one of the fancy restaurants like **Halyards**, featuring Southern seafood dishes (55 Cinema Lane; 912-638-9100; halyardsrestaurant.com; $$-$$$), or the more traditional **Georgia Sea Grill** (407 Mallery Street; 912-638-1197; georgiaseagrill.com; $$-$$$).

SUNDAY

8 *Church with a Past* 10 a.m.

It has history, it has literary significance, it has a tragic love story. But the thing to notice at Christ Church, Frederica, built in 1884 by a lumber magnate mourning the death of his wife on their honeymoon, is the thick, lambent lawn, one of the great unnoticed triumphs of Southern horticulture. **Christ Church, Frederica** (6329 Frederica Road; 912-638-8683; christchurchfrederica.org), was a setting in a novel by Eugenia Price, who is buried in the graveyard there. The oldest grave dates to

1803. Across the street is a wooded garden dedicated to Charles and John Wesley, who preached on St. Simons in the 1730s as Anglicans; they later returned to England and founded Methodism.

9 *Bicycle-Friendly* 11:30 a.m.

The exclusive **Lodge at Sea Island** (100 Retreat Avenue; 912-638-3611; seaisland.com) is off limits to all but guests and members. But if you go by bike you may be able to sneak a peek of its grounds and the ruins of Retreat Plantation's hospital, where slaves were treated. You'll also experience the island's bicycle-friendly avenues, lined with tremendous 150-year-old oaks. Rent a bike at **Ocean Motion** (1300 Ocean Boulevard; 912-638-5225), head south following the road around the tip of the island, and make a left on Frederica Road to reach the Avenue of Oaks, which leads to the guard house of the Lodge before it loops back to Frederica Road. You can ask to see the ruins just inside the grounds. If you're ambitious, venture onto the Torras Causeway, which leads to the mainland and has a bike path.

ABOVE Rent a fishing pole and drop in a line.

THE BASICS

Fly into Savannah/Hilton Head International Airport or Jacksonville International Airport. Rent a car for the 90-minute drive from either airport, and then use it to stay mobile.

King and Prince Beach & Golf Resort
201 Arnold Road
912-638-3631
kingandprince.com
$$$-$$$$
A sprawling 75-year-old full-service resort with guest rooms, villas, and cabanas.

The Lodge at Sea Island
100 Retreat Avenue
855-572-4975
seaisland.com
$$$$
Close to golf courses; 24-hour butler service.

Ocean Inn & Suites
599 Beachview Drive
912-634-2122
oceaninnsuites.com
$$
Within walking distance of the Village and the lighthouse.

GEORGIA
Hunter's Cafe
Shellman Bluff
2
Broro R.
Altamaha R.
25
341
17
SAPELO ISLAND
95
BRUNSWICK GOLDEN ISLE AIRPORT
Brunswick
Area of detail
GA.
S.C.
Savannah
Area of detail
FLA.
Jacksonville
Atlantic Ocean
10 miles
20 kilometers

Hampton River Marina Ferry
Altamaha Sound
King and Prince Golf Course
6
GEORGIA
Little St. Simons Island
5
17
25
ST. SIMONS ISLAND
LAWRENCE RD.
Hampton Cr.
Christ Church, Frederica
8
SEA ISLAND RD.
Halyards
7
FREDERICA RD.
Atlantic Ocean
F.J. TORRAS CSWY.
Area of detail
2 miles
4 kilometers

RETREAT AVE. (AVE. OF THE OAKS)
MALLERY PARK
ST. SIMONS ISLAND
ARNOLD RD.
Ocean Motion
SEASIDE GOLF COURSE
KINGS WAY
Murphy's Tavern
3
MALLERY ST.
OCEAN VILLAGE
King and Prince Beach & Golf Resort
DEMERE RD.
BEACH VIEW DR.
BUTLER AVE.
Georgia Sea Grill
9
Lodge at Sea Island
Palmer's Village Cafe
4
Ocean Inn & Suites
BEACH VIEW DR.
OCEAN BLVD.
Atlantic Ocean
St. Simons Bait & Tackle
1
St. Simons Sound
ST. SIMONS FISHING PIER
St. Simons Island Lighthouse
1/4 mile
1/2 kilometer

Savannah

Certain things about Savannah never change — it remains one of America's loveliest cities, organized around a grid of 21 squares, where children play, couples wed, and in the evenings lone saxophonists deliver a jazz soundtrack. Live oaks shade the squares; shops and cafes occupy stately old houses; ships still arrive on the Savannah River. But Savannah also savors the new. A growing emphasis on art has brought both a major expansion of the South's oldest art museum and a lively contemporary scene energized by students and instructors at SCAD, the booming Savannah College of Art and Design, expanded with a new museum built on the ruins of an antebellum rail depot. So now, the historic mansions and mossy cemeteries of traditional Savannah coexist alongside craft breweries, cool boutiques, and innovative restaurants. — BY SHAILA DEWAN AND RON STODGHILL

FRIDAY

1 *Good and Evil* 3:30 p.m.

You're in the heart of the gracious South, so embrace every cliché from the frilly to the Gothic, with some eccentric characters for good measure. Begin with a tour of the splendid **Mercer Williams House** on Monterey Square (429 Bull Street; 912-236-6352; mercerhouse.com). It was built in the 1860s for the great-grandfather of Savannah's favorite son, the songwriter Johnny Mercer, and restored by Jim Williams, the antiques dealer memorialized in a now-classic book, *Midnight in the Garden of Good and Evil*. The stern guide won't dwell on the four murder trials of Williams, who was acquitted for the shooting that took place there, and guests aren't allowed on the second floor, which is still a residence. But the guide will offer plenty of detail about the formal courtyard, the nap-ready veranda, the Continental rococo, and the Edwardian Murano glass.

2 *Georgia on Your Plate* 7 p.m.

Dress up a bit (no flip-flops) for the froufrou milieu of **Elizabeth on 37th** (105 East 37th Street; 912-236-5547; elizabethon37th.net; $$$), a Low Country restaurant housed in an early 20th-century mansion where the décor may be prissy but the food is anything but. Expect a seafood-rich menu and what is arguably Savannah's quintessential dining experience. Look for Georgia shrimp, local sea bass, or a pecan crust on the rack of lamb.

3 *Creepy Cocktails* 9 p.m.

Savannah began peacefully enough, with a friendship between Tomochichi, chief of the Yamacraw tribe, and James Oglethorpe, leader of the British settlers who founded the city in 1733. But then came war, yellow fever, hurricanes, and fires, not to mention pirates, curses, and slavery — making the place seem like one big graveyard. Savannah has turned that sordid history to its advantage: about 30 ghost tours are offered, including a haunted pub crawl. Only one, though, picks you up at your hotel in an open-top hearse, **Hearse Tours** (912-695-1578; hearseghosttours.com). While recounting some of Savannah's most notorious murders, suicides, and deathbed tales, your jocular guide might make everyone scream in unison to spook passersby, or stop for cocktails at favorite haunts. (It's legal to take your julep for a stroll.) For a different perspective take the popular, daytime **Black History Tour** (912-398-2785), led by Johnnie Brown of Freedom Trail Tours, one of the city's few black tour guides. As his bus rolls past slave cemeteries, whipping trees, and civil rights-era landmarks, you'll get a few dollops of indignation, along with a hearty serving of Savannah's powerful, if woefully undercelebrated, black narrative.

OPPOSITE Savannah, Georgia, in the heart of the gracious South, carefully preserves the elegant houses lining its central grid of oak-shaded squares.

BELOW The ornate cast-iron fountain in Forsyth Park.

SATURDAY

4 *Up-and-Coming* 10 a.m.

Venture out of the historic district to the up-and-coming Starland area, filled with galleries and studios. Start at **Non-Fiction Gallery** (1522 Bull Street; 912-662-5152), an adventurous space, affiliated with the nonprofit Art Rise Savannah, that shows contemporary artwork in diverse media. Next, proceed to **Maldoror's** (2418 De Soto Avenue; 912-443-5355; maldorors.com; $), a frame shop with the aura of a Victorian curio cabinet and a print collection to match. Rounding the corner, you'll come to **Back in the Day** (2403 Bull Street; 912-495-9292; backinthedaybakery.com), an old-fashioned bakery that inspires fervent loyalty among locals. Pick up a sandwich, like the Madras curry chicken on ciabatta, and maybe a cupcake, to take with you for lunch.

5 *Picnic with the Dead* Noon

Few cemeteries are more stately and picnic-perfect than **Bonaventure Cemetery** (330 Bonaventure Road), with its 250-year-old live oaks draped with Spanish moss as if perpetually decorated for Halloween. The cemetery, where Conrad Aiken, Johnny Mercer, and other notable residents are buried, looks out over the Intracoastal Waterway and is a gathering spot for anglers as well as mourners. Find a quiet spot to ponder fate and eat your lunch.

6 *Old Streets, New Museum* 2 p.m.

The battle took years and matched two unlikely adversaries: the **Telfair Museum of Art**, the oldest art museum in the South, which wanted to expand, and the powerful Savannah Historic District Board of Review. The result, after intense haggling, was a light-filled building that is as trim as a yacht and has won accolades for its architect,

ABOVE Elizabeth on 37th, a restaurant with Low Country cuisine, serves up seafood-rich dishes in a palatial neo-Classical-style villa built in 1900.

BELOW Hearse Tours takes visitors to the haunts of Savannah's thriving population of ghosts.

Moshe Safdie. The addition, the **Jepson Center for the Arts** (207 West York Street; 912-790-8800; telfair.org), preserved Savannah's cherished street grid by dividing the structure into two and joining it with two glass bridges while giving the museum much-needed space. The Jepson is home to *The Bird Girl*, the now-famous statue that adorns the cover of *Midnight in the Garden of Good and Evil*; she was relocated from Bonaventure Cemetery to protect her from the book's thronging fans. The original museum building (Telfair Academy, 121 Barnard Street) was put up as a mansion in 1819, and the museum also operates tours of the nearly 200-year-old **Owens-Thomas House** (124 Abercorn Street). A combination ticket covers all three.

7 *School Fair* 5 p.m.

Shopping in Savannah is increasingly sophisticated — or homogenized, depending on your point of view — with recent additions like J.Crew and Lululemon on the steadily gentrifying Broughton Street. But the most interesting retail is at **shopSCAD**, a boutique that sells the creations of the students, faculty, and staff of the Savannah College of Art and Design (340 Bull Street; 912-525-5180; shopscad.com). There is fine art — drawings, paintings, photography, and prints — as well as decorative and wearable items from a rotating cast of alumni, like hand-dyed ties by Jen Swearington or a pendant lamp by Christopher Moulder.

8 *Crab Heaven* 7:30 p.m.

Forget about crab cakes, stuffed soft shells, or crabmeat au gratin. Crab is most rewarding when it is pure and unadulterated, served in a pile on newspaper with a can of beer and a blunt instrument for whacking at the shell. That, plus some boiled potatoes and corn, is what you will find at **Desposito's** (3501 Marye Street, Thunderbolt; 912-897-9963; $$), an unadorned shack in a onetime fishing village on the outskirts of town. This is not dining; this is working, but the sweet morsels are better than any payday.

9 *Drinking In the Scene* 9:30 p.m.

Many of Savannah's finest bars close early — often when the owners feel like it — so don't wait to start on your drink-by-drink tour. Begin at the **American Legion Post 135**, south of Forsyth Park (1108 Bull Street; 912-233-9277; alpost135.com), a surprisingly shimmery, mirrored space where the clientele is a mix of age and vocation. Proceed to the **Crystal Beer Parlor** (301 West Jones Street; 912-349-1000; crystalbeerparlor.com). On the outside, it's as

ABOVE The no-frills, low-priced Thunderbird Inn plays up its retro ambience.

anonymous as a speakeasy, which it was, but inside, its high-backed booths and colorful hanging lamps are more ice cream than booze. A full menu is available. Wind up at **Planters Tavern** (23 Abercorn Street; 912-232-4286), a noisy, low-ceilinged bar in the basement of the high-dollar Olde Pink House, a dignified restaurant in a 1771 house. With a fireplace on either end of the room, live music, and boisterous locals, it's the place to be.

SUNDAY

10 *Church's Chicken* 11 a.m.

Church and food go together in the South, and they do so especially well at the **Masada Café** (2301

West Bay Street; 912-236-9499), a buffet annex to the United House of Prayer for All People. The church has several locations in Savannah; this one is a mission of sorts, catering to the poor, but the inexpensive, revolving buffet of soul food classics like fried chicken and macaroni and cheese has gained a following among food critics and locals. Get there at 11 a.m. for the Sunday service, where the music and rhythmic hand-clapping surely share some DNA with the "ring shouts" of the Gullah-Geechee people, descendants of slaves who once lived on the nearby barrier islands.

OPPOSITE Learning about art at the Jepson Center.

THE BASICS

Fly to the Savannah/Hilton Head International Airport and take a shuttle into Savannah. The historic district is easily traversed by foot. A cab or a car may be necessary for other destinations.

Mansion on Forsyth Park
700 Drayton Street
912-238-5158
kesslercollection.com/mansion
$$$
A lavish 1888 home eccentrically decorated with garish paintings and an antique hat collection.

Andaz Savannah
14 Barnard Street
912-233-2116
savannah.andaz.hyatt.com
$$$
Hip boutique hotel overlooking Ellis Square.

Thunderbird Inn
611 West Oglethorpe Avenue
912-232-2661
thethunderbirdinn.com
$$
A no-frills motel refurbished with vintage flair.

Andaz Savannah
Planters Tavern/ Olde Pink House
1/4 mile
1/2 kilometer
Savannah River
Thunderbird Inn
TELFAIR SQ.
6 Telfair Museum of Art
Jepson Center for the Arts
OGLETHORPE AVE.
Owens-Thomas House
LOUISVILLE RD.
STATE ST.
W. BOUNDARY ST.
Black History Tour of Savannah
LIBERTY ST.
COLONIAL PARK CEMETERY
E. BROAD ST.
Savannah
Crystal Beer Parlor
shopSCAD/Savannah
7 College of Art and Design
Mercer Williams House **1**
MONTEREY SQ.
GASTON ST.
Atlanta
S.C.
MARTIN LUTHER KING JR. BLVD
WALDBURG ST.
FORSYTH PARK
Mansion on Forsyth Park
GWINNETT ST.
GEORGIA
Savannah
ALA.
HENRY ST.
ANDERSON ST.
DUFFY ST.
9 American Legion Post 135
FLORIDA
MONTGOMERY ST.
BARNARD ST.
WHITAKER ST.
BULL ST.
DRAYTON ST.
ABERCORN ST.
LINCOLN ST.
HABERSHAM ST.
4 Non-Fiction Gallery
3 Hearse Tours
S.C.
Bonaventure Cemetery
16
10
Area of detail
5
Elizabeth on 37th **2**
Masada Café/ United House of Prayer for All People
80
Savannah
37TH ST.
THUNDERBOLT
8 Desposito's
Maldoror's
Back in the Day
GEORGIA
4 miles
8 kilometers

Lexington

Miles of low fences line the winding, two-lane roads of the Bluegrass Country around Lexington, Kentucky, and enclose its rolling green horse farms, where magnificent thoroughbreds rest near pristinely painted barns. Now and again, the fences break for a leafy lane leading to an age-old bourbon distillery with doors open for a tour and a tipple. Then they lead away to a quaint 19th-century town, a quintessential country inn, or a serene Shaker village. These magical fences, made of wood or of stones stacked long ago by slaves and Scotch-Irish settlers, take you back in time and away in space. But you'll be brought back soon enough by Kentucky's modern hosts serving up Southern charm and distinctly American food and drink. — BY TAYLOR HOLLIDAY

FRIDAY

1 *Horse Fixation* 1:45 p.m.

Lexington, a leisurely university city with preserved antebellum houses, calls itself the horse capital of the world. On thousands of acres of nearby farms, pampered horses graze on the local bluegrass, so called because it blooms a purplish blue. Dip into the horse world at **Kentucky Horse Park** (4089 Iron Works Parkway; 859-233-4303; kyhorsepark.com). It may seem at first like merely a giant horsy theme park, but the horse trailers in the parking lot attest to its importance for competitions as well. There are displays on the history of the horse, paeans to winners like Man o' War and Cigar, and a Parade of Breeds. (Catch it at 2 p.m.) Horse shows and races are frequent — you might catch a steeplechase. And in June, musicians arrive from far and wide for a festival of bluegrass music.

2 *Chefs of the Country* 7 p.m.

Northwest of Lexington, Route 62 cuts a path through lush countryside to charming little Midway, a railroad town of about 1,600 people where trains still run right down the middle of the main street. A gem

OPPOSITE White rail fences mark the rolling green fields of a horse farm in Kentucky Bluegrass Country.

RIGHT Woodford Reserve, one of the Kentucky bourbon distilleries where a tour is capped with a sip of the whiskey.

of a restaurant, the **Holly Hill Inn** (426 North Winter Street, Midway; 859-846-4732; hollyhillinn.com; $$$), awaits you down a nearby lane, in a house dating to 1839. Ouita Michel, the chef, and her husband, Chris, the sommelier, both graduates of the Culinary Institute of America, serve a four-course prix fixe dinner. Choices on the changing menus have included spoonbread soufflé, pork roast with figs and dates, and tile fish with Kentucky red rice.

SATURDAY

3 *Brake for Bourbon* 10 a.m.

The land around Lexington grows more than thoroughbreds. West of the city, you're in bourbon country. Several distillers have banded together to create what they call the Bourbon Trail, so spend a day learning why their product is such a source of Kentucky pride. Stop first in Versailles (pronounce it "ver-SALES"), where the stately limestone **Woodford Reserve** (7855 McCracken Pike; 859-879-1812; woodfordreserve.com) is nestled deep among farms with cupola-topped stables and miles of black-painted board fences. The only product made here is the small-batch Woodford Reserve, but visitors come by the thousands, and you'll see the entire bourbon-making process from mash to bottle. Inhale the smells of whiskey and old wood, and sip a sample.

4 *Whiskey Saga* Noon

Bardstown, a city of about 10,000 in the heart of bourbon territory, honors its debt to spirits at the **Oscar Getz Museum of Whiskey History** (114 North Fifth Street; 502-348-2999; oscargetzwhiskeymuseum. com). In the 1790s, Scotch-Irish distillers fleeing George Washington's whiskey tax and the quelling of the subsequent Whiskey Rebellion landed in an area of Virginia then called Bourbon County, which now covers several counties of northeastern Kentucky. They found perfect conditions for their trade, partly because of a layer of limestone that filters iron from the local water, and bourbon whiskey was born. In the museum, examine local artifacts including authentic moonshine stills.

5 *Lettuce or Schnitzel* 1 p.m.

You're saving room for a big dinner tonight, so go for a salad at **Kreso's Restaurant** (218 North Third Street; 502-348-9594; kresosrestaurant.com; $). Eating light here does means avoiding the schnitzel, which is a specialty. Your choice.

6 *Dip Your Own* 2 p.m.

Meander about 15 miles south on Route 49 to tiny Loretto and enter the red-shuttered, brown-clapboard buildings of **Maker's Mark** (3350 Burks Spring Road; 270-865-2099; makersmark.com). The oldest bourbon distillery in the country, dating to 1805, it is well schooled in the rules of bourbon: the mash must be at least 51 percent corn, barrels for aging must be new and made of charred white oak, alcohol must be at prescribed strengths in the years-long process of transforming grain into whiskey. The tour here shows you the cooker, mash fermentation, the still, aging rackhouses, and hand-bottling. You can dip a finger into a vat of bubbling, fermenting mash to get a taste (like sweetened cereal gone sour), and you can even hand-dip your own souvenir bottle in the trademark red wax.

7 *Jim Beam's Place* 4 p.m.

Drive back north to Bardstown and take Route 245 west to Clermont, the home of **Jim Beam** (526 Happy Hollow Road; 502-543-9877; jimbeam.com), the biggest of the bourbon distillers. Jim Beam doesn't have an extensive tour, but you'll get a good tasting. And from the porch of the Beam family's whitewashed mansion on the hill, you have a perfect view of the vapor-spewing, multibuilding factory, which has turned out millions of bottles of bourbon.

8 *Kentucky Comfort Food* 6 p.m.

For real Kentucky skillet-fried chicken, take a table at **Kurtz** (418 East Stephen Foster Avenue, Bardstown; 502-348-5983; kurtzrestaurant.com; $$), which has been satisfying hungry Kentuckians since 1937. The chicken is superb and the fixings

are traditional—mashed potatoes, cornbread, green beans with Kentucky ham. For dessert, ask for the biscuit pudding with bourbon sauce.

9 *Bourbons by the Dozen* 8 p.m.

When you're finished with the day's driving and ready to relax, sample the atmosphere and the libations at a bourbon bar, where knowledgeable bartenders serve Kentucky's favorite drink in dozens of varieties. In Bardstown, there's a classic of the genre at **Old Talbott Tavern** (107 West Stephen Foster Avenue; 502-348-3494; talbotts.com). In Lexington, try **Bluegrass Tavern** (115 Cheapside; 859-389-6664; thebluegrasstavern.com).

SUNDAY

10 *Thoroughbreds at Home* 9 a.m.

Taking tourists to the horse farms is a Lexington specialty—the local convention and visitors bureau publishes a list of tour companies and private guides (visitlex.com/idea/horse-farms.php). One good choice is a trip with the women of **Horse Farm Tours** (859-268-2906; horsefarmtours.com), who point out historical buildings in downtown Lexington on the way to a sampling of farms. If decadently luxurious stables and a 10-bedroom mansion at one farm are a reminder that thoroughbreds are a rich person's hobby, the wholesome young broodmare manager at

the next farm, attending to the mares and their wobbly, week-old foals, is proof of how intense the horse-and-human relationship can be. At the stud farm, it's all about bloodlines and breeding techniques. You'll also be whisked to the best seats in the ivy-covered limestone viewing stand at Keeneland, Lexington's

OPPOSITE Oak barrels at Woodford Reserve. On the tour, you'll see the bourbon-making process from mash to bottle.

TOP Green countryside near Loretto, on one of the winding side roads to explore near Lexington.

ABOVE Whiskey makers migrated to this part of Kentucky, then known as Bourbon County, Virginia, around 1800. Some of their tools are displayed at Maker's Mark distillery.

renowned race track—to see, perhaps, some horses in training.

11 *Plain or Crispy* 1 p.m.

Drive south from Lexington, and pick your version of local history. Route 68, through undulating hills and forested bluffs, will take you to **Shaker Village of Pleasant Hill** (3501 Lexington Road, Harrodsburg; 859-734-5411; shakervillageky.org), a home of the plain-living 19th-century Shaker sect. Wander around

34 restored buildings and stay for dinner in the restaurant. If you prefer more populist fare, head south on Interstate 75, exit at the Cumberland Gap Parkway, Route 25E, and turn right onto 25W to get to the **Harland Sanders Cafe and Museum** (688 Highway 25W, Corbin; 606-528-2163; kentuckytourism.com/harland-sanders-cafe-and-museum), located in the restaurant where the renowned Colonel Sanders cooked a lot of chickens before becoming world-famous. You can still savor his 11 herbs and spices at the KFC cafe.

ABOVE Maker's Mark, in Loretto, finishes off its bourbon bottles with signature red wax.

OPPOSITE A warehouse at the Jim Beam distillery.

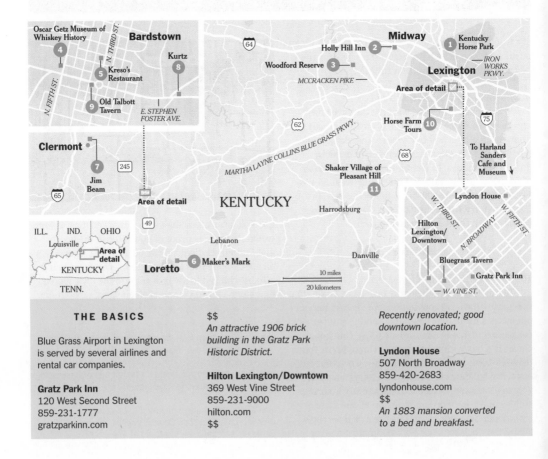

THE BASICS

Blue Grass Airport in Lexington is served by several airlines and rental car companies.

Gratz Park Inn
120 West Second Street
859-231-1777
gratzparkinn.com

$$
An attractive 1906 brick building in the Gratz Park Historic District.

Hilton Lexington/Downtown
369 West Vine Street
859-231-9000
hilton.com
$$

Recently renovated; good downtown location.

Lyndon House
507 North Broadway
859-420-2683
lyndonhouse.com
$$
An 1883 mansion converted to a bed and breakfast.

Louisville

Every May, Louisville, Kentucky, bolts into the public eye for 120 seconds — the time it takes to run the Kentucky Derby. But there is more to this courtly city on the Ohio River than the Derby. It has experienced a cultural and civic blooming, with new galleries, restaurants, and performance spaces taking their place alongside the city's already robust roster of seductions. Entire neighborhoods — Butchertown, for instance, and East Market — have been reimagined as engines of cultural and culinary expression. Regardless of the changes, Derby City retains its easy charm — a glass of fine bourbon and good conversation aren't hard to find. And for the record, it's pronounced "LOU-uh-vull."
— BY MICHAEL WASHBURN

FRIDAY

1 *Getting Acquainted* 6 p.m.

More than 45 different watering holes line the roughly two miles of the Bardstown Road-Baxter Avenue corridor, from elegant restaurants to sticky-floored dives. Sandwiched among them are cafes and galleries specializing in regional ceramics and woodwork, and shops selling vintage clothing and jewelry, musical instruments, and Louisville-themed curiosities. Stop in at the **Holy Grale** (1034 Bardstown Road; 502-459-9939; holygralelouisville.com). Located in a century-old church, this dark, snug tavern with a polished bar running its length offers a selection of fine beers, including rare drafts. The menu of small plates, with selections from poutine to kale salad, lists suggested beer pairings.

2 *Bootleggers and Grits* 8:30 p.m.

Jack Fry's (1007 Bardstown Road; 502-452-9244; jackfrys.com; $$$) opened in 1933 as a haven for bootleggers and bookies and has remained a popular dining spot, with its classic Old South atmosphere and original décor. A collection of 1930s-era photographs — including shots of the 1937 flood that devastated downtown Louisville and prompted development in the eastern, now more affluent, sections of town — adorns the walls, and a discreet jazz trio performs in the corner. These days the restaurant focuses

OPPOSITE On the track at the Kentucky Derby.

on subtle reinventions of Southern staples: shrimp and grits with red-eye gravy and country ham, for example, or lamb chops in a rosemary natural jus with shiitakes and thyme.

3 *Night Music* 10:30 p.m.

From Will Oldham and Slint to My Morning Jacket, Louisville performers have sent their music echoing around the world. Even if you're not lucky enough to catch Oldham or MMJ in one of their local appearances, you can always find something to spirit you away. **Zanzabar** (2100 South Preston Street; 502-635-9227; zanzabarlouisville.com) offers cheap whiskey for you to sip at its horseshoe-shaped bar while you catch one of the city's (or country's) comers on its intimate stage. You can also catch live music at **Lola** (gotolola.com), a cocktail lounge at **Butchertown Grocery** (1076 East Washington Street; 502-742-8315; butchertowngrocery.com) where Patrick Hallahan, the drummer for MMJ, is a part owner.

SATURDAY

4 *New Louisville* 9 a.m.

The East Market District, dubbed NuLu (new Louisville), is one of the best of the city's revitalization projects, offering antiques stores, boutiques, and galleries. Find breakfast there at **Toast on Market** (620 East Market Street; 502-569-4099; toastonmarket.com; $), where hearty options like lemon soufflé pancakes supplement the signature dish. Then explore the shops. This is a place to look for stylish clothes, interesting housewares, crafts, and quirky gifts. Galleries in NuLu show the work of regional and national artists. The neighborhood anchor **Joe Ley Antiques** (615 East Market Street; 502-583-4014; joeley.com) stocks three stories with distinctive finds.

5 *Float Like a Butterfly* 11 a.m.

Louisville's greatest son is the greatest: Muhammad Ali. The **Muhammad Ali Center** (144 North Sixth Street; 502-584-9254; alicenter.org) celebrates his singular talent as a boxer and his post-retirement humanitarian efforts, but the curators pulled no punches with the history. Sure, you can try the speed bag, but not before you're immersed in multimedia presentations that contextualize Ali's career within the civil

rights struggle. It was at its height when he burst onto the national scene as a flamboyant, uniquely gifted athlete who soon demonstrated a personal commitment to justice. The Ali Center is part of **Museum Row** (museumrowonmain.com), an eclectic confederation of museums and galleries devoted to science, blown glass art, Louisville Slugger baseball bats, historical artifacts (including armor worn by English knights), and more.

6 *Riders Up!* 2 p.m.

Churchill Downs (700 Central Avenue; 502-636-4400; churchilldowns.com) demands a visit even if you're not here for the Derby — especially if you're not here for the Derby. During other races in the spring meet, which runs for several months, a spot on Millionaire's Row costing Diddy and his ilk $68,000 on Derby Day will set you back less than $50 as you walk among the mortals. Don't worry, the ponies charge just as hard. Adjacent to the Downs, the **Kentucky Derby Museum** (704 Central Avenue; 502-637-7097; derbymuseum.org), open all year, offers an overview of the Run for the Roses and hosts several track tours, including one of the "backside," home to 1,400 thoroughbreds during racing season. After leaving the Downs, visit **Wagner's Pharmacy** (3113 South Fourth Street; 502-375-3800; wagnerspharmacy.com), fabled hangout of grooms, jockeys, and sportswriters. Barely changed since 1922, Wagner's lunch counter displays fading photos of legends — two- and four-legged — from Derby history.

7 *Whiskey Row* 6 p.m.

Doc Crow's (127 West Main Street; 502-587-1626; doccrows.com; $$) occupies the former Bonnie Bros. distillery, one of Louisville's collection of cast-iron-facade buildings in an area called Whiskey Row. Take a seat in the back room of this 1880s-era gem and enjoy oysters on the half shell with bourbon mignonette or Carolina-style pulled pork.

8 *Broadway on the Ohio* 8 p.m.

Home of the annual spring Humana Festival of New American Plays, one of the nation's foremost new-works festivals, **Actors Theatre of Louisville** (316 West Main Street; 502-584-1205; actorstheatre.org) not only provides a rigorous testing ground for new talent, but shows well-acted plays for most of the year. The festival introduced Pulitzer Prize-winning plays including *Dinner With Friends* and *Crimes of the Heart* and has sent an impressive cadre of graduates on to Broadway. If nothing at Actors Theatre strikes your fancy, check out the **Kentucky Center for the Arts** (501 West Main Street; 502-562-0100; kentuckycenter.org), which hosts touring productions as well as performances by the Louisville Orchestra and the Louisville Ballet.

9 *Borne Back Ceaselessly* 10:30 p.m.

The college crowd and some of their elders party at Louisville's overwrought, underthought **Fourth Street Live**, an urban mall featuring clubs, bars, and outlets of too-familiar national chain restaurants. Take a few steps from that chaos, however, and discover the wonderfully worn **Old Seelbach Bar** (500 South Fourth Street; 502-585-3200; seelbachhilton.com). It's rumored that when F. Scott Fitzgerald was a young military officer stationed in Louisville, he would while

ABOVE Reliving the Derby at the Kentucky Derby Museum.

OPPOSITE Interactivity at the Muhammad Ali Center.

away the hours at this stately lounge directly off the Seelbach Hotel's grand lobby. Fitzgerald gave the hotel itself a cameo in the *The Great Gatsby*, but he didn't highlight the bar in his masterpiece, preferring to keep the best for himself. At least that's how the local story goes.

SUNDAY

10 *Wake Up and Read* 10 a.m.

Wake up with a jolt from **Heine Brothers' Coffee** (1295 Bardstown Road; 502-456-5108; heinebroscoffee. com), accompanied by one of the shop's pastries. Heine Brothers, a local favorite coffee shop with a full range of barista creations made with organic fair trade coffee, has grown into a chain of a dozen stores. This location, in a lively neighborhood, shares a passageway with one of the country's last great bookstores, **Carmichael's** (1295 Bardstown Road; 502-456-6950; carmichaelsbookstore.com).

11 *Interstate Amble* 1 p.m.

Drive back toward downtown along waterway-hugging River Road and stop to walk across the **Big Four Bridge** at the 85-acre Louisville Waterfront (louisvillewaterfront.com/explore-the-park/features). A spiraling access ramp winds its way up to connect with a decommissioned train bridge, now repurposed as a mile-long stretch for pedestrians and cyclists. Enjoy the views of the city and the Ohio River. On the other side, you're in Indiana.

THE BASICS

Fly into Louisville International Airport or drive into town on interstate highways 64, 65, or 71. Once in town, you will need a car to get around.

21C Museum Hotel
700 West Main Street
502-217-6300
21cmuseumhotels.com/Louisville
$$$
A highly rated hotel-art gallery with 9,000 square feet of exhibition space.

The Brown Hotel
335 West Broadway
502-209-7346
brownhotel.com
$$
Grand old hotel open since 1923.

The Seelbach Hilton
500 Fourth Street
502-585-3200
seelbachhilton.com
$$$$
A Louisville classic.

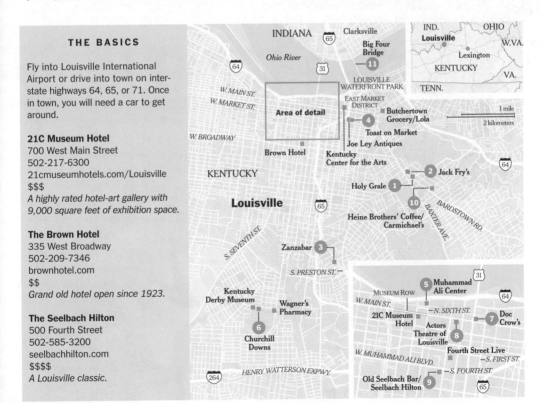

New Orleans

The weekend here begins midday on Friday when the smartly dressed lunch crowd descends upon Galatoire's restaurant in the French Quarter and, well armed with cocktails, starts its long assault on the afternoon. But a strong case could be made for the weekend starting off on Wednesday night when the Treme Brass Band settles in at the Candlelight Lounge. That is only in normal time, anyway. The season leading up to Mardi Gras fuses into one long weekend, as the streets around the city begin filling up with floats, and the living rooms of New Orleanians become littered with feathers, glue, and the makings of costumes. This is how they do it in New Orleans, a city that was four-fifths underwater after the infamous Hurricane Katrina and has survived to take up the countless parades and festivals that are part of its life. —BY CAMPBELL ROBERTSON

FRIDAY

1 *Cocktail Hour* 5 p.m.

In a city blossoming with craft-cocktail bars, best begin with a classic. The **French 75 Bar** (813 Bienville Street; 504-523-5433; arnaudsrestaurant.com/french-75) is a side chapel to **Arnaud's**, one of the old French Quarter dining palaces, and still projects an aura of French colonial charm. Order a Sazerac, the classic local drink that New Orleanians claim was the world's first cocktail, or let the bartender stir up something of his own design.

2 *No Diets* 7 p.m.

For a scenic if unhurried ride uptown, take the streetcar past the mansions and live oaks to the end of St. Charles Avenue. There is good food here. For classic south Louisiana cuisine, including a justly celebrated roast duck, head to **Brigtsen's** (723 Dante Street; 504-861-7610; brigtsens.com; $$$), situated in a homey Victorian cottage. Or for a more casual meal, cross the street to **Dante's Kitchen** (736 Dante Street; 504-861-3121; danteskitchen.com; $$), which begins dinner with spoon bread so good you want

OPPOSITE The French Quarter, the heart of old New Orleans and still its atmospheric center.

RIGHT Snake and Jake's Christmas Club Lounge, where the locals stay up late and the conversation is convivial.

to eat it with a ladle. A walk of a few blocks is worth it for **Boucherie** (1506 South Carrollton Avenue; 504-862-5514; boucherie-nola.com; $$), a Southern-flavored bistro that began its life as a food truck. Start off with the boudin balls and end with—this is real—Krispy Kreme bread pudding.

3 *Decisions* 10 p.m.

Stuffed and standing at the corner of Oak Street and South Carrollton Avenue, you have a choice. If you're in the mood for refined, you can go to **Oak** (8118 Oak Street; 504-302-1485; oaknola.com), a glossy wine bar, and conclude the evening all civilized-like with a crisp riesling. If you're restless, walk to the **Maple Leaf Bar** (8316 Oak Street; 504-866-9359; mapleleafbar.com) and join the crowd already dancing to the Dirty Dozen Brass Band or whoever is on the bill. And if you're game, turn around and head to **Snake and Jake's Christmas Club Lounge** (7612 Oak Street; 504-861-2802; snakeandjakes.com), strike up a conversation with the person sitting next to you, and see where the night goes.

SATURDAY

4 *City of the Dead* 10 a.m.

New Orleans is known for its cemeteries, built largely above ground in part because the water

table lurks only a few feet below. The variety runs from the eerily beautiful tombs of Creole grandees to a small plot on the grounds of a former plantation outside town where one of Adolf Hitler's horses is said to be buried. The best place to start looking is just outside the French Quarter in **St. Louis Cemetery No. 1** (1300 St. Louis Street), the oldest existing cemetery in the city. Explore on your own, or take a tour (1539 Jackson Avenue; 504-525-3377; saveourcemeteries.org) and study the tombs of mayors, gamblers, jazz musicians, and heroes of the War of 1812, as well as the graves of Paul Morphy, one of the greatest chess players of the 19th century; Marie Laveau, the voodoo priestess; and, potentially, Nicolas Cage, who financed the construction of a rather odd-looking pyramidal tomb presumably for his future use.

5 *Use a Fork* Noon

There's no SUBstitute for a real New Orleans po'boy, or so the bumper sticker goes, and whether your taste runs to gravy-doused roast beef or barbecued shrimp, the one at **Liuzza's by the Track** (1518 North Lopez; 504-218-7888; liuzzasnola.com; $$) is so over-stuffed that it verges on a stew. Still, the buckboard

ABOVE The Social Aid and Pleasure Clubs play at funerals and parade through town on Sunday afternoons.

bacon melt sandwich at **Cochon Butcher** (930 Tchou-pitoulas Street; 504-588-7675; cochonbutcher.com; $$) makes for a pretty good stand-in.

6 *The Lower Ninth* 2 p.m.

The destruction wrought by Katrina and the subsequent flooding go far beyond the famous Lower Ninth Ward, but it is also true that the wonders of the Lower Ninth Ward go far beyond the floodwaters. There is the pastel origami of the "Brad Pitt houses," Fats Domino's black-and-yellow mini-mansion, the beguiling steamboat houses on Egania Street, and the little museum behind Ronald Lewis's house at 1317 Tupelo Street. Call Lewis ahead (504-957-2678), and he'll arrange a visit to the House of Dance and Feathers, his private collection dedicated to the Mardi Gras Indian, the still vibrant century-plus-old tradition wherein black New Orleanians create ornate suits and parade the streets. If you have a car, you can hire a guide from lowernine.org, a nonprofit rebuilding group (504-278-1240); all the proceeds go to their work in the neighborhood. But you can also explore on a bicycle tour with **Ninth Ward Rebirth Bike Tours** (504-400-5468; ninthwardrebirthbiketours.com).

7 *Punks and Pinots* 7 p.m.

If the night is breezy and it is not too late, head over to **Bacchanal** (600 Poland Avenue; 504-948-9111;

bacchanalwine.com; $$), order a bottle of whatever they suggest, and take a seat in the courtyard under lights strung among the mulberry and oleander trees. It will only grow more crowded, which is why you should come on the early side (especially if there are a few of you). But once you've established a beachhead, there is live jazz and there is very good food, including bacon-wrapped dates and a cheese plate that you create yourself. Oh, and what the heck, maybe another bottle.

8 *Music Town* 10 p.m.

Frenchmen Street on Saturday night is like a big radio dial: you can just pop in and out of the bars and hear something different at each one. A swing band is most likely onstage at the **Spotted Cat** (623 Frenchmen Street; 504-258-3135; spottedcatmusicclub. com); over at **d.b.a.**, John Boutté may be well into a Saturday night gig (618 Frenchmen Street; 504-942-3731; dbaneworleans.com); a chanteuse is giving way to a jazz trio at the **Three Muses**

(536 Frenchmen Street; 504-252-4801; 3musesnola. com); and just beyond the foot of Frenchmen at the **Balcony Music Club** (1331 Decatur Street; 504-301-5912; balconymusicclub.com), a 10-piece is playing classic soul and R&B late into the night.

SUNDAY

9 *Down in the Treme* 10 a.m.

Shortly before **St. Augustine Catholic Church** (1210 Governor Nicholls Street; 504-525-5934; staugchurch.org) was dedicated in 1842, white and black Catholics in the area began battling to see who could buy up the most pews. When the "War of the Pews" ended, the congregation was a mix of

ABOVE Make a Sunday morning visit to St. Augustine Catholic Church, where the choir is always good and sometimes there is the bonus of a jazz Mass.

RIGHT The exterior of St. Augustine's, built in 1842. The church has been integrated from the start, when black and white Catholics competed to buy up pews.

free blacks, whites, and slaves, possibly the most integrated in the country. The church is known for its jazz Masses throughout the year, but any given Sunday the choir and the church's history make it worth a visit.

10 *Stepping Out* Noon

The boundary between parade and spectator in New Orleans is always a blurry one, especially when the second line comes down the street. Every Sunday from the fall through spring, neighborhood associations known as Social Aid and Pleasure Clubs,

formed long ago as insurance and financial assistance pools, take turns putting on parades. The brass band and the club's dancers march out front, followed by everyone else—the "second line." That is, when you go, you will be in the second line. The parades usually last a few hours, and you can hop in at any point. Check the website of radio station WWOZ (wwoz.org/new-orleans-community/inthestreet) for the route.

ABOVE Kermit Ruffins, a jazz trumpeter and singer, is a local favorite. Music is plentiful here; check the listings to see where the top acts are playing.

OPPOSITE Above-ground graves at St. Louis Cemetery No. 1. Tour here to see tombs of mayors, gamblers, jazz musicians, and heroes of the War of 1812.

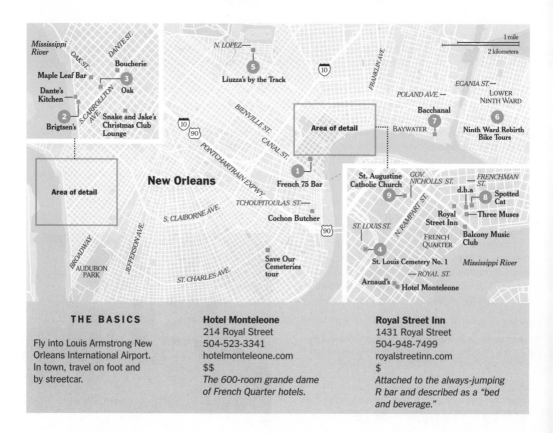

THE BASICS

Fly into Louis Armstrong New Orleans International Airport. In town, travel on foot and by streetcar.

Hotel Monteleone
214 Royal Street
504-523-3341
hotelmonteleone.com
$$
The 600-room grande dame of French Quarter hotels.

Royal Street Inn
1431 Royal Street
504-948-7499
royalstreetinn.com
$
Attached to the always-jumping R bar and described as a "bed and beverage."

Baltimore

"You can look far and wide, but you'll never discover a stranger city with such extreme style," John Waters once noted about his hometown. Maybe that's why Baltimore's trumpeted glass-and-steel Inner Harbor development, with its chain restaurants, neon-loud amusements, and brand-name shopping, feels so counterintuitive as a symbol for the city. But walk in any direction, and the city's charm reasserts itself. Indeed, Baltimore's best draws tend to be left-of-center: offbeat theater, grandly decrepit neighborhoods on the cusp of gentrification, a world-class museum devoted to outsider art, and a dive-bar culture that must be one of the nation's finest. — BY CHARLY WILDER

FRIDAY

1 *Divine Inspiration* 3 p.m.

There may be no better introduction to Baltimore than the extraordinary **American Visionary Art Museum** (800 Key Highway; 410-244-1900; avam.org), or AVAM, which is devoted to the work of self-taught and outsider artists. AVAM's collection ranges in scale and tenor from a 10-foot mirror-plated sculpture of the drag icon Divine to *Recovery*, a moving self-portrait of an anonymous British mental patient that was carved from an apple tree trunk before he committed suicide in his 30s.

2 *Crab Happy* 7 p.m.

Call it the great democratizer: it's hard to find a Baltimorean who doesn't enjoy wielding the mallet. **L.P. Steamers** (1100 East Fort Avenue; 410-576-9294; lpsteamers.com; $$) is a purist's crab house. Its waiters dump buckets of fresh-caught Old Bay-coated steamed crab onto brown paper for diners to whack, smash, pry, shuck, and suck out the tender white meat. For two people, a dozen mediums and a pitcher of Baltimore's signature beer, National Bohemian a.k.a. Natty Boh, should do the trick. Snag a table on the restaurant's upper deck and watch the sun set over one of Baltimore's best views.

OPPOSITE "The Avenue" in Hampden, whose pink flamingoes, beehived ladies, and classic cars were made famous through the films of John Waters.

RIGHT The Inner Harbor, where recreation reigns.

3 *Arts and Drafts* 10 p.m.

Several arts districts have popped up in Baltimore in the past decade. The most successful has been **Station North**, the downtown area inhabited by artists, actors, and students (and dropouts) from the nearby Maryland Institute College of Art and University of Baltimore. You can see an art show, hear local sounds, or catch a screening at the **Metro Gallery** (1700 North Charles Street; 410-244-0899; themetrogallery. net) or the **Windup Space** (12 West North Avenue; 410-244-8855; thewindupspace.com). Yet when it comes to night life, what Baltimore does best is the dive bar. There may be none better than **Club Charles** (1724 North Charles Street; 410-727-8815; clubcharles.us), a grimy, kitschy little joint with a masterful jukebox and regulars like the electro-pop ringleader Dan Deacon.

SATURDAY

4 *Greasy Spoon* 9 a.m.

Grab breakfast at **Pete's Grille** (3130 Greenmount Avenue; 410-467-7698; $), a grits-and-grease diner in a rundown neighborhood dotted with liquor stores, Chinese takeout joints, and the occasional boarded-up row house. At the counter, cops, dockworkers, students, and professionals sidle up, while career waitresses trade barbs with regulars (the Olympian Michael Phelps sometimes among them) and sling plates of fried eggs, home fries, and blueberry pancakes touted as the best in town.

able (last tour: 2:30). The top floor also houses a museum with displays related to the building and a colored-glass bottle collection.

5 *Beside the Point* 11 a.m.

Walk breakfast off with a trip to **Normals** (425 East 31st Street; 410-243-6888; normals.com), a trove of used records and books. From there, head to **Fells Point**, a historic waterfront neighborhood that has transformed over the years from salty fisherman's quarter to touristy night-life district and emerging hub for boutique shopping. Shops include **Poppy and Stella** (728 South Broadway; 410-522-1970; poppyandstella.com), a girlie emporium of accessories and shoes, and **Katwalk Boutique** (1709 Aliceanna Street; 410-669-0600), a cultish clothing boutique.

6 *Patrician Beans* 1 p.m.

Board the free shuttle bus service with the jocular title Charm City Circulator (charmcitycirculator.com; 410-350-0456) and get off in Mount Vernon, an area filled with leafy blocks of 19th-century row houses. Stroll around the original Washington Monument, completed in 1829 when the neighborhood was home to the city's most fashionable families. The Mount Vernon Place Conservancy (mvpconservancy.org) oversees the monument and organizes free concerts, screenings, and other events in the square. For a snack, stop at locavore hangout **Milk & Honey Market** (816 Cathedral Street; 410-685-6455; milkandhoneybaltimore.com; $), an organic cafe and deli.

7 *Open House* 2:30 p.m.

Go west to see works by some of Baltimore's best emerging art-makers. A 117-acre swath of downtown's west side is a state-designated arts district. Among the galleries is the **Bromo Seltzer Arts Tower** (21 South Eutaw Street; 443-874-3596; bromoseltzertower.com), the tallest building in the city when it went up in 1911, now converted to studios for photographers, architects, jewelers, and visual artists who open their studios to the public and display their work in common areas. The building is open to the public on Saturdays from 11 a.m. to 4 p.m. The original 20-ton Bromo-Selzer bottle is no longer there, but tours of the original clock tower are avail-

8 *Exotic Avenue* 6 p.m.

The northwest neighborhood of **Hampden**, traditionally working-class, is now shared by its original demographic and a younger, arty set. Hampden's quirky boutique-lined main drag, a part of 36th Street called "The Avenue," is packed with galleries and shops selling vintage clothing, books, and eccentric home décor. This is also where you'll see 20-somethings in jeans and T-shirts sharing cigarettes with "Hons," the brassy women with 10-ton beehive hairdos and cat's-eye glasses now deified as Hampden's central characters. (They're celebrated every June in Baltimore's "Honfest.") For dinner, book ahead or join the community table at a local favorite, the **Food Market** (1017 West 36th Street; 410-366-0606; thefoodmarketbaltimore.com), a grocery-turned-eatery where the open kitchen dishes out new takes on traditional Americana such as the shrimp with Andouille sausage, Cheddar grits, and Cajun thyme cream. The cocktails also warrant a thumbs up.

9 *Little Theaters* 8 p.m.

This is a city of small, feisty theater companies, like the **Vagabond Players** (806 South Broadway; 410-563-9135; vagabondplayers.org), founded in 1916 and perhaps America's oldest continuously operating community theater. In 2005, 10 University of Colorado students chose Baltimore to found a

troupe; today their **Single Carrot Theatre** (2600 North Howard Street; 443-844-9253; singlecarrot.com) stages innovative works by young playwrights.

SUNDAY

10 *The Tell-Tale House* 11 a.m.

Yet another neighborhood to undergo renewal is **Hamilton**, a northeastern area with bakeries, coffee shops, and restaurants opening along once-depressed Harford Road. Slide into a seat at the **Silver Queen Café** (5429 Harford Road; 443-345-2020; silverqueencafe.com) for a breakfast sandwich of eggs, Cheddar, and grits or strawberry, blueberry, or chocolate chip pancakes. Or, for a grittier

farewell, go west to the **Edgar Allan Poe House and Museum** (203 North Amity Street; 410-462-1763; poeinbaltimore.org), a tiny, three-story brick duplex where, in the 1830s, Poe wrote some of his chilling early stories and poems. The house, once surrounded by countryside, now stands among blighted homes and weeded lots — Poe meets *The Wire*. A fitting place to bear witness to the outsider's Baltimore, past and present.

OPPOSITE ABOVE A Dalton Ghetti pencil-tip sculpture at the American Visionary Art Museum.

OPPOSITE BELOW Night life at the Windup Space, which hosts screenings and art shows as well as music and dancing.

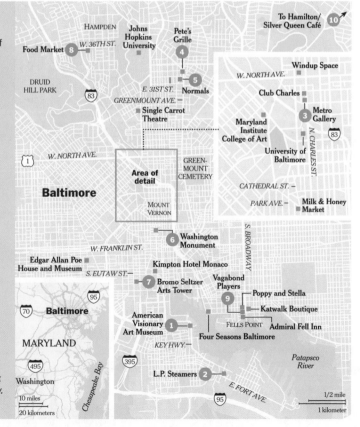

THE BASICS

By car, Baltimore is three and a half hours from New York and less than an hour from Washington. Amtrak trains are faster. Flights land at Thurgood Marshall BWI Airport.

Kimpton Hotel Monaco
2 North Charles Street
monaco-baltimore.com
443-692-6170
$$
Marble and Tiffany stained glass in a downtown location close to the harbor.

Four Seasons Baltimore
200 International Drive
410-576-5800
fourseasons.com/baltimore
$$$$
One of the luxury hotels clustered around the Inner Harbor.

Admiral Fell Inn
888 South Broadway
410-522-7380
harbormagic.com
$$$
Eighty rooms in a group of red-brick buildings from the late 18th century.

Jackson

When movie crews descended on Jackson in 2010 to film The Help, *based on Kathryn Stockett's novel about the city's maids in the 1960s, it didn't take much to recreate the scenes necessary for cinematic time travel. Local loyalty has assured the survival of mom-and-pop stores like Brent's Drugs, where you can still sit at the counter and order a chocolate malt. Time rewinds as you savor a dish of peach cobbler at one of the city's beloved dining spots. The city's population of fewer than 200,000 still gives it the familiarity of a big country town, and Mississippians' old-fashioned charm is no rumor. But much has changed as well. Today Jackson calls itself the City with Soul, and top-notch restaurants and music venues mixing many genres have joined soul-food establishments to create a relaxed marriage of old and new. — BY LAURA TILLMAN*

FRIDAY

1 *A Writer's Refuge* 3 p.m.

A stroll through the rolling hills of the historic Belhaven neighborhood is the perfect introduction to Jackson's laid-back mood. Join the couples power-walking past bungalow-style houses, parks, and front-yard vegetable gardens; and make your way to **Eudora Welty House** (1119 Pinehurst Street; 601-353-7762; eudorawelty.org), the preserved home of the Pulitzer Prize-winning author, who died in 2001. Born in Jackson, Welty lived here most of her life and made Mississippi her subject. You can tour the house, which is arranged to look as it did in the 1980s, when she was still writing and the couches, coffee tables, and chairs were stacked high with books. Outside again, take a lap around the campus of **Belhaven University** (1500 Peachtree Street; belhaven.edu) and breathe in the scent of magnolia.

2 *Living History* 4 p.m.

When Mississippi's "new" **Capitol** building (the first had architectural flaws and still stands a few blocks away) opened in 1903, electricity was an uncommon luxury in this state. That may be why the architect, Theodore Link, installed over 4,700 decorative light bulbs throughout the Beaux Arts-style building (400 High Street; 601-359-3114). On the night of the grand opening, 20,000 spectators gathered in the pouring rain outside the brightly illuminated building.

The stories associated with the Capitol provide a candid portrait of the state's history, and you can learn about more of them in a self-guided tour (or come earlier in the day for a free guided tour). The Confederate battle emblem still occupies a corner of the state's banner, and the face of the Choctaw Indian Theresa Whitecloud is at the top of the Senate rotunda.

3 *Sophisticated Southern* 7 p.m.

Jackson's historic downtown is primarily a place of business, active in the daytime, but a few ambitious restaurants are now challenging the after-dark quiet. One impressive entrant is **Parlor Market** (115 West Capitol Street; 601-360-0090; parlormarket. com; $$), which serves playful interpretations of classic Southern fare. One memorable entree on the frequently changing menu combined lamb ragout with squid ink cavatelli, lady peas, preserved lemon, pickled chilies, and mint.

4 *Honky Tonk* 9 p.m.

Head over to **Hal and Mal's** (200 Commerce Street; 601-948-0888; halandmals.com), a bar and

OPPOSITE Over 4,700 light bulbs decorate the Mississippi State Capitol, built when electricity was still a luxury.

BELOW Canned goods at the Mississippi Farmers' Market.

restaurant not far from Parlor Market. Started by a pair of brothers, Hal and Malcolm White, it has been bringing blues, jazz, and country bands to Jackson since 1985. Pictures of past acts plaster the walls, along with musicians' signatures. The bar keeps regional beers on draft.

SATURDAY

5 *A Venerable Survivor* 9 a.m.

Farish Street was the center of African-American life in Jackson during the Jim Crow era, but in recent decades the street has nearly emptied out, with a few notable exceptions. The **Big Apple Inn** (509 North Farish Street; 601-354-9371; $), which opened more than 70 years ago, is one of a handful of businesses to survive the exodus. The limited menu includes smoked sausage sandwiches and pig ear sandwiches. For breakfast, ask the cook to add an egg. Medgar Evers, the Jackson civil rights activist who in 1963 was shot in his driveway by a white supremacist, had a small office above the Big Apple Inn when he was a field officer for the N.A.A.C.P. He held meetings here with Freedom Riders, one of whom was the owner's mother. Little seems to have changed inside the restaurant since those days. A gleaming soda vending machine nods to the present, and after you taste the homemade hot sauce, you'll be grateful for this allowance.

6 *Taste of the Country* 10 a.m.

The **Mississippi Farmers' Market**, held on Saturdays at the Mississippi Fairgrounds (929 High Street; 601-354-6573), is a taste of the rest of this largely rural state. Try the hand-churned goat's milk ice cream, and buy some Mississippi-made soap, cutting boards, and cornmeal to take home.

ABOVE Preparations at the Big Apple Inn, a 70-year-old restaurant. The menu is limited, and the specialties of the house include pig ear sandwiches.

7 *Mississippi Greats* Noon

Lemuria Books (4465 I-55 North; 601-366-7619; lemuriabooks.com), a Jackson institution, has changed locations a few times since it opened in the 1970s. Don't be put off by its current site, in a shopping complex next to the highway. Once you step inside the cozy store, pick out a book, and sink into one of the plush, timeworn couches, you'll begin to feel Lemuria's magic. There are sections on everything Southern, from cooking to gardening, literature to religion. Lemuria also has a room of rare, signed books; seeing William Faulkner's signature on a limited-edition print is humbling.

8 *Fondren Finds* 3:30 p.m.

In Fondren, Jackson's hub of creative, locally owned businesses, the more you look, the more you find. At **Sneaky Beans** (2914 North State Street; 601-487-6349), a good place to stop for a cup of coffee or a craft beer, posters advertise concerts and events around town. Check out **Sal & Mookies** (565 Taylor Street; 601-368-1919) for a slice of pizza and ice cream, or **Brent's Drugs** (655 Duling Avenue; 601-366-3427), the throwback luncheonette that served as a setting in *The Help*. Next explore the shops inside the mixed-use building **Fondren Corner** (2906 North State Street) for clothing, jewelry, and gifts. Leave some time to sit on the patio at **Babalu** (622 Duling Avenue; 601-366-5757; babalums.com) and sip a Cat 5 — similar to a mojito, but with Mississippi-made Cathead Vodka instead of rum.

9 *At the Drive-In* 7 p.m.

Walker's Drive-In (3016 North State Street; 601-982-2633; walkersdrivein.com; $$$) isn't really a drive-in. It's a beloved restaurant, considered by many to serve the best meals in Jackson, and it manages to make retro diner décor elegant. At lunch, patrons crowd the booths for the redfish sandwiches, sweet potato fries, and salads. During dinner, the menu changes entirely, with entrees like lamb with mint-tzatziki sauce and appetizers like fried oysters with warm Brie and apple slaw.

10 *Positively Farish Street* 9 p.m.

Housed in a former gas station and named for a legendary Farish Street businessman, **F. Jones Corner**

(303 North Farish Street; 601-983-1148; fjonescorner. com) reincarnates the juke joint, with soul food and live music and a sign painted on the wall that says, "No Black. No White. Just the Blues." Musicians have been known to keep playing here until dawn.

SUNDAY

11 *Back to School* 1:30 p.m.

Though the locals may dispute that an oyster from anywhere but the Gulf just doesn't measure up, **Saltine** (622 Duling Avenue; 601-982-2899; jackson. saltinerestaurant.com; $$) takes a cosmopolitan approach, welcoming bivalves from the East and West Coasts, Canada, and New Zealand. In a bright, airy space in the corner of an old schoolhouse (complete with vintage lockers and repurposed chalkboards) in Fondren, Saltine channels Mississippi and Louisiana cuisine with a worldly touch. Brunch might include wood-fired Gulf oysters with citrus butter, bacon and quail egg. You could choose a side of buttermilk drop biscuits with bacon cream gravy, order a mimosa — and plan on a light supper.

ABOVE At Walker's Drive-In, where the food is some of the finest in Jackson, the décor is retro and so is the name. It isn't a drive-in and has an elegant look.

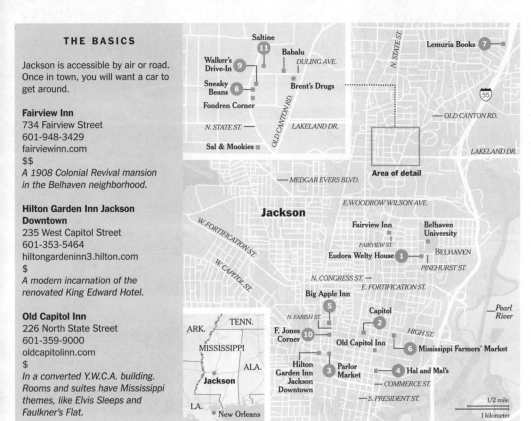

THE BASICS

Jackson is accessible by air or road. Once in town, you will want a car to get around.

Fairview Inn
734 Fairview Street
601-948-3429
fairviewinn.com
$$
A 1908 Colonial Revival mansion in the Belhaven neighborhood.

Hilton Garden Inn Jackson Downtown
235 West Capitol Street
601-353-5464
hiltongardeninn3.hilton.com
$
A modern incarnation of the renovated King Edward Hotel.

Old Capitol Inn
226 North State Street
601-359-9000
oldcapitolinn.com
$
In a converted Y.W.C.A. building. Rooms and suites have Mississippi themes, like Elvis Sleeps and Faulkner's Flat.

Asheville

Asheville calls itself the Land of the Sky, but that barely scratches the surface. This city of just over 89,000 people, nestled between the Blue Ridge and Great Smoky Mountains, is also the land of the arts, the outdoors, progressive politics, and terrific cuisine, as well as a land of colorful history distinguished by Gilded Age opulence and literary inspiration. It all unfolds against the majestic backdrop of the Blue Ridge Mountains and close to the scenic Blue Ridge Parkway. — BY JEREMY EGNER

FRIDAY

1 *He Couldn't Go Home Again* 1 p.m.

Fun fact: Asheville inspired one of the most famous phrases in American literature. Thomas Wolfe, who was from Asheville, had inspired hometown outrage with barely veiled depictions of actual Ashevillians in his 1929 novel *Look Homeward, Angel.* (The local library declined to carry it for years even as it became an American classic.) Wolfe died in 1938 but left a manuscript behind. In it, the parallels surfaced again: a fictional novelist who had written a similar book becomes a hometown pariah. Hence the title of Wolfe's posthumously published novel, *You Can't Go Home Again.* Eventually, though too late for Wolfe himself, all was forgiven. Now his former home on Spruce Street is part of the **Thomas Wolfe Memorial** (52 North Market Street; wolfememorial. com), a small but fascinating museum. Literature fans may also want to drive past the Highland Hospital site (75 Zillicoa Street) where F. Scott Fitzgerald's wife, Zelda, died in a sanitarium fire in 1948 — or even book the Fitzgerald Suite at the **Grove Park Inn** (290 Macon Avenue), where Scott stayed during his visits to her.

2 *Book Town* 3 p.m

Follow up on the literary theme with a trip to one of Asheville's intriguing downtown bookstores. **Malaprop's** (55 Haywood Street; malaprops.com) is a wonderfully atmospheric bookshop and cafe. **Battery Park Book Exchange & Champagne Bar** (1 Page Avenue; batteryparkbookexchange.com), an elegant

OPPOSITE Paths crisscross in the botanical patchwork of the Quilt Garden at the North Carolina Arboretum.

spot in the Grove Arcade, will let you sip wine while examining its stock of rare and limited-edition books.

3 *South Slope Suds* 4 p.m.

Asheville also calls itself Beer City USA, and it's hard to argue the point. Many of the best small breweries are within a few blocks of one another on the South Slope. **Burial Beer Co.** (40 Collier Avenue; burialbeer.com), in a former auto repair shop, makes terrific Belgian ales. **Green Man** (27 Buxton Avenue; greenmanbrewery.com) specializes in English styles — opt for the original taproom over the more touristy "Green Mansion" next door. The **Funkatorium** (147 Coxe Avenue; wickedweedbrewing.com) focuses on sours that range from majestic to mouth-twisting. Keep exploring, and you'll find more.

4 *Farm to Chef to You* 7 p.m.

Asheville has been doing farm-to-table since before it was a marketing point. A reliable stalwart is **Bouchon** (62 North Lexington Avenue; ashevillebouchon.com; $$), where the theme is French comfort food. Sophisticated takes on familiar dishes like beef Bourguignon and chicken cordon bleu, accompanied by French wines, keep the customers coming back. The desserts include chocolate mousse, presented on the menu with the comment, "Is this a French bistro or what?" For a nightcap, move on to **Sovereign Remedies** (29 North Market Street; sovereignremedies.com), a 21st-century cocktail bar in a former early 20th-century pharmacy.

SATURDAY

5 *Take a Hike* 9 a.m.

Western North Carolina is a hiker's paradise, with Mount Pisgah, Sam Knob and waterfalls all within an hour's drive of Asheville. But you don't have to go so far to get your nature fix. The **North Carolina Arboretum** (100 Frederick Law Olmsted Way; ncarboretum.org), roughly 10 miles southwest of downtown, packs lush seasonal gardens, actual babbling brooks, and miles of trails into 434 acres. Guided hikes are available from the rustic-but-refined visitors center, but the best thing about managed wilderness is the ability to get lost without getting, you know, actually lost.

6 *First, the Flour* Noon

Some may say that pizza is all about the crust, but **All Souls Pizza** (175 Clingman Avenue; allsoulspizza.com; $$) goes one better, taking the emphasis all the way back to the flour the crust is made from. All Souls grinds locally raised specialty grains in its own custom stone mill, preserving natural oils in the grain that most commercial millers eliminate to enhance the shelf life of flour. The result is a distinctive crust that has attracted a following, and the exceptional toppings (one pie had eggplant, goat cheese, capers, and sun gold tomatoes) aren't bad, either.

7 *River & Arts* 2 p.m.

In the mid-1980s artists began transforming more than 20 industrial buildings along a one-mile stretch of the French Broad River into work and display spaces. The **River Arts District** (riverartsdistrict.com) now hosts some 200 artists, most working in studios open to visitors. Expect to find paintings, textiles, jewelry, and more. Many of the artists clus-

ter at **Curve Studios & Garden** (6, 9, and 12 Riverside Drive; curvestudiosnc.com). Look here for beautifully crafted pottery, a North Carolina specialty.

8 *River & Arts & Snacks* 4 p.m.

Wind down at **Wedge Brewing Co.** (37 Paynes Way, Suite 001; wedgebrewing.com), specializing in local beers (Iron Rail IPA is the go-to), or a snack at the industrial chic **Bull and Beggar** (37 Paynes Way, Suite 007; thebullandbeggar.com), where you might find rabbit rillettes or grilled eggplant with yogurt and mint.

9 *Toast the Sunset* 6 p.m.

Despite its name, **SkyBar** (18 Battery Park Avenue; skybar.worldcoffeecafe.com) is essentially a glorified fire escape—three steel platforms, with rails and tables, attached to the Beaux-Arts Flatiron Building. Most evenings those terraces fill up with patrons watching the sun set over the mountains as servers bring beverages conventional (local beers) and less so (cocktails in combinations like rye whiskey, gingersnap liqueur, and vanilla tea). Enter at the World Coffee Cafe on Battery Park Avenue and wait for the antique elevator. The **Sunset Cocktail Terrace** at the Grove Park Inn (290 Macon Avenue; omnihotels.com/hotels/asheville-grove-park) also offers a picturesque end to the day.

10 *Westward Ho* 8 p.m.

Once shabby, West Asheville has become a dining destination. Many credit the **Admiral** (400 Haywood Road; theadmiralasheville.com; $$$), a gastropub hiding behind a cinderblock exterior, with kick-starting this evolution. Its menus change regularly and pursue interesting combinations, like quails with

pepper fricasee, parsley, and nasturtium. The Admiral is still the neighborhood's signature restaurant, but it's now hardly alone. **Nine Mile** (751 Haywood Road; ninemileasheville.com), for example, is a popular Jamaican cafe with inspired jerk dishes, salads, and lots of vegan options.

SUNDAY

11 *Pretend You're a Vanderbilt* 9 a.m.

Asheville's most renowned landmark, the **Biltmore Estate** (1 Lodge Street; biltmore.com) is expensive to visit and often crowded. But it's also magnificent. The main house, a 250-room limestone marvel, was designed by Richard Morris Hunt for George Washington Vanderbilt, who fell in love with the mountainous countryside and, in true Vanderbilt fashion, bought 125,000 acres of it. (The estate now stands at around 8,000 acres.) Completed in 1895, the

house is the largest private residence in the United States, with over four acres of floor space. In addition to viewing the 10,000-volume library, cavernous banquet hall, and other remnants of Gilded Age luxury, visitors can see 16th-century tapestries and works by Sargent and Renoir. The elaborate gardens were designed by Frederick Law Olmsted.

OPPOSITE TOP A studio in the River Arts District, home to 200 artists.

OPPOSITE BOTTOM All Souls Pizza.

ABOVE Working artists cluster at Curve Studios.

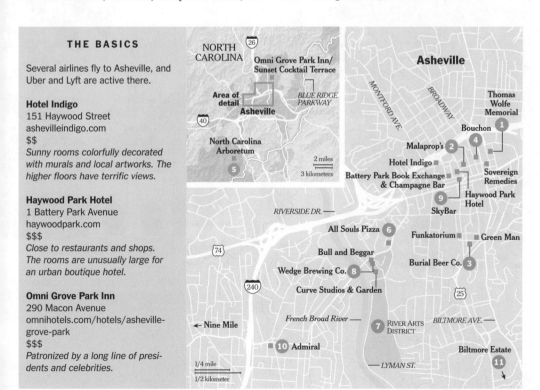

THE BASICS

Several airlines fly to Asheville, and Uber and Lyft are active there.

Hotel Indigo
151 Haywood Street
ashevilleindigo.com
$$
Sunny rooms colorfully decorated with murals and local artworks. The higher floors have terrific views.

Haywood Park Hotel
1 Battery Park Avenue
haywoodpark.com
$$$
Close to restaurants and shops. The rooms are unusually large for an urban boutique hotel.

Omni Grove Park Inn
290 Macon Avenue
omnihotels.com/hotels/asheville-grove-park
$$$
Patronized by a long line of presidents and celebrities.

NORTH CAROLINA
Omni Grove Park Inn/ Sunset Cocktail Terrace
Area of detail
Asheville
BLUE RIDGE PARKWAY
North Carolina Arboretum
2 miles
3 kilometers

Asheville
MONTFORD AVE.
BROADWAY
Thomas Wolfe Memorial
Bouchon **1**
Malaprop's **2**
4
Hotel Indigo
Battery Park Book Exchange & Champagne Bar
Sovereign Remedies
9 Haywood Park Hotel
RIVERSIDE DR.
SkyBar
All Souls Pizza **6**
Funkatorium
Green Man
Bull and Beggar
Burial Beer Co. **3**
Wedge Brewing Co. **8**
Curve Studios & Garden
French Broad River
7 RIVER ARTS DISTRICT
BILTMORE AVE.
← Nine Mile
10 Admiral
LYMAN ST.
Biltmore Estate **11**
1/4 mile
1/2 kilometer
5

Raleigh-Durham

Tell North Carolinians you're heading to the Raleigh-Durham area, locally called the Research Triangle or just the Triangle, and they will probably ask, "Which school are you visiting?" Yet the close-knit cities of Raleigh, Durham, and Chapel Hill, North Carolina, are marked by more than college bars and basketball fans. Visitors not bound for Duke (Durham), the University of North Carolina (Chapel Hill), or North Carolina State (Raleigh) come to see buzz-worthy bands, dine on food from painstaking chefs, and explore outdoor art. From its biscuits to its boutiques, the Triangle occupies a happy place between slow-paced Southern charm and urban cool.
— BY J. J. GOODE AND INGRID K. WILLIAMS

FRIDAY

1 *Art Inside Out* 2 p.m.

The collection at the **North Carolina Museum of Art** (2110 Blue Ridge Road, Raleigh; 919-839-6262; ncartmuseum.org) is on the small side by major museum standards, and that size has its advantages. The lack of tour bus crowds means unfettered access to the museum's Old Masters and contemporary heavyweights like Anselm Kiefer. The real treat is the adjacent Museum Park, more than 164 acres of open fields and woodlands punctuated by environmental art like *Cloud Chamber*, a stone hut that acts as a camera obscura with a small hole in the roof projecting inverted, otherworldly images of slowly swaying trees on the floor and walls.

2 *New Wares* 4 p.m.

New restaurants, shops, and galleries have transformed Raleigh's once declining **Warehouse District** (facebook.com/RaleighWarehouseDistrict), several blocks of old red-brick buildings a short stroll from the North Carolina Capitol Building (which is easily spotted because of its dome). Check out the exhibitions at the contemporary art museum **CAM Raleigh** (409 West Martin Street; 919-261-5920; camraleigh. org), and then drop in at **Designbox** (307 West Martin

Street; 919-834-3552; designbox.us), where several working artists and craftsmen display and sell their work. At **Videri Chocolate Factory** (327 West Davie Street; 919-755-5053; viderichocolatefactory.com), you can watch the signature product being made before buying some to take home. There's more visible craftsmanship at the **Curatory at the Raleigh Denim Workshop** (319 West Martin Street; 919-917-8969; raleighdenimworkshop.com), where you can see workers at vintage sewing machines and buy the company's high-end blue jeans as well as jewelry, accessories, and other well-made clothing.

3 *Going for the Whole Hog* 6 p.m.

Small towns and backroads, not cities, are usually thought to have a monopoly on great barbecue. What makes **The Pit** (328 West Davie Street, Raleigh; 919-890-4500; thepit-raleigh.com; $) a striking exception is the masterly practice here of the eastern North Carolina art form of whole hog cooking. Instead of trekking 100 miles to porcine capitals like Ayden and Lexington, you can dig into pilgrimage-worthy chopped or pulled pork — made from pigs purchased from family farms and cooked for 10 to 14 hours over coals and hickory or oak. Your chopped barbecued pork plate comes with two sides and greaseless hush puppies.

4 *Night at the Theater* 8 p.m.

Raleigh is not only the state's political capital, but its cultural capital as well, home of the North Carolina Symphony, North Carolina Ballet, and Theatre Raleigh. To find a performance, check

OPPOSITE The neo-Gothic Duke Chapel, a symbol of both Duke University and Durham.

RIGHT University of North Carolina basketball fans.

the schedule of the **Duke Energy Center for the Performing Arts** (2 East South Street; 919-996-8700; dukeenergycenterraleigh.com). Or drive to Durham for an event at the sparkling glass **Durham Performing Arts Center** (123 Vivian Street; 919-680-2787; dpacnc.com). You might catch a show right off Broadway or a concert — performers have included Smokey Robinson, Diana Krall, and B. B. King.

SATURDAY

5 *Homage to the Home Team* 10 a.m.

The Triangle is college basketball country, home to two of the winningest teams — Duke and North Carolina — and some of the most rabid fans in college sports history. Pay your respects by visiting the **Carolina Basketball Museum** (450 Skipper Bowles Drive, Chapel Hill; 919-962-6000; goheels.com/news/2017/6/26/general-carolina-basketball-museum.aspx) on the University of North Carolina Campus. The museum is next door to the Dean E. Smith Center arena, named for the coach who was famed for developing championship teams. Interactive exhibits replay great moments in the university's basketball history, and the Tar Heel memorabilia include Coach Smith's typewritten notes suggesting areas for improvement to a young player named Michael Jordan.

6 *Campus Gothic* Noon

The **Duke University** campus (duke.edu) is the quintessential collegiate setting, with grassy quads and lovely neo-Gothic buildings lorded over by the 210-foot spire of the stately stone Duke Chapel, which despite its modest name is an American version of a richly decorated European cathedral. Nearby are the **Sarah P. Duke Gardens** (420 Anderson Street, Durham; 919-684-3698; gardens.duke.edu), 55 meticulously maintained acres bursting with diverse flora. From the gardens, it's not far to the **Nasher Museum of Art** (2001 Campus Drive; 919-684-5135; nasher.duke.edu), a cluster of modern, monolithic structures that host impressive exhibitions. Find the Nasher's

cafe, a popular spot for weekend brunch (a reservation is a good idea).

7 *Take-Home Test* 3 p.m.

Start your souvenir shopping (or just plain shopping) in downtown Durham at **Brightleaf Square** (Main and Gregson Streets; historicbrightleaf.com), where shops occupy former tobacco warehouses. Then find some take-home gifts for your family chef, or yourself, at **Southern Season** (201 South Estes Drive, Chapel Hill; 919-929-7133; southernseason.com), a culinary superstore with all kinds of fresh foods and kitchen gadgets. Winding through the crowded aisles is half the fun.

8 *Back-Room Bites* 7 p.m.

Quiz locals about the best spot for a memorable meal, and chances are they'll direct you to the dining room of **Lantern** (423 West Franklin Street, Chapel Hill; 919-969-8846; lanternrestaurant.com; $$$), an Asian-inflected restaurant owned by the James Beard Award-winning chef Andrea Reusing. That answer gets half-credit. Full credit requires a stipulation that you seek out the restaurant's hidden back-room bar, where the same farm-focused menu is served in a more seductive space lit by votives and red paper lanterns. When ordering, consider the smaller plates — they tend to be the highlights.

9 *Big Bands* 10 p.m.

Nirvana played at the **Cat's Cradle** (300 East Main Street, Carrboro; 919-967-9053; catscradle.com) for the first time in pre-*Nevermind* 1990 to about 100 people. A year later Pearl Jam played to three times as many, filling just half the standing-room-only space. Today the Cradle, just a mile from downtown Chapel Hill, hosts acts you may be hearing more about tomorrow for low ticket prices that seem more like yesterday.

SUNDAY

10 *Drive-Thru Biscuits* 10 a.m.

There are several places in Chapel Hill that serve a distinguished Southern breakfast for an easy-to-swallow price. Diners linger over gravy-smothered pork chops and eggs at **Mama Dip's** (408 West Rose-

mary Street, Chapel Hill; 919-942-5837) and peerless shrimp and grits at **Crook's Corner** (610 West Franklin Street, Chapel Hill; 919-929-7643; crookscorner. com). But for a morning meal on the go that's equally unforgettable, roll up to the drive-through window at **Sunrise Biscuit Kitchen** (1305 East Franklin Street, Chapel Hill; 919-933-1324; sunrisebiscuits.com; $), where the iced tea is tooth-achingly sweet and the main course is fluffy, buttery, and filled with salty country ham or crisp fried chicken.

11 *Nature's Way* 11 a.m.

The **North Carolina Botanical Garden** (100 Old Mason Farm Road, Chapel Hill; 919-962-0522; ncbg. unc.edu) is popular for weddings, but the peaceful grounds are worth visiting even without an occasion

to celebrate. Follow winding paths through landscaped gardens focused on the diverse flora of the Carolinas, and past a giant chessboard with toddler-size pieces fashioned from recycled metal. Then hike the Piedmont Nature Trails in the surrounding woods.

OPPOSITE A fresh batch at Sunrise Biscuit Kitchen.

ABOVE Museum Park is 164 acres of woodland, grassy fields, and outdoor artworks adjacent to the North Carolina Museum of Art in Raleigh.

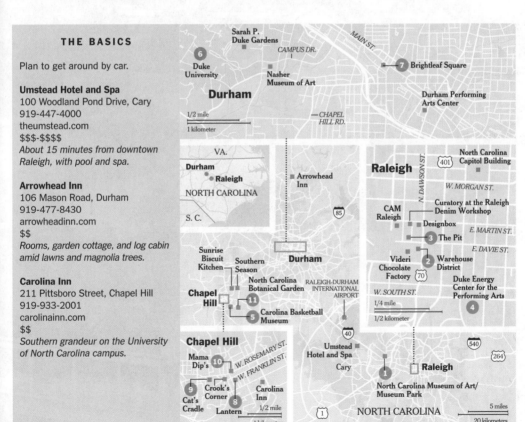

THE BASICS

Plan to get around by car.

Umstead Hotel and Spa
100 Woodland Pond Drive, Cary
919-447-4000
theumstead.com
$$$-$$$$
About 15 minutes from downtown Raleigh, with pool and spa.

Arrowhead Inn
106 Mason Road, Durham
919-477-8430
arrowheadinn.com
$$
Rooms, garden cottage, and log cabin amid lawns and magnolia trees.

Carolina Inn
211 Pittsboro Street, Chapel Hill
919-933-2001
carolinainn.com
$$
Southern grandeur on the University of North Carolina campus.

Map labels:

Sarah P. Duke Gardens · CAMPUS DR. · MAIN ST. · Duke University · 6 · Nasher Museum of Art · 7 Brightleaf Square · **Durham** · Durham Performing Arts Center · 1/2 mile · 1 kilometer · CHAPEL HILL RD.

VA. · **Durham** · Raleigh · Arrowhead Inn · **Raleigh** · 401 · North Carolina Capitol Building · NORTH CAROLINA · W. MORGAN ST. · S. C. · 85 · CAM Raleigh · N. DAWSON ST. · Curatory at the Raleigh Denim Workshop · Designbox · E. MARTIN ST. · 3 The Pit · E. DAVIE ST.

Sunrise Biscuit Kitchen · Southern Season · **Durham** · Videri Chocolate Factory · 70 · 2 Warehouse District · North Carolina Botanical Garden · RALEIGH-DURHAM INTERNATIONAL AIRPORT · Duke Energy Center for the Performing Arts · **Chapel Hill** · W. SOUTH ST. · 1/4 mile · 1/2 kilometer · 4 · 11 · Carolina Basketball Museum · 5

Chapel Hill · Mama Dip's · 10 · W. ROSEMARY ST. · W. FRANKLIN ST. · Umstead Hotel and Spa · Cary · 540 · 264 · 9 · Crook's Corner · Carolina Inn · 1 · **Raleigh** · Cat's Cradle · 8 · Lantern · 1/2 mile · North Carolina Museum of Art/ Museum Park · 1 · NORTH CAROLINA · 5 miles · 1 kilometer · 20 kilometers · 40

Charleston

The world is in love with Charleston: the antebellum mansions, the cobblestone streets, the mild climate that might bring 70-degree days in February, the scent of tea olive trees that floats in the air, the orchestra of church bells that crescendoes on Sunday morning. And in May and June, there's the Spoleto Festival, the city's artistic crown jewel. The city is a genteel and mannerly place with its complex history in plain view: stone hitching posts from the Revolutionary period, the Old Slave Mart on Chalmers Street that's now a museum. In the present, it's also a cultural hotbed and gastro-magnet, with more restaurants than there are pelicans in the harbor. — BY CHRISTIAN L. WRIGHT

FRIDAY

1 *Hit the Ground Strolling* 4 p.m.

Walking in Charleston is one of life's great pleasures, like an oyster roast or England in bloom. Stroll around the southern tip of the downtown peninsula, in the area around **St. Philip's Episcopal Church** (142 Church Street), to see the densely packed, incredibly well-preserved showcase of American history and architecture: Federal, Greek Revival, rowhouses, 18th-century wrought-iron boot scrapers on the sidewalk, and second-story porches (piazzas, in common parlance) on many a wooden "single house."

2 *Sunset and Steeple* 6 p.m.

In a city hugged by rivers, there are surprisingly few places to raise a glass by the water. Order an Aperol spritz at the **Rooftop** bar at the Vendue hotel (19 Vendue Range; thevendue.com) and admire the views of the harbor and the church spires that pock the skyline. A mix of newlyweds, girlfriends in colorful blouses, and office mates out for after-work stress relievers crowds the open-air space to drink in the unobstructed sky and its riot of color as the sun goes down.

3 *Nantucket South* 8 p.m.

The restaurant explosion in Charleston has repurposed defunct buildings, revived ill-used corners, and seduced a number of entrepreneurs "from off." Jesse Sandole — whose family opened the Nantucket fish market in 1978 — has made a success with the whitewashed brick **167 Raw** (289 East Bay Street;

167raw.com; $$). Specials are scrawled on a mirror backed by glossy white tile, otherwise decorated with framed field guides to fish. Young friends gather on high bar stools to share tart ceviche with warm tortilla chips or have a bountiful lobster roll all to themselves.

SATURDAY

4 *Breakfast Uptown* 9 a.m.

On an ungentrified corner near Hampton Park and the Citadel military college, the **Park Cafe** (730 Rutledge Avenue; theparkcafechs.com; $$) is a local favorite — see the young mother dining with her infant at an outdoor table and the flannel-clad fellow with a man bun and MacBook at the tiny bar by the takeout counter — with a breezy white interior, seasonally inspired menu, and modest prices. Breakfast here might include oyster mushroom toast or a "veggie mess" of scrambled eggs, tomato, white Cheddar, and avocado.

5 *Plantation Corridor* 11 a.m.

About 11 miles west of the peninsula, the Ashley River Road (Highway 61) becomes a narrow passage lined by oak, hickory, and palmetto trees, designated a National Scenic Byway and once a boulevard of plantations. Stop at **Drayton Hall** (3380 Ashley River Road; draytonhall.org). At the center of this 18th-century plantation sits a remarkable Georgian-Palladian

OPPOSITE St. Philip's Church and Ravenel Bridge.

BELOW The peaceful salt marsh behind Sullivan's Island.

house, preserved in a state of grand dilapidation. Like the 19th-century Aiken-Rhett House museum downtown, Drayton Hall has been maintained — with its worn paint and faded friezes — rather than restored. An hour's guided tour is like time traveling into the bittersweet, sometimes ugly history of the Lowcountry and its people, both free and enslaved.

6 *Adventures in Shopping* 2 p.m.

Gucci, Lacoste, Anthropologie, and Apple have all moved in downtown, but the independent shops give a better impression of Southern style and sensibility. Browse the shops on the rapidly changing Upper King Street, where you'll find up-to-the-minute boutiques, coastal-chic home décor, books, and artwork. If you'd rather skip the shopping and learn more about the city, visit the **Old Slave Mart Museum** (6 Chalmers Street; 843-958-6467; oldslavemartmuseum.org), in a pre-Civil War slave market building where the first sale, in 1856, was a 20-year-old woman named Lucinda. A mile to the north stands the **Emanuel African Methodist Episcopal Church** (110 Calhoun Street; emanuelamechurch.org), known as Mother Emanuel, which was thrust into the national spotlight by a 2015 mass shooting and then inspired awed admiration for its congregation's resilience.

7 *Dinner at Home* 7:30 p.m.

For an approximation of dinner at the home of a local friend, try **Chez Nous** (6 Payne Court;

cheznouschs.com; $$$$). In an off-the-beaten-path residential neighborhood, this tiny restaurant takes up two floors of a classic single house, renovated to feel as if it's in the South of France. The menu changes daily — two appetizers, two entrees, and two desserts — all worth your attention. One night's selection included endive and walnut salad; pork shank with onion, carrots, and potato purée; and gateau Basque.

8 *Nightcap* 10 p.m.

Nip into the bar at Mike Lata's colossal restaurant in a former bank, the **Ordinary** (544 King Street; eattheordinary.com) for a martini and a couple of East Coast oysters. On another weekend, you might want to come back here for dinner (or make a reservation a month in advance for its sister restaurant, FIG).

SUNDAY

9 *Beach Time* 8 a.m.

Swing by **The Daily** (652 King Street; shopthedaily. com) for gourmet coffee and a pastry. Then drive over the Arthur Ravenel Jr. Bridge — a stunning cable-stayed bridge that crosses the Cooper River — to Sullivan's Island. It will be early enough to park without a permit along a sleepy residential street. Follow one of the wooden catwalks to traverse the marsh and dunes and find the vast expanse of one of the East Coast's great beaches. Sandpipers skitter

along the gullies, springer spaniels chase the waves, and classic old beach houses on stilts share the coastline with newer modern follies.

10 *Olde Times* 10:30 a.m.

Brunch at **McCrady's Tavern** (2 Unity Alley; mccradystavern.com; $-$$) comes with a side of history: George Washington ate here in 1791. While the exposed brick and timber of the circa 1778 Georgian building along busy East Bay look unchanged, the menu is respectfully modern. Try the house's version of Charleston's hallmark she-crab soup—blue crab bisque with vermouth and tarragon—before embarking on a fried pork chop sandwich or the daintier quiche Lorraine.

11 *Art as Sanctuary* 1 p.m.

The **Gibbes Museum of Art** (135 Meeting Street; gibbesmuseum.org) incorporates a handsome

Beaux Arts building in front and a strikingly modern back section, all glass and sunlight, with a public garden that looks plucked from Paris. The Gibbes has open studios, uncluttered galleries, a permanent collection anchored by pieces from the Charleston Renaissance (1915 to 1945), and an illustrious past: In 1936, it was the first museum to exhibit Solomon R. Guggenheim's collection of modern art. (New York's Guggenheim would not open until 1939.)

OPPOSITE The Old Slave Mart, where people were once bought and sold, now tells the story from their point of view.

ABOVE Art and artifacts at the Gibbes Museum of Art.

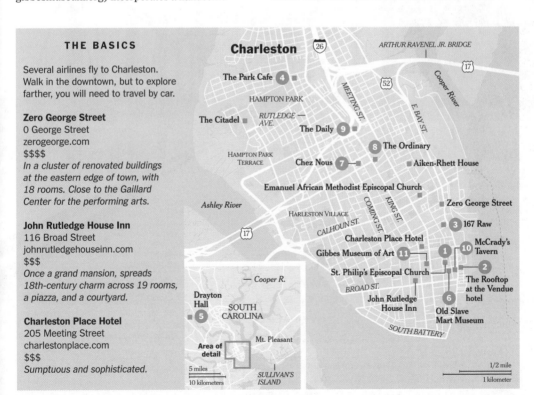

THE BASICS

Charleston

Several airlines fly to Charleston. Walk in the downtown, but to explore farther, you will need to travel by car.

Zero George Street
0 George Street
zerogeorge.com
$$$$
In a cluster of renovated buildings at the eastern edge of town, with 18 rooms. Close to the Gaillard Center for the performing arts.

John Rutledge House Inn
116 Broad Street
johnrutledgehouseinn.com
$$$
Once a grand mansion, spreads 18th-century charm across 19 rooms, a piazza, and a courtyard.

Charleston Place Hotel
205 Meeting Street
charlestonplace.com
$$$
Sumptuous and sophisticated.

The Park Cafe **4**
HAMPTON PARK
The Citadel — RUTLEDGE AVE.
The Daily **9**
HAMPTON PARK TERRACE
Chez Nous **7**
The Ordinary **8**
Aiken-Rhett House
Emanuel African Methodist Episcopal Church
Ashley River
HARLESTON VILLAGE
CALHOUN ST.
COMING ST.
KING ST.
MEETING ST.
E. BAY ST.
Zero George Street
3 167 Raw
Charleston Place Hotel
Gibbes Museum of Art **11**
1 **10** McCrady's Tavern
2
St. Philip's Episcopal Church
BROAD ST.
John Rutledge House Inn
6
The Rooftop at the Vendue hotel
Old Slave Mart Museum
SOUTH BATTERY
ARTHUR RAVENEL JR. BRIDGE
Cooper River

Cooper R.
Drayton Hall **5**
SOUTH CAROLINA
Area of detail
Mt. Pleasant
5 miles
10 kilometers
SULLIVAN'S ISLAND
1/2 mile
1 kilometer

Chattanooga

Nestled against the Tennessee River in the foothills of the Appalachian Mountains, Chattanooga has transformed itself in recent decades from an unassuming valley town to a hyper-clean, tech-savvy, and outdoorsy family destination. Come for a weekend and find hiking trails, rock climbing, museums, one of the finest educational aquariums in the world, and innumerable food and entertainment venues. Nearby are adventures like white-water rafting on the Ocoee River and hang gliding on Lookout Mountain.

— BY COLLEEN CREAMER

FRIDAY

1 *Art Stop* 2 p.m.

Start out slow at the **Hunter Museum of American Art** (10 Bluff View Avenue; huntermuseum.org) in the Bluff View Arts District overlooking the Tennessee River. Its outstanding collection—housed in an early 20th-century mansion, a modern 1970s-era building, and a contemporary structure of steel and glass—represents the sprawling artistic talent of the American soul, from the Colonial period to the present day. Look for paintings by Thomas Cole, Jasper Johns, Robert Rauschenberg and Helen Frankenthaler; photography by Lorna Simpson and Sally Mann; and glass works by Karen LaMonte and Dale Chihuly.

2 *Carb Fill-Up* 5:30 p.m.

There will soon be action verbs in your sentences, so head to nearby **Tony's Pasta Shop & Trattoria** (212 High Street; bluffviewartdistrictchattanooga.com; $), in a former carriage house of a Victorian mansion, for some fancy carb loading that won't break the bank. Just about everything here is made from scratch and time tested. Grab a seat on the upper deck under the wisteria, and scan the menu for dishes like Low Country linguine with sautéed crawfish and mushrooms, or seafood ravioli with dill sauce. Warning: It's all too easy to gorge on the olive oil dip with bits of pecorino, so go easy.

OPPOSITE Pedestrian traffic rules the beloved Walnut Street Bridge, built in 1890 and now a linear park.

RIGHT The Hunter Museum of American Art spans many eras.

3 *Cave Dweller* 9 p.m.

Avoid the tourist crush at Ruby Falls, a 145-foot underground waterfall within Lookout Mountain, by opting for the lesser-known **Ruby Falls Lantern Tour** (rubyfalls.com/special-events/lanterntours). Traversing a maze of corridors, the tours take small groups through the Lookout Mountain Caves to the falls, more than 1,000 feet below the surface. Don't look for rubies; the waterfall is named after the wife of its discoverer. Tour guides explain rock formations and at some point require participants to turn off their lanterns to experience total darkness. The falls itself is illuminated by a spectacular light show.

SATURDAY

4 *Reinventing the Whee* 9 a.m.

Zip lining is fast becoming a bucket list item for many outdoor enthusiasts, and **Zip Stream Aerial Adventure** (1720 South Scenic Highway; rubyfallszip.com), near Ruby Falls, is family-friendly—for those who can reach up to 70 inches and whose weight falls between 60 and 275 pounds. Choose from one of several courses incorporating tunnels, zigzag bridges, and swinging logs with zip lining at the end. Or just fly through the pines in a zip line-only experience.

5 *Fish Fry* Noon

This isn't the time to steer away from fried food. Family-owned **Uncle Larry's** (736 MLK Boulevard; unclelarrysrestaurant.com; $$) fries up fresh catfish to something close to sublime. Tilapia and other fish,

shrimp, and pork chops are on the menu, but it's the delicately battered catfish that keeps the locals coming back. Add on a slice of key lime cake to complete the diet fail—it's worth it.

6 *Guitar Arcadia* 2 p.m.

New to the Chattanooga Choo Choo campus on Station Street and gaining national attention for its rare vintage guitar collection, **Songbirds Guitar Museum** (35 Station Street; museum.songbirds.rocks) is a staggering compilation that appeals to both guitar connoisseurs and those who wouldn't know a Fender from a fender. The self-guided tour takes patrons through the origins of rock 'n' roll, showcasing music history from the 1930s through the 1970s. There is a collection of custom-color Stratocasters and one of the most complete sets of Gibson Firebirds, Telecasters, Esquires, and Jazzmasters in the world. In the evening, consider a visit to the museum's live venue, Songbirds South Stage.

7 *Bike-a-Bout* 3:30 p.m.

Visit bikechattanooga.com, and then find one of the numerous bike stations close to the waterfront. Bike along the river and past the diverse merchants on Broad Street and its environs. Take a nostalgic trip through Americana at the **MoonPie General Store** (429-B Broad Street; moonpie.com), a novelty gift shop where Moon Pies are still made. And at

High Point Climbing and Fitness Gym (219 Broad Street; highpointclimbing.com), watch people scaling the gym's surreal 60-foot-high outdoor climbing wall. Or scramble skyward yourself.

8 *Oysters on the House* 6 p.m.

The **Boathouse Rotisserie & Raw Bar** (1459 Riverside Drive; boathousechattanooga.com; $$-$$$) is one of the few foodie haunts in Chattanooga situated right on the Tennessee River. The massive deck that surrounds the restaurant blasts heaters that keep diners warm in cooler seasons. Menus change, but expect entrees like wood-grilled ribeye steak or garlic chicken with arugula, pineapple, tomatoes, avocado, and feta cheese, along with daily specials from the raw bar.

9 *Crafty Cocktails* 9 p.m.

Called one of the best-designed bars in the country by the Los Angeles chapter of the American Institute of Architects, the **Flying Squirrel** (55 Johnson Street; flyingsquirrelbar.com), in Chattanooga's hip Southside, is a gorgeous gastro pub built from remnants of a 115-year-old barn in McMinnville,

ABOVE Open-air summer dining on the rooftop deck at Tony's Pasta Shop & Trattoria. Tables come with a view of distant hills and the shade of a wisteria arbor.

Tennessee. The menu is well thought out, and the cocktails are award winning. The Reverend (Elijah Craig bourbon, Luxardo Maraschino liqueur, Fernet, orange cream bitters, and orange peel) was voted one of the best new cocktails by *Restaurant Hospitality* magazine.

SUNDAY

10 *Water World* 9 a.m.

The mission of the **Tennessee Aquarium** (1 Broad Street; tnaqua.org) is to connect the movement of water from the mountains to the sea with the creatures that both live in or are dependent on the world's water system. It's a well-told conservation story that includes lemurs, birds, otters, penguins, and a wondrous Butterfly Room. There are thousands of colorful reef fish, prehistoric-looking sturgeons, the nation's largest salamander, and the feared red-bellied piranha. In Stingray Bay, guests can touch sharks and stingrays. The aquarium's app tells users where experts will be throughout the day.

ABOVE Milk & Honey, on the North Shore of the Tennessee River, makes its own gelato. Nearby are shops and cafes.

BELOW Scuba divers mingle with the fish on display as they describe the underwater goings-on to young visitors at the Tennessee Aquarium.

11 *Get Connected* Noon

A few blocks from the aquarium is the entrance to the 2,376-foot-long **Walnut Street Bridge**, a Chattanooga centerpiece that is on the National Register of

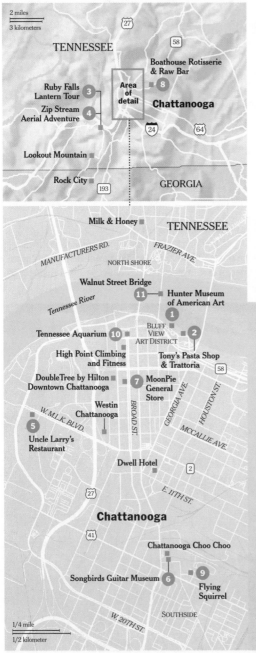

Historic Places. Built in 1890 and now a pedestrian bridge, it connects the Bluff View Arts District to the city's vibrant North Shore and is considered a "linear park," with places of rest and bits about the bridge's history stationed along the way. At night, the bridge is nearly an aphrodisiac, lit up and reflecting across the water—part City of Lights, part Bridge of Sighs. On the other side of the river, make your way to Milk & Honey (135 North Market Street; milkandhoneychattanooga.com) for homemade gelato and North Shore shops, galleries, and cafes. If you're exiting Chatt Town on the south side, veer over to **Rock City** on Lookout Mountain to where— ostensibly — one can see seven states. All you have to do is stand there and take in the vista, and this one is grand.

OPPOSITE Ruby Falls, a startling natural spectacle deep underground. An elevator takes visitors on a descent to caverns and the waterfall, more than 1,000 feet below the surface of Lookout Mountain.

THE BASICS

Chattanooga Metropolitan Airport is served by several airlines, and interstate highways provide easy connections to Nashville and Atlanta.

Dwell Hotel
120 East 10th Street
thedwellhotel.com
$$
Colorful retro-chic boutique hotel in a converted early 20th-century building.

DoubleTree by Hilton Downtown Chattanooga
407 Chestnut Street
doubletree3.hilton.com
$$
Modern high-rise close to many riverfront attractions and to the Bluff View Arts District.

Westin Chattanooga
801 Pine Street
westinchattanooga.com
$$$
Downtown near the city's convention center. Some rooms have views of Lookout Mountain.

Memphis

Memphis has strong affiliations with not one musical genre but three. It is the birthplace of rock 'n' roll and the cradle of soul, and though the blues weren't born here (that distinction goes to the rural parts of the Mississippi Delta), it was the Memphis-based musician and "Father of the Blues," W. C. Handy, who helped get those "lonesome songs" out into the world. But the Memphis story is more complicated than just blues and barbecue. Elvis Presley's Graceland is on the outskirts, up-to-date shops and restaurants keep things lively, and the past is not forgotten. A sobering civil rights museum incorporates the motel where Martin Luther King was assassinated in 1968.
— BY ELAINE GLUSAC AND COLLEEN CREAMER

FRIDAY

1 *Recording Session* 3 p.m.

For music fans, touring **Sun Studio** (706 Union Avenue; sunstudio.com) is a Memphis pilgrimage. In this modest two-story brick building, the sound engineer Sam Phillips — or, as tour guides like to tell it, his secretary Marion Keisker — discovered a young Elvis Presley. Phillips recorded the future King of Rock 'n' Roll's first single, "That's All Right," in 1954, but he was a blues fan before that and recorded other legends. In the actual studio, an unglamorous work room where more recent acts like U2 and Bonnie Raitt have recorded, guides invite tourgoers to pose holding the original Shure 55 microphone used by Elvis and other artists.

2 *Genesis* 5 p.m.

"The Mississippi Delta begins in the lobby of the Peabody Hotel," wrote the historian and journalist David L. Cohn, so take a look around and do some people-watching at the **Lobby Bar** (149 Union Avenue; peabodymemphis.com) while you order a drink. If there's too much madness downstairs, take your glass and stake a claim on the hotel's opulent mezzanine. From there, you'll get a gander at the famous Peabody ducks while absorbing the lush ambience of this classic hotel. The duck story

is a Southern Gothic gem dating from the '30s that involves a former manager and his hunting buddy, some Jack Daniel's sippin' whiskey, and the placement of live decoy ducks in the hotel's fountain.

3 *Raw and Charred* 7 p.m.

The chef duo of Andy Ticer and Michael Hudman, who have collaborated on several Italian-meets-the-South restaurants, change the pattern at **Gray Canary** (301 South Front Street; thegraycanary.com; $$), serving up oysters and wood-grilled dishes in a romantic room overlooking the distant Hernando De Soto Bridge spanning the Mississippi River. Oysters are the stars here, but other seafood gets its due — scallops, clams, octopus — along with vegetable and meat dishes.

SATURDAY

4 *Civil Rights Story* 10 a.m.

The **National Civil Rights Museum** (450 Mulberry Street; civilrightsmuseum.org), which encompasses the original Lorraine Motel where Dr. Martin Luther King, Jr. was assassinated on April 4, 1968, is an immersive multimedia experience that begins in a replica slave hold on a ship and covers five centuries of oppression and struggle. Visitors pass through rooms dedicated to the Jim Crow era; a replica of the Montgomery bus where Rosa Parks refused to give up her seat; and lunch counters where students held sit-ins in the 1960s. Transitioning to King and his civil rights activism, the emotional journey culminates outside Room 306, the well-preserved hotel room he occupied before he was shot on the balcony.

OPPOSITE Sun Studio, where musical legends were made.

RIGHT Hearty po' boys bring patrons to the Second Line.

5 *Po' Boy Fix* Noon

Sate your appetite with a generous New Orleans-style sandwich at the **Second Line** (2144 Monroe Avenue; secondlinememphis.com) in Overton Square. Lodged in an intimate bungalow with exposed brick walls and black-and-white photos, this convivial spot draws fans from around the city for substantial po' boys along with savory sides like red beans and rice.

6 *Great Outdoors* 1 p.m.

Spend a few hours in one of the city's great outdoor spaces: **Overton Park** (1914 Poplar Avenue: overtonpark.org), a 342-acre green space that includes the Brooks Museum of Art, the Levitt Shell,

the Memphis Zoo, and other attractions. Be sure to stroll through one of the park's most extraordinary spaces, the 126-acre Old Forest State Natural Area, on the National Register of Historic Places (it's over 10,000 years old), having never been tilled or farmed—rare for any space, urban or otherwise.

7 *Feed the Spirit* 6 p.m.

The Four Way (998 Mississippi Boulevard; fourwaymemphis.com; $), on the corner of Mississippi Boulevard and Walker Avenue, has been serving up soul food since 1946. The restaurant has a storied past, having served many Stax Records artists (Otis Redding, Isaac Hayes) as well as movers and shakers of the civil rights movement, and it was integrated when few restaurants were, all of which helped make south Memphis the Soulsville USA it is now. Turkey and dressing with greens, fried chicken, catfish, mac and cheese—whatever you choose will make you give thanks. And don't pass up the lemon meringue pie or fruit cobbler.

8 *Show Time* 7:30 p.m.

New and expanding performing arts venues have concentrated around Overton Square, making the

ABOVE The Lorraine Motel, a shrine to Martin Luther King.

LEFT Wall art announces the Overton Square district.

entertainment district a magnet for culture seekers. Glass walls at **Ballet Memphis** (2144 Madison Avenue; balletmemphis.org) invite onlookers to peer into rehearsals even when no performances are scheduled. A few blocks away, the acclaimed African-American repertory company **Hattiloo Theatre** (37 South Cooper Street; hattilootheatre.org) maintains an ambitious yearlong program of plays and events.

9 *Music for Every Mood* 10 p.m.

Memphis music resounds from downtown's Beale Street, lined with blues clubs, to venues across town devoted to diverse genres. Begin a progressive listening tour in Overton Square, where **Lafayette's Music Room** (2119 Madison Avenue; lafayettes.com/memphis) stages shows from bluegrass to soul in a bi-level room with a raised stage. The retro-furnished **Mollie Fontaine Lounge** (679 Adams Avenue; molliefontainelounge.com) occupies one of the original mansions on Millionaire's Row downtown, now

known as Victorian Village, with music ranging from jazz crooners to D.J.-spun house. Catch boogie fever on the lighted dance floor of the late-night, weekends-only club **Paula & Raiford's Disco** (14 South Second Street; paularaifords.com).

SUNDAY

10 *The King & Co.* 9 a.m.

Touring Elvis Presley's estate, **Graceland** (Elvis Presley Boulevard; graceland.com), home to the

ABOVE The Mollie Fontaine Lounge in Millionaire's Row.

BELOW The Mississippi and the Memphis skyline.

kitschy Jungle Room with a carpeted ceiling, remains a bucket-list trip for music fans the world over. Tours begin at the mansion, where home movies and artifacts like his-and-her wedding attire focus on Elvis's personal life. A series of exhibits survey his service in the Army, his influence on entertainers like Elton

ABOVE The well regarded African-American repertory company of the Hattiloo Theatre maintains an ambitious yearlong program of performances and events.

OPPOSITE In a city that resounds with music, Beale Street is still the place for the blues.

John and Bruce Springsteen, and his collections of showy cars and spangled jumpsuits. If the full tour is too much (or too costly), you can still visit Graceland's Meditation Garden, where Presley is buried — it's peaceful and free.

11 *Backyard Barbecue* Noon
Head back downtown for a few lazy hours at the sprawling outdoor compound **Loflin Yard** (7 West Carolina Avenue; loflinyard.com; $). Backing up to still-active train tracks, it's an acre and a half encompassing a restaurant, a cocktail bar specializing in barrel-aged drinks in a former locksmith's shop, a coach house-turned-bar, and a sun-dappled yard scattered with colorful lawn chairs. Visit the build-your-own Bloody Mary bar, grab a plate of house-smoked brisket hash, and pretend it's your own Sunday backyard barbecue.

THE BASICS

Fly into Memphis International Airport and rent a car.

Hotel Napoleon Memphis
179 Madison Avenue
hotelnapoleonmemphis.com
$$
A 1902-vintage office building repurposed with 58 guest rooms and a restaurant.

Big Cypress Lodge
1 Bass Pro Drive
big-cypress.com
$$
A rustic-themed, 103-room hotel within the riverfront Bass Pro Shop's glass pyramid, formerly a basketball arena, downtown.

The Peabody Memphis
149 Union Avenue
peabodymemphis.com
$$$
Refurbished grand old downtown hotel, dripping with tradition and known for its resident ducks.

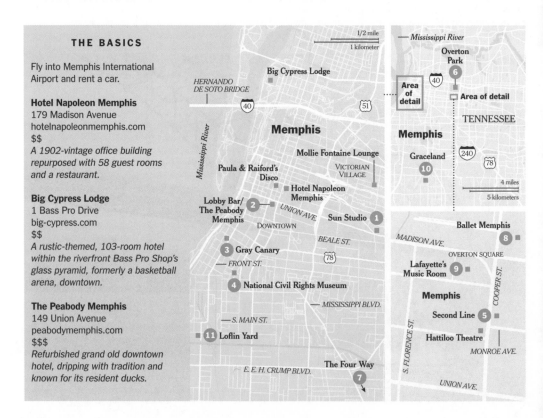

Nashville

Nashville has undergone a number of iterations in recent decades, from its longstanding position as the "home of country music" to its boozier, fun cousin "Nashvegas" to its most recent as home to one of the fastest-growing foreign-born populations in the United States (not to mention the country's No. 1 destination for bachelorette parties). Tourism aside, Nashville lures those wanting the cultural heft of larger cities on the coasts without the price tag. For this short visit, skip the party madness on Second Avenue and Broadway, and find places like the Station Inn and the Douglas Corner Cafe that showcase what Nashville is famous for: fresh, original songs and the people who give them voice. — BY COLLEEN CREAMER

FRIDAY

1 *A Fine Tribute* 5:30 p.m.

The chef Jonathan Waxman's tribute to his mother, **Adele's** (1210 McGavock Street; adelesnashville.com; $$), in the reinvented Gulch neighborhood, focuses on seasonal comfort food with little fanfare; the awards it has won, the food, and the breezy space do the talking. Situated in what was formerly the Universal Tire Center, Adele's is a fine example of the visionary dining that is blooming in Nashville. Menus have included dishes like crispy shrimp with basil and togarashi aioli; and pork loin with watermelon, jalapeño chutney, and mint. When the weather permits, the garage doors are rolled up for outdoor dining.

2 *Pickin' Pedigree* 8:30 p.m.

Everyone's favorite bar for bluegrass and roots music, the genre-bending, boxlike **Station Inn** (402 12th Avenue South; stationinn.com) sits genially amid the shiny high-rises of the Gulch, a little like an architectural Luddite — but that's part of its charm. Artists who have played its small stage include Vince Gill, Bill Monroe, Sam Bush, Ricky Skaggs, Alison Krauss, Dolly Parton, and Gillian Welch. Get there early for the 9 p.m. show.

3 *Nashville Skyline* 11 p.m.

Stay in the Gulch and top the night off with a skyline view at the **Up Rooftop Lounge** (901 Division Street; uprooftoplounge.com) atop the Fairfield Inn. The late-night snacks are tasty, and the thoughtful craft cocktails include creations like the "No Sorrow Amaro" (amaro Montenegro, Berentzen apple whiskey, Combier apricot, and lemon juice).

SATURDAY

4 *Yes, the Parthenon* 10 a.m.

Nashville's Parthenon, at **Centennial Park** (2500 West End Avenue), is the only full-size replica of the one in Athens. Built in 1897 as part of the Tennessee Centennial Exposition, it's a bit of a guilty pleasure. It took the modern-day sculptor Alan LeQuire eight years to finish the colossal 42-foot statue of Athena inside, and considerable finesse to gild her in more than eight pounds of gold leaf, part of the Parthenon's makeover in 2002. Ironically, some find out about this Parthenon during the tour of the actual Parthenon in Athens.

5 *Johnny and Patsy Together Again* 2 p.m.

If you haven't seen the Country Music Hall of Fame (countrymusichalloffame.org) on Fifth Avenue South, pencil it in for tomorrow. For now, stop at 119 Third Avenue South to see two smaller treasures. **The Johnny Cash Museum** (johnnycashmuseum.com) uses elements from the Hendersonville home of Cash and his wife June Carter, his trademark outfits, his awards, and state-of-the-art technology to help

OPPOSITE David Peterson & 1946, a bluegrass band, performing at the Station Inn in the Gulch district.

BELOW Boots for sale at a shop in the Gulch.

tell his remarkable story. At the **Patsy Cline Museum** (patsymuseum.com), in the space just above, a wall displays every 45 record Cline released. There's also a trove of handwritten letters, gowns, and jewelry, including the gold watch she was wearing on March 5, 1963, the day she died. Cline's meticulously set table in her early 1960s dining room hits hard for those who know that she would perish in a plane crash at the height of her career at the age of 30. Outside again, take a walk on the **John Seigenthaler Pedestrian Bridge** (nashvilledowntown.com/go/

ABOVE Gold records at the Country Music Hall of Fame.

BELOW Ryman Auditorium of *Grand Ole Opry* fame.

shelby-street-pedestrian-bridge) over the Cumberland River, just across the street; it's free and freeing.

6 *Vegan Soul Food* 4:30 p.m.

Opened in 2018, the **Southern V** (1200 Buchanan Street; thesouthernv.com; $-$$) has pulled off what many have attempted and at which many have failed: tasty comfort food that won't stop your heart or break the bank; it's 100 percent vegan. In a cheery, modern building in the Buchanan Arts District, the owners, Tiffany and Cliff Hancock, have put together a compelling menu that indulges the stomach while the smooth R&B in the background does the same for the spirit. Two barbecue jackfruit sliders with mac and (vegan) cheese and baked beans are $12.25; three crispy "chicken" strips with greens and green beans, $12.25.

7 *Break Out* 6 p.m.

Long a hub for budding Americana and country talent, **Douglas Corner Cafe** (2106 Eighth Avenue South; douglascorner.com) in the Melrose neighborhood has often been referred to as the "Improv" for songwriters: a small venue where many a career has been launched (Trisha Yearwood, Garth Brooks, Alan Jackson, the Kentucky Headhunters, Blake Shelton). It's one of the few venues in town that has a 6 p.m. show, so go; you never know whom you will help discover.

8 *Hush* 8:30 p.m.

With the famed Bluebird Cafe usually reserved for months in advance, the **Listening Room Cafe** (618 Fourth Avenue South; listeningroomcafe.com), which seats 300, is helping shoulder the mantle of hosting established singer/songwriters as well as young blood. Shows usually have three or four performers who take turns, with amusing banter in between. The club, which, despite its size, has an intimate feel, also offers a full dinner menu.

9 *Jazz, Too* 11 p.m.

Rudy's Jazz Room (809 Gleaves Street; rudysjazzroom.com) is like a little snifter of Remy Martin: dark, delicious, and seemingly from another era. Rudy's opened in 2017 and was modeled after Smalls Jazz Club in Greenwich Village. The club has a speakeasy feel with stone walls made warm with mood lighting and casual seating, not to mention a Steinway Model B grand piano. Local musicians, as

well as major acts from around the country, offer a smooth, urbane palate cleanser for those who may be over-twanged from recent evenings at bluegrass and country venues. On weekends, there is an 11:30 p.m. late show. Rudy's also serves New Orleans-style cuisine, craft cocktails and beers on tap.

SUNDAY

10 *Sunday Drive-By* 9 a.m.

While much of Nashville is still asleep (or in church), see what all the hoopla is about downtown and on Broadway without the frenzy or the hangover. Your 9 a.m. appointment with **Joyride** (joyrideus. com/nashville) brings you a "driver ambassador" who will take you to places of your choice. Swing by

BELOW A photo op in the Gulch district. Chic and upscale, the Gulch is a reinvented neighborhood of renovated warehouses and cool restaurants and night spots.

Tootsie's Orchid Lounge and the other honky-tonks on lower Broadway. Learn the full history of the Ryman Auditorium (the original *Grand Ole Opry* stage), and take a long look at the Country Music Hall of Fame; every curve of that structure has built-in significance, including a section that suggests the tail fin of a 1959 Cadillac. And let's face it, running around in a golf cart is fun.

11 *Brunch and More Music* 10:30 a.m.

The **Sutler Saloon** (2600 Eighth Avenue South; thesutlersaloon.com; $$) opened in 1976 and became a prominent watering hole for Nashville's music business community as well as performers. Now reopened in its original location, it offers a Sunday bluegrass brunch with live music, two kinds of sangria, and bottomless mimosas. The sweet potato pancakes with cinnamon bourbon syrup are just like what they sound like: Southern and delicious.

OPPOSITE Nashvillians will proudly tell you that their Parthenon, in Centennial Park, is the only full-size replica of the one in Athens. It dates back to 1897, but the 42-foot gilded statue of Athena inside is a modern creation.

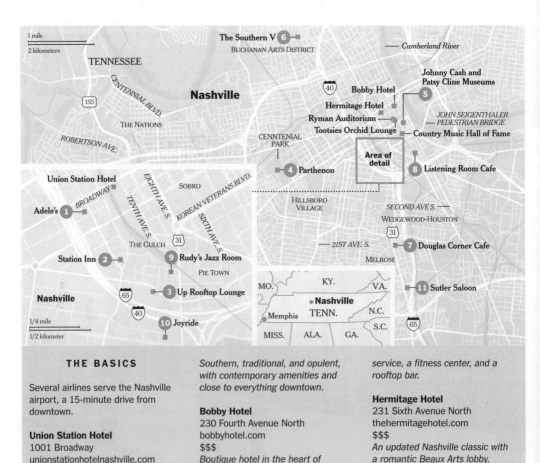

THE BASICS

Several airlines serve the Nashville airport, a 15-minute drive from downtown.

Union Station Hotel
1001 Broadway
unionstationhotelnashville.com
$$

Southern, traditional, and opulent, with contemporary amenities and close to everything downtown.

Bobby Hotel
230 Fourth Avenue North
bobbyhotel.com
$$$
Boutique hotel in the heart of downtown with 24-hour room

service, a fitness center, and a rooftop bar.

Hermitage Hotel
231 Sixth Avenue North
thehermitagehotel.com
$$$
An updated Nashville classic with a romantic Beaux Arts lobby.

Charlottesville

Charlottesville received unwanted attention in 2017 when white-supremacist demonstrators arrived to stage a rally there that turned violent, but the true spirit of the city is tolerant, warm, and free. As far as Charlottesville is concerned, Thomas Jefferson might still be living on the hill at Monticello. There and at the University of Virginia, which he founded in 1819, he is referred to as "Mr. Jefferson" with a familiarity that suggests he might stroll past, horticulture manual in hand, at any moment. To this day an inordinate number of houses and buildings in the area resemble the back of a nickel. But Jefferson was always at the cutting edge, and the traveler today can share in some of that spirit, too, thanks to the energy emanating from the university he left behind. The active music scene has produced megastars like the Dave Matthews Band. Local chefs marry grits and fried chicken with international influences. Prize-winning vineyards checker the foothills. — BY JENNIFER TUNG AND JOSHUA KURLANTZICK

FRIDAY

1 *Al Fresco Downtown* 5 p.m.

Walk through the oak-lined downtown mall, where students talk philosophy over coffee and locals gravitate for drinks. You will pass rows of restored brick buildings, street entertainers like mimes and violinists, a central plaza for public art, and al fresco cafes. Stop in just off the main mall at **Feast** (416 West Main Street, Suite H; 434-244-7800; feastvirginia.com), an artisanal cheese shop, charcuterie, and gourmet market that feels as if it could be in Paris.

2 *Old and New* 7 p.m.

Only 10 minutes from downtown Charlottesville, the **Clifton Inn** (1296 Clifton Inn Drive; 434-971-1800; thecliftoninn.com; $$$$) sits amid rolling hills and pasture land. Virginia's inns have embarked on a culinary arms race, and the Clifton has kept up. Its restaurant, inside a white-pillared *Gone With the*

OPPOSITE Monticello, Thomas Jefferson's home and a conspicuous example of his architectural prowess.

RIGHT The restaurant at the *Gone with the Wind*-style Clifton Inn is worth the drive out of town.

Wind-style Southern mansion, offers a design-your-own tasting menu featuring local ingredients. Reservations are essential. For a more casual dinner, eat in Charlottesville at **C & O** (515 East Water Street; 434-971-7044; candorestaurant.com; $$-$$$), a 110-year-old building that originally served as a railroad stop. Sit in the mezzanine, a candlelit room as dark and narrow as a mine shaft, and order dishes like local organic lamb or house-made chorizo with braised collard greens and purple potato frites.

SATURDAY

3 *The Morning Tour* 8 a.m.

A quiet Saturday morning is a good time to see Jefferson's Academical Village, the central buildings he designed at the University of Virginia. Pick up coffee at **Mudhouse** on the Main Street mall (213 West Main Street; 434-984-6833; mudhouse.com), and walk onto the grounds (Mr. Jefferson never used the word "campus," and neither does anyone else in Charlottesville). Begin at the **Rotunda** (tours, 434-924-7969; rotunda.virginia.edu), inspired by the Pantheon in Rome, which sits at the north end of the 225-foot-long Lawn. Flanking the Lawn are the Pavilions, where esteemed professors live, and dorm rooms occupied by high-achieving final-year

students ("senior" isn't a word here, either). The charming gardens behind the Pavilions, divided by undulating serpentine walls, are the professors' backyards but are open to the public.

4 *Outback* 10 a.m.

For a fascinating detour little known by outsiders, visit the university's **Kluge-Ruhe Aboriginal Art Collection**. John W. Kluge, a billionaire businessman, built perhaps the largest collection of aboriginal art outside Australia and then donated it to the University of Virginia. The free guided tour, every Saturday at 10:30 a.m., is essential to understanding these stark and sometimes inscrutable works of art (400 Worrell Drive, Peter Jefferson Place; 434-244-0234; kluge-ruhe.org).

5 *Colonial Fried Chicken* Noon

Let the lady in the bonnet and the big skirt corral you into the lunch line at **Michie Tavern**, an inn that dates back to 1784 (683 Thomas Jefferson Parkway; 434-977-1234; michietavern.com; $$$). Let more women in bonnets pile fried chicken, black-eyed peas, stewed tomatoes, and cornbread onto your pewter-style plate; then eat at a wooden table by the hearth. Once you accept full tourist status, the food is very tasty.

6 *The Back of the Nickel* 1 p.m.

Tours of historical sites are rarely billed as exciting, but Jefferson's home, **Monticello** (434-984-9800; monticello.org), actually causes goose bumps. Jefferson designed the house to invoke classical ideals of reason, proportion, and balance, and sited it on a rise ("Monticello" is from the Italian for "small hill") for a view of distant mountains. After your introduction at the new visitor center, opened in 2009, enter the house and note the elk antlers in the entrance hall, courtesy of Lewis and Clark, and the private library that once housed 6,700 books. Guides point out Jefferson's design innovations, including a dumbwaiter hidden in a fireplace, and

offer insight into the unsung lives of the slaves who kept everything going. Monticello lost its spot on the back of the nickel coin for a brief period a few years ago, but Eric Cantor, who was then a Virginia representative in Congress, ushered through legislation to guarantee that after 2006 it would be back to stay.

7 *Country Roads* 5 p.m.

Drive back toward Charlottesville and turn northeast on Route 20 to Barboursville. The drive, through an area called the **Southwest Mountains Rural Historic District**, winds up and down through green farmland sitting in the shadow of the Southwest range. Keep your eyes out for historical marker signs; the area also boasts a rich trove of African-American history (nps.gov/history/nr/travel/journey/sou.htm).

8 *Dining Amid the Ruins* 7 p.m.

There's more of Jefferson (didn't this man ever sleep?) to be seen at the Barboursville Vineyard,

ABOVE Comestibles at Feast, a stop on the oak-lined downtown mall near the University of Virginia.

BELOW Tasting at Barboursville Vineyard. The winery has a notable restaurant and a Jefferson-designed building.

where you should have made reservations well before now for dinner at the **Palladio Restaurant** (17655 Winery Road, Barboursville; 540-832-7848; bbvwine.com; $$$$). Jefferson designed the main building at the vineyard, which dates to 1814. There was a fire in the late 1880s, but you can see the ruins of his design. The restaurant features Northern Italian cooking as well as locally inspired dishes like quail with corn cakes.

9 *Miller Time* 10 p.m.

Every college town needs a few decent bars for grungy bands to play in, but in Charlottesville you wind up later seeing those bands everywhere. The Dave Matthews Band had its start here when Matthews tended bar at **Miller's** (109 West Main Street; 434-971-8511; millersdowntown.com). He

moved on, but Miller's, a converted drugstore that retains the trappings of an old-time apothecary, is still there. Get there before the college crowd packs the place.

SUNDAY

10 *Take a Hike* 10 a.m.

Drive west for 30 minutes on Interstate 64 to **Shenandoah National Park** (Exit 99). By mid-morning the early mist will have lifted. Follow signs to Skyline Drive and the Blue Ridge Parkway. For a vigorous hike, start at the Humpback Gap parking area, six miles south of the Blue Ridge Parkway's northern end. Follow the Appalachian Trail a half-mile south to a challenging spur trail that leads to a breathtaking view of the Shenandoah Valley.

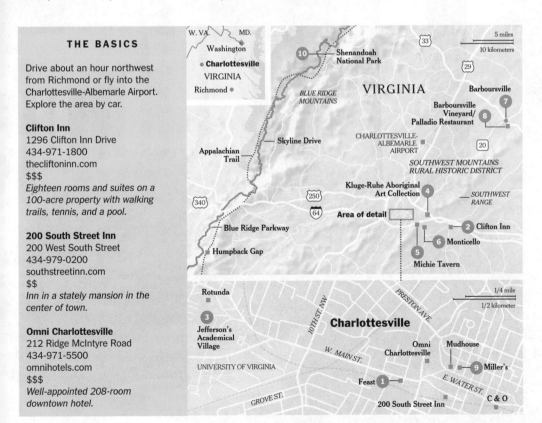

THE BASICS

Drive about an hour northwest from Richmond or fly into the Charlottesville-Albemarle Airport. Explore the area by car.

Clifton Inn
1296 Clifton Inn Drive
434-971-1800
thecliftoninn.com
$$$
Eighteen rooms and suites on a 100-acre property with walking trails, tennis, and a pool.

200 South Street Inn
200 West South Street
434-979-0200
southstreetinn.com
$$
Inn in a stately mansion in the center of town.

Omni Charlottesville
212 Ridge McIntyre Road
434-971-5500
omnihotels.com
$$$
Well-appointed 208-room downtown hotel.

Richmond

Richmond, the farthest north of the East Coast's more traditional Southern cities, once clung to its longstanding version of Southern gentility, with mansions on leafy streets and plentiful commemorations of its long-ago role as the capital of the Confederacy. In the new century, it has emerged as a more energetic and youthful place, with a surer sense of its complicated history and the diversity of its residents. With the James River as an anchor, Richmond also reveals a stark natural beauty that, no matter the season, lends a distinctive urban charm and vibrancy.
— BY JOHN L. DORMAN

FRIDAY

1 *Milestones* 2 p.m.

History feels alive and close in Richmond. The **American Civil War Museum at Historic Tredegar** (500 Tredegar Street; acwm.org) tells the story of the Civil War from the perspectives of the Union, the Confederacy, and the slaves. At the adjacent **Richmond National Battlefield Park** (470 Tredegar Street; nps.gov/rich), recorded voices read wartime accounts by local witnesses. Garland H. White, a former slave, tells of entering defeated Richmond as a Union soldier and being reunited with his mother, from whom he had been sold as a small boy. More recent history gets its due at the **Black History Museum and Cultural Center of Virginia** (122 West Leigh Street; blackhistorymuseum.org), where interactive touch screens and replica artifacts recall events from the Virginia Constitutional Convention of 1867 to lunch counter sit-ins of the 1960s.

2 *Deco, Nouveau, and More* 5:45 p.m.

Spend happy hour at the **Virginia Museum of Fine Arts** (200 North Boulevard; vmfa.museum), drinking in wine in the cafe and an extensive art collection in the galleries. Art Deco and Art Nouveau collections reside alongside American, Asian, and European art of many eras and styles. Happy hour is a TGIF affair, running on Fridays only, from 5:30 to 7:30 p.m.

3 *Go Mediterranean* 8:30 p.m.

Stella's (1012 Lafayette Street; stellasrichmond.com; $$) delivers a first-rate, refreshingly casual

Greek dining experience. Pottery lines the upper walls near the bar, and there is a lively communal table. The menu is a Mediterranean medley. The place fills up quickly, so reserve a table in advance. Stella Dikos, a co-owner, also runs Stella's Grocery across the street, where prepared meals are ready for purchase.

SATURDAY

4 *Outlook on the James* 9:30 a.m.

Created in 1851, **Libby Hill Park** (2801 East Franklin Street; richmondgov.com/parks/parkLibbyHill.aspx) is one of the first parks established in Richmond. On a high bluff in the Church Hill neighborhood, the park is surrounded by beautiful Italianate, Federal, Greek Revival, and Queen Anne houses situated on many of Richmond's original blocks. First called Marshall Square, the park was renamed for the influential landowner Luther Libby. The view of the James River from Libby Hill Park is said to have inspired the city's founder, William Byrd II, to name the city Richmond, since it reminded him of the view from the Thames River in Richmond Hill in London. An ornamental fountain at the park is a popular spot for locals and tourists alike.

5 *Pop's Kitchen* 10:30 a.m.

Pop's Market on Grace (415 East Grace Street; facebook.com/popsongrace; $), in a former Cokes-

OPPOSITE The Fan District, a bastion of old Richmond.

BELOW The casual crowd at Stella's restaurant.

bury bookstore location, is a great example of how urban spaces can be reimagined as successful purveyors of food. The interior is cozy, with a generous amount of seating, a chalkboard menu, and a lounge area with a piano. For breakfast, choose from selections like bagels, sage sausage, egg and cheese biscuits, and French toast rounds with maple syrup. The biscuits are flaky and delicious.

6 *Vintage and Vinyl* Noon

For most of the 20th century, Broad Street downtown was an economic powerhouse, with the Thalhimers and Miller & Rhoads department stores dominating the landscape. Smaller stores nearby catered to the thousands of people on foot. By the late 1990s, most of the downtown stores were gone and the pulse in this area was barely noticeable. But new life has been breathed into the area by **Steady Sounds** (facebook.com/steadysounds), a vinyl record store with a diverse selection, and **Blue Bones Vintage** (bluebonesvintage.com), a vintage clothing and accessories store. They share space at 322 West Broad Street, so you can combine your hunt for that elusive soul or punk record with a shopping spree that might include a Converse sweater. The upscale

ABOVE The Black History Museum and Cultural Center chronicles events like the lunch counter sit-ins of the 1960s.

shirtmaker **Ledbury** (315 West Broad Street; ledbury. com) operates just across the street, with a retail store and made-to-measure lounge on the first floor.

7 *Brewing Up a Sandwich* 2 p.m.

The Manchester neighborhood has many attributes, including an abundance of old factory buildings that have become housing and offices, and a budding sense of community. **Brewer's Café** (1125 Bainbridge Street; brewerscaferva.com; $) attracts new and existing residents with a bright, welcoming space and a menu of hearty sandwiches. The specialty, the Brewer's Club, combines turkey, Virginia ham, bacon, and Sriracha mayonnaise. The iced green tea or a cappuccino would go well with anything here.

8 *The James Up Close* 3 p.m.

To know Richmond well, you need to know the James River. Among several vantage points within the **James River Park System** (jamesriverpark.org), three stand out. Belle Isle has a multitude of rocks where you can view the river and its rapids. The island has biking and running trails and is a hot spot for nature lovers. In the warmer months, Pony Pasture Rapids Park is an excellent area for swimming, canoeing, and inner tubing. Exercise caution, as there can be slippery spots. Huguenot Flatwater Park, the westernmost park in the system, is one of the best launching areas for paddling.

9 *Beer and Supper* 6 p.m.

The craft beer scene has grown rapidly, especially in Scott's Addition, a former industrial area now brimming with residents. One occupant is the **Veil Brewing Co.** (1301 Roseneath Road; theveilbrewing.com), which specializes in hop-forward ales and spontaneous fermentation. Relax over a brew until it's time for **Supper** (1215 Summit Avenue; lunchorsupper.com; $$), which has an adjoining twin restaurant, Lunch. Supper serves eclectic Southern fare, and it has antler chandeliers to boot. Menu choices might include fried chicken, braised boneless short ribs, and selections like "monument" shrimp and grits, blackened shrimp topped with bacon and served over cheese grits.

SUNDAY

10 *Brunch With Nostalgia* 10 a.m.

The old Tarrant Drug Company building now houses **Tarrant's Cafe** (1 West Broad Street; tarrantscaferva.com; $$), a gem of a brunch spot. The atmosphere is nostalgic, with the original stained-glass signs and attractive wooden booths. Recent selections included French toast Foster, with cinnamon-vanilla egg batter, bananas, strawberries, and bourbon sauce, and crab cakes Benedict.

11 *Father of the Court* Noon

Built in 1790, the Federal-style **John Marshall House** (818 East Marshall Street; preservationvirginia.com/visit) was the main residence for John Marshall,

ABOVE Brewer's Café, a good spot for a hearty sandwich.

BELOW Fishing in the swift James River at Belle Isle.

the longest-serving chief justice of the United States Supreme Court and one of its most influential. In the 45-minute tour, you will learn about landmark judicial cases including Marbury v. Madison, which established the system of judicial review, and view

heirlooms from early America. The house, in the Court End neighborhood, is open for tours from March through December.

OPPOSITE Richmond is a city that loves its river.

THE BASICS

Fly into the Richmond airport or drive south from Washington for two hours (much longer at rush hour). A car is the best option for getting around town.

Quirk Hotel
201 West Broad Street

destinationhotels.com/quirk-hotel
$$
Located in a prime downtown arts district; with graceful limestone arches, a bright lobby, and a dynamic rooftop bar.

Hilton Richmond Downtown
501 East Broad Street
hilton.com

$$
Housed in the former flagship Miller & Rhoads department store; centralized location for exploring.

The Jefferson Hotel
101 West Franklin Street
jeffersonhotel.com
$$$
The definition of luxury since 1895.

MIDWEST
& GREAT LAKES

362 WINNIPEG

372

Duluth

436 the Black Hills

376

MINNEAPOLIS
St. Paul

MILWAUK

the Niobrara
River Valley

352 DES MOINES

388

OMAHA

356

344

394

Iowa's
Mississippi
river

Chicago
Neighborhoo

380 Kansas City

384

St. Louis

Oklahoma
416 City

TORONTO 422

404

*Niagara
falls*

*Chicago
y Water*

DETROIT
366

398

DETROIT
366

412

Buffalo

Cleveland

PITTSBURGH
432

CHICAGO

ndianapolis
348

99

Cincinnati
408

428

*the Laurel
Highlands*

Chicago

Chicago keeps playing to its strengths, adding parks, architectural crowd pleasers, and public art to a wealth of brilliant urban planning and adventurous building design. A raft of improvements in the last decade or so have left its 19th- and 20th-century public spaces brimming with 21st-century attractions. And it is a special treat to move through it all: on an elevated train rattling between skyscrapers, on a boat plying the river beneath low bridges, or on a bike or on foot, meandering past parks, pavilions, and sandy beaches. — BY FRED A. BERNSTEIN

FRIDAY

1 *Loop the Loop* 3 p.m.

A good place to start in Chicago is at the **Chicago Architecture Center** (111 East Wacker Drive; 312-922-3432; architecture.org), housed in a Ludwig Mies van der Rohe glass tower. The guided downtown walking tour orients newbies to the late 19th- and early 20th-century buildings that first gave Chicago its reputation as a center of great architecture, and several other walking tours will help give you a feeling for the city. You can also buy tickets here for the foundation's popular 90-minute architecture cruise, which travels the Chicago River into the city's heart, through a forest of interesting buildings. If you already know what to look for, get reacquainted with a ride on the "L," the elevated railway that defines the Loop (transitchicago.com). Get on the brown, orange, or pink line — it doesn't matter which color, as long as you sit in the first car by the front-view window — and ride around the two-square-mile area. You'll see Bertrand Goldberg's spectacular **Marina City**, with a design inspired by corncobs; the **Trump International Hotel and Tower**; Frank Gehry's **Pritzker Pavilion** band shell; and Louis Sullivan's **Auditorium Building**, now part of Roosevelt University.

2 *Gilded Fare* 8 p.m.

A number of good midprice but high-style restaurants have opened in Chicago in the past few years. A favorite is **Gilt Bar** (230 West Kinzie Street;

OPPOSITE Chicago's urban canyons and the Willis Tower.

RIGHT The view down from the Willis Tower Skydeck.

312-464-9544; giltbarchicago.com; $$), a casual restaurant that isn't casual about its cooking. The menu features New American dishes like blackened cauliflower with capers and ricotta gnocchi with sage and brown butter. After dinner, head downstairs for a drink at the Library, a cozy basement bar and restaurant lined with bookshelves and decorated in red velvet, golden lighting, and dark wood.

3 *Choose Your Bubbly* 11 p.m.

There are so many clubs on Ontario Street, just north of the Loop, that it's sometimes known as Red Bull Row. For something unusual, try **Pops for Champagne** (601 North State Street at Ohio; 312-266-7677; popsforchampagne.com), a sleek, upscale lounge with a roundish bar and nearly 200 different kinds of champagne and sparkling wine to sample. European lounge music wafts from the speakers as smartly dressed men and women laugh beneath dim (read: flattering) lights.

SATURDAY

4 *Eggs Plus* 9 a.m.

Couldn't get to dinner at Frontera Grill, the nouvelle Mexican restaurant owned by the celebrity chef Rick Bayless? No worries. Just head over to **Xoco** (449 North Clark Street; 312-661-1434; rickbayless.com;

$), another Bayless restaurant. Breakfast is served till 10 a.m.; expect a line after 8:30. Favorites include scrambled egg empanada with poblano chili, and an open-face torta with soft poached egg, salsa, cheese, cilantro, and black beans.

5 *Off-Label Strip* 11 a.m.

The Magnificent Mile area is filled with flagships (Gucci, Vuitton—you know the list). But there are still

ABOVE Girl & the Goat, chef Stephanie Izard's restaurant on Randolph Street just west of downtown.

BELOW Aqua, a new addition to Chicago's skyscraper collection, was designed by Jeanne Gang.

some independent stores you won't find at your hometown mall. **Ikram** (15 East Huron Street; 312-587-1000; ikram.com) is the stylish boutique that counts Michelle Obama among its customers, with fashion-forward labels like Maison Margiela. East Oak Street has a couple of cool shops, including **Independence** (No. 47; 312-675-2105; indepedence-chicago.com), which sells a finely curated array of American-made menswear and accessories, as well as its own brand of shoes and boots.

6 *Grand Piano* 1 p.m.

Chicago knows how to mix neoclassical architecture with contemporary design, and no place in town does it better than the **Art Institute of Chicago** (111 South Michigan Avenue; 312-443-3600; artic.edu). Its celebrated Modern Wing, designed by Renzo Piano, is a luminous space containing a magnificent set of galleries for 1900–1950 European art (Picasso, Giacometti, and Klee are among the big names) and up-to-the-minute contemporary art, and a capacious room for the museum's design collection. Arrive in time for lunch and check out **Terzo Piano**, the stunning rooftop restaurant with views of the Pritzker Pavilion in Millennium Park across the street.

7 *Bridges to Tomorrow* 4 p.m.

From the museum, walk over the pedestrian bridge, also designed by Piano, to **Millennium Park,** which is best known for the big, reflective *Cloud Gate* sculpture (known to locals as the Bean) and the newer Crown Fountain, a combination of video, fountain, and sculpture. At the south end of the park is the **Lurie Garden**, which is magical during the summer and works in the winter as well, when colorful blooms are replaced by the captivating shapes of downy seed heads and silver panicles. Then, take Millennium Park's serpentine Frank Gehry-designed BP Bridge to the edge of **Maggie Daley Park** to see the latest stage in the evolution of Chicago's front yard.

8 *Livestock Menu* 7 p.m.

Chicago was once the meatpacking capital of the world, and it still knows what to do with meat. Take **Girl & the Goat** (809 West Randolph Street; 312-492-6262; girlandthegoat.com; $$), a much-blogged-about restaurant where the *Top Chef* winner Stephanie Izard takes livestock parts seriously. The often-updated menu has included the likes of lamb

ribs with grilled avocado and pistachio piccata, and braised beef tongue with masa and beef vinaigrette. But you don't have to be a carnivore. If you are vegetarian, there is something for you, too — perhaps chickpeas three ways, and for dessert, potato fritters with lemon poached eggplant and Greek yogurt. The soaring dining room, designed by the Chicago design firm 555 International, is warm and modern, with exposed beams, walls of charred cedar, and a large open kitchen.

9 *Funny Bone* 10 p.m.

You won't find big names at the **The Comedy Bar** (500 North LaSalle Street; 312-836-0499; comedybar. com). But a hit-or-miss roster of itinerant comedians will be looking for laughs, including some who heckle

BELOW The Pritzker Pavilion and its Frank Gehry-designed band shell, in Millennium Park.

the audience in language that Grandma would not consider polite. There's more comedy at **UP** (230 West North Avenue; 312-662-4562; upcomedyclub.com) in the Old Town neighborhood, roughly two miles north of the Loop. UP is the Second City improv group's foray into standup.

SUNDAY

10 *Wheels Up* 10 a.m.

At Millennium Park, rent bikes from **Bike and Roll** (312-729-1000; bikechicago.com) for a ride up the shore of Lake Michigan. You'll pass Navy Pier, skyscrapers by Mies van der Rohe, and hundreds of beach volleyball courts that make this the Malibu of the Midwest on summer and fall weekends. Along the way, you'll see Lincoln Park, with a pavilion by the Chicago architect Jeanne Gang — another example of how the city is updating its open spaces.

ABOVE *Cloud Gate*, signature sculpture of Millennium Park.

OPPOSITE One way to see great Chicago architecture is to ride the "L," the elevated railway that defines the Loop.

THE BASICS

From O'Hare International Airport to the Loop, take the L's Blue Line, about a 40-minute ride. From Midway International Airport, use the Orange Line, about a 30-minute journey.

Langham Chicago
330 North Wabash Avenue
312-923-9988
chicago.langhamhotels.com
$$$$
In the former IBM Building designed by Mies van der Rohe.

Hotel Allegro
171 West Randolph Street
312-236-0123
allegrochicago.com
$$
A 483-room hotel in the bold style of Kimpton hotels.

Wit Hotel
201 North State Street
312-467-0200
thewithotel.com
$$
Chic hotel with a popular rooftop bar.

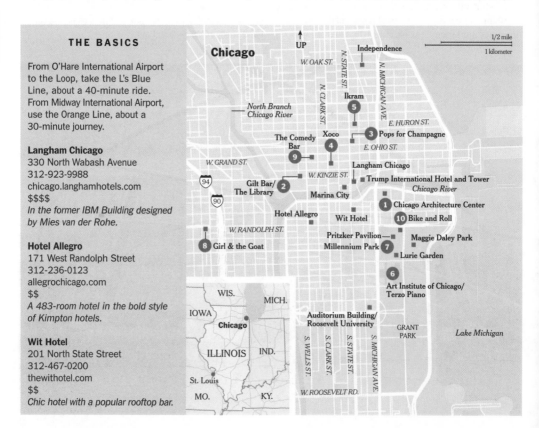

Chicago by Water

Expensive water-view condos and gleaming commercial towers line the Chicago River in downtown Chicago, close to its connection to Lake Michigan. Long ago the river was a polluted dumping ground, but now kayakers ply its waters and tour boats glide along as guides explain some of the wealth of interesting architecture on the banks. For an intimate, easygoing exploration of the river, with stops to look deeper at some of what's close by on land, create your own tour by water taxi. From late spring through fall, two taxi companies operate on the river, running distinct, though partly overlapping, routes. One ventures out into Lake Michigan. The boats operate like buses, following scheduled routes that take you to standard tourist stops. Hop on and off at will, and see the heart of the city from a different point of view.
— BY RUSSELL WORKING

FRIDAY

1 *Know Your River* 3 p.m.

Get your bearings at the **Michigan Avenue Bridge**. Stop on the pedestrian walkway, gaze down the river into the heart of the city and then back the other way toward Lake Michigan. You may spot a water taxi — yellow for Chicago Water Taxi or blue for Shoreline. Inside the ornately decorated stone tower at the southwest corner of the bridge is the **McCormick Tribune Bridgehouse & Chicago River Museum** (99 Chicago Riverwalk; 312-977-0227; bridgehousemuseum.org), where you can see the inner workings of a drawbridge and learn about river history, including the arrival of Jean Baptiste Point du-Sable, a black French pioneer, in the 1780s. At the north end of the bridge, duck down to the lower level and find the **Billy Goat Tavern** (430 North Michigan Avenue; 312-222-1525; billygoattavern.com), a reporters' watering hole for generations and the inspiration for the *Saturday Night Live* "cheeseburger" sketches with John Belushi as the single-minded counter man.

2 *Down by the Docks* 4 p.m.

Still at the bridge's north end, walk down to water level to see where the taxis leave. For **Chicago Water Taxi** (400 North Michigan Avenue; 312-337-1446; chicagowatertaxi.com for routes and prices), go down the stairs by the **Wrigley Building** and follow the signs to the taxi dock. For **Shoreline Water Taxi** (401 North Michigan Avenue; 312-222-9328; shorelinesightseeing.com), take the steps down on the northeast side of the bridge. There's no reason to take a water taxi anywhere today, but if you'd like to have the names and histories to go with some of the buildings you'll see on your taxi tour tomorrow, one option is to cross the bridge, walk down the steps on the southern side, and find the dock for the **Chicago Architecture Foundation**'s 90-minute architecture cruise. (To minimize waiting, buy tickets in advance; check caf.architecture.org or go to the foundation's shop at 224 South Michigan Avenue.) It's a pleasant, breezy introduction to the heart of the city. Another way to prepare is with a guidebook; a good one is Jennifer Marjorie Bosch's *View From the River: The Chicago Architecture Foundation River Cruise* (Pomegranate Communications).

3 *Mellow Out* 8 p.m.

Relax and plan your strategy for tomorrow over dinner at **State and Lake** (201 North State Street; 312-239-9400; stateandlakechicago.com; $$), a restaurant that's at least as much about the beverages as the food. The dining choices include small plates, salads, and substantial entrees like ribeye steak or salmon. Linger over one of the wines or a draft or bottled beer.

SATURDAY

4 *Squint at the Corncobs* 9 a.m.

Return to the Michigan Avenue dock and catch a Chicago Water Taxi headed west. Out on the river, glide along for a while, squinting upward at the skyscrapers in the morning light. There are dozens of landmarks, including the **Marina City** towers at 300 North State Street, designed to resemble corncobs; the sprawling **Merchandise Mart** at North Wells Street, built in 1930; and the **Civic Opera House** on North Wacker Drive, constructed in the Art Deco armchair form and nicknamed Insull's Throne after the tycoon who commissioned it.

OPPOSITE The Merchandise Mart, built in 1930, hulks over the Chicago River, a highway for water taxis.

5 *Waterside* 10 a.m.

Get off at the LaSalle stop and walk across the river on the Clark Street bridge to find the **Riverwalk** (explorechicago.org). Explore for a while, passing outdoor cafes and kiosks that thrive in the summer season. You're also close here to the area around State and Randolph Streets that is home to several major theaters and the Joffrey Ballet.

6 *Brunch With a View* Noon

A pleasant place for brunch, right across from the Riverwalk, is the **Kitchen** (316 North Clark Street; 312-836-1300; thekitchenbistros.com; $$), where the elevated view of the river and the Loop is an appetizer. Tables under cheerful orange umbrellas are lined up on a narrow balcony overlooking the river. For indoor seating, ask for a table near the loft-size windows. (The people-watching is good, too, in this bustling brasserie.) Check the menu for the Farmer's Breakfast or Smoked Salmon Toast. When you're ready to venture out again, return to the LaSalle Street stop to pick up another taxi and continue west on the river.

7 *Do Look Down* 1:30 p.m.

After the river bends south, alight at the spot near the **Willis Tower** (233 South Wacker Drive; 312-875-0066; willistower.com), once known as the Sears Tower, where both taxi lines stop. Ride the elevator to the Skydeck (theskydeck.com). Take the dare—venture out onto one of the glass-floored retractable bays to join the other sightseers scaring themselves silly by staring 1,353 feet straight down at the street. Across the river is Union Station, a cavernous rail terminal. Its Beaux Arts Great Hall has been featured in several films, including *The Untouchables*.

8 *Chinatown* 3:30 p.m.

Continue south on the Chicago Water Taxi to **Ping Tom Memorial Park** (named for a Chinese-American civic leader), and proceed on foot under an ornate gate into **Chinatown**, where you'll find hole-in-the-wall restaurants and stores selling barrels of ginseng or aquariums full of live frogs. Stop in at the one-room **Dr. Sun Yat-Sen Museum** (2245 South Wentworth Avenue, third floor; open until 5 p.m.), dedicated to the revolutionary who played a leading role in overthrowing the Qing Dynasty — the last of the Chinese emperors — in 1911. The photos inside include some from Sun's visit to Chicago at around that time. At **Chinatown Square**, an outdoor mall just south of the park, you'll find stores selling green tea and Chinese cookies. For an early dinner, take a short walk to **Yan Bang Cai** (228 West Cermak Road; 312-842-7818; yanbangcaichicago.com; $), which serves the food of Sichuan province.

9 *Honky-Tonk Bard* 7 p.m.

There's enough going on at the **Navy Pier** (navypier.com) to keep you busy all weekend. Reach it from the Michigan Avenue dock of the Shoreline Water Taxi. (And as you debark, take note of the schedule; you don't want to miss the last taxi back.) The pier is 50 acres of parks, promenades, restaurants, carnival-like stalls, and souvenir shops,

with fireworks on summer Saturday nights. There's also an indoor garden, a stained-glass museum, and the **Chicago Shakespeare Theater** (800 East Grand Avenue; 312-595-5600; chicagoshakes.com), where you might find local fare in addition to the serious drama. Several years ago Second City's *Rod Blagojevich Superstar* included an appearance by Blagojevich himself, then already smarting from the scandal that cost him the Illinois governorship and eventually landed him in prison. He recited lines from *Henry V* and invited the cast for dinner, adding, "We'll be serving tarantulas."

SUNDAY

10 *Feeding the Spirit* 10 a.m.

From either Michigan Avenue or the LaSalle stop, it's a short walk to the **House of Blues** (329 North Dearborn Street; 312-923-2007; houseofblues.com; $$$), where the Sunday-morning Gospel Brunch includes buffet choices like blackened catfish, jambalaya, fried chicken, and omelets,

OPPOSITE ABOVE The Billy Goat Tavern, open since 1934.

OPPOSITE BELOW Aboard the Shoreline Water Taxi.

ABOVE The view from the Chicago River up at the Clark Street Bridge.

along with exhilarating African-American worship and music.

11 *Lakeside Dinosaurs* Noon

For a nice ride out into Lake Michigan, take the Shoreline taxi to the Navy Pier, change boats, and go to the lakeside museum campus that is home to the **Field Museum**, **Shedd Aquarium**, and **Adler Planetarium**. All are worth serious time, but for generations of children, the must-see has

been the Field's dinosaur skeletons, including a Tyrannosaurus rex found in South Dakota in 1990 and nicknamed Sue.

ABOVE The Shedd Aquarium and the Adler Planetarium at Grant Park, on Lake Michigan. Get there from downtown on the Shoreline Water Taxi. Both Shoreline and Chicago Water Taxis cater to commuters and tourists alike.

OPPOSITE Marina City, two corncob-shaped towers.

THE BASICS

The Chicago River, in the heart of downtown, is the north and west boundary of the Loop. When you're not on a water taxi, take the "L" (that's "El" to some) or land-bound cabs.

Fairmont Chicago Millennium Park
200 North Columbus Drive
312-565-8000
fairmont.com/chicago
$$
Recently renovated; a short walk to the Michigan Avenue bridge.

Radisson Blu Aqua Hotel Chicago
221 North Columbus Drive
312-565-5258
radissonblu.com/en/
aquahotel-chicago
$$
Upscale version of a Radisson in a prime spot — where the Chicago River meets Lake Michigan.

Hotel Chicago
333 North Dearborn Street
312-245-0333
thehotelchicago.com
$$
Stylish hotel beneath Marina City towers.

Map labels:

1/2 mile
1 kilometer

N. WELLS ST.
N. LASALLE DR.
N. CLARK ST.
N. DEARBORN ST.
N. STATE ST.

N. MICHIGAN AVE.

Chicago Water Taxi

Area of detail below

Marina City **4**

2

Billy Goat Tavern

Shoreline Water Taxi

Chicago Shakespeare Theater

Radisson Blu Aqua Hotel Chicago

Navy Pier **9**

Civic Opera House

3

State and Lake

1

Fairmont Chicago Millennium Park

McCormick Tribune Bridgehouse & Chicago River Museum

S. WACKER DR.

W. CONGRESS PKWY.

7

Willis Tower/ Skydeck

E. JACKSON DR.

Lake Michigan

Chicago Architecture Foundation

S. LAKE SHORE DR.

— Chicago River

Shedd Aquarium

Adler Planetarium

W. ROOSEVELT RD.

Chicago

Field Museum **11**

Ping Tom Memorial Park

8

W. 18TH ST.

CHINATOWN

Chinatown Square

Yan Bang Cai

W. CERMAK RD.

Dr. Sun Yat-Sen Museum

S. WENTWORTH AVE.

S. MICHIGAN AVE.

Merchandise Mart

N. DEARBORN ST.

N. CLARK ST.

Kitchen

Hotel Chicago

N. STATE ST.

6

Riverwalk **5**

House of Blues **10**

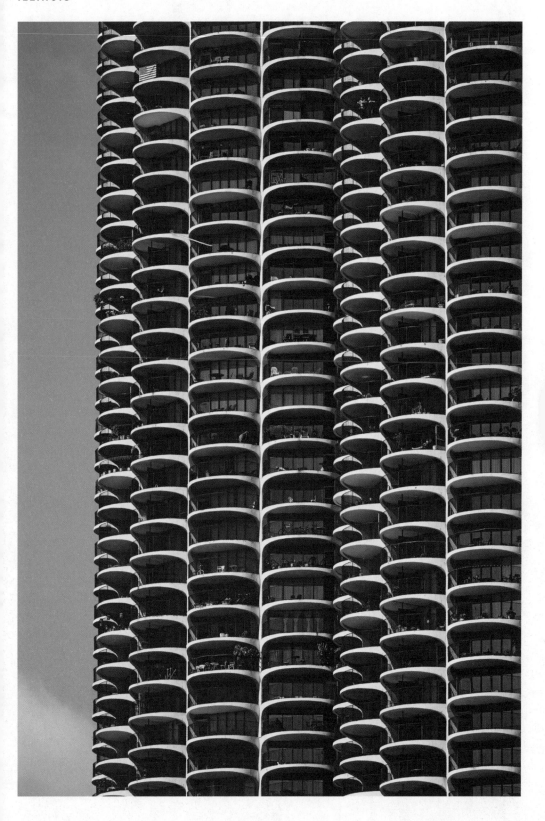

Chicago Neighborhoods

The notion that Chicago is a city of neighborhoods seems silly and obvious at first. Aren't all cities? But a weekend here, wandering the nooks far from the tourists swarming Navy Pier near downtown or ogling the masterpieces at the Art Institute of Chicago, explains the distinction. Cross a single street, from one neighborhood into the next, and you will often find a suddenly changed style of architecture, a distinct language on the signs and, in the street, an utterly different feel. Sadly, a single getaway weekend will never allow enough time to make your way through the vast patchwork of Chicago's neighborhoods. But there is time enough to explore a few, and enough to come away understanding why this is, indeed, a city of neighborhoods. — BY MONICA DAVEY

FRIDAY

1 *The Glamour! The Art!* 3 p.m.

The Magnificent Mile, just north of the Loop along Michigan Avenue, is a neighborhood too full of the city's most glamorous, high-end shops to feel like a neighborhood at all. But in the blur of sales and shopping bags, the **Museum of Contemporary Art** (220 East Chicago Avenue; 312-280-2660; mcachicago.org) makes the Magnificent Mile worth seeing, even for those who hate to shop.

2 *Go West* 5 p.m.

Due west of downtown, the West Loop neighborhood and its surroundings, once distinguished by meat-packing companies, warehouses, and factories, has been transformed into a place of lofts and galleries. There's good shopping in small stores and boutiques, restaurants with exposed old brick walls, and breweries. **City Winery** (1200 West Randolph Street; 312-733-9463; citywinery.com/chicago) really is a winery, as well as a restaurant and live music venue. Venture on into Ukrainian Village, where the churches have domes and some signs are still in Cyrillic script, to **Old Lviv** (2228 West Chicago Avenue; 773-772-7250; facebook.com, search Old Lviv; $). A small, out-of-the-way spot, it's the place to go for authentic borscht and pirogi. Or dine nearby at

OPPOSITE Performers at Constellation on the North Side.

Roister (951 West Fulton Market; roisterrestaurant. com; $$), an upscale casual restaurant that celebrates the global and the local in an eclectic, inventive mix of dishes, from Wagyu beef to shrimp and grits.

3 *Night People* 10 p.m.

Logan Square, on the northwest side of Chicago, is a locus of interesting, grown-up drinking. **Billy Sunday** (3143 West Logan Boulevard; 773-661-2485; billy-sunday.com), named for the last-century temperance crusader (and onetime Chicago White Stockings outfielder), is a cocktail bar where the drinks have names like Bucket of Bottles and Mom Jeans. Ordering the Box Lunch brought no lunch at all — just a concoction of goat's milk, spices, sherry, and wormwood liqueur.

SATURDAY

4 *Head North* 10 a.m.

Lakeview, north of downtown, is a neighborhood of young people, not far from Wrigley Field and the always popular Cubs, Lake Michigan, and a million places to shop. Settle in for a hearty brunch at **Southport Grocery and Cafe** (3552 North Southport Avenue; 773-665-0100; southportgrocery.com; $$), where you might find choices like pancakes made with bread pudding or French toast stuffed with apples, cream cheese, and streusel.

5 *To Sweden and Beyond* Noon

It's a short hop to Andersonville, traditionally the Swedish quarter. It's booming now with families, a substantial gay population, restaurants that serve diverse cuisine, and the kinds of shops that sell vintage housewares. The Swedish Bakery and the Swedish American Museum Center seem surrounded and joined by arrivals from other places. At the **Hopleaf Bar** (5148 North Clark Street; 773-334-9851; hopleaf.com; $$), pause to choose a sampling from nearly 300 beers, many of them Belgian, and munch on moules frites.

6 *Check Your Chakras* 2 p.m.

The dress code in Wicker Park is flannel and denim, and fine old buildings mix with an upscale bohemian cachet. Milwaukee Avenue is dotted

with stylish boutiques selling new and vintage clothing, accessories, and home décor. For book browsing with a glass of wine or an espresso drink, stop in at **Volumes Bookcafe** (1474 North Milwaukee; volumesbooks.com), where cafe tables mingle with the bookshelves. If chakra crystals are your thing, detour to **Ruby Room** (1743 West Division; 773-235-2323; rubyroom.com), a haute New Age spa, salon, and inn where you might measure your electromagnetic field or attend a meditation class.

7 *Under the Eagle's Eye* 5 p.m.

Logan Square is a remnant of Chicago's late 19th-century beautification movement, with broad boulevards and grand turn-of-the-20th-century mansions. After a long decline, it has picked up again in recent years, but its still affordable rents, an alternative to now pricey Wicker Park and Bucktown, make it a magnet for creative types running everything from hip hair salons to an international film series. A statue of an eagle by Evelyn Longman stands where two of the grandest boulevards meet, and nearby, **Longman & Eagle** (2657 North Kedzie Avenue; 773-276-7110; longmanandeagle.com; $$) serves refined pub food to a friendly clientele. It doesn't take reservations, so be prepared to wait.

8 *Show Time* 9 p.m.

For an intriguing take on up-to-the-minute music, seek out **Constellation** (3111 North Western Avenue; constellation-chicago.com), a venue opened in Roscoe Village by the drummer, composer, and Pitchfork Music Festival producer Mike Reed. With influences as varied as Duke Ellington and John Cage, it defines its mission as promoting "forward-thinking" jazz, improvisation, and contemporary classical music. For entertainment in a nostalgic setting, see a movie at the **Music Box** (3733 North Southport Avenue; 773-871-6604; musicboxtheatre. com), a grand old Lakeview neighborhood theater (complete with an organ) that opened in 1929 and shows an eclectic mix, from cutting-edge independent films to old, comforting classics.

SUNDAY

9 *Get Thee to the Fernery* 9 a.m.

Craving peace and quiet? Start the morning in the fern room at the **Garfield Park Conservatory** (300 North Central Park Avenue; 312-746-5100; garfieldconservatory.org), an exquisite building opened in 1908 on the Far West Side. A Green Line L train or cab will carry you through tougher-looking neighborhoods to within a few steps of the conservatory. Once inside, a waft of warm, humid air and the smell of plants will greet you. Relax and breathe.

10 *Southern Exposures* 11 a.m.

Head south to the Pilsen neighborhood, which once was mainly home to Bohemians, Irish, and Germans and is now one of the city's largest Mexican-American communities. Start with a cup of coffee or Mexican hot chocolate and a vegetarian brunch at **Cafe Jumping Bean** (1439 West 18th Street; 312-455-0019; facebook.com/18thStpilsen; $). Then wander past bakeries and art galleries a few blocks toward the **National Museum of Mexican Art** (1852 West 19th Street; 312-738-1503; nationalmuseumofmexicanart.

org), which has made a name for itself both with its fine art displays and with its exhibitions that confront political and cultural issues. Nearby at the **Maxwell Street Market** (800 South Desplaines Street; maxwellstreetmarket.us), Latin music blares and shoppers browse a four-block stretch of stalls on Sundays.

11 *Obama Country* Noon

South of downtown is Hyde Park, home to the University of Chicago, Frank Lloyd Wright's Frederick C. Robie House (5757 South Woodlawn Avenue; flwright.org/visit/robiehouse), and the stellar **Museum of Science and Industry** (5700 Lake Shore Drive; msichicago.org), with its trademark U-505

submarine, and model train with 1,400 feet of track. It's easy to see why Barack and Michelle Obama settled in this leafy, walkable neighborhood before moving to Washington. Their house, on South Greenwood Avenue between 50th and 51st Streets, isn't open, but you can take a selfie outside.

OPPOSITE Relaxing at Cafe Jumping Bean in Pilsen.

ABOVE A seller at the Maxwell Street Market.

THE BASICS

The best ways to get around Chicago are by L train, by bus, and by foot, reserving cabs for late nights or lazy moments.

The LondonHouse
85 East Wacker Drive
312-357-1200
$$
An upscale hotel in a Beaux-Arts building in the Loop with a popular rooftop bar.

Wicker Park Inn
1331 North Wicker Park Avenue
773-486-2743
wickerparkinn.com
$$
Attractive bed-and-breakfast in Wicker Park.

The James
55 East Ontario Street
312-337-1000
jameshotels.com/chicago
$$$
High-design boutique hotel on the Near North Side.

Indianapolis

Indianapolis, Indiana's capital city, may be best known outside the state for sports — professional basketball and football teams, the headquarters of the National Collegiate Athletic Association, and, of course, the Indianapolis Motor Speedway, home of the Indy 500. But there's much more — a new sculpture park, a downtown canal walk, a library dedicated to Kurt Vonnegut, and the multiethnic influences of thriving populations of recent immigrants. It's all mixed in with the old Indianapolis standbys of hearty Midwestern food and Hoosier hospitality and charm. — BY JOHN HOLL

FRIDAY

1 *A Cocktail With That Scotch* 6:30 p.m.

Start with a drink downtown at one of the city's oldest restaurants, **St. Elmo Steak House** (127 South Illinois Street; 317-635-0636; stelmos.com; $$$), where for more than a century patrons have sidled up to the tiger oak bar — first used in the 1893 Chicago World's Fair — for martinis and single malts. Settle in under the gaze of the Indiana celebrities whose photos adorn the walls (David Letterman, Larry Bird) and try St. Elmo's not-for-the-faint-of-heart signature dish: the shrimp cocktail. The jumbo shrimp are served smothered in horseradish cocktail sauce made every hour to ensure freshness and a proper sinus assault. If you can see through the tears in your eyes, you'll probably notice one of the tuxedoed bartenders having a quiet chuckle at your expense.

2 *New Indiana* 7 p.m.

While downtown has been rejuvenating itself with new development, areas out toward the suburbs have been transformed by immigration, with Pakistanis, Salvadorans, Burmese, and an assortment of other groups mingling comfortably. To see a bit of what this melting pot has brought to Indianapolis dining, drive a few miles to **Abyssinia** (5352 West 38th Street, in the Honey Creek Plaza; 317-299-0608; abyssinianindy.weebly.com; $), an Ethiopian restaurant decorated with Haile Selassie portraits and Ethiopia tourism posters. The authentic, well-cooked cuisine incorporates lots of lentils as well as goat in

berbere sauce, house-made injera bread, and sambusas, the Ethiopian version of samosas. The place draws Africans, Indians, vegans, and plenty of longtime Indianans who like a culinary adventure.

3 *Blues and Bands* 10:30 p.m.

Indianapolis has had a blues scene for generations, and it's still alive and kickin' at the **Slippery Noodle Inn** (372 South Meridian Street; 317-631-6974; slipperynoodle.com). Housed in a two-story building constructed as a bar and roadhouse around 1850, the Noodle attracts a lively crowd (including, back in the day, the Dillinger Gang) and nationally known blues musicians like Country Joe McDonald and Ronnie Earl. But it's the local bands that make the place rock, so hoist a pint of the Indiana-brewed Upland IPA and groove on the dance floor to the thumping bass.

SATURDAY

4 *Monumental Efforts* 10 a.m.

Start a walking tour in the heart of downtown at the neo-classical **Soldiers and Sailors Monument** (1 Monument Circle; 317-232-7615), a 284-foot-tall obelisk dating back to 1902. Look over the Civil War museum in the base and then take the elevator or brave the 330 stairs to the top. Back on the ground, it's a short walk down West Market Street to the **Indiana Statehouse**, a suitably domed and columned structure built in 1888. A few blocks north is the **Freemasons' Scottish Rite Cathedral** (650 North Meridian Street; 317-262-3100; aasr-indy.org), actually a meeting hall, not a church. It's a tour de force of ornate decoration with a 212-foot tower, 54 bells, and stained-glass windows. Most guided tours are on weekdays, but a good look at the castle-like exterior gives you the idea.

5 *Duckpins* Noon

Order a salad to keep it light at the **Smokehouse on Shelby** (317-685-1959; $) in the 1928 **Fountain Square Theatre Building** (1105 Prospect Street; fountainsquareindy.com), so that you can follow up with a chocolate malt or a strawberry soda from the restored 1950s soda fountain, rescued from a defunct Woolworth's. Then rent a lane and some shoes at one

OPPOSITE The Canal Walk in downtown Indianapolis.

of the two duckpin bowling alleys in the building. The one upstairs still uses the original 1930s equipment. Downstairs has '50s-vintage bowling.

6 *Bless You, Mr. Vonnegut* 1:30 p.m.

Growing up in Indianapolis, Kurt Vonnegut absorbed an Indiana worldview that informed many of his novels, even when the references to Midwestern virtues and values were ironic. Indianapolis acknowledges its famous literary son at the **Kurt Vonnegut Memorial Library** (340 North Senate Avenue; 317-652-1954; vonnegutlibrary.org), which displays mementoes including his typewriter, his World War II Purple Heart, and rejection letters sent to him by editors in the days before he became famous. The library also has a collection of books, articles, films, and papers, and it sponsors readings and other literary events.

7 *White River Junction* 3 p.m.

Stroll along the canal and through the green spaces of **White River State Park** (801 West Washington Street; 317-233-2434; inwhiteriver.wrsp.in.gov) on the city's west side. You can take your pick of several museums and the Indianapolis Zoo, but a more unusual destination here is the headquarters of the National Collegiate Athletic Association. The **N.C.A.A. Hall of Champions** (317-916-4255; ncaahallofchampions.org) has displays on 23 men's and women's sports, a theater showing memorable college sports moments, and interactive simulators that take you on a virtual trip into a game.

8 *Hoosier Heartland* 6 p.m.

For a real taste of Hoosier country (Indianans wear the Hoosier nickname proudly), grab some hors d'oeuvres and a bottle of wine and drive about 40 minutes northeast of the city, past farmland and cornfields, till you come to **Bonge's Tavern** (9830 West 280 North, Perkinsville; 765-734-1625; bongestavern.com; $$), a country roadhouse that opened in 1934. The restaurant does not take

reservations for fewer than 10 people, so arrive early and be ready to wait 90 minutes or more. Part of the Bonge's experience is chatting with other patrons while sitting on rocking chairs on the enclosed porch, maybe sharing some of the wine and snacks you so thoughtfully brought. Once inside, order the Perkinsville Pork, a juicy, pounded-flat, Parmesan-crusted loin that is worth waiting for.

9 *Basketball Bar* 10 p.m.

High school basketball is practically a religion in Indiana, and there is no more famous team than the 1954 squad from small Milan High School. It won the statewide championship on a final shot by Bobby Plump, who quickly became a folk hero. The story formed the basis for the 1986 film *Hoosiers*. Today, Plump and his family operate a bar, **Plump's Last Shot** (6416 Cornell Avenue; 317-257-5867; facebook. com/Plumps-Last-Shot-54782431600), a hoops-memorabilia-filled hangout in the Broad Ripple neighborhood and the perfect place to catch a game on TV. Sports-mad as Indianapolis may be, however, it also has a healthy respect for the arts. When the **Indianapolis Symphony Orchestra** (indianapolissymphony. org) was threatened financially, the owners of the Colts and the Pacers, the city's two pro teams, were major donors to a successful fund drive to save it.

SUNDAY

10 *Sculpture Hike* 9 a.m.

Explore and play amid 100 acres of outdoor art at the **Virginia B. Fairbanks Art & Nature Park** (4000

Michigan Road; 317-923-1331; discovernewfields.org/do-and-see/places-to-go), adjoining the Indianapolis Museum of Art. Aside from large, lighthearted, and interactive artworks (there's no "no-touch" rule here), the park satisfies a Sunday morning wanderer's wants with woods, grass, wetlands, and a lake.

11 *Start Your Engines* Noon

Naturally you want to get a look at the **Indianapolis Motor Speedway** (4790 West 16th Street; 317-492-6784; indianapolismotorspeedway.com), home of the Indianapolis 500. The **Hall of Fame Museum** within the racetrack grounds displays vintage race cars, trophies, and more than two dozen cars that won the race, including the very first winner (in 1911), a Marmon

Wasp. The narrated bus ride around the fabled oval may be the closest you ever come to racing in the old Brickyard, but unfortunately the driver never gets above 30 miles an hour. You will get up-close views of the famed racing pagoda, Gasoline Alley, and the last remaining strip of the track's original brick surface, 36 inches wide, which now serves as the start/finish line.

OPPOSITE ABOVE The first winner of the Indianapolis 500, on display at the Indianapolis Motor Speedway.

OPPOSITE BELOW Take the dare and order the super-spicy horseradish shrimp cocktail at the century-old St. Elmo Steak House.

THE BASICS

Fly into the Indianapolis airport or drive about three hours south from Chicago. For getting around in the city, you will need a car.

The Alexander
333 South Delaware Street
317-624-8200
thealexander.com
$$
Stylish hotel; part of CityWay, a downtown residential, retail, and office development.

Conrad Indianapolis
50 West Washington Street
317-713-5000
conradindianapolis.com
$$
Luxurious outpost of the Hilton chain.

JW Marriott Indianapolis
10 South West Street
317-860-5800
jwindy.com
$$$
A 34-story swoosh of Indianapolis Colts-blue glass.

Map labels:
2 miles / 4 kilometers
Plump's Last Shot 9
To Bonge's Tavern/ Perkinsville
E. 56TH ST.
Virginia B. Fairbanks Art & Nature Park/ Indianapolis Museum of Art
N. MERIDIAN ST.
N. COLLEGE AVE.
E. 46TH ST.
31
421
Abyssinia
2
65
LAFAYETTE RD.
10
E. 38TH ST.
Indianapolis
70
465
11
Indianapolis Motor Speedway/ Hall of Fame Museum
74
Area of detail
Smokehouse on Shelby/ Fountain Square Theatre Building
465
36
5
31
70
SOUTHERN AVE.
Downtown Indianapolis
Freemasons' Scottish Rite Cathedral
N. CAPITOL AVE.
421
40
INDIANA UNIVERSITY/ PURDUE UNIVERSITY
N. MERIDIAN AVE.
Kurt Vonnegut Memorial Library 6
Soldiers and Sailors Monument/ Civil War Museum
MICH.
Chicago
N.C.A.A. Hall of Champions
White River
Indiana Statehouse
Indianapolis Symphony Orchestra
4
Indianapolis
ILL.
OHIO
Conrad Indianapolis
7
JW Marriott Indianapolis
W. WASHINGTON ST.
1 St. Elmo Steak House
INDIANA
White River State Park
S. DELAWARE ST.
1/4 mile / 1/2 kilometer
S. ILLINOIS ST.
The Alexander
Slippery Noodle Inn 3
KY.

Des Moines

In Iowa's landscape of small towns and farms, Des Moines is the Big City — the state's capital; its business, civic, and cultural hub; and an evolving center of urban pleasures. Well-designed new buildings and a popular sculpture park have revitalized the downtown, theaters and galleries are thriving, and the refurbished East Village area is crowded with restaurants, coffeehouses, shops, and clubs. Des Moines is starting to stay up late. Still, the countryside never feels far away, in miles or in mind-set. And for 10 days every August, there's the Iowa State Fair, renowned for its blue-ribbon agricultural exhibits, butter sculptures, and pork chops on a stick. — BY BETSY RUBINER

FRIDAY

1 *Sculpture on the Lawn* 3 p.m.

Drivers entering Des Moines from the west once sped past a motley collection of worn-out buildings and abandoned auto dealerships, but that vista has been replaced by a five-block landscape of green parkland, meant to be enjoyed on foot. There are curving pathways, benches, and thick grass, but what makes this park outstanding are two dozen contemporary sculptures — by Willem de Kooning, Louise Bourgeois, Richard Serra, and Sol Lewitt, among others — arranged on an undulating lawn. The **John and Mary Pappajohn Sculpture Park** (between Locust Street and Grand Avenue, 13th and 15th Streets; desmoinesartcenter.org; audio tour at 515-657-8264 and online), named for the venture capitalist and his wife who donated the sculptures, covers two formerly dreary blocks. Two arresting pieces: *Nomade*, by the Spanish sculptor Jaume Plensa, a 27-foot-tall hollow human form made of a latticework of white steel letters, and *Glass Colour Circle* by the Berlin-based Olafur Eliasson, a walk-in structure made of 23 nine-foot-tall, 1,200-pound glass panels in various colors, illuminated by lantern light that casts a hazy rainbow.

2 *Transformed Core* 5 p.m.

The park is at the front door of the striking **Des Moines Central Library**, designed by the London architect David Chipperfield. A two-story, 110,000-square-foot building, it is sheathed in glass reinforced by copper mesh that gives it a beguiling glow and makes it a warm anchor to downtown. In the downtown core, many in the dense assortment of office buildings are linked by sheltering sky walks, especially welcome in winter. Along the Des Moines River, a 1.2-mile loop called the **Principal Riverwalk** incorporates gardens, more sculpture, pedestrian bridges, and an outdoor ice rink, **Brenton Skating Plaza** (520 Robert D. Ray Drive; 515-284-1000; brentonplaza.com). Downriver is **Principal Park**, a handsome Triple A ballpark surrounded by old buildings converted into condominiums.

3 *Center Stage* 7 p.m.

An ornate Masonic temple built in 1913 was in danger of being torn down before it was taken over by a local real estate developer, Harry Bookey, who converted it into the **Temple for Performing Arts** (1011 Locust Street; 515-246-2300; templeforperformingarts.com), a recital hall with a richly decorated grand hall and a theater hosting plays and performances. **Centro** (1003 Locust Street; 515-248-1780; centrodesmoines.com; $$),

OPPOSITE A photo opportunity beneath *T8*, by Mark di Suvero, at the John and Mary Pappajohn Sculpture Park.

BELOW Bread for sale at La Mie, a bakery and restaurant. Quiches, sandwiches, and tartines are on the lunch menu.

the bustling ground-floor restaurant, is an enduring symbol of the re-energized downtown. Centro expresses its "Italian urban" theme in choices like lobster ravioli, chicken saltimbocca, and tofu gnocchi, and it has an appealing drinks menu and wine list. Stroll the nearby blocks of the **Court Avenue Entertainment District** for more night life.

SATURDAY

4 *Farm Fresh* 9 a.m.

On Saturday mornings in the months from May through October, the **Downtown Farmers Market** (desmoinesfarmersmarket.com) takes over a chunk of downtown around the intersection of Fourth and Court Avenues. There are spring morels, rhubarb, and asparagus; summer tomatoes, sweet corn, and raspberries; fall apples, squash, and pumpkins; plus a mishmash of ethnic foods (Salvadoran, Indian, Laotian, Afghan) and specialty items (Mennonite pies, elk jerky, buffalo bologna). Don't miss the Dutch Letters — S-shaped pastries filled with almond paste. If you're here on a day when there's no market, take a tour of the **Iowa State Capitol** (515-281-5591; legis.iowa.gov/resources/tourCapitol), one of the country's most beautiful state capitol buildings. Its gilded dome rises grandly over downtown, and inside are marble and carved wood, mosaics, paintings, and other ornate decoration.

5 *Artful Inside and Out* 10:30 a.m.

In 1948 Eliel Saarinen's flat-roofed stone building appeared; in 1968 I.M. Pei's heavy geometric concrete addition; in 1985 Richard Meier's towering wing, clad in white porcelain-coated metal panels.

ABOVE The dome of the Iowa State Capitol rises grandly over downtown Des Moines. Inside, tour guides point out details of the ornate interior decoration.

OPPOSITE ABOVE Transacting business on a Saturday morning at the Downtown Farmers Market.

Combined, they make up the **Des Moines Art Center** (4700 Grand Avenue; 515-277-4405; desmoinesartcenter.org), west of downtown. It's a showcase for contemporary art as well as architecture, with works by Edward Hopper, John Singer Sargent, Louise Bourgeois, Carl Milles, Maya Lin, and Andy Goldsworthy.

6 *Iowa Patisserie* 1 p.m.

La Mie (841 42nd Street; 515-255-1625; lamiebakery.com; $), in a commercial strip on the edge of an old residential neighborhood, specializes in breads (baguette, focaccia, olive ciabatta, rye) and pastries (tarts, macarons, cheesecakes, cookies). It's also the right stop for a classy brunch or lunch (quiche, tartines, sandwiches), with tables and booths beyond the pastry counter.

7 *The Village* 2 p.m.

A once-dying neighborhood east of the Des Moines River, at the foot of the Capitol's golden dome, was reborn as the **East Village**, drawing new, young residents and sprinkled with stylish restaurants, boutiques, galleries, and specialty shops. Do not miss **Sticks** (400 East Locust Street; 515-282-0844; sticksgallery.com), which sells one-of-a-kind hand-painted wood furniture that's made in Des Moines. Stop at **Gong Fu Tea** (414 East Sixth Street; 515-288-3388; gongfu-tea.com), a tranquil Asian-inspired teahouse. **Raygun** (505 East Grand Avenue; 515-288-1323; raygunsite.com) sells cheeky Iowacentric T-shirts such as one aimed at one of the state's famed college towns with the message "Iowa City: All our creativity went into this name."

8 *Dine Beneath the Doors* 8 p.m.

Alba (524 East Sixth Street; 515-244-0261; albadsm.com; $$), an East Village favorite, serves contemporary American food in a minimalist space decorated with colorful paintings and a motley collection of wood-paneled doors hanging from the ceiling. The menu changes often; typical entrees are pan-roasted chicken breast, herb-rubbed hanger steak, and paella. After dinner, stop off at **Wooly's** (504 East Locust Street; 515-244-0550; woolysdm. com), for live music performed in a former Woolworth's store.

SUNDAY

9 *Down on the Farms* 10 a.m.

Experience the evolution of Iowa farming by touring **Living History Farms** (2600 111th Street; Urbandale; 515-278-5286; lhf.org), an open-air museum in a suburb west of the city. A trail connects three period farms that look, feel, and smell like the real McCoy, with authentic crops and livestock as well as interpreters demonstrating chores. The 1700 Ioway Indian Farm has bark lodges and lush gardens of corn, beans, and squash. The 30-acre 1850 Pioneer Farm has a plain log house and hard-working oxen. The 40-acre 1900 farm has a pretty white frame house and the next stage of animal muscle — draft horses.

10 *A Prescription for Ice Cream* Noon

For lunch at an old-fashioned soda fountain, head to **Bauder Ice Cream** (3802 Ingersoll Avenue; 515-255-1124), formerly Bauder Pharmacy, serving ice cream in all its guises, including an irresistible peppermint bar, as well as doughnuts and sandwiches. There are tinted medicine bottles behind the prescription counter, upholstered stools, and a handful of booths. But it isn't a self-conscious throwback — it just hasn't changed much since it opened here in 1916.

THE BASICS

Downtown Des Moines is about 10 minutes by taxi from Des Moines International Airport.

Renaissance Savery Hotel
401 Locust Street
515-244-2151
marriott.com
$$
Renovated hotel, originally opened in 1919, in a Georgian Revival building.

Des Moines Marriott Downtown
700 Grand Avenue
515-245-5500
marriott.com
$$
Pool, downtown location, and flashy City Center Lounge.

Des Lux
800 Locust Street
515-288-5800
desluxhotel.com
$$
Luxury hotel with fitness center; near the sculpture park.

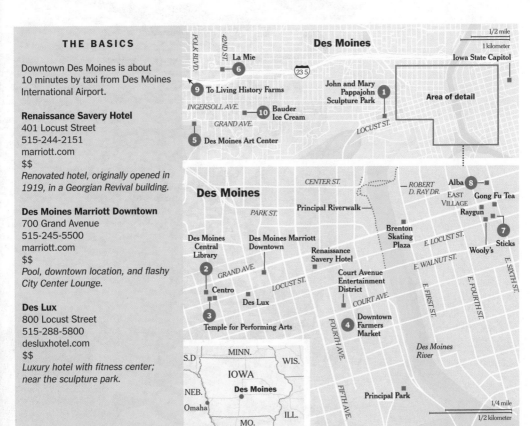

Iowa's Mississippi River

"For 60 years the foreign tourist has steamed up and down the river between St. Louis and New Orleans… believing he had seen all of the river that was worth seeing or that had anything to see," Mark Twain lamented in Life on the Mississippi. *The visitors were missing an "amazing region" to the north, he wrote. They were missing "extraordinary sunsets" and "enchanting scenery." They were missing Iowa. Today, tourists do find Iowa's Mississippi riverfront, thanks partly to modern confections like riverboat casinos and a water park resort, but much of this shore still feels undiscovered. Set out for a weekend car trip on quiet back roads, and you'll find the real life of the Mississippi amid green hilltops and fields, in small villages and busy cities, and on the wide river itself.*
— BY BETSY RUBINER

FRIDAY

1 *Skimming the River* 4 p.m.

Start your Mississippi River explorations in Davenport, about 1,775 miles upstream from the Gulf of Mexico. With no flood wall (though there are perennial arguments about whether to build one), downtown Davenport has a feeling of intimacy with the river, and you can get even closer on the **Channel Cat Water Taxi** (foot of Mound Street at the river; 309-788-3360; gogreenmetro.com/231/Channel-Cat), a small ferry with several stops. From its benches you may see blocks-long grain barges, speedboats, 19th-century riverbank mansions, and egrets on small wooded islands.

2 *Field of Dreams* 7 p.m.

One of the best points to enjoy Davenport's un-usual eye-level river view is **Modern Woodmen Park** (209 South Gaines Street; 563-324-3000; milb.com/quad-cities), the riverfront minor-league baseball field. If the River Bandits are playing at home, have some hot dogs or cheese steak as you take in a game. (There's also a tiki bar.) The park has a small corn-field where, when the stalks are high enough, the Bandits emerge at game time like the ghostly players in *Field of Dreams*, which was filmed in Iowa. If it's not a game night, seek a more substantial dinner at **Front Street Brewery** (208 East River Drive; 563-322-1569; frontstreetbrew.com; $). Look on the menu for walleye, a favorite Midwestern native fish.

SATURDAY

3 *A River Still Traveled* 10 a.m.

Drive down to the levee at **Le Claire** to see a nicely preserved example of the craft used for traveling the river in Twain's day. The *Lone Star* is an 1860s sternwheel steamboat in dry dock at the **Buffalo Bill Museum** (199 North Front Street; 563-289-5580; buffalobillmuseumleclaire.com). Nearby, S.U.V.s towing today's pleasure boats pull up to a launching ramp, disgorging day trippers toting kids, coolers, and life jackets. After the families have sped off, you may see them again, picnicking on an island. A block from the river, along Cody Road—named, as is the museum, for Le Claire's favorite son, William Cody—inviting shops and restaurants rejuvenate old brick storefronts.

4 *From the Heights* Noon

You're passing some of the world's most expen-sive farmland—fertile valley acreage conveniently close to river transportation on the grain barges—as you head north on Routes 67 and 52 to Bellevue. The town lives up to its name with sweeping views from the high bluffs at **Bellevue State Park** (24668 High-way 52; 563-872-4019; iowadnr.gov). A display in the

OPPOSITE Success in the form of a smallmouth bass, pulled from the Mississippi at McGregor.

RIGHT Rolling farmland along Highway 52 between Bellevue and St. Donatus.

park's nature center recalls an early industry in these river towns: making buttons from mussel shells. In the pretty riverside downtown, check out the pizza at **2nd Street Station** (116 South Second Street; 563-872-5410) and stop for a look at **Lock and Dam No. 12** (Route 52 at Franklin Street). Locks are a common feature on the Upper Mississippi, where tugs push as many as 15 barges at a time, carrying as much freight as 870 tractor trailers or a 225-car train.

5 *Luxembourgers* 2:30 p.m.

Stop for a quick glance around tiny **St. Donatus**, where one of America's rarer ethnic groups, immigrants from Luxembourg, arrived in the 1800s and built limestone and stucco buildings. For some classic Iowa landscape, walk up the Way of the Cross path behind the Catholic church and look across the valley at patches of hay and corn quilting the hills. You may smell hogs. Or is it cattle?

6 *Gawk at the Gar* 3 p.m.

Spend some time in **Dubuque**, Davenport's rival Iowa river city. At the **National Mississippi River Museum and Aquarium** (350 East Third Street; 563-557-9545; rivermuseum.com), a Smithsonian affiliate, huge blue catfish, gar, and paddlefish swim in a 30,000-gallon tank; a boardwalk goes through reclaimed wetlands inhabited by herons and bald eagles; and a model shows havoc caused by a 1965 flood. Downtown, Dubuque feels like an old factory town, with Victorian mansions (several converted into inns), brick row houses flush to the street, and many a church and corner tap. Ride the **Fenelon Place Elevator** (512 Fenelon Place; fenelonplaceelevator. com), a funicular that makes a steep climb to a bluff top where Wisconsin and Illinois are visible across the river.

7 *American Pie* 6 p.m.

Follow Highway 52 and the County Route C9Y, the Balltown Road, through a peaceful valley up and up onto a ridge with views worthy of a painting by Grant Wood (an Iowan): wide open sky, a lone pheasant in a field, alternating rows of crops, grazing cows, and tidy farms with stone houses, weathered red barns, and blue silos. Your goal is **Balltown**, which has about 65 residents and one famous restaurant, **Breitbach's** (563 Balltown Road, Route C9Y; 563-552-2220; $-$$). It has been open since 1852 and is justly famed for its fried chicken, barbecued ribs, and fresh pie.

ABOVE Lock and Dam No. 12 spanning the river at Bellevue.

OPPOSITE ABOVE The Fenelon Place Elevator in Dubuque climbs a steep bluff to a panoramic river view.

OPPOSITE BELOW Riverside baseball in Davenport.

SUNDAY

8 *A "T" Too Far* 10 a.m.

Forty miles north of Dubuque, Highway 52 brings you to the river at **Guttenberg**, a lovely town settled by German immigrants in the 1840s and named after the inventor of moveable type, Johannes Gutenberg. (Word has it that an early typographical error accounts for the extra T.) Admire the downtown's well-preserved pre-Civil War-era limestone buildings and stroll at mile-long **Ingleside Park**. A few miles farther on, stop at **McGregor**, where boaters hang out by the marina and locals eat bratwurst and drink beer on riverview restaurant decks. McGregor is also the home of the **River Junction Trade Company** (312 Main Street, McGregor; 866-259-9172; riverjunction.com), which makes reproductions of Old West gear, sometimes selling to Hollywood production companies.

9 *Pike's Other Peak* 11 a.m.

Even if you're getting weary of river panoramas, stop at **Pikes Peak State Park** (32264 Pikes Peak Road, McGregor; 563-873-2341; iowadnr.gov) to see one from the highest bluff on the Mississippi. Like Pikes Peak in Colorado, this spot is named for the explorer Zebulon Pike. Scouting for federal fort locations in 1805, Pike thought this peak was an ideal spot, and although the fort ended up across the river in Wisconsin, you can understand his reasoning. Look out at a swirl of green forested islands and mud-brown river pools. To the north, suspension bridges connect to Wisconsin. To the south, the Wisconsin River empties out at the place where in 1673 the

explorers Jacques Marquette and Louis Jolliet first saw the Mississippi.

10 *Mound Builders* 1 p.m.

At **Effigy Mounds National Monument** (151 Highway 76, Harpers Ferry; 563-873-3491; nps.gov/efmo), 2,526 acres of grounds are dotted with mysterious prehistoric burial and ceremonial mounds, some as old as 2,500 years. The Indians of the Upper Midwest built large numbers of mounds shaped

like animals, most often bears and birds that lived along the Mississippi. Why they were built and who was meant to see them — since the best views are from the sky — remains unknown. Take the two-mile Fire Point Trail up a 360-foot bluff, through forests and past mounds. At the top, a clearing reveals a Mississippi that seems wild — with forested banks and islands, a soupy marsh, and hawks soaring above a bluff — until out of nowhere a speedboat zips by, breaking the silence.

ABOVE A houseboat anchored near McGregor.

OPPOSITE Downtown McGregor, a promising stop for Mississippi River souvenir hunters.

THE BASICS

The Mississippi River is a three-hour drive west from Chicago. The Quad City International Airport serves Davenport.

Hotel Blackhawk
200 East Third Street, Davenport
563-322-5000
hotelblackhawk.com
$$
Stylishly decorated landmark hotel, reopened in 2010 after extensive renovation.

Hotel Julien Dubuque
200 Main Street, Dubuque
563-556-4200
hoteljuliendubuque.com
$$
Boutique décor, pool, and spa in a hotel with history back to Abraham Lincoln's day.

The Landing
703 South River Park Drive, Guttenberg
563-252-1615
thelanding615.com
$
Rooms and suites in a renovated stone riverfront warehouse.

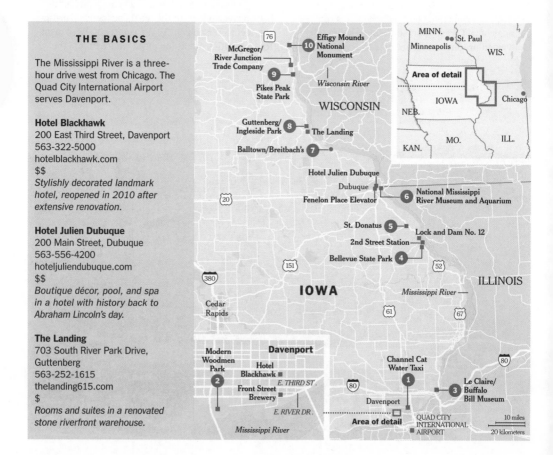

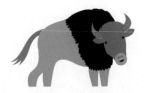

Winnipeg

Once known as "the Chicago of the North," Winnipeg (population 780,000) is a smaller version of the Windy City, with similar broad avenues, century-old architecture, and indie-style art and music. Winnipeg is geographically isolated (it's a thousand miles in either direction to the next large city), so it's a place that has learned how to generate its own entertainment. There are four distinct seasons, all arriving with exclamation marks. (If Winnipeg were portrayed in a stage play, the weather would be one of the main characters.) Culture is the city's principal export industry. Burton Cummings and the Guess Who, Carol Shields, Guy Maddin, Bachman-Turner Overdrive, Neil Young, the Royal Winnipeg Ballet, and countless painters, writers, and actors have grown up out of its cracked sidewalks.

— BY JAKE MACDONALD

FRIDAY

1 *Straight to the Heart* 3 p.m.

Winnipeg was shaped by its rivers, and the two main waterways, the Red River and the Assiniboine, meet in the heart of the city. At the confluence, called the Forks, you'll find a village of restored warehouse buildings, cobblestone avenues, busking musicians, charcoal grills, restaurants, and little shops purveying exotic clothes and handicrafts. For a half-hour tour of the city's waterways by boat, check out **Splash Dash Tours** (204-783-6633; splashdash.ca). Boats leave the Forks Harbor every 15 minutes from 10 a.m. to sunset. Boat captains provide commentary and historical insights along the route — a great way to explore the city's neighborhoods.

2 *Italy on the Forks* 7 p.m.

The vast Forks Market emporium evolved from horse stables for rail companies at the turn of the last century. On the ground floor, tucked within a stone arch, is **Passero** (147-1 Forks Market Road; 204-219-7300; passerowinnipeg.com; $$$), from a Peg City favorite chef, Scott Bagshaw. The interior's ribbed wood walls resemble a whalebone. The

cuisine is Italian, with the emphasis on small plates like a ricotta gnocchi with wild mushrooms and black garlic. A specialty is the beef tartare, concealed within a thinly shaved white radish — like a rose.

3 *River Shimmer* 9 p.m.

At the Forks a paved riverwalk winds off along the waterfront in either direction. Colored lanterns and city lights swim on the water on a summer night, and boats cruise past in the darkness. It's a bucolic and safe inner-city stroll, populated with skaters, lovers, and families. Some of the biggest catfish on the continent live in this river, and here and there you'll see anglers sitting on the bank, waiting for a tug.

SATURDAY

4 *First, the Flapjacks* 8:30 a.m.

Seek out the **Original Pancake House** (1 Forks Market Road; 204-947-5077; originalpancakehouse.ca; $$), a local institution founded over half a century ago. Great coffee comes from a bottomless vat, and lovely morning light pours through all-glass walls. The pride of the house is the oven-baked apple pancake topped with cinnamon-sugar glaze, with sausages on the side.

5 *Sailors and Fur Traders* 10 a.m.

Three centuries ago, much of the interior of North America was governed by a private corporation, its currency being the "MB" (Made Beaver) and its fortified headquarters at trading posts along Hudson Bay and the river network to the south. The Hudson's Bay Company, established in 1670 and soon rich on the fur trade, is still the oldest corporation in North America, and its Fort Garry eventually grew into the city of Winnipeg. At the **Manitoba Museum** (190 Rupert Avenue; 204-956-2830; manitobamuseum.ca), the company gets its due and the early history of the continent comes to life. Visitors can enter a gallery that recreates the English port of Deptford, circa 1668, and climb aboard a seaworthy replica of the HMS *Nonsuch*, the sailing ship that conducted the first trading voyage to North America. In other galleries, aboriginal families make camp in the woods, and an immense polar bear pads across snow under the Northern Lights.

6 *Lunch With the Bears* 1 p.m.

A short drive or bus ride takes you to **Assiniboine Park** (55 Pavilion Crescent; 204-927-6000; assiniboinepark.ca), a vast estate of lawn, ponds, and forest with a conservatory, a miniature steam train, and a zoo. Before exploring the grounds, stop at the **Tundra Grill** (204-927-8040; $$) and have lunch while watching polar bears through a 150-foot-wide wall of windows. Later, before you leave the park, find the statue of a soldier and a bear cub near the entrance and take the time to learn the story behind it. A young lieutenant heading off to World War I in 1914 adopted a black bear cub and named it for his hometown — Winnipeg, or Winnie for short. It became his unit's mascot, and in 1919 he donated it to the London Zoo. It was a popular attraction, and a boy named Christopher Robin named his teddy bear after it. You can guess the rest: the boy's father was A. A. Milne, and the bear was immortalized as Winnie the Pooh.

7 *Date Night* 7:30 p.m.

There are a couple of sushi restaurants in town more expensive than **Blufish** (179 Bannatyne Avenue; 204-779-9888; blufish.ca; $$), but this is the place that locals regard as the ultimate in delicate Japanese cuisine. Small and elegant, it is quiet enough for intimate conversation, and the exquisite tidbits of sashimi, ben roll, and tuna tataki awaken

the nerve endings like Sonny Rollins playing the sax. Winnipeg males seeking to impress their dates reserve Table One.

8 *Action After Dark* 9:30 p.m.

You're in the heart of the Exchange District, a neighborhood of historical buildings, art galleries, and offbeat boutiques. A few blocks west of Blufish is the **Old Market Square**, an open-air park with live world music and thronging crowds on warm nights. Across the street is the **King's Head** (120 King Street; 204-957-7710; kingshead.ca), a loud, crowded pub with designer beers on tap, a good supply of pool tables, and a rowdy Celtic dance band doing its best to blow the roof off.

SUNDAY

9 *Brunch at the Fort* 10 a.m.

The **Fort Garry Hotel** (222 Broadway; 204-942-8251; fortgarryhotel.com), Winnipeg's grandest and oldest, puts on a magnificent brunch every Sunday

---

ABOVE Autumn on the Assiniboine Riverwalk. Winnipeg is a city of rivers, and the Forks, where the Assiniboine meets the Red, is a favorite playground.

OPPOSITE ABOVE "The Great Buffalo Hunt," a diorama at the Manitoba Museum in Winnipeg.

morning. The building is an outstanding example of the "neo chateau" style of architecture that was established in New York at the Plaza Hotel and spread across Canada with a chain of palatial railway hotels. The Fort Garry has a ghost, of course, who seldom comes for breakfast but is occasionally spotted in the hallways.

10 *Rebellion Gone Wrong* 11 a.m.

Right behind the hotel are the remains of the fort where Louis Riel, a leader in the French-descended Métis community, hatched a plan to rebel against the Canadian government of 1870 and start a new nation. Riel apparently agreed with the old revolutionary dictum that you have to break a few eggs to make an omelet, and ordered the death of a local loudmouth named Thomas Scott. By some accounts, the firing squad was drunk and the execution was a messy affair with the not-quite-dead Scott shouting from

inside his coffin. Is Thomas Scott the hotel ghost? Is he still upset at Louis Riel?

11 *The French Quarter* Noon

Immediately east of the Forks is the **Esplanade Riel**, a futuristic-looking pedestrian cable bridge that crosses the river and leads into Winnipeg's **French Quarter**, the home of the largest Canadian French population outside Quebec. Its citizens are proudly francophone, and the shops and cafes have a French flavor. Visit the nearby cemetery and the grave of Louis Riel (tourismeriel.com), who was eventually charged with treason and hanged but is now celebrated as the Father of Manitoba.

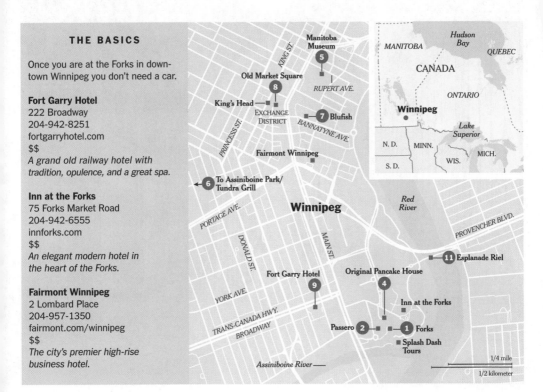

THE BASICS

Once you are at the Forks in downtown Winnipeg you don't need a car.

Fort Garry Hotel
222 Broadway
204-942-8251
fortgarryhotel.com
$$
A grand old railway hotel with tradition, opulence, and a great spa.

Inn at the Forks
75 Forks Market Road
204-942-6555
innforks.com
$$
An elegant modern hotel in the heart of the Forks.

Fairmont Winnipeg
2 Lombard Place
204-957-1350
fairmont.com/winnipeg
$$
The city's premier high-rise business hotel.

Detroit

Detroit might be one of the most misunderstood cities in America. Founded in 1701, it boomed in the mid-20th century and declined in the Rust Belt years. But it remained defiantly proud, and now a new energy is transforming it once again. The Motown sound, embraced around the world, still resonates. Downtown, and in the Midtown and New Center neighborhoods, economic and residential growth has been exponential. The Pistons and the Red Wings are playing in a new arena. And at its core, residents old and new are injecting a remarkable vibrancy into the city. — BY JOHN L. DORMAN

FRIDAY

1 *Studio Sounds* 2:30 p.m.

At the **Motown Museum** (2648 West Grand Boulevard; motownmuseum.org), you'll be encouraged to sing and dance to the Temptations hit "My Girl" (written by Smokey Robinson and Ronald White) in front of complete strangers. And you won't care one bit. With $800 and a dream, the songwriter Berry Gordy started Motown Records in 1959, and the rest is history. From Mary Wells and Stevie Wonder to the Jackson 5 and Marvin Gaye, with countless legends in between, the museum captures the label's early years perfectly. Studio A, where the Supremes first sang "Stop in the Name of Love," contains an 1877 Steinway grand piano.

2 *Room for Squares* 4 p.m.

A thick, crunchy crust, cut into squares, defines Detroit-style pizza. Since 1946, **Buddy's Pizza** (17125 Conant Street; buddyspizza.com; $) has made a delectable deep-dish pie. This location, the original, radiates a homey charm and makes a variety of pizzas to choose from. Add a Vernors Float, which features vanilla ice cream and Vernors, a Detroit original that imparts new meaning to the name "ginger ale."

3 *Night at the Museum* 6 p.m.

Boasting one of the finest collections of art in the world, the **Detroit Institute of Arts** (5200 Woodward Avenue; dia.org) has more than 100 galleries, featuring works from artists as varied as Mary Cassatt and Hughie Lee-Smith. Diego Rivera's *Detroit Industry* frescoes are a fitting tribute to the city's industrial,

working-class roots. On Fridays, the museum remains open until 10 p.m., with live music and special workshops.

4 *Midwestern Mixology* 10:30 p.m.

Standby (225 Gratiot Avenue; standbydetroit. com), with its intimate, speakeasy feel, has helped elevate Detroit's previously limited cocktail scene into a creative movement. Located off the Belt, an artsy downtown alley connecting Grand River and Gratiot Avenues, it offers roughly 50 cocktails. Between the exceptional drinks and the welcoming staff, you'll be in good hands.

SATURDAY

5 *Changing Gears* 10 a.m.

Tucked in a somewhat forgotten industrial neighborhood, the **Ford Piquette Avenue Plant** (461 Piquette Avenue; fordpiquetteplant.org) is one of the most significant car factories ever built. This was where the first Model T was constructed. In the early 20th century, Studebaker had a plant next door. The exceptional guided tour gives you a sense of the plant's huge role in American automotive history. Among an extensive selection of cars, you'll find a 1904 curved dash Oldsmobile body, largely

OPPOSITE The grand interior of the Fisher Building, part of the rich architectural legacy from Detroit's gilded era.

BELOW The conservatory in Belle Isle Park. An aquarium and a museum of the Great Lakes are also in the park.

considered to be the first mass-produced gasoline vehicle, along with some of the first Cadillacs and a classic 1965 Ford Mustang.

6 *Lunch That Satisfies* Noon

Get serious with lunch by choosing one of the hearty local favorites. The signature sandwich at the Corktown fixture **Mudgie's Deli & Wine Shop** (1413 Brooklyn Street; mudgiesdeli.com; $$) is, aptly, the Mudgie: house-roasted Michigan-raised beef brisket and turkey breast, housemade cream cheese, and various fixings, served warm on an onion roll. Or get any one of the other two dozen hearty sandwiches on offer from a deli consistently

voted Detroit's best. **Taqueria El Rey** (4730 West Vernor Highway; taqueria-elrey.com; $), a cash-only Mexicantown restaurant, has some of the best tacos anywhere. And **Lafayette Coney Island** (118 West Lafayette Boulevard; facebook.com/Lafayette-Coney-Island-143071722397988; $), purveys the classic Detroit experience, a hot dog (or two) topped with chili, mustard, and onions.

7 *Gilded Detroit* 1 p.m.

The **Guardian Building** (500 Griswold Street; guardianbuilding.com), a financial district sky-scraper with an amalgam of Art Deco and Mayan Revival styles, features a three-story vaulted lobby with locally crafted Pewabic tiles and an intricate mural of Michigan. The architect Albert Kahn designed the **Fisher Building** (3011 West Grand Boulevard; thefisherbuilding.com), another Art Deco gem in the New Center neighborhood. You can tour either building, courtesy of Pure Detroit (shop.puredetroit.com), and learn more about the city's gilded era. Both also contain Pure Detroit retail stores, which sell T-shirts, hats, and magnets

ABOVE Cars weren't all black at the start of the Model T era. This collection is at the Ford Piquette Avenue Plant.

LEFT Color and pattern vie for attention in the lobby of the Guardian Building, an Art Deco and Mayan Revival gem.

to show your Detroit pride. Close to the Guardian building is the **Monument to Joe Louis**, the African-American boxer who was the heavyweight champion of the world from 1937 to 1949. Dedicated in 1986, five years after his death, the fist-shaped monument weighs 8,000 pounds and is suspended in a traffic island at the busy intersection of Jefferson and Woodward Avenues. You can't miss it.

8 *Retail Renaissance* 3:30 p.m.

Detroit's retail scene is alive and growing. The luxury brand **Shinola**, based in Detroit, has a minimalist Midtown store (441 West Canfield Street; shinola.com) featuring its trademark watches, bikes, and leather accessories. The men's clothing designer **John Varvatos**, a Detroit native, opened a snazzy, guitar-filled branch of his namesake store in the

BELOW The Belle Isle Aquarium displays underwater life in a building designed by the architect Albert Kahn.

Lower Woodward Avenue Historic District (1500 Woodward Avenue; johnvarvatos.com), joining the upscale retailers Bonobos, Moosejaw, and Warby Parker. For a quirky change of pace, do some exploring at the mammoth **John K. King Books** (901 West Lafayette Boulevard; johnkingbooksdetroit.com), where you need a map (there's one online) to navigate the used books on seemingly every subject.

9 *Jazz Composition* 8:30 p.m.

Baker's Keyboard Lounge (20510 Livernois Avenue; theofficialbakerskeyboardlounge.com; $), one of the oldest jazz clubs in the world, exudes a coziness that only heightens the stellar musical performances. Luminaries including Ella Fitzgerald, Miles Davis, and Cab Calloway performed here, and the bar surface resembles a keyboard. The Southern-inflected menu includes entrees like smothered pork chops, meat loaf, and catfish, and sides like yams and black-eyed peas.

atmosphere is festive, so naturally the space fills up fast. That's why you're going early.

11 *Maritime Mode* 10:30 a.m.
Located on Belle Isle Park, a 982-acre island park in the Detroit River, the **Dossin Great Lakes Museum** (100 The Strand, Belle Isle; detroithistorical.org) showcases the history of the Great Lakes. There are simulations and hands-on exhibits, as well as artifacts like the pilot house of the *William Clay Ford*, a Great Lakes freighter, and *Miss Pepsi*, a circa-1950 hydroplane. When you leave the museum, enjoy the rest of the park, including its aquarium and conservatory.

SUNDAY

10 *Crowd Pleaser* 8:30 a.m.
Dime Store (719 Griswold Street, Suite 180; eatdimestore.com; $$) is the rare creative brunch spot that can win over skeptics. Breakfast staples like steel-cut oatmeal and brioche French toast can be paired with more adventurous items like the lemon curd waffle and bacon avocado omelet. The

ABOVE Hitsville U.S.A., the heart of the Motown Museum.

OPPOSITE A bird's-eye view of illuminated downtown Detroit.

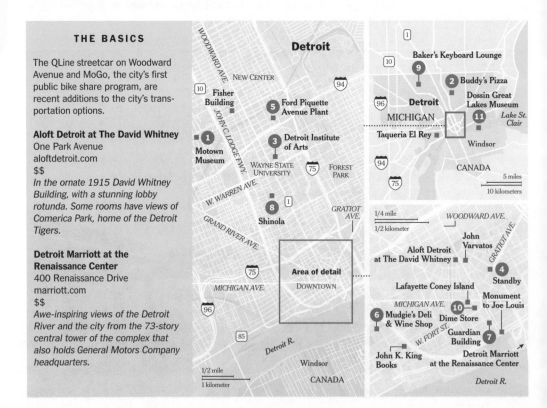

THE BASICS

The QLine streetcar on Woodward Avenue and MoGo, the city's first public bike share program, are recent additions to the city's transportation options.

Aloft Detroit at The David Whitney
One Park Avenue
aloftdetroit.com
$$
In the ornate 1915 David Whitney Building, with a stunning lobby rotunda. Some rooms have views of Comerica Park, home of the Detroit Tigers.

Detroit Marriott at the Renaissance Center
400 Renaissance Drive
marriott.com
$$
Awe-inspiring views of the Detroit River and the city from the 73-story central tower of the complex that also holds General Motors Company headquarters.

Duluth

Believe it. Minnesota bakes in the summer. And when temperatures hit the 90s, many Minnesotans head for Duluth, a city on the westernmost tip of Lake Superior that is cooled to comfort by lakeshore breezes. Built into bluffs overlooking this largest of the Great Lakes, Duluth was shaped by its long role as the port gateway to Minnesota's Iron Range (although many outside Minnesota know it best as the childhood home of Bob Dylan). Bed-and-breakfasts and museums now occupy spacious Victorian mansions built by mining and lumber barons. And Canal Park, once an abandoned warehouse district, is a vibrant waterfront area of shops, bars, and restaurants. — BY PAT BORZI

FRIDAY

1 *Lakefront Ramble* 5 p.m.

Acquaint yourself with **Canal Park** and the harbor by strolling the **Lakewalk**, a three-mile path along the Lake Superior shore. Whether you go the whole way or only part of it, rest your feet and enjoy the view from the courtyard deck of the **Fitger's Brewery Complex** (600 East Superior Street; fitgers.com), a mile from Canal Park. A big brewery from 1859 until 1972, Fitger's was converted into shops, nightclubs, restaurants, and a luxury hotel and now houses a microbrewery, **Fitger's Brewhouse** (218-279-2739). Have a drink and watch the hulking ore boats inch in and out of the harbor. Too tired to walk back? Hop the **Port Town Trolley** (duluthtransit.com/riderguide/porttowntrolley), which serves Canal Park and the downtown hotels until about 7 p.m. in summer.

2 *What, No Ping?* 7 p.m.

They use real wooden bats in the Northwoods League, whose 12 teams are made up of top-level players from colleges around the United States and Canada. The Duluth Huskies play at cozy **Wade Municipal Stadium** (101 North 35th Avenue West; 218-786-9909; northwoodsleague.com), a Works Progress Administration relic that opened in 1941. Tickets are cheap, and families have a great time.

3 *Ironman Gelato* 10 p.m.

Sometimes the iron ore didn't make it out of Duluth, and one reminder of those days is **Clyde Iron Works** (2920 West Michigan Street; 218-727-1150;

clydeparkduluth.com), once a foundry complex that turned out heavy equipment for logging and construction. Today it's a cavernous space that holds a restaurant, bakery, and events hall. Catch some live music, a late dinner, and drinks. Or at least dig into a homemade baked dessert or gelato.

SATURDAY

4 *Breakfast at Mom's* 10 a.m.

Few places in Duluth do breakfast as well as the **Amazing Grace Bakery Café** (394 South Lake Avenue; 218-723-0075; amazinggraceduluth.com; $), in the basement of the **DeWitt-Seitz Marketplace** in Canal Park. The funky interior is a hoot. If your mother ever had plastic tablecloths with designs of oranges, apples, and peaches on them, she'd love this place. Try French toast, muffins, or scones.

5 *Crime Scene* 11:30 a.m.

Of all the captains of industry who once called Duluth home, Chester A. Congdon was one of the richest. **Glensheen** (3300 London Road; 218-726-8910; glensheen.org), his baronial 39-room lakefront

OPPOSITE Glensheen, a baronial mansion on the Lake Superior waterfront, belonged to Chester A. Congdon, one of Duluth's captains of industry. If your tour guide doesn't bring it up, ask about the double murder committed at the estate in 1977.

BELOW The former Fitger's Brewery Complex now holds shops, restaurants, a hotel, and a microbrewery.

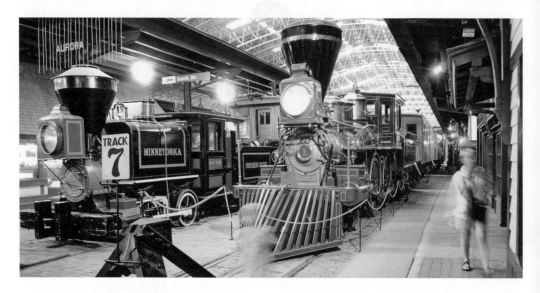

mansion on almost eight acres, was completed in 1908. The basic tour of the main house's lower floors takes about an hour. An expanded tour includes the Arts and Crafts collection on the third floor. At one time tour guides were discouraged from discussing the double murder committed at the estate in 1977. An intruder smothered the 83-year-old heiress to the Congdon family fortune with a pink satin pillow and beat her night nurse to death with a candlestick holder. Most guides now mention the crime, but you may not hear about it unless you ask.

6 *A View from the Wall* 2 p.m.

    Grandma's Saloon & Grill (522 Lake Avenue South; 218-727-4192; grandmasrestaurants.com/retail.htm) is a popular Canal Park destination. Its deck overlooks the century-old Aerial Lift Bridge, where the roadway rises in one piece to let ore and grain boats pass. But it's more fun to grab a single-scoop waffle cone at **Grandma's Ice Cream Boxcar**, the grill's ice cream and soda stand across the parking lot, and join the crowd along the canal wall and watch these huge vessels go by. Wave to the deckhands—they'll wave back—but don't be the one who jumps when the ship sounds its horn.

7 *The Iron Boats* 3:30 p.m.

    The doomed ore freighter *Edmund Fitzgerald*, sunk in a storm on Lake Superior in 1975 and immortalized in song by Gordon Lightfoot, departed from Superior, Wisconsin, across the harbor from Duluth. To get a sense of proportion, tour the immense *William A. Irvin*, a 610-foot retired laker that is 110 feet shorter than the Fitzgerald. The flagship of U.S. Steel's Great Lakes Fleet from 1938 to 1978, the *Irvin* (350 Harbor Drive; 218-722-7876; decc.org/william-a-

irvin) is named for the former U.S. Steel president who occasionally sailed on it himself. The tour takes you through the engine room, the immense hold that could handle up to 14,000 tons of iron ore and coal, and the officers' and crew's quarters. Note the contrast of the stark crew's rooms with the stunning walnut-paneled staterooms for big-shot passengers.

8 *Tequila Sunset* 7 p.m.

    The tough part at **Little Angie's Cantina and Grill** (11 East Buchanan Street; 218-727-6117; littleangies. com; $) is scoring a table at its elevated deck, Canal Park's best perch for people-watching. But in cool weather, the dining room is a lively spot, decorated with Southwest artifacts that match the Tex-Mex fare (and 60-plus tequilas). Its margaritas come in three sizes. The largest, the 45-ounce mucho, goes well with chicken fajitas (and maybe a tableful of friends ready to share a few sips). On Saturday nights, part of the fun comes from the live music, with local solo artists and small bands playing both country and alternative rock.

SUNDAY

9 *On the Rails* 10 a.m.

    Hop the trolley to the Depot, also known as the **Lake Superior Railroad Museum** (506 West Michigan Street; 218-727-8025; lsrm.org), and relive Duluth's rich railroad history. Beneath the former Union Depot,

ABOVE The Lake Superior Railroad Museum has an extensive collection of old locomotives and train cars.

OPPOSITE Take the Lakewalk from Canal Park to reach Fitger's, a landmark impossible to miss.

which in its heyday handled seven railroads and up to 50 trains a day, lies one of the country's most extensive collections of old locomotives, coaches, and other equipment. The admission price also gets you into the rest of the St. Louis County Heritage and Arts Center, which includes a children's museum and a gallery.

10 *Just an Embryo* Noon

The **Electric Fetus** (12 East Superior Street; 218-722-9970; electricfetus.com/Venue/10092) is a record shop as eccentric as its name suggests. If you absolutely have to get your toddler a Dead Kennedys T-shirt, this is the place to find it. The original Fetus opened in Minneapolis in 1968, and in many ways this branch remains stuck in time: for starters, the store smells

like incense. The Fetus is known for offering CDs across every genre, and even if you don't buy anything on your way out of town, you should get a laugh out of looking at the buttons and head-shop merchandise.

THE BASICS

Fly into Duluth International Airport or drive two and a half hours from Minneapolis. You will need a car to venture beyond downtown and Canal Park.

South Pier Inn on the Canal
701 South Lake Avenue
218-786-9007
southpierinn.com
$$-$$$
Water views near the lift bridge on the Duluth Harbor canal.

Suites Hotel at Waterfront Plaza
325 Lake Avenue South
218-727-4663
thesuitesduluth.com
$$
Former home of Marshall-Wells, once billed as the world's largest hardware distributor.

Fitger's Inn
600 East Superior Street
218-722-8826
fitgers.com
$$
Has the feel of a grand old Western hotel, with 19th-century furnishings and an ornate cashier's cage.

Glensheen 5

1 mile
2 kilometers

MINNESOTA 61

Area of detail

Duluth

Clyde Iron Works

South Pier — Inn on the Canal

3 CANAL PARK

Lake Superior

2 Wade Municipal Stadium

Superior

WISCONSIN

CANADA

N.D. MINN. Lake Superior

Duluth •

Minneapolis WIS.

S.D. St. Paul

IOWA

Lake Superior Railroad Museum 9

St. Louis County Heritage and Arts Center

1/4 mile
1/2 kilometer

Fitger's Brewery Complex/ Fitger's Brewhouse/ Fitger's Inn

N. THIRD AVE. E.

E. FIRST ST.

N. FIRST AVE. E.

E. SUPERIOR ST.

10 Electric Fetus

Lake Superior

Duluth

35

Suites Hotel at Waterfront Plaza

Port Town Trolley

William A. Irvin 7

Amazing Grace Bakery Café/ DeWitt-Seitz Marketplace 4

CANAL PARK

Little Angie's 8 Cantina and Grill

E. BUCHANAN ST.

Grandma's Saloon & Grill 6

Grandma's Ice Cream Boxcar

HARBOR DR.

LAKE AVE. S.

1 Lakewalk

AERIAL LIFT BRIDGE —

Minneapolis-St. Paul

Minnesotans take pride in their humility, but make an exception when it comes to showing folks around. And they have a lot to show. There is a depth of cultural amenities to Minneapolis and its not-so-twin city St. Paul that will surprise a first-time visitor. And please remember, when they ask you at the coffee shop, "How you doing, today?" they really want to know.
— BY DAVID CARR

FRIDAY

1 *By the Falls of Minnehaha* 5 p.m.

On a hot summer day, there is convenient and diverting respite at **Minnehaha Park** (4825 South Minnehaha Park Drive; 612-721-8990; minneapolisparks.org). Don't go there expecting Niagara; rather, you'll find a quaint urban park with both landscaped and wild elements, a surprisingly good seafood restaurant (the Sea Salt Eatery; seasalteatery. wordpress.com), and, of course, the 53-foot Falls of Minnehaha that Henry Wadsworth Longfellow wrote about in *The Song of Hiawatha*. Now, Longfellow never actually saw the falls—he was inspired by the writing of others—but why put such a fine point on it?

2 *Intermission With a View* 7 p.m.

Many cities in the middle of the country chirp reflexively about their "great theater," but Minneapolis lives up to its rhetoric with strong independent companies. Among them is the **Guthrie Theater** (818 South Second Street; 612-377-2224; guthrietheater.org), a first-rate repertory theater with a recently built facility featuring a cantilevered bridge to nowhere. Step out and you can see all the way to the city's industrial northeast. Inside, you can take in a well-acted play.

3 *To the Warehouses* 8 p.m.

People are of two minds about Minneapolis's warehouse district. There are those who live for the street-filling frolic of a Friday night, and many who would drive miles to avoid it. A point for the former is

the **112 Eatery** (112 North Third Street; 612-343-7696; 112eatery.com; $$), where you can avoid the mob by going to the upstairs bar for the tagliatelle with foie gras meatballs. Afterward, liquid diversions can commence. Start at the **Monte Carlo** (219 Third Avenue North; 612-333-5900; montecarlomn.com). Lawyers, politicos, and media types congregate here amid a mind-boggling, and potentially mind-bending, array of alcohol. Move on to **Lee's Liquor Lounge** (101 Glenwood Avenue; 612-338-9491; leesliquorlounge. com), just west of downtown, where Trailer Trash may be playing. You can face-plant at the nearby and artful Chambers hotel, or just have a nightcap on the rooftop then cab back to your own hotel.

SATURDAY

4 *You Going to Eat That?* 10 a.m.

Tell room service to keep it quiet when they deliver coffee. Or if you are feeling ambitious, go to **Al's Breakfast** in Dinkytown (413 14th Avenue Southeast; 612-331-9991; alsbreakfastmpls.com), hard by the east-bank campus of the University of Minnesota. Wait against the wall for one of 14 stools while eyeing the food of the patron whose stool you are coveting. Minnesota is a friendly place, but don't ask for a bite of his blueberry pancakes. Order the hash browns and forswear ever eating so-called home fries again.

OPPOSITE AND RIGHT The Walker Art Center, devoted to modern and contemporary art, and Claes Oldenburg's *Spoonbridge and Cherry* in its sculpture garden.

5 *Necklace of Blue* 11:30 a.m.

So many lakes right in the city, but which one is for you? If you wear socks with sandals and think walking is a sport, **Lake Harriet** is for you. If you are prone to nudity and like swimming at night, then it's **Hidden Beach at Cedar Lake**. The rest of us can go to **Lake Calhoun**. Wheels of any kind, most commonly rollerblades, take you around it, but why not go to the boathouse and rent a canoe (wheelfunrentals.com)? Avoid the sailboats and windsurfers by paddling under the bridge into Lake of the Isles, which is sort of swampy to walk around, but lovely from the water.

6 *Spoon Feeding* 2:30 p.m.

The **Walker Art Center** (725 Vineland Place; 612-375-7600; walkerart.org) has one of the best contemporary art collections between the coasts, but why not stay outside for a little artist-designed mini-golf? At the sculpture garden, one might be tempted to climb into the giant spoon by Claes Oldenburg and Coosje van Bruggen. Don't. Motion detectors were installed after locals decided to memorialize their love with nocturnal visits. **Café Lurcat** (1624 Harmon Place; 612-486-5500; cafelurcat.com; $$), across the walking bridge, has excellent small plates.

7 *Ambulatory Retail* 4:30 p.m.

Shopping in Minnesota is usually reductively assigned to the Mall of America, but there is a strollable necklace of stores along Grand Avenue in St. Paul where down-home and style make nice. **Bibelot** (No. 1082; 651-222-0321; bibelotshops.com) has been featuring cool local stuff for four decades, and **Cooks of Crocus Hill** (No. 877; 651-228-1333;

ABOVE The Guthrie Theater in Minneapolis.

RIGHT Kitchenware at Cooks of Crocus Hill, one of the stores that make for good shopping on Grand Avenue.

OPPOSITE So many lakes in Minneapolis — which to choose on a summer day? This beach lover picked Lake Calhoun.

cooksofcrocushill.com) is the foodie perennial that just won't quit. If you get hungry or thirsty, you can always walk into **Dixie's on Grand** (No. 695; 651-222-7345; dixiesongrand.com) for some Southern-inspired fare.

8 *The North Star* 7 p.m.

As in many urban areas, the ineffable epicenter of cool migrates on a schedule known only to a select few. In Minneapolis, the indigenous tribe of artists, musicians, and wannabes have forsaken Uptown for Northeast, where trendy restaurants and bars have taken root. **Brasa Premium Rotisserie** (600 East Hennepin Avenue; 612-379-3030; brasa.us) is a new-ish favorite where precious food localism comes without a dear price. Another is **331 Club** (331 13th Avenue Northeast; 612-331-1746; 331club.com), with a neighborhood vibe even a visitor can't miss. Yes, you should try the Hot Polack, a mix of jalapeños, kraut, and bratwurst. And if you like speakeasys with secret entrances, find the **Back Bar** at **Young Joni**. Open the door in the alley alongside the restaurant (165 13th Avenue Northeast; 612-345-5719; youngjoni.com), and you'll find a moodily lit lounge and excellent cocktails.

9 *Here Comes a Regular* 11 p.m.

The Replacements may not drink anymore at the **CC Club** (2600 Lyndale Avenue South; 612-874-7226;

ccclubuptown.com). And Tom Arnold was 86'ed for the last time a while ago. But the venerable club remains a nexus for the city's down and dirty rock scene. Plus, there's a killer jukebox and no live music to try to talk over.

SUNDAY

10 *Over the River* 9 a.m.

Head over the river and check out St. Paul's **City Hall** (15 Kellogg Boulevard West; stpaul.gov), where *Vision of Peace*, a 60-ton onyx statue, towers over a lobby done in black Zigzag Moderne. And try to grab a booth at **Mickey's Diner** (36 West Seventh Street; 651-698-0259; mickeysdiningcar.com).

11 *A Historic Visit* Noon

History museums in fairly young places like Minnesota can be dreary, but not so at **Paisley Park** (7801 Audubon Road, Chanhassen; 612-474-8555; officialpaisleypark.com), where Prince lived and worked from 1987 until his death in 2016. Book your tour ahead of time, view the Purple One's studios, view his many costumes, guitars, and motorcycles, and you'll see: the man who warned us to act our age, not our shoe size, was Minnesota Nice.

THE BASICS

Take light rail or drive from the airport to downtown. There are cabs, but you will want a car to get beyond downtown.

Le Méridien Chambers Minneapolis
901 Hennepin Avenue
612-767-6900
lemeridienchambers.com
$$-$$$
Gorgeous, beautifully designed hotel with good food, lovely rooms, and a wonderful lounge.

The Depot Renaissance Hotel
225 Third Avenue South
612-375-1700
thedepotminneapolis.com
$$
Retrofitted in the historic Depot.

hotel340
340 Cedar Street, St. Paul
651-280-4120
hotel340.com
$$
Comfortable modern rooms in a lavishly detailed 1917 landmark building.

Kansas City

Kansas City, Missouri, is known for its barbecue, bebop, and easy-does-it Midwestern charm. Still a jazz mecca, the place where Charlie Parker, Lester Young, and Count Basie all got their start, it also has a newer and broader cultural richness. A buzzing revitalized downtown includes gleaming residential towers, a popular streetcar handy for visitors and residents alike, and the Kauffman Center for the Performing Arts, a sleek modern home to the symphony, opera, and ballet. Yet while Kansas City is no backwater, its best asset may still be an unvarnished grit traceable all the way back to its days as the jumping-off point to the West on the Santa Fe Trail. — BY CHARLY WILDER

FRIDAY

1 *Crossroads Redefined* 2 p.m.

Industrial stagnation and suburban exodus in the 1960s left the Crossroads neighborhood nearly deserted. But now it is the **Crossroads Arts District** (kccrossroads.org), a stop on the KC Streetcar route and home to fashionable lofts in buildings like the former Western Auto offices as well as some 70 galleries. A pioneering mainstay is **Sherry Leedy Contemporary Art** (2004 Baltimore Avenue; 816-221-2626; sherryleedy.com). The **Belger Arts Center** (2100 Walnut Street; 816-474-3250; belgerartscenter.org), the project of a local family foundation, has varying exhibitions that have included 3D and 4D works. If it's the first Friday of the month, many galleries hold open houses until about 9 p.m.

2 *Sauce It Up* 6 p.m.

Debates over the best barbecue rouse as much passion here as religion or politics. Some swear by the old guard like Gates Bar-B-Q (gatesbbq.com) and Arthur Bryant's (arthurbryantsbbq.com), both of which have multiple branches. Others make the quick trip across the state line into Kansas City, Kansas, to a relative newcomer, **Joe's Kansas City Bar-B-Que** (3002 West 47th Avenue; 913-722-3366; oklahomajoesbbq.com; $). It serves pulled pork and beef brisket piled high on white bread, in a sauce that may just be the perfect amalgam of sweet, smoke, and vinegar.

OPPOSITE Kansas City's Crossroads district.

3 *Under the Safdie Domes* 8 p.m.

Arts lovers in Kansas City raised the funds to build the $326 million **Kauffman Center for the Performing Arts** (1601 Broadway; 816-994-7200; kauffmancenter.org), designed by Moshe Safdie, which opened in 2011. Placido Domingo, Itzhak Perlman, and the jazz artist Diana Krall performed on opening night, and the building quickly won rave reviews from architecture critics, music critics, and the people of Kansas City. Its two clamshell domes hold an 1,800-seat theater for the city's ballet and opera companies and a 1,600-seat concert hall for the symphony orchestra. It's a rare Friday night when there's nothing going on here. Check the schedule in advance, and enjoy the performance.

SATURDAY

4 *Park Life* 10 a.m.

Kansas City is said to have more fountains than any other city except Rome. (This is difficult to prove, but with about 200 of them, it certainly has a good claim.) One of the loveliest can be found at **Jacob L. Loose Park** (51st Street and Wornall Road), a Civil War site, where the Laura Conyers Smith Fountain, made of Italian stone, is encircled by thousands of roses in some 150 varieties. The park is popular with picnicking families and bongo-playing teenagers on furlough from the suburbs.

5 *Contemporary Greens* Noon

If last night's barbecue has you yearning for a salad, head to **Café Sebastienne**, an airy, glass-covered restaurant at the **Kemper Museum of Contemporary Art** (4420 Warwick Boulevard; 816-561-7740; kemperart.org/cafe; $$). Seasonal greens come with cucumber, red onion, grape tomatoes, sheep's milk cheese, and grilled pita. After lunch, pop inside for a quick look at the Kemper's small but diverse collection of modern and contemporary works by artists like Dale Chihuly and Louise Bourgeois, whose gigantic iron spider sculpture looms over the front lawn.

6 *Art in a Cube* 1:30 p.m.

In 2007, the **Nelson-Atkins Museum of Art** (4525 Oak Street; 816-751-1278; nelson-atkins.org) was thrust into the national spotlight when it

opened a new wing designed by Steven Holl. The Bloch Building — which holds contemporary art, photography, and special exhibitions — consists of five translucent glass blocks that create what Nicolai Ouroussoff, the architecture critic of *The New York Times*, described as "a work of haunting power." The museum's suite of American Indian galleries shows an assemblage of about 200 works from more than 68 tribes.

7 *18th Street Couture* 4 p.m.

The Crossroads cultural awakening extends beyond art and into fashion. At **Birdies** (116 West 18th Street; 816-842-2473; birdiespanties.com), for example, occupying a former film storage unit on West 18th Street, Peregrine Honig and Danielle Meister hand-pick lingerie and swimwear. Across the street is **Coki Bijoux Fine Jewelry** (115 West 18th Street; 913-339-8829; cokibijoux.com), where Coki Reardon, who studied jewelry making in Paris in the 1990s, sells pieces that include those she modeled on forms found in nature, often working with stones, wire, and metalwork, as well as her French-inspired designs.

8 *Midwest Tapas* 7 p.m.

Stay in the Crossroads to sample modern Mediterranean-style tapas at **Extra Virgin** (1900 Main Street; 816-842-2205; extravirginkc.com; $$-$$$), whose chef and owner is Kansas City's culinary titan, Michael Smith. The fare is more playful and adventurous than in his formal restaurant (called simply Michael Smith) next door. And if the loud, euro-chic décor, replete with a floor-to-ceiling *La Dolce Vita* mural, seems to be trying a little too hard, the crowd of unbuttoned professionals enjoying inspired dishes like crispy pork belly with green romesco and

chickpea fries doesn't seem to mind. The menu is diverse, as is the wine list.

9 *'Round Midnight* 10 p.m.

The flashy new **Kansas City Power and Light District** (1100 Walnut Street; powerandlightdistrict. com) offers a wide range of bars, restaurants, and clubs, but it can feel like an open-air fraternity party. When midnight strikes, head to the **Mutual Musicians Foundation** (1823 Highland Avenue; 816-471-5212; mutualmusiciansfoundation.org). The legendary haunt opened in 1917, and public jam sessions are held every Saturday until dawn. For a small cover, you can catch impromptu sets by some of the city's undiscovered musicians in the same room where Charlie Parker had a cymbal thrown at him in 1937.

SUNDAY

10 *Viva Brunch* 10 a.m.

As any resident will tell you, Mexican food is a big deal here. Look for an inventive take on it at **Port**

Fonda (4141 Pennsylvania Avenue; 816-216-6462; portfonda.com; $$). For brunch, the originality translates into eggs with chorizo, borracho beans, pico de gallo, and fresh corn tortillas, or Huevos Benedictos — poached eggs, biscuits, pork belly tomatillo-chile jam, and hollandaise.

11 *Homage to the Greats* 11 a.m.
The **American Jazz Museum** and **Negro Leagues Baseball Museum** (1616 East 18th Street; 816-474-8463 and 816-221-1920; americanjazzmuseum.com and nlbm.com) share a building in the 18th and Vine Historic District, once the heart of the city's African-American shopping area. The jazz museum, with listening stations to bring the music to life, pays

tribute to legendary jazz stars including Charlie Parker, Louis Armstrong, Duke Ellington, and Ella Fitzgerald. The baseball museum is dedicated to the leagues where black stars like Satchel Paige, Josh Gibson, and Kansas City's own Buck O'Neil played until the integration of Major League Baseball in 1947. It was in Kansas City in 1920 that the first of them, the National Negro League, was founded.

OPPOSITE ABOVE The translucent glass Bloch Building, designed by Stephen Holl, at the Nelson-Atkins Museum of Art. The building is the museum's contemporary wing.

OPPOSITE BELOW Sample modern Mediterranean-style tapas at Extra Virgin, owned by the Kansas City chef Michael Smith.

THE BASICS

The shiny new KC Streetcar (kcstreetcar.org) will get you around downtown in comfort. Elsewhere, drive or use ride-sharing or taxis.

The Raphael
325 Ward Parkway
816-756-3800
raphaelkc.com
$$
Historic 1928 building, now with black marble bathrooms and flat-screen televisions.

Sheraton Kansas City at Crown Center
2345 McGee Street
816-841-1000
marriott.com
$$
Close to the National World War I Museum and Memorial and to imposing Union Station, now a museum as well as a rail station.

Hilton President Kansas City
1329 Baltimore Avenue
816-221-9490
hilton.com
$$
Downtown landmark built in 1926.

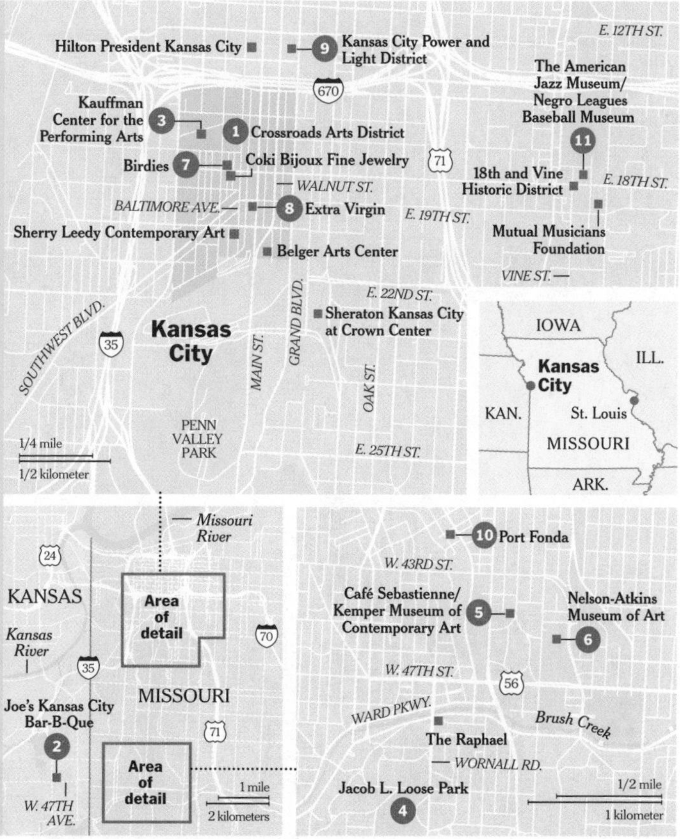

St. Louis

St. Louis, Missouri, is more than just a Gateway to the West. It's a lively destination in its own right, full of inviting neighborhoods, some coming out of a long decline and revitalized by public art, varied night life, and restaurants that draw on the bounty of surrounding farmland and rivers. The famous arch, of course, is still there, along with plenty of 19th-century architecture and an eye-opening amount of green space. Add to that a mix of Midwestern sensibility and Southern charm, and you've got plenty of reason to stay a while. — BY DAN SALTZSTEIN

FRIDAY

1 *Out in the Open* 4 p.m.

The new jewel of downtown St. Louis is **Citygarden** (citygardenstl.org), a sculpture park the city opened in 2009, framed by the old courthouse on one side and the Gateway Arch on the other. The oversize public art, by boldface-name artists like Mark di Suvero and Keith Haring, is terrific, but the real genius of the garden's layout is that it reflects the landscape of the St. Louis area: an arcing wall of local limestone, for instance, echoes the bends of the Mississippi and Missouri Rivers, which join just north of town.

2 *Up in the Sky* 6 p.m.

If you've never been to the top of the 630-foot **Gateway Arch** (gatewayarch.com), the four-minute ride up in a uniquely designed tram system is a must. And even if you have, it's worth reminding yourself that yes, that water down there is the Mississippi River, and that city spreading out beyond it is where a lot of optimistic Easterners slogged their first miles into the West. Eero Saarinen designed the arch, made of stainless steel, and it was completed in 1965. Besides providing a helicopter-height view, it's an elegantly simple artwork that endures.

3 *Soulard BBQ* 7:30 p.m.

Historic Soulard (pronounced SOO-lard) is one of those neighborhoods experiencing a renaissance thanks in part to several new restaurants. One relative newcomer is the casual, rustic (and tiny) **Wood Shack Soulard** (1862 South 10th Street; 314-833-4770;

thewoodshacksoulard.com; $$), a barbecue/smokehouse, where the chef chooses different woods according to the meats he serves. Try the pulled pork, for example, with house ham, creamy mustard, and Comté cheese.

4 *Analog Underground* 9:30 p.m.

Jazz and blues are part of the St. Louis legacy, and one of the best places to hear the tradition play on is **BB's Jazz, Blues, and Soups** (700 South Broadway; 314-436-5222; bbsjazzbluessoups.com), a club in an old brick building a few blocks from the river and the Gateway Arch. In addition to the music, you'll find a variety of beers. And yes, there really is soup, and its house-made goodness is a point of pride.

SATURDAY

5 *Cupcakes and Blooms* 9 a.m.

In the leafy neighborhood of Shaw, stately architecture mixes with hip spots like **SweetArt** (2203 South 39th Street; 314-771-4278; sweetartstl.com), a mom-and-pop bakery where you can eat a virtuous vegan breakfast topped off by a light-as-air cupcake. Shaw is named for Henry Shaw, a botanist and philanthropist whose crowning achievement is the

OPPOSITE St. Louis's signature, the Gateway Arch designed by Eero Saarinen. Take the tram to the top, and you'll be riding up 630 feet on an elegant work of art.

BELOW The Missouri Botanical Garden.

Missouri Botanical Garden (4344 Shaw Boulevard; 314-577-5100; mobot.org). Founded in 1859, it is billed as the oldest continuously operating botanical garden in the nation. It covers an impressive 79 acres and includes a large Japanese garden and Henry Shaw's 1850 estate home, as well as his (slightly creepy) mausoleum.

6 *Taste of Memphis* 1 p.m.

St. Louis-style ribs are found on menus across the country, but it's a Memphis-style joint (think slow-smoked meats, easy on the sauce) that seems to be the consensus favorite for barbecue in town. Just survey the best-of awards that decorate the walls at **Pappy's Smokehouse** (3106 Olive Street; 314-535-4340; pappyssmokehouse.com; $-$$). Crowds line up for heaping plates of meat and sides, served in an unassuming space (while you wait, take a peek at the smoker parked out back on a side street). The ribs and pulled pork are pretty good, but the winners might be the sides — bright and tangy slaw and deep-fried corn on the cob.

7 *Green Day* 3 p.m.

St. Louis boasts 105 city-run parks, but none rivals **Forest Park** (explorestlouis.com/things-to-do/neighborhoods/forest-park), which covers more than 1,200 acres smack in the heart of the city. It opened in 1876, but it was the 1904 World's Fair that made it a world-class public space, spawning comely buildings like the Palace of Fine Art, which now houses the Saint Louis Art Museum. The Jewel Box, a towering, contemporary-looking greenhouse, dates back to 1936 but was renovated in the early 2000s. For an overview, rent a bike from the park visitor's center at 5595 Grand Drive (914-367-7275) and just meander.

8 *Eat Your Vegetables* 8 p.m.

The Midwest isn't all about meat. Vegetables are treated almost reverentially at **Vicia** (4260 Forest Park Avenue; 314-553-9239; viciarestaurant.com; $$),

whose name comes from the genus for a common Missouri cover crop. In a sleek, airy space, the husband-and-wife team of Tara and Michael Gallina curate an inventive greens-focused menu with dishes like a milk-brined cauliflower with smoked tomatoes, wheat berries, and Cheddar, wrapped in Italian ham. The drinks take up the green theme, too, and almost become dishes in themselves. Try the rhubarb rye with zucca, Punt e Mes, and cherry shrub.

9 *Royale Treatment* 10 p.m.

Tower Grove is home to a handful of fine watering holes, including the **Royale** (3132 South Kingshighway Boulevard; 314-772-3600; theroyale.com), where an Art Deco-style bar of blond wood and glass is accompanied by old photos of political leaders (John F. Kennedy, Martin Luther King Jr., the late Missouri governor Mel Carnahan). But it's the extensive cocktail list, with drinks named after city neighborhoods (like the Carondelet Sazerac), and a backyard patio that keep the aficionados coming. There's plenty of craft beer, too.

SUNDAY

10 *The Home Team* 10 a.m.

Take a number for one of the small, worn wooden tables at **Winslow's Home** (7213 Delmar Boulevard;

BELOW In the impressive and sprawling Forest Park, the Palace of Fine Art, a leftover from the 1904 world's fair, now houses the Saint Louis Art Museum.

314-725-7559; winslowshome.com; $). It's more than just a pleasant place for brunch and espresso; it doubles as a general store that carries groceries, baked goods, books, and kitchen items like stainless-steel olive oil dispensers. Have a hearty breakfast and then take time to browse.

11 *Art Class* Noon

Washington University gets high marks for its academics. But the campus, with its rolling green hills and grand halls, is also home to terrific contemporary art. See its collection at the **Mildred Lane Kemper Art Museum** (1 Brookings Drive; 314-935-4523; kemperartmuseum.wustl.edu). Designed by the Pritzker Prize-winning architect Fumihiko Maki, it's charmingly cramped and vaguely organized by theme — so you'll find a Jackson Pollock cheek

by jowl with a 19th-century portrait of Daniel Boone. You'll also find ambitious contemporary art exhibitions curated by Washington University faculty. Like much of St. Louis, the Kemper may not be flashy, but it's full of gems.

OPPOSITE ABOVE Oversize public art finds space at Citygarden, a downtown sculpture park.

ABOVE The extensive cocktail list at the Royale in the Tower Grove area features drinks — the Carondelet Sazerac, for one — that are named after city neighborhoods.

THE BASICS

Lambert International Airport is served by major airlines. For getting around in town, it's best to have a car.

Moonrise Hotel
6177 Delmar Boulevard
314-721-1111
moonrisehotel.com
$$
Pleasant boutique vibe and a central location.

Four Seasons St. Louis
999 North Second Street
314-881-5800
fourseasons.com/stlouis
$$$-$$$$
Part of a striking riverside complex that also includes a casino.

St. Louis Union Station
1820 Market Street
314-621-5262
stlunionstationhotel.com
$$
In the grand old downtown railroad station.

Map of St. Louis area showing locations:

IOWA · ILL. · Kansas City · KAN. · St. Louis · MISSOURI · ARK.

DR. MARTIN LUTHER KING DR. · NATURAL BRIDGE AVE.

N. SKINKER BLVD.

10 Winslow's Home

Moonrise Hotel
DELMAR BLVD. — N. KINGSHIGHWAY BLVD.

11 Mildred Lane Kemper Art Museum
LINDELL BLVD.
Pappy's Smokehouse · MARTIN LUTHER KING JR. BRIDGE

WASHINGTON UNIVERSITY

St. Louis Art Museum · 7 Forest Park · 6 · Four Seasons St. Louis · Citygarden · 1

64 · 40 · 8 · Vicia · St. Louis Union Station · 70

MCCAUSLAND AVE. · MANCHESTER AVE. · SweetArt · Gateway Arch · 2

5 · BB's Jazz, Blues, and Soups · 4 · POPLAR ST. BRIDGE

44 · Missouri Botanical Garden · S. 39TH ST. · Wood Shack Soulard · 3

TOWER GROVE PARK · SOULARD

Royale · 9 · St. Louis

S. KINGSHIGHWAY BLVD. · MORGAN FORD RD. · S. GRAND BLVD. · VIRGINIA AVE. · Mississippi River

55

East St. Louis

6 miles / 10 kilometers
—Missouri R.
MISSOURI · ILLINOIS
270
170
Area of detail
255
— Mississippi R.
MISSOURI · ILLINOIS

1 mile / 2 kilometers

The Niobrara River Valley

To the uninitiated, Nebraska conjures a certain image: a treeless prairie steamrolled pancake-flat, stretching to the horizon. But tucked in a north-central patch of the state is the Niobrara River Valley, filled with a surprising collection of conifers and hardwoods, 200-foot sandstone bluffs, and spring-fed waterfalls. The Niobrara starts in eastern Wyoming and flows across Nebraska for more than 400 miles, emptying into the Missouri River. Seventy-six miles, starting just east of Valentine, are designated as national scenic river (nps.gov/niob). The rapids are mostly riffles, and the water is knee-deep in most spots, inviting a journey by canoe. And although a good float on the river is the center of your trip, there is more to see on land nearby. — BY HELEN OLSSON

FRIDAY

1 *Spurs and Saddles* 2 p.m.

In Valentine (population 2,820), red hearts are painted on the sidewalks and ranchers in cowboy hats roll down Main Street in dusty pickups. Browse the jeans, chaps, hats, ropes, and saddles at **Young's Western Wear** (143 North Main Street; 402-376-1281; discountwesternwear.com), purveyor of all things cowboy. The store has 5,000 pairs of cowboy boots, in snakeskin, elephant, stingray, ostrich, and — if you must — cow leather. Take time to stop by your float-trip outfitter to make sure your reservations are in order for tomorrow. A handful of outfitters in Valentine rent canoes, kayaks, and giant inner tubes and can shuttle you or your car from point to point. One is **Little Outlaw** (1005 East Highway 20; 402-376-1822; outlawcanoe.com). If you canoe or kayak, you can run 22 miles from the Fort Niobrara Refuge to Rocky Ford in a day. A lazy float in a tube takes twice as long, so tubers might get only as far as Smith Falls by day's end.

2 *Under the Waterfall* 3:30 p.m.

This will be a weekend of outings far from restaurants, so get to know the options in Valentine for picking up provisions. One good bet is **Scotty's**

Ranchland Foods (108 Highway 20; 402-376-3114; scottysranchlandfoods.com), a family-owned grocery store with a deli, fresh produce, and organic items. Stow your choices (on ice, preferably) in your car and drive 23 miles south on Highway 97 through the Sandhills, past grazing cattle, massive spools of rolled hay, and spinning windmills, to **Snake River Falls**. (This Snake River is a tributary of the Niobrara.) Descend the trail through sumac and yucca to the base and crawl behind the 54-foot-wide falls to marvel at the gushing torrent inches away. Look for the cliff swallows' mud nests clinging to the limestone cliffs around the falls.

3 *Prairie Beach* 5:30 p.m.

Three miles down Highway 97 is **Merritt Reservoir** (402-389-0672; outdoornebraska.gov/merrittreservoir), a deep emerald lake rimmed by white sand beaches. Bury your toes in the warm sugar sand and look for the tiny tracks of sand toads. Anglers pull walleyes, crappies, and wide-mouth bass from the depths, and jet skiers trace arcs on the surface. When it's time to be hungry, pull out your picnic lunch and enjoy it at lakeside.

4 *Yes, It's the Milky Way* 9 p.m.

Because of its remote location (about 25 miles southwest of Valentine), the **Merritt Reservoir** is a

OPPOSITE Floating on the Niobrara near Valentine, Nebraska.

RIGHT An elk in the Valentine National Wildlife Refuge.

prime spot for stargazing. "On a clear, moonless night, no kidding, it's so bright the Milky Way casts a shadow," said John Bauer, owner of the Merritt Trading Post and Reservoir. In late July or early August, amateur astronomers gather here for the annual Nebraska Star Party. They camp on the beach and crane their necks staring into the cosmos. If you're camping at the reservoir, you can gaze until sunrise. Otherwise, get back on the road by 10 or so and let the stars light your way back to Valentine.

SATURDAY

5 *Downriver With a Paddle* 9 a.m.

Grab sandwiches for later (choices for picnic supplies include Henderson's IGA and Subway, as well as Scotty's Ranchland). Meet your outfitter at Cornell Bridge in the **Fort Niobrara National Wildlife Refuge**. Whatever your craft of choice — canoe, kayak, or inner tube — this is where you'll put in and float away on the shallow Niobrara. Over the eons, the Niobrara (pronounced nigh-oh-BRAH-rah) has cut more than 400 feet through a series of rock formations, pinkish-red, chalky white, and gray. Drifting in it is not unlike floating through an enormous block of Neopolitan ice cream. Beach your craft whenever you like and go for a swim or take a walk on shore. On the banks, wade through cold streams and search for small waterfalls tucked inside canyons. A recent National Park

Service study found more than 230 falls, most only a few feet high, tumbling into the river along a 35-mile stretch in this part of the Niobrara.

6 *In the Mist* Noon

Twelve miles downriver, just past Allen Bridge, watch for signs along the riverbank for **Smith Falls State Park**. Stop to eat the picnic lunch you packed this morning. Stretch your legs with a short hike to the Smith Falls, Nebraska's tallest. Follow the trail across the steel truss Verdigre Bridge and up a winding boardwalk to the falls, where water plunges 63 feet over a bell-shaped rock. Surrounded by moss and mist, red cedar and bur oak, you'd be surprised to find that just a quick hike will take you to the dry, windswept Sandhills Prairie. The cool, moist environment in the river valley not only nurtures these familiar trees, but has preserved ancient species, like the giant paper birch that died out in the rest of Nebraska as the climate grew hotter and drier thousands of years ago. Animal life thrives here too: turkey vultures ride the thermals, sandpipers perch on sandbars, dragonflies dart above the water's surface.

ABOVE Stars, trailing across the sky in a time-lapse photograph, at the Merritt Reservoir, a lake south of Valentine. The remote reservoir is a prime stargazing spot.

OPPOSITE Sunset at the Merritt Reservoir.

7 *Floating Party Zone* 1:30 p.m.

By now, you are probably passing flotillas of summertime tubers from Iowa, Missouri, Kansas, and Nebraska—young things in bikinis and shorts, broiling in the sun and imbibing mightily. As bald eagles soar overhead, hip-hop may be thumping from boom boxes. Stuart Schneider, a park ranger, patrolled the river one late summer day, passing out mesh bags for empties. "On a busy Saturday, we can get 3,000 people," he said. "My favorite time on the river is the fall," he added. "The water is clear, there are no bugs, and the leaves can be spectacular." And, of course, the students are back in school.

8 *Time to Take Out* 4:30 p.m.

Having paddled 22 miles, you can take out at **Rocky Ford**, where your outfitter will retrieve you and your canoe and shuttle you back to your car. Beyond Rocky Ford, there are Class III and IV rapids. Unless you have a death wish, exit here.

9 *Meat Eater's Paradise* 7 p.m.

Back in Valentine, reward yourself with a big center-cut sirloin at **Peppermill** (502 East Highway 20; 402-376-2800; peppermillvalentine.com; $$). You're in cattle country after all. (Thursdays are livestock auction day in Valentine, where the buyers sit 10 deep on bleachers.) Of course, there isn't a menu in town that doesn't have chicken-fried steak. Peppermill is no exception.

SUNDAY

10 *Fuel Up* 10 a.m.

Have breakfast in Valentine at the **Bunkhouse Restaurant & Saloon** (109 East Highway 20; 402-376-1609; $). Under various names and owners, the Bunkhouse building has been serving grub since the 1940s. Slide into a booth and load up with a sirloin steak and eggs (when in Rome, you know…) or a stack of Joe's pancakes. Try a side order of Indian

fry bread with powdered sugar or honey. Rest assured the window you gaze out won't have the unseemly imprint of Valentine's infamous "Butt Bandit." The man who, for more than a year, left greasy prints of his nether regions on the windows of Valentine businesses was arrested in 2008.

11 *Birder's Paradise* 11 a.m.
Twenty miles south of Valentine, you'll find the **Valentine National Wildlife Refuge** (fws.gov/valentine). Where the Ogallala Aquifer nears the surface, bright blue lakes and marshes sparkle like jewels in the green grass. Hundreds of bird species have been sighted here: sharp-tailed grouse, blue-winged teal, long-billed curlews. Just beyond the park's main headquarters, a trail mowed through the grass rises up to a rusting fire tower. From that perch, gaze at the Sandhills, which spread out like a turbulent sea in a hundred shades of green, blue, and gold. It's time to reflect that the only pancake you've seen in Nebraska came with syrup and a generous pat of butter.

ABOVE A view of West Long Lake in the Valentine National Wildlife Refuge.

OPPOSITE At Snake River Falls, near the Merritt Reservoir, adventurers can climb behind the cascade. This Snake River is a tributary of the Niobrara.

THE BASICS

Valentine is a three-and-a-half-hour drive from Rapid City, South Dakota. Canoe, kayak, or tube on the river and drive nearby.

Trade Winds Motel
1009 East Highway 20, Valentine
402-376-1600

tradewindslodge.com
$
Locally owned, retro, and tidy.

Merritt Trading Post and Resort
Highway 97, 26 miles south of Valentine
402-376-3437
merritttradingpost.com
$

Cabins and campsites, catering to the fishing crowd at the Merritt Reservoir.

The Niobrara Lodge
803 East Highway 20
402-376-3000
niobraralodge.com
$$
Cozy but modern.

Omaha

As the birthplace of both Warren Buffett and TV dinners, Omaha is a pragmatic, come-as-you-are sort of place — but one with a hip cultural swagger it has earned. With a steady stream of musicians, visual artists, designers, and chefs opting to stay and create here (or seeking refuge from the high rents of Brooklyn, Chicago, or the Bay Area), Omaha has become known for something other than its steaks: it is fertile creative ground. This growth has burnished the reputation of a city with already well-regarded museums, gardens, and zoo. Pedestrian-friendly downtown development has led to a revitalized riverfront, a concert hall, a convention center, and a ballpark hosting the annual College World Series. There's even a one-stop hipster district anchored by Saddle Creek Records, the indie-rock exporter of the "Omaha sound." Of course, in places like the Old Market, visitors can still glimpse the distinctly American mix of the Old West and the Old World that makes Omaha feel like part hearty frontier town and part arty downtown. — BY ANNA BAHNEY

FRIDAY

1 *The Mighty Mo* 4 p.m.

Stroll along the Missouri River, once a vital waterway for the native Omaha tribe. The **Lewis and Clark Landing** (515 North Riverfront Drive; 402-444-5900; cityofomaha.org/parks), a 23-acre park with walking trails along the river, marks the site where the historic expedition landed in 1804. Less than a half-mile north is the graceful **Bob Kerrey Pedestrian Bridge** (705 Riverfront Drive), a 15-foot-wide footbridge spanning the Missouri. Walkers can cross into Iowa and then return to Nebraska, following the river trails south to **Heartland of America Park** (800 Douglas Street) and the **Gene Leahy Mall** (1302 Farnam), both of which border the Old Market.

2 *The Old Is New* 5 p.m.

The vibrant brick streets of the **Old Market** are lined with buildings bearing the fading advertisements

OPPOSITE The sinuous Bob Kerrey Pedestrian Bridge crosses the Missouri River to Iowa.

RIGHT Downtown and the riverfront.

for rugs, fruit, and stoves — goods these late 19th-century brick buildings once warehoused. Now they are bustling with galleries, bars, boutiques, and sidewalk cafes. Slip into **La Buvette** (511 South 11th Street; 402-344-8627; labuvetteomaha.com) for some Old World gastronomy, selecting from among 800 wines, 30 cheeses, and fresh breads. Saunter through shops selling books, music, jewelry, clothing, and art. A dozen galleries are located in the Old Market, a couple of them in the **Passageway**, a grotto-like hideaway of spots tucked into balconies and archways.

3 *Unfussy Feast* 8 p.m.

The **Grey Plume** (220 South 31st Avenue; 402-763-4447; thegreyplume.com; $$), in the revitalized Midtown neighborhood, has impressed diners with an exquisite farm-to-table, fine-dining experience that is neither precious nor pretentious. Everything here has a story — the floorboards are from a barn, the peaches were preserved last summer, the rabbit comes from a farm near Lincoln. The chef, Clayton Chapman, a prodigal native who returned to Omaha via Chicago and France, turns out some of Omaha's finest food — a bright steelhead trout with crème fraiche spätzle, for example, or tender Wagyu beef with maitake mushroom and parsnip.

4 Scotch Honor 10 p.m.

Drop by the homey **Dundee Dell** (5007 Underwood Avenue; 402-553-9501; dundeedell.com), an unassuming yet formidable bar in the residential neighborhood of Dundee. What seems like an ordinary pub slinging fried pickles and fish and chips beneath large-screen TVs is also known for one of the largest collections of single-malt Scotch whiskies in the world. The Scotch menu, which lists more than 700 single malts and includes two maps of Scotland, runs 15 pages. Beer drinkers may have to do their homework, too: a dozen kinds are on tap and hundreds of varieties are in bottles.

SATURDAY

5 Sit a Spell 9 a.m.

Take your appetite to **Big Mama's Kitchen** (3223 North 45th Street; 402-455-6262; bigmamaskitchen. com; $), where Patricia Barron (a.k.a. Big Mama) serves it old school in what is actually an old school. Big Mama's gained local fame for the oven-fried chicken and sweet-potato-pie ice cream served at lunch and dinner, but it turns out made-from-scratch classics for breakfast, too, like biscuits and gravy, breakfast casseroles, buttermilk pancakes, and pork chop with eggs.

6 Wild Kingdom 10 a.m.

Prepare for adventure at Omaha's **Henry Doorly Zoo and Aquarium** (3701 South 10th Street; 402-733-8401; omahazoo.com). Meander over suspension bridges and along trails in the Lied Jungle, an eight-story-high indoor habitat amid lush trees and waterfalls, where three-toed sloths hang and pygmy hippos waddle. In the aquarium, walk the ocean floor in a transparent 70-foot-long tunnel as sharks

ABOVE Inside the Desert Dome, one of many habitats to explore at the Henry Doorly Zoo and Aquarium.

RIGHT Civic pride in a wall mural.

(in 900,000 gallons of water) dart above your head. Then explore the Desert Dome, the bat caves, and the butterfly habitat, and take in an IMAX film.

7 All Aboard 1 p.m.

Transport yourself to bygone days when the country traveled by train at the **Durham Museum** (801 South 10th Street; 402-444-5071; durhammuseum.org), housed in the former Omaha Union Station, a stunning 1931 Art Deco jewel. The museum has history and science exhibitions including trains, but the real delight is wandering the station. The 160-foot-long hall is crowned with ornate ceilings that soar 65 feet above the rose and yellow patterned terrazzo floor. Take it in over a hot dog or sandwich from the lunch counter at the Soda Fountain — and don't forget the thick chocolate malt or cherry phosphate.

8 Future Perfect 3 p.m.

Bemis Center for Contemporary Arts (724 South 12th Street; 402-341-7130; bemiscenter.org) has supported contemporary artists from around the world through residencies in Omaha since the 1980s. The center mounts exhibitions of contemporary work by both established and emerging artists. Whatever is on, chances are you've never seen anything like it.

9 Have What Jack Had 8 p.m.

Johnny's Cafe (4702 South 27th Street; 402-731-4774; johnnyscafe.com; $$) appeared in the film *About Schmidt*, starring Jack Nicholson and directed by Omaha's native bard of Midwestern middle-class mediocrity, Alexander Payne.

Nicholson's character sat at the right end of the bar after excusing himself from his own retirement party in the banquet room. But this steakhouse was a favorite long before he bellied up. Opened in 1922 by Frank Kawa, whose family still runs it, the place served meat where it could not get any fresher: right next to the stockyards. The stockyards closed in 1999, but the delicious steaks are still hand-cut and aged on site.

10 *Do NoDo* 9 p.m.

When the growing indie-music label Saddle Creek Records needed both new offices and a viable rock club, the young music execs made a pragmatic decision to build their own. The resulting club is **Slowdown** (729 North 14th Street; 402-345-7569; theslowdown.com), a sleek but chill lounge, bar, and performance space owned by Saddle Creek that is now an anchor of North Downtown, or NoDo. **Film Streams** (1340 Mike Fahey Street; 402-933-0259; filmstreams.org), a nonprofit cinema, shows first-run and repertory films, and nearby are a coffee house and design, bike, and apparel shops.

SUNDAY

11 *Native Nature* 10 a.m.

Wander the gardens, fields, and trails at **Lauritzen Gardens** (100 Bancroft Street; 402-346-4002; lauritzengardens.org). Situated on 100 acres high on the bluffs overlooking the Missouri River, the garden offers more than 15 seasonal or themed plots, from English gardens to woodland walks. Pause among the native wildflowers in the serene Song of the Lark Meadow, named after Willa Cather's story of the same name, to see if you can hear the call of a meadowlark.

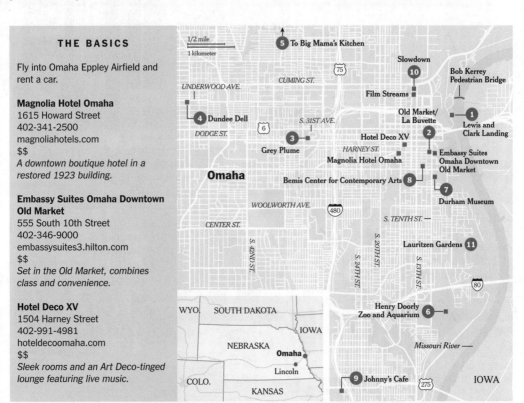

THE BASICS

Fly into Omaha Eppley Airfield and rent a car.

Magnolia Hotel Omaha
1615 Howard Street
402-341-2500
magnoliahotels.com
$$
A downtown boutique hotel in a restored 1923 building.

Embassy Suites Omaha Downtown Old Market
555 South 10th Street
402-346-9000
embassysuites3.hilton.com
$$
Set in the Old Market, combines class and convenience.

Hotel Deco XV
1504 Harney Street
402-991-4981
hoteldecoomaha.com
$$
Sleek rooms and an Art Deco-tinged lounge featuring live music.

1/2 mile
1 kilometer

5 To Big Mama's Kitchen

Slowdown

75

CUMING ST.

10

Bob Kerrey
Pedestrian Bridge

UNDERWOOD AVE.

Film Streams

4 Dundee Dell

S. 31ST AVE.

Old Market/
La Buvette

1

Lewis and
Clark Landing

DODGE ST.

6

3

Hotel Deco XV

2

Omaha

Grey Plume

HARNEY ST.

Magnolia Hotel Omaha

Embassy Suites
Omaha Downtown
Old Market

Bemis Center for Contemporary Arts 8

7

Durham Museum

WOOLWORTH AVE.

480

S. TENTH ST.

CENTER ST.

S. 20TH ST.

S. 13TH ST.

Lauritzen Gardens 11

S. 42ND ST.

S. 24TH ST.

80

WYO. SOUTH DAKOTA

Henry Doorly
Zoo and Aquarium 6

IOWA

NEBRASKA

Omaha

Missouri River

Lincoln

9 Johnny's Cafe

275

IOWA

COLO.

KANSAS

Buffalo

Is it the influx of immigrants from countries like Myanmar and Bhutan or the uptick in cultural investments? The transformation of the waterfront or the revitalization of local institutions? Or is it simply the food? Like many small American cities, Buffalo, which had early booms from various industries, including railways, shipyards, and steel manufacturing, is shedding its rusty roots and experiencing a bona fide renaissance. No longer merely the portal to nearby Niagara Falls, Buffalo is a modern and multifaceted city, more than ready for its moment.
— BY AMY M. THOMAS

FRIDAY

1 *Above It All* 3 p.m.
A good place to begin your visit to Buffalo is above it. **City Hall** (65 Niagara Square; buffalony. gov), a majestic 32-story Art Deco tower, has a free public observation deck that offers 360-degree views of Lake Erie and Canada, the city's old factories and grain silos, and a scattershot of the surrounding 19th- and 20th-century architecture. To get there, enter the domed lobby, where murals illustrate themes like peace, industry, and pioneer life. Then take the elevator to the 25th floor and walk up the remaining three flights. Before circling the outdoor catwalk, read the placards on the inside perimeter for a deeper appreciation of the city you're about to spend a weekend exploring.

2 *Climb a Wall* 5 p.m.
Buffalo RiverWorks (359 Ganson Street; buffaloriverworks.com) is a recreational complex occupying several structures of a former grain-milling facility along the Buffalo River, including old grain silos that now have 35-, 40- and 50-foot climbing walls, both inside and outside. Experts are on hand to harness you in and help guide you, whatever your level. If wall-climbing is too daunting, do some loops on the indoor roller rink, rent a kayak or water-bike on the river, or just grab a home-brewed brown ale and watch all the action.

3 *Wing It* 8 p.m.
It's hard to get a bad chicken wing in Buffalo. And while everyone has an opinion on whose is best,

you can't go wrong at **Anchor Bar** (1047 Main Street; anchorbar.com; $), which served its first batch of deep-fried wings doused in a "special sauce" in 1964 and is widely credited with starting the whole wings trend. You'll likely have to wait, so pass the time checking out the bric-a-brac: license plates, photos, and trophies, not to mention Harleys hanging from the ceiling. Wings come in many varieties, all served with celery and blue cheese. There's also standard bar fare like burgers and wraps, as well as a solid Buffalo-style thick crust pizza.

SATURDAY

4 *A Fresh Start* 9 a.m.
Head toward **Canalside** (canalsidebuffalo.com), the revitalized area along the Buffalo River where the Erie Canal once came to an end. This is a busy place, with concerts, fitness classes, children's story hours, a naval museum, history cruises, and more. Rent a paddle boat or kayak, practice yoga on a paddleboard, stroll the boardwalk, and make time to visit *Sharkgirl*, the half-shark, half-girl sculpture created by the artist Casey Riordan Millard that has become a selfie sensation.

5 *International Flavor* 11:30 a.m.
Pop across town and see another side of Buffalo's changing face. Housed in a simple garage-like space,

OPPOSITE Shea's Buffalo, a landmark theater.

BELOW Shopping in the restored Market Arcade.

West Side Bazaar (25 Grant Street; westsidebazaar. com; $) is a small business incubator run by the city's booming immigrant and refugee populations. Browse the stalls where vendors sell craft items and then dive into a smorgasbord of international flavors at the casual cafeteria-style dining section. Ethiopian injera topped with spicy lentils and vegetables? Sweet and sour Thai tom yum soup? The world is your oyster.

6 *Tour a Classic* 1 p.m.

Move onto a different kind of cultural experience in the regal Parkside neighborhood. The magnificent **Martin House** (125 Jewett Parkway; martinhouse. org), a prairie house tour de force by Frank Lloyd

Wright, has been restored after 21 years and $50 million of effort. The house has a fascinating history of opulence, abandonment, and resurrection, explained in the Toshiko Mori-designed glass pavilion and in guided tours. Upon entering the 15,000-square-foot main house, catch the epic view of a towering *Winged Victory* sculpture in the conservatory, visible at the end of a dramatic 175-foot pergola. Also inside are furniture, decorative elements, and art glass designed for the house by Wright. Just outside are two smaller houses and a carriage house, more elements of what is really a sprawling family compound, all designed by Wright early in the 20th century.

7 *Stroll and Shop* 3 p.m.

Shopping in the city center is small-scale and local, best illustrated on Elmwood Avenue, where young families and college students provide the buzz. Check out **Blue Sky Design Supply** (No. 978; blueskydesignsupply.com), for housewares and home decor; **Half & Half** (No. 1088; facebook.com/pg/halfandhalf1088), with men's and women's clothing; and **Talking Leaves** (No. 951; facebook.com/talkingleavesbooks), an idiosyncratic bookseller.

ABOVE The Martin House, a tour de force of a prairie house designed by Frank Lloyd Wright.

LEFT Old grain silos house breweries and climbing walls.

Try the sponge candy, a local treat, at **Watson's Chocolates** (No. 738; watsonschocolates.com). There are more shops nearby at the **Market Arcade** (617 Main Street; facebook.com/shopsatmarketarcade), but they play second fiddle to the arcade itself, a Beaux-Arts and neo-Classical space that's all Corinthian columns, Palladian windows, and sculpted bison heads, diffused with natural light from a frosted glass skylight.

8 *Cocktail Culture* 6 p.m.

Ease into evening with a well-crafted, cheekily named cocktail at the nearby **Buffalo Proper** (333 Franklin Street; buffaloproper.com). The mustachioed barmen in plaid and the twee mix of taxidermy and mismatched vintage glasses makes this place feel like Buffalo by way of Brooklyn.

9 *Modern Mexican* 7:30 p.m.

Finish the day back on the west side with more worldly flavors — this time contemporary Mexican at **Las Puertas** (385 Rhode Island Street; laspuertas-buffalo.com; $$$). The chef, Victor

Parra Gonzalez, serves up surprising selections like guacamole dusted with crushed crickets (crickets optional); creamy mole verde topped with vegetables, sesame seeds, and queso cotija cheese; or tender duck with poached pears, heirloom carrots, and quinoa. The intimate space and simple white interior act like a blank canvas, letting the elegantly plated dishes stand out.

SUNDAY

10 *Start With Art* 10 a.m.

The modestly sized **Albright-Knox Art Gallery** (1285 Elmwood Avenue; albrightknox.org), one of

TOP Small shops and galleries line Elmwood Avenue.

ABOVE A vendor and her wares at the West Side Bazaar, a small business incubator and shopping spot run by the city's growing immigrant and refugee population.

the oldest museums in the nation, packs a punch. Starting in 1863 with a painting by Albert Bierstadt, it has amassed an impressive permanent collection of everything from photography to abstract expressionism and also hosts about six major temporary exhibitions each year. Then journey across the street to the **Burchfield Penney Art Center** (1300 Elmwood Avenue; burchfieldpenney.org), which is devoted to the work of the 20th-century artist Charles Burchfield, whose singular, not quite abstract view of the natural world made him a true American original.

11 *Plush Brunch* 12:30 p.m.

A coffeehouse, larder, and more, **Rowhouse Bakery & Restaurant** (483 Delaware Avenue; rowhousebuffalo.com; $$) delivers all the things a modern foodie wants. There are all kinds of nooks for enjoying your turmeric smoothie or macchiato: near a fireplace in the cocktail lounge, in a book alcove overlooking the three-story atrium, or perched at a counter in a clean white cafe. But with its plush chairs and ornamental fireplaces, the refined dining room is your best bet for digging into a salmon gravlax tartine with crème fraiche or a breakfast pizza with Cheddar, tomato, egg, and sausage.

ABOVE Recreation rules on the repurposed waterfront.

OPPOSITE *Sharkgirl*, a photo op at Canalside.

THE BASICS

The Buffalo Niagara Airport is 20 minutes from downtown. To get around, rent a car, use ride sharing, or rent a bicycle from Reddy Bikeshare.

Mansion on Delaware Avenue
414 Delaware Avenue
mansionondelaware.com
$$$
Boutique luxury and butler service in an elegant oversized house built in 1869, with preserved architectural and interior details.

Hotel Henry
444 Forest Avenue
hotelhenry.com
$$
Clever update in a former mental hospital designed by the 19th-century American architect H.H. Richardson.

Westin Buffalo
250 Delaware Avenue
westinbuffalo.com
$$
Central location downtown, with two restaurants, a spa, and fitness center.

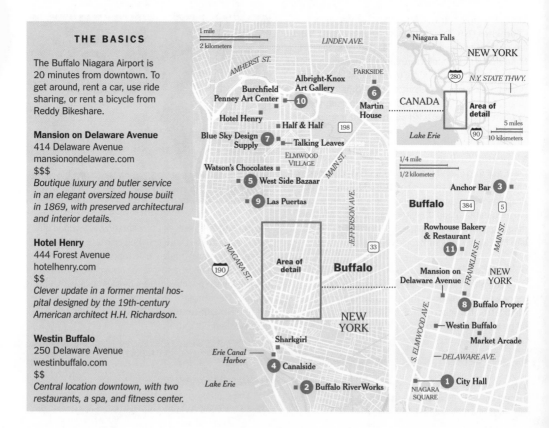

Niagara Falls

To grasp the might of Niagara Falls, you have to see and feel it close up, with the spray hitting your face and the thunder of the water drowning out all other sound. Niagara is not by any particular statistic the largest waterfall in the world, but there is a good case to be made that it is the most impressive. The falls are very tall, very wide, and gracefully shaped. They drop in a single long descent and run year round with a massive, unimaginable volume. They are majestic and beautiful. They are also international, shared by the United States and Canada. Niagara Falls, Ontario, has the wide-angle vista and more commercial attractions; Niagara Falls, New York, has a close-up view of the roaring Niagara River and a more natural feeling. The border is easy to cross, especially on foot, so why limit yourself to one side or the other? Hop back and forth to get the best of both Niagaras.

— BY BARBARA IRELAND

FRIDAY

1 *Feet Across the Border* 5 p.m.

Cars sometimes line up for hours to cross the international border at the **Rainbow Bridge**, a few hundred yards downriver from the falls. But on the walkway it's a breeze — a 10-minute stroll for one dollar in American or Canadian currency (niagarafallsbridges.com). Customs agents at each end are pedestrian-friendly, though you must have your passport. If you're staying on the American side, make your first crossing now. If your hotel is in Canada, wait until tomorrow. Either way, this is one of the most scenic saunters you will ever take.

2 *Brinkmanship* 6 p.m.

Push into the crowds on the riverfront walkway in Canada and see the whole geological spectacle at once. The imposing cascade on the left, 850 feet wide, is the **American Falls**. The supercharged one on the right, nearly half a mile wide, is the **Horseshoe Falls**, often called the Canadian Falls even though the international border actually runs through it. Stop at the Horseshoe brink and wait your turn to be

OPPOSITE Niagara Falls State Park offers jaw-dropping up-close views of both the American and Canadian Falls.

doused at the rail by spray from thousands of tons of water plunging down every second. Impressed? This thundering mass is only half of the river's natural flow. The other 50 percent (75 percent in the off-season) is channeled away underground to hydroelectric plants.

3 *Wine and Bacon* 7 p.m.

From the terrace at **Queen Victoria Place Restaurant** (6345 Niagara Parkway; 905-356-2217; niagaraparks.com/dining; $$$), the tourist hordes below seem far away. Relax and sample one of Canada's Niagara Region wines or an Ontario-brewed craft beer. For a casual dinner, try the signature burger, made with Canadian beef and local Woolwich's goat cheese. Afterward, explore shady **Queen Victoria Park**, where gracious landscaping reflects the English style.

4 *Over the Top* 9 p.m.

You want to hate **Clifton Hill**, a garish strip of funhouses, glow-in-the-dark miniature-golf palaces, 4-D theaters, wax museums, and noisy bars. But tackiness on this level cries out to be experienced. So watch a multinational crowd shovel tickets into blinking game machines at the Great Canadian Midway. Observe the story-high monster chomping a hamburger atop the House of Frankenstein. Shop for maple candy and a moose puppet. And climb aboard the **SkyWheel** Ferris wheel (4950 Clifton Hill; cliftonhill.com) for five vertiginous revolutions and a view of the colored lights projected nightly on the falls. (Oh right, there are waterfalls here. Remember?)

SATURDAY

5 *The Central Park* 10 a.m.

Frederick Law Olmsted and Frederic Church were among the 19th-century champions of a radical idea, public parks at Niagara Falls, erasing a clutter of factories and tourist traps. The Free Niagara movement succeeded on both sides of the border, and on the American side Olmsted designed landscapes at the crest of both waterfalls and on Goat Island, which separates them. Explore the woods and walkways of the resulting **Niagara Falls State Park** (716-278-1796; niagarafallsstatepark.com) to find what remains of the essential experience of Niagara. The

brink of the thunderous Horseshoe on Goat Island is the show-stopper, and newly redesigned walkways and vista points make the most of it. For an enticing mix of quiet glades and furious rapids, venture out on the tiny **Three Sisters Islands**.

6 *Wings Optional* 1 p.m.

Every table has a falls view at the seasonal **Top of the Falls** restaurant (in the state park; 716-278-0337; $$), where the locally inspired casual menu includes Buffalo chicken wings, salads, burgers, and wraps. In the off-season, walk out of the park for Saturday lunch at **Savor** (28 Old Falls Street; nfculinary.org/savor), the restaurant of the Niagara Falls Culinary Institute.

7 *Why the Waterfall?* 2 p.m.

You'll hunt in vain on both sides of the river for a straightforward geological explanation of Niagara Falls. At the **Niagara Gorge Discovery Center** in the state park, look selectively at the displays to tease out the basic facts. What's falling is the water of the Great Lakes. The falls are on the move upriver, naturally receding as much as 6 feet a year. There's a giant whirlpool where they took a sharp turn 40 centuries ago. (A Canadian attempt at explaining Niagara, a film called *Niagara's Fury*—niagaraparks.com/niagara-falls-attractions/niagaras-fury.html—is entertaining for children but not especially informative, mixing cartoon stereotypes with snippets of

textbook language.) Outside the Discovery Center, trails head toward the deep Niagara Gorge below the falls, where hikers get within a few feet of the largest standing waves in North America.

8 *The Close-Up* 3 p.m.

The **Maid of the Mist** tour boats (maidofthemist. com) have been thrilling customers since 1846. Chug out to the base of the Horseshoe on one of these sturdy craft, struggle to look up 170 feet to the top through the torrents, and you'll grasp the power of what brought you here. At the end of the ride, you can hang on to your flimsy slicker and take a wet but exhilarating hike to the base of the American Falls. You'll no longer find the *Maid* in Canada, but the **Hornblower Niagara Cruises** (niagaracruises.com) provide the same thrill. For a different daring view, ride the **Mistrider Zipline** (wildplay.com/niagarafalls) out over the gorge on the Canadian side of the river.

9 *Culinary Canada* 7 p.m.

AG, the soothing, stylish restaurant in the **Sterling Inn & Spa** (5195 Magdalen Street, Niagara Falls, Ontario; 289-292-0000; sterlingniagara.com; $$$), serves imaginative dishes using seasonal Canadian ingredients, paired with local wines. One summer menu included basil-and-potato-encrusted Lake Huron trout and pork tenderloin stuffed with macerated Niagara fruit. The desserts are good, too, but if you're not up for one, you can get by on the eye candy of the red, white, and crystal dining room.

SUNDAY

10 *Vineyards Haven* 10 a.m.

Leave the falls behind and drive north along the river in Canada on the lovely **Niagara Parkway**. Beyond placid Queenston, where an American attack was turned back in the War of 1812, the Niagara turns tame, and wineries, peach orchards, manor-like houses, and an inviting bicycle path line the road. The tasting rooms pour chardonnays, pinot noirs, and the regional specialty, ice wine. At **Inniskillin** (on the Parkway at Line 3; 905-468-2187; inniskillin.com/Niagara),

tours and signboards explain grape-friendly local conditions. **Reif Estate** (15608 Niagara Parkway; 905-468-7738; reifwinery.com) has a gimmicky but pleasant Wine Sensory Garden. **Peller Estates** (just off the parkway at 290 John Street West; 905-468-4678; peller.com) pairs its vintages with a posh restaurant. Between the reds and whites, stop in at the **Kurtz Orchards Gourmet Marketplace** (16006 Niagara Parkway; 905-468-2937; kurtzorchards.com), where you can munch enough free samples of breads, tapenades, jams, cheeses, and nut butters to take you all the way to dinner.

OPPOSITE Slickers are essential equipment for exploring the Cave of the Winds at the American Falls.

THE BASICS

By car, Niagara Falls is eight hours from New York City, 90 minutes from Toronto, and 45 minutes from the Buffalo Niagara airport. At the falls, walk and take trolleys and people movers. For exploring, drive a car.

Sterling Inn & Spa
5195 Magdalen Street, Niagara
Falls, Ontario
289-292-0000
sterlingniagara.com
$$$
A boutique-hotel oasis at the edge of the tourist maelstrom.

Doubletree Fallsview Resort & Spa
6039 Fallsview Boulevard, Niagara
Falls, Ontario
905-358-3817
niagarafallsdoubletree.com
$$
On a hill overlooking the falls.

The Giacomo
222 First Street, Niagara Falls,
New York
716-299-0200
thegiacomo.com
$$$
Renovated Art Deco building.

CANADA

Toronto

ONTARIO

Lake Ontario

40 miles
60 kilometers

Niagara Falls • • **Niagara Falls**

Rochester

• Buffalo

390

Lake Erie

90

NEW YORK

1/2 mile
1 kilometer

AG/
Sterling
Inn & Spa

Clifton
Hill

RIVER RD.

Niagara River

ROBERT
— MOSES
PKWY.

9

4

Niagara
Gorge
Discovery
Center

7

SkyWheel

Mistrider
Zipline

1

Rainbow Bridge

Doubletree
Fallsview Resort
& Spa

Hornblower
Niagara Cruises

Maid of the Mist tour boats

8

Queen Victoria
Place Restaurant

3

Savor

The Giacomo

American
Falls

Top of the Falls

6

5

Niagara Falls State Park

GOAT ISLAND

Queen
Victoria
Park

2

Horseshoe
Falls

Three Sisters Islands

UNITED STATES
CANADA

Lake Ontario

Niagara-on-
the-Lake

Peller
Estates ■

Kurtz Orchards
Gourmet
Marketplace

Reif Estate ■

— RIVER RD.

Inniskillin
■

10

Niagara
Parkway

CANADA

NEW
YORK

Queenston

405

190

Whirlpool
■

Niagara Falls

Area of
detail

Niagara River

2 miles
3 kilometers

Cincinnati

With the quiet momentum of a work in progress, Cincinnati, Ohio, is finding an artsy swagger, infused with a casual combination of Midwest and Southern charm. The city center, for decades rich with cultural and performing arts venues, now offers a renovated Fountain Square area and a gleaming new baseball stadium with views of the Ohio River. Transformations are taking place in surrounding areas and across the river in the neighboring Kentucky cities of Newport and Covington — with cool music venues, funky shopping outlets, and smart culinary options. While it looks to the future, the city also honors its historic role in the antislavery movement with its National Underground Railroad Freedom Center. — BY KASSIE BRACKEN

FRIDAY

1 *Tranquility and Eternity* 4 p.m.

A graveyard may not be the most obvious place to start a trip, but **Spring Grove Cemetery and Arboretum** (4521 Spring Grove Avenue; 513-681-7526; springgrove.org) is not your average resting place. The arboretum, designed in 1845 as a place for botanical experiments, features 1,200 types of plants artfully arranged around mausoleums and tranquil ponds. Roman- and Greek-inspired monuments bear the names of many of Cincinnati's most prominent families, including the Procters and the Gambles, whose business, begun in the 1830s, still dominates the city. Admission and parking are free, and the office provides printed guides and information about the plant collection.

2 *Where Hipsters Roam* 6 p.m.

The Northside district has blossomed into a casually hip destination for shopping and night life, particularly along Hamilton Avenue. Vinyl gets ample real estate at **Shake It Records** (4156 Hamilton Avenue; 513-591-0123; shakeitrecords.com), a music store specializing in independent labels; if you can't find a title among the 40,000 they carry, the owners will track it down for you. For a bite, locals swear by **Melt**

Eclectic Cafe (4100 Hamilton Avenue; 513-818-8951; facebook.com/MeltEclecticCafe; $), a quirky restaurant serving melted sandwiches, salads, soups, and a popular black bean chili. Order the Joan of Ark, a melt with peppers, blue cheese, and caramelized onions atop braised brisket, and retreat to the patio.

3 *Local Bands, Local Beer* 9 p.m.

Saunter next door to find 20-somethings in skinny jeans mingling with 30-somethings in flip-flops at **Northside Tavern** (4163 Hamilton Avenue; 513-542-3603; northsidetav.com/cinci), a prime spot for live music. Sip a pint of Cincinnati's own Christian Moerlein beer and listen to jazz, blues, and acoustic rock acts in the intimate front bar. Or head to the back room, where the best local bands take the larger stage. Wind down with a crowd heavy with artists and musicians at the **Comet** (4579 Hamilton Avenue; 513-541-8900; cometbar.com), a noirish dive bar with an impossibly cool selection on its jukebox and top-notch burritos to satisfy any late-night cravings.

SATURDAY

4 *The Aerobic Arabesque* 9:30 a.m.

The fiberglass pigs in tutus that greet you outside the **Cincinnati Ballet** (1555 Central Parkway; 513-621-5219) might indicate otherwise, but don't be fooled: the Ballet's Open Adult Division program (cballet.org/academy/adult) is a great place to get lean. Start your Saturday with a beginning ballet class (90 minutes, under $20), as a company member steers novices through basic movements. More experienced dancers might try the one-hour Dancefix

OPPOSITE The John A. Roebling Suspension Bridge over the Ohio River connects Cincinnati to its Kentucky suburbs.

RIGHT The revitalized Over-the-Rhine neighborhood.

class, which combines hip-hop and jazz, "from Latin to lyrical." Regulars know the moves, so pick a spot in the back and prepare to sweat.

5 *A Bridge to Brunch* 11:30 a.m.

If John Roebling's Suspension Bridge looks familiar, you might be thinking of his more famous design in New York. (Cincinnati's version opened in 1867, almost two decades before the Brooklyn Bridge.) It's a pedestrian-friendly span over the Ohio River, providing terrific views of the skyline. Cross into Covington, Kentucky, and walk a few blocks to the **Keystone Bar & Grill** (313 Greenup Street; 859-261-6777; keystonebar.com; $-$$), where alcohol-fueled partying gives way to brunch on weekend mornings. You'll be well nourished for the walk back.

6 *Tracing a Legacy* 2 p.m.

The **National Underground Railroad Freedom Center** (50 East Freedom Way; 513-333-7500; freedomcenter.org) is a dynamic testament to Cincinnati's place in the antislavery movement. Multimedia presentations, art displays, and interactive timelines trace the history of the global slave trade as well as 21st-century human trafficking. Leave time for the genealogy center, where volunteers assist individuals with detailed family searches.

7 *Sin City, Updated* 5 p.m.

For decades, Cincinnatians scoffed at their Kentucky neighbors, but that has been changing in the last few years, especially with the revitalization of Newport, a waterfront and historic housing district. Stroll to **York Street Café** (738 York Street, entrance on Eighth Street; 859-261-9675; yorkstonline.com; $$), an 1880s-era apothecary transformed into a three-story restaurant, music, and art space, where wood shelves are stocked with kitschy memorabilia. Browse a bit before scanning the menu for bistro fare like a Mediterranean board (an array of shareable appetizers) or a delicate fresh halibut with spinach and artichoke. Leave room for the excellent

homemade desserts, including the strawberry buttermilk cake.

8 *Stage to Stage* 7 p.m.

Cincinnati Playhouse in the Park (962 Mount Adams Circle; 513-421-3888; cincyplay.com), which has been producing plays for five decades, offers splendid vistas of Mount Adams and a solid theater-going experience. A lesser-known but equally engaging option can be found at the **University of Cincinnati College-Conservatory of Music** (Corry Boulevard; 513-556-4183; ccm.uc.edu/theatre). Students dreaming of Lincoln Center perform in full-scale productions of serious drama and opera. Check the online calendar for show times and locations.

9 *Ballroom Bliss* 10 p.m.

Head back to Newport's Third Street and its bars and clubs. A standout, **Southgate House Revival**, is set in a big converted church (111 East Sixth Street, Newport; 859-431-2201; southgatehouse.com) with stained glass and multiple spaces for several acts to play on the same date. On a typical Saturday night, music fans of all ages and sensibilities roam among its multiple stages and bars.

SUNDAY

10 *Neighborhood Reborn* 11 a.m.

As the epicenter of 19th-century German immigrant society, the neighborhood known as Over-the-Rhine once teemed with breweries, theaters, and social halls. Though it fell into disrepair and parts remain rough around the edges, an $80 million

revitalization effort has slowly brought back visitors. Walk down Main Street between 12th and 15th Streets to find local artists' galleries and the **Iris BookCafé** (1331 Main Street; 513-381-2665; irisbookcafeotr. com), a serene rare-book shop with an outdoor sculpture garden. A few blocks away, Vine Street between Central Parkway and 13th Street offers new boutiques including the craft shop **MiCA 12/v** (1201 Vine Street; 513-421-3500; shopmica.com), which specializes in contemporary designers.

11 *Designs to Take Home* 1 p.m.
    Before heading home, find inspiring décor at **HighStreet** (1401 Reading Road; 513-723-1901; highstreetcincinnati.com), a spacious and sleek design store. The owners have carefully composed a cosmopolitan mix of textiles, clothing,

and jewelry by New York and London designers as well as local artists, showcased in a creatively appointed space. A free cup of red flower tea makes it all the more inviting.

OPPOSITE ABOVE Spring Grove Cemetery and Arboretum.

OPPOSITE BELOW Northside, an area for shopping and night life.

ABOVE The National Underground Railroad Freedom Center. Cincinnati was a stop for many who escaped slavery.

THE BASICS

Fly into Cincinnati/Northern Kentucky International Airport, a 25-minute drive from downtown. A rental car is recommended.

Hilton Cincinnati Netherland Plaza
35 West Fifth Street
513-421-9100
hilton.com
$$
561 renovated rooms in a landmark building, the Art Deco Carew Tower.

The Westin Cincinnati
21 East Fifth Street
513-621-7700
starwoodhotels.com
$$
Downtown with views of Fountain Square from many rooms.

Cincinnatian Hotel
601 Vine Street
513-381-3000
cincinnatianhotel.com
$$
Updated rooms in a classic hotel dating to 1882.

Cleveland

"You Gotta Be Tough" was a popular T-shirt slogan worn by Clevelanders during the 1970s, when their city was beset by industrial decline and population flight. These days it still helps to be at least a little tough; a fiercely blue-collar ethos endures in this part of Ohio. But instead of abandoning the city, entrepreneurs and bohemian dreamers alike have put down roots. "The Land," as the prodigal son LeBron James calls Cleveland, is back with a revitalized downtown, sophisticated restaurants, and industrial-turned-arty neighborhoods, while a strong base of cultural institutions has always endured. Spend the weekend and catch the vibrant spirit. — BRETT SOKOL AND ELAINE GLUSAC

FRIDAY

1 *Hello, Cleveland!* 3 p.m.

Staring at Lady Gaga's meat dress or Michael Jackson's glove hardly evokes the visceral excitement of rock music, but the **Rock and Roll Hall of Fame** (1100 East Ninth Street; 216-781-7625; rockhall.com) has a wealth of interactive exhibits in addition to its displays of the goofier fashion choices of rock stardom. In a meandering building designed by I. M. Pei, the museum traces the evolution of rock to its early roots in gospel and blues, and lets visitors discover the influences of popular artists. (Who knew the Beach Boys influenced the Ramones?)

2 *Pit Master* 8 p.m.

The chef Michael Symon is synonymous with Cleveland's culinary prowess via his popular restaurant Lola, as well as his appearances on the television shows Iron Chef America and The Chew. Now another Symon restaurant, **Mabel's BBQ** (2050 East Fourth Street; 216-417-8823; mabelsbbq.com; $$), downtown, makes the case for Cleveland-accented barbecue, using Eastern European spices on the meats and local Bertman Ball Park Mustard in the sauce. Exposed brick walls, warehouse-height ceil-

ings, and long communal tables create the informal industrial vibe. Have a succulent sandwich with sides like baked beans, coleslaw, or broccoli salad. Or consider sharing sizable dishes from piles of crispy pig ears, to a half-pound of fatty brisket, to a mess of kielbasa and spare ribs piled with sauerkraut. The bar specializes in bourbon and beer.

3 *How About a Highball?* 10 p.m.

Discerning drinkers head for the **Velvet Tango Room** (2095 Columbus Road; 216-241-8869; velvettangoroom.com), inside a one-time Prohibition-era speakeasy and seemingly little changed. The bitters are house-made, and the bartenders pride themselves on effortlessly mixing a perfect classic, like a Bourbon Daisy or Pink Lady, or a more newfangled drink, if that's your pleasure. Live jazz performers keep the vibe smooth.

SATURDAY

4 *Sip and Look Up* 10 a.m.

Many grocery stores have coffee bars and cafes, but few occupy a place in Clevelanders' hearts like **Heinen's Grocery Store** downtown (East Ninth Street and Euclid Avenue; 216-302-3020; heinens.com/downtown). This branch of Heinen's, a local chain specializing in prepared foods, is in the 1908 Cleveland Trust Company Building. Its 85-foot-high leaded-glass ceiling is bordered by 13 murals depicting local history by the painter Francis Davis Millet, who died on the *Titanic*.

OPPOSITE The Cleveland Museum of Art in the culture-saturated University Circle district.

RIGHT At the Velvet Tango Room, the bitters are house-made and the cocktails are precisely mixed.

5 *Vintage Shopping* 11 a.m.

Find more vintage architecture put to modern use at the **Arcade** (401 Euclid Avenue; theclevelandarcade.com), one of three elegant glass-topped, blocklong malls in the area that are modeled on classic shopping arcades like those in Paris and Milan. This one, with five floors and scrolling iron balconies, is largely occupied by a hotel. The two across the street, the former Colonial (1898) and Euclid (1911) Arcades, now operating as the **5th Street Arcades** (530 Euclid Avenue; 5thstreetarcades.com), warrant browsing. The shops sell souvenirs, local art and fashion, jewelry, and sweet treats.

6 *Eating Ohio City* 1 p.m.

Just west of downtown, Ohio City, which was annexed by Cleveland in 1854, still attests to the heritage of its original European immigrant population, particularly in the historic **West Side Market** (1979 West 25th Street; 216-664-3387; westsidemarket.com), a 1912 landmark bustling with shoppers and more than 100 vendors of produce, meat, cheese, and baked goods. Pick up some edibles and take a perch on the second-story mezzanine for a view over the market and its vaulted brick ceiling. As an artisan culinary district, Ohio City also offers possibilities beyond the market. Try a scoop at **Mitchell's Ice Cream** (1867 West 25th Street; 216-861-2799; mitchellshomemade. com), or an Eliot Ness amber lager at **Great Lakes Brewing** (2516 Market Avenue; 216-771-4404; greatlakesbrewing.com).

7 *From Steel to Stylish* 3 p.m.

The steelworkers who once filled the Tremont neighborhood's low-slung houses and ornately topped churches have largely vanished, now replaced by restaurants, galleries, and stores. At one of the shops, **Tremont Scoops** (2362 Professor Avenue; 216-781-0352; tremontscoops.com), you can choose among 24 flavors of ice cream, dairy or vegan, and four kinds of cones, including gluten-free.

8 *Cleveland Stage* 7:30 p.m.

Downtown's **Playhouse Square** (playhousesquare. org) calls itself the country's largest performing arts center outside of New York, with nine theaters in a one-block radius, many staging touring productions. If you prefer music to theater, book a date with the renowned **Cleveland Orchestra** (clevelandorchestra. com). When it's not touring the world, the orchestra performs most of the year in Severance Hall, an opulent, 1931-vintage concert hall. In the summer, catch it with the picnic crowd at Blossom Music Center, about 25 miles south of the city.

SUNDAY

9 *Locavore Brunch* 10:30 a.m.

Many of the ingredients that go into the dishes at **Spice Kitchen + Bar** (5800 Detroit Avenue; 216-961-9637; spicekitchenandbar.com; $$) come from the restaurant's 13-acre farm in Cuyahoga Valley National Park, about 20 miles south of town. Brunch fare ranges from apple cinnamon beignets to Korean fried chicken and waffles.

ABOVE The Rock and Roll Hall of Fame, repository of John Lennon's "Sgt. Pepper" suit and Michael Jackson's glove.

OPPOSITE Home cooks and chefs both stock their kitchens at the West Side Market, a good stop for Saturday morning.

10 *Free Impressionists* Noon

For decades, the University Circle district has housed many of the city's cultural jewels, including Severance Hall, the majestic Georgian residence of the Cleveland Orchestra, and the Cleveland Institute of Art Cinematheque, one of the country's best repertory movie theaters. At the **Cleveland Museum of Art** (11150 East Boulevard; 216-421-7350; clevelandart.org), already famed for its collection of Old Masters and kid-friendly armor, exhibits in the newer Rafael Viñoly-designed East Wing have put the spotlight on more modern fare, including Impressionist paintings. A special inducement: admission to the museum's permanent collections is free. Nearby, the **Museum of Contemporary** **Art Cleveland** (11400 Euclid Avenue; 216-421-8671; mocacleveland.org) has a stunning home designed by the Iranian-born London architect Farshid Moussavi.

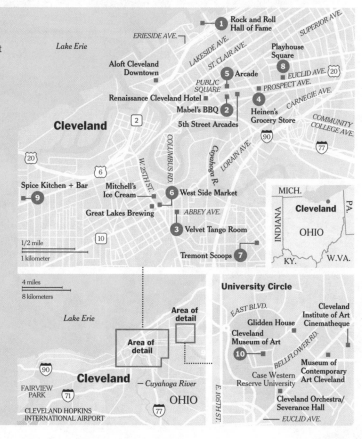

THE BASICS

Several major airlines have frequent flights to Cleveland. A light rail system connects the airport with downtown and University Circle. A car is needed for reaching most other neighborhoods.

The Glidden House
1901 Ford Drive
216-231-8900
gliddenhouse.com
$$
Quaint rooms in a 1910 mansion on the Case Western Reserve University campus.

Renaissance Cleveland Hotel
24 Public Square
216-696-5600
marriott.com
$$-$$$
A renovated elegant downtown classic, now a Marriott property.

Aloft Cleveland Downtown
1111 West 10th Street
216-400-6469
aloftclevelanddowntown.com
$$
Bright, colorful, and contemporary.

Oklahoma City

It shouldn't take more than a day for the song—who doesn't know that song?—to clear your head. Yes, a constant wind does seem to come sweepin' down the plain (more accurately, the red-dirt prairie). But amid the grand urban projects, gleaming museums, and air of new sophistication in today's Oklahoma City, the only folks yelling "Ayipioeeay" are likely to be visitors. Hints of what's behind the revitalization pop up everywhere: oil rigs, even on the State Capitol grounds. Even so, newcomers to town might wonder at first where they are. A generally flat cityscape, friendly hellos, and Chicago-style downtown architecture suggest the Midwest. Jazz, blues bars, and barbecue joints speak of the South. But the wide vistas and the American Indian shops (Oklahoma has 38 sovereign tribes), pickups, and cowboy hats tell another story: this is the West.

— BY FINN-OLAF JONES

FRIDAY

1 *Bricks and Bronzes* 4 p.m.

The Oklahoma River waterfront has come alive since 1999, when a canal was completed to attract visitors. In the lively Bricktown district, old warehouses now hold restaurants, clubs, and shops. Catch the bold spirit by checking out the **Centennial Land Run Monument** (Centennial Avenue; visitokc.com/listings/oklahoma-land-run-monument/467), an eye-popping, larger-than-life-size commemoration of the great Land Run of 1889, when 10,000 people rushed into town on a single day. Its series of ultra-realistic bronze statues, by the sculptor Paul Moore, shows pioneers, horses, and wagons caught in motion as they charge into the fray and ford a river. Together, they make up one of the largest freestanding bronze sculptures in the world. Nearby, duck inside for a look at some of the 300 banjos in the **American Banjo Museum** (9 East Sheridan Avenue; 405-604-2793; americanbanjomuseum.com), ranging from lavishly decorated Jazz Age beauties to replicas of slaves' homemade instruments.

OPPOSITE Taxi boats on the canal in Bricktown, a happening Oklahoma City neighborhood.

RIGHT Oil has been good to Oklahoma, and derricks appear all over town, even on the grounds of the State Capitol.

2 *Wasabi on the Range* 7 p.m.

If you're in the mood for steak, you will never have far to look in Oklahoma City. But even if you're not, have dinner at the **Mantel Wine Bar & Bistro** (201 East Sheridan Avenue; 405-236-8040; themantelokc.com; $$). The menu honors the regional theme with several beef entrees, but also offers interesting alternatives like duck breast with cranberry port wine sauce or wasabi-encrusted tuna.

3 *You'll Never Bowl Alone* 9 p.m.

Check out the night life in Bricktown, where taxi boats ferry merrymakers to the teeming home-grown jazz and blues joints. One of the livelier spots is **HeyDay Lower Bricktown** (200 South Oklahoma Avenue; 405-602-5680; heydayfun.com), an entertainment complex with a 10-lane bowling alley. Rent some hip-looking high-top bowling shoes, grab a beer or a specialty cocktail, and bowl the night away.

SATURDAY

4 *Feed Your Inner Cowboy* 11 a.m.

South of the river, the century-old Oklahoma National Stockyards are still used for enormous cattle auctions several times a week, but there's another kind of show one block farther up at **Cattlemen's Steakhouse** (1309 South Agnew Avenue; 405-236-0416;

cattlemensrestaurant.com; $$). Long lines form for lunch and dinner (no reservations taken), so try breakfast. "Usually it's just the old-timers that want this," a waitress said when one out-of-towner succumbed to curiosity and ordered the calf brains. For the record, it looks like oatmeal, has a slight livery aftertaste, and isn't half bad. But wash it down with a couple of mugs of hot coffee and a plate of eggs and magnificently aged and tenderized steak.

5 *Dress Your Inner Cowboy* 12:30 p.m.

Cross the street to **Langston's Western Wear** (2224 Exchange Avenue; 405-235-9536; langstons. com) for your dungarees and boots. Down the block, **Oklahoma Native Art and Jewelry** (2204 Exchange Avenue; 405-604-9800; oklahomanativearts.com) carries a broad variety of items from Oklahoma's tribes. White pottery pieces with horse hairs burned onto their surfaces — a centuries-old technique — in Jackson Pollock-like swirling patterns are made by the store's owner, Yolanda White Antelope, a member of the Acoma tribe. Then wander into the **National Saddlery Company** (1400 South Agnew Avenue; 405-239-2104; nationalsaddlery.com) for a hand-tooled saddle — prices run from about $1,500 for a base model to $30,000 for a masterpiece with

silver trimmings. Down the street, **Shorty's Caboy Hattery** (1007 South Agnew Avenue; 405-232-4287; shortyshattery.com) will supply you with a custom-made cattleman's hat described by Mike Nunn, who manned the counter one day, as "the only hat that will stay on your head in Oklahoma wind."

6 *Where the West Is Found* 2 p.m.

James Earle Fraser's famous 18-foot statue of an American Indian slumped on his horse, *The End of the Trail*, greets you in the lobby of the **National Cowboy and Western Heritage Museum** (1700 Northeast 63rd Street; 405-478-2250; nationalcowboymuseum.org). Beware. You may think you can cover it in a couple of hours, but a whole day could be too little to reach the end of this trail. Exhibits in tentlike pavilions around a central courtyard cover everything about cowboys from their roots in Africa and England to how they operate on contemporary corporate ranches. Examine a replica of a turn-of-the-century cattle town; guns including John Wayne's impressive personal arsenal; and Western art including works by Frederic Remington, Albert Bierstadt, and Charles M. Russell.

7 *Cosmopolitans* 7 p.m.

The city's new economy has attracted a whole new class of settler, business types from world financial capitals, usually male and accompanied by stylish spouses. Find them — and a pre-dinner cocktail — in

the noirish-cool **Lobby Cafe and Bar** (4322 North Western Avenue; 405-604-4650; willrogerslobbybar. com) in the newly renovated Will Rogers Theatre, which looms over an affluent corridor of North Western Avenue. The street continues up to Tara-sized mansions dotting Nichols Hills. For dinner, drive a few blocks to **The Hutch** (6437 Avondale Drive; 405-842-1000; hutchokc.com; $$), formerly the Coach House, where the concept is "modern tavern cuisine," such as braised short ribs, grilled beef filet, and roasted salmon, with custom cocktails. The Hutch retained its predecessor's chef and mixologist, and they have creatively reimagined the menu.

8 *Dances With Bulls* 10 p.m.

Find friends fast at **Cowboys OKC** (2301 South Meridian Avenue; 405-686-1191; cowboysokc.com),

formerly Club Rodeo. Modern cowgirls and cowboys of every age group and shape can be found hootin' and hollerin' at this acre-sized honky-tonk south of downtown near the airport. Fellow carousers will help you figure out the dance moves to go with country

ABOVE Shorty's Caboy Hattery. The cattleman's hat, they'll tell you at Shorty's, is the only kind that will stay on your head in an Oklahoma wind.

BELOW A view of downtown Oklahoma City from the fountain in front of City Hall.

sounds. The mood may turn real cowpokey when dance-floor lights go dark to be replaced by spotlights on a tennis-court-sized rodeo ring, where revelers migrate with their beers to watch hopefuls try to hang onto bucking bulls for longer than eight seconds. The loudest cheers have been known to go to the orneriest bulls.

SUNDAY

9 *The Memorial* 10 a.m.

All longtime residents of Oklahoma City seem to know exactly where they were at 9:02 a.m. on April 19, 1995, when Timothy McVeigh detonated an explosives-filled truck beneath the Alfred P. Murrah Federal Building, killing 168 people and damaging 312 surrounding buildings. At the **Oklahoma City National Memorial** (620 North Harvey Avenue; 405-235-3313; oklahomacitynationalmemorial.org)

that now covers the site, a gently flowing reflecting pool and two massive gates preside over 168 empty bronze chairs—one for each victim, the 19 smaller ones denoting children. Absorb the quiet, and the message.

10 *Under Glass* 11 a.m.

The **Oklahoma City Museum of Art** (415 Couch Drive; 405-236-3100; okcmoa.com) boasts the world's most comprehensive collection of glass sculptures by Dale Chihuly, starting with the 55-foot-tall centerpiece at the front door. Savor the mesmerizing play of light, color, and fantastic shapes, a fitting goodbye to a town that never seems shy about grabbing your attention.

OPPOSITE *The End of the Trail*, by James Earle Fraser, at the National Cowboy and Western Heritage Museum.

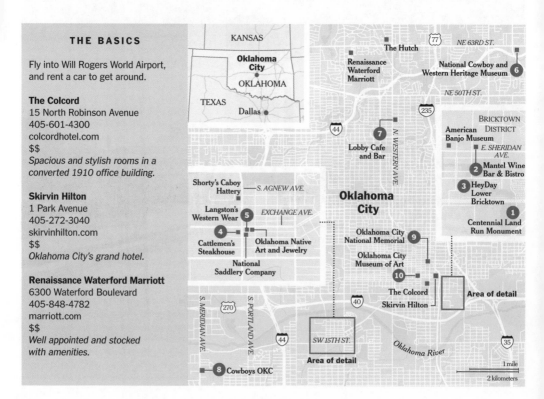

THE BASICS

Fly into Will Rogers World Airport, and rent a car to get around.

The Colcord
15 North Robinson Avenue
405-601-4300
colcordhotel.com
$$
Spacious and stylish rooms in a converted 1910 office building.

Skirvin Hilton
1 Park Avenue
405-272-3040
skirvinhilton.com
$$
Oklahoma City's grand hotel.

Renaissance Waterford Marriott
6300 Waterford Boulevard
405-848-4782
marriott.com
$$
Well appointed and stocked with amenities.

Toronto

Known for its diversity and livability, Toronto feels less like a metropolis than a patchwork of distinct neighborhoods linked by a live-and-let-live ethos and a vibrant street culture. There's a plentiful supply of innovative restaurants, a full range of cultural offerings, and a smorgasbord of ethnically distinct shops, not to mention Lake Ontario beachfront and that most traditional of Canadian institutions, the Hockey Hall of Fame. While a long weekend offers only enough time to scratch the surface, it doesn't take long to succumb to Toronto's charms. — BY JEREMY EGNER

FRIDAY

1 *Shopping Diversity* 2 p.m.

Despite the singular name, **Kensington Market** (kensington-market.ca) is actually a proudly multicultural neighborhood encompassing about ten disparate blocks of shops, services, grocers, and restaurants. You could have a fine afternoon just focusing on Baldwin Street, prospecting for quirky gifts, delicious baked goods, coffee, and hockey jerseys. Venture farther to the longstanding spice, produce, cheese, and tea shops that give the neighborhood, a national historic site, its vital and diverse character. Look for the colorful Victorians on Augusta Avenue and the No. 8 Hose Station, built in 1878, on College Street at Bellevue.

2 *Catalonia in Little Italy* 5 p.m.

Bar Raval (505 College Street; thisisbarraval. com) is a great spot for an afternoon break, but it will be ready for you whenever you need it. This cozy, gorgeous Barcelona-style pintxos and tapas bar is open every day from early to late, offering coffee and sweet and savory pastries in the morning, along with Spanish cheeses, Galician tinned seafood, and succulent charcuterie throughout the day. The wine list is well curated but the real star is the Gaudí-esque interior — all whimsically swooping mahogany millwork that will have you staring at the ceiling as you sip your Rioja.

3 *New Dining Faves* 7 p.m.

Toronto is crazy about izakayas, casual Japanese gastro pubs, and one of the best is **Imanishi Japanese Kitchen** (1330 Dundas Street West; imanishi.ca; $$).

This low-slung spot in Little Portugal is less boisterous than many izakayas, the better to sit at the reclaimed wood bar with a yozu Tom Collins and focus on elegant snacks like bright, citrusy tai carpaccio and crispy sweet corn tempura fritter. Still peckish, somehow? Head down Dundas Street West to order from the game-heavy menu at **Antler** (1454 Dundas Street West; antlerkitchenbar.com; $$). A boar, bison, and deer burger will affirm your spot at the top of the food chain.

SATURDAY

4 *Go to (Another) Market* 8 a.m.

Located in Toronto's Old Town, the **St. Lawrence Market** (92-95 Front Street East; stlawrencemarket. com) opens at 5 a.m. on Saturdays; you'll want to get there as early as you can to beat the crowds. Ontario farmers have been selling produce at this spot since 1803, but the modern version, named the world's top food market a few years ago by National Geographic, includes bakeries, delis, cheesemongers, sweets makers, and a local legend, **Carousel Bakery** (stlawrencemarket.com/vendors/vendor_detail/56), with its renowned peameal bacon sandwich. (That's Canadian bacon to you Americans.) Its humble charms beguiled Anthony Bourdain and Emeril Lagasse, among other culinary celebrities.

OPPOSITE Queen Street West, a go-to strip for trendy boutiques, galleries, bars, and restaurants.

BELOW A burger at Antler might mix boar, bison, and deer.

5 *Island Getaway* 10 a.m.

One of Lake Ontario's gifts to Toronto is Toronto Island (torontoisland.com), a hot spot in the summer and a placid one in winter. It's actually a series of small islands connected by small bridges, making up a four-mile-long car-free getaway. Take a 10-minute ferry ride from the foot of Bay Street at Queen's Quay (torontoislandferryfinder.com) and then walk. You'll enjoy incredible city views, acres of parkland, and a 1.5-mile boardwalk. **Rectory Café** (102 Lakeshore Avenue; facebook.com/TheRectoryCafe; $$), just off the boardwalk, is open year round — the salads are the standouts.

6 *Distill Life* 2 p.m.

The 47 buildings that make up the **Distillery Historic District** (thedistillerydistrict.com), the oldest dating to the 1850s, would be notable even if nothing was in them. Together, they make up what's billed as the largest collection of Victorian industrial architecture in North America. But beginning in the early 2000s, the once-dilapidated former site of the Gooderham & Worts Distillery was resurrected as a 13-acre cultural district. The cobbled lanes are lined with an array of artisan workshops, and the factory buildings host shops and artists' studios. Worthy dining options include **El Catrin** (18 Tank House Lane; elcatrin.ca; $$), a cavernous modern Mexican cantina with excellent ceviche and a two-story fever

dream of a mural by the Mexican street artist Oscar Flores. A truffle (or four) at **Soma Chocolatemaker** (32 Tank House Lane; somachocolate.com) makes a fine chaser.

7 *Tagspotting* 5 p.m.

Street art has evolved from its illicit origins to become a source of civic pride in Toronto, thanks largely to the efforts of groups like StreetARToronto. There are head-turning splashes all over the city, but the most concentrated display is along Rush Lane, a stretch just south of Queen Street West, between Spadina and Portland, known as **Graffiti Alley** (instagram.com/explore/locations/283630). Stylistically, the works are by turns macabre (elaborate skulls), whimsical (cartoon characters), and fantastical (an undersea array covering most of a building). Most are stunning. You'll never look at a can of spray paint the same way again.

8 *Do I Drink It? Or …?* 6 p.m.

BarChef (472 Queens Street West; barcheftoronto.com) is to mixology what CERN was to your high school physics class. Created by the modernist cocktail wizard Frankie Solarik, this dimly lit booze

ABOVE Get to the St. Lawrence Market, a food emporium, early in the morning to beat the Saturday crowds.

laboratory turns out multisensory concoctions that dazzle the eyes before they tickle the taste buds. Consider the hickory-smoked vanilla Manhattan that actually smokes, and the rotating creations (Spring Thaw, the Essence of Fall) served amid foliage and soil. Over the top? Absolutely, with prices to match. But when's the last time you got to drink a season?

9 *Canadian Cooking* 8 p.m.

A walk down Queen Street West takes you through a frenetic strip of bars, boutiques, galleries, and restaurants. A good destination is **Montgomery's** (996 Queen Street West; montgomerysrestaurant.

ABOVE Pandemonium, a book and record store on Dundas Street West in the hip Junction neighborhood.

BELOW Graffiti Alley south of Queen Street West, starting at Spadina Avenue. Toronto street art has evolved to become a source of civic pride.

com; $$), a farm-to-table restaurant with a stripped-down aesthetic. The rotating menu focuses on Ontarian and Canadian ingredients prepared with unassuming sophistication.

SUNDAY

10 *Hit the Junction* 10 a.m.

A longstanding prohibition on alcohol sales in the Junction neighborhood was overturned in 1997, and the area, named for its proximity to an intersection of four railroads, has since emerged as one of the hippest districts in the city. Coincidence? Standout shops on Dundas Street West include **Gerhard Supply** (No. 2949; gerhardsupply.com) for men's wear and denim;

Opticianado (No. 2919; opticianado.com), offering a chic assortment of new and vintage eyeglass frames; and **Pandemonium** (No. 2920; pandemonium.ca) for new and used books and vinyl. Find brunch at **3030 Dundas West** (No. 3030; 3030dundaswest.com).

11 *Castle in a Time Warp* 2 p.m.

Completed in 1914 for the financier Sir Henry Mill Pellatt, the 64,700-square-foot **Casa Loma** (1 Austin Terrace; casaloma.ca) is both majestic and slightly

terrifying. Tours offer glimpses of many of the house's 98 rooms, with opulent art and furnishings, as well as spectacular views of the city from the upper floors. Outside, stroll around the exterior and check out the skyline vista from the Baldwin Steps, just around the corner.

OPPOSITE Old buildings including the pillared Union Station mingle with skyscrapers on Front Street.

THE BASICS

The Union Pearson Express rail link connects Toronto Pearson International Airport to Union Station downtown, a 25-minute trip.

Le Germain Hotel Toronto
30 Mercer Street
legermainhotels.com/en/
torontomercer

$$$$
Boutique hotel in the downtown entertainment district, across from the Second City comedy theater.

Cambridge Suites Toronto
15 Richmond Street East
cambridgesuitestoronto.com
$$$
All-suite hotel centrally located downtown, close to subways and

attractions like the St. Lawrence Market.

Hotel Ocho
195 Spadina Avenue
hotelocho.com
$$
In a former Chinatown textile factory from 1902; designed by local cutting-edge Design38.

The Laurel Highlands

In the Laurel Highlands of southwestern Pennsylvania, cornfields undulate between forested slopes and rivers spill downward in a rush of whitewater, luring fishermen and rafters. These green hills gave Frank Lloyd Wright the setting for Fallingwater, his cantilevered masterpiece of a house set over a swiftly flowing creek. Nearby, another client hired Wright to design Kentuck Knob, a quirky counterpart. And a bit north in Acme, a Wright ranch house saved from demolition in Illinois arrived in pieces, completing the setting for a Wrightian weekend. Balancing the architectural immersion with a little history and some outdoor adventures creates a memorable experience under the shiny leaves of the mountain laurel.

— BY BETHANY SCHNEIDER AND BARBARA IRELAND

FRIDAY

1 *A Matter of Necessity* 4 p.m.

Everybody has to start somewhere, and George Washington's first battlefield command was in 1754 at what is now **Fort Necessity National Battlefield** (off Route 40 in Farmington; 724-329-5805; nps.gov/fone). The reconstruction of the fort that Washington's forces threw together in their moment of necessity (they were about to be attacked) is terrifying in its meagerness. Sure enough, the French and their Indian allies made mincemeat of the British led by Colonel Washington, then just 22. But other victories came later, and the French and Indian War made Washington's reputation. Rangers evoke the feel of combat in the era when these highlands were virgin forest, delivering dramatic lines like "Half King, Washington's Indian ally, washed his hands in the brains of the French commander."

2 *Dinner With History* 7 p.m.

Wash your own hands in something more appropriate as you tidy up for dinner. Find it at the **Eastwood Inn** (661 Old Lincoln Highway; 724-238-6454; theeastwoodinn.com; $$$), in Ligonier, a classic steakhouse with period charm, where lamb chops

from the nearby Jamison Farm are grilled simply and served with mint jelly and a choice of such anachronistic accompaniments as baked potato and an iceberg wedge. The restaurant was once a stagecoach stop, in the 1880s, then a speakeasy during Prohibition and retains a soupçon of secrecy: There's no sign; you must buzz to be let in.

SATURDAY

3 *The Masterwork* 8:15 a.m.

Arrive in plenty of time for your in-depth tour at **Fallingwater** (1491 Mill Run Road, Mill Run; 724-329-8501; fallingwater.org; tours must be purchased several weeks in advance). You're up early, but it's worth it; this tour, longer than the basic version, allows more time inside the house and more leisure to absorb the complexity of its construction. Projecting airily over a waterfall on Bear Run Creek, its platforms mimicking the striations of the local rock, the house still looks as strikingly original and eerily perfect for its setting as it did when it was completed in 1939. Instantly famous, it resuscitated the faltering career of its creator, Frank Lloyd Wright, who was then 72. No matter how many times you've seen it, Fallingwater is breathtaking. On one bright May day, a middle-aged visitor from Scotland, dressed in a blue anorak, stood with tears flowing down his cheeks at his first sight of it. The guide assured him this was normal.

OPPOSITE Frank Lloyd Wright's Fallingwater, the famed masterwork cantilevered over a waterfall in the woods of the Laurel Highlands.

RIGHT The Cucumber Falls at Ohiopyle State Park.

4 *Lingering for Lunch* Noon

Fallingwater's inviting grounds, not to mention various vantage points for your perfect photo, will keep you busy until lunchtime, so stay for a sandwich at the cafe. The shopping is good, too. At the Fallingwater Museum Store, even the souvenir mugs are classy.

5 *A Bike in the Forest* 1 p.m.

In Confluence, a tiny, charming town wedged between the tines of three converging rivers, you'll find the gateway to the most beautiful 11 miles of the 150-mile **Great Allegheny Passage** rail trail (atatrail.org), following an old railroad bed. Rent a mountain bike or a recumbent (easy on the body if you're not a regular cyclist) from one of the village outfitters, and glide through the dreamy woodland of **Ohiopyle State Park** (dcnr.state.pa.us/stateparks/findapark/ohiopyle).

6 *Nature's Water Park* 3 p.m.

Cool down in daredevil style at the **Natural Waterslides**, still in the park, just south of Ohiopyle on Route 381. Sit in the stream, and it barrels you across smooth rocks and through a curving sluice, producing an adrenaline rush and maybe a few bruises. Dry off by **Cucumber Falls** around the corner on Route 2019, a bridal veil that splashes into a pool the pale green and rusty red of a glass of Pimm's. When you feel refreshed, cycle back to Confluence and drop off your bike.

7 *Going Usonian* 7:30 p.m.

Make your way over hill and dale to secluded **Polymath Park** (187 Evergreen Lane, Acme; 877-833-7829; franklloydwrightovernight.net), a quiet, tree-shaded resort whose intriguing business plan centers on architectural preservation. You made your dinner reservations here long ago, so take a little time now to explore the shaded drives and find the **Duncan House,** one of the modest houses that Frank Lloyd Wright designed for the middle class and christened Usonians. Rescued from its original site in Illinois,

where it was threatened with teardown, it was moved to Pennsylvania in thousands of numbered pieces and, after some cliffhanger misadventures, painstakingly reassembled here. The house is vastly more modest than the tour de force of Fallingwater, but it bears the unmistakable marks of Wright's ingenuity. It is available for short-term rentals, so be respectful of the tenants who may be inside and view it from a distance. (Unless, of course, you are the lucky tenant this weekend yourself, in which case you are already well into a uniquely memorable experience.) Wind along the other drives to find three more houses, designed by Wright apprentices and also available as lodging.

8 *Food of the Polymaths* 8 p.m.

The fare runs to entrees like pecan-crusted brook trout and wood-fired filet mignon at **Tree Tops Restaurant** (877-833-7829; treetopsrestaurant.net; $$-$$$) on the Polymath Park grounds. Soak in the atmosphere and share the evening with the other Wright groupies who will have found their way to this quiet spot. If the night is right, you can exchange some stories.

SUNDAY

9 *His Lordship's Getaway* 10 a.m.

Kentuck Knob (723 Kentuck Road, Chalk Hill; 724-329-1901; kentuckknob.com), in another wooded

OPPOSITE ABOVE AND RIGHT Wright's Duncan House, re-assembled in Polymath Park after facing destruction on its original site in Lisle, Illinois, is available for short-term stays.

OPPOSITE BELOW A swivel gun demonstration at Fort Necessity National Battlefield, where Colonel George Washington lost a battle at age 22.

setting, represents the middle ground of your Wright weekend: less renowned than the spectacular Fallingwater, but far more impressive than the Duncan House. A stone-and-cypress hexagon with a balcony ending in a stone prow, it is full of eccentric angles and unexpected viewpoints that add up to the usual Wrightian mastery. Wright designed it as a hillside home for a local ice cream magnate, but the current owner is a British lord who not only lets the public traipse through but also displays his

collectibles, from Claes Oldenburg sculptures to bullets from Custer's Last Stand. Take the tour and then take your time on the grounds.

10 *Tuck It In* 1 p.m.

Locals praise the food at the **Out of the Fire Cafe** (3784 State Route 31, Donegal; 724-259-8887; outofthefirecafe.com; $$), and it's a good spot for a substantial Sunday lunch: pan-seared jumbo lump crab cakes with fried green tomatoes, corn salsa, and avocado mousse, perhaps, or house-smoked salmon salad with spinach and portobellos. Tuck it away, and it should get you all the way back home.

THE BASICS

The Laurel Highlands are southeast of Pittsburgh. The country roads can be confusing. Arm yourself with maps, a GPS unit, and a cellphone.

The Duncan House
187 Evergreen Lane, Acme
877-833-7829
franklloydwrightovernight.net
$$$$
Designed by Frank Lloyd Wright. Stay overnight and pretend he built it just for you.

Summit Inn Resort
101 Skyline Drive, Farmington
724-438-8594
summitinnresort.com
$$
Porch rockers and mountain views.

Hampton Inn Uniontown
698 West Main Street, Uniontown
724-430-1000
hamptoninn.com
$$
One of several chain options.

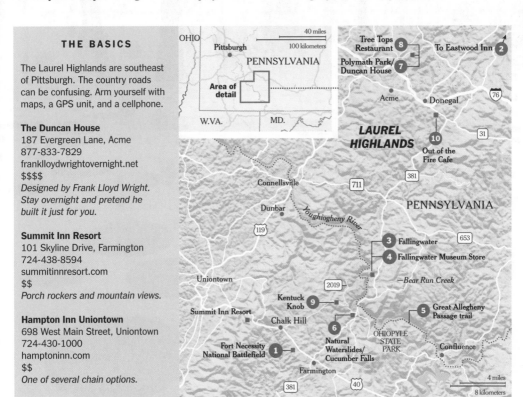

Pittsburgh

Pittsburgh has undergone a striking renaissance from a down-and-out smokestack town to a gleaming cultural, educational, and technological oasis. There are great restaurants, excellent shopping, breakthrough galleries, and prestigious museums. The convergence of three rivers and surrounding green hills makes a surprisingly pretty urban setting, and with abandoned steel mills long since torn down or converted to other uses, more of the natural beauty of this part of Pennsylvania has emerged. If the Pirates are in town, head to the waterfront ballpark. Besides seeing the game, you'll have an excuse to explore downtown and take in the river views.

— BY JEFF SCHLEGEL

FRIDAY

1 *Gridiron and Steel* 4 p.m.

Get to know what makes the city tick at the **Senator John Heinz History Center** (1212 Smallman Street; 412-454-6000; pghhistory.org), which chronicles past and present glories from United States Steel to the Pittsburgh Steelers. This is actually a twofer: the main museum is devoted to everything from the Heinz food empire to the city's polyglot population. The upper two floors are occupied by the Western Pennsylvania Sports Museum.

2 *Waterfall Dining* 7 p.m.

The martini menu changes almost as often as the seasonal specials at **Soba** (5847 Ellsworth Avenue; 412-362-5656; soba.kitchen; $$$), a pan-Asian restaurant with a Victorian exterior and a Zen-like interior that features a two-story wall of cascading water. Scan the menu for dishes like lobster maki and seafood and tandoori-grilled salmon. The wine list is extensive, and the vibe is upscale and trendy, but not in an overbearing way. If you arrive early, grab a special martini, perhaps made with ginger-infused vodka, on the rooftop deck.

3 *Brillo Pad* 10 p.m.

Brillobox (4104 Penn Avenue; 412-621-4900; brillobox.net) feels like an arty bar in New York's East Village — apt, considering that it was founded by an artist couple who came back home to Pittsburgh from New York to contribute to the city's growing arts scene. If the name of their establishment reminds you of Andy Warhol, you're on the right track. Pittsburgh is Warhol's hometown, and the Andy Warhol Museum on the North Shore holds 12,000 of his works. Brillobox, in the hipster haven Bloomfield district, catches some of his adventurous spirit with art-film screenings, spoken-word performances, and live music held upstairs in a room decked out in velvet wallpaper and murals. But you can just hang loose in the downstairs bar with its eclectic jukebox that has Patsy Cline, Snoop Dogg, and Girl Talk, the mashup D.J. star from the nearby Polish Hill neighborhood.

SATURDAY

4 *Nosh 'n' Stroll* 10:30 a.m.

By night, the formerly industrial **Strip District** is filled with partygoers bouncing between bars and clubs. But on Saturday mornings, the parallel thoroughfares of Penn Avenue and Smallman Street (roughly between 16th and 26th Streets) are turned into a sprawling outdoor market with international food kiosks that serve Middle Eastern kebabs, Italian sausages, and Greek baklava. Shop for produce, clothing, and vintage knickknacks as accordionists and

OPPOSITE The Mattress Factory on the North Side, home to room-size installations from artists like Yayoi Kusama.

BELOW The Duquesne Incline, a funicular first opened in 1877, takes passengers to Mount Washington for a view of the city.

mariachi bands provide a festive soundtrack. Take a breather with a cup of coffee and a mele, a fruit-filled pastry, at **La Prima Espresso Bar** (205 21st Street; 412-281-1922; laprima.com), where the old men sitting at the outdoor tables look like they've been sipping espresso and playing cards for eternity.

5 *No Beds Here* 1 p.m.

If you haven't already been there, don't miss the **Andy Warhol Museum** (117 Sandusky Street; 412-237-8300; warhol.org). For more radical contemporary art, beat a new path in the Mexican War Streets neighborhood to the **Mattress Factory** (500 Sampsonia Way; 412-231-3169; mattress.org). Housed in a former mattress factory, the museum is dedicated to room-size art installations.

6 *Hard-to-Find Items* 3 p.m.

Some of the city's funkiest shopping can be found in the **16:62 Design Zone** (lvpgh.com/explore/shop-dine), which spans the Strip District and Lawrenceville neighborhoods. It has more than 100 locally owned shops that focus on design, home décor, contemporary art, clothing, and architecture. Among the more interesting is the nonprofit **Society for Contemporary Craft** (2100 Smallman Street; 412-261-7003; contemporarycraft.org), a gallery and store that showcases handmade crafts like jewelry by national and local artists.

7 *Grab the Camera* 6 p.m.

The best views of Pittsburgh are from Mount Washington, and the best way to get there — or at least the most fun — is up the **Duquesne Incline** (1197 West Carson Street; 412-381-1665; duquesneincline. org). One of two surviving hillside cable cars from the 1870s, it takes three minutes to climb 800 feet to Grandview Avenue. There's a neat little history museum at the top that has old newspaper clippings, but the real spectacle is the view of downtown Pittsburgh, where the Allegheny and Monongahela Rivers meet to form the Ohio.

8 *City Under Glass* 7 p.m.

While you're up there, Grandview Avenue is also home to a cliff-hugging restaurant row. For seafood to go with the river views, make reservations for the **Monterey Bay Fish Grotto** (1411 Grandview Avenue; 412-481-4414; montereybayfishgrotto.com; $$$). This tri-level restaurant sits atop a 10-story apartment building. Jackets aren't required, but nice clothes are apropos. Fresh fish is flown in daily, and the menu changes often. On one visit the specials included a charcoal-grilled Atlantic salmon with fresh peppered strawberries in a red-wine sauce.

9 *Off-Downtown Theater* 9 p.m.

Generally regarded as Pittsburgh's most innovative theater company, the **City Theatre** (1300 Bingham Street; 412-431-2489; citytheatrecompany. org) stages challenging plays that aren't likely to be staged in the downtown cultural district. Housed in a pair of former churches in the South Side Flats neighborhood, it has both a 272-seat mainstage and a more intimate 110-seat theater. After the show, stop in at **Dee's Cafe** (1314 East Carson Street; 412-431-1314; deescafe.com), a comfortable, jam-packed dive that is part of what by some counts is the country's longest continuous stretch of bars.

SUNDAY

10 *Brunch and Bric-a-Brac* 11 a.m.

One of the city's more unusual brunch spots is the **Zenith** (86 South 26th Street; 412-481-4833; zenithpgh.com; $-$$), a combination art gallery,

vintage clothing store, antiques shop, and vegetarian restaurant. For those who can't stomach tofu, brunch includes traditional staples like eggs, pancakes, and French toast. It gets busy, so to avoid the line, get there before it opens at 11.

11 *Brain Food* 12:30 p.m.

The Oakland district teems with intellectual energy from the University of Pittsburgh, Carnegie Mellon University, and several museums. Start out at the Nationality Rooms at the **Cathedral of Learning** (4200 Fifth Avenue; 412-624-6000; nationalityrooms.pitt.edu), a 42-story Gothic-style tower on the Pittsburgh campus with 27 classrooms, each devoted to a different nationality. Then head

over to the renowned **Carnegie Museum of Art** (412-622-3131; cmoa.org) and **Carnegie Museum of Natural History** (carnegiemnh.org), both at 4400 Forbes Avenue, for Degas and dinosaurs. Before leaving, pick up a handy walking tour of Oakland and public art in the neighborhood.

OPPOSITE ABOVE The unassuming exterior of the Andy Warhol Museum on Sandusky Street. Warhol was from Pittsburgh, and the museum holds thousands of his works. Those on display are spread over six floors of gallery space.

OPPOSITE BELOW A table with a view out over the city at the Monterey Bay Fish Grotto, a dining spot on the Grandview restaurant row.

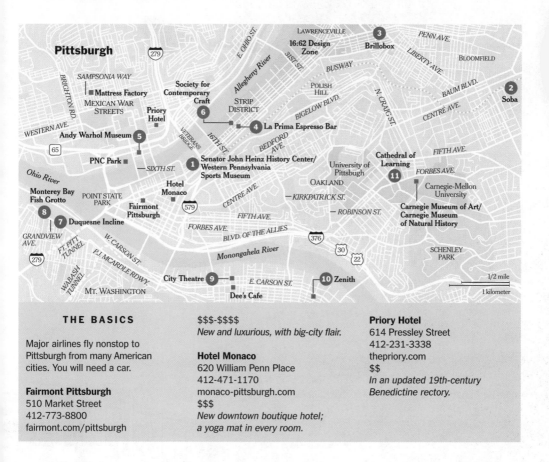

THE BASICS

Major airlines fly nonstop to Pittsburgh from many American cities. You will need a car.

Fairmont Pittsburgh
510 Market Street
412-773-8800
fairmont.com/pittsburgh

$$$-$$$$
New and luxurious, with big-city flair.

Hotel Monaco
620 William Penn Place
412-471-1170
monaco-pittsburgh.com
$$$
New downtown boutique hotel; a yoga mat in every room.

Priory Hotel
614 Pressley Street
412-231-3338
thepriory.com
$$
In an updated 19th-century Benedictine rectory.

The Black Hills

Everything may, as they say, be big in Texas, but everything is positively monumental in the southwest corner of South Dakota, in and around the Black Hills. The caves are unusually cavernous, the badlands especially bad; the archaeological sites turn up mammoths. Giant faces gaze from more than one mountain. Drive through this sometimes hilly, sometimes flat, sometimes grassy, sometimes downright lunar landscape, and it will seem that every crossroad has a sign pointing to an outsize attraction, a national monument, or some other officially remembered site. — BY PAUL SCHNEIDER

FRIDAY

1 *Old Men of the Mountain* 2 p.m.

Begin at **Mount Rushmore National Memorial** (13000 Highway 244, Keystone; 605-574-3171; nps.gov/moru). Never mind that Teddy Roosevelt doesn't altogether fit in the group, or that the former republican solemnity of the place has been woefully squandered by the addition of imperial arches and triumphal gewgaws at the entrance. And never mind if you are re-enacting a childhood visit to the place. A visit to Abe and the boys is a fitting start to your zigzagging tour through country where communal gawking and commemoration are de rigueur.

2 *Would Crazy Horse Approve?* 4 p.m.

Just outside Custer, appropriately, is the **Crazy Horse Memorial** (12151 Avenue of the Chiefs, Crazy Horse; 605-673-4681; crazyhorsememorial.org), which when completed, its builders say, will be the largest sculpture on the planet. All of the presidential men on Rushmore would fit on the head of Crazy Horse, an Oglala Lakota chief, which has gradually been emerging from a granite mountain since 1948. The memorial already has what must be one of the world's largest interpretive centers, with all of the requisite snack and souvenir opportunities. The

nonprofit, family-run place is somehow unnerving, as much a monument to monument makers and monument marketers as to the man who, with Sitting Bull, defeated George Armstrong Custer at the Little Bighorn. What Crazy Horse, who never permitted a photograph of himself to be taken, would have thought of laser shows projected on his graven image is anybody's guess, but Buffalo Bill Cody would have eaten it up.

3 *Comfort Food* 6 p.m.

Drive into **Hot Springs** and take a quick walk around its eye-catching downtown of carved pink sandstone buildings. Yes, there really are hot springs here, once visited as healing waters and today marketed more as a theme park for children (evansplunge.com). As evening deepens, find your way to the **Vault** (329 North River Street; 605-745-3342; thehotspringsvault.com; $), in one of those fine old buildings — this one dating from 1905 — for pub food and beer or soda.

SATURDAY

4 *Platters and Provisions* 8 a.m.

You're setting out for a long day of exploring, so have a hearty breakfast at **Daily Bread Bakery & Café** (431 North River Street, Hot Springs; 605-745-7687;

OPPOSITE The face of Crazy Horse, an Oglala Lakota chief, at the Crazy Horse Memorial, which has been gradually emerging from a granite mountain since 1948.

RIGHT Sunset falls on Badlands National Park, an arid wilderness of singular beauty.

ABOVE The famous sculptures of the Mount Rushmore National Memorial. The heads of the four presidents are 60 feet high, with 20-foot noses.

facebook.com; $). This is a bakery with fresh bread, cakes, and cookies, but it is also a restaurant with a full breakfast menu: omelets, pancakes, chipotle bacon, hash browns, and all the Midwest favorites. Be sure to pick up water, as well as snacks, before leaving town. When hunger strikes again, you may be far from the nearest restaurant.

5 Boys Will Be Boys 9 a.m.

Even nature seems to be in the business of turning out stone memorials to fallen behemoths. On the southern outskirts of Hot Springs, a mass grave for mammoths is slowly emerging from an ancient sink hole called the **Mammoth Site** (1800 U.S. 18 Bypass, Hot Springs; 605-745-6017; mammothsite.com). The effect is intensely sculptural: a mass of femurs and fibulas, skulls and tusks, backbones and pelvises, some just beginning to show in bas relief, some nearly freed from the surrounding matrix, some displayed behind glass. A few other animals have turned up in the hole, but it's mostly mammoths that ventured in and couldn't get out. And of those, nearly all seem to have been young males, the population most inclined, some mammoth experts have theorized, to risk-taking behavior.

6 The Underground 11 a.m.

Crystal lovers may prefer nearby Jewel Cave National Monument, which is one of the world's largest cavern systems, but **Wind Cave National Park** (visitor center on Route 385, 11 miles north of Hot Springs; 605-745-4600; nps.gov/wica) is only marginally less labyrinthine, with 134 miles of mapped passages. It is also where Crazy Horse and his fellow Lakota believed a trickster spirit first convinced humans into coming above ground sometime back at the beginning of the world, which seems more in keeping with the monumental theme. Take along a jacket (it's chilly down there), and choose the tour that descends through the natural entrance rather than the elevator.

7 Slow Roads 2 p.m.

Take your time for an afternoon meander through some of the most beautiful parts of the Black Hills. Travel north on Route 87 through **Custer State Park** (4605-255-4515; custerstatepark.info), where there's a celebrated herd of buffalo. (For help finding them, ask at the park entrance.) Turn right, toward Keystone, on Route 16A, which will take you through an improbable number of hairpin turns and one-lane tunnels in turreted mountains. For more of the same, check out the more crowded Route 87, the renowned **Needles Highway**. Either way, when you re-emerge, make your way north to Rapid City.

8 Beef and a Nice Red 8 p.m.

Cattle ranching country is close by, and at the **Delmonico Grill** (609 Main Street, Rapid City; 605-791-1664; delmonicogrill.com; $$$), beef is the specialty. Order the classics, like straightforward New York strip and filet mignon, or something more unusual, like ribeye with poblano chiles, crimini mushrooms, caramelized onions, and poblano cream sauce. (Cattle consumption is not required: the menu also includes some seafood and pasta.) The wine list is extensive, with California heavily represented.

SUNDAY

9 *Not So Bad* 9 a.m.

The baddest parts of **Badlands National Park**—desiccated, vaguely Martian landscapes formed by erosion—aren't the whole story. Find an alternative on the **Sage Creek Rim Road** (in a convertible if you were smart enough to rent one), which overlooks rolling grasslands that stretch to the horizon. To get to it, leave I-90 at Exit 131, drive south on Route 240, which loops west just before the town called Interior, and turn left at the sign a few miles past the

Pinnacles Overlook. Stop at the Sage Creek primitive campground, where you can just walk off into the wide-open wilderness in whatever direction suits your fancy, following buffalo trails and creek beds.

10 *Cold War Firepower* 1:30 p.m.

At the **Minuteman Missile National Historic Site** (605-433-5552; nps.gov/mimi), you can peer into an open silo containing one of the missiles that the United States once had ready for launch to the Soviet Union. It's difficult even to absorb the startling fact that the single bomb that armed this missile had two-thirds of the power of all the weapons expended in World War II. If you want to visit the launch control room, a fortified bunker, show up early; tickets are in demand.

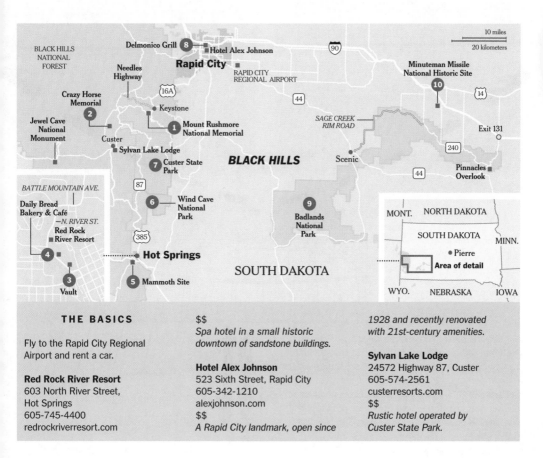

THE BASICS

Fly to the Rapid City Regional Airport and rent a car.

Red Rock River Resort
603 North River Street,
Hot Springs
605-745-4400
redrockriverresort.com

$$
Spa hotel in a small historic downtown of sandstone buildings.

Hotel Alex Johnson
523 Sixth Street, Rapid City
605-342-1210
alexjohnson.com
$$
A Rapid City landmark, open since

1928 and recently renovated with 21st-century amenities.

Sylvan Lake Lodge
24572 Highway 87, Custer
605-574-2561
custerresorts.com
$$
Rustic hotel operated by Custer State Park.

Milwaukee

There's plenty about modern-day Milwaukee that would be unrecognizable to Laverne and Shirley from Happy Days *and their own spinoff sitcom, both set here in the '50s and '60s. Oh, the area still appreciates its beer and bratwurst: delis carry a mind-boggling variety of sausage, and bars are known to have 50-plus brands of brew. But Milwaukee also has 95 miles of bike lanes, parks lacing the shores of Lake Michigan, and a revitalized riverfront where sophisticated shops coexist with remnants of an industrial past. Modern Milwaukee is defined less by the Rust Belt than by its lively downtown and a signature museum so architecturally striking that it competes for attention with the art it holds.*
— BY MAURA J. CASEY

FRIDAY

1 *Hog Heaven* 4 p.m.

Roar on over to the **Harley-Davidson Museum** (400 West Canal Street; 877-436-8738; h-dmuseum.com), which celebrates the 1903 birth of the signature product of Milwaukee residents William Harley and Arthur Davidson. The motorcycles on display include the first two Harley-Davidson models from 1903 and 1905, a 1920 Sport model marketed to women, and the 1932 Servi-Car used for commercial deliveries and credited with keeping the company solvent during the Great Depression. Harley-Davidson has been setting aside at least one motorcycle every year since 1915, and the resulting collection tells the story of a machine, America, and the open road in the 20th century — an absorbing tale whether or not you ride.

2 *Snake Chasers* 6 p.m.

There's more to Milwaukee than beer, but beer undeniably helped build the city. At one point in the 19th century, 150 breweries flourished here, some established by German immigrants whose names were Pabst, Miller, and Schlitz. So to better appreciate all that history and perhaps take a sip yourself, tour the

Lakefront Brewery (1872 North Commerce Street; 414-372-8800; lakefrontbrewery.com), housed in a century-old former utility building with soaring, 30-foot-high ceilings. You'll learn about how beer is made and taste a few of Lakefront's winning brews, including the Snake Chaser, an Irish-style stout made in honor of St. Patrick's Day. The guides are very funny, so for the laughs alone, it's worth the trip.

3 *Slavic Feast* 8 p.m.

For authentic Eastern European flavors, you can't do better than **Three Brothers Bar and Restaurant** (2414 South St. Clair Street; 414-481-7530; $$), a Milwaukee institution that has been serving Serbian cuisine since 1954. Where else could you order roast suckling pig with rice and vegetables, served with home-pickled cabbage? Or a chicken paprikash followed by an incredibly light seven-layer walnut torte? The dining room has the unpretentious feel of a neighborhood tavern.

SATURDAY

4 *A Ward Updated* 10 a.m.

Many cities have warehouse districts that have become revitalized; Milwaukee has the **Historic Third Ward** (historicthirdward.org), made up of the blocks between the Milwaukee River and Jackson Street. A century ago, this was a manufacturing center. Now it is a magnet for shoppers, with old brick warehouses converted into boutiques and restaurants. For distinctive fashions, search no farther than **Five Hearts Boutique** (153 North Milwaukee Street;

OPPOSITE Inside the Quadracci Pavilion, designed by Santiago Calatrava, at the Milwaukee Art Museum.

RIGHT Lake Michigan and the Milwaukee skyline.

414-727-4622; shopfivehearts.com). And for an eclectic array of gifts, cards, home furnishings and artifacts, and sundry odds and ends, linger in **Mod Gen** (211 North Broadway; 414-963-1657; modgenmke.com), whose name is short for "modern general store."

5 *Sausage and Cheese* Noon

Before finding a spot to hang out in one of the city's lovely waterfront parks, pack a picnic on Old World Third Street, the center of German life in 19th-century Milwaukee. The **Wisconsin Cheese Mart** (215 West Highland Avenue; 414-272-3544; wisconsincheesemart.com), which opened in 1938, sells hundreds of varieties of cheese. A few doors down is **Usinger's** (1030 North Old World Third

Street; 414-276-9105; usinger.com), sausage makers since 1880. There are 70 varieties, including a lean summer sausage.

6 *Spreading Wings* 2 p.m.

The **Milwaukee Art Museum** (700 North Art Museum Drive; 414-224-3200; mam.org) may have opened in 1888, but the eye-catching Quadracci Pavilion, designed by Santiago Calatrava and opened in 2001, has become a symbol of modern Milwaukee. With its movable wings expanded to their full, 217-foot span, the building looks either like a large white bird landing on Lake Michigan or the tail of a white whale emerging from the water. There's art, too: extensive collections of folk, central European and Germanic, and post-1960 contemporary.

7 *What Is the Fonz Reading?* 5 p.m.

While you're in the waterfront area, walk a couple of blocks to the west side of the Wells Street Bridge for a look at the **Bronzie Fonzie**, a life-size statue of the Fonz, the iconic television character from *Happy Days*. It's a favorite spot for a photo-

ABOVE The Harley-Davidson Museum.

LEFT Up and Under Pub, a home of the blues.

OPPOSITE Updated tradition at the Lakefront Brewery.

graph, so smile and remember: two thumbs up for the camera. Then while away some time at the **Boswell Book Company** (2559 North Downer Avenue; 414-332-1181; boswellbooks.com), a sprawling shop that has long hours, a huge Wisconsin section, and readings by nationally known authors.

8 *Third Coast Custard* 7 p.m.

The "Third Coast," a term not always familiar along the Atlantic and Pacific shores, refers in the Midwest to the coasts of the Great Lakes — the United States alone has 5,000 miles of shoreline along them. The homey restaurant **Jack Pandl's Whitefish Bay Inn** (1319 East Henry Clay Street, Whitefish Bay; 414-964-3800; jackpandls.com; $$$), a 20-minute drive north along Lake Michigan, has been serving favorites of the Inland Sea since 1915. Try the broiled whitefish fillet or the broiled or fried walleyed pike fillet, both Great Lakes staples. For a dessert that's pure Milwaukee, drive out to

Leon's (3131 South 27th Street; 414-383-1784), which has been serving its decadently rich frozen custard since 1942 and is said to have been the inspiration for Arnold's in *Happy Days*.

9 *Blues in the Night* 9:30 p.m.

East Brady Street, which stretches for about eight blocks from Lake Michigan to the Milwaukee River, was a hippie hangout in the 1960s. Today, its well-preserved buildings and 19th-century Victorian homes are a backdrop to one of the city's liveliest neighborhoods. During the day, boutiques and small stores draw shoppers. At night, restaurants and bars keep the street lively. A good spot for music is the **Up and Under Pub** (1216 East Brady Street; 414-270-0029; theupandunderpub.com), which proclaims itself the blues capital of Milwaukee. With high ceilings, an antique bar and a couple of dozen beers on tap, it offers live blues, rock, and reggae until 2 a.m. If you'd rather avoid alcohol, **Rochambo Coffee and**

Tea House down the street (1317 East Brady Street; 414-291-0095; www.rochambo.com) offers dozens of teas and stays open until midnight.

SUNDAY

10 *Lakeside Brunch* 10 a.m.

The Knick (1030 East Juneau Avenue; 414-272-0011; theknickrestaurant.com; $$) is busy and breezy on Sunday mornings, with an outdoor patio near Lake Michigan overlooking Veterans Park. For a memorable breakfast, try the crab hash, a mixture of crabmeat, onions, and hash browns topped with two eggs, or the banana pecan pancakes, dripping with whiskey butter and served with maple syrup.

11 *Wisconsin Tropics* 1 p.m.

Rain or shine, the **Mitchell Park Horticultural Conservatory** (524 South Layton Boulevard; 414-257-5611; county.milwaukee.gov/EN/Parks/Explore/The-Domes) offers perennial respite. Affectionately known as the Domes, the conservatory is housed in three 85-foot-high, beehive-shaped buildings with different climates: the Floral Dome has more than 150 floral displays; the Arid Dome mimics the desert, with an oasislike pool surrounded by cactuses; and the Tropical Dome has 1,200 rainforest plants, tropical birds flying overhead, and a 30-foot waterfall.

OPPOSITE Green space along the waterfront.

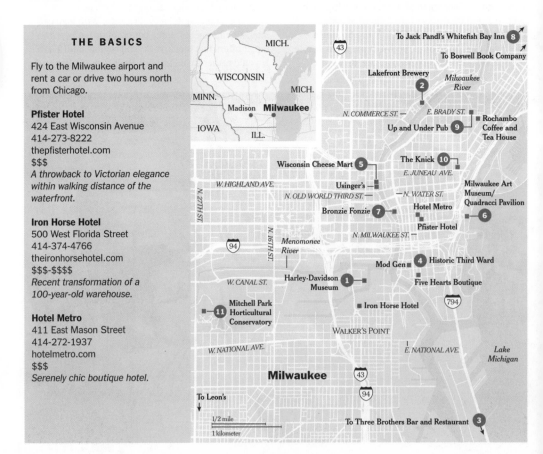

THE BASICS

Fly to the Milwaukee airport and rent a car or drive two hours north from Chicago.

Pfister Hotel
424 East Wisconsin Avenue
414-273-8222
thepfisterhotel.com
$$$
A throwback to Victorian elegance within walking distance of the waterfront.

Iron Horse Hotel
500 West Florida Street
414-374-4766
theironhorsehotel.com
$$$-$$$$
Recent transformation of a 100-year-old warehouse.

Hotel Metro
411 East Mason Street
414-272-1937
hotelmetro.com
$$$
Serenely chic boutique hotel.

448 Banff   452 CALGARY

JACKSON HOLE
564   568 The Tetons

500

Boise

Salt Lake City
560   556 PARK CITY

Aspen

WELCOME TO Fabulous
LAS VEGAS
504

550 MOAB

496

TELLURID

456   the Grand Canyon

TELLURID

472

SCOTTSDALE
468   Albuquer

SEDONA

462

phoenix   tucson
478

SOUTHWEST
& ROCKY MOUNTAINS

Boulder
486

492

Denver

514 Santa Fe

STOCK

FORT
WORTH

532

526 Dallas

AUSTIN

Texas Hill Country
546

520

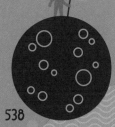

538

Houston

542 SAN ANTONIO

Banff

There are higher towns in the Canadian Rockies, but Banff in almost any season feels about as close to heaven as one can get. In winter, the S.U.V.s rolling into town are loaded with skiing and snowboarding gear; in the warmer seasons, this is a place to get close to the wilderness by bike, on horseback, or, best of all, on foot. The glacier-fed rivers and lakes are an electrifying aqua-tinted blue, and the breathtaking mountain scenery is highlighted by the dark boughs of matchstick-straight lodgepole pines. When you've seen enough snowy peaks and waterfalls for the day, sample Banff's other side: grand hotels, fine restaurants, shopping, and spas. And thanks in part to the Banff Centre for the Arts, the town has a cultural life that few resort towns enjoy.
— BY BRUCE HEADLAM AND BARBARA IRELAND

FRIDAY

1 *First Steps* 3:30 p.m.

Pick up maps and hiking advice from the knowledgeable and cheerful staff at the **Banff Visitor Centre** (224 Banff Avenue; 403-762-1550; pc.gc.ca/en/pn-np/ab/banff/visit/installations-facilities), and then warm up your hiking muscles with a walk along rugged **Lake Minnewanka**, nicknamed the Devil's Lake for the creature that is supposed to live in its cold waters. Drive north out of Banff for 15 minutes, following the signs to the lake, and then park near the launch of Lake Minnewanka Boat Tours. Follow the path along the west side of the lake, then take the trail to the bridge at Cascade River. Drink in the mountain scenery while looking out for bighorn sheep along the shore and listening for the howls of distant wolves. If the Lake Minnewanka trail is closed (as it sometimes is when bears are active), stay in Banff and walk the serene **Fenland Trail** (off Mount Norquay Road; friendsofbanff.com/blog/hike/fenland-trail) through sun-dappled woods.

2 *Western Gourmet* 8 p.m.

If you're not easily intimidated by graduate-level cuisine and encyclopedic wine lists, try the **Eden** restaurant in the **Rimrock Resort Hotel** (300 Mountain Avenue; 403-762-3356; banffeden.com; $$$$). In its well-appointed dining rooms overlooking the town, Eden offers tasting menus with multiple courses that incorporate Canadian ingredients into French-style cooking. The attentive waiters — more like consultants, really — walk you through each course, and the sommelier will match your meal with a bottle from the restaurant's vast cellar. Those who prefer their food and surroundings a little rougher (and prices a little lower) can try **Grizzly House** (207 Banff Avenue; 403-762-4055; banffgrizzlyhouse.com; $$$$), a Western-kitsch restaurant where you can cook your own combination of exotic game (buffalo, rattlesnake, ostrich) over hot rocks at your table.

SATURDAY

3 *Day Breaks* 8 a.m.

Early morning — before the tour buses are herded into town — is the quietest time of day in Banff, so get up early and take a leisurely walk to breakfast at **Melissa's Missteak** (218 Lynx Street; 403-762-5511; melissasmissteak.com; $$). The crowd will already be assembling in Melissa's big main room, which looks like the inside of an especially large log cabin. The Swiss apple pancake may not be authentically Western, but it's a great way to start the day.

4 *Happy Trails* 9:30 a.m.

Walk south on Banff Avenue, turn left just before the downtown bridge, and find the paved walking

OPPOSITE The landmark Fairmont Banff Springs Hotel.

BELOW Have a drink and a casual dinner, or in season get your hockey fix, at the Elk & Oarsman.

trail marked **Bow Falls**. The trail follows the Bow River past the falls (a favorite site for wedding photographs) and then briefly joins with a paved road before descending into the Bow Valley. The trail will carry you through the deep forest, then up a moderately steep incline to Tunnel Mountain. The path forks in places, but there is no need to have a Robert Frost moment: all the trails converge eventually. Follow Tunnel Mountain Road east to the Banff Hoodoos, free-standing pillars that have separated from the mountain's side. After walking back to town on Tunnel Mountain Road, get a grand perspective on the **Banff Gondola** (403-762-2523; explorerockies.com/banff-gondola). Drive to the base station, take the eight-minute ride to the upper terminal and then follow the Vista Trail up to Sanson Peak. Admire the views from all sides.

5 *Soak It Up* Noon

Time to ease your sore muscles. Follow the signs from the gondola parking lot to the historic **Banff Upper Hot Springs** (403-762-1515; hotsprings.ca) and slip into one of the 105-degree outdoor pools, fed by naturally heated spring water. Lie back and enjoy the spectacular mountain scenery.

6 *Afternoon Tea* 2 p.m.

Afternoon tea, a splendid British tradition, has never looked quite so splendid as it does at the **Fairmont Banff Springs** hotel, the magnificent former railroad lodge known locally as the castle. Tea is served every afternoon in the Rundle Lounge. Sit back in the overstuffed chairs with a pot of the hotel's own blend, some scones, pastries, and, of course, cucumber sandwiches, and enjoy the serene view of the Bow Valley. The hotel recommends booking

in advance (405 Spray Avenue; 403-762-2211; fairmont.com/banff-springs; $$$) for a window seat, but every table has its rewards. Allow yourself a few extra minutes to poke around the hotel's nooks, especially the baronial dining halls (you may see the place settings going in for a wedding dinner) and exquisite wine bars, and to pick up a package of tea from the hotel's pantry shop.

7 *Mountain Shopping* 4 p.m.

If you're short on workout clothes and cold-weather wear, Banff is the place to stock up. Several stores sell clothing and gear for the outdoor sports that this town so loves; even the local Gap honors the fleece-and-Lycra theme. Budget some serious time to investigate **Monod Sports** (129 Banff Avenue; 403-762-4571; monodsports.com), which has been catering to fans of the Canadian Rockies since 1949. Its four floors are stocked with clothing and supplies from parkas and biking shorts to fly-fishing rods and ice axes.

8 *Elk on the Lawn* 6 p.m.

Wander toward the **Banff Centre** (107 Tunnel Mountain Drive; 403-762-6100; banffcentre.ca), watching for the giant elk that gather on the grounds year-round. In addition to holding book, film, and television festivals, the center puts on challenging music and opera performances by visiting artists. Try the box office (in the Eric Harvie Theatre; open late the day of performances) for last-minute tickets.

9 *Elk on the Plate* 8 p.m.

Find sustenance and conviviality at **Elk & Oarsman** (119 Banff Avenue, second floor;

403-762-4616; elkandoarsman.com; $$), a pub with a wood-beamed ceiling where everyone seems to gather. Seth Rogen look-alikes swill the crisp house lager, and triathletes are quick to crack a smile and start a conversation. Try the elk burger, Canadian bacon pizza, or poutine (regular, pulled pork, or elk, of course), and stick around for live music.

SUNDAY

10 *The Spring That Started It All* 9:30 a.m.

On a winter visit, you would be taking today to go to Lake Louise for some skating or skiing. But on a summer trip, rent a bicycle (there are several rental spots around this mountain bike-crazy town) and pedal south to the end of Cave Avenue to the **Cave and Basin National Historic Site** (311 Cave Avenue; 403-762-1566; pc.gc.ca/en/lhn-nhs/ab/caveandbasin), the hot spring cave that first drew tourists to Banff more than 100 years ago. Take the tour, and see the original cave entrance. Then go back outside and continue on the 4.5-mile trail along the Bow River until you get to the bike racks at the last point before you're required to continue on foot. Climb the trail to the **Sundance Canyon**, a magical glen with a cascading stream falling next to your upward path.

OPPOSITE Banff is an all-weather resort, with year-round beauty and seasonal sports. This skater is on Lake Louise.

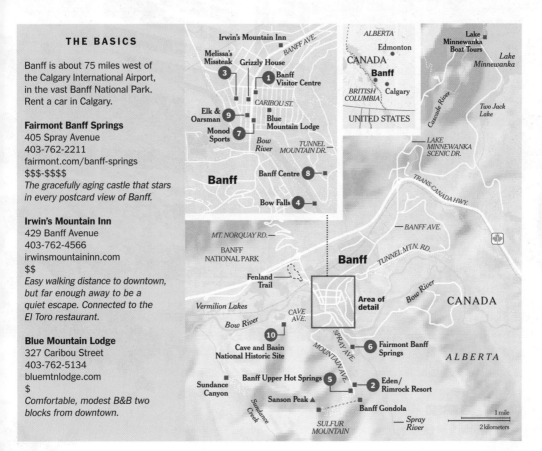

THE BASICS

Banff is about 75 miles west of the Calgary International Airport, in the vast Banff National Park. Rent a car in Calgary.

Fairmont Banff Springs
405 Spray Avenue
403-762-2211
fairmont.com/banff-springs
$$$-$$$$
The gracefully aging castle that stars in every postcard view of Banff.

Irwin's Mountain Inn
429 Banff Avenue
403-762-4566
irwinsmountaininn.com
$$
Easy walking distance to downtown, but far enough away to be a quiet escape. Connected to the El Toro restaurant.

Blue Mountain Lodge
327 Caribou Street
403-762-5134
bluemtnlodge.com
$
Comfortable, modest B&B two blocks from downtown.

Calgary

There was a time, not so many years ago, when the only reasons most tourists would bother venturing into Calgary was for the famous Stampede, a two-week rodeo festival in July, or in winter for a Flames hockey game. But this rugged city in central Alberta underwent an energetic revitalization brought on by a long oil boom; its population increased by tens of thousands every year for well over a decade, bringing the number of residents to more than a million. For visitors, all this activity means a revived downtown core with restaurants whose chefs — and prices — could vie with those in Toronto or Montreal; spruced-up outlying neighborhoods; and urban boutique hotels. But perhaps most surprising is that the Heart of the New West, as Calgary is billing itself these days, is becoming known as a center of culture, with sophisticated museums and diverse options for music and live theater. — BY SUSAN CATTO

FRIDAY

1 *Sandstone Downtown* 3 p.m.

Founded in the 19th century as an outpost of the Northwest Mounted Police, Calgary soon found prosperity based on sandstone quarries, and the honey-hued sandstone buildings lining the **Stephen Avenue Walk**, a pedestrian mall between First Street Southwest and Sixth Street Southwest, date from the late 1880s. Today the street is a brick pedestrian strip filled with shops and restaurants, a good place to get acquainted with the city and start your weekend.

2 *Cocktails and Petroleum* 5 p.m.

At the fashionable **Metropolitan** (317 Seventh Avenue Southwest; 403-263-5432; themet.ca) at the top of Stephen Avenue's sandstone row, mingle with casually dressed young professionals meeting for after-work drinks. Listen for shop talk about the petroleum business. Many of the patrons are probably recent arrivals from someplace else, drawn by the oil boom. Oil was discovered in this area in 1914, and a boom-bust cycle repeated itself in the 1920s, 1950s, 1980s, and again in the mid-2010s.

OPPOSITE Skating in the sunshine at the Olympic Plaza.

RIGHT The Kensington Riverside Inn, a boutique hotel.

During prolonged busts, the city hollows out; during prolonged booms, it is the Houston of Canada, complete with cowboy hats and swagger. Calgary is home to Canada's biggest oil and gas companies and the administrative headquarters of the oil sands extraction projects centered 470 miles north in Fort McMurray, Alberta.

3 *Steak Special* 7 p.m.

Calgary is not only Canada's energy capital, but its beef capital, too, surrounded by grasslands perfect for grazing cattle. While you're here, you have to have at least one steak dinner. There are plenty of steakhouses to choose from, including **Charbar** (618 Confluence Way Southeast; 403-452-3115; charbar.ca; $$$), where the chef uses an Argentine-style wood-fired grill, and **Saltlik** (101 Eighth Avenue Southwest; 403-537-1160; saltlik.com; $$$). But you'll find steak from Alberta beef at most fine-dining restaurants in town.

4 *Your Kind of Sound* 10 p.m.

Visitors to Calgary can easily fill their nights with music. Live bands play in bars around town: **Ironwood Stage & Grill** (1229 Ninth Avenue Southeast; 403-269-5581; ironwoodstage.ca) programs everything from bluegrass and folk to jazz and Bruce Springsteen tributes. And the **Calgary Philharmonic Orchestra** (calgaryphil.com) maintains a busy schedule.

SATURDAY

5 *Blackfoot Country* 10 a.m.

The **Glenbow Museum** (130 Ninth Avenue Southeast; 403-268-4100; glenbow.org) is both art gallery and history museum, emphasizing the history of Alberta, including display areas dedicated to the province's original inhabitants, the Blackfoot Indians. The Glenbow also has an incongruous but beautiful collection of early Asian sculpture. The museum shop, which carries jewelry, carvings, and beadwork, has a fine collection of books on Blackfoot history and culture.

6 *Going Upscale* Noon

As condominiums have sprung up along the Bow River, neighborhoods on the edge of downtown are becoming destinations, too. **Kensington**, just over the Louise Bridge, is prime shopping and strolling territory, geared to a population prosperous enough to afford neighborhood restaurants that serve entrees like lobster lasagna but young enough to desire a bit of bohemia. Lunch is easy to find in a pub or bistro, and the array of stores includes **Livingstone and Cavell Extraordinary Toys** (1124 Kensington Road Northwest; 403-270-4165; extraordinarytoys.com), which, though small, lives up to its name, and a shop of the favorite local chocolatier **Bernard Callebaut** (1123 Kensington Road Northwest; 403-283-5550; bernardcallebaut.com).

7 *Riverside Park* 2 p.m.

Calgary, though sprawling, lives day to day in a beautiful setting on the high plains along the Bow and Elbow Rivers, with the snowy Canadian Rockies off in the distance. The best way to get in touch with the city's natural side is along 130 miles of bikeways and pathways that line Calgary's rivers, meander through parks, and crisscross the city. A good place to start is **Prince's Island Park** (First Avenue and Fourth Street Southwest; 403-268-2489; calgary.ca/CSPS/Parks), which runs along the Bow River

and is the scene of festivals and open-air theater in summer. Despite the views of downtown on one side and Kensington on the other, the park isn't too urban — signs warn visitors to give a wide berth to coyotes. In 2013, the rivers showed their aggressive side in massive flooding, but the city soon recovered.

8 *Dinner in Red* 6:30 p.m.

Inglewood, often cited as the next Kensington, is an increasingly upscale district with blocks of antiques stores, home furnishing shops, and quirky boutiques. It's also the home of **Rouge** (1240 Eighth Avenue Southeast; 403-531-2767; rougecalgary.com; $$$-$$$$), a romantic high-end French restaurant in a red Victorian-era house surrounded by a lawn and trees. On the menu, expect Canadian beef, lamb, and probably elk, and fish from Canadian waters. For a splurge, order the chef's tasting menu with wine pairings.

9 *Theater Town* 8 p.m.

The downtown **Arts Commons** (225 Eighth Avenue Southeast; 403-294-7455; artscommons.ca) houses — with style — several theater groups. Theatre Calgary (theatrecalgary.com) has presented professional productions since 1968. Downstage (downstage.ca) and One Yellow Rabbit (oyr.org) tend toward the provocative. Alberta Theatre Projects (atplive.com) specializes in new Canadian plays.

ABOVE The Calgary skyline at dusk.

BELOW Mountain biking at Canada Olympic Park.

10 *Your Inner Olympian* 10 a.m.

How about trying the luge, biking down a mountain, and riding a zip line off a ski jump, all in one place? A legacy of the 1988 Calgary Winter Games, the **Canada Olympic Park** (88 Canada Olympic Road Southwest; 403-247-5452; winsport.ca), 15 minutes west of downtown, has a high thrill quotient, including solo rides on a luge track. Three zip lines include the Monster Zipline, which shoots harnessed passengers from the top of the ski-jump tower. Chairlifts are turned over to mountain bikers, while milder adventure options include mini-golf, a climbing wall, and a bungee trampoline.

11 *Jurassic Side Trip* Noon

Alberta's badlands are home to Canada's biggest dinosaur finds, so if you have budding paleontologists in your family, consider driving 80 miles northeast to the **Royal Tyrrell Museum** (1500 North Dinosaur Trail, Drumheller; 403-823-7707; tyrrellmuseum.com). After your trek, you will find more than 40 dinosaur skeletons as well as galleries devoted to the excavation of fossils and long-extinct underwater creatures. In the town of Drumheller, murals of dinosaurs decorate downtown buildings, and at the end of Main Street you'll find an 86-foot-high fiberglass Tyrannosaurus rex (four times bigger than life size). Climb 106 stairs up into the beast's mouth for a panoramic view of the Canadian Badlands.

THE BASICS

A car will come in handy, but Calgary is small enough to enjoy on foot much of the time.

Le Germain Hotel Calgary
899 Centre Street Southwest
877-362-8990
germaincalgary.com
$$
Calgary outpost of a Quebec-based chain of stylish boutique hotels.

Hotel Arts
119 12th Avenue Southwest
403-266-4611
hotelarts.ca
$$
Art installations in the lobby and minimalist chic bedrooms.

Kensington Riverside Inn
1126 Memorial Drive Northwest
403-228-4442
kensingtonriversideinn.com
$$
Just across the Bow River from downtown.

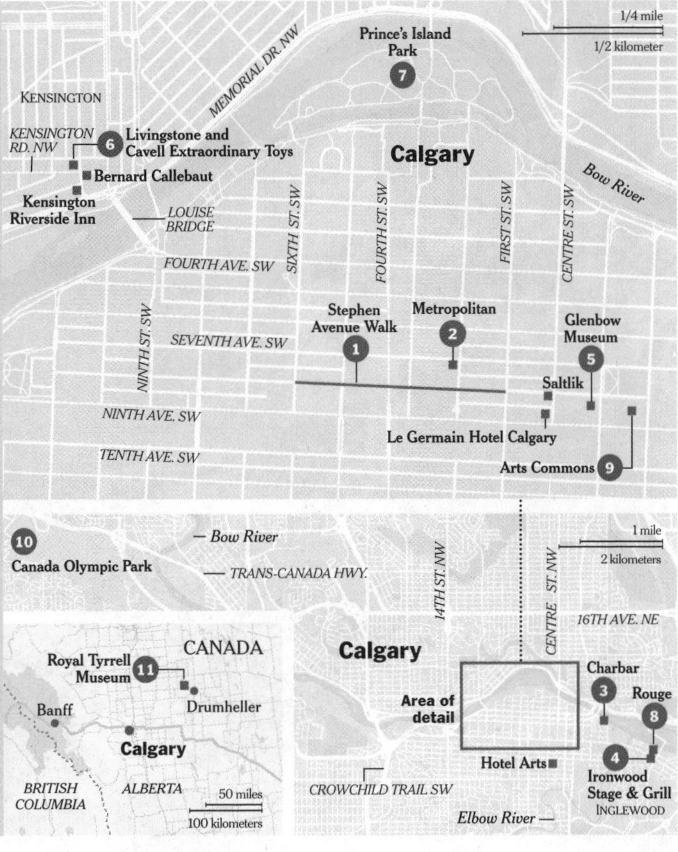

The Grand Canyon

More than a mile deep at its most majestic, the Grand Canyon can still drop the most jaded of jaws. The sun sparkling across the exposed rock, the delicate curl of the Colorado River, the birds chirping in the pinyon pines — and then a bus grinds past you on a hunt for the best postcards in the park. Yes, the Grand Canyon is big in every way, including the category of tourist trap. Over four million people visit this remote corner of Arizona each year, and the experience can be a bit death-by-gift-shop if you don't plan ahead — a necessity even if crowds and kitsch are your thing. During peak season, May through September, hotel rooms sell out months in advance, ditto for those mule rides, and certain rafting trips can be a yearlong wait or more. Ah, wilderness!
— BY BROOKS BARNES

FRIDAY

1 *The Main Event* 5 p.m.

Save the best for last? Not on this trip. After driving the 81 miles from Flagstaff, Arizona, the destination where most air travelers land, head to **El Tovar Hotel** (Grand Canyon Village; 928-638-2631, extension 6380; grandcanyonlodges.com). The historic lodge, purposely built at such an angle that guests must leave their rooms to see more than a glimpse of the splendor, features one of the easiest access points to the canyon rim. Stretch your legs with a walk along the eastern portion of the 13-mile **Rim Trail**, which may leave you out of breath at 7,000 feet above sea level. Resist the temptation to go off the trail; park officials say about one person a year falls and dies and others are injured.

2 *Eat Hearty, Folks* 7:30 p.m.

El Tovar may look familiar — the exterior of the hotel had a cameo in *National Lampoon's Vacation,* the 1983 road-trip movie. Clark Griswold, a.k.a. Chevy Chase, pulls up in his pea-green station wagon and robs the front desk. He should have at least eaten dinner first. The restaurant at **El Tovar** (928-638-2631,

extension 6432; $$$) is by far the best in the area. As twin fireplaces blaze, relax with an Arizona Sunrise (orange juice, tequila, and grenadine) and take in the wall-mounted Hopi and Navajo weavings. For dinner, start with a salad or corn chowder and then choose something wilderness-appropriate (buffalo ribeye? rainbow trout?) for the main course.

3 *Star Struck* 10 p.m.

If dinner got a bit pricey, take comfort in a free show afterward. Because there is so little pollution here — the nearest large cities, Phoenix and Las Vegas, are both 200 miles or more away — the night sky is crowded with stars. Pick up one of the free constellation-finder brochures in the lobby of El Tovar and gaze away. Bonus points for anybody who can spot the Lesser Water Snake.

SATURDAY

4 *Sunrise Sonata* 5 a.m.

The canyon's multiple layers of exposed rock are glorious in the morning light; download the soundtrack to *2001: A Space Odyssey* as a dawn complement — the combination heightens the experience even further. Take a morning run or walk along the Rim Trail heading west, and keep your eyes peeled for woodpeckers making their morning

OPPOSITE Looking into the canyon from the Rim Trail.

RIGHT The lobby at the Bright Angel Lodge.

rounds. Don't bother trying to make it to Hermit's Rest, a 1914 stone building named for a 19th-century French-Canadian prospector who had a roughly built homestead in the area. These days, it's—you guessed it—a gift shop and snack bar.

5 *Hop On* 10 a.m.

Those famous mules? Ride one if you want—they can take more time than you may be willing to spend on a weekend trip here—but be aware that they walk scary narrow ledges and come with a daunting list of rules. (Reads one brochure: "Each rider must not weigh more than 200 pounds, fully dressed, and, yes, we do weigh everyone!") An alternative is to tour the canyon aboard an Eco-Star helicopter, an energy-efficient model built with extra viewing windows. There are several tour companies that offer flights; one with a newish fleet and friendly service is **Maverick Helicopters** (Grand Canyon National Airport on Highway 64; 928-638-2622; maverickhelicopter.com). The tours are personal —seven passengers maximum—and are priced according to the length of the trip. (None are cheap.) Ask the pilot to point out the Tower of Ra, a soaring butte named for the Egyptian sun god.

6 *Pack a Picnic* Noon

The nearest town and the location of the heliport, Tusayan, Arizona, is a disappointing collection of fast-food restaurants, motels, and souvenir shops. Get out of Dodge and pick up lunch at the deli counter tucked inside the general store at **Market Plaza** (located a mile or two inside the park gates; 928-638-2262). It's nothing fancy—pastrami sandwiches and the like—but it will at least save you from an order of junk food.

7 *Desert View* 1 p.m.

Hitting the **Desert View Watchtower** (26 miles past Market Plaza on Highway 64 East; scienceviews.com/parks/watchtower.html) at midday will keep you clear of the throngs that assemble here for sunrise and sunset. From the historic tower, constructed in 1932, you can see the Painted Desert, a broad area of badlands where wind and rain have exposed stratified layers of minerals, which glow in hues of violet, red, and gold. Park rangers give daily talks about the area's cultural history.

8 *Play Archaeologist* 3 p.m.

Outdoorsy types will want to do another hike —more power to them. For those who have had enough of the canyon for one day, another of this area's cultural treasures still waits to be explored.

ABOVE The Wukoki Pueblo at the Wupatki National Monument near Flagstaff.

About 800 years ago, **Wupatki Pueblo National Monument** (about 34 miles north of Flagstaff on Highway 89; 928-679-2365; nps.gov/wupa) was a flourishing home base for the Sinagua, Kayenta Anasazi, and Cohonina peoples. The remnants of 100 rooms remain, including a space that archaeologists identified as a ball court similar to those found in other sites left by pre-Columbian cultures.

9 *Who Screams?* 5:30 p.m.

If heights aren't your thing, you can relax now: you've made it through the hard parts of touring the Grand Canyon. Regroup after the drive back to the Grand Canyon National Park with ice cream on the patio at **Bright Angel Lodge** (about two blocks west of El Tovar; 928-638-2631; grandcanyonlodges.com), which features an old-fashioned soda fountain. There are multiple ice cream flavors to choose from, plus other fountain specialties — try a strawberry milkshake. Inside the lodge, a rustic motel, is a newsstand, one of the few in the park.

10 *Dinner and a Dance* 7 p.m.

Apart from the dining room at El Tovar, Grand Canyon food can be alarmingly bad. But walk inside the Bright Angel Lodge and give the **Arizona Room** ($$) a whirl. The dishes can be a mouthful in name — chili-crusted, pan-seared wild salmon with fresh melon salsa and pinyon black bean rice pilaf, for example — if not exactly in quality. After dinner, hang out around the stone fireplace in the lobby. With any luck, you will catch one of the randomly presented Hopi dancing demonstrations.

BELOW The Desert View Watchtower, built in 1932.

SUNDAY

11 *Wild Side* 10 a.m.

Kaibab National Forest, 1.6 million acres of ponderosa pine that surrounds the Grand Canyon, is a destination on its own for nature lovers and camping enthusiasts. After saying goodbye to the world's most famous hole in the ground, stop on the way back to Flagstaff to explore the **Kendrick Park Watchable Wildlife Trail** (Highway 180, about

20 miles north of Flagstaff; wildlifeviewingareas.com). Elk, badgers, western bluebirds, and red-tailed hawks are relatively easy to see, along with short-horned lizards and a variety of other forest creatures. The Grand Canyon area is also home to scorpions, tarantulas, rattlesnakes, and Gila monsters—but those are (mostly) confined to the canyon itself.

ABOVE A Navajo hoop dancer performing in costume at the canyon's South Rim.

OPPOSITE Mule trains take tourists bumping down into the canyon along the Bright Angel Trail. Other sightseeing options include helicopter rides and rigorous hikes.

THE BASICS

Fly to Flagstaff, Arizona, and rent a car at the airport.

El Tovar Hotel
Off Village Loop in Grand Canyon Village
303-297-2757
grandcanyonlodges.com/lodging/el-tovar
$$$-$$$$
By far the most upscale lodging in the area; centrally located and recently renovated.

Bright Angel Lodge & Cabins
Near El Tovar
928-638-2631
grandcanyonlodges.com/lodging/bright-angel
$$
A cabin-style motel built in the 1930s that is bare-bones but surprisingly comfortable.

Red Feather Lodge
300 Highway 64
928-638-2414
redfeatherlodge.com
$$
As good a motel as any of the many in the Tusayan area.

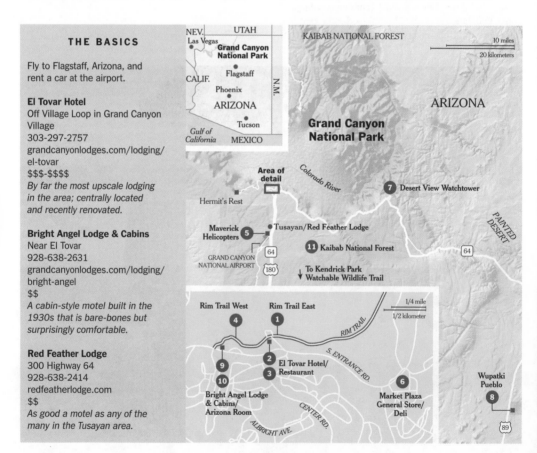

Phoenix

With one of the fastest growth rates in the United States, Phoenix, Arizona, seemed to come out of nowhere to rank in the first years of the 21st century as the nation's fifth-largest city. Although the go-go trend came to a crashing halt when the housing bubble collapsed in 2008 and 2009, the city never lost its appeal, and the housing market rebounded. The southern Arizona heat makes it an inferno in the summer, but the other nine months of the year are gorgeous and sunny. That means that three-fourths of the time, Phoenix, with its resorts, restaurants, contemporary shops, Southwest culture, and desert and mountain landscape, is perfect for exploring.
— BY RANDAL C. ARCHIBOLD AND AMY SILVERMAN

FRIDAY

1 *One Man's Castle* 3 p.m.

All sorts of people, some of them rich and famous, once flocked to Phoenix for health reasons, at least before smog became a big problem. But perhaps none was stranger than Boyce Luther Gulley, an architect from Seattle, who arrived in 1930 to recover from tuberculosis and, while he was at it, built a "castle" largely from found objects. The **Mystery Castle** (800 East Mineral Road; mymysterycastle.com), a trippy monument to Gulley's imagination, is adorned with all sorts of stuff, including tree branches for chairs, crooked windows, and Indian artifacts.

2 *Tacos and Mariachi* 6 p.m.

The border is just three hours away by car and more than a third of the city's residents are Latino, so Mexican food rules. Phoenicians argue over the best restaurants, but it is hard to top **Garcia's Las Avenidas** (2212 North 35th Avenue; 602-272-5584; garcias-las-avenidas-phoenix-3.sites.tablehero.com; $), a family-run place known for its traditional menu and cavernous setting. A mariachi band often drifts from table to table, belting out ballads. No, the menu

is not daring, but the plates come heaping with home-style favorites like tacos and enchiladas that won't damage the wallet. The juicy carnitas de puerco are worth a try.

3 *Hollywood in Phoenix* 8 p.m.

The juggernaut of downtown construction in the frenetic days of the real estate boom — projects included a convention center expansion, a hotel, and condominiums — spared a few jewels, including the historic **Hotel San Carlos** (202 North Central Avenue). Hollywood stars like Mae West and Marilyn Monroe stayed in this 1928 Italian Renaissance-style landmark, which still exudes an air of European refinement. Walk inside for a look around, and then move on to the **Crescent Ballroom** (308 North Second Avenue; 602-716-2222; crescentphx.com), where you can have a drink and listen to live bands.

SATURDAY

4 *Up Close at Camelback* 8 a.m.

Camelback Mountain sits in the middle of metropolitan Phoenix, and the Echo Canyon Trail in the **Echo Canyon Recreation Area** (phoenix.gov/parks/trails/locations/camelback-mountain/trails) is its most renowned hike there. Locals call it the Scenic Stairmaster, and they'll warn you that this is no dawdle — the hike is 1.2 miles, and about 1,200 feet up, one way, and recommended only for very experienced hikers. (Be sure to bring plenty of water.) On a clear day, you can see the Salt River Pima-Maricopa Indian Community to the east and Piestewa Peak (formerly

OPPOSITE Saguaros at the Desert Botanical Garden, an oasis of towering cacti, aromatic flowers, and verdant plants in the middle of the urban grid.

RIGHT Phoenix sprawls out in the desert below a lookout point in South Mountain Park.

known as Squaw Peak) to the west. You might also see cottontail rabbits, rattlesnakes, or coyotes. For more child-friendly hiking, try some of the many miles of trails at **South Mountain Park** (phoenix.gov/parks/trails/locations/south-mountain/trail-descriptions-and-map), which at 16,000 acres is sometimes called the country's largest municipal park.

5 *Hiker's Reward* 11 a.m.

Gaze up at the mountain you just conquered from a patio table at **La Grande Orange Grocery** (4410 North 40th Street; 602-840-7777; lagrandeorangegrocery.com; $). You'll fit in comfortably at this little fine-foods market and pizzeria whether you've showered post-hike or not. The menu offers salads, burgers,

and sandwiches along with mostly vegetarian pizzas, such as the baby artichoke with goat cheese and tomatoes.

6 *Hiker's Rejuvenation* Noon

Step into the lobby of the **Arizona Biltmore Resort & Spa** (2400 East Missouri Avenue; 602-955-6600; arizonabiltmore.com) to appreciate the Frank Lloyd Wright-inspired architecture fully. Even on the hottest day, you'll instantly feel cooled by the structure of Biltmore Block, precast concrete blocks that make up the high-ceilinged main building. The Biltmore welcomes nonguests at its spa, so wrap yourself in a thick terry robe and head to a treatment room. (Reservations recommended.) Shopaholics may want to stick around afterward to seek out **Biltmore Fashion Park** (2502 East Camelback Road; 602-955-8400; shopbiltmore.com), a largely open-air mall stocked with high-end stores.

7 *Art Spaces* 2 p.m.

A cluster of galleries, boutiques, and restaurants in rehabilitated bungalows and old commercial buildings along once-forlorn Roosevelt Street have

ABOVE Seclusion at the Royal Palms Resort.

LEFT Camelback Mountain rises up beyond the cactus at the Desert Botanical Garden.

led to the area's christening as the Roosevelt Row Arts District (RoRo). Examine the local and regional contemporary art at **Modified Arts** (407 East Roosevelt Street; 602-462-5516; modifiedarts. org) and adventurous pieces at **eye lounge** (419 East Roosevelt Street; 602-430-1490; eyelounge. com). Take a look at **monOrchid** (214 East Roosevelt Street; 602-253-0339; monorchid.com), which does double duty as an art space and a wedding venue. And walk around the corner to the front of **MADE Art Boutique** (922 North Fifth Street; 602-256-6233; madephx.com), which carries books, ceramics, craft items, and jewelry.

8 *The Original Residents* 3:30 p.m.

American Indian culture runs deep here, with several active tribes and reservations in the region. Just about all of them have contributed displays or materials to the **Heard Museum** (2301 North Central Avenue; 602-252-8840; heard.org), renowned for its

collection of Native American art. The museum shop is also a great place to buy gifts.

9 *Steak and the Fixings* 7 p.m.

Phoenicians love a good steak as much as the next westerner, and since 1955, many in search of a chunk of beef and a bottle of wine have flocked to **Durant's** (2611 North Central Avenue; 602-264-5967; durantsaz.com; $$$). The steaks come in several cuts, from Delmonico and strip to the "humble T-bone," and the rest of the menu hits all the familiar notes: shrimp cocktail, oysters Rockefeller, stuffed baked potatoes, surf and turf. The place is well stocked with regular customers, but you may not be the only newcomer dropping in.

BELOW A pool at the Arizona Biltmore Resort & Spa. You don't have to be a hotel guest to use the spa, so schedule a treatment after a morning of hiking.

10 *Beer, Bands and Art* 10 p.m.

For a craft beer or glass of organic wine to top off the night in a lively setting, head to the 1922 bungalow that houses the **Lost Leaf** (914 North Fifth Street; 602-258-0014; thelostleaf.org), opened in 2007. The brick-walled bar, which hosts local bands or D.J.s

ABOVE Mystery Castle, built from a little of everything.

OPPOSITE The Hotel San Carlos, built in 1928.

nightly, offers life-drawing classes, and artists who display their work keep 100 percent of their sales.

SUNDAY

11 *Urban Desert* 10 a.m.

Driving through central Phoenix, you're more likely to see imported pine trees than saguaros, the giant native cactuses. The **Desert Botanical Garden** (1201 North Galvin Parkway; 480-941-1225; dbg.org) is the perfect place to get your dose of desert life without ever leaving a brick pathway. Spread across 50 acres in Papago Park, the garden is an oasis of towering cacti, aromatic flowers, and surprisingly verdant plants in the middle of the urban grid.

THE BASICS

Phoenix, 350 miles east of Los Angeles, is served by multiple airlines. On the ground, a car is essential.

Royal Palms Resort
5200 East Camelback Road
602-840-3610
royalpalmshotel.com
$$$
Palms, gardens, and fountains help create a feeling of seclusion amid the Phoenix sprawl.

Arizona Biltmore Resort & Spa
2400 East Missouri Avenue
602-955-6600
arizonabiltmore.com
$$$$
Eight swimming pools, a golf course, and well-reviewed restaurants.

Sheraton Phoenix Downtown
340 North Third Street
602-262-2500
sheratonphoenixdowntown.com
$$$
A 31-story, 1,000-room tower that opened in 2008.

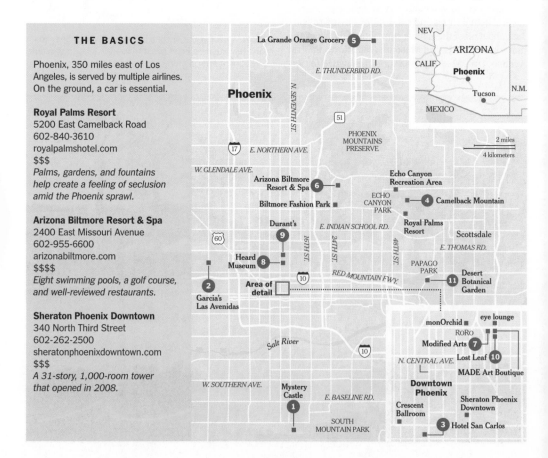

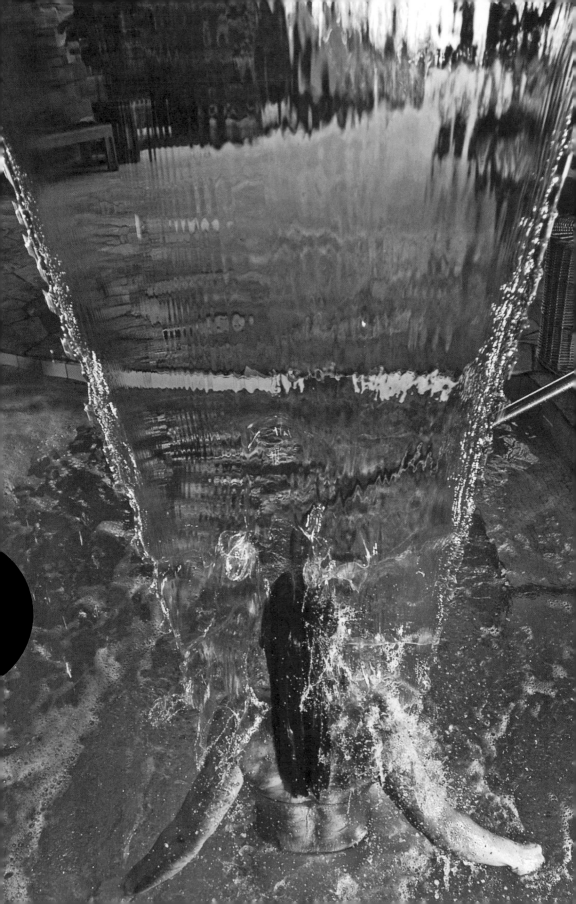

Scottsdale

It might be tempting a curse from the golf gods to enter the Scottsdale city limits without a set of clubs. But it's easy to spend a full weekend here far from the fairways. Just east of Phoenix, Scottsdale was once home to the Hohokam Indians; the town was founded in the 1880s by Winfield Scott, an Army chaplain who bought land to farm sweet potatoes. Today, Scottsdale is associated less with farming than with Frank Lloyd Wright, massage therapists, affluent second-home owners, and posh resorts. Wright's influence can be seen in much of the city's architecture as well as in his own Arizona headquarters, Taliesin West. Golf, if you wish. Or eat, explore, and then float in an infinity pool, contemplating your next cocktail.

— BY JENNIFER STEINHAUER

FRIDAY

1 *Enchilada Central* 7:30 p.m.

Much of Scottsdale may look as if it sprang up yesterday, but there are a few vestiges here and there of an earlier era. **Los Olivos** (7328 East Second Street; 480-946-2256; losolivosrestaurants.com; $), one of the oldest restaurants in the original area known now as Old Town, is still family run and has a personality all its own; the building itself looks like a piece of folk art, with a sculpture of a Mayan head rising from the roof. Inside, there's a lively central dining and bar area and a Blue Room that risks aquamarine overload. The food is solid Tex-Mex.

2 *Exotic Vintages* 10 p.m.

Kazimierz World Wine Bar (7137 East Stetson Drive; 480-946-3004; kazbar.net), known as the Kaz Bar, has all the trappings of hipness — no sign over the door (which is in the back), sofas, and a crowd of varying ages and sexual orientations. There are wines from dozens of nations available — yes, this is the place to find that elusive Thracian Valley

merlot from Bulgaria. Expect live music or a D.J., too. Cavelike and dimly lit, Kaz Bar makes for good people watching.

SATURDAY

3 *A Plan over Pancakes* 9 a.m.

The coffee is strong and the buttermilk pancakes are yummy at **Cafe ZuZu** in the Hotel Valley Ho (6850 East Main Street; 480-421-7997; hotelvalleyho.com; $). Sit in the supermodern chairs or comfy booths and plot potential misadventures.

4 *Desert Produce* 11 a.m.

For a sense of how irrigation can make a desert bloom, mingle with the locals shopping at the **Old Town Farmers Market** (Brown Avenue and First Street; arizonafarmersmarkets.com). Along with the Arizona oranges and vegetables, expect a variety of other artisan and homemade products vying for your attention: apricot walnut bread, vegan desserts, barbecue sauce, bee pollen, cherry pepper relish, organic cider, tamales, hot doughnuts, and more.

5 *Taste of the East* 1 p.m.

While you are in the neighborhood, do as the local residents do and hit **Malee's Thai Bistro** (7131 East Main Street; 480-947-6042; maleesonmain.com; $), a softly lighted room that muffles the sun-drenched action outside. The best bets are the tofu spinach

OPPOSITE Splashing in the open-air waterfall at the spa in the Fairmont Scottsdale Princess. Scottsdale resorts cater to an affluent clientele.

RIGHT The Old Town Farmers Market, where local growers show off the variety of plants and produce that a well-watered desert can provide.

pot stickers, Evil Jungle Princess (a pile of chicken doused in coconut cream with mushrooms and fresh mint), and the reliable pad Thai.

6 *A Bit of the Old West* 2 p.m.

Stay in Old Town for a stroll and a little browsing. There are scores of galleries displaying everything from works of the masters to Native American jewelry to large contemporary paintings by local artists. You'll also find questionable Western-themed statuary, store names with puns (Coyo-T's), and the obligatory wind chimes and dried chile peppers lilting and listing in the breeze. Check out **Mexican Imports** (3933 North Brown Avenue; 480-945-6476) for all the South of the Border kitsch you've always wanted. Nearby is **Old Town Jewels** (4009 North Brown Avenue; 480-970-8065; oldtownjewels.com), which has been selling Native American jewelry and accessories since 1984.

7 *Boot Up* 3:30 p.m.

For western wear — especially boots — the traditional stop in Scottsdale is **Saba's** (sabas.com), which has two stores in Old Town, nearly across the street from each other. For the complete look, you'll have to visit both. The one at 7254 Main Street (480-949-7404) sells only boots; the one at 3965 Brown Avenue (480-947-7664) has clothing and hats.

8 *There's Always the Rub* 5 p.m.

The ways to get pummeled, peeled, and rubbed in Scottsdale are endless, and there seems to be an almost Constitutional obligation to submit. From the shoulder rubs at the most commonplace hair salons to the aquatic watsu massage at the gorgeous **Sanctuary Camelback Mountain Resort**

& Spa (5700 East McDonald Drive; 855-245-2051; sanctuaryoncamelback.com), there is something for every (reasonably generous) budget. Right in the middle is the **VH Spa for Vitality and Health** at the Hotel Valley Ho (hotelvalleyho.com), where the Back, Neck, Shoulders massage was heaven.

9 *Serenity, Inside and Out* 7 p.m.

Start dinner right at **Elements** (at the Sanctuary resort; sanctuaryoncamelback.com/dining/elements; $$$) by angling for just the right seat on the patio at the Jade Bar, where you can watch the sunset while eavesdropping on first-daters as you munch on wasabi-covered peanuts. This moment is best paired with an Asian pear cucumber and ginger martini or a glass of sparkling rosé. You will want to ask for a window booth inside the restaurant, where the chef

cooks up seasonal fare as you take in Paradise Valley. The view is really the main course, but there have been some standout offerings on the changing menu, like grilled salmon, carrot and millet pot stickers, or a diabolical banana fluffernutter sundae. The Zen-like setting with stone and fireplaces is serene.

SUNDAY

10 *The Architect's Place* 10:30 a.m.

Do not miss **Taliesin West**, the international headquarters for the Frank Lloyd Wright Foundation and the winter campus for the Frank Lloyd Wright School of Architecture (12621 Frank Lloyd Wright Boulevard; 480-860-2700; franklloydwright.org).

Troubled by poor health, Wright took up half-year residence in this 600-acre "camp" in 1937, and the complex was built by apprentices. Take the 90-minute tour, which takes you through the living quarters, working areas, and outdoor spaces that incorporate indigenous materials and organic forms. Then there's all that Asian art.

OPPOSITE ABOVE Taliesin West, built by Frank Lloyd Wright as a community of architects and apprentices. Its low-slung buildings on 540 acres of desert attract 120,000 visitors a year for tours.

OPPOSITE BELOW Year-round Arizona sunshine makes for steady activity at outdoor pools, like this one at the Fairmont.

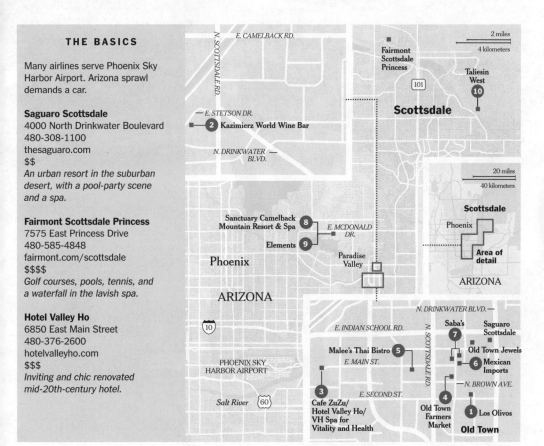

THE BASICS

Many airlines serve Phoenix Sky Harbor Airport. Arizona sprawl demands a car.

Saguaro Scottsdale
4000 North Drinkwater Boulevard
480-308-1100
thesaguaro.com
$$
An urban resort in the suburban desert, with a pool-party scene and a spa.

Fairmont Scottsdale Princess
7575 East Princess Drive
480-585-4848
fairmont.com/scottsdale
$$$$
Golf courses, pools, tennis, and a waterfall in the lavish spa.

Hotel Valley Ho
6850 East Main Street
480-376-2600
hotelvalleyho.com
$$$
Inviting and chic renovated mid-20th-century hotel.

Sedona

Ask five people to sum up Sedona, Arizona, and you'll probably get five wildly different responses. Art lovers enthuse over the galleries specializing in Southwestern tableaus. Shopaholics rave about boutiques selling Western duds and Native American jewelry. Pessimists rue the rash of T-shirt shops, while enlightenment-seekers wax spiritual about the "vortexes." And outdoor enthusiasts rhapsodize about hiking among red rock spires and ancient Indian ruins. All of this is great news for visitors, who can sample it all in a quirky city that some call the most beautiful place in the United States. — BY KERIDWEN CORNELIUS

FRIDAY

1 *Red Rock Rover* 4 p.m.

Sedona's cinematic red rocks have been zipping across your windshield like scenes from a Hollywood Western as you've driven toward town. Now it's your turn to ride off into the sunset. Turn up Airport Road to Airport Saddleback — you want the tiny parking lot on the left, not the chockablock Airport Vista farther up the road. Slip on hiking boots and hit the **Airport Loop Trail** for close encounters with the towering crimson sandstones: Bell Rock, Courthouse Butte, Coffee Pot Rock, and the Cockscombe. It's a 90-minute ramble, but if your energy flags, just turn back and scramble up Overlook Point, a good spot to watch paprika-red sunsets.

2 *Shopping for Dinner* 7 p.m.

It's hard to find authentic Southwestern food in Sedona, but there are good restaurants. One is **René Restaurant at Tlaquepaque** (336 State Route 179; 928-282-9225; renerestaurantsedona.com; $$$), where tenderloin of antelope, rack of lamb, and cilantro scallops are signature dishes. It's in the **Tlaquepaque Arts & Crafts Village** (tlaq.com), a Spanish-colonial-style shopping arcade with fountains and muscular sycamores. The shops and galleries are worth a look. Peek in the window of Kuivato Glass Gallery, which sells glass sculptures and jewelry, as well as ceramics and watercolors.

3 *Cocktail by the Fire* 9:30 p.m.

Sedona isn't known for its night life. Most bars shut down at 10 p.m. For a little atmosphere to go

with your nightcap, swing by **SaltRock Southwest Kitchen** inside the **Amara Resort and Spa** (100 Amara Lane; 928-282-4828; amararesort.com). Sample a cocktail or a reposado from the lengthy tequila list as you lounge on the patio, gazing at the infinity pool with the red rocks just beyond. The outdoor fire pit is just as picturesque.

SATURDAY

4 *Break an Egg* 9 a.m.

Kick-start your day in classic Sedona fashion with breakfast at the **Coffee Pot Restaurant** (2050 West Highway 89A; 928-282-6626; coffeepotsedona.com; $), which serves 101 "famous" omelets. Locals and tourists pack this kitschy joint, so you may have to browse the gift shop for jewelry and coffee mugs while waiting for a table. But once you're seated, the friendly waitresses are swift and might even leave the coffeepot on your table for convenient refills. Overwhelmed by the omelet choices? Try the hearty huevos rancheros, smothered in green chili. If you have kids, dare them to order the peanut butter, jelly, and banana omelet.

OPPOSITE The red sandstone rocks of Sedona.

BELOW The Chapel of the Holy Cross sits atop one of Sedona's famous vortexes, revered as sites of psychic energy.

5 *Southwest Inspiration* 10 a.m.

Galleries dot the city. The biggest of them is **Exposures International** (561 State Route 179; 928-282-1125; exposuresfineart.com), a sprawling space overflowing with paintings, sculpture, jewelry, and more. Check out Bill Worrell's prehistoric-art-inspired sculptures. Other interesting galleries can be found at **Hozho Center**, including **Lanning Gallery** (431 State Route 179; 928-282-6865; lanninggallery. com), which specializes in contemporary art. To learn more about the local art scene, visit the **Sedona Arts Center** (15 Art Barn Road; 928-282-3809; sedonaartscenter.com), a nonprofit gallery that holds exhibits and poetry readings.

6 *A Creek Runs Through It* 1 p.m.

Sedona is cradled in a fragrant riparian valley through which Oak Creek gently runs. Weather permitting, dine creekside at **Etch Kitchen & Bar** at **L'Auberge de Sedona** (301 L'Auberge Lane; 928-282-1661; lauberge.com; $$$), a contemporary American restaurant. The menu includes dishes like roasted chicken with quinoa. Cottonwoods rustle, the creek burbles, and ducks waddle between the linen-draped tables.

7 *Spirited Away* 2:30 p.m.

You can't get far in Sedona without hearing about the vortexes, places where the earth supposedly radiates psychic energy. Believers claim that they induce everything from heightened energy to tear-inducing spiritual enlightenment. Whether you're a skeptic or a believer, a guided tour of the vortexes by **Earth Wisdom Jeep Tours** (293 North State Route 89A; 928-282-0254; earthwisdomjeeptours.com) is definitely scenic. If vortexes aren't your thing, go

ABOVE Rust-colored cliffs, shaded by oxidation of their iron-laced stone, tower above Enchantment Resort.

BELOW Earth Wisdom tours explore local history, geology, Native American culture, and vortexes.

OPPOSITE Oak Creek, the gentle stream running through the valley that cradles Sedona.

anyway. This tour also explores the area's history, geology, and Native American culture, and there are other tours to choose from. You'll learn how the rocks became rust-colored: add a dash of iron, let it oxidize for several million years, and voilà!

8 *Cactus on the Rocks* 6 p.m.

A prickly pear margarita — made from a local cactus — is the must-drink cocktail in Sedona, and one of the best spots to try it is the terrace at **Tii Gavo** at **Enchantment Resort** (525 Boynton Canyon Road; 928-282-2900; enchantmentresort.com). Tii Gavo means gathering place in the Havasupai Indian language, and in this restaurant well-heeled spa-lovers rub elbows with hikers fresh off the trail. Afterward, move inside to the **Che-Ah-Chi** (928-282-2900; $$$; reservations required for nonguests). With its American Indian pottery and views of Boynton Canyon, this restaurant is well known to Sedona's celebrity visitors. The wine list

is extensive and far-ranging, but consider one of the local Echo Canyon reds.

9 *A Galaxy Far, Far Away* 9:30 p.m.

Thanks to strict ordinances on light pollution, the dark skies over Sedona are ideal for stargazing (or U.F.O. spotting). Take a cosmic journey with **Sedona Star Gazing** (928-203-0006; eveningskytours.com). You'll be led by an astronomer who can point out those elusive constellations as well as an eyeful of spiral galaxies and the rings of Saturn.

SUNDAY

10 *Rock Your World* 6 a.m.

Soar over Sedona valley in a hot-air balloon at sunrise for jaw-dropping views of rose-tinted buttes. **Northern Light Balloon Expeditions** (928-282-2274; northernlightballoon.com) offers three- to four-hour trips that include a Champagne breakfast picnic in

climb up a doughlike outcropping for commanding views of Casner Canyon.

11 *Morning Spiritual* 10 a.m.

Peek inside the **Chapel of the Holy Cross** (780 Chapel Road; 888-242-7359; chapeloftheholycross. com), a modernist icon that looks like a concrete spaceship jutting out of the craggy boulders. Designed in 1932 by Marguerite Brunswig Staude (but not built until 1956), the chapel is sandwiched between soaring concrete walls that bookend a gigantic glass window with a 90-foot-tall cross. Prayer services are held on Monday evenings, so don't worry about interrupting when you make your visit this morning. This spot affords spectacular photo ops and another chance to have a psychic moment. The chapel sits on — you guessed it — a vortex.

a remote spot (about $220). If you prefer to stay earthbound, pack your own picnic and set out on the 3.6-mile **Broken Arrow Trail**. A Red Rock Day Pass (redrockcountry.org) allows entry to a number of natural areas and is available at most Sedona hotels and many stores. Hike along red rocks stained with desert varnish, weave through cypress forests, and

ABOVE Inside Tlaquepaque Arts & Crafts Village, a Spanish-colonial-style shopping arcade.

OPPOSITE Poolside at the Enchantment Resort.

THE BASICS

Fly to Phoenix, rent a car, and drive north for about two hours.

Enchantment Resort
525 Boynton Canyon Road
928-282-2900
enchantmentresort.com
$$$
Adobe casitas, nature walks, a Native American culture program, and stargazing.

L'Auberge de Sedona
301 L'Auberge Lane
855-702-0063
lauberge.com
$$$$
Blends log cabin style with a touch of France.

Lantern Light Inn
3085 West Highway 89A
928-282-3419
lanternlightinn.com
$$
Attractive bed-and-breakfast with fireplaces, fountains, and patios.

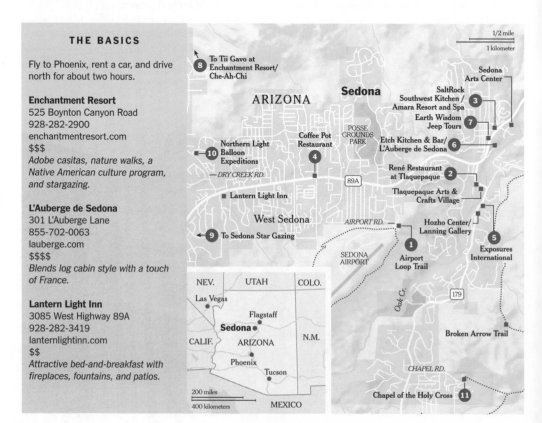

Tucson

To complement its natural beauty — a national park in its midst and mountains on four sides — Tucson has poured hundreds of millions of dollars into its downtown, saving older buildings and retooling them as movie houses and museums. Elsewhere in the city, astonishingly individualistic examples of mid-20th-century Modernist architecture are scattered among the highways and strip malls, some of them most noticeable when their neon signs come on at night. And with a deep-rooted Hispanic community, tides of Mexican immigrants, and students from the University of Arizona who never left after graduation, the city has a youthful and multicultural glow.

— RICHARD B. WOODWARD

FRIDAY

1 *Jet Age Graveyard* 4 p.m.

Tucson's bone-dry climate is easy on all kinds of metal bodies. The city is a hunting ground for used-car buyers as well as home to one of the world's largest airplane graveyards. A sample of the 4,000 or so stranded military and civilian aircraft can be viewed by driving along the fence on Kolb Road by the Davis-Monthan Air Force Base. For a closer look, the **Pima Air & Space Museum** (6000 East Valencia Road; 520-574-0462; pimaair.org) offers tours with frighteningly knowledgeable guides who can run down all the specs on the SR-71 "Blackbird" spy plane.

2 *Hear That Whistle Blow* 6 p.m.

The Southern Pacific railroad reached Tucson in 1880, and the moaning whistle of trains can still be heard day and night. For a front-row seat to the passing leviathans, head to **Maynard's Market and Kitchen** (400 North Toole Avenue; 520-545-0577; maynardstucson.com; $$). Less than 50 feet from the tracks, this former depot attracts an upscale crowd that comes for the wines (from the store next door) and the reasonably priced menu. But just as inviting as the pizzas and strip steaks

OPPOSITE Saguaro National Park, a favorite Tucson playground when the summer sun isn't blazing.

RIGHT Terror remembered: a cold war artifact, the top of a missile, at the Titan Missile Museum outside Tucson.

are the sights and sounds of the rattling plates and glasses.

3 *Tucson Nights* 8 p.m.

Tucson has a jumping band scene on weekends, a sleepier one the other five days. On warm nights, the noise of music pumps through the open doors of restaurants and bars along Congress Street. The center of the action is often the historic **Rialto Theatre** (318 East Congress Street; 520-740-1000; rialtotheatre.com). A nonprofit showcase vital to downtown's renewal, it books major acts but has no stylistic agenda.

SATURDAY

4 *Roadrunner* 9 a.m.

When the summer sun isn't blazing, Tucsonians head outdoors. A prime destination is the **Saguaro National Park** (3693 South Old Spanish Trail; 520-733-5155; nps.gov/sagu), which embraces the city on two sides. To walk among fields of multi-armed cactus giants, drive west about a half-hour along a snaking road. Look for an unmarked parking lot a few hundred feet beyond the Arizona-Sonora Desert Museum. This is the start of the **King Canyon Trail** (saguaronationalpark.com/favorite-trails.html), put in by the Civilian Conservation Corps in the 1930s and the path for a refreshing morning hike. A covered picnic area is at mile 0.9. Fitter types can proceed 2.6 miles to Wasson Peak, the highest point in the Tucson Mountains.

5 *Modern Mexican* Noon

Tucson thinks highly of its Mexican restaurants, and one place that it can justly be proud of is **Cafe Poca Cosa** (110 East Pennington Street; 520-622-6400; cafepocacosatucson.com; $$$). Don't be put off by its location (in an ugly office building) or the décor (a vain attempt to import some glam L.A. style). The place has attracted national attention for a novel take on Mexican cuisine, which emphasizes fresh and regional. Try the daily sampler (el plato Poca Cosa) of three dishes chosen by the chef. Expect an exotic mole and perhaps a zinger like a vegetarian tamale with pineapple salsa. Dinner reservations are essential for weekends.

6 *Picture This* 1:30 p.m.

One of the most impressive collections of 20th-century North American photographs can be found at the **Center for Creative Photography** (1030 North Olive Road; 520-621-7968; ccp.arizona.edu), in a hard-to-find building on the University of Arizona campus. Containing the archives of Ansel Adams, Edward Weston, Garry Winogrand, W. Eugene Smith, and more than 40 other eminent photographers, it also runs a first-rate exhibition program.

7 *The Buy and Buy* 3:30 p.m.

Phoenix-style shopping has arrived at **La Encantada**, a mall in the foothills of the Santa Catalinas, with Tiffany and Louis Vuitton (2905 East Skyline Drive, at Campbell Avenue; 520-299-3566; laencantadashoppingcenter.com). North of downtown at the **Plaza Palomino** (2960 North Swan Road), local merchants carry more idiosyncratic items like funky handmade jewelry and crafts.

8 *Eyes on the Desert Sky* 5 p.m.

The surrounding mountains are heavenly for stargazing. The **Kitt Peak National Observatory** (Tohono O'odham Reservation; 520-318-8726; noao.edu), about 90 minutes southwest of the city and 6,900 feet above sea level, says it has more optical research telescopes

than anywhere in the world. Aside from serving professional astronomers, it also has generous offerings for amateurs. One of these, the Nightly Observing Program, begins an hour before sunset and lasts four hours. An expert will show you how to use star charts and identify constellations and will give you a peek through one of the mammoth instruments. (Dinner is a deli sandwich; remember to wear warm clothing.) Reserving a month in advance is recommended, but you may get lucky and find an opening the same day.

9 *More Cosmos* 10:30 p.m.

For a nightcap, head to the boisterous **Club Congress** (on the ground floor of the Hotel Congress, 311 East Congress Street; 520-622-8848; hotelcongress.com/club), a nightclub with five different bar areas. The beats of live bands often send crowds of dancers spilling out into the lobby of the hotel. Finish the night across the street at the cozy **Good Oak Bar** (316 East Congress; 520-882-2007; goodoakbar.com) with a locally made craft beer or creative cocktail and maybe a basket of frites.

SUNDAY

10 *Early Bird* 9 a.m.

The **Epic Cafe** (745 North Fourth Avenue; 520-624-6844; epiccafe.com; $) is a happening spot

ABOVE Dirk J. Arnold's *Gateway Saguaro*, a neon landmark.

BELOW The Kitt Peak National Observatory. For nighttime stargazing, reserve well in advance.

at almost any hour. This neighborhood hub on the corner of University Boulevard is open from 6 a.m. to 9 p.m. and serves an eclectic menu of sandwiches, sweets, and drinks to a clientele of laptop-toting would-be intellectuals and dog owners who jam the sidewalk tables. Grab a cup of the excellent coffee and a vegan seed cookie. If it tastes like delicious bird food, that's because it is.

11 *Missile America* 10 a.m.

For a terrifying yet educational reminder of the cold war, drive about 30 minutes south of downtown on Interstate 19 to the **Titan Missile Museum** (1580 West Duval Mine Road, Sahuarita; 520-625-7736; titanmissilemuseum.org). The nuclear silo housed

a single intercontinental ballistic missile equipped with a warhead 700 times more powerful than the Hiroshima bomb. The museum tour lasts an hour. Much of it is underground, behind eight-foot-thick blast walls, and it ends with a peek at the 103-foot weapon, with its warhead removed.

ABOVE At Maynard's Market and Kitchen, in a former depot, glasses rattle as trains go by less than 50 feet away.

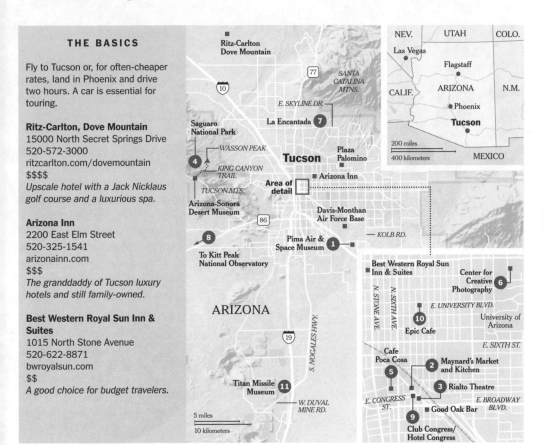

THE BASICS

Fly to Tucson or, for often-cheaper rates, land in Phoenix and drive two hours. A car is essential for touring.

Ritz-Carlton, Dove Mountain
15000 North Secret Springs Drive
520-572-3000
ritzcarlton.com/dovemountain
$$$$
Upscale hotel with a Jack Nicklaus golf course and a luxurious spa.

Arizona Inn
2200 East Elm Street
520-325-1541
arizonainn.com
$$$
The granddaddy of Tucson luxury hotels and still family-owned.

Best Western Royal Sun Inn & Suites
1015 North Stone Avenue
520-622-8871
bwroyalsun.com
$$
A good choice for budget travelers.

Map labels:

Ritz-Carlton Dove Mountain
SANTA CATALINA MTNS.
77
10
E. SKYLINE DR.
La Encantada 7
Saguaro National Park
WASSON PEAK
Tucson
Plaza Palomino
4
KING CANYON TRAIL
Area of detail
Arizona Inn
TUCSON MTS.
Arizona-Sonora Desert Museum
86
Davis-Monthan Air Force Base
8
Pima Air & Space Museum 1
KOLB RD.
To Kitt Peak National Observatory

NEV. UTAH COLO.
Las Vegas
Flagstaff
CALIF. ARIZONA N.M.
Phoenix
Tucson
200 miles
400 kilometers
MEXICO

ARIZONA
S. NOGALES HWY.
19
Titan Missile Museum 11
W. DUVAL MINE RD.
5 miles
10 kilometers

Best Western Royal Sun Inn & Suites
Center for Creative Photography 6
N. STONE AVE.
N. SIXTH AVE.
E. UNIVERSITY BLVD.
10
Epic Cafe
University of Arizona
E. SIXTH ST.
Cafe Poca Cosa 5
Maynard's Market and Kitchen 2
Rialto Theatre 3
E. CONGRESS ST.
9 Good Oak Bar
E. BROADWAY BLVD.
Club Congress/ Hotel Congress

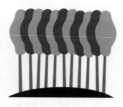

Aspen

Aspen emphatically lives up to its reputation as a winter playground for the jet-set crowd—but it's more than that. It's a multifaceted gem with acres of surrounding wilderness. Spend as many of the precious daylight hours you can exploring and tramping. But there is also plenty to do outside of the wilderness experience: shopping, trying out a few excellent restaurants, and, yes, skiing. Don't waste your time and money or risk your safety trying to keep up with the billionaires from Brazil or the daredevils from Australia. With some strategic choices, you can experience this sublime and compact winter wonderland in comfort and style without a credit-card hangover.

— BY HANNAH SELIGSON

FRIDAY

1 *Top of the Mountain* 1 p.m.

Start your weekend atop **Aspen Mountain**, which the locals refer to as Ajax, with a snowshoe tour (aspensnowmass.com/plan-your-stay/winter-activities) led by the Aspen Center for Environmental Studies. At over 11,000 feet, you'll orient yourself to the stunning surroundings: Highland Bowl, Hayden Peak, and Smuggler Mountain. One extremely knowledgeable guide pointed out animal tracks, gave mini history lessons and supplied cookies and hot chocolate.

2 *Après Ski* 3:30 p.m.

Après ski (or simply après) is to Aspen what teatime is to England: an indispensable daily ritual that is taken seriously. The sacred window between the closing of the ski lifts and nightfall is a time for drinking and noshing. **Chair 9** at the **Little Nell** (675 East Durant Avenue; thelittlenell.com), the five-star hotel at the foot of Aspen Mountain, is a reasonably priced establishment devoted to this pastime. Order a draft beer or a glass of bubbly, and toast to your first day at altitude while nibbling on some Parmesan fries and empanadas. Live music or a D.J. every day.

3 *Dinner by the Board* 7 p.m.

A welcome and needed addition to the sometimes stuffy Aspen dining scene, **Meat & Cheese** (319 East Hopkins Avenue; meatandcheeseaspen.

com; $$$) is the hipster casual spot that serves boards of (you guessed it) top-notch meat and cheese. Start with a cheese board (let your server do the picking; there are no bad cheeses here) and then move on to the succulent and juicy local rotisserie chicken board.

SATURDAY

4 *Ski Time* 11 a.m.

Buy a ski pass (at the ticket booth in the plaza at South Hunter Street and East Durant Avenue) that you can use at four mountains—Highlands, Buttermilk, Aspen, and Snowmass—and ride the gondola up Aspen Mountain to hit the slopes. More confident skiers can stay on Aspen Mountain, which has no green trails and is dominated by advanced skiers. Make good use of the secondary lifts because the gondola takes 14 minutes to get to the top. For families with children just learning and those looking for more manageable terrain, take the free public bus about 10 minutes to **Buttermilk Mountain** (aspensnowmass.com/our-mountains/buttermilk), three miles from downtown Aspen. In the words of a local, "There is no better place to cruise around on groomers." But even experienced

OPPOSITE A skier at Aspen Highlands. Renowned as a resort where billionaires gather to strap on skis, Aspen can also be affordable for snow lovers on tighter budgets.

BELOW Skiers and snowboarders congregate on Aspen Mountain as a gondola glides by overhead.

skiers can have fun on the mountain's challenging blue trails. Both Aspen and Buttermilk Mountains run ambassador programs—free tours that orient skiers and snowboarders to the mountains. Tours meet and leave from the guest services cabins on both mountains.

5 *Work the Kinks Out* 3 p.m.

Aspen has a hedonistic streak, so splurge with a massage at the **Remède Spa** at the **St. Regis** (315 East Dean Street; stregisaspen.com), which has a lot of practice working out the kinks and tight spots, inevitable byproducts of winter sports. Go early or stay longer to take advantage of the spa's oxygen room, hot tub, cold plunge, and sauna.

6 *Shopping Sampler* 4:30 p.m.

Many Aspen stores can be found in other major cities, so focus on what isn't easy to find back home. **Kemo Sabe** (217 South Galena Street; kemosabe.com), for instance, is a cowboy store that sells its trademark boots for prices starting at over $500 and going up from there. Check out the belt buckles, which are made by the same buckle maker who made them for *The Lone Ranger*. For the style-conscious, **Stefan Kaelin Ski & Golf** (416 East Cooper Avenue; stefankaelin.com) sells runway-worthy ski outfits that are both pricey and beautiful. And for a high-end example of the cannabis stores in Aspen, a growing part of the town's retail offerings, head for the impec-

cably professional **Silverpeak Apothecary** (520 East Cooper Avenue; silverpeakapothecary.com).

7 *Alpine Dining* 7:30 p.m.

La Creperie du Village (400 East Hopkins Avenue; lacreperieduvillage.com; $$$) is a cozy French alpine bistro known for its fondue, crepes, and raclette, a dish of melted cheese, boiled potatoes, cornichons, and cured meat. The dish is served with a tabletop grill and is the main draw. Also popular is the fondue, which comes in a cheese and beef variation. Save room for a dessert crepe.

8 *Nostalgia Nightcap* 10 p.m.

Since 1892, thirsts have been slaked on the premises of the **Red Onion** (420 East Cooper Avenue; 970-925-9955; redonionaspen.com), a dageurrotype-ready saloon with exposed brick walls, a copper-hammered ceiling, and more than 300 varieties of whiskey behind the inlaid-wood bar, plus more than 10 local drafts. Oh, and the bullet hole there from the storied past? Ask the bartender to show you where it is.

SUNDAY

9 *Cross-Country* 9 a.m.

Caffeinate and fortify with coffee and quiche at **Paradise Bakery and Cafe** (320 South Galena Street; paradisebakery.com) before heading out for a cross-country ski outing. If you thought you would only

enjoy Aspen vertically, you were mistaken. The sleeper, and most budget-conscious among Aspen's outdoor activities, the **Aspen Cross Country Center** (39551 West Highway 82; utemountaineer.com/our-store/aspen-cross-country-center) is easily reached on the free public bus to Buttermilk (Truscott stop). The Aspen Snowmass Nordic Trail System's 90 kilometers of free trails are accessible from the center, but a one-hour, five-kilometer loop is more than enough to get the heart rate going.

10 *Aspen and the Arts* 2 p.m.

The **Aspen Art Museum** (637 East Hyman Avenue; aspenartmuseum.org), designed by Shigeru Ban, is as much a work of art as its contents. A vari-

ety of rotating multimedia exhibitions are presented, by artists who have included Yves Klein and Miranda July. Don't miss the sculpture garden on the top floor, facing Aspen Mountain.

OPPOSITE Après ski at a local bar. Aspen scrupulously honors this ritual of food and drink after the ski lifts close.

ABOVE The Aspen Art Museum, designed by Shigeru Ban, proves this ski town isn't just about skiing.

THE BASICS

Fly into Aspen/Pitkin County Airport, three miles from downtown Aspen, or Denver International Airport, 125 miles away but often a less expensive alternative.

Hotel Aspen
110 Main Street
hotelaspen.com
$$$
A cozy, no-frills option with a great location in the center of the town. Service is friendly and there is free breakfast as well as a daily wine reception.

St. Regis Aspen Resort
315 East Dean Street
stregisaspen.com
$$$$
A haven of luxury close to the base of Aspen Mountain.

Hotel Jerome
330 East Main Street
hoteljerome.com
$$$
Built in 1889 as Colorado's first hotel with electricity and indoor plumbing; now sumptuously updated.

100 miles
150 kilometers

Denver
● **Aspen**

COLORADO

2 miles
3 kilometers

82
Aspen

Buttermilk Mountain
4

■ Aspen Cross Country

Area of detail

Aspen Mountain snowshoe tour 1

Silver Queen gondola

■ Hotel Aspen

W. MAIN ST.

■ Hotel Jerome

Aspen

N. SPRING ST.

W. HOPKINS AVE.

Meat & Cheese
3

E. MAIN ST.

W. HYMAN AVE.

S. MONARCH ST.

S. MILL ST.

7 La Creperie du Village

6 Kemo Sabe

E. HOPKINS AVE.

S. ASPEN ST.

Red Onion 8

Silverpeak Apothecary ■

Stefan Kaelin Ski & Golf

E. DURANT AVE.

Paradise Bakery and Cafe

9

■ Aspen Cross Country Center

E. HYMAN AVE.

10 Aspen Art Museum

S. HUNTER ST.

E. COOPER AVE.

S. ORIGINAL ST.

Remède Spa/
St. Regis Aspen Resort
5 ■

S. MILL ST.

Chair 9 at The Little Nell 2

Silver Queen gondola

1/8 mile
1/4 kilometer

Boulder

A crowd of 4,000 gathered at the base of Boulder's Flatirons in July of 1898 to celebrate the opening of the Colorado Chautauqua, part of a national movement promoting "wholesome, pleasurable study in sylvan surroundings," according to the brochure, as well as "abundant recreational opportunities." These days, Boulder offers the same formula. It has a college-town base of 30,000 students at the University of Colorado Boulder, 45,000 acres of protected open space, and 300-plus days that see the sun, with an outdoorsy populace of former Deadheads, many now business owners and endurance athletes. The resulting Boulder Bubble is an exceptionally easygoing place to hang out. Who even needs the legal marijuana?
— BY MELISSA COLEMAN

FRIDAY

1 *Join the Bicycle Brigade* 3 p.m.

The bicycle is obligatory in the People's Republic of Boulder. Students and C.E.O.s ride to school or work—even after cycling circuits up Flagstaff Mountain. The city has miles of routes. Check out the 5.5-mile Boulder Creek Path, a bike trail following the creek from Stazio Fields near 55th to the intersection of Four Mile and Boulder Canyons. **Boulder B-cycle** (boulder.bcycle.com) manages dozens of bike-share stations—simply insert a credit card for 30-minute increments or daily, monthly, and annual passes, and return to any station. Gearheads will prefer the wider range of frames at **University Bicycles** (839 Pearl Street; ubikes.com), based on Ninth and Pearl since 1985, for town, mountain, road, or kids' rentals. Your bike may become your best friend for the weekend, and using it will promote that Boulder glow.

2 *Farm to Table on the Mall* 5 p.m.

Pearl Street Mall's four blocks of brick walkway from 11th to 15th Streets and the surrounding area are the shopping, eating, and drinking heart of town. Alfresco and farm-to-table dining can be found at the Kitchens, the hip nexus of three dining spots initiated in 2004 by Kimbal Musk, brother to the space-travel entrepreneur Elon Musk. **The Kitchen** (1039 Pearl Street; thekitchenbistros.com; $$-$$$) is a community bistro with an urban crispness to the décor and locally sourced vegetable and meat dishes. The **Kitchen Next Door** ($) is the walk-in, pub-style option, with an equally tasty menu at pub prices. Return after hours for craft cocktails and an upscale night-life scene at the **Kitchen Upstairs**.

3 *Peace, Love, Dessert* 6:45 p.m.

Grab a quickie dessert at **Piece, Love & Chocolate** (805 Pearl Street; pieceloveandchocolate.com). Behind a kitschy, flower-bedecked storefront, this retail ode to the cocoa bean offers handmade truffles in over 50 flavors, sipping chocolate, and extravagant wedding cakes.

4 *Music and More* 7:30 p.m.

Once described by Theodore Roosevelt as "the most American thing in America," the Chautauqua Movement, a circuit of summer adult education camps with lodging and lectures, faded with the takeover of radio and film in the 1930s, but the **Colorado Chautauqua** (900 Baseline Road; chautauqua.com) at the top of the town is one of the few still alive and well. Amenities include lodging and a dining hall, but the big draw is the May to September schedule of music, film, theater, dance, and lectures at the 1,300-seat Chautauqua Auditorium, a barnlike structure built in 1898. William Jennings Bryan spoke here, as did Al Gore and the Rev. Jesse Jackson.

OPPOSITE Hikers at the base of a peak in the aptly named Flatiron Mountains, a favorite symbol of Boulder.

RIGHT Cyclists are everywhere in Boulder, and the city supports their passion with miles of bike trails.

5 *Boulder's Backyard* 8 a.m.

Emblematic of Boulder's milieu are the burgundy rock formations of the five Flatiron Mountains, rising into the true-blue Colorado sky like back plates of a giant stegosaurus. The Mesa Trail forms the north-south spine of the interconnected trails that run along the base. Consult the **Ranger Cottage** at Chautauqua for route possibilities. Fairly steep access trails aside, the well-worn paths are mostly horizontal and offer vistas as well as sheltered stretches of ponderosa forest. You'll encounter trail runners, rock climbers, tourists in flip-flops, and lots of dogs.

6 *Not Just Lunch* 11 a.m.

Here's one way to combine recreation, learning, and lunch in the Chautauqua spirit. Depart from the Enchanted Mesa Trail at Chautauqua to connect with the Mesa Trail to the National Center for Atmospheric Research (NCAR) Trailhead on Table Mesa, about a four-mile hike. Then take a self-guided tour of the exhibit area inside NCAR's **Mesa Laboratory** (1850 Table Mesa Drive; scied.ucar.edu/visit), a modernist I.M. Pei building where scientists study climate change and space weather. Next hike a few miles down the NCAR Road or get an Uber for a ride to **Under the Sun Eatery & Pizzeria** (627A South Broadway; mountainsunpub.com/underthesun), in the Table Mesa Shopping Center. The wood-fired oven turns out roast chicken and pizzas, and Southern Sun Pub & Brewery is upstairs.

7 *Tubin' It* 1 p.m.

Boulder Creek, from its headwaters up Boulder Canyon to its confluence with the South Platte River, is a draw for wading, fishing, and tubing. If you've never been tubing before, now is the time. Rent or

TOP Students, families, couples, and tourists all join the jumble at the Pearl Street Mall in the heart of town.

ABOVE Running a trail at the Colorado Chautauqua, a retreat and cultural center that's been active since 1898.

take a tour from **Whitewater Tube Co.** (2709 Spruce Street; whitewatertubing.com), and ask about shuttle service. Starting near Eben G. Fine Park, you will shoot down gentle drops and frothy falls for up to seven miles afloat.

8 *That Special Feeling* 3 p.m.

Time to relax. Watering holes on the Mall include the roof deck at the **Rio Grande Mexican Restaurant** (1101 Walnut Street; riograndemexican.com), with views of the Flatirons. If you plan to sample the edible and smokable weed at the **Native Roots Boulder** marijuana dispensary (1146 Pearl Street; nativerootsboulder.com), you must do so before Boulder's legal closing time of 10 p.m.

9 *Colorado Rock* 8 p.m.

Red Rocks Amphitheater is only 45 minutes away in Morrison, which means headline musicians often spill over to Boulder. The **Fox Theatre** (1135 13th Street; foxtheatre.com), a standup drink and dance club in the college hub of the Hill with a capacity of only 625, has hosted the Dave Matthews

Band, Phish, Willie Nelson, and Bonnie Raitt. Whoever's playing, the Fox is sure to rock late on weekend nights. The Art Deco **Boulder Theater** (2032 14th Street; bouldertheater.com), a former opera and movie house presiding over the Mall, has seen the likes of Johnny Cash, Lucinda Williams, and Lyle Lovett.

SUNDAY

10 *Brunch, Creole-Style* 10 a.m.

Ensconced in a homey yellow Victorian on 14th Street since 1980, **Lucile's Creole Cafe** (2124 14th Street; luciles.com; $) is often referred to as the

TOP The National Center for Atmospheric Research, where scientists study climate change and space weather.

ABOVE Brave the Sunday lines for a table at Lucile's Creole Cafe, a much-loved spot for brunch and a Bloody Mary.

best brunch spot in town (there's even a song about it by the Little Women). Brave the lines (they can be long) for New Orleans beignets covered in a blizzard of powdered sugar or a Cajun breakfast with hollandaise sauce over eggs, red beans, and grits. Don't forget a Bloody Mary or two.

11 *Or Brunch, Tajik-Style* 10 a.m.

For a completely different take on brunch, pass up Lucile's and try the fare at **Boulder Dushanbe Teahouse** (1770 13th Street; boulderteahouse.com; $$). Its hand-painted Persian ceilings and ceramic panels were created by Tajikistan artisans in Central Asia, shipped in crates, and reconstructed near Boulder Creek in 1998. This intimate sanctuary with a sculptural pond is now a gem of a restaurant run by Three Leaf Concepts. For Tea Time, reserve in advance and return between 3 and 5 p.m.

ABOVE Quiet time at Boulder Dushanbe Teahouse.

OPPOSITE Boulder Creek invites tubing with miles of gentle drops, and anyone can rent a tube and join in.

THE BASICS

Most major airlines serve Denver International Airport, which is a 45-minute drive from Boulder in light traffic.

Colorado Chautauqua
900 Baseline Road
chautauqua.com
$-$$$
Cottages built in the early 1900s for Chautauqua guests. Full kitchens, screened porches. Lodge rooms are also available.

St. Julien Hotel & Spa
900 Walnut Street
stjulien.com
$$$
Luxury option downtown near the Pearl Street Mall. Includes the 10,000-square-foot Spa at St. Julien.

Hotel Boulderado
2115 13th Street
boulderado.com
$$$
Opened in 1909; in the heart of the shopping and restaurant district.

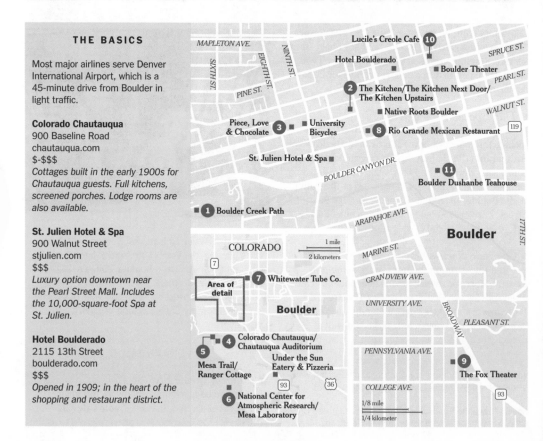

Denver

The signs of Denver's economic high times as a pot boomtown and bastion of progressive urban policies are everywhere. There are the inconspicuous marijuana dispensaries that dot neighborhoods. But once you've noticed them, there is the B-cycle bike-share program, among the most affordable and best-run systems in the country, and the newly renovated Union Station, which has taken a still-in-use 1881 train station and made it the focal point of the thriving LoDo neighborhood. And more stunning public spaces than one city has a right to.
— BY FREDA MOON AND ERIC WILSON

FRIDAY

1 *Larimer Square to Santa Fe* 3 p.m.

To see a bit of old Denver, shop the boutiques in the 19th-century buildings of Larimer Square, where in rougher days saloons and stores catered to gold miners. Gold was first discovered in Colorado in the 1850s, and prospectors staked their claims in what is now Denver's downtown. If you're shopping for art, a wealth of remarkable galleries is concentrated in Lower Downtown (LoDo) and also along Santa Fe Drive. For novices, one of the most accessible is **Artists on Santa Fe** (747 Santa Fe Drive; 303-573-5903; artistsonsantafe.com), a warren of studios where sculptors and painters will explain their work. On the first and third Friday of each month, the Santa Fe Arts District (denversartdistrict.org) hosts a festive art walk, with studios, galleries, and antiques shops overflowing with people and music.

2 *Where Isn't the Beef?* 7 p.m.

There's no getting around Denver's culinary specialty, red meat, the starring attraction at Old West-themed grill joints all over town. Count the Wild West species represented in the form of taxidermy on the walls (or on the menu) of **Buckhorn Exchange,** billed as Denver's oldest restaurant (1000 Osage Street; 303-534-9505; buckhornexchange.com; $$$). Here, steak can be ordered by the pound. Another option is to drive to **The Fort,** 18 miles southwest in Morrison (19192 Highway 8; 303-697-4771; thefort.com; $$$), where thousands of buffalo entrees are served annually in a 1960s rendition of an 1830s fur-trading fort.

3 *Mayan Movie Time* 9 p.m.

Wind down the evening with a movie at the Art Deco **Mayan Theater** (110 Broadway; 303-744-6799; landmarktheatres.com/denver/mayan-theatre). Built in 1930, this three-screen movie palace is one of three remaining theaters in the country built in the elegant Mayan Revival style. It has a full bar-cafe and shows independent, art house, and arty mainstream movies.

SATURDAY

4 *The Urban Outdoors* 9 a.m.

Coloradans are passionate about the outdoors, even in the city. Denver has more than 100 miles of pedestrian and bicycle paths, and you can get to one of the most popular, the **Cherry Creek Path,** right downtown. Hop on the MallRide, a free bus service along 16th Street, at the Civic Center. Hop off at Larimer Street and walk a couple of blocks southwest on Larimer to find the steps down to the creek level. Take the path north, staying alert for occasional glimpses of the snow-capped Rockies, and arrive at **Confluence Park,** where the creek meets the South Platte River. This is the historic center of Denver, the spot where the city had its start. Continue on the path until you've had enough, and then return.

OPPOSITE The Denver Art Museum's new Hamilton building, designed by Daniel Libeskind.

BELOW Dinner at outdoor tables in Larimer Square.

5 *Amusement Food* Noon

For an unusual lunch, order the wild boar, rattlesnake and pheasant, Alaskan reindeer, or duck cilantro hot dog at **Biker Jim's Gourmet Dogs** (2148 Larimer Street; 720-746-9355; bikerjimsdogs.com; $). The menu also includes sides, like charred tahini cauliflower and deep-fried pickles; Boylan's Natural Fountain sodas; and craft beer. In the increasingly trendy Highland neighborhood, **Little Man Ice Cream** (2620 16th Street; 303-455-3811; littlemanicecream.com) operates in a 28-foot-tall milk can, reminiscent of the doughnut- and hot-dog-shaped restaurants of vintage Americana. Its dozens of flavors include choices like bhakti chai, French toast, and pomegranate chia seed.

6 *Juxtapositions* 2 p.m.

The **Denver Art Museum** (100 West 14th Avenue Parkway; 720-865-5000; denverartmuseum.org), with its Daniel Libeskind-designed add-on, remains the Museum District's not-to-miss institution. The jutting addition looks like an Imperial Cruiser from *Star Wars,* and once inside, the vertigo-inducing floor plan will make you long to get your feet back on earth. But the museum's juxtaposition of many styles and eras, from the work of contemporary art stars to Native American artifacts, is compelling, and your inner ears will soon adjust.

7 *History Report* 4 p.m.

Despite being the home of the mega-brewery Coors, Colorado has one of the most varied and exciting craft beer scenes in the country. Walk to the South Broadway corridor and take a seat on the partly enclosed rooftop (open year-round) at **Historians Ale House** (24 Broadway; 720-479-8505; historiansalehouse.com), where typically at least 75 percent of its 40-tap

ABOVE Union Station, built in 1914 and newly rejuvenated, anchors Denver's LoDo neighborhood.

RIGHT Denver's oldest restaurant, the Buckhorn Exchange.

list is local. The five-ounce option makes it possible to sample breweries from around the state.

8 *Foundry Fine Dining* 8 p.m.

Opened in 2013 in a former 19th-century foundry that is now an upscale public market called the Source, **Acorn** (3350 Brighton Boulevard; 720-542-3721; denveracorn.com; $$) calls itself "eclectic American." *Bon Appétit* once called it one of the best new restaurants in the country. Menu highlights have included oak-grilled octopus with gnocchi, braised artichokes, house-made chorizo and salsa verde, and tomato-braised meatballs with grits, burrata, and basil. If Acorn's celebrity makes a table hard to come by, try **ChoLon** (1555 Blake Street; 303-353-5223; cholon.com; $$$), an inventive, Asian-influence bistro in LoDo.

SUNDAY

9 *Bagel or Bust* 10 a.m.

Rosenberg's Bagels & Delicatessen (725 East 26th Avenue; 720-440-9880; rosenbergsbagels.com; $) has taken the quest for a decent New York-style bagel west of the Mississippi to heroic heights. Its owner, Josh Pollack, tested and replicated the New York City water supply, which is widely credited with the unique properties of the city's bagels and pizza. The sizable effort and expense have paid off. The bagels are chewy and flawless. Sandwiches (like the delicious Heebster: scallion cream cheese, whitefish salad, and wasabi flying fish roe) are worth the calorie splurge.

10 *Horizontal Mile* 11 a.m.

The **Mile High Flea Market** (88th Avenue; milehighmarketplace.com) could just as well be named the Mile Wide Flea Market. Browse its hundreds of tightly packed, pastel-colored stalls, and sample street fare like corn on the cob with butter and Parmesan.

11 *A Fighter to Remember* 1 p.m.

In the 1890s, Margaret Tobin Brown, a social climber with a rich husband and an outsize personality, acquired a mansion in Denver on what was then called Pennsylvania Avenue. Later mythologized as Molly Brown, she survived the sinking of the *Titanic* and ran for United States Senate when women could vote only in Colorado and a few other states. Tour the **Molly Brown House Museum** (1340 Pennsylvania Street; 303-832-4092; mollybrown. org) and imagine her standing on the front porch like Debbie Reynolds in *The Unsinkable Molly Brown*, hollering, "Pennsylvania Avenue, I'll admit you gave me a nose full of splinters, but it's all good wood from the very best doors!"

ABOVE The Molly Brown House Museum.

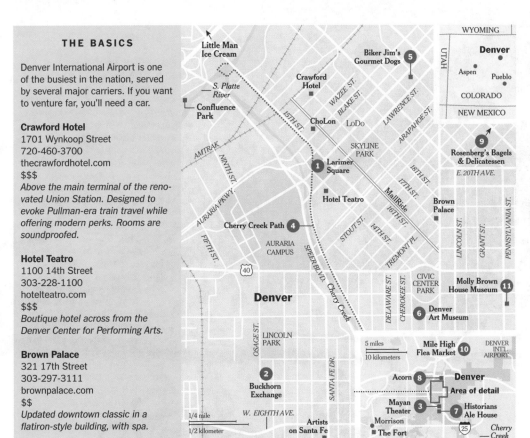

THE BASICS

Denver International Airport is one of the busiest in the nation, served by several major carriers. If you want to venture far, you'll need a car.

Crawford Hotel
1701 Wynkoop Street
720-460-3700
thecrawfordhotel.com
$$$
Above the main terminal of the reno-vated Union Station. Designed to evoke Pullman-era train travel while offering modern perks. Rooms are soundproofed.

Hotel Teatro
1100 14th Street
303-228-1100
hotelteatro.com
$$$
Boutique hotel across from the Denver Center for Performing Arts.

Brown Palace
321 17th Street
303-297-3111
brownpalace.com
$$
Updated downtown classic in a flatiron-style building, with spa.

Telluride

There are steeper ski resorts than Telluride. There are ski resorts that get more snow. But few places are friendlier and prettier than this town at the end of a box canyon in the tall San Juan Mountains. Beauty and great skiing keep pulling the money here, and that keeps refreshing the scene. But it's the people who make this place interesting — a quirky stew of Patagonia-clad men who look as if they came straight from base camp; flushed women direct from their 10-mile runs; still others reciting poetry in bordello-wear at a Colorado Avenue bar; and gray-ponytailed hippies who play "Sugar Magnolia" so often you'd think Jerry Garcia never went to that great jam fest in the sky. — BY CHRISTOPHER SOLOMON

FRIDAY

1 *A Ski Is Born* 3 p.m.

Pete Wagner, an engineer who designed better ways to fit golf clubs to golfers, wondered why skis were basically an off-the-shelf purchase. So in 2006 he opened **Wagner Custom Skis** (wagnerskis.com) in Placerville, a rough little mining burg 15 miles downstream from Telluride. Success bloomed, and you'll find it now closer to the action at 620 Mountain Village Boulevard. The company customizes everything from a ski's base material to the central core — maple? white ash? — to the graphics you see in the lift line. Tours of the shop are free (weekday afternoons by appointment), but skis are pricey. They're said to be worth every penny.

2 *Après-Ski at Altitude* 5 p.m.

The best thing about Mountain Village, the affluent stepchild of Telluride that sits above the town at 9,540 feet, is that the gondola to town runs until midnight. Another bright spot is **Siam's Talay Grille** (119 Lost Creek Lane, Mountain Village; innatlostcreek.com), offshoot of the popular Siam-Telluride. Dip into the alpine pagoda-décor bar when the lifts shut down for a drink and a snack.

3 *Good, Fresh Mexican* 8 p.m.

Follow the locals to **La Cocina de Luz** (123 East Colorado Avenue; lacocinatelluride.com; $$) on the main drag, Colorado Avenue. This casual joint in an old bank, complete with vault door, uses mostly organic ingredients and also offers some vegan and gluten-free options. Step up to the counter and order the combo with a chile relleno — order it "Christmas" (with both red and green chile) — with a side of refried Anasazi beans. The food here is simple, fresh, and bright; and the margaritas are strong.

SATURDAY

4 *Starter Feast* 7:30 a.m.

There is nothing extravagant about the **Butcher & Baker Cafe** (201 East Colorado Avenue; butcherandbakercafe.com; $), a locals' favorite. It's a clean, well-lighted place, a one-time pool hall with worn wood floors and big storefront windows through which floods the morning sun — so welcome on a winter morning in this deep, dark valley. They make their own breads here, and pastries, sauces, and pickles. Place your order at the counter. Take a billiard ball as your number. Feast on the good, simple fare — a huge breakfast sandwich, or eggs just as sunny as ordered, beside a track of deeply tanned bacon.

5 *Hit the Slopes* 9 a.m.

"Telluride really is a skier's mountain," the ski-maker Pete Wagner said. "Great terrain, and there's never anyone on it." In good snow conditions, experts often head for the billy-goat descents in Prospect Bowl; those who want a mellower day shouldn't miss

OPPOSITE Winter cyclists cruise over snow on fat bikes.

BELOW Downtown Telluride and its mountain backdrop.

See Forever, a meandering ridgetop groomer with views into adjoining Utah. Once you're warmed up, try Bushwacker, a black diamond that is groomed almost nightly; dive-bombing the run is vintage Telluride. You can rest those oxygen-deprived legs on Chair 9, one of the few lifts that aren't high-speed.

6 *Lunch at Treeline* Noon

Tucked among the subalpine fir at 11,966 feet, **Alpino Vino** (12100 Camels' Garden Road, on See Forever Trail, below the top of Chair 14; tellurideskiresort.com/events-activities/dining; $$$) lays claim to being the highest fine-dining restaurant in North America. The thick-walled stone hut and its outside deck recall an Alpine rifugio. On a still, sunny day, with the toothy San Juans smiling all around, it feels like the best of Europe—with Gstaad prices. But to be fair, the grilled cheese sandwich, with double-cream Colorado cheese and pesto and arugula, might be the most savory you've tasted.

7 *Bike to Beer* 2 p.m.

Try out a fat bike, one of those two-wheelers with cartoonishly big tires and names like the Moonlander that are able to cruise atop the snow. On the tour run by **Paragon Outdoors** (213 West Colorado Avenue; bootdoctors.com; reservations required), participants ride along the flat, groomed snow trails of the box canyon's scenic floor, skirting aspen, Engelmann spruce, and the winter trickle of the San Miguel River. Go in the afternoon and stop to visit the exceptional

ABOVE Alpino Vino offers fine dining with a European feeling at 11,966 feet above sea level.

RIGHT The Butcher & Baker Cafe, a good breakfast spot.

Telluride Brewing Company (156 Society Drive; telluridebrewingco.com). Or save your alcohol allowance for cocktails at **Altezza** (136 Country Club Drive, Mountain Village; thepeaksresort.com/dining), where the view from the bar is one of the best in town.

8 *Alpine Passeggiata* 5:30 p.m.

Historic Colorado Avenue, though just a few blocks long, is one of the great main streets in the West. Strolling the wide sidewalks in an alpine passeggiata as the alpenglow fades is a singular pleasure. Skip the stores selling silk-screened onesies and check out **CashmereRED** (221 East Colorado Avenue; cashmerered.com). Caci Grinspan works with a 150-year-old Scottish mill to create some of the most cloudlike sweaters, scarves, and blankets you've ever touched.

9 *Mountain Hip* 8 p.m.

There (627 West Pacific Avenue; therebars.com; $$) has all the marks of Brooklyn hipsterdom. On my visit, the drinks list was like a bookmark in a tattered

copy of Orwell's *1984* and the menu looked like a page torn from a comic book, the comics' conversation bubbles filled not with exclamations but with lists of pork rillette tostadas and crispy spicy duck steamed buns. But this place pulls it off, in no small part because of the charismatic bartenders who are the small room's workhorses, entertainers, and maître d's. There may be better food in town, but there's no place you'd rather be.

SUNDAY

10 *Fire Stoking* 10 a.m.

The **New Sheridan Hotel** (231 West Colorado Avenue; newsheridan.com) is a classic brick hotel that dates from the town's mining days. To get you out the door and keep your fires stoked on a Rocky Mountain

morning, the hotel's **Chop House Restaurant** ($$) serves brunch from 8 a.m. until 2 p.m., with options like a pistachio-encrusted trout spinach salad or a poached egg and sherry vinaigrette.

11 *Kick and Glide* Noon

Most come for the downhill thrills, but the Telluride area has six Nordic ski areas, with about 20 miles of groomed trails. Flag down the free Galloping Goose town bus and take it to the trailhead of the valley floor, where trails wend beside the San Miguel River. If you have a car, drive about 13 miles to the trails at Priest and Trout Lakes, with the most varied terrain and best snow conditions. If you rent gear at **Telluride Nordic Center at Town Park** (500 East Colorado Avenue; telluridetrails.org), your money helps maintain the trails you use.

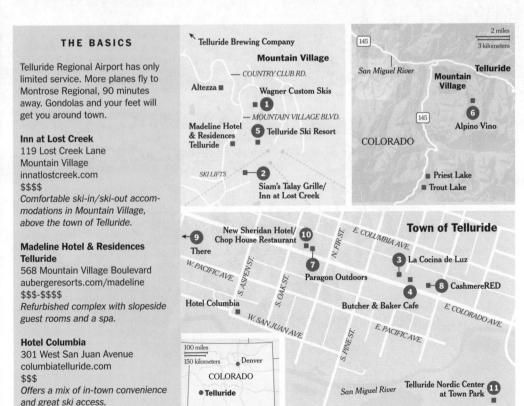

THE BASICS

Telluride Regional Airport has only limited service. More planes fly to Montrose Regional, 90 minutes away. Gondolas and your feet will get you around town.

Inn at Lost Creek
119 Lost Creek Lane
Mountain Village
innatlostcreek.com
$$$$
Comfortable ski-in/ski-out accommodations in Mountain Village, above the town of Telluride.

Madeline Hotel & Residences Telluride
568 Mountain Village Boulevard
aubergeresorts.com/madeline
$$$-$$$$
Refurbished complex with slopeside guest rooms and a spa.

Hotel Columbia
301 West San Juan Avenue
columbiatelluride.com
$$$
Offers a mix of in-town convenience and great ski access.

Telluride Brewing Company
Mountain Village
— COUNTRY CLUB RD.
Altezza ■
Wagner Custom Skis
1
— MOUNTAIN VILLAGE BLVD.
Madeline Hotel & Residences Telluride ■
5 Telluride Ski Resort ■
SKI LIFTS
2
Siam's Talay Grille/ Inn at Lost Creek

145
2 miles
3 kilometers
San Miguel River
Mountain Village
Telluride
145
6
Alpino Vino
COLORADO
■ Priest Lake
■ Trout Lake

9 ← New Sheridan Hotel/ Chop House Restaurant
10
E. COLUMBIA AVE.
Town of Telluride
There
W. PACIFIC AVE.
S. ASPEN ST.
N. FIR ST.
7
Paragon Outdoors
S. OAK ST.
3 La Cocina de Luz
8 CashmereRED
4
Hotel Columbia
Butcher & Baker Cafe
E. COLORADO AVE.
W. SAN JUAN AVE.
S. PINE ST.
E. PACIFIC AVE.
100 miles
150 kilometers   • Denver
COLORADO
• Telluride
San Miguel River
Telluride Nordic Center at Town Park **11** ■

Boise

Boise, once ruled by the bait-and-bullet crowd, has embraced the Lycra lifestyle. Sitting at the junction of the arid plateau of the high desert and the western foothills of the Rocky Mountains, Boise, Idaho's capital, offers all the outdoor advantages of more ballyhooed Western towns but with less ballyhoo. Boise may have a population of more than 200,000, but it is still a mining and farming town at heart, and it attracts active professionals and young families who will tell you that theirs is a great hometown—just don't let too many people know. They wouldn't want those trailheads or hot springs to get too crowded. A rejuvenated downtown and a budding arts community mean that after a day of rafting on the Payette River, mountain biking in the foothills, or carving at Bogus Basin Ski Resort you don't have to turn in once the sun fades behind the Snake River.

— BY MATTHEW PREUSCH

FRIDAY

1 *The Idaho Story* 4 p.m.

It's best to educate before you recreate, so check out the pioneer days reconstructions and Lewis and Clark artifacts at the **Idaho State Museum** (610 North Julia Davis Drive; 208-334-2120; history.idaho.gov/museum) in **Julia Davis Park**. From there, walk down the **Boise River Greenbelt** (parks.cityofboise.org), a much-loved and gloriously scenic corridor of parks and trails snug against the Boise River. It stretches for 25 miles, but you won't be going that far tonight.

2 *Big Game* 7 p.m.

Emerge at the **Cottonwood Grille** (913 West River Street; 208-333-9800; cottonwoodgrille.com; $$) to reward yourself with drinks and dinner. Have a cocktail or a glass of wine on the patio overlooking the river and the cottonwoods. Check out the game menu. This is your chance to try elk sirloin, buffalo with cabernet sauce, or Muscovy duck. If you're

feeling more conventional, there's always the pasta or Idaho trout.

SATURDAY

3 *Breakfast Builders* 8 a.m.

Put your name on the list at **Goldy's Breakfast Bistro** (108 South Capitol Boulevard; 208-345-4100; goldysbreakfastbistro.com; $$) and stroll two blocks north to the domed Capitol to contemplate the statue of Governor Frank Steunenberg. He was killed in 1905 by a bomb planted near his garden gate; the perpetrators were enraged by his rough handling of labor uprisings in upstate mines. But don't let that assassination ruin your appetite. Return to Goldy's and examine the menu to see which elements of the build-your-own breakfast you'd like to have with your scrambled eggs. Red flannel hash? Black beans? Salmon cake? Blueberry pancake? Be creative.

4 *Bumper Crop* 10 a.m.

Join stroller-pushing Boiseans gathered near the Capitol dome at the **Capital City Public Market** (280 North Eighth Street; capitalcitypublicmarket. com). Browse amid the lettuces—not to mention the fruit, flowers, desserts, and art glass—and reflect that Idaho grows more than potatoes.

5 *Basque Brawn* 11 a.m.

A century ago, Basque shepherds tended flocks in the grassy foothills around Boise. Today the mayor and many other prominent Idahoans claim Basque heritage. Learn about aspects of the Basques' culture,

OPPOSITE Rafting on the South Fork of the Payette River north of Boise.

RIGHT Join the Boiseans browsing amid carrots and lettuces near the Capitol dome at the Capital City Public Market.

including their love of a stirring strongman competition, at the **Basque Museum and Cultural Center** (611 Grove Street; 208-343-2671; basquemuseum.com). Don't drop the theme when you leave the museum in search of lunch. Grab a table at **Bar Gernika Basque Pub & Eatery** (202 South Capitol Boulevard; 208-344-2175; bargernika.com; $). The lamb grinder is a safe bet, but for something more spirited, brave the beef tongue in tomato and pepper sauce. Wash it down with Basque cider.

6 *Rapid Transit* 1:30 p.m.

Join the weekend exodus of pickups hauling A.T.V.s and Subarus bearing bikes as they head over the brown foothills of the Boise Front to outdoor adventure. Drive 45 minutes north to Horseshoe Bend and hook up with **Cascade Raft and Kayaking** (7050 Highway 55; 208-793-2221; cascaderaft.com) for a half-day raft trip through Class III and IV rapids on the Lower South Fork of the Payette River. There's also a milder trip with Class II and III rapids. If even that seems like whiter water than you're up for, stay in town, buy an inner tube, and join lazy locals floating down the relatively placid Boise River for six miles

ABOVE Downtown and the Boise Mountains.

OPPOSITE Hikers, runners, and cyclists share the 130 miles of paths in the Ridge to Rivers trail system.

between **Barber Park** (4049 Eckert Road) and **Ann Morrison Park** (1000 Americana Boulevard). Avoid the river if the water is high.

7 *How about a Potato-tini?* 7 p.m.

Swap your swimsuit for town wear and find an outdoor table on the pedestrian plaza outside the overtly cosmopolitan **Red Feather Lounge** (246 North Eighth Street; 208-429-6340; bcrfl.com; $$), where the focus is on post-classic cocktails like a Tangerine Rangoon: Plymouth gin, fresh tangerine juice, and homemade pomegranate grenadine. Pair that with pan-roasted halibut or potato confit pizza, and you might forget that you're in laid-back Boise. That is, until you spot the guy in running shorts and a fanny pack sitting at the bar.

8 *Bard by the Boise* 8 p.m.

Borrow a blanket from your hotel and find a spot on the lawn at the **Idaho Shakespeare Festival**, overlooking the Boise River east of town (5657 Warm Springs Avenue; 208-336-9221; idahoshakespeare.org), which runs June to September. It features productions of Shakespeare as well as more contemporary works at an outdoor amphitheater. As the sun sets and the stars come out, you might start to think that Boise's status as one of the most isolated metro areas in the lower 48 states is not a bad thing.

SUNDAY

9 *Pedal for Your Coffee* 9 a.m.

Head to **Idaho Mountain Touring** (1310 West Main Street; 208-336-3854; idahomountaintouring.com), rent a full-suspension mountain bike, and head north on 13th Street to Hyde Park, a neighborhood of bungalows and tree-lined streets. Park your bike with the others in front of **Java Hyde Park** (1612 North 13th Street; 208-345-4777) and make your way past the dogs tied up outside to order your favorite caffeinated creation.

10 *Up, Down, Repeat* 10 a.m.

Fortified, and perhaps jittery, remount your rented ride and pedal a few blocks farther up 13th Street to **Camel's Back Park** (1200 West Heron Street). Look for the trailhead east of the tennis courts, one of many entrances to the Ridge to Rivers trail system (ridgetorivers.org), a single- and double-track network that covers 80,000 acres between the Boise Ridge and Boise River. Climb the Red Cliffs Trail to open vistas of the Treasure Valley below, then loop back down on the rollicking Lower Hulls Gulch Trail. Repeat as necessary.

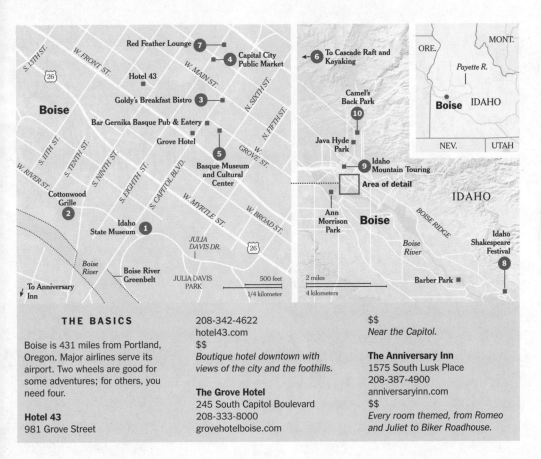

THE BASICS

Boise is 431 miles from Portland, Oregon. Major airlines serve its airport. Two wheels are good for some adventures; for others, you need four.

Hotel 43
981 Grove Street

208-342-4622
hotel43.com
$$
Boutique hotel downtown with views of the city and the foothills.

The Grove Hotel
245 South Capitol Boulevard
208-333-8000
grovehotelboise.com

$$
Near the Capitol.

The Anniversary Inn
1575 South Lusk Place
208-387-4900
anniversaryinn.com
$$
Every room themed, from Romeo and Juliet to Biker Roadhouse.

Las Vegas

For tourists, Las Vegas is ever the chameleon. New restaurants, shows, clubs, and hotels are constantly reinventing Sin City with the aim of getting repeaters back to the gaming tables. The momentum slowed temporarily after a lone gunman attacked an outdoor concert crowd in 2017, leaving 58 people dead, hundreds wounded, and the city shaken. But the locals adopted the defiant motto "Vegas Strong," and tourists and conventioneers came back, lured as always by the bright lights and swinging style.
— BY ELAINE GLUSAC

FRIDAY

1 *Buy or Browse* 3 p.m.

Las Vegas shops make up a parade of high-end global brands designed to tempt high rollers. The **Crystals at CityCenter** mall (3720 Las Vegas Boulevard South; simon.com/mall/the-shops-at-crystals) exemplifies the mode with swimsuits from Eres, clothing from Stella McCartney, and accessories from Porsche Design. But the center, with sharp and soaring angles, designed by the architect Daniel Libeskind to resemble a quartz crystal, has an artistic side, too. Pick up a free CityCenter Fine Art walking tour brochure from the concierge at Aria or Vdara, the two neighboring resorts, for a self-guided tour of the public art collection in and around the building, including a sculpture by Henry Moore; *Big Edge*, a stack of boats wired in a web, by the artist Nancy Rubins; and several ice pillars that slowly melt each day, only to be refrozen each night, from the designers of the Bellagio fountains.

2 *Haute Perch* 6 p.m.

Since Wolfgang Puck arrived in 1992, celebrity chefs have flocked to the Strip. But most local observers agree that the food scene didn't really improve until the French guys arrived—the chefs Joël Robuchon and Guy Savoy, principally. Their namesake restaurants remain bastions of formality,

OPPOSITE The Las Vegas Strip, where ostentation can never be overdone.

RIGHT A performance of Cirque du Soleil's Beatles-based show at the Mirage.

but **L'Atelier de Joël Robuchon** (3799 Las Vegas Boulevard South; 702-891-7358; mgmgrand.com; $$$$), the 33-seat à la carte restaurant next door to Joël Robuchon in the MGM Grand, offers a more affordable meal and relaxed setting. Reserve a seat at the black granite bar, raise a glass to Robuchon, who died in 2018, and watch the chefs prepare dishes like quail stuffed with foie gras or steak tartare with frites.

3 *Circus Circuit* 9:30 p.m.

Move over, showgirls. The pervasive **Cirque du Soleil** performances—at several different hotels—and the mammoth ads everywhere make Cirque something like the Starbucks of the entertainment circuit here. Its Vegas extravaganzas have included shows based on the lives and music of Michael Jackson and the Beatles; the saga of a magical ringmaster visiting a haunted theater with trapeze artists, jump ropers, and strongmen; and the adult-themed *Absinthe*, with circus acts, some nudity, and lots of risqué humor. Tickets for all of the Cirque shows are available at cirquedusoleil.com.

SATURDAY

4 *Downward Dolphin* 8:30 a.m.

Las Vegas is a multitasking kind of town. It's only fitting, then, that while you practice yoga, you should

be able to watch dolphins. That's the combination offered in the hourlong **Yoga Among the Dolphins** at the Mirage Las Vegas (3400 Las Vegas Boulevard South; mirage.com). Students adopt yoga poses in a subterranean room with glass windows looking into the dolphin pools in Siegfried & Roy's Secret Garden and Dolphin Habitat. Curious bottlenose dolphins peer through the glass at you while you hold your Warrior I position.

5 *All That Glows* 11 a.m.

Before the Strip's Eiffel Tower replica and pseudo Manhattan skyline, Las Vegas marketed itself via neon signs. The **Neon Museum** (770 Las Vegas Boulevard North; 702-387-6366; neonmuseum.org)

celebrates the showy signage in a collection of more than 150 pieces, most still vibrant though not operational in their resting place in the outdoor "Neon Boneyard." Casino castoffs include signs from the Golden Nugget, Binion's, and the defunct Stardust and Moulin Rouge; a bright yellow duck that once advertised a used car lot; and a "Free Aspirin & Tender Sympathies" sign that was used to market a gas station. Book an hourlong guided tour; visitors are not allowed to wander here on their own.

6 *Made Men* 12:30 p.m.

The **Mob Museum** (300 Stewart Avenue; 702-229-2734; themobmuseum.org) covers a more notorious aspect of Las Vegas history. Occupying a 1933 former federal courthouse and post office where one of the anti-Mafia Kefauver Committee hearings was held, the Mob Museum lays out the history of organized crime across America with interactive exhibits, including the chance to simulate firing your own Tommy gun. Eventually it narrows its focus to Las Vegas, where a number

ABOVE AND LEFT The Crystals at CityCenter, designed by Daniel Libeskind to resemble a quartz crystal, takes the shopping mall to a new level in flamboyant Las Vegas style. Inside are shops including Tiffany's and Prada; a public art collection; and a Wolfgang Puck pizzeria.

of crime syndicates funneled their energies after legal crackdowns elsewhere. The tour through the three-story building thoughtfully offers the squeamish a chance to opt out of some of the more graphic galleries, featuring photos of mob hits, and winds up in a theater screening a documentary on Hollywood's fascination with gangsters.

7 *Go Fish* 2 p.m.

Estiatorio Milos (3708 Las Vegas Boulevard South; 702-698-7930; milos.ca/restaurants/las-vegas; $$$), a spinoff of the Greek seafood-focused restaurants run by the chef Costas Spiliadis in Montreal, New York, and other cities, is a mandatory midday stop, serving a three-course prix fixe lunch that manages to be relatively healthy in a town that equates fine dining with excess. Appetizer/entree/dessert combinations include dishes like a Greek mezze plate, grilled whole bass, and walnut cake. You'll eat well and still be ambulatory for the next stop.

8 *Dip or Strip* 4 p.m.

Poolside clubs known as day clubs have become the afternoon indulgence du jour at hotels up and down the Strip, primarily patronized by the trim and toned under-30 set. At the **Aria Resort & Casino Las Vegas**, you can party with the bikini-clad, water-gun-armed crowds at the adults-only **Liquid Pool Lounge** (3730 Las Vegas Boulevard South; 702-590-9979; liquidpoollv.com). Or, for a quieter experience, seek serenity in the 81,000-square-foot **Spa at Aria** (aria.com), which has 62 treatment rooms, heated stone beds, a salt room, a steam room, a sauna, and an outdoor pool.

9 *Omakase Hour* 8 p.m.

The chef Nobu Matsuhisa and partners have their own hotel-within-a-hotel in a separate tower at Caesars Palace Hotel & Casino. Anchoring the Nobu Hotel just off the Caesars casino floor is a large branch of **Nobu** restaurants (3570 Las Vegas Boulevard South; 702-785-6677; nobucaesarspalace.com/restaurants.html; $$$$). Cushion-like fixtures that hang above the dining room like U.F.O.'s emit flattering light. The vast menu encompasses tiradito (Peruvian raw fish salad) and ceviche, wagyu steaks and brick-oven-baked chicken, skewered meats and, of course, sushi.

10 *Club House* 10 p.m.

There are limitless places to party in Las Vegas. For drinks overlooking the dancing fountains at the Bellagio resort, **Hyde** (3600 South Las Vegas Boulevard South; bellagio.com/en/nightlife/hyde.html),

designed in sleek style, morphs from sunset cocktail calm to late-night bash. **Hakkasan Las Vegas Restaurant and Nightclub** in the MGM Grand (3799 Las Vegas Boulevard South; hakkasanlv.com) sprawls over five levels of nightclubs and dancing.

SUNDAY

11 *Top Gear* 10:30 a.m.

In the city that sells itself on wish fulfillment, sitting behind the wheel of a high-performance car as it hurtles down a fast desert track is a perfect fit. **Speedvegas** (14200 Las Vegas Boulevard South;

702-874-8888; speedvegas.com) stables the latest exotic models, like the Ferrari 458 Italia and Lamborghini Huracán, designed to appeal to your inner F1 driver. The company used to organize driving trips to Red Rock Canyon 23 miles away, but the 50 m.p.h. speed limit felt too restrictive. So it built a 1.5-mile banked racetrack with 12 curves, 15 gear changes, and a straightaway where cars reach a top speed of 135 m.p.h.

ABOVE The Neon Museum celebrates a Las Vegas cliché, the bright, brash signs that light the nighttime on the Strip. In its collection are castoffs from casinos and oddities like a yellow duck that once advertised a used-car lot.

OPPOSITE A downsized Eiffel Tower and Arc de Triomphe at the Paris Las Vegas hotel. Gleaming in front is a desert extravagance, the Bellagio's pond.

THE BASICS

Las Vegas is a four-hour drive from Los Angeles. Its airport is served by the major airlines. Along the Strip, walk or use taxis, buses, and the monorail. Elsewhere, drive a car.

The Cosmopolitan
3708 Las Vegas Boulevard South
702-698-7000
cosmopolitanlasvegas.com
$$$
In a multibillion-dollar development, with hotel interiors designed by David Rockwell.

Aria Resort & Casino
3730 Las Vegas Boulevard South, in CityCenter
702-590-7111
aria.com
$$$
In CityCenter, with 4,000 rooms and every amenity (some with extra fees).

SPRING MOUNTAIN RD.

Yoga Among the Dolphins/
Mirage Las Vegas

15 **4**

DEAN MARTIN DR.

Neon Museum **5**

Mob Museum **6**

NEVADA **Las Vegas** Area of detail

4 miles
8 kilometers

215

Speedvegas **11**

9 Nobu/
Caesars Palace Hotel & Casino

FLAMINGO RD.

10 Hyde/
Bellagio

7 Estiatorio Milos/
The Cosmopolitan

Las Vegas

1 Crystals at
CityCenter

HARMON AVE.

8 Aria Resort & Casino
Las Vegas/
Liquid Pool Lounge/
Spa at Aria

2 L'Atelier de Joël Robuchon/
MGM Grand/
Hakkasan Las Vegas
Restaurant and Nightclub

LAS VEGAS BLVD. S.

PARADISE RD.

TROPICANA AVE.

604

ORE. | IDAHO

NEVADA | UTAH

Las Vegas

CALIF. | ARIZ.

1/4 mile
1/2 kilometer

MCCARRAN
INTERNATIONAL
AIRPORT

Albuquerque

New Mexico's biggest city has come back into its own. Thanks to tax breaks and great scenery, the TV and film industry is well established: scenes for Joss Whedon's film The Avengers *were shot here, and TV watchers recognize Albuquerque as the backdrop for* Breaking Bad *and its prequel,* Better Call Saul. *For visitors, the sprawl can seem daunting, but it is tempered by new bike paths. On the main drag, Central Avenue, neon signs from Route 66's heyday glow over revitalized, pedestrian-friendly neighborhoods. And along the banks of the Rio Grande, farmland provides a quiet oasis, not to mention heirloom beans, corn, and more to feed the city's vibrant organic movement.* — BY ZORA O'NEILL

FRIDAY

1 *Mother Road* 3 p.m.

At night, Albuquerque's revived downtown can be a bleary seven-block bar crawl. By day, though, you can appreciate the ornate buildings financed by the railroad boom, like the exuberant Pueblo Deco **KiMo Theatre** (423 Central Avenue Northwest; 505-768-3522; cabq.gov/kimo), which opened as a movie palace in 1927 and is now the city's public arts center. Enter through the business office to admire cow skull wall sconces and pueblo drum chandeliers. Nearby, drop in at classic shops like **Skip Maisel's** (510 Central Avenue Southwest; 505-242-6526; skipmaisels.com), an emporium of American Indian crafts that's just the place to pick up a turquoise-and-silver bolo tie. Look for the '30s murals above the display windows, by artists from surrounding pueblos. The **Man's Hat Shop** (511 Central Avenue Northwest; 505-247-9605; manshatshop.com) is stacked to the ceiling with 10-gallons, fedoras, and more. A short drive south, stop off to see what's showing at the **National Hispanic Cultural Center** (1701 Fourth Street Southwest; 505-246-2261; nhccnm.org).

2 *Healing Potions* 6 p.m.

Go early to get a seat along the edge of the roof deck at the **Parq Central** hotel, a renovated 1926 hospital for railroad employees, tuberculosis patients, and the mentally ill. The menu at its **Apothecary Lounge** (806 Central Avenue Southeast; 505-242-0040; hotelparqcentral.com) notes the place is "not a licensed pharmacy." Instead, it prescribes potions like a dreamy margarita made with prickly-pear juice and elderflower liqueur. As the sun sets, watch the east-side Sandia ("Watermelon") Mountains turn a luscious shade of pink.

3 *Home Grown* 8 p.m.

For a taste of old-school Albuquerque, head to **Golden Crown Panaderia** (1103 Mountain Road Northwest; 505-243-2424; goldencrown.biz; $), for empanadas, Mexican-style bolillos, and pizza with a crust of blue corn or green chili (or chile, as it's usually spelled in New Mexico). Salads are tossed with greens snipped from a tangled indoor garden. For dessert, get a classic anise-laced biscochito cookie and a double-shot espresso milkshake.

4 *Beer and Atmosphere* 10 p.m.

The drinking wing of **Marble Brewery** is called Marble Pub (111 Marble Avenue Northwest; 505-243-2739; marblebrewery.com), and it is a consummate New Mexican bar: benches, banjo players or salsa drummers, and lots of dogs. Rehydrate, after dancing, with a goblet of barrel-aged ale. Over in the Nob Hill district, east of the University of New Mexico, the longer-established brewpub **Kellys** (3222 Central Avenue Southeast; 505-262-2739; kellysbrewpub.com) is set in a 1939 Ford dealership and service station. Find a seat outside, weather permitting, by the vintage gas pumps and watch the fashion parade: flip-flops, graying ponytails, lavish tattoos.

SATURDAY

5 *Family-Style Breakfast* 9 a.m.

The chef's credentials include Chez Panisse and the Zuni Café, but his mother greets you at the counter, and the eatery is named for his daughter. **Sophia's Place** (901 Park Avenue Southwest; 505-916-5496), which has undergone several iterations around town, has developed a cult following for its New Mexican spin on Mexican dishes. Wake up to gems like the breakfast burritos (with salsa or chili

OPPOSITE Hot-air balloon traffic is heaviest during the annual Albuquerque International Balloon Fiesta, but ballooning is popular all year round.

(2711 Fourth Street Northwest; 505-344-6266; $).
Its recipe hasn't changed in decades, nor has its
décor — the combination won it a James Beard
America's Classic award. Try the carne adovada
as a turnover, wrapped in flaky dough and fried.

SUNDAY

9 *Up in the Air* 5:45 a.m.

Since 1972, when the first Balloon Fiesta convened,
Albuquerque has been hot-air-balloon heaven, with
friendly winds and ample sunshine. Take a dawn flight
with **Rainbow Ryders** (5601 Eagle Rock Avenue Northeast; 505-823-1111; rainbowryders.com). The bird's-
eye view takes in the Sandias and dormant volcanoes,
but most remarkable is the sensation of drifting just a
few feet above the muddy waters of the Rio Grande.
Replenish afterward at the **Grove** (600 Central Avenue
Southeast; 505-248-9800; thegrovecafemarket.com; $)
with pancakes or a chocolate-date scone.

10 *Church Music* 10 a.m.

Free espresso fuels the congregation at
Chatter Sunday (at Las Puertas; 1512 First Street
Northwest; 505-244-0290; chatterabq.org/sunday),
a Sunday-morning chamber music and poetry
series. Founded in 2008 by the cellist Felix Wurman,

and potatoes), huevos divorciados or the lemon
ricotta pancakes, a house specialty.

6 *Rolling on the River* 10:30 a.m.

Sixteen paved miles of biking bliss, the Paseo
del Bosque trail in the city's lowlands hugs the Rio
Grande. Pick up your wheels at **Routes Bicycle
Tours & Rentals** (2113 Charlevoix Street Northwest;
505-933-5667; routesrentals.com). The shop is a
seven-minute ride to the Bosque via Mountain Road,
which passes through a neighborhood of centuries-
old adobe houses. One destination is **Los Poblanos
Farm Shop** (4803 Rio Grande Boulevard Northwest;
505-344-9297; lospoblanos.com), the store at Los
Poblanos inn and organic farm. Lavender lotions
and soaps are a specialty.

7 *Clang, Clang, Clang* 3 p.m.

Even if a faux-trolley tour bus doesn't normally
appeal to you, hop aboard the adobe-look **ABQ Trolley**
(800 Rio Grande Boulevard Northwest; 505-200-2642;
abqtrolley.com). The two owner-operators (one
talks and the other drives and rings the bell) return
happy waves from locals and blast Chuck Berry as
they cruise Route 66. The tour features locations for
Breaking Bad and tales of a young Bill Gates, who
co-founded Microsoft here with Paul Allen before
he moved back to Seattle. Special outings feature
recitals of Albuquerque lore, talks on public art, ghost
stories around Halloween, and tours to see holiday
luminarias, the paper-bag lanterns that cast a glow
on winter nights.

8 *Red Meat* 6 p.m.

Carne adovada — pork stewed in earthy New
Mexican red chili — is the lifeblood of **Mary & Tito's**

ABOVE Pick up a 10-gallon hat from the Man's Hat Shop.

BELOW Fresh baked at Golden Crown Panaderia.

OPPOSITE KiMo Theatre, designed in Pueblo Deco style.

just two years before his death, it was originally called the Church of Beethoven. Wurman's vision of a weekly ritual without the strictures of religion has become one of the city's best-loved musical events. Arrive early to score the best seats in the converted warehouse with a specially created live chamber music space.

11 *Sweet and Hot* 1 p.m.

The decades-old **Frontier Restaurant** (2400 Central Avenue Southeast; 505-266-0550; frontierrestaurant.com; $) occupies the better part of a city block. The Frontier's walls are adorned with portraits of John Wayne, and its booths are occupied by every social stratum of the city. Standard order at the counter: breakfast burrito with bacon, fresh-squeezed orange juice, and a killer sweet roll dripping with molten cinnamon goo. You can even take a frozen pint of New Mexico green chili home on the plane.

THE BASICS

The Albuquerque International Sunport is about a 10-minute drive from downtown.

Los Poblanos Inn
4803 Rio Grande Boulevard
Northwest
505-344-9297
lospoblanos.com
$$
Agriturismo, New Mexican style, set on an organic farm. Rooms balance brick and adobe with Alexander Girard textiles.

Andaluz
125 Second Street Northwest
505-242-9090
hotelandaluz.com
$$
Built in 1939 by the New Mexico native Conrad Hilton and recently renovated. Rooms have faux-Moorish doorways and Frette linens.

Bottger Mansion of Old Town
110 San Felipe Street Northwest
505-243-3639
bottger.com
$$
Victorian inn with period decorations.

Map labels:

COLORADO
Santa Fe
ARIZONA
Albuquerque
NEW MEXICO
MEXICO
TEXAS

COORS BLVD. NW
Los Poblanos Farm Shop
Los Poblanos Inn
Rio Grande
MONTANO RD. NW
RIO GRANDE BLVD. NW
FOURTH ST. NW
SECOND ST. NW
45
Albuquerque
Rainbow Ryders **9**
85
25
6 Paseo del Bosque trail
8 Mary & Tito's
CORONADO FWY.
Golden Crown Panaderia
10 Chatter Sunday
ABQ Trolley **7**
3
40
Routes Bicycle Tours & Rentals
MOUNTAIN RD. NW
Bottger Mansion of Old Town
Area of detail
4 Marble Brewery
Frontier Restaurant
11
5
Andaluz
CENTRAL AVE.
Man's Hat Shop
FIFTH ST. NW
Sophia's Place
The Grove
2
Kellys
Skip Maisel's
Parq Central/ Apothecary Lounge
SIXTH ST. SW
CENTRAL AVE.
1
KiMo Theater
National Hispanic Cultural Center
1 mile
GOLD AVE. SW
2 kilometers

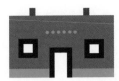

Santa Fe

The Plaza, the heart of old Santa Fe, New Mexico, hasn't changed much since the Spanish settled here 400 years ago, and it's possible to focus a trip entirely on the historic town center, where Native American handicrafts are for sale on every corner. But surrounding it is an increasingly cosmopolitan city. The rest of Santa Fe now offers contemporary art spaces, hot Asian restaurants, and a park designed by a pair of trailblazing architects. Santa Fe is worth loving not just for what it was, but for what it is.
— BY FRED A. BERNSTEIN

FRIDAY

1 *Public Space* 3 p.m.

For a beautifully curated introduction to Santa Fe, visit the **New Mexico History Museum** (113 Lincoln Avenue; 505-476-5200; nmhistorymuseum.org), which includes a gripping display about Los Alamos, where the Manhattan Project was conducted in secret during World War II. A large courtyard with ancient walls and shady trees separates the museum from the adobe Palace of the Governors (palaceofthegovernors. org), the Spanish seat of government in the early 1600s. Now a small museum of Colonial and Native American history, it is the oldest continuously occupied public building in the United States.

2 *White Walls and Wine* 7 p.m.

You'd have to be crazy to pay for a glass of white wine on Fridays. Canyon Road, which angles up from the center of town, has more than 100 galleries, and there are openings every Friday night. According to canyonroadarts.com, the largest category is contemporary representational (think brightly colored paintings of the desert). At **Ventana Fine Art** (400 Canyon Road; 800-746-8815; ventanafineart. com) you'll find works by dozens of artists from Santa Fe and beyond. The backyard sculpture garden is a great place to marvel at New Mexico's amazingly clear sky and savor its piñon-infused air before heading to dinner.

3 *Ahi Moment* 9 p.m.

Martín Rios is a hometown boy made good. Born in Mexico and raised in Santa Fe, he apprenticed at the Eldorado Hotel and the Inn of the

Anasazi — two local stalwarts — and made a brief appearance on *Iron Chef* before opening his own place, **Restaurant Martín** (526 Galisteo Street; 505-820-0919; restaurantmartin.com; $$). The main draw is the food — dishes like ahi tuna tartare and duck breast with smoked bacon polenta and Marcona almonds offer hints of the Southwest, with a dash of global aspiration. But the homey décor makes you want to stick around even after finishing the bittersweet chocolate truffle cake.

SATURDAY

4 *Spice Market* 10 a.m.

The **Santa Fe Farmers' Market** (1607 Paseo de Peralta; 505-983-4098; santafefarmersmarket.com) dates back a half-century and now has a permanent building in the revitalized Railyard district. Everything sold here, including dried chilies, yogurt, and grass-fed meats, is produced in northern New Mexico. The market is part of a bustling district that includes the new Railyard Park by the architect Frederic Schwartz and the landscape architect Ken Smith, both Manhattanites whose taste is anything but quaint. As you wander around, be on the lookout for the **Rail Runner** (nmrailrunner.com), a gleaming passenger train that pulls in from Albuquerque in late morning.

OPPOSITE The Sangre de Cristo Mountains form a backdrop for residences designed by Ricardo Legorreta.

BELOW Don Gaspar Avenue in downtown Santa Fe.

5 *Sustainable Salads* Noon

Santa Fe residents care — as you learned roaming the Farmers' Market — where their food comes from. No wonder **Vinaigrette** (709 Don Cubero Alley; 505-820-9205; vinaigretteonline.com; $$) is an enduring favorite. The brightly colored cafe has a menu based on organic greens grown in the nearby town of Nambé. Choose a base — Caesar, Cobb, and Greek are possibilities — then add diver scallops or hibiscus-cured duck confit. Add a glass of wine for a satisfying meal.

6 *O'Keeffe Country* 1 p.m.

Georgia O'Keeffe's famous landscapes of the New Mexico desert assure that she will always be identified with Santa Fe, and the **Georgia O'Keeffe Museum** (217 Johnson Street; 505-946-1000; okeeffemuseum.org), right off the plaza, holds more than 1,000 of her works. The **New Mexico Museum of Art** (107 West Palace Avenue; 505-476-5072; nmartmuseum.org), which emphasizes art produced in or related to New Mexico, is also worth a visit. Besides providing a cool afternoon of art appreciation, the museums have stores that offer an alternative to costly shopping and tourist kitsch.

7 *Riding the Spur* 4 p.m.

Thanks to Santa Fe's sometimes depressing sprawl, it's getting harder and harder to find wide-open spaces. But drive (or bike) to the corner of

Galisteo Street and West Rodeo Road, where there's a small parking lot. Then begin pedaling due south, in the direction of Lamy (about 12 miles away). What starts as an asphalt path morphs into a dirt bike trail that swerves around a 19th-century rail spur. There are some pretty steep hills, but they're short, and the momentum from a downhill is usually enough to handle the next uphill. (If only life were like that!) The scenery is always gorgeous, especially in late afternoon, when the sun is low in the sky. **Mellow**

ABOVE The Rail Runner train connects Santa Fe to Albuquerque.

BELOW The New Mexico Museum of Art, near the plaza.

Velo (132 East Marcy Street; 505-995-8356; mellowvelo.com) rents mountain bikes.

8 *Tapas With Strangers* 8 p.m.

La Boca (72 West Marcy Street; 505-982-3433; labocasantafe.com; $$) is one of downtown Santa Fe's most popular restaurants—thanks to its contemporary tapas, plus dishes like cannelloni filled with cod, garlic cream, and parsley pesto. You may find yourself sharing tips on what to order—and even forkfuls of delicious food—with strangers.

SUNDAY

9 *Free-Range Peacocks* 10 a.m.

For a big breakfast and an early start, drive south on Cerrillos Road about 10 miles past the Interstate, until you arrive at the **San Marcos Café** (3877 State Road 14; 505-471-9298; $$). Dozens of peacocks, turkeys, and hens roam the property (which also houses a feed store), providing an Old

MacDonald-like backdrop for crowd-pleasers like eggs San Marcos, a cheese omelet in a bath of guacamole, beans, and salsa. While you're at the Railyard, check out **SITE Santa Fe** (1606 Paseo De Peralta; 505-989-1199; sitesantafe.org), a huge, multi-leveled contemporary art space with provocative installations that change regularly.

10 *Kitsch to Contemporary* Noon

If you ever thought that item you found at a roadside stand was one of a kind, **Jackalope** (2820 Cerrillos Road; 505-471-8539; jackalope.com),

ABOVE Pancho Villa's death mask at the History Museum.

BELOW The Santa Fe Farmers' Market.

a sprawling indoor-outdoor flea market, will disabuse you of that notion. There are hundreds of every-thing—look for items like punched-copper switch plates and tote bags that depict Michelle Obama smiling on a swing.

11 *Bring Your Own Adobe* 1 p.m.

It's difficult to spend time in Santa Fe without thinking about buying a home (or second home) here. So check out **Zocalo** (Avenida Rincon;

505-986-0667; zocalosf.com), a striking development by the Mexican architect Ricardo Legorreta, who also designed the Visual Arts Center of the Santa Fe University of Art and Design (santafeuniversity. edu). He is known for crisp geometry and super-bright colors—a welcome sight in this city of browns and terra cottas. To appreciate Zocalo, you don't really have to be in the mood to buy. Consider this real estate voyeurism, combined with a crash course in contemporary architecture.

ABOVE The Railyard district draws crowds to its shops, restaurants, and farmers' market.

OPPOSITE Outside the San Marcos Café.

THE BASICS

Santa Fe has a tiny airport with limited service. Most visitors fly into Albuquerque and drive about an hour to Santa Fe.

Hotel St. Francis
210 Don Gaspar Avenue
505-983-5700
hotelstfrancis.com
$$
Billed as the oldest hotel in Santa Fe. Fully renovated in 2009.

The El Rey Court
1862 Cerrillos Road
505-982-1931
elreycourt.com
$$
Retro-chic 1930s-style motel with nicely furnished rooms.

Hilton Santa Fe Buffalo Thunder
20 Buffalo Thunder Trail
505-455-5555
hiltonbuffalothunder.com
$$
Part of a casino complex 15 minutes north of town.

COLORADO

Santa Fe

ARIZONA

Albuquerque

NEW MEXICO

Georgia O'Keeffe Museum **6**

New Mexico History Museum **1** — LINCOLN AVE.

8 La Boca

E. MARCY ST.

New Mexico Museum of Art

Palace of the Governors

7 Mellow Velo

E. PALACE AVE.

N. GUADALUPE ST.

W. ALAMEDA ST.

Hotel St. Francis

AGUA RFIA ST.

Santa Fe Farmers' Market **4**

DON GASPAR AVE. —

Santa Fe

Santa Fe River

Ventana Fine Art

CERRILLOS RD.

— GALISTEO ST.

CANYON RD.

2

3 Restaurant Martín

DELGADO ST. —

SITE Santa Fe

SANTA FE RAILYARD PARK

5 Vinaigrette

PASEO DE PERALTA

500 feet

1/4 kilometer

Hilton Santa Fe Buffalo Thunder

84

SANTA FE NATIONAL FOREST

285

599

Area of detail

Rio Grande

Zocalo **11**

Area of detail

Santa Fe River

El Rey Court

Santa Fe

NEW MEXICO

25

9 San Marcos Café

14

CERRILLOS RD.

Visual Arts Center/ Santa Fe University of Art and Design

10 Jackalope

25

5 miles

10 kilometers

1 mile

2 kilometers

Austin

The sprawling capital of Texas just keeps growing as new residents come from around the country, eager to join in the culture of a college town known for its liberal leanings and rich music scene. Along with all the new Austinites, dozens of new shops, restaurants, bars, and hotels have appeared, along with high-rise condos and high-tech flagships. Every March, the South by Southwest Festivals only add to the bustle. If you're a first-time visitor, take time for the city's must-sees, like Lady Bird Lake, the State Capitol, and the enormous bat colony that lives under the Ann W. Richards Congress Avenue Bridge. With all the excitement in Austin, you might also find yourself considering moving here for good. — BY EVAN RAIL

FRIDAY

1 *The New South* 4 p.m.

While South Congress Avenue, a.k.a. SoCo, has been a countercultural favorite for generations, new shops keep refreshing this colorful strip south of the Colorado River. This is the place to browse for cool jeans, rare and collectible vinyl records, women's indie-designer clothing, and quirky souvenirs. In the midst of it all is the sleek **South Congress Hotel** (1603 South Congress Avenue), whose lobby bar has become a destination in and of itself.

2 *French Fare* 8 p.m.

With a name like **Hopfields** (3110 Guadalupe Street; hopfieldsaustin.com; $$), it might sound like this place is all about the suds, but go inside and you'll find more. Locals love this central Austin gastropub for such French-inspired fare as steak frites with Dijon mustard, house-made pâtés, and the Pascal burger (with Camembert, cornichons, whole grain mustard, and caramelized onions), which many call the city's best.

3 *Fowl Play* 9:30 p.m.

Betting on its hometown's claim as the Live Music Capital of the World, **Geraldine's** (605 Davis Street; geraldinesaustin.com), the stunning fourth-floor bar and restaurant inside the Hotel Van Zandt, offers live concerts 365 days a year. Geraldine's (named after a neighborhood guinea fowl that moved on to the great farmyard in the sky after being hit

by a car in 2014) offers killer views of the downtown skyline as well as up-close views of musicians performing everything from modern indie-rock to traditional blues and country. If you want to extend the night, check out the numerous watering holes on nearby Rainey Street. One of many popular Austin destinations now operating inside Rainey's historic bungalows is **Javelina** (69 Rainey Street; javelinabar.com), a friendly roadhouse with communal tables and outdoor seats that face the evening parade.

SATURDAY

4 *Java Upgrade* 10 a.m.

Austin's burgeoning barista scene offers plenty of options for a morning pick-me-up, from old favorites like the original location of **Caffé Medici** (caffeemedici.com) on West Lynn Street to newer spots like **Radio** (4204 Manchaca Road; radiocoffeeandbeer.com). This is a good morning for exploring shops and restaurants in the South Lamar neighborhood, so start at **Picnik** (1700 South Lamar Boulevard; picnikaustin.com), a coffee trailer that serves high-grade java, including

OPPOSITE The Texas Capitol and South Congress Avenue.

BELOW In Austin, a guitar is always the right accessory.

upgraded options with grass-fed butter and medium-chain triglyceride oil. The pastry case includes Paleo-inspired treats — that morning poppy seed muffin might be delicious, and it's also gluten-free, grain-free, and free of refined sugar.

5 *Guitars to Go* 11 a.m.

Take inspiration from local musical talent and shop for instruments as souvenirs. From South Lamar, start out at **South Austin Music** (1402 South Lamar Boulevard; southaustinmusic.com), a favorite for electric guitars and effects. Then head north across the river to **Austin Vintage Guitars** (4306 Red River Street; austinvintageguitars.com), which offers

collectible models from brands like Fender, Gibson, Rickenbacker, and Danelectro, as well as guitar picks, slides, and T-shirts in a spacious shop.

6 *New 'Cue* Noon

In the old days, lovers of great barbecue knew to leave Austin for smoke pits in nearby towns like Lockhart and Driftwood. Then came East Austin's Franklin Barbecue, frequently called the best in the country, but often too crammed to get into. You can get a more reliable snack at **Micklethwait Craft Meats** (1309 Rosewood Avenue; 512-791-5961; craftmeatsaustin.com; $$), which serves fall-apart smoked brisket, massive beef ribs, and flavorful specialty sausages. The backyard party vibe is another draw. Afterward, clear the smoke from your palate with a tasting tour at **Blue Owl** (2400 East Cesar Chavez Street No. 300; blueowlbrewing.com), a brewery specializing in sour beers and ales.

7 *Art Hungry* 3 p.m.

Artists' studios are dotted around the city. Art Austin (artaustin.org) maintains an online gallery guide that can lead you to some of the new local work. For a broader view, check out the Jones Center down-

ABOVE There's plenty to choose from at South Austin Music.

LEFT A clothing shop on South Congress, a.k.a. SoCo.

town (700 Congress Avenue), one of two locations of the **Contemporary Austin** (thecontemporaryaustin. org). The other, which has more limited opening hours, is the beautiful villa and sculpture park **Laguna Gloria** (3809 West 35th Street).

8 *My Beautiful Laundromat* 7 p.m.

 Launderette (2115 Holly Street; launderetteaustin. com; $$) extends contemporary Mediterranean cuisine to include influences from regions like North Africa and the Levant, as well as American cuisine. The result is a menu that might range from beet hummus to potato gnocchi to a burger with challah. Launderette really is in a former laundromat, but the quality of the food quickly makes that irrelevant.

9 *Craft Cocktails* 10 p.m.

 Check out the expanding bar scene in downtown's Warehouse District, surrounding Republic Square, with a sampling of craft cocktails at the new **Roosevelt**

Room (307 West 5th Street; therooseveltroomatx. com), which lists its mixed drinks by era of origin. (The Manhattan originated in the 1860s, the menu informs you, and the Freddy Fudpucker is from 1970s Los Angeles). The house cocktails tend toward the exotic. Intimate booths and videos projected on the wall give an underground character to the long, dark space. To see how this place compares with an older favorite, move on to **Péché** (208 West 4th Street; pecheaustin.com), just two blocks away, where the focus is on high-grade absinthes.

ABOVE At Javelina, have a drink in a repurposed bungalow.

BELOW Street art mingles with cool shops in SoCo.

SUNDAY

10 *Taco BBQ* 11 a.m.

There's no better morning-after restorative than **Valentina's** (11500 Manchaca Road; valentinastexmexbbq.com; $), which combines classic Texas barbecue with authentic Mexican fare. Fans followed this food trailer's move from downtown to a parking lot in South Austin, lining up for potato-egg-and-cheese breakfast tacos

ABOVE Micklethwait Craft Meats thrives on a well-deserved reputation for succulent barbecue.

OPPOSITE Cycling in bluebonnet season.

with house-made chorizo as well as lunch tacos like the smoked-brisket taco, topped with guacamole and a mild tomato-serrano salsa, and the pulled "pollo" chicken taco, dressed with spicy tomatillo-habanero sauce.

11 *Wildflower Country* 1 p.m.

Texas is proud of the masses of wildflowers, and you can find out why at the **Lady Bird Johnson Wildflower Preserve** (4801 La Crosse Avenue; wildflower.org), a University of Texas research center that is also a public botanical garden and spa. If you're curious about Lady Bird and her husband, check out the **Lyndon Baines Johnson Library and Museum** (2313 Red River Street; lbjlibrary.org). The permanent exhibition includes a multimedia-enhanced parallel journey through President Johnson's life, including a display on his sudden elevation to the presidency after the assassination of John F. Kennedy and an animatronic version of Johnson telling jokes.

THE BASICS

To get around town, use a rental car or a service like Uber or Lyft.

South Congress Hotel
1603 South Congress Avenue
southcongresshotel.com
$$$
Located on one of the city's coolest shopping strips.

Hotel Van Zandt
605 Davis Street
hotelvanzandt.com
$$$
Just off the Rainey night-life scene, with its own live-music venue.

The Driskill
604 Brazos Street
driskillhotel.com
$$$
The grande dame of Austin hotels.

5 miles
10 kilometers

Austin
Laguna Gloria

Lady Bird Johnson
Wildflower Preserve — Area of detail

11

Driftwood TEXAS

N.M. OKLA.
TEXAS Dallas
Austin Houston
San Antonio
MEXICO Gulf of Mexico

HYDE PARK W. 45TH ST.
1
Hopfields **2** Austin Vintage Guitars
111

Lyndon Baines Johnson
Library and Museum

EAST AUSTIN

Caffé Medici Jones Center/ The Contemporary Austin
7

Roosevelt Room **9** The Driskill Micklethwait Craft Meats
6

Colorado R.— Péché Franklin Barbecue

Geraldine's/ Hotel Van Zandt **3** Javelina Blue Owl

South Austin Music **8**
5

Picnik **4** Launderette

BARTON HILLS

343

— SOUTH LAMAR BLVD.

SOUTH LAMAR

Valentina's Radio
10

290

S. FIRST ST.

S. CONGRESS AVE.

35

South Congress Hotel
1

Austin
TEXAS

1 mile
2 kilometers

Dallas

Dallas may not be a world-class city, but it's pulling out all the stops to get there. Rich with oil money, it has pumped millions of dollars into civic projects, including the AT&T Performing Arts Center, a recent addition to the 68-acre Arts District. Meanwhile, glamorous subterranean bars and edgy Asian restaurants are giving the city a cosmopolitan aura. But when it comes to entertainment, its No. 1 attraction is still the Cowboys and their $1.2 billion football stadium featuring one of the largest retractable roofs and one of the largest high-definition televisions in the world.
— BY LUISITA LOPEZ TORREGROSA

FRIDAY

1 *Architecture Park* 3 p.m.

See what Dallas is happily showing off these days. Go on a walking tour of the **Dallas Arts District** (thedallasartsdistrict.org), a 19-block area straddling downtown office skyscrapers and uptown luxury hotels. A prime attraction of the district is the **AT&T Performing Arts Center** (2403 Flora Street; 214-954-9925; attpac.org), a four-venue complex for music, opera, theater, and dance in a parklike setting. A drum-shaped opera house was designed by Norman Foster and a cube-shaped theater is by Rem Koolhaas. To take it all in, find a bench at the **Nasher Sculpture Center** (2001 Flora Street; 214-242-5100; nashersculpturecenter.org), a museum designed by Renzo Piano with a lush garden that features works from a collection including Rodin, Henry Moore, and George Segal.

2 *Trendsetter Cocktails* 7:30 p.m.

Size up the city's trendsetters and assorted poseurs in their alligator boots and butter-soft tailored jackets at the **Rattlesnake Bar**, a plush lounge with mahogany-paneled walls and chocolate-brown leather sofas at the **Ritz-Carlton,**

Dallas (2121 McKinney Avenue; 214-922-4848; ritzcarlton.com/dallas). Order the Dean's Margarita with organic agave nectar, nibble on jalapeño elk corndogs, and watch heads turn whenever a posse of lanky blondes in skinny jeans and designer heels sidles up to the bar.

3 *Southwest Supreme* 8 p.m.

Not so long ago, Dallas was a culinary wasteland, save for its famous barbecue. But in recent years, celebrity chefs like Nobu Matsuhisa, Tom Colicchio, and Charlie Palmer have planted their flags here, joining a fresh crop of hometown talent. At the top is **Fearing's** (2121 McKinney Avenue; 214-922-4848; fearingsrestaurant.com; $$$$), a casual but chic restaurant in the Ritz-Carlton that serves imaginative Southwest-rooted cuisine. Opened in 2007, Fearing's gained national acclaim at the time: Zagat named it No. 1 in domestic hotel dining, and Frank Bruni, then the restaurant critic for *The New York Times*, called it one of the country's top 10 new restaurants outside New York. Expect dishes like lobster coconut bisque and wood-grilled Australian lamb chops on pecorino polenta.

4 *Party High* 10:30 p.m.

There are still men's clubs, honky-tonks, and jukebox joints in Dallas, but the city's night life has gotten decidedly sleeker and flashier, with

OPPOSITE Vertigo can be a concern for swimmers at the Joule Hotel. Cantilevered out from the building, the rooftop pool juts out 10 stories above the sidewalk.

RIGHT Size up the city's trendsetters and assorted poseurs in their alligator boots at the Rattlesnake Bar, a plush watering hole at the Ritz-Carlton.

TWO x TWO x TEN

Celebrating Ten Years of Two by Two for AIDS and Art
presented by Deloitte LLP

velvet-roped discos and bottle-service lounges. If you want a stellar view of the stars and the city's bright lights, go to the rooftop bar of the **Joule** hotel (1530 Main Street; 214-748-1300; thejouledallas.com). It features bedlike sofas and cocoonlike chairs arrayed along a slender, cantilevered swimming pool that juts out 10 stories above the sidewalk. Or, for an even better view, go to **FiveSixty**, Wolfgang

ABOVE A contemplative viewer takes in a sculpture at the Dallas Museum of Art. The city's rich cultural life reveals itself in museums and performing arts.

BELOW Forty Five Ten, the epitome of chic Dallas boutiques. The prices are shocking, but it's worth a visit.

Puck's Asian-style restaurant in the glowing ball atop the 560-foot-high **Reunion Tower** (300 Reunion Boulevard; 214-571-5784; wolfgangpuck.com). The rotating bar, which serves a dozen kinds of sake, offers magnificent views of a skyline edged in colorful lights and the suburban sprawl beyond.

SATURDAY

5 *Morning Glory* 10 a.m.

Need a breath of fresh air after a late night out? Head to the **Katy Trail** (entrance at Knox Street at Abbott Avenue; 214-303-1180; katytraildallas.org), a 3.5-mile greenway that winds through the city's wooded parks and urban neighborhoods. Built along old railroad tracks, the trail is a favorite of young and old, bikers and runners, stroller-pushing parents and dog walkers.

6 *Slower Food* Noon

Chicken-fried everything may be a staple in Texas, but in Dallas organic salads and other light fare are just as popular. A trendy spot is **Rise No. 1** (5360 West Lovers Lane; 214-366-9900; risesouffle.com; $$), a charming bistro with a grass-green facade that serves up wonderful soufflés — a slow-paced antidote to Dallas's manic drive-and-shop lifestyle. Try the truffle-infused mushroom soufflé with a glass of dry white.

7 *Retail Overload* 2 p.m.

Shopping is a sport here, and there are more stores than just Neiman Marcus. For slow-paced window shopping, stroll around **Inwood Village** (West Lovers Lane and Inwood Road; inwoodvillage.com), a landmark 1949 shopping center with an eclectic range of signature stores. Retail highlights include **Rich Hippie** (5350 West Lovers Lane, No. 127; 214-358-1968; richhippie.com) for retro and avant-garde clothing. Two miles away lies another landmark plaza, this one from 1931: **Highland Park Village** (hpvillage.com). One of its chic boutiques is **Forty Five Ten** (No. 60; 214-252-0150; fortyfiveten.com; also downtown at 1615 Main Street), where there's high style for both men and women. The prices are shocking but hey, this is Dallas.

8 *Mex-Mex* 8 p.m.

One of the most popular Dallas spots for original Mexican fare is **La Duni Latin Cafe** (4620 McKinney Avenue; 214-520-7300; laduni.com; $$), which offers terrific dishes like tacos de picanha (beef loin strips on tortillas). For Tex-Mex in a party atmosphere, with mariachi bands, hefty margaritas, and house-made tortillas, travel to East Dallas for **Mexico Lindo** (7515 East Grand Avenue; 214-319-9776; mexicolindodallas.com; $$).

9 *Night Moves* 10 p.m.

There are plenty of ways to close out the evening in Dallas. You could mingle with a well-dressed crowd and enjoy a classic cocktail and some jazz or sultry vocalizing at the urbane **Library Bar** in the Landmark Restaurant of the Warwick Melrose Hotel (3015 Oak Lawn Avenue; 214-224-3152; landmarkrestodallas.com). For indie bands, try **Dada Dallas** (2720 Elm Street; dadadallas.com), in

BELOW AT&T Stadium, home of the Dallas Cowboys and the focus of the city's energy on home-game Sundays.

the Deep Ellum neighborhood. Or stay up late at **J.R.'s Bar & Grill** (3923 Cedar Springs Road; 214-528-1004; jrsdallas.com), a cavernous gay club

ABOVE The Morton H. Meyerson Symphony Center in the 19-block Arts District.

OPPOSITE Fearing's, a chic, casual restaurant with imaginative Southwest-rooted cuisine. Celebrity chefs have planted their flags in Dallas, joining a fresh crop of hometown talent.

with a scuffed dance floor, where nothing gets going before midnight.

SUNDAY

10 *Sports Madness* 11:30 a.m.

If it's Sunday in Dallas and you can't get to the Cowboys' AT&T Stadium, do as the locals do and hit a sports bar. There are dozens in town, if not hundreds, but a favorite is **Christie's** (2811 McKinney Avenue; 214-954-1511; christiessportsbar.com). It has a patio, a pool table, and, yes, 62 HDTVs and three 120-inch projection screens that show nothing but sports, day and night. When the Cowboys play, the joint is bedlam.

THE BASICS

Fly into busy Dallas-Fort Worth Regional Airport. Rent a car for exploring.

Ritz-Carlton, Dallas
2121 McKinney Avenue
214-922-0200
ritzcarlton.com/dallas
$$$$
Reliable luxury, a fine restaurant, and a spa.

The Joule
1530 Main Street
214-748-1300
thejouledallas.com
$$$$
Trendy spot with a chic basement cocktail bar and a rooftop bar with a pool.

The Belmont
901 Fort Worth Avenue
214-393-2300
belmontdallas.com
$$
A moderate-priced alternative restored to bring back 1940s charm while providing modern amenities.

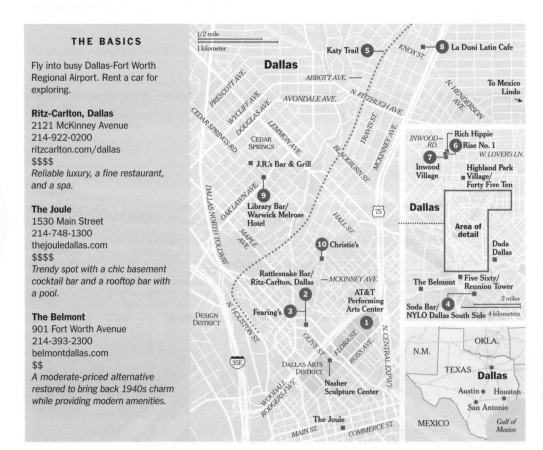

Fort Worth

How much art can you look at in one weekend? Of all American cities that might pose this dilemma, Fort Worth, Texas, traditionally a cow town overshadowed by neighboring Dallas, might be the least expected. But with oil-wealthy patrons eager to build its cultural endowment with sought-after artworks and interesting contemporary architecture to hold them, Fort Worth has become a place to go for art immersion. If you fear museum fatigue, take heart. The city's public art galleries don't overwhelm; they're on a uniformly intimate scale. And there's enough cowboy spirit left in town to give you a break from high culture whenever you want to take one. — BY RICHARD B. WOODWARD

FRIDAY

1 *Sundance* 5 p.m.

Fort Worth is dominated by a few families, none mightier than the billionaire Bass clan, famous for giving generously to George W. Bush's campaigns and for revitalizing the north end of the city. See some of their handiwork in **Sundance Square** (sundancesquare. com). Starting with two square blocks they bought in 1978, it has expanded to more than 35 square blocks dominated by a pair of Brutalist skyscrapers designed by Paul Rudolph in the 1970s and now holding the headquarters of the Bass businesses. David Schwarz, the family's favorite architect, has contributed buildings in the Texas Deco style (blending Art Deco with state symbols like the star), including Bass Performance Hall, a home to opera, symphony, touring Broadway shows, and the quadrennial piano competition begun by and named after a local hero, Van Cliburn.

2 *Romance of the West* 6 p.m.

Take your time looking at the 38 oil paintings by Frederic Remington and Charles Russell at the **Sid Richardson Museum** in Sundance Square (309 Main Street; 817-332-6554; sidrichardsonmuseum. org). The museum displays only a tiny sample of the romantic taste of Sid Richardson, a millionaire

oilman and Bass relative who collected work on Indian and cowboy themes. If you'd like a different take on Western tradition, take a 10-minute drive to the **National Cowgirl Museum and Hall of Fame** (1720 Gendy Street; 817-336-4475; cowgirl.net), which celebrates Western women, from ranchers to celebrity pop stars.

3 *Saloon Chef* 7 p.m.

Chef Tim Love's **Lonesome Dove Western Bistro** (2406 North Main Street; 817-740-8810; lonesomedovebistro.com; $$$), near Fort Worth's traditional economic heart, the Stockyards, is a very modern pairing of *Iron Chef* cooking and cowboy chic. The décor is reminiscent of an Old West saloon, with a long bar and a tin ceiling, and the staff may be wearing cowboy hats. It's hard to say what the cattle drivers who used to come through Fort Worth would make of the cuisine, including dishes like beef tenderloin stuffed with garlic and accompanied by plaid hash and a Syrah demi-glace.

SATURDAY

4 *Breakfast for All* 9 a.m.

Don't be dismayed if there's a long line at the **Paris Coffee Shop** (704 West Magnolia Avenue; 817-335-2041; pariscoffeeshop.net; $). It seats more than 100, so tables turn over quickly. A Fort Worth institution since the Depression era, it seems to cater to everyone in town. Who could resist a place that offers green tea as well as cheese grits and has ads on the menu for everything from music lessons to bail bondsmen?

OPPOSITE *High Desert Princess*, by Mehl Lawson, outside the National Cowgirl Museum and Hall of Fame.

RIGHT Breakfast at the Paris Coffee Shop.

5 *Art of America* 10 a.m.

This is your day for serious art appreciation in the **Cultural District**, about five miles west of Sundance. Start at the **Amon Carter Museum of American Art** (3501 Camp Bowie Boulevard; 817-738-1933; cartermuseum.org). Carter, who made his fortune in newspapers and radio, was a Fort Worth booster who hated Dallas so much he reportedly carried his lunch when forced to visit, to keep from spending money there. His bequest financed what is now one of the leading collections of American art in the country, especially strong in Western paintings, 19th-century photographs, and Remington sculptures. The museum's original 1961 building by Philip Johnson was expanded in the late '90s.

6 *Art and Water* Noon

The **Modern Art Museum of Fort Worth** (3200 Darnell Street; 817-738-9215; themodern.org) has been an island of tranquility since it opened a new building in 2002. The architect, Tadao Ando, oriented the building around a shallow pool so that several of the wings extend outward and seem to float on the water. Have brunch at its **Café Modern** (817-840-2157; themodern.org/cafe; $$), which attempts to serve dishes worthy of the setting—consider the Moroccan chicken salad or mushroom goat cheese crepes. Then explore the galleries, arrayed with a select group of postwar and contemporary works—usual suspects like Jackson Pollock and Dan Flavin, as well as rarities in American museums, like the German Minimalist sculptor Ulrich Rückriem. Whether in the sunlit bays beside the water, where you may find a lead floor piece by Carl Andre, or in a cul-de-sac where a wooden ladder-like sculpture by Martin Puryear reaches between floors, the building is still very much the star.

7 *Art and Light* 3 p.m.

The **Kimbell Art Museum** (3333 Camp Bowie Boulevard; 817-332-8451; kimbellart.org) provides an unrivaled museum experience combining first-rate architecture and first-rate art. From the street, the 1972 building, designed by Louis I. Kahn, offers a plain travertine exterior that will not prepare you for the

soaring harmonies inside. To step into the lobby is to enter a Romanesque church of a museum. Long slits and diffusing louvers in the barrel-vaulted ceiling allow the light to both cut spaces dramatically and softly spill over them. The collections, from all periods and places, are noteworthy for both aesthetic quality and historical depth. A pre-Angkor Cambodian statue is less a representative object than a stunningly beautiful one. European paintings — with master-pieces by Bellini, Mantegna, Caravaggio, Velázquez, de la Tour, Goya, Cézanne — are mostly presented without glass.

8 *Steak and Wine* 7 p.m.

You're not finished yet with cowboy-inspired cooking. **Reata** (310 Houston Street; 817-336-1009; reata.net; $$$) is Texas big, spread over several floors of an old building in the heart of Sundance Square. The fourth-floor bar has a panoramic skyline view. Reata's entrees run to steaks and chops, its wine list is extensive, and its desserts are tempting and calorie-laden.

9 *Hang With the Herd* 9 p.m.

Billy Bob's Texas (2520 Rodeo Plaza; 817-624-7117; billybobstexas.com), housed in a former cattle barn and touted as the world's largest honky-tonk, should be visited at least once, and perhaps only once. Walk around and select your entertainment option: play pool or the 25-cent slot machines, watch live

bull riding in a ring or sports on TV, eat barbecue or popcorn, shop for cowboy hats, try your luck at outmoded carnival games, drink at any of 32 bars, or dance and listen to country music on the two musical stages. A few hours at Billy Bob's may not measure up to an afternoon viewing Fort Worth's art collections. But as you merge with the herd (capacity is more

OPPOSITE ABOVE AND ABOVE The Modern Art Museum and the Kimbell Art Museum are islands of tranquility that invite contemplation of both the architecture and the artworks.

OPPOSITE BELOW AND BELOW Pool playing and bull riding at Billy Bob's, an outsize honky-tonk in a former cattle barn. It can entertain 6,000 Texans at a time.

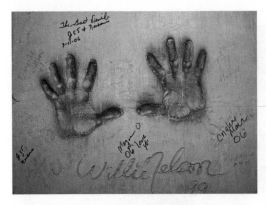

than 6,000), sipping bourbon and watching the gliding two-steppers on the dance floor, it feels like a much more authentic and less imported experience —much more like Texas.

SUNDAY

10 *Texans Also Garden* 11 a.m.
Spend some peaceful hours at the **Fort Worth Botanic Garden** (3220 Botanic Garden Boulevard;

817-392-5510; fwbg.org), home to more than 2,500 species of native and exotic plants that flourish in its 23 specialty gardens. A favorite, the Japanese Garden, is a treat for the senses with koi-filled pools, stonework, and waterfalls. If it's springtime, expect flowering trees and migrating birds—perhaps, if you're lucky, a tree full of cedar waxwings on their way north.

ABOVE Country musicians' handprints on the walls at Billy Bob's are Fort Worth's answer to movie stars' footprints in concrete in Hollywood. These were made by Willie Nelson.

OPPOSITE Texas exuberance on the dance floor.

THE BASICS

Fly into Dallas/Fort Worth International Airport or drive from Dallas. Get around by car.

Renaissance Worthington
200 Main Street
817-870-1000
marriott.com
$$$
In Sundance Square, with 474 rooms and 30 suites at a variety of prices.

The Ashton
610 Main Street
817-332-0100
theashtonhotel.com
$$
Attractive boutique hotel with 39 rooms.

Omni Fort Worth
1300 Houston Street
817-535-6664
omnihotels.com
$$$
Skyline views and a rooftop garden.

Map labels:
OKLA.
N.M. ARK.
Fort Worth
Dallas LA.
TEXAS
San Antonio
MEXICO
Houston
Gulf of Mexico

9 Billy Bob's Texas
3 Lonesome Dove Western Bistro
35W
N. MAIN ST.
Sundance Square 1
E. FIRST ST.
Renaissance Worthington
2 Sid Richardson Museum
W. THIRD ST.
8 Reata
The Ashton
MAIN ST.
HOUSTON ST.
W. NORTHSIDE DR.
West Fork Trinity River
199
WHITE SETTLEMENT RD.
Kimbell Art Museum
7
Fort Worth
Area of detail
Amon Carter Museum of American Art
W. SEVENTH ST.
HOUSTON ST.
Modern Art Museum of Fort Worth/ Café Modern
6
Omni Fort Worth
CAMP BOWIE BLVD.
GENDY ST.
5 Cultural District
National Cowgirl Museum and Hall of Fame
10 Fort Worth Botanic Garden
30
PENNSYLVANIA AVE.
287
Paris Coffee Shop
4
Clear Fork Trinity River
W. ROSEDALE ST.
1/2 mile
1 kilometer
W. MAGNOLIA AVE.

Houston

Houston has had to prove its resilience after the devastating Hurricane Harvey floods of 2017, and although the job of recovery was too massive to be completed quickly, for the most part the city has met the challenge and is ready for visitors. It may help that it is the fourth-largest city in the United States — too big and too important to languish — and the youngest, with more millennials than boomers. It is also among the most ethnically and culturally diverse, which explains the amazing gastronomic mix that a tourist can find there — from taco stands, chicken and waffle joints, and all manner of barbecue to Greek, Persian, and Vietnamese cuisine. Enriched by immigration and philanthropy, the city's ever-growing museums strike a balance between an expansive global outlook and strong local support. And despite its forest of skyscrapers, Houston is surprisingly green, with hundreds of parks. — BY ANDREW FERREN

FRIDAY

1 *Look Up* 5 p.m.

The artist James Turrell's *Sky Space* (skyspace. rice.edu) on the campus of Rice University is the perfect place to contemplate the heavens, framed with precision by a wafer-thin roof with a large aperture in the middle. Visitors sit in a pavilion below, looking up at the opening and marveling at Turrell's deft manipulation of light as day turns to night in a Technicolor extravaganza that lasts roughly 45 minutes to an hour. *Sky Space* is open from 5:30 a.m. (for the sunrise light sequence) until 10 p.m. every day except Tuesdays. Reservations are free and typically required for the sunset light sequence only.

2 *Greek Revival* 7 p.m.

Helen Greek Food and Wine (2429 Rice Boulevard; helengreek.com; $$-$$$) in Rice Village, takes Greek food local with a menu that makes use of regional produce. Huge Gulf shrimp "saganaki" are grilled and bathed in a peppery, fennel-spiked, fresh tomato sauce with feta and halloumi cheeses. Greek diner standards like the gyro are elevated with oven-

roasted Texas pork, and delicate spanakopita are bursting with freshly sautéed spinach. Desserts are revelatory, from a delicate feta mousse with olive oil and thyme shortbread to the decadent Texas pecan baklava sundae. The all-Greek wine list will open your eyes and your palate (not to mention your wallet) to the variety and quality of Greek tipples.

3 *Choose Your Poison* 11 p.m.

Cactus or grapes? Step into one of Houston's growing array of one-booze-only bars. Located downtown and serving more than 40 types of agave-based spirits, the **Pastry War** (310 Main Street; thepastrywar. com) is all about the wonders of tequila and mezcal, starting with the house margarita. Around the corner is **La Carafe** (813 Congress Avenue; facebook.com/ La-Carafe-107567809270676), a timeworn (it's among the city's oldest bars), wine-only joint that remains a perennial favorite.

SATURDAY

4 *Breakfast, Por Favor* 9 a.m.

Come with a newspaper and be prepared to stand in line at **Laredo Taqueria** (915 Snover Street; laredotaqueria.com; $), where the breakfast tacos run from egg and potato to chicharrón (pork skin). Start to burn some of those calories with a stroll to Buffalo Bayou Park, which lost trees and landscaping to the floods but was quickly a site of restoration work to recover its running paths, bike trails, and playgrounds. The bayou was the heart of the city when it was founded in 1836.

OPPOSITE James Turrell's *Sky Space* at Rice University.

RIGHT Surveying the goodies at Common Bond bakery.

5 *A Fine Display* 10:30 a.m.

With a vast art collection and roster of special exhibitions that vividly reflect the city's cultural mix and civic aspirations, the **Museum of Fine Arts Houston** (1001 Bissonnet; mfah.org) mixes Latin American, Islamic, Indian, and Texan art with European and American works from many eras. There's also an Isamu Noguchi-designed sculpture garden and one of the most cleverly curated museum shops in America. And since some Houstonians don't donate just their art but their homes as well, swing by one of the city's upscale enclaves, River Oaks, to visit the museum's collections of decorative arts in two gorgeous house museums — **Rienzi** (1406 Kirby Drive) and **Bayou Bend** (6003 Memorial Drive).

6 *Get Crabby* 2 p.m.

You might not get past the appetizers at **Goode Co. Seafood** (2621 Westpark Drive; goodecompany. com; $$), which feels like a laid-back beachtown diner with a train car stuck on the front of it. One starter was the Campechana, zingy tomato salsa with chunks of avocado and shrimp. Follow it up with a fried flounder po' boy and a slice of margarita Key lime pie.

7 *Style Mile* 4 p.m.

Houston is famously scattershot, with no single center of style gravity but rather little constellations of like-minded shops, cafes, and restaurants. One place for sartorial inspiration is the stretch of Westheimer Road between West Avenue and River Oaks. **Tootsies** (No. 2601; tootsies.com) is a 35,000-foot "boutique" with major designer collections, and down the street are smaller and edgier shops specializing in niche brands and personalized styling. Men can work the

other side of the street to find **Billy Reid** (No. 2702; billyreid.com) or drive a few blocks west to **Sid Mashburn** (2515 River Oaks Boulevard; sidmashburn. com) in an upscale strip mall — that's not a pejorative term in Houston.

8 *State of Grace* 8:30 p.m.

With Houston's smart set table-hopping and air-kissing away, you'd never know that the dining room at **State of Grace** (3258 Westheimer Road; stateofgracetx.com; $$$) was formerly a dry cleaner and nail salon. There's a clubby dining room, a raw bar ringed by tables for two, and a long bar for drinking or dining. The menu conveys Houston's new eclecticism with selections like lobster hush puppies, Wagyu beef carpaccio, pork schnitzel, and roast duck carnitas. Linger after dinner for inventive cocktails.

SUNDAY

9 *Uncommon Baked Goods* 10 a.m.

There's a Sunday morning rush hour around **Common Bond** (1706 Westheimer Road; wearecommonbond.com; $-$$), a top-shelf bakery where breakfast options range from a bialy with cream cheese and caramelized onions to adventurous egg dishes. For dessert grab some house-made macarons. Then step into **Space Montrose** (space-montrose.myshopify.com) next door for a wide array of local and international handicrafts like

ABOVE The Isamu Noguchi-designed sculpture garden, an inviting outdoor space at the Museum of Fine Arts Houston.

OPPOSITE Have a snack in a bungalow at Bistro Menil.

Texas-made ceramic coasters or a Texas-shaped Christmas ornament made from the state's license plates. If slightly older crafts are your thing, seek out the cluster of quirky antiques shops along Westheimer near Dunlavy.

10 *Arty Lunch* 1:30 p.m.

The **Menil art campus** (1533 Sul Ross Street; menil.org) is home to the renowned Menil Collection, Rothko Chapel, Cy Twombly Gallery, and Dan Flavin Installation at Richmond Hall. To fortify yourself

before setting out to conquer all that art, find **Bistro Menil** (1513 West Alabama Street; bistromenil.com; $$). Set in a quaint little bungalow facing Renzo Piano's masterful building for the Menil Collection, it has a menu strong on savory nibbles like eggplant "fries" with anchovy aioli or chicken and artichoke crepes.

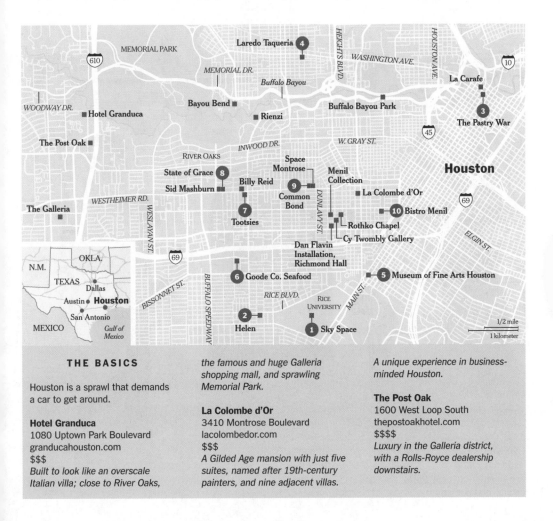

THE BASICS

Houston is a sprawl that demands a car to get around.

Hotel Granduca
1080 Uptown Park Boulevard
granducahouston.com
$$$
Built to look like an overscale Italian villa; close to River Oaks,

the famous and huge Galleria shopping mall, and sprawling Memorial Park.

La Colombe d'Or
3410 Montrose Boulevard
lacolombedor.com
$$$
A Gilded Age mansion with just five suites, named after 19th-century painters, and nine adjacent villas.

A unique experience in business-minded Houston.

The Post Oak
1600 West Loop South
thepostoakhotel.com
$$$$
Luxury in the Galleria district, with a Rolls-Royce dealership downstairs.

San Antonio

San Antonio, the United States' seventh-largest city, features a threesome of popular attractions: the River Walk (a meandering canal lined with restaurants and bars), Market Square (said to be the largest Mexican-style market outside of Mexico), and the Alamo (no explanation necessary). Beyond those obvious tourist stops, this old city also offers Latino art, 19th-century-style shopping, salsa dancing, and plenty of that famous Texas hospitality.

— BY DAN SALTZSTEIN

FRIDAY

1 *Shopping as It Was* 3 p.m.

La Villita Historic Arts Village (418 Villita Street; lavillitasanantonio.com), just off the River Walk, still feels like the little village it once was but is now crammed with artisanal shops, many of which are housed in lovely mid-19th-century buildings. At **Villita Stained Glass** (Building 1; 210-223-4480; sparkleonsa.com), opened in 1982, you will find a range of stained-glass panels, vases, boxes and lamps; glass jewelry; kaleidoscopes; and mosaic mirrors and frames, many made by local artists. The owner is often found creating lampwork beads in the back of the shop. The **Copper Gallery** (Building No. 11; 210-271-3856) sells everything copper; a gorgeous set of hammered ewers was one fine example.

2 *Dinner at Supper* 5:30 p.m.

The 1883 Pearl Brewery stopped making beer in 2001, the same year developers drew up a mixed-use plan for a 22-acre riverside site known as Pearl. The district now hosts a rich cache of good restaurants and the retro-chic Hotel Emma. For dinner, head to the hotel and cross the steampunk-inspired lobby to **Supper** (136 East Grayson; 210-448-8351; supperatemma.com; $$$). Its chef, John Brand, champions not just farm-to-table fare, but root-to-stem cooking. Sit near the open kitchen to watch

the rotisserie char vegetables while you dine. One evening's menu listed toasted cauliflower and sun-choke soup and a smoked quail dish with pickled corn relish.

3 *Salsa in Southtown* 9 p.m.

South Alamo Street, a short but colorful jumble of galleries, shops, and restaurants, is the main strip of the Southtown neighborhood, a diverse and welcoming pocket that's cherished by many locals. Let the beat and the warm bodies pull you into **Rosario's Café y Cantina** (910 South Alamo Street; 210-223-1806; rosariossa.com), a festive Mexican restaurant that pulsates with live salsa music and energetic dancing on Friday nights, especially on each month's First Friday, when the neighborhood sponsors a street fair of art and music. In a town famous for its margaritas, Rosario's are among the tastiest.

SATURDAY

4 *Brewery Without Beer* 10 a.m.

Start your Saturday by heading back to the Pearl district, where, in addition to its restaurants and a branch of the Culinary Institute of America, there are a growing number of shops, including the **Tiny Finch** (302 Pearl Parkway; 210-253-9570; thetinyfinch.com), which sells textiles, jewelry, arty accessories, and home goods. A few doors up the street is the **Twig Book Shop** (306 Pearl Parkway; 210-826-6411; thetwig.com), an airy spot that offers a nice variety of bestsellers and Texas-themed

OPPOSITE Plan your visit to the Alamo, a potent symbol not only of San Antonio but of all Texas, for early morning, before the day's onslaught of eager tourist crowds.

RIGHT San Antonio, with its enduring cross-border influences, is a natural home of Mexican and Southwestern cuisine.

publications. There is also a Saturday-morning farmers' market, **Pearl Weekend Market** (atpearl. com/farmers-market) with local vendors selling cheeses, salsa, herbs, nuts, baked goods, and all kinds of produce. The Sunday market emphasizes artisanal and prepared foods. Stroll and savor the aromas.

5 *Burgers With Conscience* Noon

Don't oversample at the market, because one of the more unusual dining places in town is a few minutes away in the Five Points neighborhood. **The Cove** (606 West Cypress Street; 210-227-2683; thecove.us; $) is a restaurant, car wash, coin laundry, and music spot. Its sloppy and satisfying Texas Burger (with refried beans, chips, grilled onion, avocado, and salsa) won mention in *Texas Monthly*. The Cove is also notable for its dedication to S.O.L. — sustainable, organic, local — ingredients, and it practices what it preaches with dishes like grilled tilapia tacos or a salad of roasted organic beets, goat cheese, and walnuts.

6 *Spirit of the Smithsonian* 2 p.m.

San Antonio has a broad visual art scene that ranges from contemporary to folk, with a special concentration on Latino work. There's a First Friday art walk; nonprofit centers like **Artpace** (artpace. org); and the **McNay Art Museum** (mcnayart.org), which has an impressive collection especially strong in modern and contemporary art. At the **San Antonio Museum of Art** (200 West Jones Avenue; 210-978-8100; samuseum.org), the Nelson Rockefeller Wing for Latin American Art has both folk art from across the Americas and splashy contemporary paintings.

7 *Her Name Is Rio* 5 p.m.

After the Alamo, the most popular attraction in town is probably the **River Walk**, a five-mile stretch of paths that snakes through downtown along the canals (thesanantonioriverwalk.com). Sure, it's touristy, but if you avoid the often overpriced restaurants and bars that line it, a stroll can be lovely, particularly as the sun sets and hanging lights illuminate picturesque bridges.

8 *Eating Up North* 7 p.m.

To satisfy a Tex-Mex craving, head out of town to the Far North area, where you'll see the full extent of San Antonio's sprawl. Amid miles of highway loops, malls, and planned communities, find family-friendly **Aldaco's Stone Oak** (20079 Stone Oak Parkway; 210-494-0561; aldacosrestaurants.com; $$), which serves big portions in a large, noisy space. A patio looks toward Texas Hill Country. After your shrimp enchiladas, follow the green glow at Plaza Ciel, a nearby strip mall, to the **Green Lantern** (20626 Stone Oak Parkway; 210-497-3722; facebook.com/ TheGreenLanternSA), a San Antonio contribution to the cocktail trend. There's no sign, but the low-lighted room and well-mixed classic and innovative drinks attract young professionals.

SUNDAY

9 *The Tourist's Mission* 10 a.m.

If you're a first-timer in San Antonio, or you just love the story of the Texans who fought to the death and want to hear it again, Sunday morning can be a good time to hit the **Alamo** (Alamo Plaza; thealamo.org). You won't lack for company — 2.5 million people a year visit this holiest of Texas

civic shrines — and the parking may cost you. But the old walls are still there, and admission is free.

10 *Brisket Brunch* Noon

Texas's most beloved barbecue is served about an hour north in Hill Country, but the **Smokehouse** (3306 Roland Avenue; 210-333-9548; thesmokehousebbqsa.com; $) represents San Antonio proudly. You'll smell the proof from the parking lot: this is the real deal. Friendly staff members work the 40-foot-long mesquite-wood pits. Order a sandwich or a platter by the pound, including the succulent, charred-on-the-outside brisket.

11 *For the Birds* 2 p.m.

Walk off those calories at **Brackenridge Park** (3910 North St. Mary's Street), a 340-plus-acre green space on the west side of town. The park's sunken Japanese Tea Garden offers a bit of serenity, while the bustling **San Antonio Zoo** (sazoo.org) is particularly child-friendly, with an aviary where visitors can feed, and play with, brightly colored lorikeets. A different sort of Texas hospitality, but an entertaining one for sure.

OPPOSITE Creative decorating on the River Walk, the beloved pathway that snakes for four miles through downtown.

ABOVE A lorikeet gets up close and personal with a visitor at San Antonio Zoo's aviary.

THE BASICS

Major airlines serve San Antonio's busy airport. In the city, get around by car.

Hotel Valencia Riverwalk
150 East Houston Street
210-227-9700
hotelvalencia-riverwalk.com
$$$
A friendly staff, comfortable beds, and valet parking offset the dark, moody décor.

Riverwalk Vista Inn
262 Losoya Street
210-223-3200
riverwalkvista.com
$$
Individually designed rooms in the historic Dullnig building.

JW Marriott San Antonio Hill Country Resort & Spa
23808 Resort Parkway
210-276-2500
jwsanantonio.com
$$$
Upscale accommodations.

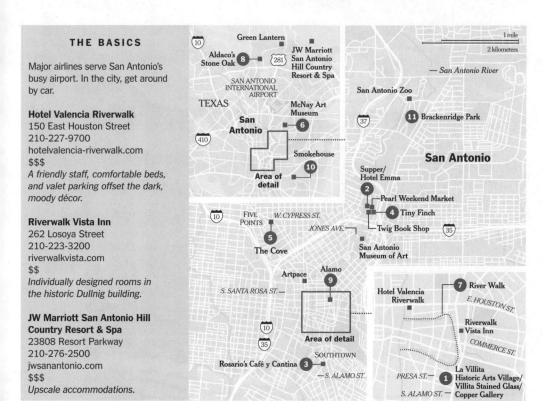

Texas Hill Country

To get a feeling for the Texas Hill Country, where cool mingles with tradition, and industriousness and idleness are equally esteemed values (depending on the time of day), head out among the limestone knolls full of live oak groves and cypress-lined creeks, and to the gritty pin-dot towns built largely of native stone. Here you'll find a delicious tension between rural and refined. Inns and restaurants are bringing a clever touch to Lone Star hospitality and mythology, and with the vineyards and boutique farms (lavender, olives), some people make comparisons to Napa Valley or even Provence. But those assessments ignore something fundamental: the Hill Country—being Texas at its finest—is like nowhere else in the world.

— BY JEANNIE RALSTON

FRIDAY

1 *Water Music* 3 p.m.

For a dramatic Hill Country landscape, many visitors go to Enchanted Rock, an enormous meatloaf-shaped piece of granite outside of the central town of Fredericksburg. **Pedernales Falls State Park** (2585 Park Road 6026, Johnson City; 830-868-7304; tpwd.state.tx.us/state-parks/pedernales-falls), just east of Johnson City, is less known but equally spectacular. Cutting through a shallow canyon here, the Pedernales River tumbles down a series of limestone shelves, with the water collecting in turquoise pools among giant boulders. The soundtrack—the rumble of cascading water—is just as exhilarating as the view.

2 *The Meat Master* 7 p.m.

At **Cooper's Old Time Pit Bar-B-Que** (604 West Young Street, Llano; 325-247-5713; coopersbbqllano. com; $$), one of the premier barbecue joints in Texas, let your fingers do the ordering. Stop at one of the pickup-bed-size grills on the front patio and point at your meat of choice: mesquite-smoked brisket, cabrito, prime rib, pork ribs, sausage—or all of the above. Inside, dig in at picnic tables surrounded by mounted deer heads—another reminder you're in serious carnivore country.

3 *Raise a Glass* 10 p.m.

The best Hill Country night life is in Fredericksburg, and the choicest spot is **Lincoln Street Wine**

Market (111 South Lincoln Street, Fredericksburg; 830-997-8463; lincolnst.com), which maintains a Texas-big selection of 300-plus types of wine. The atmosphere is pleasantly unpretentious, every wine is available by the glass, and on weekends there's live music on the patio.

SATURDAY

4 *Guten Morgen* 9 a.m.

On top of the strong Mexican influence that's usual in Texas, the Hill Country has a German overlay, thanks to immigrants who arrived starting in the 1830s. Get a taste of this heritage at the **Old German Bakery and Restaurant** (225 West Main Street, Fredericksburg; 830-997-9084; oldgermanbakeryandrestaurant.com; $). For breakfast, try crepelike German pancakes, potato pancakes, or apple strudel.

5 *Presidential Treatment* 10 a.m.

History buffs will love the superbly packaged **National Museum of the Pacific War**

OPPOSITE Tarry in Luckenbach for good Texas music.

BELOW Cooper's Old Time Pit Bar-B-Que in Llano.

(pacificwarmuseum.org) in downtown Fredericksburg, but to immerse yourself in the specific history and beauty of this part of Texas, head to the **LBJ Ranch** at Lyndon B. Johnson National Historical Park (199 State Park Road 52, Stonewall; 830-868-7128; nps.gov/lyjo), off Highway 290 in Stonewall. The 36th president spent about 25 percent of his term at what was called the Texas White House, and it's easy to see why. Your driving permit (available at the state park adjacent to the national park) comes with a CD that describes what you're seeing as you meander around the 674 acres: Johnson's reconstructed birthplace, the one-room school where he learned to read, and his grave in the family cemetery. After Lady Bird Johnson's death in 2007, the National Park Service opened part of the family home, where you'll still find traces of Johnson's power among the late-'60s furnishings, like the presidential seal on the big man's chair.

6 *Blanco Boffo* Noon

The geographic hub of Blanco—a town still geared more to working ranchers than to tourists—is the imposing 127-year-old stone courthouse, which appeared in the Coen brothers' remake of *True Grit*. But the social hub is the **Redbud Cafe** (410 Fourth Street, Blanco; 830-833-0202; redbud-cafe.com; $), on the main square, where you can order everything from fat burgers to portobello sandwiches to Middle Eastern salads. Try one of the eight beers on tap from the Blanco-based Real Ale Brewing Company. On the wall is a chart left over from the building's many years as a hardware store that recorded monthly rainfall levels from 1900 to 1999. Adjoining the restaurant is **Brieger Pottery**, which sells hefty but graceful stoneware crafted by the Redbud's owners, Jan and Jon Brieger.

7 *Strike Nine* 1 p.m.

The **Blanco Bowling Club Cafe** (310 Fourth Street; 830-833-4416; blancobowlingclub.com) is one of the few places in the Hill Country where German nine-pin bowling is still played. By advance appointment with the bartender, you can try your skill on lanes that are throwbacks to pre-automated times (the pinsetter is usually a local teenager). Follow your game with another treat: the cafe's pies with meringue piled high like airy volcanoes.

8 *Wine Time* 4 p.m.

These days wineries are almost as common in the Hill Country as those ranch windmills that look like tall tin daisies. You can't go to them all—and still expect to operate a car—so head to the two best. The wood-and-stone tasting room at **Becker Vineyards** (464 Becker Farms Road, Stonewall; 830-644-2681; beckervineyards.com) is surrounded by 46 acres of grapes and lavender. **Grape Creek Vineyards** (10587 East U.S. Highway 290, Fredericksburg; 830-644-2710; grapecreek.com) echoes Tuscany with stucco and stone buildings capped by red-tile roofs.

9 *Sirloin or Sushi?* 7 p.m.

Get a taste of nouveau Texas cuisine, with a twist, at **August E's** (203 East San Antonio; 830-997-1585; august-es.com; $$$$), in Fredericksburg. The décor is contemporary Asian, and the seasonal menu reflects the Thai roots of its chef-owner Leu Savanh, who combines traditional and fusion preparations of locally sourced meats, including wild game, and produce. Choices might include filet mignon with whipped potatoes, grilled asparagus, and sautéed wild mushrooms with Bordelaise sauce, or a pair of whole quail stuffed with wild rice, house-made sausage, cranberries, and pine nuts. There is a sushi menu as well.

10 *Willie Sang Here* 10 p.m.

Luckenbach, Texas (412 Luckenbach Town Loop, Fredericksburg; 830-997-3225; luckenbachtexas. com), isn't just the title of the Waylon Jennings and Willie Nelson anti-stress, anti-materialism anthem. It's a real place off Farm to Market Road 1376—a few old buildings including a general store and a dance hall in a clearing among the trees. If you stay a while—which you should since you'll hear a lot of good Texas music—you'll be glad that the only glitz comes from the party lights strung around the dance

hall. After a night here two-stepping across the worn wood floor, you'll feel you've hit on something genuine that can only be found in Texas, and you will be right.

SUNDAY

11 *Comfort Food* 11 a.m.

A good spot for brunch, with a bit of history, is **Po Po** (829 FM 289; 830-537-4194; poporestaurant.com; $$), in nearby Boerne. The building dates back to 1929, when it was a dancehall, with bootleggers peddling moonshine outside. House specialties are fried chicken, chicken fried steak, and fresh seafood, and portions are big enough to share. You can't miss the décor: over 2,500 commemorative plates adorn the walls. Fortified, drive on to **Comfort**, and its historic district, packed with buildings from the 1800s, many of them designed by the architect Alfred Giles.

Wander through the shops, and finish with a prickly pear cactus drink (nonalcoholic) at **Comfort Pizza** (802 High Street; 830-995-5959; comfortpizza.com), a renovated stone filling station that bears a word across its awning that should sum up how you'll feel at this point: "Comfortable."

OPPOSITE The beauty of the Hill Country lures Texans out of their cities, especially Dallas and San Antonio, for trips amid green hills and quiet creeks.

ABOVE Quintessential Texas: trying out a seat atop a longhorn. Luckenbach is a real place, not just the title of a Waylon Jennings and Willie Nelson song.

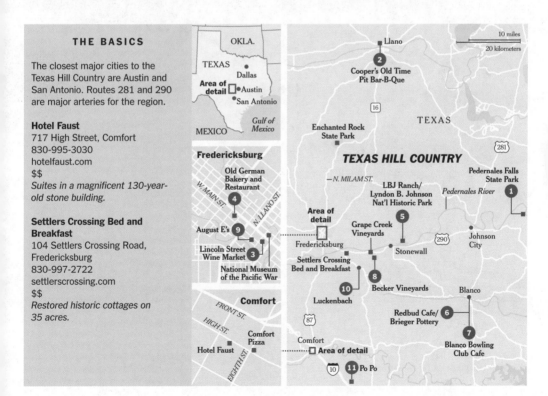

THE BASICS

The closest major cities to the Texas Hill Country are Austin and San Antonio. Routes 281 and 290 are major arteries for the region.

Hotel Faust
717 High Street, Comfort
830-995-3030
hotelfaust.com
$$
Suites in a magnificent 130-year-old stone building.

Settlers Crossing Bed and Breakfast
104 Settlers Crossing Road, Fredericksburg
830-997-2722
settlerscrossing.com
$$
Restored historic cottages on 35 acres.

Moab

It's hard not to become a dime-store philosopher in Moab. With its dipping green valleys and great red rocks piercing the wide blue sky, this tiny town in southeastern Utah can be a heady study in perspective. One minute you're sipping coffee on Main Street, tucked safely between the wild, barren Canyonlands National Park and the magnificent stony surrealism of Arches National Park. A short drive later, you're thousands of dizzying feet above civilization, the wind whipping you senseless. The startling beauty of this terrain is enough to leave even the most seasoned traveler frozen in the sand, blinking in disbelief. — BY CINDY PRICE

FRIDAY

1 *A Delicate Balance* 3 p.m.

You can look at a million photos of the **Delicate Arch** (and you will), but nothing prepares you for the real deal. At **Arches National Park** (Highway 191; 435-719-2299; nps.gov/arch), take the mile-and-a-half hike up steep, uneven slick rock to hit the landmark just before sunset (bring a flashlight and plenty of water). The massive arch doesn't come into view until the last second, and when it does, it is unforgettable. It's perched on the brink of an enormous sandstone bowl, and you can edge your way around and stand beneath it for a picture, but be forewarned — though the ground there is wider than a big-city sidewalk, the combination of steep dropoff, gusty wind, and gleaming sun makes for a dizzying few seconds.

2 *The Barroom Floor* 8 p.m.

It's no Las Vegas, but Moab knows how to kick it. Swing by **La Hacienda** (574 North Main Street; 435-259-6319; $), a townie favorite, for tasty fried fish tacos. Then hit **World Famous Woody's Tavern** (221 South Main Street; 435-259-3550; facebook.com/woodystavernmoab), where everyone from local hipsters to vacationing Dutch couples pull on cold drafts. Some say the floor is painted red to cover up

OPPOSITE The Delicate Arch, perched on the brink of an enormous sandstone bowl at Arches National Park.

RIGHT After a uranium mining bust in the 1980s, Moab reinvented itself as an outdoor recreation spot.

bloodstains from brawls, but don't be put off — aside from foosball, Woody's is fairly docile these days.

SATURDAY

3 *Rough Riders* 8:30 a.m.

There are gentler ways to take in the lay of the land, but some scenic tours are just too tame. At the **Moab Adventure Center** (225 South Main Street; 435-259-7019; moabadventurecenter.com), you can book a Hummer Safari — a guide does the driving — that will take you in and out of rock canyons and up rough and steep sandstone hills (don't think about what it's going to be like coming down). Moab is also popular with mountain bikers — if that's your thing, check out **Moab Cyclery** (391 South Main Street; 435-259-7423; moabcyclery.com) or another local bike outfitter for rentals and day trips.

4 *Old School* 12:30 p.m.

In a town where scenery looms large, it's easy to drive past the unassuming **Milt's Stop & Eat** (356 Millcreek Drive; 435-259-7424; miltsstopandeat.com; $). But this little diner, which has been doling out fresh chili and shakes since 1954, comes through where it counts. Pull up to the counter and order a mouthwatering double bacon cheeseburger. It's a greasy-spoon chef-d'oeuvre, with aged-beef patties and thick slices of smoked bacon. A creamy chocolate malt will have you cursing the advent of frozen yogurt.

5 *Hole Sweet Hole* 1:30 p.m.

In 1945, Albert Christensen built his wife, Gladys, the home of their dreams—in the middle of a rock. Part kitsch memorial, part love story, **Hole N" the Rock** (11037 South Highway 191; 435-686-2250; theholeintherock.com) is surely a tourist trap, but a heartwarming one. Even the steady drone of a

ABOVE Main Street and its rugged backdrop.

BELOW Heading for a cold draft at Woody's Tavern.

OPPOSITE ABOVE A heartwarming tourist trap.

OPPOSITE BELOW A sunset over Moab.

gum-smacking tour guide can't dispel the sheer marvel of this 5,000-square-foot testament to one man's obsession. It took Albert 12 years to hand-drill the place, and Gladys another eight to give it a woman's touch. Each room is lovingly decorated with knickknacks or Albert's taxidermy. Outside, wander over to the inexplicable but equally delightful petting zoo filled with llamas, emus, and wallabies.

6 *Main Street* 3:30 p.m.

Like most small towns with attitude, Moab has a main street that's pretty darn cute. Start your walk with an iced coffee and a fresh slice of quiche at **EklectiCafé** (352 North Main Street; 435-259-6896; $). For a quick lesson on local topography, check out the area relief map at the **Museum of Moab** (118 East Center Street; 435-259-7985; moabmuseum.org). The artifacts on display include dinosaur bones and tracks, ancient pottery, mining tools, and a proud pioneer's piano—all part of the Moab story.

7 *World's Biggest Stage Set* 6 p.m.

Head out of town, hang a right at Scenic Byway 128, drive 18 miles, and take a right on La Sal Mountain Road toward Castle Valley. The pretty, winding route leads to **Castle Rock**—a dead ringer for Disney's Big Thunder Mountain Railroad and the star of old Chevrolet commercials. Turn around at Castleton Tower and drop into **Red Cliffs Lodge** (Milepost 14, Highway 128; 435-259-2002; redcliffslodge.com) for a free wine tasting at the **Castle Creek Winery**. Afterward, check out the **Movie Museum** in the basement—a small homage to the many films shot in Moab, including *Rio Grande* and *Indiana Jones and the Last Crusade*.

8 *Local Brew* 8 p.m.

You've tasted the wine. Now sample the ale. The **Moab Brewery** (686 South Main Street; 435-259-6333; themoabbrewery.com; $) has a variety of hearty brews, plus its own homemade root beer. The dinner menu has plenty of beef and chicken, including barbecue, balanced by a cheese-heavy "Very Veggie" section and a promise that the frying is done in zero-trans-fat oil.

SUNDAY

9 *Dawn on the Cliffs* 7 a.m.

There are few reasons to endorse waking up at 7 on a Sunday, but a sunrise at Dead Horse Point passes the test. Hit the **Wicked Brew Drive Thru** (1146 South Main Street; 435-259-0021; wickedbrewmoab.com) for an espresso-laced eye-opener, and then take the winding drive up Route 313 to the 2,000-foot vantage point at **Dead Horse Point State Park** (435-259-2614;

utah.com/dead-horse-point-state-park). Watch the sun break over the vast, beautiful Canyonlands. To the west, look for Shafer Trail, the dusty road where Thelma and Louise sealed their fate in the 1991 Ridley Scott film.

10 *Rapid Observations* 10:30 a.m.

In the '70s, before Moab became known as the mountain-biking capital of the world, whitewater rafting was the big buzz. **Red River Adventures** (1140 South Main Street; 435-259-4046; redriveradventures.com)

offers trips that take it easy through Class II and III rapids, and others that go for Class IV. If you'd rather try a different form of sightseeing, the company also offers rock climbing and horseback trips.

ABOVE Scenery looms large for Moab, tucked between Canyonlands and Arches National Parks.

OPPOSITE Cycling along Scenic Byway 128 outside of town. The local terrain is legendary among mountain bikers, and outfitters in Moab will provide bicycles and gear.

THE BASICS

Fly to Salt Lake City, rent a car, and drive 235 scenic miles southeast to Moab.

Sunflower Hill Inn
185 North 300 East
435-259-2974
sunflowerhill.com
$$
Lovely restored inn with 12 rooms.

Gonzo Inn
100 West 200 South
435-259-2515
gonzoinn.com
$$
Colorful retro-style hotel.

Red Cliffs Lodge
Milepost 14, Highway 128
435-259-2002
redcliffslodge.com
$$-$$$
Overlooking the Colorado River 20 minutes out of town.

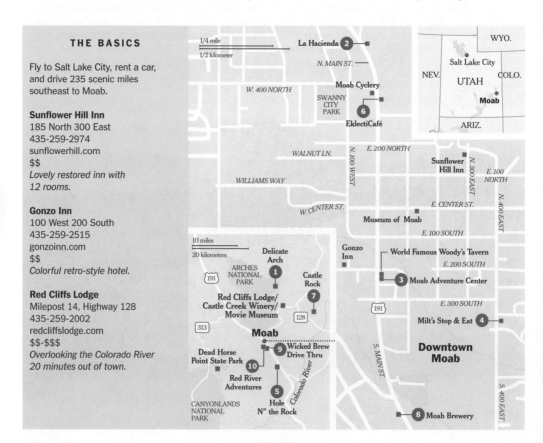

Park City

To ski or not to ski. That's the luxurious question in Park City, Utah, the rare ski resort that offers lively diversions on and off the slopes. Historic Main Street still evokes a silver mining town, with local delis mixed in among upscale restaurants and fashion boutiques. And thanks to constant refinements, the powdery slopes remain a favorite of hard-core ski bums — not to mention the United States Ski Team, which calls Park City home — and the fur-trimmed celebrities who invade during the Sundance Film Festival. But the town's greatest asset may be location: Park City is 30 minutes from Salt Lake City and a short hop to several of the most popular slopes in the Rockies.
— BY DENNY LEE

FRIDAY

1 *Foraging on Main* 4:30 p.m.

As dusk shrouds the Wasatch Range, the Old West-style storefronts of Main Street light up with the hubbub of shoppers and après-skiers. Wedged among the ski shops and real estate windows are some stylish stores. **Flight Boutique** (545 Main Street; 435-604-0806; flightclothingboutique.com) carries such brands as Elizabeth & James and Theory. Another fashionable spot is **Cake Boutique** (577 Main Street; 435-649-1256; cakeparkcity.com), which carries brands like Rag & Bone. If you'd rather skip the shopping and sample local culture, go to the **Kimball Art Center** (1401 Kearns Boulevard; 435-649-8882; kimballartcenter.org), the region's nonprofit arts anchor, which is housed in a historic stable.

2 *Dining Camp* 6 p.m.

A secret to having a high-end ski vacation without all the high prices is to eat where the locals eat. Meet them around the communal tables at the sprawling, rustic-chic **Boneyard Saloon & Kitchen** (1251 Kearns Boulevard; 435-649-0911; boneyardsaloon.com; $$), located in an old lumberyard, which serves classic comfort food like the chicken dumpling potpie or a fried Brussels sprout Caesar salad, while the wood-fired grill turns out wild-caught blackened salmon along with steaks, burgers, and ribs. For a change of scene, check out the on-site Wine Dive, with 16 wines on tap plus an extensive bottle selection and more than 100 draft and bottled beers. Oh, and spirits too.

3 *Show Time* 8 p.m.

Channel Sundance's glamour at the **Egyptian Theatre** (328 Main Street; 435-649-9371; egyptiantheatrecompany.org), the pharaoh-themed landmark in the middle of town. When the 1926 theater isn't used for red-carpet premieres, it features concerts, comedy acts, and other live performances. Check its website for coming shows. For a more cinematic experience, the **Park City Film Series** (1255 Park Avenue; 435-615-8291; parkcityfilmseries.com) offers a stellar lineup of indie films at the Park City Library.

SATURDAY

4 *Town Lift* 9 a.m.

One of the underappreciated things about Park City is that the entire town is practically ski in/ski out. A triple lift on Main Street whisks riders to the **Park City Mountain Resort** (parkcitymountain.com), so if you're staying in town, there's no need for parking or shuttles. There are 3,300 acres of terrain to cover, so it's a good idea to check the morning's grooming reports before clicking in. Warm up on the Crescent and King Con mountain zones before tackling the black diamonds.

5 *Dine In/Ski Out* 1 p.m.

The town lift goes both ways, so if you're hankering for more than just burgers and pizzas, skip the

OPPOSITE The bobsled run at the Utah Olympic Park.

BELOW A marquee for the Sundance Film Festival.

slopeside cafeterias and ski into town for a more civilized lunch. Casual comfort food is plentiful on and off historic Main Street. At **Windy Ridge Cafe** (1250 Iron Horse Drive; 435-647-0880; windyridgecafe.com), mac and cheese with bacon and an open-faced hot turkey sandwich on sourdough with mashed potatoes are specialties of the house. After lunch, just hop back onto the lift. Trails can get packed along the lower runs, so work your way to the right side of the trail map.

6 *Getting Steamed* 5 p.m.

After an exhausting day of skiing, there's nothing like heading to a sauna and massage. **Main & Sky**, one of Park City's luxury condo hotels (201 Heber Avenue; 435-658-2500; skyparkcity.com) boasts a spa and wellness center, where scrubs, wraps, and facials are also on offer. Afterward, you can head down to the rustic bar at the Tavern restaurant for a predinner drink. Another option is **Spa Montage** in Deer Valley (9100 Marsac Avenue; 435-604-1300; spamontage.com), a Roman-style wellness center with steaming whirlpools, volcanic saunas, massage services, and a quiet room for a little nap.

7 *Western Beef* 8 p.m.

As Utah's first distillery since Prohibition, the **High West Distillery and Saloon** (703 Park Avenue; 435-649-8300; highwest.com; $$) gets high marks for its small-batch whiskeys and vodkas. But it also gets props for its Western-inspired menu, which includes nouveau cowboy fare like dry-aged bison with a porcini sauce and pan-seared trout. Ask your server which whiskey would pair well with your meal. Another option, for those seeking a different

vibe, is **Shabu** (442 Main Street; 435-645-7253; shabuparkcity.com; $$$), a stylish Park City mainstay that specializes in "freestyle Asian" cuisine, Instagram-ready plate presentations, and a killer sake martini.

8 *Rough and Tumble* 10 p.m.

The brothels and casinos are long gone, but party seekers won't have any trouble finding a bar stool or a dance floor to keep the night going. An old reliable is the **No Name Saloon** (447 Main Street; 435-649-6667; nonamesaloon.net), a packed and friendly spot with the motto "Helping People Forget Their Names Since 1903." For a younger singles crowd, follow the cologne trail to **Downstairs** (625 Main Street; 435-226-5340; downstairspc.com), a throbbing disco. Expect

ABOVE Main Street is achingly picturesque but can also be jammed with S.U.V.s.

BELOW On the mountain after a confectioner's sifting of Utah's famous light snow.

bottle service, waitresses who dance on tables, and guys who fist-pump to rap music.

9 *Go for the Gold* 9:30 a.m.

See how the pros do it. Built for the 2002 Winter Olympics, the vertiginous **Utah Olympic Park** (3419 Olympic Parkway; 435-658-4200; olyparks.com) remains an active training center for Olympic-class skiers. Call ahead to see if anyone is barreling down the K120 Nordic ski jump. Or catch some air yourself: the park offers Sunday ski clinics for intermediate skiers. Speed demons, however, will gravitate toward another sport: the Comet Bobsled. The mile-long track offers 80-mile-per-hour speeds and up to five

G's of force. Those with heart problems are strongly urged to stand on the sidelines.

10 *Grander Canyons* Noon

If you have time to ski only one other part of the resort, point your tips toward **Canyons**, to the north. Canyons, now combined with Park City Mountain Resort, has undergone huge upgrades in recent years, with 182 trails and 4,000 acres of skiable terrain — so wide that it had trouble fitting it all on a trail map. Start at the Orange Bubble lift, a covered, heated chairlift that feels like riding inside a pair of toasty ski goggles, protected from the wind and snow. At the summit lookout, direct your gaze at Iron Mountains. It's a veritable winter wonderland.

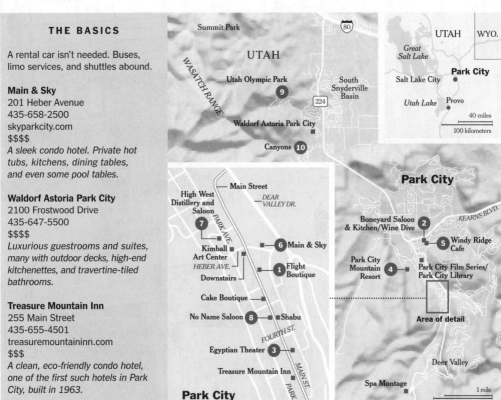

THE BASICS

A rental car isn't needed. Buses, limo services, and shuttles abound.

Main & Sky
201 Heber Avenue
435-658-2500
skyparkcity.com
$$$$
A sleek condo hotel. Private hot tubs, kitchens, dining tables, and even some pool tables.

Waldorf Astoria Park City
2100 Frostwood Drive
435-647-5500
$$$$
Luxurious guestrooms and suites, many with outdoor decks, high-end kitchenettes, and travertine-tiled bathrooms.

Treasure Mountain Inn
255 Main Street
435-655-4501
treasuremountaininn.com
$$$
A clean, eco-friendly condo hotel, one of the first such hotels in Park City, built in 1963.

Salt Lake City

Sprawling and rapidly growing, Salt Lake City, Utah, is more complicated and cosmopolitan than most outsiders know. It's also more beautiful. Situated directly below the towering Wasatch Front, the city has a spectacular natural backdrop, beautiful 1900s neighborhoods, and one of the nation's most inviting college campuses at the University of Utah. Salt Lake City is still the headquarters of the Mormon Church and the place to go to see Mormon monuments. But it also has a rejuvenated downtown, a bold new natural history museum, interesting restaurants, and an open-door stance toward refugees and immigrants that has brought a variety of newcomers to town.
— BY JAIME GILLIN AND CHRISTOPHER SOLOMON

FRIDAY

1 *City Structure* 4 p.m.

Chart your own downtown tour. The **Main Library** (210 East 400 South; 801-524-8200; slcpl.org), which was an early and influential venture in the city center revitalization, is a curving glass structure designed by the architect Moshe Safdie. Step inside. There are fireplaces on every floor and a rooftop garden with views of the city and the Wasatch Mountains. Downtown has bloomed with new businesses, including shops and galleries, but the single biggest catalyst of change is **City Creek Center** (50 South Main Street; shopcitycreekcenter.com), a sprawling, 23-acre development with residential towers, office space, and a shopping mall, all financed by an arm of the Mormon Church. A handsome monument to consumption, the mall has more than 100 stores, including the likes of Tiffany, Nordstrom, and Coach. There are also Las Vegas-like fountains (music! jets of flame!), a retractable glass roof that closes in inclement weather, and a river that runs through it (O.K., a stream, the reimagined City Creek) with actual trout.

2 *Hungry in Utah* 7 p.m.

There's been an explosion of places to eat in downtown Salt Lake. Ryan Lowder, a local chef and restaurateur who worked in the Jean-Georges Vongerichten and Mario Batali empires in Manhattan, opened the **Copper Onion** (111 East Broadway; 801-355-3282; thecopperonion.com; $$), which serves American food with what he calls "a pretty decent Mediterranean influence" and lots of house-made ingredients, from the noodles in the popular beef stroganoff to some cheeses. Lowder's second restaurant, **Plum Alley** (111 East Broadway; 801-355-0543; plumalley.com; $), named for a now-vanished street that was once part of a thriving Chinatown, is "white guys cookin' Asian food," Lowder said wryly. Look for ramen with house-made noodles and a bone broth or locally raised beef with coconut milk curry and bean sprouts.

3 *Open City* 9 p.m.

Since local liquor laws loosened in 2009, night spots have proliferated. **The Red Door** (57 West 200 South; 801-363-6030; thereddoorslc.com) has dim lighting, a great martini list, and kitschy revolution décor — yes, that's a Che Guevara mural on the wall. **Squatters Pub Brewery** (147 West Broadway; 801-363-2739; squatters.com) is one of several microbreweries now operating downtown.

SATURDAY

4 *Botanical Bliss* 9 a.m.

The **Red Butte Garden** (300 Wakara Way; 801-585-0556; redbuttegarden.org), nestled in the Wasatch foothills above the University of Utah campus, has a rose garden, 3.5 miles of walking trails,

OPPOSITE The Moshe Safdie-designed Public Library.

BELOW The University of Utah's Red Butte Garden and Arboretum has 3.5 miles of walking trails.

and morning yoga in the Fragrance Garden. For a wake-up hike, ask the front desk for directions to the Living Room, a lookout point named for the flat orange rocks that resemble couches. Sit back and absorb the expansive views of the valley, mountains, and the Great Salt Lake.

5 *Skulls and Moccasins* 11 a.m.

A state with such tremendous natural assets deserves a museum of natural history fit to contain it. Now it has one—the **Natural History Museum of Utah** at the Rio Tinto Center (301 Wakara Way; 801-581-6927; nhmu.utah.edu), next to Red Butte Garden. Sheathed in copper and designed to blend with the mountainside, the dramatic building houses 10 galleries of fearsome skulls, ancient moccasins, and interactive displays. Ramps let you see eye-to-eye with giant monsters in the dinosaur hall. And continuing research isn't far away here: visitors stare through glass windows and watch scientists cleaning dinosaur bones. Outside, there's a view of downtown, in the flat land below, and the big Utah sky.

6 *Diverse Palate* 2 p.m.

Salt Lake City has growing contingents of Latinos, Pacific Islanders (particularly Samoan and Tongan), and refugees from Tibet, Bosnia, and Somalia. One place to taste this kind of imported flavor is **Himalayan Kitchen** (360 South State Street; 801-328-2077; himalayankitchen.com; $$), a down-home dining room with turmeric-yellow walls and red tablecloth tables, where you might find Nepali goat curry or Himalayan momos, steamed chicken dumplings served with sesame seed sauce. For Middle Eastern food, go to **Mazza** (912 East 900 South; 801-521-4572; mazzacafe.com; $$), the second location of an established Salt Lake City original.

7 *A Taste of Marmalade* 3 p.m.

Branch out into some different neighborhoods. To see more of the city as it once was, wander the **Marmalade Historic District**, home to many original pioneer homes from the 19th century, or go on a walking tour with **Preservation Utah**, formerly the Utah Heritage Foundation (801-533-0858; preservationutah. org). In the mini-neighborhood called **15th and 15th** (1500 East and 1500 South), get a sense of the city's gracious middle-class residential districts dating from the mid-20th century. Stop in at the charming **King's English Bookshop** (1511 South 1500 East; 801-484-9100; kingsenglish.com), a creaky old house filled with books and cozy reading nooks.

8 *Italian Hour* 7 p.m.

Salt Lake City has plenty of appealing Italian restaurants, but the most vibrant may be **Valter's Osteria** (173 West Broadway; 801-521-4563; valtersosteria.com; $$$$), not least because of its gregarious, Tuscany-born namesake, Valter Nassi, who says he reinterprets classics from his mother's kitchen. Those might include house-made lasagna in a light meat sauce, or a fennel-crusted duck breast in a Cognac and grape sauce. The service is similarly Old World, with outdoor dining in season. And maybe you want a house-made gelato for dessert? A roomier restaurant for good Italian food is **Caffe Molise** (404 South West Temple; 801-364-8833; caffemolise.com; $$). Its location near Abravanel Hall, home of the Utah Symphony, makes it a favorite destination for music lovers.

9 *Live From Utah* 9 p.m.

As the only sizable city between Denver and Northern California, Salt Lake City gets many touring bands passing through. Hear established and up-and-coming acts at places like the **Urban Lounge** (241

South 500 East; 801-746-0557; theurbanloungeslc.com) and **Kilby Court** (741 South Kilby Court; 801-364-3538; kilbycourt.com). If you want to make your own sweet music, stop by **Keys on Main** (242 South Main Street; 801-363-3638; keysonmain.com), a piano bar where the audience sings along.

SUNDAY

10 *Voices on High* 9 a.m.

Almost every Sunday morning the 360 volunteer members of the Mormon Tabernacle Choir sing at the **Mormon Tabernacle** in Temple Square (801-240-4150; mormontabernaclechoir.org). The egg-shaped hall, with its 150-foot roof span, is an acoustical marvel, and the nearly 12,000-pipe organ is among the largest in the world. You can join the live audience at the concert broadcast from 9:30 to 10 a.m., but you need to be in your seat by 9:15. Afterward, drop in at one of the Temple Square visitors' centers (visittemplesquare.com) and then take a look around. The square is 35 acres, the epicenter of the Mormon Church, and its monumental scale is a spectacle in itself.

OPPOSITE ABOVE A light-rail trolley system runs through downtown past Temple Square and Mormon monuments.

OPPOSITE BELOW A congenial stop for readers is the King's English Bookshop, in an old house with cozy nooks.

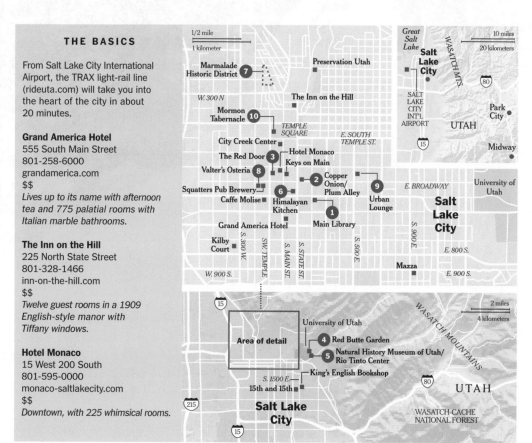

THE BASICS

From Salt Lake City International Airport, the TRAX light-rail line (rideuta.com) will take you into the heart of the city in about 20 minutes.

Grand America Hotel
555 South Main Street
801-258-6000
grandamerica.com
$$
Lives up to its name with afternoon tea and 775 palatial rooms with Italian marble bathrooms.

The Inn on the Hill
225 North State Street
801-328-1466
inn-on-the-hill.com
$$
Twelve guest rooms in a 1909 English-style manor with Tiffany windows.

Hotel Monaco
15 West 200 South
801-595-0000
monaco-saltlakecity.com
$$
Downtown, with 225 whimsical rooms.

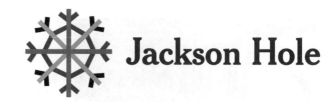

Jackson Hole

When the first mountain men crossed into Jackson Hole from the Yellowstone Park area, they were flabbergasted by its epic beauty. Before them lay a flat plain fenced in by snow-clad peaks soaring a mile up from the valley floor. That beauty is still here, but in winter, it is not the only lure. This is powder country — the valley's microclimate produces considerable precipitation within a generally dry climate — and those conditions combine with the favorable tilt of the mountain slopes to create excellent skiing and boarding. Add to that a recent five-year overhaul of Jackson Hole Ski Resort's lift system and the resort's luxurious modern facilities, plus the proximity of the valley town of Jackson, and it's easy to see why Jackson Hole has almost a cult following among skiers.

— BY FINN-OLAF JONES AND TOM PRICE

FRIDAY

1 *The Local Mountain* 3 p.m.

While the big ski resort that drew you here closes at 4 p.m., you can still get in a little skiing this afternoon at the more intimate **Snow King Mountain** (400 East Snow King Avenue, Jackson; 307-201-5464; snowkingmountain.com), which stays open until 7 p.m. thanks to lots of floodlights. Snow King, beloved by locals, almost never has lift lines and charges a bargain rate for night skiing. Exhibition ski run, with its steep, long, unbroken fall line, is where generations of Olympians cut their teeth; beginners and intermediate skiers hit their stride under the Rafferty lift. If you arrive early enough, take a good look around. From the summit here, the view stretches 50 miles to Yellowstone.

2 *Sleigh Ride* 6:30 p.m.

At **Spring Creek Ranch** (1600 North East Butte Road; 307-733-8833; springcreekranch.com), which straddles East Gros Ventre Butte, cowhands will pull thick blankets over you for a horse-pulled sleigh ride to the top of the butte. After gaping at what must be one of the best views on the continent, sleigh back

OPPOSITE A seasoned skier tries out expert terrain at the Jackson Hole Mountain Resort.

RIGHT The town of Jackson seen from Snow King Mountain.

down to dinner at the Ranch's **Granary Restaurant** ($$$-$$$$), a popular Friday night destination with live jazz. (The ride and dinner come as a package.) The chef excels at Jackson Hole high-altitude cuisine with dishes like Cajun-spice elk tenderloin and rainbow trout with black truffles — all served at the edge of the butte with the stars twinkling above the Teton Range and moose, mule deer, and elk grazing among the cabins outside.

SATURDAY

3 *Breakfast at the Top* 9 a.m.

From Teton Village, the **Jackson Hole Aerial Tram** (jacksonhole.com) will whisk you through spectacular scenery up 4,139 feet to the 10,450-foot summit of Rendezvous Mountain. There's been a "big red box" on this mountain since 1966, but the beloved original was retired and replaced by this newer, larger, more streamlined version, which holds 100 people. Once at the top, join the morning ski patrol and eager skiers for waffles — with brown sugar butter or with peanut butter and bacon — in the cozy confines of the seemingly permanently ice-encrusted **Corbet's Cabin** (307-739-2688; jacksonhole.com/dining/on-mountain-dining.html; $). Situated right next to the tram, Corbet's offers convenience along with its delicious options to fuel a day on the slopes.

4 Skiing the Tetons 9:30 a.m.

Jackson Hole Mountain Resort (Teton Village; jacksonhole.com) is unlike any other ski mountain. There's that favorable microclimate, and in addition, this side of the valley was created by tectonic tilting, resulting in slopes rising straight out of the prairie like an upended table. The skier's choices range from gentle slopes to cliffs, and from spacious bowls to narrow chutes. The Casper high-speed quad lift opens up the vast intermediate and beginner slopes. For advanced skiers, Corbet's Couloir, Rendezvous Mountain, and the unusually accessible backcountry skiing (they even have testing devices for your personal avalanche gear at the gates) remain legendary.

5 Slopeside Lunch 1 p.m.

You may be skiing in some of the best wilderness cowboy country in the world, but that's all the more reason to eat well, even at the top of the slopes. **Piste Mountain Bistro** (top of Bridger Gondola, Teton Village; 307-732-3177; jacksonhole.com/piste-mountain-bistro.html; $$$), next to the summit of the Bridger Gondola, is popular for its shared plates and signature cocktails served in its cheerful dining room or on the terrace, which has killer views at 9,000 feet. You're here at lunchtime, so you might sample its confit duck wings and mac and cheese with pulled pork, or perhaps a grilled cheese and seasonal salad for a worthy ski break. The restaurant goes to local sources for its food and even for a lot of its beverages.

6 Change of Pace 5 p.m.

When it's time for relaxation and a massage to ease those tired muscles, you'll have several spas to choose from. The **Four Seasons Spa** (7680 Granite Loop Road, Teton Village; 307-732-5000; fourseasons.com/jacksonhole) promises altitude-adjusted treatments using local materials like hawthorne berries, sage, willow bark, and smooth stones from the Snake River. The **Snake River Lodge** (7710 Granite Loop Road, Teton Village; 855-342-4712; snakeriverlodge.com) advertises a 17,000-square-foot spa and rooms with mountain views. **Chill Spa** at the Hotel Terra (3335 West Village Drive, Teton Village; 307-201-6065; hotelterrajacksonhole.com) lives up to its name with a heated outdoor infinity pool.

7 Moose Music 8 p.m.

Dig into an elk steak, accompanied by a local beer, at the **Mangy Moose Restaurant and Saloon** (3295 Village Road, Teton Village; 307-733-4913; mangymoose.com; $$), which looks almost as self-consciously rustic as its name. Primarily a steakhouse, this place also offers salads, burgers, and truffle fries, and it's a consistent favorite with Jackson Hole insiders. As the evening wears on, the locals crowd in for the live music, which includes national and local acts.

SUNDAY

8 Swimming With Django 11 a.m.

The whole valley bubbles with underground thermal activity that makes for exotic swimming holes. Drive out to the tiny town of Kelly, turn right at Gros Ventre Road, and you'll find a small parking lot next to the **Kelly Warm Springs** (intersection of Lower Gros Ventre Road and Gros Ventre Road, Kelly). Steam will be wafting into the valley. Film buffs might recognize the springs from the movie

ABOVE Corbet's Cabin, a cozy restaurant near the top of the Jackson Hole Mountain Aerial Tram.

BELOW Simon Gudgeon's bronze *Isis*, a work on the sculpture trail at the National Museum of Wildlife Art.

Django Unchained, which was filmed here. It's a stunning scene — wilderness and the towering Tetons. Wade into the 80-degree water and swim with the hundreds of tropical fish that improbably have found their way here — legend has it that this is a favorite spot for locals to dump their aquariums.

9 *Bronze Buffalo* 1 p.m.

A hillside quartzite building designed to resemble a ruined Scottish castle overlooking the plains where herds of elk graze is the setting for the **National Museum of Wildlife Art** (2820 Rungius Road; 307-733-5771; wildlifeart.org). The collection, primarily American and European paintings and sculpture, has objects created as far back as 2500 B.C. If you're prepared for an easy outdoor hike, follow the three-quarter-mile sculpture trail that meanders across the terrain where impressive animal forms like Simon Gudgeon's bronze *Isis* seem to be meditating on the Gros Ventre Range across the valley. The view can also be savored over a lunch of bison gyros in the museum's Palate restaurant ($$).

ABOVE Kelly Warm Springs are good for a winter swim.

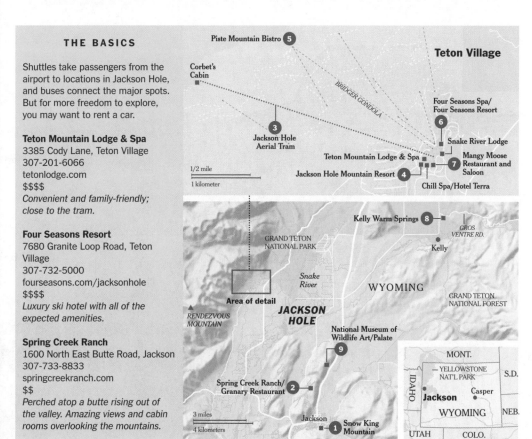

THE BASICS

Shuttles take passengers from the airport to locations in Jackson Hole, and buses connect the major spots. But for more freedom to explore, you may want to rent a car.

Teton Mountain Lodge & Spa
3385 Cody Lane, Teton Village
307-201-6066
tetonlodge.com
$$$$
Convenient and family-friendly; close to the tram.

Four Seasons Resort
7680 Granite Loop Road, Teton Village
307-732-5000
fourseasons.com/jacksonhole
$$$$
Luxury ski hotel with all of the expected amenities.

Spring Creek Ranch
1600 North East Butte Road, Jackson
307-733-8833
springcreekranch.com
$$
Perched atop a butte rising out of the valley. Amazing views and cabin rooms overlooking the mountains.

Piste Mountain Bistro **5**

Teton Village

Corbet's Cabin

BRIDGER GONDOLA

Four Seasons Spa/ Four Seasons Resort **6**

3 Jackson Hole Aerial Tram

Snake River Lodge

1/2 mile

1 kilometer

Teton Mountain Lodge & Spa

Jackson Hole Mountain Resort **4**

Mangy Moose Restaurant and Saloon **7**

Chill Spa/Hotel Terra

Kelly Warm Springs **8**

GROS VENTRE RD.

GRAND TETON NATIONAL PARK

Kelly

Snake River

WYOMING

GRAND TETON NATIONAL FOREST

Area of detail

RENDEZVOUS MOUNTAIN

JACKSON HOLE

National Museum of Wildlife Art/Palate

9

Spring Creek Ranch/ Granary Restaurant **2**

3 miles

4 kilometers

Jackson

Snow King Mountain **1**

MONT.

YELLOWSTONE NAT'L PARK

S.D.

IDAHO

Casper

Jackson

WYOMING

NEB.

UTAH

COLO.

The Tetons

The three iconic peaks of the Tetons — 13,770-foot Grand Teton and the mountains flanking it on either side — have been a landmark since the days of the French fur trade and probably for centuries before that. While they once guided long-distance travelers struggling through the Rockies on horseback, today they are a symbol of the beauty of the American West and an invitation to lovers of hiking, fishing, and adventure sports. The town of Jackson, at the edge of Grand Teton National Park, has avoided becoming a sprawling tourist trap thanks to a quirk of geography: hemmed in by public land, it has no room to expand. New money has been drawn to Jackson, but it has added cosmopolitan flair without loss of respect for the town's Old West tradition. — BY TOM PRICE AND FINN-OLAF JONES

FRIDAY

1 *Western Style* 4 p.m.

Get oriented with a ramble around Jackson's town square, which is framed by four arches made from elk horns gathered in nearby forests (the animals shed them annually). Then check out some of the nearby shops. If you want to blend in, the local look is "cowpine," and that's what you'll find at **Stio** (10 East Broadway; 307-201-1890; stio.com), which blends elegance with modern insulating technology under its own brand. In Gaslight Alley, at 125 North Cache Street, you can pick up books on local lore at the **Valley Bookstore** (307-733-4533; valleybookstore.com); jewelry, pottery, and rugs from Native American artists at **Crazy Horse** (307-733-4028; crazyhorsejewelry.com); and glass belt buckles (by the designer and owner John Frechette) and other Western-themed gifts at **Made** (307-690-7957; madejacksonhole.com).

2 *Log Cabin Gourmet* 7 p.m.

Climb the steps to the **Snake River Grill** (84 East Broadway; 307-733-0557; snakerivergrill.com; $$$-$$$$) and settle down at one of the tables in the log-walled dining room. Its log-cabin-chic décor,

OPPOSITE A settler's barn remains in a historic district in Grand Teton National Park.

RIGHT Rivers and natural ponds thread through the park and other publicly owned wilderness nearby.

extensive wine list, and master chef put Jackson Hole on the culinary map. Warm up with one of the house cocktails, like Spike's Paper Plane, a concoction of Wyoming Whiskey small-batch bourbon, Amaro Meletti, Aperol and lemon, and then it's onward to the kind of fare rarely unloaded from the back of a chuck wagon, including local beef ribeye with sautéed green beans and soy-mustard steak sauce or grilled Idaho trout with romano beans and fried lemon.

3 *Star Bright* 10 p.m.

After dinner, stroll north, toward the **National Elk Refuge**, which abuts town. If the season is right, you may find southbound geese asleep on the grass roof of the visitors center (532 North Cache Street; 307-733-9212; fws.gov/refuge/national_elk_refuge/). But look up higher. Away from the lights and neon, you'll have a striking view of the night sky.

SATURDAY

4 *Preparations* 9 a.m.

For all its worldliness, Jackson is a tiny town of about 9,000 full-time residents, and it's easy to pick up snacks or a meal with a minimum of wandering around. Get your caffeine ration, along with granola or a breakfast sandwich, at **Jackson Hole Coffee Roasters** (50 West Broadway; 307-200-6099;

jacksonholeroasters.com). Then take a five-minute drive to **Jackson Whole Grocer and Cafe** (1155 South Highway 89; 307-733-0450; jacksonwholegrocer.com) to pick up food for a picnic later in the day.

5 *And Wear a Helmet* 10 a.m.

Get fitted for a mountain bike rental at **Hoback Sports** (520 West Broadway; 307-733-5335; hobacksports.com), buy a trail map, and start pedaling. Ride east toward the 20-mile Cache Creek-Game Creek loop through the **Bridger Teton National Forest**. Take either the smooth dirt road or the parallel single-track Putt-Putt Trail, winding along a shaded stream. At the Game Creek turnoff, crank up a short steep climb, and you'll be rewarded with a five-mile descent down sage- and aspen-covered hills before connecting with a paved path back to town.

6 *Drive-By Shooting* 2 p.m.

Relax with a behind-the-wheel wander through **Grand Teton National Park** (307-739-3300; nps.gov/grte). Best bet for scenic photos: loop north on Route 191 past the Snake River Overlook, where you can frame the river that carved the valley and the mountains behind it in one shot. Then head south along Teton Park Road past Jenny Lake. On your way back, stop at **Dornan's** in the town of Moose (200 Moose-Wilson Road; 307-733-2415; dornans.com) for cocktails on the deck, about as close as you can get to the Tetons and still have someone bring you a drink.

7 *Contemporary Plus* 7 p.m.

At **The Kitchen** (155 North Glenwood Street; 307-734-1633; thekitchenjacksonhole.com; $$$), an Asian-inflected bistro in a casual, contemporary,

Scandinavian-like space, you can start with sashimi and move on to venison pho or an organic burger. For drinks, there's a wide selection of sakes and 19 different types of tequila.

8 *Two-Stepping* 9 p.m.

Sidle up to a saddle bar stool at the **Million Dollar Cowboy Bar** (25 North Cache Street; 307-733-2207; milliondollarcowboybar.com) — the bucking bronco of Jackson Hole's night life since 1937 — for a bottle of the local brew or a fire cider (whiskey, cider, and cinnamon) amid knobbled pine beams and Wild West artifacts, including a stuffed grizzly killed bare-handed by one C. Dale Petersen. Look over the spur collection and 70 years' worth of other accumulated Westernalia. Around the corner, the **Silver Dollar Bar & Grill** (in the Wort Hotel; 50 North Glenwood; 307-733-2190; worthotel.com) is another cowpoke scene, with fiddling bands and guys in suspenders dancing with tight-jeaned women beneath the curved pink lights of the "Cowboy Deco"-style bar.

SUNDAY

9 *Never Toasted* 8 a.m.

Join the lineup for coffee at **Pearl Street Bagels** (145 West Pearl Avenue; 307-739-1218). Purists, rejoice; even after pranksters nailed a dozen toasters to Pearl Street's pink facade several years ago, it still serves its bagels warm from the oven but always untoasted. And with bagels this fresh and good, it seems a little unfair to quibble.

10 *The Compleat Angler* 10 a.m.

Not every full-service hotel is likely to have a director of fly-fishing, but this is Jackson Hole, and you'll find one at the **Four Seasons Resort** (7680 Granite Loop Road, Teton Village; 307-732-5000; fourseasons.com/jacksonhole). In the resort's handmade wooden dory, he'll take you down one of the secluded braids of the Snake River and offer expert advice on how to reel in some of the Snake's 2,500 fish per mile. You don't have to be a guest, even first-timers are welcome, and it's safe to feel very surprised if you don't land a fish. A day trip will set you back several hundred dollars, and if it's a couple of hundred too many, you can look for a less expensive guide back in town.

OPPOSITE ABOVE Night life beckons in Jackson.

OPPOSITE BELOW Fishing the Snake River. Jackson attracts a well-to-do crowd that loves getting outdoors.

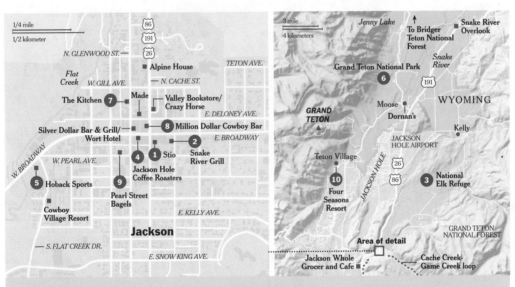

SOUTHWEST

THE BASICS

Arrive at Jackson Hole Airport and rent a car.

Cowboy Village Resort
120 South Flat Creek Drive
307-733-3121
townsquareinns.com/
cowboy-village
$$

Two-room, two-bed cabins with lots of logs and knotty pine.

Alpine House
285 North Glenwood Street
307-739-1570
alpinehouse.com
$$
An upscale 22-room B&B a few blocks from the town square.

Wort Hotel
50 North Glenwood Street
307-733-2190
worthotel.com
$$$$
First opened in 1941. Its popular Silver Dollar Bar has 2,000 inlaid silver dollars.

Anchorage

Anchorage sits between mountains and saltwater in a setting that is hard to improve upon. "And they haven't," a cynic might say of the state's largest city. True, this municipality of 300,000 (its sprawling boundaries make it physically far larger than that population would suggest) will not win any urban-planning contests. But you do not come all this way for architecture tours or adventures in molecular gastronomy. You come to Anchorage for Alaska, and to meet the welcoming Alaskans: both are sui generis, outsize and unforgettable. Home to the railroad, a ship terminal, and what may be the world's largest seaplane base, Anchorage is a great place to settle in for a weekend and to use as a jumping-off point for adventures near and far. — BY CHRISTOPHER SOLOMON

FRIDAY

1 *Drink In the View* 5 p.m.

Anchorage residents say they take visiting friends for a drink at the **Crow's Nest** (939 West Fifth Avenue; captain-cook.com/dining/crows-nest) on the 20th floor of the Hotel Captain Cook. The service is excellent, as are the views of the water and mountains. Situated in the center of the restaurant, the bar is elevated several feet, so you get an unobstructed view over diners while you sip your Sazerac and drink in the view.

2 *South, Up North* 7:30 p.m.

The menu at **South** (11124 Old Seward Highway; southak.com; $$-$$$) is all over the map, offering everything from tapas to the Butter Burger, which is what it sounds like. You usually cannot go wrong with Alaskan staples like seared salmon with roasted local potatoes. South takes pride in its "Barcelona-style" gin and tonics, enhanced by herbs and berries. There's a wide selection of wines as well.

SATURDAY

3 *Fuel Up* 8 a.m.

Head to the Spenard neighborhood and grab a cappuccino at **Kaladi Brothers Coffee** (1340 West Northern Lights Boulevard; kaladi.com), excellent local coffee roasters. Then wander a few doors down to **Middle Way Café** (No. 1200; middlewaycafe.com;

$$), a popular local joint in a strip mall. There is something here for everyone, including avocado toast topped with meats like Alaskan reindeer sausage.

4 *Head for the Hills* 10 a.m.

The Chugach Mountains, Anchorage's eastern backdrop, hold many hiking options, from the steep-and-gorgeous Bird Ridge to the fun scramble of O'Malley Peak. If you want to take a quick hike to amazing views, and don't mind crowds, head to **Flattop Mountain**, (Chugach State Park; dnr.alaska. gov/parks/units/chugach), among the most popular hikes in the state. The summit requires a 200-foot scramble. But you don't need to do that to enjoy views of Denali and the mountains, with the waters of the Turnagain Arm and the buildings of the city laid at your feet (not to mention feasts of dwarf blueberries in late summer). Want a guide to provide commentary or to calm your bear-anoia? Contact **Ascending Path** (907-783-0505; ascendingpath.com).

5 *Baked Bliss* 1 p.m.

"First-timers get a cookie," said the young woman behind the counter at **Fire Island Rustic Bakeshop** (1343 G Street; fireisland-bread.com; $), presenting a pretty great chocolate chip. You like this place even before ordering a hearty sandwich, sweet and savory scones, or the bread pudding studded

OPPOSITE Downtown rises above the Ship Creek area.

BELOW Wild Scoops sells ice cream flavored with local ingredients like blueberries and birch syrup.

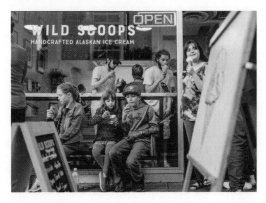

with golden raisins. And, of course, there's a variety of tempting breads.

6 *Spin the Seashore* 2 p.m.

Outside is where Anchorage shines. Even if you have only an hour or two, the best, quickest escape is to hop on the **Tony Knowles Coastal Trail** (anchoragecoastaltrail.com), a beloved public trail that winds along the waters of Knik Arm and Cook Inlet for 11 miles. Rent a bike downtown at **Pablo's Bicycle Rentals** (415 L Street; pablobicyclerentals.com), catch the paved trail a block away, and start pedaling toward wooded Kincaid Park (itself home to about 15 miles of single-track mountain-bike trails). The mostly flat trail soon enters glades of ferns and birch where you might see a moose or a black bear. The tide flats over your shoulder are your constant companion. So is the smell of alder trees. It is the smell of Alaska.

7 *Scream for Ice Cream* 4:30 p.m.

Anchorage rarely gets hot — the average high temperature in August is 64 degrees. But that is warm enough for ice cream. Drop by **Wild Scoops** (429 E Street; wildscoops.com) and fear not: the line moves fast. Flavors feature local ingredients, like blueberries from Talkeetna and Alaskan birch syrup. A scoop of the Alaska spruce tip will transport you to a stroll through a damp spring forest.

8 *A Little Mermaid* 6 p.m.

The **Bubbly Mermaid Champagne and Oyster Bar** (417 D Street; facebook.com/akfreshseafood) hits the mark between trendy and twee. The centerpiece of the tiny space is the bar, formed from a chunk of a former fishing boat. Ask the blue-eyed mermaid stand-ing in the bow to pour you a sparkling wine from almost a dozen open bottles. Study the wall for the nearly three dozen hot and cold oyster offerings like the warm St. Jacques (with a scallop, shiitake, and Mornay) or the cold Hipster shooter (with kale, sriracha, and Pabst Blue Ribbon beer). But the place also serves oysters plain, from sweet British Columbia Kusshis to Hump Islands from Ketchikan that taste like a gulp of fresh saltwater. For all the fun experiments on the wall, a great oyster needs no clothes.

9 *Strip Mall Surprise* 8:30 p.m.

You may think Google Maps has steered you wrong as your search for the best seafood in town ends at a strip mall near the airport. But Anchorage is a city of strip malls that occasionally harbor surprises. Beyond the parking lot lies an oddly quiet, candlelit space that serves great seafood: **Kincaid Grill** (6700 Jewel Lake Road; kincaidgrill.com; $$$). You will pay for that excellence, but what are you here for, if not fresh-caught halibut or Kodiak Island scallops?

SUNDAY

10 *Outer Alaska* 9 a.m.

There's a saying here: "Alaska is 30 minutes outside of Anchorage." Grab a coffee and drive 40 miles southeast along the Alaska Scenic Byway that skirts Turnagain Arm, to the resort village of Girdwood, home of Alyeska Resort. Housed in a Swiss-feeling chalet at the bottom of the ski hill, with sunlight and reggae music filtering down through the blond rafters, is **Jack Sprat** (165 Olympic Mountain Loop; jacksprat.net; $$). The motto here is "fat and lean world cuisine," and the inspired brunch menu skips around the globe.

11 *No Binoculars Needed* 11 a.m.

The drive along Turnagain Arm is one of the most spectacular in the United States. Drive 11 more miles to the end of the arm until you reach another Alaskan must-see: animals. The **Alaska Wildlife Conservation Center** (alaskawildlife.org) is a sanctuary of more than 200 acres that takes in injured wild animals that cannot be returned to nature—creatures such as Venetie, an orphaned lynx found as a kitten after a wildfire. The nonprofit facility has animals in large enclosures, from musk oxen to brown bears. Signs are full of smart, gee-whiz factoids. (Musk ox qiviut, or underwool, is apparently one of the warmest fibers on earth.)

OPPOSITE Hikers take on a steep ascent in the Chugach Mountains. Below them is the icy water of Turnagain Arm.

ABOVE Scones, cookies, and sandwiches with a variety of breads are all on the menu at Fire Island Rustic Bakeshop.

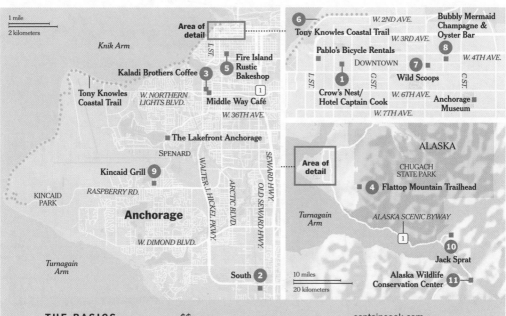

THE BASICS

Fly into Ted Stevens Anchorage International Airport and rent a car. Be sure to pack your hiking shoes.

The Lakefront Anchorage
4800 Spenard Road
millenniumhotels.com

$$
A 248-room, lodge-style hotel on the shore of the busy seaplane base of Lake Hood, not far from downtown and very close to the airport. Relax on the deck and watch floatplanes come and go.

Hotel Captain Cook
939 West Fifth Avenue

captaincook.com
$$-$$$
With 546 rooms in three towers, a dozen shops, and several dining spots on multiple decks, this hotel feels a bit like one of the big cruise ships whose passengers stay here upon reaching Alaska. Murals of Captain Cook's journeys are charmingly retro.

Homer

As you round the final bend on the Sterling Highway in Alaska and reach the town of Homer, the view of Kachemak Bay stops you dead. Across the water, jagged mountains cut by fjords lead right to the rocky coastline, and forests lead to alpine tundra, then glaciers that glint in the sunlight. On the Homer side of the bay, fields full of purple lupine, white yarrow, and goldenrod lead to beaches. Snow-capped volcanoes across a nearby inlet come into view. Homer is called the End of the Road, the Halibut Fishing Capital of the World, or the Cosmic Hamlet by the Sea, depending on whom you happen to ask. Located on the Kenai Peninsula, a 220-mile drive south of Anchorage, Homer is a small town of homesteaders and artists, fishermen and ex-hippies, with a sprinkling of outlaws and seers. These categories frequently overlap, creating a funky, dynamic community that is a bit eccentric even by Alaskan standards. — BY MARIA FINN

FRIDAY

1 *Across the Water* 4:30 p.m.

The road on the Homer Spit, a four-mile-long sliver of land jutting into the bay, leads to the boat harbor and **Kachemak Bay Ferry** (907-226-2424; alaska.org/detail/danny-j-tours). Catch the ferry, the *Danny J*, for a ride across Kachemak Bay to **Halibut Cove**, a small community that has no roads, only wooden boardwalks. The *Danny J* includes a wildlife tour at Gull Island, a bird sanctuary, at noon and a 5 p.m. service that takes people to Halibut Cove for the evening. Before dinner at the Saltry restaurant, stroll the boardwalks and drop in at the **Halibut Cove Experience Fine Art Gallery** (907-296-2215; halibutcoveexperience.com), which shows the works of Halibut Cove artists. Some of this area's local artists also fish commercially, a way of life reflected in their work.

2 *Taste of the Bay* 6:30 p.m.

The **Saltry** restaurant (907-399-2683; thesaltry. com/saltry.htm; $$$) in Halibut Cove serves seafood caught locally and vegetables grown in a

patch out back. There is seating indoors or outside on a covered deck that overlooks the moored boats. The Saltry has a brief list of wines to go with its main event, the seafood. Try a huge appetizer platter of tart pickled salmon or mildly spiced halibut ceviche, and an entree of grilled halibut or Pacific cod brandade.

3 *Beer on the Spit* 9 p.m.

To while away a few hours in an atmosphere of conviviality (if not urbanity), drop in at the **Salty Dawg Saloon** (4380 Homer Spit Road; 907-235-6718; saltydawgsaloon.com), a dive bar and Alaska institution. It's the place where tourists and locals drink, sing, and get silly together.

SATURDAY

4 *Tempting Aromas* 8 a.m.

Anyone cutting back on carbs should avoid **Two Sisters Bakery** (233 East Bunnell Avenue; 907-235-2280; twosistersbakery.net) in Homer's Old Town near Bishop's Beach. But the salty ocean air carrying wafts of pecan sticky buns, savory Danishes, and fresh-brewed coffee makes this place hard to resist.

5 *Natural Alaska* 10 a.m.

Get into the forest on an early guided hike at the **Wynn Nature Center** (East Skyline Drive; 907-235-6667; akcoastalstudies.org/guided-tours/wynn-nature-center.html), which is part of the nonprofit Center for Alaskan Coastal Studies, established in 1982. The bears and moose may be elusive, but the wildflowers and trees stay in place, ready for your guide's interpretation. (The coastal studies center also offers full-day nature tours from its Peterson Bay Field Station, Memorial Day through Labor Day, including a forest hike, talks about indigenous peoples and fantastical rock formations, and a glimpse of the sea life exposed at low tide.)

6 *Lunch and a Book* Noon

You'll be back in town in time for lunch at the cozy **Wild Honey Bistro** (106 West Bunnell Avenue; 907-435-7635; wildhoneybistro.com; $$), which offers a choice of sweet and savory crepes, soups, and

pastries. Afterward, browse the **Old Inlet Bookshop** (3487 Main Street; 907-235-7984; oldinletbookshop. com), located in a log cabin a block away.

7 *Paddling the Bay* 2 p.m.

From the Homer harbor, take a water taxi ride across the bay to **Yukon Island**, where you can launch a kayak into the smooth waters of Kachemak Bay. There, translucent jellyfish pulse below the sea's surface and bald eagles perch on

ABOVE The beach at Kachemak Bay.

BELOW A fresh catch of halibut is prepared for market on a dock along the Homer Spit.

OPPOSITE Catch the ferry to Halibut Cove.

rocky balustrades. On clear days the volcanoes Iliamna and Augustine can be seen. Take a half-day tour with **True North Kayak Adventures** (5 Cannery Row Boardwalk, Homer Spit Road; 907-235-0708; truenorthkayak.com). Alison O'Hara, a founder and a longtime guide in Kachemak Bay, teaches how to approach the sea otters resting in kelp beds and identifies the seabirds. You may see porpoises, whales, and seals. (There are also full-day and three-quarter-day options.)

8 *The Homestead* 8 p.m.

For a breathtaking view on the deck or in the solarium above the kitchen and bar, take a seat at **Finn's Pizza** (4287 Homer Spit Road, Cannery Row Boardwalk; 907-235-2878; finnspizza.co; $$), opened in 2000, and order a thin-crusted pizza baked in the wood-fired oven. Most of the ingredients for the pizzas and salads come from local farms. A local favorite: the Blue Pear, with organic pears, mozzarella, pine nuts, and Gorgonzola.

SUNDAY

9 *Cosmic Cuisine* 7:30 a.m.

Brother Asaiah Bates, a follower of South Asian mysticism, arrived in Homer in 1955 from California. He and others with him vowed not to wear shoes or cut their hair until world peace had been achieved and world hunger eradicated. They were called Barefooters. Although the group broke up, Brother Asaiah stayed on, becoming a local sage. He dubbed Homer "the Cosmic Hamlet by the Sea," and although he died in 2000, a small cafe, the **Cosmic Kitchen** (510 East Pioneer Avenue; 907-235-6355; cosmickitchenalaska.com; $), shows that his legacy lives on in many forms, even in the breakfast burrito. A homemade salsa bar offers condiments for the burritos or huge plates of huevos rancheros accompanied by fresh hash browns.

10 *Head of the Bay* 8:30 a.m.

Just about the only way to get to the head of Kachemak Bay is on horseback. **Trails End Horse Adventures** (53435 East End Road; 907-235-6393) takes visitors down a steep switchback that leads to the beach, and then past the Russian Orthodox village of Kachemak Selo. The tour continues on to the Fox River Flats. Turning toward the Homer Hills, the horses follow a narrow path flanked by elderberry bushes that open into a breathtaking site

that was a Barefooters homestead in the 1950s and is now abandoned. Bald eagle chicks peer down from cottonwood trees, and clusters of wildflowers dot the open fields. It feels like timeless Alaska.

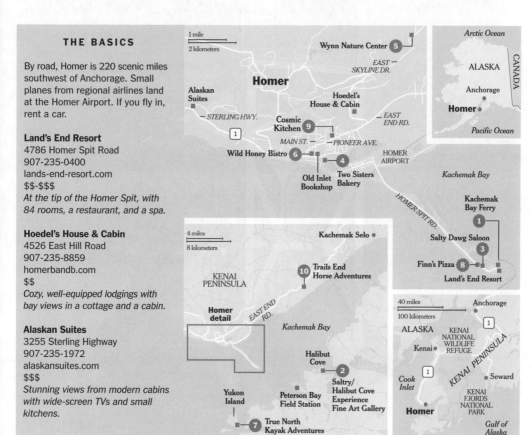

THE BASICS

By road, Homer is 220 scenic miles southwest of Anchorage. Small planes from regional airlines land at the Homer Airport. If you fly in, rent a car.

Land's End Resort
4786 Homer Spit Road
907-235-0400
lands-end-resort.com
$$-$$$
At the tip of the Homer Spit, with 84 rooms, a restaurant, and a spa.

Hoedel's House & Cabin
4526 East Hill Road
907-235-8859
homerbandb.com
$$
Cozy, well-equipped lodgings with bay views in a cottage and a cabin.

Alaskan Suites
3255 Sterling Highway
907-235-1972
alaskansuites.com
$$$
Stunning views from modern cabins with wide-screen TVs and small kitchens.

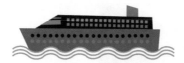

Juneau

Residents of Juneau, Alaska, brag that their town is the most beautiful state capital city in America, and they have a strong argument. Juneau is inside the Tongass National Forest, part of the world's largest temperate rainforest. Old-growth groves and glaciers lie within the municipal limits, snow-capped mountains loom overhead, and whales and other marine wildlife are a short boat ride away. The town itself is a working state capital with a utilitarian feel, but gold rush-era buildings, art galleries, quality regional theater, and fresh seafood make pleasant complements to Juneau's stunning surroundings. — BY CORNELIA DEAN

FRIDAY

1 *Back to the Ice Age* 3 p.m.

Nature beckons. But some preparations are required. On your way into town, stop at **Western Auto-Marine** (5165 Glacier Highway; 907-780-4909; juneauoutfitters.com) for a pair of brown rubber, calf-high Xtratuf Boots, a must-have item in any Alaskan's wardrobe. Thus prepared, start your Juneau explorations at the entrance to **Switzer Creek** and **Richard Marriott Trails** (midway on Sunset Street). On the hillside, evergreens in even ranks give way to a hodgepodge of trees of different species, sizes, and shapes. This change marks the boundary between second-growth timber, on land logged decades ago, and an old-growth forest, untouched since the end of the last ice age. Hike up the trail — it's not too strenuous — and discover for yourself why environmentalists are so keen to save these ancient woods, home to an amazingly rich variety of plant and animal life. (Keep to the wooden planks at the base of the trail, and be glad you have your boots. The bog, or muskeg, is plenty wet.)

2 *Fish Don't Get Fresher* 6:30 p.m.

Locals say Juneau is not much of a restaurant town because so many people dine on fish they catch themselves. But when they want fish prepared for them,

they head to the **Hangar on the Wharf Pub & Grill** (2 Marine Way; 907-586-5018; hangaronthewharf. com; $$-$$$). The building's exterior of plain blue clapboard isn't designed to impress, but the harbor-side location offers dazzling views of the Gastineau Channel and the mountains of Douglas Island west of downtown. There's halibut on the menu, of course, and salmon (guaranteed wild-caught) and king crab.

3 *Indoor Drama* 8 p.m.

Take in a play at the **Perseverance Theatre**, a nonprofit repertory company across the Gastineau Channel on Douglas Island (914 Third Street, Douglas; 907-364-2421; perseverancetheatre.org). A pillar of Juneau's cultural life since 1979, Perseverance stages high-quality classic and contemporary plays, and the prices are low.

SATURDAY

4 *Seeing Sea Life* 9 a.m.

What better way to start your Saturday than with some close-up views of Juneau's wildlife? A number of companies offer whale-watching trips from Auke Bay, a short car (or bus) ride north of downtown. Find one offering a trip up the Lynn Canal to **Berners Bay**, and you are sure to see Steller sea lions basking on a rocky haul-out, harbor seals bobbing in the water, and harrier hawks, geese, and ducks. Also watch for eagles nesting along the shores. Most companies guarantee you will see whales; chances of spotting humpbacks are best in late spring when the herring-like fish called eulakon ("hooligan" in a local Native language) are running.

OPPOSITE A navigational buoy near Juneau makes a convenient perch for Steller sea lions and a bald eagle.

RIGHT Cruise ships turn their sterns toward town at the end of daylong stops in Juneau's harbor.

5 *Up North, Down South* Noon

Back in town, enjoy a taste of old Juneau at the **Triangle Club** (251 Front Street; 907-586-3140; triangleclubbar.com; $). Order a hot dog and some Alaskan Amber, one of the local beers brewed and bottled right in town. If the Triangle looks a bit louche for your tastes, try **El Sombrero** around the corner (157 South Franklin Street; 907-586-6770; facebook.com/ElSombreroJuneau; $$), a Juneau institution. This modest place has been dishing out generous helpings of Mexican standards since the oil boom began in the 1970s.

6 *They Came First* 1:30 p.m.

For some historical perspective, visit the **Alaska State Museum** (395 Whittier Street; 907-465-2901; museums.state.ak.us), which houses a collection covering the Athabascans, Aleuts, and other Alaska Natives, the state's history as a Russian colony, and the gold rush that helped create Juneau. The museum's store stocks Native crafts including baskets, prints, and dolls. Keep walking farther from the port and you'll come upon what is probably Juneau's least-known gem: the lichen-covered tombstones in **Evergreen Cemetery** (601 Seater Street; 907-364-2828). Joseph Juneau and Richard Harris, the prospectors who founded the city, are buried here, and the cemetery was also the site of the funeral pyre of Chief Cowee, the Auk who led them to Juneau's gold.

7 *Arts and Crafts* 3 p.m.

When cruise ships are in town, the locals say they stay out of "waddling distance" of the piers. And with good reason: most of the shops that line the streets of downtown are filled with mass-produced "Native" items for the tourist trade. But not all. The **Juneau Artists Gallery** (175 South Franklin Street; 907-586-9891; juneauartistsgallery.net), a co-operative shop, sells jewelry, prints, pottery, drawings, and other work. Be sure to chat with the gallery staff—each is an artist and a member of the co-op. For apparel a little more exotic than the ubiquitous Alaska-themed sweatshirt, try **Shoefly & Hudsons** (109 Seward Street; 907-586-1055; shoeflyalaska.com), which offers unusual designs in footwear, handbags, and accessories. (People in Juneau say it was one of Sarah Palin's favorite shops when she was the governor.) But the city's most unusual retail outlet is **William Spear Design** (174 South Franklin Street; 907-586-2209; wmspear.com), a purveyor of tiny enamel pins, zipper pulls, and other items—many with edgy political messages.

8 *On the Page* 4:30 p.m.

If your shopping interests run more toward the written word, you are in luck: Juneau is friendly to independent bookstores. One in downtown is the **Observatory** (299 North Franklin Street; 907-586-9676; observatorybooks.com), perched up the hill from the harbor. From a tiny blue house not much younger than the town itself, the shop's proprietor, Dee Longenbaugh, offers an extensive stock of books on Alaska, particularly the southeast region, as well as a collection of maps and charts.

9 *Alaskan Bounty* 7 p.m.

In 2015, chefs from the **Rookery Café** (111 Seward Street; 907-463-3013; therookerycafe.com) won a national seafood cook-off with dishes made, nose to tail, from a wild Alaskan sockeye salmon. The

ABOVE AND BELOW Spectacular scenery courtesy of Juneau's in-town glacier, the Mendenhall Glacier. Downstream, Nugget Falls cascades from the glacial melt, while upstream the glacier itself holds onto its frozen grandeur.

restaurant, centered by a long wooden communal table, brings that ethos to its inventive menu in dishes that include cured Alaskan pork tenderloin, locally grown radishes, and of course, salmon collars. After dinner, get back into the gold rush mood with a game of pool and an Alaskan pale ale in the bar of the **Alaskan Hotel** (167 South Franklin Street; 907-586-1000; thealaskanhotel.com).

SUNDAY

10 *Coffee and a View* 9 a.m.

Grab a coffee and a pastry at the downtown location of the **Heritage Coffee Company** chain (130 Front Street; 907-586-1087; heritagecoffee.com) before donning your boots and heading out to Juneau's in-town glacier, the **Mendenhall Glacier**, off Glacier

Spur Road. Dress warmly—cool air flows constantly off the 12-mile stream of ice, and it is typically five or 10 degrees cooler here than in town. In part because of global warming, the glacier is retreating perhaps as much as 100 feet a year. Even from the visitor center (8510 Mendenhall Loop Road; 907-789-0097), you can see the kinds of rock and soil it deposited as it moved inland. But if you are feeling energetic, try the Moraine Trail for a first-hand look at what glaciers leave behind.

ABOVE A food truck transaction near the waterfront.

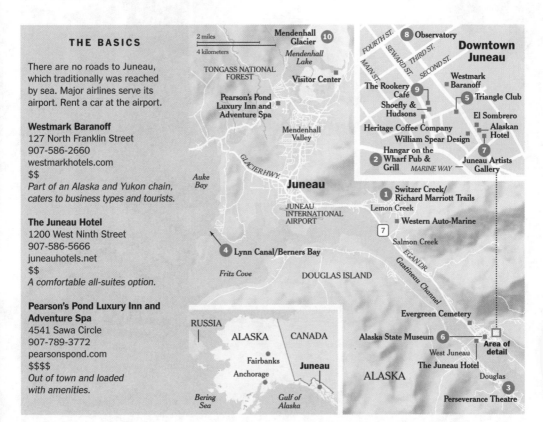

THE BASICS

There are no roads to Juneau, which traditionally was reached by sea. Major airlines serve its airport. Rent a car at the airport.

Westmark Baranoff
127 North Franklin Street
907-586-2660
westmarkhotels.com
$$
Part of an Alaska and Yukon chain, caters to business types and tourists.

The Juneau Hotel
1200 West Ninth Street
907-586-5666
juneauhotels.net
$$
A comfortable all-suites option.

Pearson's Pond Luxury Inn and Adventure Spa
4541 Sawa Circle
907-789-3772
pearsonspond.com
$$$$
Out of town and loaded with amenities.

2 miles
4 kilometers

Mendenhall **10** Glacier

Mendenhall Lake

TONGASS NATIONAL FOREST

Visitor Center

Pearson's Pond Luxury Inn and Adventure Spa

Mendenhall Valley

GLACIER HWY.

Auke Bay

Juneau

JUNEAU INTERNATIONAL AIRPORT

4 Lynn Canal/Berners Bay

Fritz Cove

DOUGLAS ISLAND

FOURTH ST.
SEWARD ST.
THIRD ST.
MAIN ST.
SECOND ST.

8 Observatory

Downtown Juneau

The Rookery Café **9**

Shoefly & Hudsons

Heritage Coffee Company

William Spear Design

Hangar on the **2** Wharf Pub & Grill *MARINE WAY*

Westmark **■** Baranoff

5 Triangle Club

El Sombrero

■ Alaskan Hotel

7

Juneau Artists Gallery

1 Switzer Creek/ Richard Marriott Trails

Lemon Creek

■ Western Auto-Marine

7

Salmon Creek

EGAN DR.
Gastineau Channel

Evergreen Cemetery

Alaska State Museum **6**

West Juneau

The Juneau Hotel

ALASKA

Area of detail

Douglas

3

Perseverance Theatre

RUSSIA

ALASKA   CANADA

Fairbanks

Juneau

Anchorage

Bering Sea   *Gulf of Alaska*

Vancouver

It happens before you know it: Suddenly, you're smitten with Vancouver—its endless coastline, its glassy downtown, the extravagant nature that surrounds and permeates it. It's also a food lover's kind of place: You could spend days sampling local variations on everything from sushi to lasagna to vegetarian concoctions that can transform an heirloom tomato into something decadent, and barely scratch the surface of the constantly evolving restaurant scene. On the cultural front, a commitment to public art has turned some areas into sculpture gardens. And in this city of many ethnicities, First Nations art and culture are becoming more and more visible. — BY SUZANNE MACNEILLE

FRIDAY

1 *Urban Jungle* Noon

Stanley Park (vancouver.ca/parks-recreation-culture/stanley-park) is the oldest and largest of the more than 230 parks in Vancouver: 1,000 acres of forest, wetlands, and beaches (and a few manmade attractions—among them, an aquarium and a handful of restaurants). On mild weekends, some areas are more hectic than bucolic; by mid-morning, swarms of bicyclists and skaters race around the park's peripheral trail (its views, like the one near Siwash Rock, are spectacular). But most of the park is quiet, threaded with trails. On a guided walk, Candace Campo, a First Nations co-owner of **Talaysay Tours** (talaysay.com), identified salmon berry bushes, skunk cabbage, and other plants, noting that taking "only what is needed"—for food, clothing, medicine, and shelter—has long been a given in indigenous cultures.

2 *On the Water* 2 p.m.

On the opposite end of the park spectrum is tiny **Cardero Park** (1601 Bayshore Drive), with its views across the harbor to the mountains beyond. Stroll east, past lawns where people hunch over books or picnics. Not far away, on West Pender Street, the **Heritage Asian Eatery** (1108 West Pender Street; eatheritage.ca; $$) offers communal tables and a concise, pleasing menu.

3 *Chinatown and Beyond* 3:30 p.m.

West Pender changes as you head east into an area that itself wavers, block by block, from trendy to seedy to touristy. Eventually you'll reach Chinatown, which has its gritty areas but is also home to food markets, restaurants, and the serene **Dr. Sun Yat-Sen Classical Chinese Garden** (578 Carrall Street; vancouverchinesegarden.com). Not far from the flaring tiled roofs of the Millennium Gate, a totem rises above **Skwachàys Lodge** (29 West Pender Street; skwachays.com), an indigenous artists' residence and boutique hotel. In the beautifully lit gallery, contemporary works draw on ancient images and beliefs.

4 *Literary Chaos* 4:45 p.m.

MacLeod's Books (455 West Pender Street; facebook.com/pages/MacLeods-Books/126095490890770) is a vintage bookstore par excellence. Inside, pure, lovely literary chaos awaits: precarious stacks and overstuffed shelves of history books, novels, rare editions of Kipling and Wilde, pamphlets on Chinook jargon, and endless art tomes. Browse there, and then wander into the nearby Gastown neighborhood, its narrow streets thick with shoppers, restaurant-seekers, and the occasional panhandler. Yes, it's touristy, but this is also the historic heart of the city, a place where loggers and seafaring types once communed. Amid the current frenzy, **Purebread** (159 West Hastings Street; purebread.ca) offers irresistible treats, like a thick slice of buttermilk coconut cake, that can be wrapped up for later.

5 *Ice Wine and Sablefish* 7:30 p.m.

Watch the sky fade above False Creek from the quiet terrace at **Ancora Waterfront Dining and Patio** (1600 Howe Street; ancoradining.com; $$$), where the choices on the Japanese-Peruvian menu run to crispy prawn causa or sablefish in aji panca glaze. Regional ice wines may be paired with desserts like coconut panna cotta.

SATURDAY

6 *On English Bay* 10 a.m.

Denman Street is lined with restaurants, galleries, and shops. Get a coffee and pastry to go at **Delany's Coffee House** (1105 Denman Street; delanyscoffee.com/denman-street) and head past

OPPOSITE Bicycling on the peripheral trail in Stanley Park.

the bronze statues of laughing men, collectively known as *A-maze-ing Laughter*, to English Bay. Find a comfortable log on the breezy beach, and eat breakfast to a soundtrack of waves and gulls.

7 *Hug the Coast* Noon

Rent a bike near English Bay and go east on the waterside bike path, past the Inuit Inukshuk rock sculpture; a peaceful, somber AIDS memorial in the form of steel panels engraved with names; and other installations. Once you cross Burrard Bridge, keep close to the shore. Consider visits to the **Museum of Vancouver** (1100 Chestnut Street; museumofvancouver. ca), with an in-depth, multimedia exhibition on Musqueam First Nation culture, and **Kitsilano Beach Park** (1499 Arbutus Street), favored by families, view-seekers, occasional film crews (this is Hollywood North, after all), and admirers of big, frothy weeping willows (download a tree map at kitstreemap.com). Take a detour down residential streets; when you reach the 1865 Old Hastings Mill Store Museum, turn back, this time taking the long way around False

Creek (keep an eye out for dragon boats). If you can face the crowds, Granville Island has many shops, galleries, and, in the **Public Market** (granvilleisland. com/public-market), excellent food stalls.

8 *Cantonese Feast* 6:30 p.m.

It's not difficult to find a reason to hop on the Canada Line train (thecanadaline.com) for the short trip to nearby Richmond with its largely Chinese population. There are temples, like the imperial-style International Buddhist Temple, which welcomes visitors; midday dim-sum feasts; and tea shops where you can find rare and expensive pu-erh teas. And then there is dinner at **Chef Tony** (101-4600 No. 3 Road; cheftonycanada.com; $$$-$$$$), blazingly bright beneath elaborate light fixtures. A screen flashed through one night's menu: stewed pumpkin and short ribs, stir-fried sea cucumbers, fried purple rice with eel, and on and on. Expect to stay long.

9 *Waterfront Wandering* 8:30 p.m.

Back on the downtown waterfront, wander past hotels and bars, some offering live music. You might stop at the Fairmont Pacific Rim hotel for a drink at the pastel-hued, plant-filled **Botanist** (1038 Canada Place; botanistrestaurant.com), a glamorous restaurant and bar with a "cocktail lab" equipped with things like centrifuges and ice-sculpting tools. Or head a few blocks inland to the small, smart bar of **Royal Dinette** (905 Dunsmuir Street; royaldinette. ca). As long as you're at this excellent farm-to-table restaurant, order dessert to go with your drink.

ABOVE A First Nations boat in the Museum of Anthropology.

LEFT Siwash Rock, seen from the sea wall in Stanley Park.

SUNDAY

10 *Breakfast in the Neighborhood* 9 a.m.

At **Forage** (foragevancouver.com; $$), a sleek little restaurant in the artsy West End **Listel Hotel** (1300 Robson Street; thelistelhotel.com), just about everything is house-made, from the spiced pear jam to the candied bacon. After breakfast, stroll around the neighborhood. Vancouver has many wonderful buildings—from the Art Deco Marine Building to the Colosseum-like Central Branch of the Vancouver Public Library—but the West End is special, with verdant streets and graceful heritage houses. An online map for a West End Architectural Walk is at the website vancouver.ca.

11 *A Fitting Setting* 11 a.m.

The wooded campus of the **University of British Columbia** (ubc.ca/our-campuses/vancouver) holds many surprises: a suspended walkway through a forest canopy; a Japanese tea garden; a reconciliation pole by the Haida master carver James Hart; and a longhouse that serves as a student center. Near the water, the **Museum of Anthropology** (6393 Northwest Marine Drive; moa.ubc.ca) has thousands of First Nations artifacts. Its splendid Great Hall, with a soaring glass wall, is a powerful setting for canoes, carved poles, house posts, and other traditional objects.

ABOVE The sweet creations may be irresistible at Purebread, a bakery in the Gastown district.

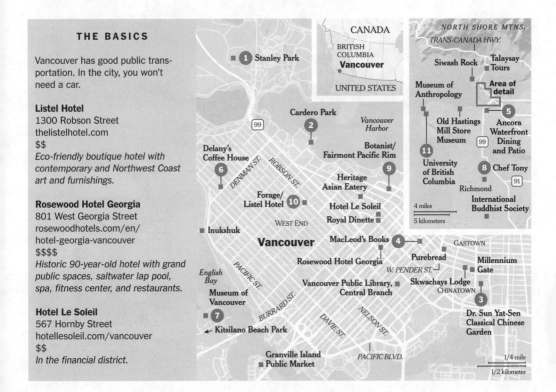

THE BASICS

Vancouver has good public transportation. In the city, you won't need a car.

Listel Hotel
1300 Robson Street
thelistelhotel.com
$$
Eco-friendly boutique hotel with contemporary and Northwest Coast art and furnishings.

Rosewood Hotel Georgia
801 West Georgia Street
rosewoodhotels.com/en/
hotel-georgia-vancouver
$$$$
Historic 90-year-old hotel with grand public spaces, saltwater lap pool, spa, fitness center, and restaurants.

Hotel Le Soleil
567 Hornby Street
hotellesoleil.com/vancouver
$$
In the financial district.

CANADA
BRITISH COLUMBIA
Vancouver
UNITED STATES

NORTH SHORE MTNS.
TRANS-CANADA HWY.

Stanley Park ·1·

Siwash Rock · Talaysay Tours ·
Museum of Anthropology
Area of detail

Cardero Park
Vancouver Harbor
·2·

Old Hastings Mill Store Museum · 99 · Ancora Waterfront Dining and Patio ·5·

Delany's Coffee House ·6·
DENMAN ST. ROBSON ST.
Botanist/ Fairmont Pacific Rim
University of British Columbia ·11·
·8· Chef Tony
Richmond 91

Heritage Asian Eatery ·9·
International Buddhist Society

Forage/ Listel Hotel ·10·
Hotel Le Soleil
Royal Dinette
4 miles
5 kilometers

Inukshuk ·
WEST END

Vancouver
MacLeod's Books ·4·
GASTOWN

Rosewood Hotel Georgia
Purebread
Millennium Gate

English Bay
PACIFIC ST.
W. PENDER ST.
Skwachays Lodge
CHINATOWN

Museum of Vancouver ·7·
Vancouver Public Library, Central Branch
·3·

BURRARD ST.
DAVIE ST.
NELSON ST.

Kitsilano Beach Park
Dr. Sun Yat-Sen Classical Chinese Garden

Granville Island Public Market
PACIFIC BLVD.
1/4 mile
1/2 kilometer

Victoria

Victoria, British Columbia's compact, eminently walkable capital city, is set amid the breathtaking beauty and bounty of Vancouver Island. Beyond the picture-perfect downtown waterfront, the city is an exhilarating blend of cultures, from Canadian and First Nations to Chinese and European (especially British). There are three universities, thriving arts and cultural institutions, significant historic preservation, and a celebrated local food scene. Victoria has Canada's mildest climate — that means year-round forest visits, biking, and golf; gardens galore (daffodils in February); even beehives downtown. There is wildness too: "bear jams" disrupting traffic, cougar sightings, soaring eagles, towering ancient trees, log-strewn beaches, and distant snowy peaks.
— BY SUZANNE CARMICK

FRIDAY

1 *Early Days* 3 p.m.

To explore the Old Town, start at Bastion Square and Wharf Street, overlooking the harbor, where James Douglas founded Fort Victoria in 1843 as an outpost of the Hudson's Bay Company. This area became the heart of commerce, industry, and government, swelling in size after the 1858 Fraser Gold Rush. Next to the Old Victoria Customs House is a grassy overlook with a display telling the history of British settlement and the indigenous Lekwungen people. Check out the lively **Bastion Square** pedestrian area of shops, restaurants, and cafes; then browse through **Munro's Books** (1108 Government Street; munroboooks.com), co-founded in 1963 by the Nobel Prize-winning Canadian writer Alice Munro. Detour through Trounce Alley (note the 125-year-old gaslights), and walk east on Fort Street to **La Taqueria** (766 Fort Street; lataqueria.com) to snack on tacos amid festive music and colorful tiles.

2 *On the Waterfront* 6 p.m.

The Inner Harbour is where seaplanes, water taxis, kayak outfitters, whale-watching tours, restaurants, and festivals can all be found. Sit under the trees and watch the boats and passersby; then head to the chateau-style **Fairmont Empress** (721 Government Street; fairmont.com/empress-victoria), one of several luxury hotels built across Canada by the Canadian Pacific Railway Company at the turn of the century. Take a look at its Q restaurant and bar, with coffered ceiling, gold and purple accents, and portraits of Queen Victoria. Nearby are the majestic provincial Parliament buildings, spectacularly illuminated at night. **Thunderbird Park** (675 Belleville Street; tourismvictoria.com) is a quiet spot with a recreated First Nations house and totem poles.

3 *The Art of Dining* 8 p.m.

Little Jumbo (506 Fort Street; littlejumbo.ca; $$-$$$) feels like a warm embrace; the exposed brick, aged wood, and glowing copper ceiling take you back in time. The restaurant, which has received accolades for everything from design to food and drinks, is a homage to two New York City saloon owners in the 1860s who championed the art of dining and mixology. Entrees feature creative presentations of beef, salmon, and duck. Order British Columbian wines with your meal.

SATURDAY

4 *Urban Oasis* 9 a.m.

Fol Epi bakery (732 Yates Street; folepi.ca) is known for its wild-yeast breads, made from milled-on-site organic flours and baked in brick ovens. Choose from an array of loaves, pastries, and quiches; then think ahead to a packable lunch of sandwiches. Walk down Douglas Street to **Beacon Hill Park** (100 Cook Street). Its 200-acre landscape varies from manicured and natural gardens to forest, swampland, lakes, Garry oaks, and camas fields (originally planted by the Lekwungen, who harvested the edible bulbs), and includes a children's farm and a 127-foot totem pole. Make time to tour the nearby **Emily Carr House** (207 Government Street; emilycarr.com), home of the early 20th-century painter of forests and First Nations scenes whose unique modernist vision continues to earn greater accolades with the passing decades.

OPPOSITE Bastion Square makes a good starting point for exploring Victoria's Old Town, which dates to the 19th century. It's now an inviting streetscape for strolling amid restaurants, shops, and glowing gaslights.

5 *Along Dallas Road* Noon

Dallas Road, a scenic stretch on the southern shore of the city, draws walkers, joggers, bikers, and dogs. Start at **Ogden Point** (gvha.ca/ogden-point-terminal), where interpretive kiosks explain murals depicting Coast Salish First Nations culture. Walk out to the lighthouse, watching for sea otters and seals. Farther east, cross the road to **Ross Bay Cemetery** (oldcem.bc.ca/cem_rb.htm), where you'll find some of the city's oldest heritage trees. If you have extra time, consider returning later to drive farther on this road, which takes other names but continues along the dramatic rocky coast. Good stops are Oak Bay, where you'll find art galleries and British-style pubs and teahouses; Willows Beach; and Mount Douglas Park, where the panoramic view is remarkable.

6 *To the Garden* 2 p.m.

From the cemetery, head to the exquisite **Abkhazi Garden** (1964 Fairfield Road; conservancy.bc.ca), tucked away on a quiet block behind rhododendrons and Garry oaks. The tranquil gardens, with their several distinct outdoor "rooms," were designed to harmonize with the rocky glacial outcroppings and native trees on the hilly property, which includes rock ponds (with mallards and turtles) and the 1950s Modernist summerhouse and former home (now teahouse) of the couple whose love story started it all.

7 *Afternoon Art* 4 p.m.

At the **Art Gallery of Greater Victoria** (1040 Moss Street; aggv.ca), seven modern gallery spaces adjoin an 1889 mansion. On permanent display are works by Emily Carr and an impressive Asian collection and garden. There are amber and ivory carvings, a Japa-

ABOVE The Fairmont Empress, Victoria's landmark hotel, overlooks the harbor and dominates the skyline.

LEFT Traditional carvings in the First Peoples gallery of the Royal BC Museum. The fascinating exhibits in this museum are worth many hours of exploration.

nese Shinto shrine, and a Chinese Ming dynasty bell presented to Victoria in 1903.

8 *Chinatown* 6 p.m.

The 19th-century gold rushes and Canadian Pacific Railway construction drew thousands of Chinese immigrants to Victoria, where they settled above Johnson Street. Today, Canada's oldest Chinatown is a National Historic Site, a small, colorful (especially red, for luck), vibrant community of narrow streets and alleyways, shops and restaurants, beyond the resplendent Gates of Harmonious Interest. The Victoria Chinese Public School (636 Fisgard Street), built in 1909, is still used to teach Chinese language classes. Climb the stairs to the top floor of the **Yen Wo Society** building (1713 Government Street)

BELOW Browsing at Munro's Books. The Nobel Prize-winning author Alice Munro was one of the store's founders.

to see the oldest active Chinese temple in Canada, honoring the sea deity Tam Kung.

9 *Down-to-Earth Dinner* 8 p.m.

OLO (509 Fisgard Street; olorestaurant.com; $$) serves up serious farm-to-table fare with a nod to the region's cultural diversity. The name means hungry in Chinook, and the space is comfortable and rustic, with warm light emanating from hanging spheres of loosely wound wooden strips. One typical meal included Hakurei turnip salad, garganelli pasta with a meaty sauce, and a dreamy dessert of rhubarb, salmonberries, and elderberry ice cream. Pair your meal with a local wine.

SUNDAY

10 *Local Brunch* 10 a.m.

There is pleasant outdoor seating along a pedestrian way at **Agrius** (732 Yates Street;

agriusrestaurant.com; $$), where brunch follows the restaurant's theme of organic and local. Look for such offerings as buckwheat and rye pancakes, egg dishes with cured salmon, house-made lamb sausage, and fried oysters.

11 *Totems and Streetscapes* 11 a.m.
You could spend hours in the **Royal BC Museum** (675 Belleville Street; royalbcmuseum.bc.ca), a stellar repository of natural and human history with a singular collection of British Columbia First Nations archaeological materials. The First Peoples gallery includes a totem hall and ceremonial house, an interactive language display, and a collection of argillite (black shale) carvings from the island of Haida Gwaii, while the Old Town recreates period streetscapes and trades — a cannery, hotel, sawmill — even the ship quarters of George Vancouver, who charted the British Columbia coasts for the British in the 1790s.

ABOVE La Taqueria, a good stop in the Old Town. Walking is the way to get around this part of the city, one of its most pedestrian-friendly areas.

OPPOSITE The Old Victoria Customs House, on the waterfront, recalls the era when ships crowded the harbor and Victoria was Canada's leading Pacific Ocean port.

THE BASICS

Seaplanes and more conventional aircraft arrive in Victoria from Vancouver and Seattle. Ferries come from Vancouver and nearby islands, as well as Seattle.

Best Western Plus at Carlton Plaza
642 Johnson Street
bestwesterncarltonplazahotel.com
$$$
In Victoria's Old Town.

Dashwood Manor Seaside Bed and Breakfast
1 Cook Street
dashwoodmanor.com
$$$-$$$$
Step out the door to the waterfront path or Beacon Hill Park.

Oak Bay Beach Hotel
1175 Beach Drive
oakbaybeachhotel.com
$$$
A 1927 seaside manor house with 239 guest rooms and a spa.

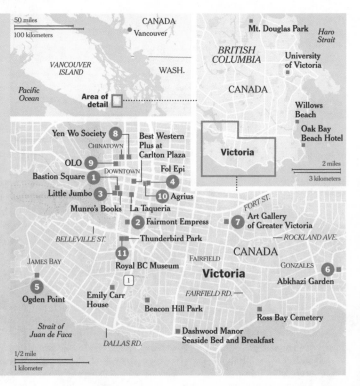

Whistler

Whistler, North America's biggest ski resort, invites a listing of statistics. A mile of vertical drop, 37 lifts, 8,100 skiable acres, 200 runs spread across its two mountains, Whistler and Blackcomb. In 2010, the Winter Olympics, lured by all that snow, brought skiers to town from around the planet. But this steep mountain valley is home to a diversity that has nothing to do with international competitions. Walk down the main promenade and see everyone from rich urban castaways and old-school hippies to stylish French-speaking Québécois and weathered dropouts shouldering skis the size of ironing boards. It makes Whistler feel worldly and cosmopolitan, even when gold medals aren't being handed out.

— BY CHRISTOPHER SOLOMON

FRIDAY

1 *Cultural Powder* 4 p.m.

Before you hit the snow, pay homage to the ground underneath: for thousands of years, Whistler Valley was the hunting and berry-picking grounds of the Squamish and Lil'wat First Nations. Explore the rich history of the land you'll be skiing at the **Squamish Lil'wat Cultural Center** (4584 Blackcomb Way; 866-441-7522; slcc.ca). While the hand-carved canoes, baskets, and smoked-salmon bannocks (kind of a local panini) are diverting, what really makes this 30,000-square-foot museum shine are the friendly aboriginal "youth ambassadors," who welcome visitors with native songs and totem-carving exhibitions.

2 *Carbo Load* 8 p.m.

It's easy to spend money in Whistler. Those watching their loonies should follow the local ski bums to **Pasta Lupino** (4368 Main Street, Whistler Village North; 604-905-0400; pastalupino.com; $$). Tucked away at the edge of the resort, the small, cheery restaurant serves fantastic fresh pastas with homemade Bolognese and Alfredo sauces. And the budget-friendly prices for pastas, soup or salad, and freshly baked focaccia make it easy to indulge.

3 *Pre-Ski Cocktails* 10 p.m.

Maybe it's all the snow, but Whistler doesn't skimp when it comes to watering holes. They run the spectrum from hockey sports bars to "ice" bars where you can chill your drink between sips. For the latter, head to the august **Bearfoot Bistro** (4121 Village Green; 604-932-3433; bearfootbistro.com; $$$$). There you can have your flute of B.C. bubbly with a side of tinkling piano music and appetizers by Melissa Craig, an award-winning chef. For a more boisterous setting, stomp your Sorel boots over to **Crystal Lounge** (4154 Village Green; 604-938-1081; facebook.com/WhistlersCrystalLounge), a basement bar in the village center with live music and big TVs. It's packed with local skiers and boarders eating chicken wings and drinking pitchers of beer.

SATURDAY

4 *Where to Schuss* 8 a.m.

Which mountain, Whistler or Blackcomb? Skiers used to have to pick one, but thanks to the **Peak 2 Peak Gondola**, this whole behemoth resort is now within easy reach. If the snow is good, Whistler will be packed, so here's a plan. In the morning, avoid the crowded Village Gondola at Whistler and go to

OPPOSITE The Peak 2 Peak Gondola links Whistler and Blackcomb Mountains, the two peaks whose 8,100 skiable acres make Whistler North America's largest ski area.

BELOW Quattro at Whistler, a spot for Italian cuisine.

Blackcomb's base area to ride the Wizard Express and Solar Coaster Express lifts. The lines are shorter, and they get you right up Blackcomb Mountain. Warm up on the gentle Jersey Cream run and check the lighted boards to see which mountaintop lifts are open. When you reach the top, take your pick of ego powder runs like Showcase or the mettle-testing Couloir Extreme. When you're ready, swoop across to Whistler on the Peak 2 Peak, which is an event in itself: the cabins, which fit 28 passengers, dangle up to 1,427 feet high over a span of almost three miles.

5 *Belgian Waffles and BBQ* Noon

Come lunchtime, the huge lodges can feel like rush hour. So seek out the lesser-known on-mountain restaurants. On Blackcomb, the **Crystal Hut** (604-938-7527; facebook.com, search Crystal Hut) is a small log cabin near the top of the Crystal Chair that serves Belgian waffles all day and lunch specialties from a wood-burning oven. On Whistler, the **Chic Pea** (604-905-2383) near the top of the Garbanzo Express lift serves toasted sandwiches, pizza, and barbecue.

6 *Heaven on Skis* 2 p.m.

If the sun is smiling, head over to **Blackcomb's 7th Heaven** area, which has great views and is warmed by the afternoon's rays. It also has something for everyone: long, bumpy runs like Sunburn and Angel Dust, harder-to-reach powder stashes like Lakeside Bowl, and lingering intermediate groomers like Hugh's Heaven and Cloud Nine, which seem to meander to the valley floor.

7 *Boards at the Source* 4 p.m.

Independent ski and snowboard makers like Igneous Skis and Never Summer Snowboards have sprung up all over in recent years. One of the oldest is **Prior Snowboards and Skis** (104-1410 Alpha Lake

ABOVE The new timber-and-stone Nita Lake Lodge.

LEFT The shooting range for biathletes at Whistler Olympic Park, a sprawling Nordic playground.

Road; 604-935-1923; priorskis.com), founded in 1990 in Whistler. Every Wednesday at 5 p.m. and Saturday at 4 p.m., the company offers free one-hour tours of the factory floor. See how fiberglass layers are glued with epoxy and pressed together under enormous heat and pressure to create a springy, responsive snow toy.

8 *Playtime for All* 6:30 p.m.

A ski resort demands a break for parents, so drop the kids off for the nightly Climb & Dine program for kids — three hours of supervised rock climbing and pizza — at the **Core** (4010 Whistler Way; 604-905-7625; whistlercore.com), a climbing gym and fitness center. (For a kid-pleasing event for all to share, extend your stay until Sunday evening for the Fire and Ice Show in Skier's Plaza, a ski acrobatics extravaganza with flaming hoops and fire dancers; whistler.com/events).

9 *Dinner for Grownups* 7 p.m.

Yes, you had Italian last night, but this is different. The snug and romantic **Quattro at Whistler** (Pinnacle Hotel Whistler, 4319 Main Street; 604-905-4844; quattrorestaurants.com; $$$) serves entrees like glazed wild salmon with orange, honey, pickled fennel, and baby arugula. And yes, there is pasta

ABOVE Nordic skiing maneuvers on the biathlon course at Whistler Olympic Park.

BELOW At Prior Snowboards and Skis, see how fiberglass layers are bonded together under enormous heat and pressure to create a springy, responsive snow toy.

with accompanying ingredients like duck leg confit, prawns, and Australian lamb.

10 *What Wipeout?* 9:30 p.m.

Everyone from weary locals to visiting ski-film royalty (sometimes just returned from nearby backcountry heli-skiing) ends up at the **Garibaldi Lift Company** (4165 Springs Lane; 604-905-2220), fondly known as GLC. The crowd is big and rowdy, favoring beer by the pitcher. Count on a band or D.J. playing, a fire roaring, and hockey on the flat screen. With its floor-to-ceiling windows overlooking the slopes, the GLC is the kind of place to embellish the day's stories and make outsize promises for tomorrow.

SUNDAY

11 *Nordic Dreams* 11 a.m.

Yesterday you barreled down Whistler Mountain pretending to be Lindsey Vonn. Now go for the Walter Mitty experience. About 12 miles southwest of the resort, in the Callaghan Valley, is the **Whistler Olympic Park** (5 Callaghan Valley Road; 604-964-0060; whistlerolympicpark.com), a sprawling Nordic playground. Strap on cross-country skis, toss a firearm over your shoulder, and become a biathlete for an hour. Or try the skeleton, rocketing down an icy track at the **Whistler Sliding Centre** (4910 Glacier Lane; 604-964-0040; whistlerslidingcentre.com).

ABOVE A bright day on Blackcomb Mountain.

OPPOSITE Drop the kids off at the Core, a gym and fitness center that has a rock-climbing wall.

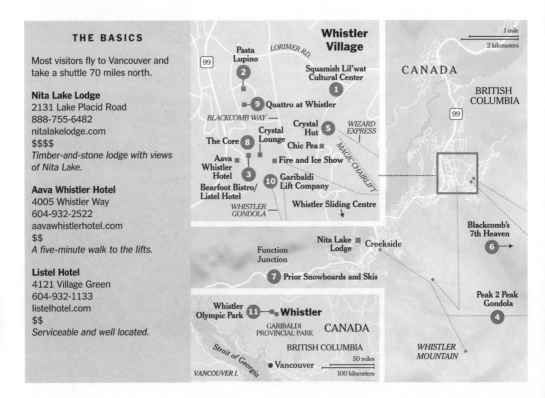

THE BASICS

Most visitors fly to Vancouver and take a shuttle 70 miles north.

Nita Lake Lodge
2131 Lake Placid Road
888-755-6482
nitalakelodge.com
$$$$
Timber-and-stone lodge with views of Nita Lake.

Aava Whistler Hotel
4005 Whistler Way
604-932-2522
aavawhistlerhotel.com
$$
A five-minute walk to the lifts.

Listel Hotel
4121 Village Green
604-932-1133
listelhotel.com
$$
Serviceable and well located.

Berkeley

More than four decades ago, Alice Waters, a pioneer of farm-fresh California cuisine, opened Chez Panisse in a jewel-box Craftsman-style building just north of downtown Berkeley. Other outstanding food purveyors followed, expanding and elevating the dining options available in newly stylish pockets of downtown. They're all worthy, grown-up stops to pepper a weekend spent exploring this vibrant college community, rich as ever with music, independent bookstores, and cafe culture. Rest assured that the hippie spirit is alive and well in the barefoot buskers and longhaired denizens biking through town. — BY BONNIE TSUI

FRIDAY

1 *Canopy to Campanile* 4 p.m.

Begin with an idyllic stroll under the canopy of old-growth oaks, redwoods, and 200-foot eucalyptus trees on the beautiful University of California campus. The famous Campanile, at 307 feet, is the third-tallest carillon and clock tower in the world. For a singular view, buy a day pass to the rooftop swimming pool in the **Hearst Gymnasium** (Bancroft Way and Bowditch; 510-642-7796; recsports.berkeley. edu/facilities/pools/hearst-pool/) and take a plunge. From the sun-warmed marble deck, the Campanile punctuates a tree-level sight line.

2 *Taste of Tokyo* 5:30 p.m.

A half-block from the eucalyptus grove, step off the student-clogged stretch of Center Street and through the black-and-white curtains at **Ippuku** (2130 Center Street; 510-665-1969; ippukuberkeley. com). A top-notch selection of sake, shochu, and craft beer anchors the front bar, and the warm staff is happy to introduce novices to the savory pleasures of casual izakaya-style snacking: chicken gizzard skewers, bacon-wrapped mochi, corn fritters, soft-cooked eggs in dashi broth.

3 *Mexico With a Twist* 8 p.m.

John Paluska has an interesting pedigree for a restaurateur: for 17 years, he was the manager for the band Phish. His **Comal** (2020 Shattuck Avenue; 510-926-6300; comalberkeley.com; $$) is an upscale Mexican restaurant and cocktail bar with an emphasis on Oaxacan-inspired cuisine:

white shrimp ceviche, roasted chicken with black beans, rich mole sauces. Cocktails can be fierce: the Jack Satan is made with "infierno tincture." The music is always good.

SATURDAY

4 *Stair Masters* 10 a.m.

The hill areas of Berkeley were developed in the early 20th century with long, winding blocks, and pathways sprang up to offer shortcuts between them. These days, there is an extensive system of 136 pedestrian paths, historic staircases, and walkways. They include greenways, bike paths, and leafy, meandering steps up to parks, gardens, trails, and rock-climbing areas; for example, the 183 concrete steps up **Tamalpais Path** lead past a waterfall and fern grotto to a redwood-framed view of Mount Tamalpais itself. The Berkeley Path Wanderers Association (berkeleypaths.org) puts out a terrific map of all the secret routes and corridors; pick up a copy at one of the locations listed on the website and set out on your own, or sign up for one of the group's regular guided walks.

5 *Cheesy Music Fix* Noon

The **Cheese Board Collective** (1504 and 1512 Shattuck Avenue; cheeseboardcollective.coop/pizza) has been a worker-owned-and-operated business

OPPOSITE At Moe's Books, the stock spills off the tables and all of Berkeley streams in the door.

BELOW Chez Panisse Cafe, still earning its fame.

since 1971. It has expanded to include a bakery, an espresso bar, and an inventive pizzeria, but at heart it's still a cheese shop, so be sure to check in at the cheese counter — there is a rotating selection of 300 to 400 cheeses you can taste — before heading to the pizzeria for lunch and live music.

6 *View From the Top* 2 p.m.

One of the most magnificent views of San Francisco Bay can be found at the **Lawrence Hall of Science** (1 Centennial Drive; lawrencehallofscience. org), the university's science museum and educational research center, just a five-minute drive uphill from the main campus. Take a walk around the expansive pedestrian plaza for a look at the shifting panorama of San Francisco and its bridges. The outdoor sculpture garden, perfect for picnics, has telescopes facing the bay. A few minutes farther up the road is **Tilden Regional Park** (Tilden Regional Park; ebparks.org/parks/tilden); its 2,000-plus acres are crisscrossed with hiking trails and include a botanical garden and showcase farm.

7 *Snake Pit* 5 p.m.

For a shopping experience not easily duplicated, drop in at the **East Bay Vivarium** (1827C Fifth Street; 510-841-1400; eastbayvivarium.com), perhaps the city's strangest attraction. But don't come with a fear of snakes: the massive gallery

and store, which specializes in reptiles, amphibians, and arachnids, is like a living nightmare. Strolling through, you'll pass gargantuan boas and more scorpion species than you'd ever imagined.

8 *Culture Clubs* 7 p.m.

Berkeley's downtown arts district has serious street cred. It's home to the **Freight & Salvage Coffeehouse** (2020 Addison Street; 510-644-2020; freightandsalvage.org), which hosts folk and bluegrass luminaries; the Tony Award-winning Berkeley Repertory Theater; and the **Pacific Film Archive** in the new Berkeley Art Museum (2155 Center Street; 510-642-0808; bampfa.berkeley. edu). The new museum building was planned with

OPPOSITE ABOVE Sather Gate, leading into the central campus of the University of California.

OPPOSITE BELOW The pool in the Hearst Gymnasium.

the film collection in mind, and its theaters offer eclectic moviegoing experiences in space designed for them.

9 *A Star Is Reborn* 10 p.m.

If you haven't made a reservation, late night at **Chez Panisse Cafe** (1517 Shattuck Avenue; 510-548-5049; chezpanisse.com; $$) is a good time for walk-ins. After a devastating fire, the legendary restaurant reopened with a face-lift, and the food is as good and the service as pitch-perfect as always — attuned to a clientele that may arrive in formal attire or flip-flops. One cafe dinner menu

included corn and goat cheese pudding soufflé, skirt steak with borlotti beans, and a nectarine galette that tasted just like summer.

SUNDAY

10 *Hit the Books* 11 a.m.

Book lovers have their choice in Berkeley. For easygoing browsing and serendipity, spend time at **Moe's Books** (2476 Telegraph Avenue; 510-849-2087; moesbooks.com), founded in 1959 and piled high with used volumes. Moe's is a place to wander for hours, flipping through choices from out-of-print tomes on 1950s African history to kabbalah manuals. There's another philosophy at **Mrs. Dalloway's** (2904 College Avenue; 510-704-8222; mrsdalloways. com), where the stock is new and the selection is carefully curated. Both stores have frequent in-store readings.

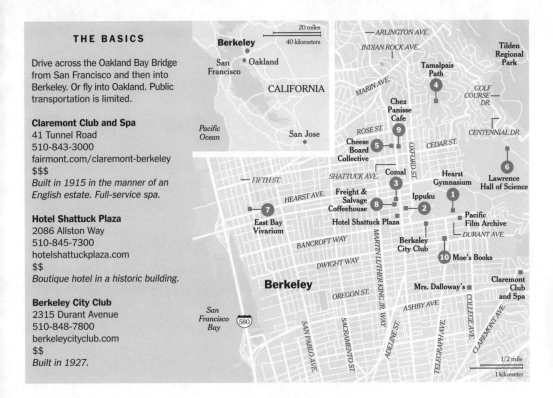

THE BASICS

Drive across the Oakland Bay Bridge from San Francisco and then into Berkeley. Or fly into Oakland. Public transportation is limited.

Claremont Club and Spa
41 Tunnel Road
510-843-3000
fairmont.com/claremont-berkeley
$$$
Built in 1915 in the manner of an English estate. Full-service spa.

Hotel Shattuck Plaza
2086 Allston Way
510-845-7300
hotelshattuckplaza.com
$$
Boutique hotel in a historic building.

Berkeley City Club
2315 Durant Avenue
510-848-7800
berkeleycityclub.com
$$
Built in 1927.

Big Sur

Running southward from Carmel, 150 miles south of San Francisco, to San Simeon, Big Sur's mass of tight mountains pushes brazenly against the Pacific swell. Kelp forests sway at the feet of the rugged sea cliffs. Deep valleys shelter some of California's southernmost redwoods. Writers, artists, dreamers, and hippies have all been drawn here; Henry Miller described it as "a region where one is always conscious of weather, of space, of grandeur and of eloquent silence." Although the rich and famous are now building homes here, the geography prevents sprawl and most of the development is invisible, preserving the feeling of solitude. Big Sur still rewards serendipity, but this is no place to rely upon it: the few lodgings fill quickly. Make your reservations well in advance, allow plenty of time for the drive, and then let the ocean and the mountains take over.
— BY GREGORY DICUM

FRIDAY

1 *View from the Road* 2 p.m.

The only way into and through the Big Sur coast is along winding, breathtaking **California Highway 1**. Its construction here in the 1930s was controversial (sheer cliffs and constant rockfalls attest to the project's audacity), but today it is a testament to the ambition of New Deal public works projects. Though Big Sur is as much an idea as a place, you will know you have arrived when, driving south from Monterey, you cross **Bixby Bridge**. A marvel of concrete spanning a deep coastal gorge, it has appeared in a thousand car commercials, and it's worth a stop if you're into infrastructure: turn out at either end of the span. Other viewpoints abound on the road, so keep your camera at the ready and expect to stop frequently.

2 *Waterside* 5 p.m.

Though the Pacific is everywhere in Big Sur, the enfolding coast guards access like a jealous lover. Beaches nestle in coves backed by fearsome cliffs, and in only a few places is it easy — or even possible — to set foot on them. **Pfeiffer Beach** is one. Take a sharp right turn a quarter-mile south of the Big Sur Ranger Station onto the unmarked Sycamore Canyon Road, and follow it down to a bay sheltered from the ocean's full force by chunky offshore rocks. The fine tan sand here is streaked with purple minerals. Wander in the warm sun and test a toe in the cold water. On one sunny late afternoon, handfuls of college students basked in sweatshirts and sunglasses like style-conscious sea lions. An arch in the rocks serves as a proscenium for the lowering sun and the backlit orange seawater splashes of gentle swells.

3 *Sunset Sustenance* 7 p.m.

Big Sur has remarkably few dining options for a place so visited. Fortunately, some of them are sublime. The **Sur House at the Ventana Big Sur** (48123 Highway 1; 831-667-2331; ventanabigsur.com; $$$) takes locally sourced ingredients — halibut from coastal fishermen, seasonal organic vegetables, Sonoma duck — and turns them into a finely wrought cuisine that celebrates California's Central Coast. Get a table by the big windows, or outside, and enjoy a view of the sun dropping into the rippling waves. Unless it's foggy, of course.

OPPOSITE McWay Falls pours 80 feet onto a perfect, though inaccessible, beach around a blue Pacific cove.

BELOW A yurt at Treebones Resort, a mid-priced lodging option. Land-use restrictions both keep Big Sur beautiful and limit places to stay.

SATURDAY

4 *Grandpa's Eggs Benedict* 9 a.m.

One of Big Sur's heartiest breakfasts is at **Deetjen's Big Sur Inn** (48865 Highway 1; 831-667-2378; deetjens. com; $$), this coast's original roadhouse. The inn dates to the 1930s, when Grandpa Deetjen built a redwood barn here that grew into a cluster of cabins. The restaurant, open to all, has an unpretentious but efficient and friendly feel that seems the epitome of Big Sur at its best. Eggs Benedict are a specialty, but there's a varied menu that also includes smoked salmon and huevos rancheros. If you're lucky, you can eat by the fire, but resist the urge to sit there all day: it's time to work off that breakfast.

5 *The Redwoods Are Waiting* 10 a.m.

State parks are strung up and down the coast. Many offer short hikes to astounding coastal vistas, while others permit access to the rugged mountain

ABOVE A cabin in a redwood grove at Deetjen's, an inn that dates to the 1930s.

RIGHT At Pfeiffer Big Sur State Park, trails lead through dense redwood groves to open ridges and mountaintops.

OPPOSITE Pfeiffer Beach, one of the few accessible Big Sur beaches. Most are below fearsome cliffs.

wilderness of the interior. At **Pfeiffer Big Sur State Park** (26 miles south of Carmel on Highway 1), trails lead through dense, damp groves of redwoods and oaks to coastal overlooks and a waterfall, and up to open ridges and mountaintops. The Oak Grove Trail gives hikers a taste of the diversity of Big Sur landscapes and, with luck, the wildlife: Big Sur is a place where once nearly extinct California condors have been reintroduced.

6 *Go for the View* 1 p.m.

Nepenthe (48510 Highway 1; 831-667-2345; nepenthe.com; $$–$$$) has long been a favorite tourist aerie. It is worth a visit on a sunny day for the magnificent views and cheery crowd, although

the food is undistinguished. Think of it as the price of admission.

7 *Waterfall to the Sea* 2 p.m.

Julia Pfeiffer Burns State Park (on Highway 1; 831-667-2315; parks.ca.gov), not to be confused with Pfeiffer Big Sur State Park, is an all but requisite stop. From the parking area it's an easy stroll to view McWay Falls. The 80-foot-high cataract pours onto a perfect, though inaccessible, beach around a blue Pacific cove. It's the image most likely to come to mind later as you reminisce about Big Sur.

8 *Enlightenment* 3 p.m.

"There being nothing to improve on in the surroundings," Miller wrote of Big Sur in 1957, "the tendency is to set about improving oneself." He could have been describing the **Esalen Institute** (55000 Highway 1), a sort of New Age Harvard founded in 1962, whose campus tumbles down toward a precipitous cliff above the ocean. Seekers and celebrities come for "energy" and Atlantis, registering for workshops in yoga, meditation, and various kinds of self-realization. Participants stay overnight. To get a taste of the place in a shorter time—and work away any lingering stress that has managed to survive Big Sur so far—book a massage (831-667-3002; esalen.org/page/welcome-esalen-healing-arts; time slots limited and reservations essential). It will give you a rare opportunity to enter the Esalen grounds without committing to a longer stay. You're allowed to arrive an hour early and stay an hour afterward to experience the hot springs.

9 *The Soak* 5:30 p.m.

By now you've emerged refreshed from your bodywork and are soaking (nudity optional but de rigueur) in the **Esalen Hot Springs Baths** (esalen.org/page/esalen-hot-springs). Esalen is known for these legendary tubs. Hugging a seaside cliff, the complex of baths momentarily captures natural hot springs before they pour into the Pacific. Indoors, there are concrete walls, warm and grippy sandstone floors, and floor-to-ceiling windows looking out to sea. Outdoor soaking pools and a living roof lend the baths a sense of belonging in the landscape. From the hot water, bathers can look down on sea otters lounging in the kelp. If your brief soak isn't enough, sign up to return between 1 a.m. and 3 a.m., when the baths are open to the public. The hours are inconvenient (the nighttime drive over corkscrew Highway 1 will instantly undo the baths' restorative effects), but breakers below shake the cliff and thousands of stars shine out of a black sky, giving the place the feel of a celestial point of embarkation.

10 *Above It All* 8 p.m.

On the ridgeline hundreds of feet above Pfeiffer Beach, the **Post Ranch Inn** perches in unobtrusive luxe, its cottages spread tactfully over rolling acres of grass and woods. But like the rest of Big Sur, the inn has a charm that has as much to do with its attitude as with the landscape — not every thousand-dollar-a-night resort has an in-house shaman. Even if your wallet places you in a different category from the establishment's target clientele, you will find a welcoming spirit at the inn's restaurant, the **Sierra Mar** (831-667-2800; postranchinn.com; $$$$; reservations required). Seek a table on the outdoor deck and order the four-course prix fixe dinner.

OPPOSITE A hot spring pool at the Esalen Institute, where you can seek enlightenment or just a relaxing massage.

SUNDAY

11 *Literary Nexus* 11 a.m.

The **Henry Miller Memorial Library** (48603 Highway 1; 831-667-2574; henrymiller.org) maintains a reference collection of Miller's work, a bookshop, and a big wooden deck where visitors can enjoy coffee and Wi-Fi. Special events include readings, concerts, art shows, performances, and seminars. It's hardly monumental — little more than a house in the woods before a grassy yard strewn with sculptures and bric-a-brac that might be sculptural. Like much of the rest of Big Sur, the library is a casual place where lounging and artistic pursuit go hand in hand.

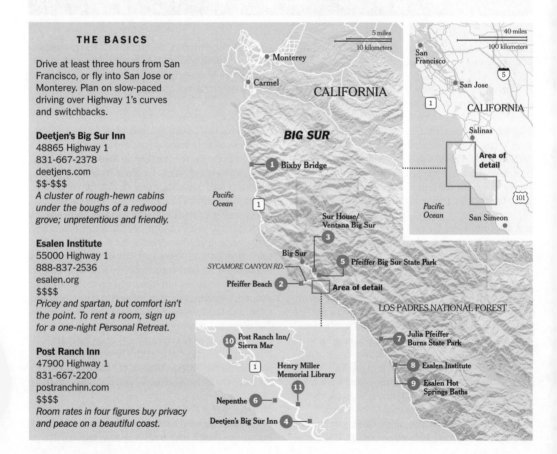

THE BASICS

Drive at least three hours from San Francisco, or fly into San Jose or Monterey. Plan on slow-paced driving over Highway 1's curves and switchbacks.

Deetjen's Big Sur Inn
48865 Highway 1
831-667-2378
deetjens.com
$$-$$$
A cluster of rough-hewn cabins under the boughs of a redwood grove; unpretentious and friendly.

Esalen Institute
55000 Highway 1
888-837-2536
esalen.org
$$$$
Pricey and spartan, but comfort isn't the point. To rent a room, sign up for a one-night Personal Retreat.

Post Ranch Inn
47900 Highway 1
831-667-2200
postranchinn.com
$$$$
Room rates in four figures buy privacy and peace on a beautiful coast.

Carmel

With its architectural mishmash of storybook English cottages and Swiss Alpine chalets, the small California town of Carmel-by-the-Sea resembles a Disneyland version of Europe. You half expect a bereted Parisian to saunter out of one of the ridiculously cute Euro-themed bistros. But walk a few blocks to Carmel's steep, sandy beach and the view is pure California: a rugged Pacific coastline spangled with rocky outcroppings, ghostly cypress trees, and the electric green slopes of the famed Pebble Beach golf course. The one-square-mile village has no street lights, parking meters, or numbered addresses, but you wouldn't call it low-key. Once a bohemian outpost for people like Jack London, Carmel today is prime real estate, and the surrounding valley is abuzz with top-notch restaurants, boutique wineries, and upscale shops. — BY JAIME GROSS

FRIDAY

1 *Cocktails with Clint* 6 p.m.

Carmel has had its share of boldfaced residents, but few more enduring or beloved than Clint Eastwood, who was the town's mayor from 1986 to 1988 and still lives in the area. You might catch a glimpse of him at his restaurant at **Mission Ranch** (26270 Dolores Street; 831-624-6436; missionranchcarmel.com), his 22-acre property just outside of town, where he's been known to eat with his family and greet old-timers at the piano bar. Order a glass of wine and snag a seat on the heated restaurant patio overlooking a striking tableau: sheep meadows, rolling hills, and the shimmering ocean in the distance.

2 *California French* 8 p.m.

For an intimate dinner with plenty of foodie appeal, try **Aubergine** (Seventh Avenue and Monte Verde Street; 831-624-8578; auberginecarmel.com; $$$$), the award-winning restaurant at the Relais & Châteaux hotel L'Auberge Carmel. The menu changes daily, reflecting the availability of fresh local produce with dishes like roasted lamb with cranberry bean cassoulet.

OPPOSITE The Point Lobos State Natural Reserve.

RIGHT A landscape painter at Bernardus Winery in vineyard country near Carmel-by-the-Sea.

SATURDAY

3 *Biking for a View* 8 a.m.

Beat the gawking motorists and entry fee for cars by waking early and biking the **17-Mile Drive**, the jaw-dropping corniche that hugs the rocky coastline between Carmel and Pacific Grove. **Adventures by the Sea** (299 Cannery Row, Monterey; 831-372-1807; adventuresbythesea.com) rents bikes and is an easy five miles from the drive's most scenic stretches, which are lined with sandy beaches, golf courses, and a 250-year-old cypress tree sprouting from a seaside boulder.

4 *Mission Museum* 11 a.m.

The **San Carlos Borroméo del Rio Carmelo Mission** (3080 Rio Road; 831-624-1271; carmelmission.org) was founded at its present site in 1771 by Father Junípero Serra and was once the headquarters for the entire California mission system. Known more simply as the Carmel Mission, the site includes a poppy-filled garden, an abalone-strewn cemetery, and a stone basilica with original 18th-century artworks. At the Mission's **Convento Museum**, you can peer into Father Serra's spartan living quarters — with a table, a chair, and a highly uncomfortable-looking wooden bed — and check out his book collection, identified as "California's first library."

5 *Lunch In-Town* 1 p.m.

Pick up lunch at Carmel's best food shops. **Bruno's Market and Deli** (Sixth Avenue and Junipero Avenue; 831-624-3821; brunosmarket.com) has gourmet tri-tip and barbecued chicken sandwiches. The **Cheese Shop** (Carmel Plaza, Ocean Avenue and Junipero Avenue, lower level; 831-625-2272; thecheeseshopinc.com) stocks picnic fixings, wine, and about 300 cheeses. They'll let you taste as many as you like, or they can assemble a customized cheese plate that you can nibble at the cafe tables out front.

6 *Poodles and Scones* 2 p.m.

In a town known for being dog-friendly, the **Cypress Inn** (Seventh Avenue and Lincoln Street; 831-624-3871; cypress-inn.com) takes the cake with poop bags at the door, bone-shaped biscuits at the front desk, and a *Best-in-Show*-worthy tea service. In addition to serving scones and crustless cucumber sandwiches, the tea service draws a head-spinning parade of Shih Tzus, toy poodles, and other impeccably groomed pups taking tea with their equally well-coiffed owners. Reservations are recommended.

7 *Stuff for Home* 4 p.m.

The 42 hidden courtyards and alleys of Carmel shelter a plethora of stylish galleries and fashionable boutiques. Spend a lazy afternoon wandering and browsing. One shop not to miss is the **Carmel Drug Store** (Ocean Avenue and San Carlos Street; 831-624-3819; carmeldrugstore.com), which has been selling handmade Swiss combs, grandma colognes, and Coca-Cola in glass bottles since 1910. Another high spot is the working studio and gallery of **Steven Whyte**, a local sculptor (Dolores Street

ABOVE The Cheese Shop stocks picnic fixings, wine, and about 300 different cheeses.

RIGHT A heron at Point Lobos State Natural Reserve.

between Fifth and Sixth Avenues; 831-620-1917; stevenwhytesculptor.com) who makes hyper-realistic cast-bronze portraits.

8 *Casual Flavors* 8 p.m.

For dinner, make a beeline for one of Carmel's über-charming French or Italian restaurants. **La Bicyclette** (Dolores Street at Seventh Avenue; 831-622-9899; labicycletterestaurant.com; $$$) resembles a rustic village bistro. The compact menu spans Europe with dishes like beef with Gorgonzola-red wine sauce or German sausage with homemade sauerkraut. Also worth a try is **Cantinetta Luca** (Dolores Street between Ocean and Seventh Avenues; 831-625-6500; cantinettaluca.com; $$$), an Italian restaurant popular for its wood-fired pizzas, homemade pastas, predominantly Italian wine list, and a dozen types of salumi aged on site in a glass-walled curing room.

SUNDAY

9 *Sea Life* 11 a.m.

Legend has it that Robert Louis Stevenson hit on the inspiration for the 1883 novel *Treasure Island* while strolling the beach near Point Lobos. Retrace his steps at **Point Lobos State Natural Reserve** (Route 1, three miles south of Carmel; 831-624-4909;

parks.ca.gov), a majestic landscape with 14 meandering trails. Don't forget binoculars: you can spot sea otters, seals, and sea lions year-round, and migrating gray whales December through May. Scuba divers take note: 60 percent of the reserve's 554 acres lies underwater, in one of the richest marine habitats in California. Scuba diving, snorkeling, and kayaking reservations can be booked through the park's website.

10 *Sip the Valley* 1 p.m.

Thanks to its coastal climate and sandy, loamy soil, Carmel Valley is gaining renown for its wines. Most of the tasting rooms are clustered in Carmel Valley Village, a small town with a handful of restaurants and wineries 12 miles east of Carmel. **Bernardus** (5 West Carmel Valley Road; 831-298-8021; bernardus.com), the granddaddy of area

wineries, is known for the breadth and quality of its wines. A relative newcomer, **Boekenoogen Wines** (24 West Carmel Valley Road; 831-659-4215; boekenoogenwines.com), is a small family-owned winery with a few varietals. Teetotalers can opt for a different kind of relaxation at **Bernardus Lodge** (415 West Carmel Valley Road; 831-658-3560; bernarduslodge.com). Its spa treatments have been known to include chardonnay facials.

ABOVE Cycling on the winding 17-Mile Drive, which hugs the rocky coastline between Carmel and Pacific Grove.

THE BASICS

Carmel-by-the-Sea is a scenic two-hour drive south of San Francisco.

L'Auberge Carmel
Seventh Avenue and Monte Verde Street
831-624-8578
laubergecarmel.com
$$$$
Winding staircases lead to 20 rooms, many with Japanese soaking tubs.

Cypress Inn
Seventh Avenue and Lincoln Street
831-624-3871
cypress-inn.com
$$$
Co-owned by Doris Day, whose songs are piped through the hotel.

Carmel Valley Ranch
1 Old Ranch Road
831-625-9500
carmelvalleyranch.com
$$$$
Fireplaces, terraces, golf course.

Carmel-by-the-Sea

FIFTH AVE.
SAN CARLOS ST.
MISSION ST.
JUNIPERO AVE.
500 feet
1/4 kilometer

Steven Whyte
SIXTH AVE.
Bruno's Market and Deli 5
ORE.
CALIF.
San Francisco NEV.
Area of detail
Los Angeles

LINCOLN ST.
OCEAN AVE.
Cheese Shop
Cantinetta Luca
Cypress Inn 6
Carmel Drug Store 7
La Bicyclette
8

SEVENTH AVE.
2
Aubergine/ L'Auberge Carmel
DOLORES ST.
EIGHTH AVE.
MONTE VERDE ST.
NINTH AVE.
To Mission Ranch 1

Monterey Bay
Pacific Grove
Adventures by the Sea
1
3
17-Mile Drive
Pebble Beach golf course
MONTEREY PENINSULA AIRPORT
68
5 miles
10 kilometers
Area of detail
Carmel Valley Ranch
Bernardus Lodge
Bernardus
4
9
Point Lobos State Natural Reserve
San Carlos Borroméo del Rio Carmelo Mission/ Convento Museum
CARMEL VALLEY RD.
10
Boekenoogen Wines
Carmel Valley
Pacific Ocean
1
CALIFORNIA

Lake Tahoe

Straddling the Nevada-California border, Lake Tahoe's immense cobalt blue oval stands out against the Sierras like a colossal eye staring into heaven. Even on a busy summer weekend, when 200,000 visitors flood the 72 miles of lakeshore to frolic against a backdrop of soaring evergreens and crystalline waters, it never feels frantic. Perhaps that's because there are so many facets to the place. Lake Tahoe has two distinctive areas: the north side, where cowboy-chic cabins and semi-isolated shops and cafes overlook a quiet shoreline; and South Tahoe, which glitters with casinos, clubs, and a slew of new upscale boutique hotels hovering in the fresh mountain air. There's nothing quite like a weekend spent circling the lake — an ambitious undertaking, but Tahoe's wilderness spirit and surprising contrasts are compelling enough to pull you into its adventurous orbit.
— BY CINDY PRICE AND FINN-OLAF JONES

FRIDAY

1 *Deeper Shades of Blue* 3 p.m.

Cobalt, azure, electric, sapphire. Describing the true color of Lake Tahoe is a task worthy of a thousand poets. But blue as it is, it is also cold. Even in late summer, the water averages 65 to 70 degrees, given the many mountain streams that flow into it. Judge for yourself on a guided kayak trip out of Sand Harbor, Nevada, with the **Tahoe Adventure Company** (530-913-9212; tahoeadventurecompany.com), which offers individual tours that are part geology lesson and part history lesson. Paddle out past the children cannonballing off the rocks, and learn about the lake's underlying fault lines — and the tsunami that may have burst forth there sometime in the last 10,000 years.

2 *Drama on the Sand* 7 p.m.

Shake yourself dry, slip on your flip-flops, and head up the beach to the **Lake Tahoe Shakespeare Festival** (Sand Harbor State Park, Nevada; 775-832-1616;

OPPOSITE Set high in the Sierra Nevada, Lake Tahoe is the largest alpine lake in North America.

RIGHT For accessible and breathtaking mountain views, Lake Tahoe is hard to beat.

laketahoeshakespeare.com). Patrons pile up on the inclined sand banks, carrying towels, wine, and fat dinner spreads. You can bring your own, or check out the food court and beer garden. The plays are staged at dusk, the lake deftly employed as a silent witness to the unfolding action. If you miss the play, you don't have to miss the beautiful park.

3 *Truckin' the North Shore* 10 p.m.

The old railroad town of Truckee, California, with its upscale hippie vibe, is the cultural and night-life nexus of the North Shore. Just off Donner Pass Road, the colorful town's main drag, you enter the crosshairs of Truckee night life: **Moody's Bistro Bar and Beats** (10007 Bridge Street; 503-587-8688; moodysbistro.com). A sleek, hip, jazzy bar tucked into a cozy niche of the Victorian-era Truckee Hotel, Moody's features spirited whatever-happens-happens local musical acts. Paul McCartney, a regular vacationer to Tahoe, has joined in a couple of times.

SATURDAY

4 *Ghosts of the Settlers* 9:30 a.m.

Explore the dark side of Manifest Destiny by revisiting one of the most famous unfortunate events in American history: the passage of the Donner Party, 87 California-bound settlers who were trapped in the Sierra Nevada during the winter of 1846-47 by an apocalyptic blizzard, many of them on the site of what is now the **Donner Memorial State Park** (Donner Pass Road, west of Truckee, California; 530-582-7894; parks.ca.gov). Caught without shelter or

supplies, they took refuge as they could by what is now called Donner Lake. The pedestal of a Pioneer Monument in the park shows the height of the snow that winter: 22 feet. Desperate rescue attempts failed, and some of the pioneers resorted to cannibalism (though diaries and recollections disagreed violently on the grim details); 46 survived. Today the park's Emigrant Trail Museum slide show dramatizes the tragedy. In warm-weather contrast to the privations of these forebears, you can hike eight miles of trails, camp, fish, and enjoy the abundance.

5 *Rump Row* 1 p.m.

Head for Lake Tahoe and Tahoe City, California, where you will be 6,225 feet above sea level. Find your way through town and take a right just past Fanny Bridge (called "rump row" for the line of backsides that forms as people lean over the railing to stare at the Truckee River and its fish). Find **Bridgetender Tavern and Grill** (65 West Lake Boulevard, Tahoe City; 530-583-3342; $) home to one of the juiciest cheeseburgers on the lake. In winter, it's a popular spot for skiers warming up from a day on the slopes. In summer, have lunch on the generous outdoor patio that winds along the Truckee. Then head to the **Truckee River Raft Company** (185 River Road, Tahoe City; 530-584-0123; truckeeriverraft.com) for a lazy afternoon on the river.

6 *The Drive to Dinner* 6 p.m.

Route 89, the road that twists down the west shoreline to South Lake Tahoe, has a haunting grandeur reminiscent of the movie *The Shining*. This is especially true at sunset at the **Inspiration Point** turnoff, 35 miles south of Northstar, overlooking Emerald Bay. From this spot 600 feet above the shore you can watch the shadows of the Sierras engulf the lake's electric blue waters and the stone teahouse atop the crags of Fanette's Island, rising like a ghost ship. Then it's on to dinner in a tiny alpine gingerbread cabin hidden in one of South Lake Tahoe's back lanes, the seven-table **Cafe Fiore** (1169 Ski Run Boulevard, South Lake

Tahoe; 530-541-2908; cafefiore.com; $$$). The chef, Gilberto Ramos, prepares Italian classics like veal scaloppine with wild mushrooms.

7 *Vegas by the Lake* 10 p.m.

The antidote to the sporting mountain life is a stroll from the tree-shrouded streets of South Lake Tahoe across the Nevada state line into the neon-lit mini Vegas-by-the-lake casino strip. There, the nonstop drinking, gambling, and indoor smoking is probably a lot closer to the original 49ers' vision of Tahoe than communing with nature. Start at the mirrored high-rise of **Harveys Resort Casino** (18 Lake Tahoe Boulevard, Stateline, Nevada; 775-588-2411; harveystahoe.com) for old-school casino action, right down to surf-and-turf meals on the panoramic 19th floor. Then head up the block to the **Hard Rock Hotel & Casino** (50 Highway 50; 844-588-7625; hardrockcasinolaketahoe.com) and check out signature retro bands like the Stone Foxes or the English Beat. To end the night on a Day-Glo note, cross the street to Opal Ultra Lounge in the **MontBleu Resort Casino & Spa** (55 Highway 50; 775-588-3515; montbleuresort.com), where strobes, a body painter, go-go dancers, and bachelorette parties swirl on the red concrete floor.

BELOW Warming up at the Bridgetender Tavern and Grill.

SUNDAY

8 *Now That's Venti* 10 a.m.

Ride the touristy but must-do **Heavenly Gondola** (Heavenly Mountain Resort; 4080 Lake Tahoe Boulevard, South Lake Tahoe; 775-586-7000; skiheavenly.com), a ski lift that doubles as a sight-seeing excursion in summer. Hop on board when it opens and cruise 2.4 miles up the mountain to the observation deck. Grab a very decent mocha at the cafe and soak in the stunning views of the Carson Valley and the Desolation Wilderness — not to mention that big blue thing in the center.

9 *Sandwiches and Sand* Noon

Gather provisions at the **PDQ Market** (6937 West Lake Boulevard, Tahoma; 530-525-7411), where you can order a tasty sandwich on fresh jalapeño or pesto bread. Then head for the shore.

Trying to pick the right Tahoe beach is a bit like plucking a date off the Internet. **Zephyr Cove** (zephyrcove.com) is young and likes to party. **Meeks Bay** (meeksbayresort.com) is into poetry and long walks. **D. L. Bliss State Park** (parks.ca.gov) is a camping ground with coves for swimming and lazing. The water at all of them is an astonishing blue that will remind you of the Caribbean. Until you dip your hand in, of course.

OPPOSITE ABOVE Learning about the lake on a kayaking tour with Tahoe Adventure Company.

ABOVE A ski lift does summer duty ferrying sightseers.

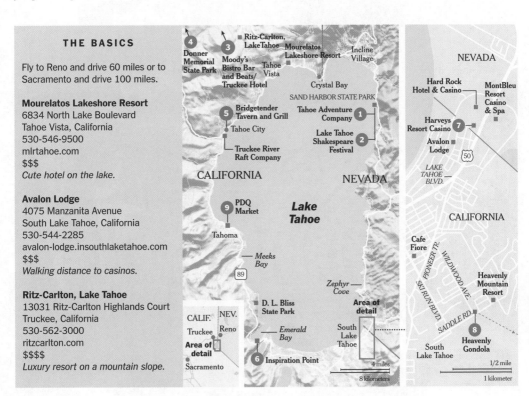

THE BASICS

Fly to Reno and drive 60 miles or to Sacramento and drive 100 miles.

Mourelatos Lakeshore Resort
6834 North Lake Boulevard
Tahoe Vista, California
530-546-9500
mlrtahoe.com
$$$
Cute hotel on the lake.

Avalon Lodge
4075 Manzanita Avenue
South Lake Tahoe, California
530-544-2285
avalon-lodge.insouthlaketahoe.com
$$$
Walking distance to casinos.

Ritz-Carlton, Lake Tahoe
13031 Ritz-Carlton Highlands Court
Truckee, California
530-562-3000
ritzcarlton.com
$$$$
Luxury resort on a mountain slope.

Los Angeles

Angelenos like to tell visitors, "It's a great place to live but I wouldn't want to visit here." Granted, it's tough to decide what to see and do in a city that encompasses 470 square miles. Fortunately, there is always an under-the-radar restaurant, a funky theater, or a splashy store to discover. And you never have to leave the iconic landmarks behind. — BY LOUISE TUTELIAN

FRIDAY

1 *Stop and Shop* 4 p.m.

The hilly Los Feliz area, just northeast of Hollywood, is an old neighborhood with an impeccably hip pedigree. A walk along North Vermont Avenue turns up an intriguing trove of vintage clothes, handmade jewelry, antique textiles, books, and much more. **Otherwild Goods and Services** (1768 North Vermont Avenue; 323-546-8437; otherwild.com), stocks an eclectic mix of locally made clothes, gifts, jewelry, and its very popular "The Future Is Female" sweatshirts. The store also hosts dance and music performances, classes, readings, and comedy nights. **Skylight Books** (1818 North Vermont Avenue; 323-660-1175; skylightbooks.com) caters to the many artists, writers, musicians, and actors in the neighborhood—and anyone else who loves a carefully curated arts bookstore. Browse the stacks and you'll see a monograph on Richard Meier next to a tome on *Mad* magazine posters. And don't step on Franny, the resident cat.

2 *Friendly Fare* 6 p.m.

Little Dom's (2128 Hillhurst Avenue; 323-661-0055; littledoms.com; $$-$$$) is the best of homey and hip, a bar/bistro with an inventive menu. The fare is mostly Italian-American, but since the executive chef, Brandon Boudet, hails from New Orleans, there's a dash of the South as well. Pappardelle with house-made sausage? No problem. But Boudet also serves up a succulent fried oyster sandwich with hot sauce mayo, y'all.

3 *Bright Lights, Big City* 8 p.m.

Get the big picture at the **Griffith Park Observatory** (2800 East Observatory Avenue; 213-473-0800; griffithobservatory.org), with its view of the entire Los Angeles basin. Visitors line up for a peek into a massive Zeiss telescope with a 12-inch reflector that reveals celestial sights like the rings of Saturn. The Samuel Oschin Planetarium shows employ laser digital projection and state-of-the-art sound. A show about the brilliant aurora borealis — accompanied by Wagner's *Ride of the Valkyries* — is a cosmic experience.

4 *Alive and Swingin'* 10 p.m.

Made famous by the 1996 movie *Swingers*, the **Dresden** (1760 North Vermont Avenue; 323-665-4294; thedresden.com/lounge.html) is a welcome throwback to a still earlier era, with its upscale 1960s rec room décor and stellar bartenders. You're here to see Marty and Elayne, jazz musicians who have performed pop, standards, and the occasional show tune, with a changing array of guest artists, in the lounge since 1982. The crowd is a cocktail shaker of twenty-somethings on dates, middle-aged couples with friends, and college kids. Somehow, it all goes down very smoothly.

SATURDAY

5 *From Canyon to Canyon* 10 a.m.

Joni Mitchell doesn't live here anymore, but Laurel Canyon retains its '70s image as a

OPPOSITE The endless sprawl of Los Angeles. In a city of 470 square miles, there's always something to do.

BELOW At the Griffith Park Observatory, stargazers line up for a peek at celestial sights like the rings of Saturn.

self-contained artistic enclave (albeit a more expensive one now). Its social hub is the **Canyon Country Store** (2108 Laurel Canyon Boulevard; 323-654-8091), a grocery/deli/liquor store marked by a flower power-style sign that pays homage to its hippie roots. Sip organic oak-roasted espresso at the Canyon Coffee Cart, buy a picnic lunch, and head for the high road — Mulholland Drive.

ABOVE Skylight Books in Los Feliz, just northeast of Hollywood, caters to writers, artists, musicians, and actors.

BELOW The crowd at the Dresden, where Marty and Elayne perform on weekends, is a cocktail shaker of 20-somethings on dates, clumps of middle-aged friends, and college kids.

The serpentine road follows the ridgeline of the Santa Monica Mountains, and every curve delivers a spectacular vista of the San Fernando Valley and beyond. Drop down into **Franklin Canyon Park** (2600 Franklin Canyon Drive; 310-858-7272; lamountains.com), 605 acres of chaparral, grasslands, and oak woodlands with miles of hiking grounds. Heavenly Pond is a particularly appealing picnic spot.

6 *The Hills of Beverly* 1 p.m.

The stores range from Gap to Gucci, but you don't need deep pockets to enjoy Beverly Hills. **Prada** (343 North Rodeo Drive; 310-278-8661; prada.com), designed by Rem Koolhaas, delivers a jolt of architectural electricity. The 50-foot entrance is wide open to the street, with no door. A staircase peopled with mannequins ascends mysteriously. On the top level, faux security scanners double as video monitors and luggage-carousel-style shelves hold merchandise. At the **Paley Center for Media** (465 North Beverly Drive; 310-786-1091; paleycenter. org/visit-visitla), enter your own private TV land. At the center's library, anyone can screen segments of classic TV and radio shows, from *The Three Stooges* to *Seinfeld* as well as documentaries and specials. When it's time to cool your heels, head for the **Beverly Cañon Gardens** (241 North Cañon Drive), a public park masquerading as a private

Italian-style garden. Adjacent to the Montage Hotel, the Gardens have plenty of benches, tables, and chairs, and a large Baroque fountain adding a splashing soundtrack.

7 *Full Exposure* 4 p.m.

The incongruous setting of corporate high-rises is home to the under-appreciated **Annenberg Space for Photography** (2000 Avenue of the Stars; 213-403-3000; annenbergspaceforphotography.org), an oasis of images. One enthralling group show was by nature photographers shooting under Arctic oceans, on a volcano, and deep within Florida swamps. Another featured photographs by Herb Ritts, Mary Ellen Mark, Chuck Close, and other documentarians of beauty and style. The space itself is open and airy, with an iris-like design on the ceiling to represent the aperture of a lens.

8 *Unleashed* 6 p.m.

Don't knock it till you've tried it. Only a restaurant unequivocally named **Animal** (435 North Fairfax Avenue; 323-782-9225; animalrestaurant.com; $$-$$$) can sell diners on dishes like pig ear with chili, lime, and a fried egg, or rabbit legs with mustard and bacon. A longstanding landmark of the snout-to-tail culinary revival, the place is nondescript with no name on the storefront (it's four doors up from Canter's Deli), but once you've tried the fat

pork-belly sliders with crunchy slaw on a buttery brioche bun, you'll beat a path there again.

9 *The Silent Treatment* 8 p.m.

Dedicated to finding and screening classic and unusual films (can you say, Bo Svenson in *Snow Beast*?), the 228-seat **New Beverly Cinema** (7165 Beverly Boulevard; 323-938-4038; thenewbev.com) is like a quirky film class held in a 1920's-vintage theater. The schedule is curated by none other than the primo pulp filmmaker himself, Quentin Tarantino. Only 16mm and 35mm prints are shown (no digital projection allowed!), some from Tarantino's own personal collection.

SUNDAY

10 *Breakfast by the Beach* 10 a.m.

Berries and Brussels sprouts abound at the **Santa Monica Farmers' Market** (2640 Main Street; Santa Monica; 310-458-8712; smgov.net/portals/ farmersmarket), but there are also 10 stands where local restaurateurs sell dishes prepared on the spot. Among the best are Arcadie's sweet or

ABOVE Basking poolside at the eco-chic Palomar boutique hotel on Wilshire Boulevard, near the University of California at Los Angeles.

savory crepes, Carbon Grill's hefty burritos, and the Victorian's custom omelets. A live band might be playing any genre from jazz to zydeco. Finish with a scone from the Rockenwagner bakery stand and munch it on the beach, only a block away.

11 *Secret Waterways* 1 p.m.

One of the loveliest walks in west Los Angeles is one visitors hardly ever take: a stroll among the **Venice canals**. The developer Abbot Kinney dug miles

of canals in 1905 to create his vision of a Venice in America. The decades took their toll, but the remaining canals were drained and refurbished in 1993. The surrounding neighborhood is now on the National Register of Historic Places. Charming footpaths crisscross the canals as ducks splash underneath. On the banks, mansions stand next to small bungalows. Residents pull kayaks and canoes up to their homes. It's quiet, serene, and hidden. Hollywood? Where's that?

ABOVE Spindly palms and an evening sky in Los Feliz.

OPPOSITE Despite its high-rises and packed freeways, Los Angeles has room for places that can feel remote, like this trail in the Santa Monica Mountains.

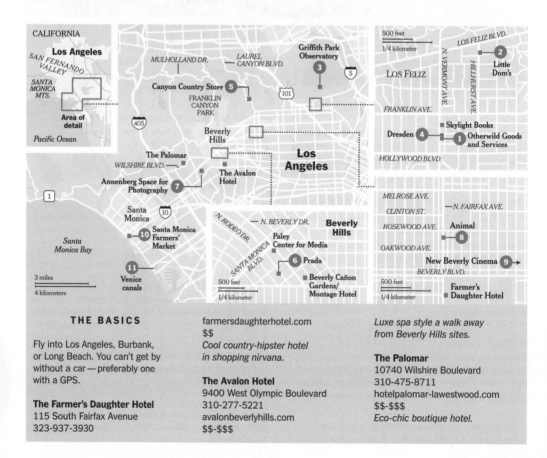

THE BASICS

Fly into Los Angeles, Burbank, or Long Beach. You can't get by without a car—preferably one with a GPS.

The Farmer's Daughter Hotel
115 South Fairfax Avenue
323-937-3930

farmersdaughterhotel.com
$$
Cool country-hipster hotel in shopping nirvana.

The Avalon Hotel
9400 West Olympic Boulevard
310-277-5221
avalonbeverlyhills.com
$$-$$$

Luxe spa style a walk away from Beverly Hills sites.

The Palomar
10740 Wilshire Boulevard
310-475-8711
hotelpalomar-lawestwood.com
$$-$$$
Eco-chic boutique hotel.

Downtown Los Angeles

The sprawl, the scale, all that freeway time — for many, Los Angeles is an acquired taste. But not downtown. New York-like in its density and mishmash, the long-blighted center has become an accessible, pedestrian-friendly destination in recent years; Angelenos walk around en masse, using their actual legs. The immense L.A. Live entertainment complex is largely responsible for this comeback, but the studiously vintage bars and imaginative restaurants that seem to open every other day are also part of the revival. Skid Row and the drifts of homeless camps haven't vanished altogether, and the grittiness still varies by block. But this part of town is alive again, in ways that make sense even to an outsider.
— BY CHRIS COLIN

FRIDAY

1 *Do the Crawl* 4 p.m.

The Downtown Art Walk — a party-in-the-streets bonanza that draws thousands of revelers the second Thursday of every month — is one way to experience the area's robust art scene. But you can do your own art walk anytime, and you should. Lured by low rents, a number of impressive galleries have found a home here, many of them on Chung King Road, a pedestrian alley strung with lanterns in Chinatown. For starters, look in at **Charlie James Gallery** (No. 969; 213-687-0844; cjamesgallery.com), then **Coagula Curatorial** (No. 974; 323-480-7852; coagulacuratorial.com). The shows are intimate and occasionally provocative, featuring a broad array of contemporary artists: William Powhida, Orly Cogan, and others.

2 *The City at Its Brightest* 7:30 p.m.

Whether you're catching a Lakers game, touring the Grammy Museum, or attending a concert at the Nokia Theater, there is always something splashy to do at the 27-acre, $2.5 billion sports and entertainment behemoth that is **L.A. Live**

OPPOSITE Broadway in downtown Los Angeles, a pedestrian-friendly destination rebounding from 20th-century decline.

RIGHT Fabric in the Fashion District, a 100-block mix of wholesale-only shops and designer retail discounts.

(800 West Olympic Boulevard; 213-763-5483; lalive.com). Just strolling the Tokyo-ish Nokia Plaza — 20,000 square feet of LED signage — is diverting. An array of restaurants and bars is clustered at the periphery, but many visitors prefer just to stroll around this giant pedestrian zone, trying to take it all in.

3 *A Late, Great Bite* 10 p.m.

Make a reservation before you hire a ride to **Bestia** (2121 East Seventh Place; 213-514-5724; bestiala.com; $$$). It's off the beaten path in a far-flung section of the artists district. But the Italian-inspired food makes it worth the trip, and it's open until midnight on weekends. Brave diners might try dishes like the Stinging Nettle Papardelle, which delivers mushroom ragu, poached egg, and crème fraîche along with the fried nettles. The entrees will make meat lovers happy, and your dessert might include sour cherry shortcake with chamomile flower cream.

SATURDAY

4 *On the Nickel* 9 a.m.

The maple bacon doughnut is a stand-out on the breakfast menu at the **Nickel Diner** (524 South Main Street; 213-623-8301; nickeldiner.com; $). The rest is mostly well-executed diner food. What's remarkable is the location — this block was once one of Skid Row's most notorious. It's a testament to downtown's revival that the intersection of Main

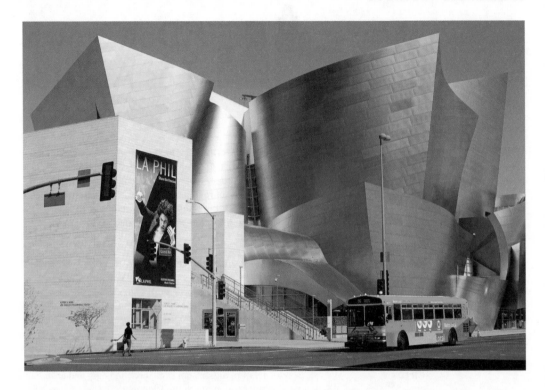

and Fifth (hence "Nickel") could become home to a place where people line up for tables.

5 *Nice Threads* 10:30 a.m.

The 100-block **Fashion District** mixes high and low seamlessly. Though many shops sell wholesale only, you can still find a wide selection of deeply discounted designer clothes, fabric, and accessories. The jumbled shops and warehouses at Ninth and Los Angeles Streets are a start. Feel free to bargain. Don't miss the rowdier **Santee Alley** (thesanteealley.com), a chaotic open-air bazaar where cheap meets weird in a thoroughly Los Angeles way. Energetic vendors hawk the impressive (perfect knock-off handbags) and the odd (toy frogs emblazoned with gang insignias). Find a higher-end experience around the corner at **Acne Studios** (855 South Broadway; 213-243-0960; acnestudios.com), a branch of a Swedish fashion brand. Dripping with 21st-century cool, it draws shoppers to the Art Deco spaces of the Eastern Columbia

Building. For an expedition tailored to your particular agenda, contact **Urban Shopping Adventures** (213-683-9715) for a guided shopping trip.

6 *Accessible Architecture* 1 p.m.

The arrival of the conductor Gustavo Dudamel at the Los Angeles Philharmonic brought new crowds to the symphony, but the stage where it performs, the **Walt Disney Concert Hall** (111 South Grand Avenue; 323-850-2000; laphil.com) deserves a visit even without a ticket. Designed by Frank Gehry, it's a deconstructivist celebration of all that is big, curvy, and shiny. Bring a picnic and wind your way along the semi-hidden outer staircase up to an excellent city vista and rooftop garden oasis. Free guided tours and self-guided audio tours are available most days. Check first (musiccenter.org) for schedules.

7 *Korean Feast* 7 p.m.

Angelenos debate about where to find the best Korean barbecue, but judging from the celebrity photos and the happy crowds, one winner is **Park's** (955 Vermont Avenue, just west of downtown; 213-380-1717; parksbbq.com; $$$). Join its perpetual party of families, salarymen, and hipsters as they talk over the open grills where hyperkinetic waiters cook, for example, bulgogi beef, shrimp, and octopus accompanied by kimchi, chile paste, pickled roots, and other tasty sides.

ABOVE Find the outdoor stairway on Frank Gehry's Walt Disney Concert Hall and climb its curves to a rooftop garden.

OPPOSITE ABOVE Drinks at Seven Grand, one of the retro bars inspired by downtown's colorful history.

OPPOSITE BELOW The Nickel Diner, a busy spot in a revived area that not so long ago was part of Skid Row.

8 *Pick a Show, Any Show* 8:30 p.m.

If you're downtown for a performance, chances are it's a sprawling affair at L.A. Live. But a handful of smaller settings offer funkier alternatives. The **Redcat Theater** (631 West Second Street; 213-237-2800; redcat.org) plays host to all manner of experimental performances — one Saturday in winter featured theater, dance, puppetry, and live music from a Slovene-Latvian art collaboration. The **Mayan** (1038 South Hill Street; 213-746-4674; clubmayan.com), an ornate old dance club most nights, occasionally hosts mad events like Lucha VaVoom, which combines burlesque and Mexican wrestling. And the **Smell** (247 South Main Street; thesmell.org), a likably grimy, volunteer-run space, hosts very small bands circled by swaying teenagers.

9 *Drink as if It's Illegal* 10:30 p.m.

Was Los Angeles a hoot during Prohibition? No need to guess, thanks to a slew of meticulously old-timey newfangled bars that exploit the wonderful history of old Los Angeles. From upscale speakeasy (the **Varnish**; 118 East Sixth Street; 213-265-7089; thevarnishbar.com) to converted-power-plant chic (the **Edison**; 108 West Second Street; 213-613-0000; edisondowntown.com) to an old bank vault (the **Crocker Club**; 453 South Spring Street; 213-239-9099; crockerclub.com), these spiffy places do set decoration as only Los Angeles can. And fussily delicious artisanal cocktails are as plentiful as you'd imagine. The well-scrubbed will also enjoy the swanky **Seven Grand** (515 West Seventh Street, second floor; 213-614-0736; sevengrandbars.com), while the well-scuffed may feel more at home at **La Cita Bar** (336 South Hill Street; 213-687-7111; lacitabar.com).

SUNDAY

10 *Big Art* 11 a.m.

Contemporary art galleries are de rigueur, but Los Angeles was in the vanguard. Its **Museum of Contemporary Art** (main location, 250 South Grand Avenue; 213-626-6222; moca.org), opened in 1979. Stop in to see what's behind its reputation for a fine collection and exciting special exhibitions.

11 *Broad Art* 1 p.m.

Cross the street for a cool take on Sunday brunch (Otium restaurant; otiumla.com; $$) and an even more contemporary view of contemporary art, both at the **Broad** (221 South Grand Avenue; 213-232-6200; thebroad.org). The Los Angeles philanthropists Eli and Edythe Broad (pronounced brode), who have long supported the arts and the development of the Grand Avenue Arts District, opened this museum in 2015 to display their own extensive art collection. The honeycombed facade is striking, and works inside range from Andy Warhol to Jeff Koons and up-to-the-minute multimedia pieces.

ABOVE If an art piece is much older than the first baby boomer, you're not likely to find it in the Museum of Contemporary Art, which is rich in works by Rothko, Oldenburg, Lichtenstein, and Rauschenberg.

OPPOSITE Downtown skyscrapers aglow in the Los Angeles night. About half a million people go to work every day in downtown's clusters of office towers and civic buildings. In the off hours, it's now also a place to play.

THE BASICS

Walking works better than it used to, but you may still want a car.

Ritz-Carlton, Los Angeles
900 West Olympic Boulevard
213-743-8800
ritzcarlton.com/en/hotels/california/
los-angeles
$$$$
Half of a gleaming new two-hotel complex rising above L.A. Live.

JW Marriott Los Angeles L.A. Live
900 West Olympic Boulevard
213-765-8600
lalivemarriott.com
$$-$$$
The other half of the same hotel complex.

Ace Hotel Downtown Los Angeles
929 South Broadway
213-623-3233
acehotel.com/losangeles
$$$
Hipster update of 1920s building with movie palace still inside.

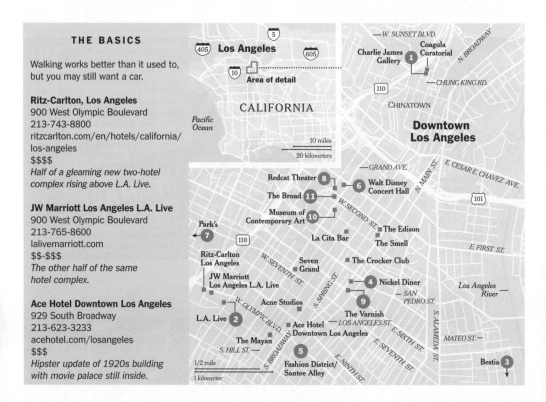

Hollywood

LOS ANGELES

Hollywood is one of those rare places that live up to their stereotypes, right down to the sign. But with minimal effort, it can offer a whole lot more. This pedestrian-friendly district represents both Los Angeles's past, with icons like the Capitol Records building, and the city's future—multiethnic, vertical, dense. A recent renaissance means there are now million-dollar condos, trendy restaurants, celebrity watering holes, and a world-class movie theater. But there are still tattoo parlors, sex shops, and homelessness. Tying it all together is the Hollywood Walk of Fame, where it is hard not to be at least momentarily tickled (Hello, Mister Rogers) or merely confused (Who the heck was that?). It remains a place that only Los Angeles could produce.
— BY JENNIFER STEINHAUER

FRIDAY

1 *Costume Change* 4 p.m.

Before you unpack your bags, prepare to fill them up. Hollywood is awash in vintage clothing stores, many of them filled with remnants from television and movie sets past. **Golyester** (450 South La Brea Avenue; 323-931-1339; golyester.com) has amazingly preserved purses, negligees ($278 was the price for one two-piece Christian Dior number), gowns (on one visit, a white leather dress with fur trim) and more. Of special interest are the shoes — finds like gold sling-backs, emerald stilettos, or elegant Herbert Levine pumps. Down the street is **The Way We Wore** (334 South La Brea Avenue; 323-937-0878; thewaywewore.com) with more vintage treasures. Keep going to **Cafe Midi** (148 South La Brea Avenue; 323-939-9860; cafemidi.com), where you can have a cappuccino and take in the Moroccan ceramic bowls and candles in the adjacent store.

2 *Planet Thai* 7:30 p.m.

There are upscale bistros and giant tuna rolls aplenty in the neighborhood, but Angelenos love Hollywood for Thai food. Reasonable minds can quibble over the best, which tends to be high on authentic flair, low on atmosphere, and budget-priced. Good examples are the **Sapp Coffee Shop** (5183 Hollywood Boulevard; 323-665-1035) and **Ruen Pair** (5257 Hollywood Boulevard; 323-466-0153). For a slightly more

upscale ambience, check out **Bulan Thai Vegetarian Kitchen** (7168 Melrose Avenue; 323-857-1882; bulanthai.com), a chic spot that's hot with the yoga crowd. Look for menu items like busaba pumpkin, mock duck curry, and mushroom tom kah.

3 *Hockney Night* 10 p.m.

Nothing is more echt Hollywood than the **Tropicana Pool** (7000 Hollywood Boulevard; 323-466-7000; hollywoodroosevelt.com), nestled beneath tall palms at the Hollywood Roosevelt Hotel. The pool and its louche cocktail bar have played host to Clark Gable and Marilyn Monroe, and celebrity sightings are still common. But the real treat is the pool itself. At night it's covered with translucent flooring, enabling you to sip cocktails while admiring the abstract underwater mural painted by David Hockney.

SATURDAY

4 *Is That Tom Cruise?* 8:30 a.m.

Los Angeles is a morning town, so get going at **Square One Dining** (4854 Fountain Avenue; 323-661-1109; squareonedining.com; $$), a cheerful local spot that focuses on farmers' market produce. Order some French toast with banana citrus caramel or the transporting pressed egg sandwich with tomato

OPPOSITE The evening lights near Sunset Boulevard.

BELOW From behind the famous Hollywood sign, the glittering lights below promise a world of celebrities, mansions, palm tree-lined boulevards, and movie studios.

and arugula. Stare at the Scientology headquarters across the street, among the more relevant fixtures in Hollywood, and try to see who is going in and coming out of its parking structure.

5 *Green Space* 11 a.m.

Many a native Angeleno knows not of **Barnsdall Art Park** (4800 Hollywood Boulevard; 323-660-4254; barnsdallartpark.com), a public space donated to the city by the eccentric oil heiress Aline Barnsdall in 1927. Beyond having one of the best views of the Hollywood sign and grass upon which to sit (a rare thing in Los Angeles), the site is home to the **Los Angeles Municipal Art Gallery**, which exhibits the work of local artists; a small municipally owned theater, and Frank Lloyd Wright's **Hollyhock House**, which was originally commissioned by Barnsdall as her home.

6 *Food (and Music) for the Soul* 2 p.m.

You thought you went to Hollywood to eat raw food? That's West Hollywood. Before your afternoon walking tour, load up on carbs at **Roscoe's House of Chicken and Waffles** (1514 North Gower Street; 323-466-7453; roscoeschickenandwaffles.com; $-$$). The beloved soul-food chain is known for its half chicken smothered with gravy and served with two waffles. From Roscoe's, it's a fast walk to **Amoeba Records** (6400 Sunset Boulevard; 323-245-6400; amoeba.com), one of the last great independent record stores in the country, where new and used CDs and DVDs are found by the mile. There are also live in-store performances (with a special emphasis on up-and-coming Los Angeles bands).

7 *High-Tech Movie* 5 p.m.

Keep walking. Now you are headed to the **ArcLight Cinema** (6360 West Sunset Boulevard; 323-615-2550; arclightcinemas.com), which has one of the best projection and sound systems in the country, plus comfy chairs. Catch the latest popcorn flick, obscure retrospective, or independent picture with every serious cinema buff in town.

8 *Peru in Hollywood* 8 p.m.

Turn the corner on North Vine, and end up in a tiny spot where the spare décor is made up of small replicas of Lima's famous balcones, or balconies. Known for its ceviches, **Los Balcones del Peru** (1360 North Vine Street; 323-871-9600; losbalconesperu. com; $) is a charming restaurant, down the block from a pawn shop, where families, couples, and guys who prefer a place on one of the tiger-patterned bar stools all feed. Start with chicha morada (a fruit drink made with corn water), then hit the lomo saltado (beef sautéed with onions) or tacu tacu con mariscos (refried Peruvian beans with shrimp).

9 *Dark Nights* 11 p.m.

End the evening at the **Woods** (1533 North La Brea Avenue; 323-876-6612; vintagebargroup.com/ the-woods.php), which, as the name implies, has an outdoorsy theme. The sleek bar has lots of cedar and elk antler chandeliers hanging from the star-encrusted ceiling. As you scope out the young crowd and peruse the juke box, have one of the signature mint juleps or a seasonal drink like the pumpkin pie shot.

SUNDAY

10 *Celebrity Dog Walkers* 9:30 a.m.

Two blocks north of Hollywood Boulevard is one of the most scenic, unusual urban parks in the country, **Runyon Canyon**. The 130-acre park offers steep, invigorating hikes with views of the San Fernando Valley, the Pacific, Catalina Island (on clear days), and the Griffith Observatory. The area

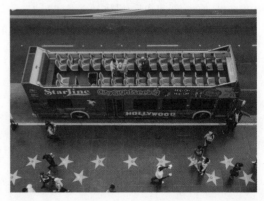

is popular with dog owners (including celebrities), who take advantage of the leash-free policy. Mixed in among the wild chaparral are the crumbling estates of Carman Runyon, a coal magnate who used the property for hunting, and George Huntington Hartford II, heir to the A&P fortune. Parking can be tricky, so enter from the north, off Mulholland. You'll find a parking lot and start the hike going downhill.

11 *Walk This Way* Noon

You can't leave Hollywood without strolling down Hollywood Boulevard on the **Hollywood Walk of Fame** (hollywoodchamber.net). Take in the hundreds of stars embedded in the sidewalks, just to see how many you recognize. Afterward, stop at **Hollywood Burger** (6250 Hollywood Boulevard;

323-378-5668; hollywood-burger.com) for a burger or milkshake. It will make you remember Hollywood with fondness.

OPPOSITE ABOVE The retro exterior of the Cinerama Dome at the ArcLight Cinema complex, built in 1963.

OPPOSITE BELOW A tour bus at the Walk of Fame.

ABOVE Roscoe's House of Chicken and Waffles keeps its soul-food promise: gravy and waffles come with the chicken.

THE BASICS

Fly into Los Angeles, Long Beach, Ontario, or Burbank. For touring, you can get by without a car.

The Hollywood Roosevelt
7000 Hollywood Boulevard
323-856-1970
hollywoodroosevelt.com
$$$
Can be loud, but historic as a favorite of stars in Hollywood's early days. All the night life you'll ever want.

Mama Shelter Los Angeles
6500 Selma Avenue
323-785-6666
mamashelter.com/en/los-angeles
$$
A friendly, nontraditional hotel with a rooftop bar in a prime location.

Magic Castle Hotel
7025 Franklin Avenue
323-851-0800
magiccastlehotel.com
$$-$$$
A longtime favorite of families; rooms have full kitchens.

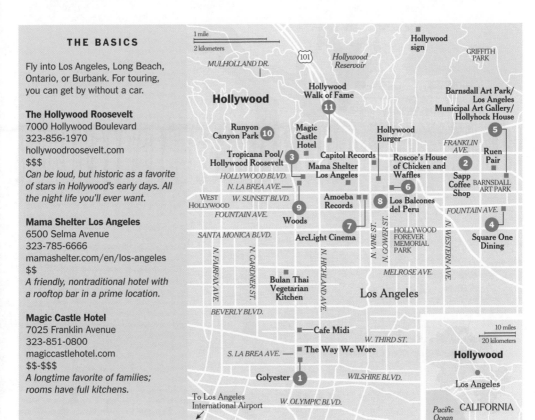

Malibu

The laid-back, sun-drenched sparkle of celebrity-filled Malibu was darkened when a devastating 2018 wildfire charred the hills, killed at least three people, and destroyed structures including some celebrities' trophy homes. But landscapes recover quickly in California, and the glamour of Malibu was not extinguished. The staggering natural beauty of the sea as it meets the mountains remains indestructible, chic shops and restaurants survive, and Malibu's 13,000 residents still welcome pleasure seekers to sunbathe, surf, and sip the local wine. — BY LOUISE TUTELIAN

FRIDAY

1 *The Wind, the Waves...* 5 p.m.

What's so appealing about Malibu's little slice of coast? Visit **Point Dume State Preserve** (Birdview Avenue and Cliffside Drive; 310-457-8143; parks.ca.gov), and you'll see. A modest walk to the top of this coastal bluff rewards you with a sweeping view of the entire Santa Monica Bay, the inland Santa Monica Mountains, and, on a clear day, Catalina Island. A boardwalk just below the summit leads to a platform for watching swooping pelicans and crashing waves. To feel the sand between your toes, drive down Birdview Avenue to Westward Beach Road and park at the very end of the lot on your left. You'll be looking at Westward Beach, a gem that most visitors miss. Strike a yoga pose. Sigh at will.

2 *Chasing the Sunset* 7 p.m.

Little known fact: Most of Malibu faces south, not west. That means sitting down at just any seaside restaurant at dusk won't guarantee seeing a sunset over the water. But the aptly named **Sunset Restaurant** (6800 Westward Beach Road; 310-589-1007; thesunsetrestaurant.com) is a sure bet, with just the right orientation. Claim a white leather banquette, order a carafe of wine and select a tasting plate of cheeses, and settle in for the light show.

3 *Shore Dinner* 9 p.m.

If you're going to spot a celebrity, chances are it will be at **Nobu Malibu** (3835 Cross Creek Road, in the Malibu Country Mart; 310-317-9140; noburestaurants.com/malibu/home; $$$), one of the famed chef Nobu Matsuhisa's many restaurants. The sushi is sublime,

and the entrees measure up. Reservations are essential. The front room is convivial but noisy; the subtly lighted back room is quieter.

SATURDAY

4 *Walk the Pier* 9 a.m.

The 780-foot-long **Malibu Pier** (23000 Pacific Coast Highway; 888-310-7437; malibupiersportfishing.com) is the most recognizable (and, arguably, only) landmark in town. Take a morning stroll out to the end, chat with the fishermen, and watch surfers paddle out. You'll be walking on a piece of Malibu history. The pier was originally built in 1905 as a loading dock for construction material, and it was a lookout during World War II. It crops up in numerous movies and TV shows.

5 *Bronze for the Ages* 10 a.m.

The **Getty Villa** (17985 Pacific Coast Highway; 310-440-7300; getty.edu) is just over the city's southern border in Pacific Palisades, but no matter: it shouldn't be missed. The museum, built by J. Paul Getty in the 1970s to resemble a first-century Roman country house, contains Greek, Roman, and Etruscan vessels, gems, and statuary, some dating back to 6500 B.C. On the second floor is a rare life-size Greek bronze, *Statue of a Victorious Youth*, a prize of the

OPPOSITE Beach and pier at Malibu, the little slice of Pacific coast that celebrities like to call their own.

BELOW Kai Sanson, a surfing instructor, initiates students into the ways of the waves.

museum. In the outside peristyle gardens, watch the sun glint off bronze statues at the 220-foot-long reflecting pool. Admission is free, but parking is limited, so car reservations are required.

6 *Magic Carpet Tile* 1 p.m.

Even many longtime Angelenos don't know about the **Adamson House** (23200 Pacific Coast Highway; 310-456-9575; adamsonhouse.org), a 1930 Spanish Colonial Revival residence that's a showplace of exquisite ceramic tiles from Malibu Potteries, which closed in 1932. Overlooking Surfrider Beach with a view of Malibu Pier, the house belonged to a member of the Rindge family, the last owners of the Malibu Spanish land grant. Take a tour and watch for the Persian "carpet" constructed entirely from intricately patterned pieces of tile. Other highlights: a stunning star-shaped fountain and a bathroom tiled top to bottom in an ocean pattern, with ceramic galleons poised in perpetuity on pointy whitecaps in a sea of blue.

7 *Vino With a View* 4 p.m.

The drive to **Malibu Wines** (31740 Mulholland Highway; 818-865-0605; malibuwines.com) along the serpentine roads of the Santa Monica Mountains is almost as much fun as tipping a glass once you get there. Set on a serene green lawn, the tasting room is really an attractive covered outdoor counter. Sidle up and choose a flight of four styles. Or buy a bottle and lounge at one of the tables. Though its buildings were damaged in the 2018 fire, Malibu Wines survived, along with its collection of exotic animals, including Stanley the giraffe.

8 *Can You Say Olé?* 7 p.m.

In the chic **Malibu Lumber Yard** shopping arcade (the piles of two-by-fours are long gone) you'll find **Café Habana Malibu** (3939 Cross Creek Road; 310-317-0300; habana-malibu.com), the West Coast hermana of famed Café Habana in the West Village in New York and Habana Outpost in Brooklyn. The sleek, solar-powered bar and cafe serves Mexican/Cuban

fare from 11 a.m. to — most nights — an unheard-of 1 a.m. in early-to-bed L.A. (There's Wednesday karaoke and a nightclub vibe after dark.) Locals tout the fish tacos and charred cheese-covered corn on the cob, and the killer margaritas and mojitos. Yes, the guacamole is the price of a diner entree, but the star-sightings are free.

SUNDAY

9 *Ride the Surf* 10 a.m.

Surf shops offering lessons and board rentals line the Pacific Coast Highway (P.C.H. in local lingo), but Kai Sanson of **Zuma Surf and Swim Training** (949-742-1086; zumasurfandswim.com) takes his fun seriously. Sanson, a Malibu native, will size you up with a glance and gear the instruction to your skills. There's a price for the lessons, but they come with Sanson's tales of growing up in Malibu. Locals also give high marks to **Malibu Makos Surf Club** (310-317-1229; malibumakos.com).

10 *Brunch in Style* Noon

Put on your oversize sunglasses if you're going to **Geoffrey's Malibu** (27400 Pacific Coast Highway; 310-457-1519; geoffreysmalibu.com; $$$). Geoffrey's (pronounced Joffreys) is the hot meeting spot for

ABOVE The curve of the Pacific beach in Malibu. The houses lining the waterside are worth millions.

BELOW Tasting the reds at Malibu Wines.

the well-heeled with a hankering for a shiitake mushroom omelet or lobster Cobb salad. Its Richard Neutra-designed building overlooks the Pacific, and every table has an ocean view. Or if you want something a bit more chill, head to **Ollo** (23750 Pacific Coast Highway in the Malibu Colony Plaza; 310-317-1444; ollomalibu.com; $$) and load up on the generous — and locally sourced — pancakes, huevos rancheros, etc., while lounging in the dining room or sunning on the patio in the ocean breeze.

11 *Shop Like a Star* 2 p.m.

Whether it's diamonds or designer jeans you're after, the open-air **Malibu Country Mart** (3835 Cross Creek Road; malibucountrymart.com) is the place

to cruise for them. Its more than 50 retail stores and restaurants include Ralph Lauren, 7 for All Mankind, and John Varvatos. In an adjacent space is the luxe **Malibu Lumber Yard** shopping complex (themalibulumberyard.com), with stores like Alice + Olivia and AllSaints Spitalfields.

ABOVE The Getty Villa museum, built by J. Paul Getty to resemble a first-century Roman country house.

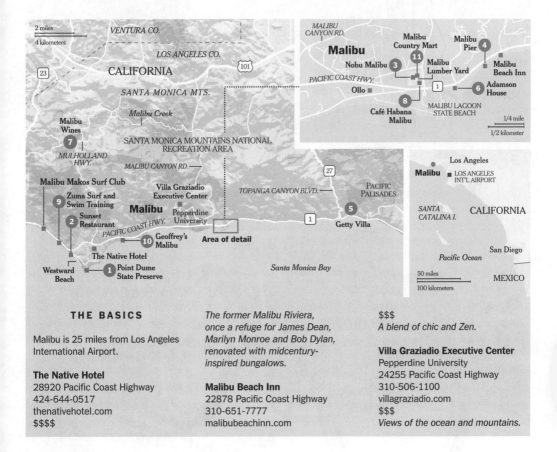

THE BASICS

Malibu is 25 miles from Los Angeles International Airport.

The Native Hotel
28920 Pacific Coast Highway
424-644-0517
thenativehotel.com
$$$$

The former Malibu Riviera, once a refuge for James Dean, Marilyn Monroe and Bob Dylan, renovated with midcentury-inspired bungalows.

Malibu Beach Inn
22878 Pacific Coast Highway
310-651-7777
malibubeachinn.com

$$$
A blend of chic and Zen.

Villa Graziadio Executive Center
Pepperdine University
24255 Pacific Coast Highway
310-506-1100
villagraziadio.com
$$$
Views of the ocean and mountains.

Marin County

Crossing the Golden Gate Bridge from San Francisco, you arrive in Marin even before landing on solid ground. The end of the bridge hangs over the county line (which is at the water's edge on the north shore of the Golden Gate strait), and this introduction is fitting since Marin itself feels suspended — ethereal, privileged, a place apart from the rest of the Bay Area. Fearing the perils of suburban sprawl, Marin invested early and often in conservation. Outside of a handful of small cities (San Rafael and Novato the largest among them), the county is a surprisingly rural landscape of cattle ranches, rolling hills, redwood groves, houseboat communities, and roadhouses. It is among the wealthiest counties in the country, but Marin also has small towns, like Bolinas and Fairfax, that retain an endearing Northern California eccentricity.
— BY FREDA MOON

FRIDAY

1 *Sentinel of the Bay* 1 p.m.

The spectacular entrance to Marin County, the **Marin Headlands** lies just beyond the Golden Gate Bridge. At the National Park Service visitors center (Field Road, Building 948, Sausalito; 415-331-1540; nps.gov/goga/marin-headlands.htm), drivers and hikers pick up a map guiding them to abandoned wartime gun emplacements and sweeping views of beaches where surfers paddle blue-green waves as red-tailed hawks soar overhead. Battery Townsley was the Bay Area's most secretive fortification; in the 1940s, it held two massive battleship guns and housed more than 100 soldiers in a network of 26 underground rooms.

2 *Dead and Alive* 5 p.m.

Phil Lesh of the Grateful Dead modeled **Terrapin Crossroads** (100 Yacht Club Drive, San Rafael; 415-524-2773; terrapincrossroads.net), in San Rafael's Canal district, after Levon Helm's Midnight Rambles in Woodstock, N.Y. This music

OPPOSITE Marin County's small towns and scenic trails are a contrast to nearby San Francisco.

RIGHT Pedaling on the Lagunitas Lake loop trail. Marin claims to be the birthplace of mountain biking.

space, restaurant, and bar on the waterfront often hosts jam sessions featuring Lesh and his friends. At happy hour, you'll find an exceptional list of Northern California draft beers, pizza from a flaming wood-fired oven, and appetizers like spice-rubbed fish tacos filled with locally caught fish, avocado, cilantro lime slaw, and spicy chipotle aioli.

3 *For the Soul* 7 p.m.

Occupying an imposing lime green building in downtown San Rafael, **Sol Food** (901 Lincoln Avenue, San Rafael; 415-451-4765; solfoodrestaurant.com; $) is a bright, plant-filled space with communal tables and Puerto Rican classics like shrimp sautéed in a garlic, onion, and tomato sauce, with mofongo (mashed green plantains), salad, and fresh avocado. Sol Food serves no alcohol; order the mango ice tea or Mexican Coke. Save room for dessert at **Fairfax Scoop** (63 Broadway Boulevard, Fairfax; 415-453-3130), an elevator-size ice cream shop where there's almost always a line.

4 *Fairfax for All* 9 p.m.

For an after-dinner drink, head over to **123 Bolinas** (123 Bolinas Road, Fairfax; 415-488-5123; 123bolinas.com), a wine bar across from Bolinas Park that serves small plates, local beer, and regional wines. The bar top is carved from a 100-year-old fallen oak, the furniture is built of reclaimed barn siding, and there's a U.F.O.-shaped fireplace. For something more casual, head to the cycle-centric beer-and-sausage spot **Gestalt Haus Fairfax** (28 Bolinas Road, Fairfax; 415-721-7895),

which has board games, a CD jukebox, cyclocross posters on the walls, and 30 or so tap beers. Then sample one of the several lively spots in downtown Fairfax, a 7,500-person town that claims to have had live music every night for more than 30 years.

SATURDAY

5 *Head for the Hills* 9:30 a.m.

Start the day with beignets and chicory coffee at the homey, New Orleans-inspired **Hummingbird** (57 Broadway Boulevard, Fairfax; 415-457-9866). Then go mountain biking; Marin proclaims itself the sport's birthplace. Stop by **Sunshine Bicycle Center** (737 Center Boulevard, Fairfax; 415-459-3334; sunshinebicycle.com) to rent a high-performance bike, grab a map, and get directions to the Lagunitas Lake loop (known locally as the Gentleman's Loop), a relatively nontechnical trail that travels past lakes and through chaparral, oak groves, and meadows.

6 *Coastal Picnic* 2 p.m.

Stop into the **Cowgirl Creamery** (80 Fourth Street, Point Reyes Station; 415-663-9335; cowgirlcreamery.com), which sells exceptional cheeses, like triple-cream Red Hawk and Mt. Tam, along with baguettes, charcuterie, and wine, in a restored barn in downtown Point Reyes Station. Then head to **Hog Island Oyster Company** (20215 Highway 1, Marshall; 415-663-9218; hogislandoysters. com), where the shuck-your-own oyster picnic gets you a picnic table and grill, rubber shucking gloves and knife, oyster condiments (lemon, hot sauce, and freshly grated horseradish), and views of Tomales Bay. There are two three-hour time slots each day, and reservations are required, often weeks in advance. For bivalves without the elbow grease (or the planning), go to **Marshall Store** (19225 Highway 1, Marshall; 415-663-1339; themarshallstore.com; $$), a waterfront seafood shack with dockside tables that serves barbecued oysters in chorizo butter, smoked oysters on crostini, and grilled fish tacos.

7 *Down to Drakes* 4 p.m.

Take the **Estero Trail** (nps.gov/pore), one of Point Reyes's lesser-known hikes, through grasslands, the remnants of a Christmas tree farm, and an egret rookery. Then descend to a wooden bridge across a narrow inlet of Drakes Estero, an estuary that's a breeding ground for seals. From the bridge, you may spot leopard sharks gliding back and forth at the water's surface. If time allows, continue to Sunset Beach, for a total round-trip hike of eight miles.

8 *Get Fresh* 8 p.m.

Saltwater (12781 Sir Francis Drake Boulevard, Inverness; 415-669-1244; saltwateroysterdepot.com; $$), in the small town of Inverness, is an unusual restaurant that, when founded in 2012, was partly crowd-source-financed and had a partnership with a community shellfish farm that trained "underserved youth" to work in the oyster industry. Today at the 55-seat bistro, local fishermen are invited to sell their catch directly at the kitchen door. The menu changes with the harvest and includes artfully executed dishes like local halibut with trumpet mushrooms, farro, Brussels sprouts and butternut squash, and crispy lamb tongue with lentils and fingerling potatoes.

SUNDAY

9 *To Market, to Market* 8 a.m.

The Sunday **Marin Farmers Market** (10 Avenue of the Flags, San Rafael; agriculturalinstitute.org) in San Rafael has nearly 200 vendors selling everything from radishes to prepared foods at the **Marin Civic**

Center, Frank Lloyd Wright's last major commission. Pick up breakfast: perhaps a savory pie or enchilada, or waffles from a food truck.

10 *Over the Hill* 10 a.m.

Take your picnic breakfast and join the slow Sunday parade of drivers winding their way over **Mount Tamalpais**. The views, which sweep from the bay west to Stinson Beach, are worth the crawl. On the coast, stop in at the **Bolinas Museum** (48 Wharf Road, Bolinas; 415-868-0330; bolinasmuseum.org), which opens at noon and comprises a regional history museum, three contemporary art galleries, and a permanent collection of works by West Marin artists. Another option, for those averse to the drive, is the breathtaking 1.7-mile walk through the **Tennessee Valley** to the cliff-flanked Tennessee Beach. And if you

have never been to **Muir Woods**, the cathedral-like grove of giant redwoods that is one of California's most revered remnants of its original landscape, this is your chance.

11 *Waterfront Living* 1 p.m.

Tucked away on a dead-end street beside a marina, **Fish** (350 Harbor Drive, Sausalito; 415-331-3474; 331fish.com; $$$) serves a decadent Dungeness crab roll. After you've finished yours, walk the waterfront for a glimpse of Sausalito's well-appointed houseboats.

OPPOSITE ABOVE Hog Island Oyster Company.

OPPOSITE BELOW 123 Bolinas, a wine bar that serves small plates and beer as well as local wines.

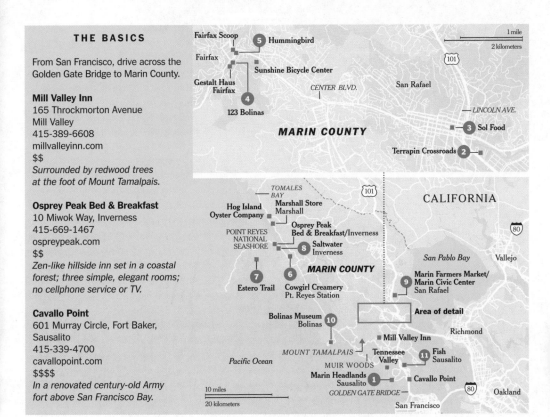

THE BASICS

From San Francisco, drive across the Golden Gate Bridge to Marin County.

Mill Valley Inn
165 Throckmorton Avenue
Mill Valley
415-389-6608
millvalleyinn.com
$$
Surrounded by redwood trees at the foot of Mount Tamalpais.

Osprey Peak Bed & Breakfast
10 Miwok Way, Inverness
415-669-1467
ospreypeak.com
$$
Zen-like hillside inn set in a coastal forest; three simple, elegant rooms; no cellphone service or TV.

Cavallo Point
601 Murray Circle, Fort Baker,
Sausalito
415-339-4700
cavallopoint.com
$$$$
In a renovated century-old Army fort above San Francisco Bay.

The Mendocino Coast

*Since the '60s and '70s, when a flood of artists, hippies, and back-to-the-landers brought the cosmopolitan counterculture to this corner of Northern California, the Mendocino coast has made appearances on many a television show (*Murder, She Wrote, *most notably, where the small village of Mendocino was the stand-in for a fictional New England town) and movies (*Overboard, *for one). Once a collection of working-class logging, fishing, and ranching communities, the Coast — as it's called by residents — has become a stand-in for California's left-coast eccentricities. It is also widely known for its intoxicants — its celebrated wine, beer, and marijuana. But what really makes this stretch of oceanfront real estate so stirring is its profound windswept natural beauty, which seems to have inspired the local residents to a fierce independence.*
— BY FREDA MOON

FRIDAY

1 *Firehouse Firewater* 5 p.m.

For local lore and a drink, pull up a stool at **Beacon Light by the Sea** (7401 South Highway 1; 707-877-3311), high on a hill near Elk, population 200. Part bar, part museum of oddities, "Bobby's place" is run by the Greenwood Ridge fire chief, R.D. Beacon, in a back room of his remote fire station. You'll be greeted by his big dog and a grand piano. Break away at sunset for a walk on Navarro Beach, where sand castles and driftwood sculptures litter the pebble-strewn shoreline and bonfires burn on clear nights.

2 *Enchanté* 8 p.m.

For dinner, continue up the coast to **Ledford House** in Albion (3000 North Highway 1; 707-937-0282; ledfordhouse.com; $$), a French country bistro in the new California style (local farms, local wines, international influences), with a deck and tall Pacific-facing windows. A husband-wife, maître d'-executive chef team turns out formidable renditions of classics

like cassoulet and steak au poivre. The dining room is homey, and there's live jazz every night.

SATURDAY

3 *Spiritual Sustenance* 8 a.m.

Rise early to explore Mendocino village and the wild coast at its edge. Wander the streets of the village, a cluster of low white frame Victorian buildings and old wooden water towers, many of which have been repurposed to house shops, art studios, and even lodging. Take note of the **Mendocino Art Center** (45200 Little Lake Street, Mendocino; 707-937-5818; mendocinoartcenter.org), in case you want to come back later to its galleries. Venture out on the narrow footpaths of **Mendocino Headlands State Park**, which wraps around the village at the water's edge, and walk along the rocky, wind-lashed headlands to the picturesque Blowhole. Nearby, there's an imposing Tiki sculpture; locals place offerings in the mouth of the carved kahuna. Or watch the swells come ashore from the driftwood "Love Bench" above Portuguese Beach.

4 *Bialy in the Morning* 9 a.m.

For a light breakfast, linger over espresso and a house-made bialy at **GoodLife Cafe and Bakery** (10483 Lansing Street; 707-937-0836; goodlifecafemendo.com).

OPPOSITE Paths at Mendocino Headlands lead out to the edges of rocky promontories.

RIGHT Watercraft at rest outside Liquid Fusion Kayaking, where novices can take lessons in sea kayaks.

For a bigger meal, drive to **Eggheads** (326 North Main Street; 707-964-5005; fortbraggrestaurants.com/eggheads; $$) in Fort Bragg—a cramped *Wizard of Oz*-themed diner with menu items like Neptune Dorothy, a supremely rich Dungeness crab eggs Benedict.

5 *Seaworthy* 10 a.m.

All who have witnessed the frothing Pacific know that its name—from the Spanish for peaceful—is a misnomer. Here, the sea is as violent as it is beautiful. **Liquid Fusion Kayaking** (32399 Basin Street, Fort Bragg; 707-962-1623; liquidfusionkayak.com) in Noyo Harbor teaches novices to ride the white water with a three-hour surf kayaking session. For a more leisurely paddle, rent a Polynesian-style outrigger at **Catch a Canoe & Bicycles Too** (1 South Big River Road, Mendocino; 707-937-0273; catchacanoe.com) and glide up Big River.

6 *Take Out* 1 p.m.

At **Jenny's Giant Burger** (940 North Main Street, Fort Bragg; 707-964-2235; $), a classic roadside stand with vinyl stools, pick up a cheeseburger and a chocolate malt to go. Drive north to **MacKerricher State Park** (24100 MacKerricher Road, Fort Bragg; 707-937-5804; parks.ca.gov) to eat beside cattail-lined, fish-stocked Lake Cleone. Then walk south along the former log-haul road to where the pavement disintegrates into the sand dunes at **Inglenook Fen Ten Mile Dunes Preserve**. Another approach is to rent a bike in town and ride the length of the trail, crossing the nearly century-old Pudding Creek Trestle, an elegant lattice bridge that is now a pedestrian and bike path.

7 *Coastal Counterculture* 3 p.m.

Back in Fort Bragg, climb the stairs to **Triangle Tattoo & Museum** (356B North Main Street, Fort Bragg; 707-964-8814; triangletattoo.com), where Madame Chinchilla and Mr. G have compiled exhibitions dedicated to Maori tattoos, circus skin art,

and vintage ink machines. Billed as the "world's largest permanent sea glass exhibit," the little but colorful **International Sea Glass Museum** (17801 North Highway 1, Fort Bragg; 707-357-1585; internationalseaglassmuseum.com) celebrates the lustrous detritus the ocean leaves on Mendocino beaches. There's more shopping in Fort Bragg's compact downtown, including the **Bookstore and Vinyl Cafe** (137 East Laurel Street; 707-964-6559), which has a lovingly curated selection of used books.

8 *Beer Country* 5 p.m.

The **Taproom** at the **North Coast Brewing Company** (444 North Main Street, Fort Bragg; 707-964-3400; northcoastbrewing.com) has wooden booths and a 12-beer sampler that includes the brewery's flagship Red Seal Ale. For a wider selection of regional beers, plus excellent New York-style pizza, head to **Piaci Pub and Pizzeria** (120 West Redwood Avenue, Fort Bragg; 707-961-1133; piacipizza.com). Or travel south to the **Wine Bar[n]** at Glendeven Inn (8205 North Highway 1, Little River; 707-937-0083; glendeven.com), which pours a wide variety of local wines by the glass each afternoon.

9 *In Good Company* 7 p.m.

Until 2002, Fort Bragg was a company town with a coastline consumed by a sprawling lumber mill. Now the historic downtown is in revival mode. A welcome addition is **Mayan Fusion** (418 North Main Street; 707-961-0211; mayanfusionftbragg.com; $$), where southern Mexican cuisine meets nouveau California in tapas plates such as salbutes (a house-made masa tortilla with lettuce, tomato, guacamole, pickled onion, and queso fresco), or an entree of crispy cod tacos with Mayan slaw, served with rice and beans.

10 *All That Jazz* 8:30 p.m.

For live music and an after-dinner latte, go to **Headlands Coffeehouse** (120 Laurel Street; 707-964-1987; headlandscoffeehouse.com), a local institution with a monthly art show and a loyal

ABOVE Llamas amble at Glendeven Inn, south of Mendocino. If you're not staying at the inn, drive out in the evening to sample vintages in its wine bar.

following that has helped to revitalize Fort Bragg's once-decaying downtown. Just across the alley, **Cucina Verona** (124 East Laurel Street; 707-964-6844; cucinaverona.com) is an Italian restaurant-cafe with a welcoming bar and a well-considered wine list.

SUNDAY

11 *The Long Road Home* 10 a.m.

Take Highway 1 out of Mendocino County, stopping at **Queenie's Roadhouse Cafe** (6061 South Highway 1, Elk; 707-877-3285; queeniesroadhousecafe. com; $$) for breakfast food like organic allspice-laced corned beef hash or waffles with fresh fruit and yogurt dressing. Continue south to Point Arena, stopping at the 115-foot **Point Arena Lighthouse** (pointarenalighthouse.com). Rebuilt in 1907 after an

earlier lighthouse was damaged in the same great 1906 earthquake that also devastated San Francisco, the current structure is said to have been the first steel-reinforced concrete lighthouse in the country. Three miles south of town, take the overgrown path to **Schooner Gulch State Beach** for one final walk along the water's edge.

ABOVE The view from Ledford House, a French country bistro in Albion, is out over the Pacific Ocean. The fare is farm-to-table, with local foods and wines.

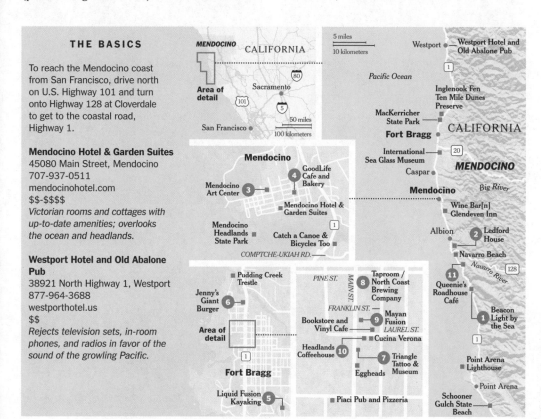

THE BASICS

To reach the Mendocino coast from San Francisco, drive north on U.S. Highway 101 and turn onto Highway 128 at Cloverdale to get to the coastal road, Highway 1.

Mendocino Hotel & Garden Suites
45080 Main Street, Mendocino
707-937-0511
mendocinohotel.com
$$-$$$$
Victorian rooms and cottages with up-to-date amenities; overlooks the ocean and headlands.

Westport Hotel and Old Abalone Pub
38921 North Highway 1, Westport
877-964-3688
westporthotel.us
$$
Rejects television sets, in-room phones, and radios in favor of the sound of the growling Pacific.

MENDOCINO CALIFORNIA

Area of detail

Sacramento

San Francisco

50 miles
100 kilometers

5 miles
10 kilometers

Westport — Westport Hotel and Old Abalone Pub

Pacific Ocean

Inglenook Fen
Ten Mile Dunes
Preserve

MacKerricher
State Park

Fort Bragg CALIFORNIA

International
Sea Glass Museum

Caspar

MENDOCINO

Mendocino Big River

Wine Bar[n]
Glendeven Inn

Albion Ledford House

Navarro Beach Navarro River

Mendocino

GoodLife
Cafe and
Bakery

Mendocino
Art Center

Mendocino Hotel &
Garden Suites

Mendocino
Headlands
State Park

Catch a Canoe &
Bicycles Too

COMPTCHE-UKIAH RD.

Pudding Creek
Trestle

Jenny's
Giant
Burger

Area of
detail

Fort Bragg

Liquid Fusion
Kayaking

PINE ST.

MAIN ST.

Taproom /
North Coast
Brewing
Company

FRANKLIN ST.

Mayan
Fusion

Bookstore and
Vinyl Cafe

LAUREL ST.

Cucina Verona

Headlands
Coffeehouse

Triangle
Tattoo &
Eggheads Museum

Piaci Pub and Pizzeria

Queenie's
Roadhouse
Café

Beacon
Light by
the Sea

Point Arena
Lighthouse

Point Arena

Schooner
Gulch State
Beach

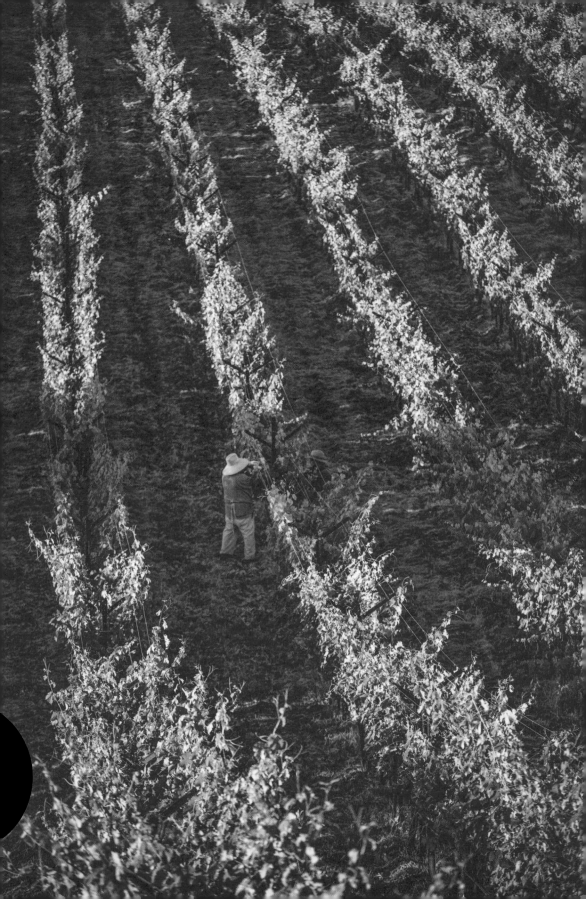

Napa Valley

Napa Valley, a delightful landscape of wildflowers and grapevines spread across miles of rolling hills, has been immortalized in film, literature, and European wine competitions. As the first and only Agricultural Preserve in the United States, and the first officially designated viticultural area, this small section of Northern California harbors some of the most hallowed wineries and restaurants in the country. Deadly wildfires burned across the North Coast in 2017, but the majority of Napa's wineries and vineyards (which served as firebreaks) were spared, and the valley was soon back on its feet. — BY PAOLA SINGER

FRIDAY

1 *Hearty Pairing* 2 p.m.

In Napa County, permits are required to serve food during tastings, which explains why most wineries dispense little more than crackers during their wine flights. But a handful of estates are offering more substantial pairings. At **B Cellars** (703 Oakville Cross Road, Napa; bcellars.com), the glass-walled tasting room surrounds a big open kitchen doling out small plates like rabbit rillettes and roasted squash with pickled beets and ricotta. Each dish complements a specific wine; the lineup includes single varietals and blends made from top vineyards within the valley. In nearby Rutherford, **Round Pond Estate** (875 Rutherford Road, Napa; roundpond.com) has several food-and-wine options, from a boozy multicourse Sunday brunch to a lighter pairing showcasing vegetables plucked from the winery's gardens. At both wineries, make an appointment well in advance.

2 *Quintessential Stroll* 4 p.m.

Yountville may be the most picturesque small town in the valley, with its pruned trees and brick buildings housing boutiques, bakeries, and Michelin-starred restaurants. You may not have a reservation at Thomas Keller's The French Laundry (spots are almost impossible to come by), but you can admire the restaurant's famous vegetable gardens across the street. Then walk over to another Yountville classic, **V Marketplace** (6525 Washington Street; vmarketplace.com), an enclosed market with cobblestone walkways and shops selling local goods, art, and food. One of California's most attractive tasting

rooms, **Stewart Cellars** (6752 Washington Street; stewartcellars.com) is nearby.

3 *The Night Is Young* 7:30 p.m.

Blue Note Napa (1030 Main Street, Napa; bluenotenapa.com), a spinoff of New York City's well-known jazz club, operates inside a venerable opera house, hosting acts like the Japanese pianist Keiko Matsui and the Hawaiian guitar virtuoso Willie K as well as emerging local musicians. An eclectic menu that spotlights California's agricultural bounty is on the playbill too. For a slightly quieter night out, nearby **Gran Eléctrica** (1313 Main Street, Napa; granelectrica.com) serves traditional Mexican bites and creative margaritas in a festive space featuring art inspired by Mexico's Day of the Dead holiday. A few blocks away, **Miminashi** (821 Coombs Street, Napa; miminashi.com) offers wines, sakes and Japanese whiskeys, along with a Rolodex of 125 cocktails.

SATURDAY

4 *Pastoral Breakfast* 9 a.m.

Farmstead at Long Meadow Ranch (738 Main Street, St. Helena; longmeadowranch.com) looks like the set of a movie about farmers turned interior decorators. This idyllic destination is anchored by a restored Gothic Revival residence that houses an old-time general store stocked with olive oils, jams,

OPPOSITE Tending to the vines in a Napa Valley vineyard.

BELOW A table for olive oil tasting at Round Pond Estate.

scented candles, and canvas bags, and a bar offering wine and whiskey flights. Steps away, inside a former plant nursery, is a stylish restaurant serving seasonal dishes sourced from Long Meadow Ranch's working farm in Rutherford. A patio nearby is the site of an outdoor cafe that opens at 7 a.m. Grab a spot at one of the weathered wooden tables, beneath the shade of a massive blue spruce, and enjoy a cup of Stumptown coffee and freshly baked pastries.

5 *Time to Detox* 11 a.m.

Calistoga, at the northern end of the region, has been drawing mud-bath enthusiasts for decades to its geothermal springs. If you want to relax the old-fashioned way (submerged in a pool of warm mud), your best option is **Indian Springs** (1712 Lincoln Avenue; indianspringscalistoga.com), a Mission Revival lodge and spa whose mud pools contain volcanic ash. For a more modern experience, book a treatment at the **Calistoga Motor Lodge and Spa** (1880 Lincoln Avenue; calistogamotorlodgeandspa.com). This mid-century hotel, rejuvenated by the Manhattan design firm AvroKO, has a chic, pastel-hued spa with claw-foot tubs for salt baths and a mud bar where you can mix your own concoction before slathering it on and reposing on a gardenside chaise.

6 *Lunch at the C.I.A.* 2 p.m.

The **Culinary Institute of America at Copia** (500 First Street, Napa; ciaatcopia.com), planned by the Napa pioneers Robert and Margrit Mondavi, and Julia Child, is an 80,000-square-foot foodie wonderland where visitors can take cooking and wine-tasting classes; see the personal cookware collection of Williams-Sonoma's founder, Chuck Williams; or kick back at the restaurant ($$), where a team of

ABOVE The Buddha Pond at Indian Springs, a resort with geothermal springs that also offers mud baths.

LEFT A tableau at B Cellars. One of the figures on the lawn is a sculpture, the other is a visitor imitating it.

chefs behind a sleek open kitchen prepare American classics like steak Diane.

7 *Private Collection* 4:30 p.m.

Drive up to Mount Veeder, about 20 minutes from the town of Napa, to see impressive contemporary art at the **Hess Collection** (4411 Redwood Road, Napa; hesscollection.com). The founder, Donald Hess, a Swiss businessman and wine producer who began collecting art in the 1960s, was an early patron of several blue-chip artists. His museum, on the second and third floors of this boulder-walled winery, displays works by the likes of Francis Bacon, Gerhard Richter, Anselm Kiefer, and Robert Motherwell.

8 *Farm to Fork* 8 p.m.

Northern California was at the forefront of the farm-to-table movement that flourished in the early 2000s, and Napa is still a haven for sustainably produced, locally sourced food. Casual yet polished, the **Charter Oak** (1050 Charter Oak Avenue, Saint Helena; thecharteroak.com; $$) is part of a new generation of restaurants honoring this now traditional formula. Much of the food, served family-style, comes from a huge open-flame grill.

TOP A lounge at Stewart Cellars in Yountville.

ABOVE Diners at Charter Oak, a farm-to-table restaurant.

SUNDAY

9 *Boomtown* 10 a.m.

Downtown Napa once played second fiddle to more scenic locales such as Yountville and St. Helena, but has come into its own. The **Oxbow Public Market** (610 First Street; oxbowpublicmarket.com) is a must-see destination and a good place to get coffee and a pastry. Few food markets can compete with the variety and quality of the offerings inside this light-filled, 40,000-square-foot structure, where you can see bakers, chocolatiers, butchers, and fishmongers at work. For a sit-down breakfast with views, head to the rooftop restaurant at the **Archer Hotel**

(1230 First Street, Napa; archerhotel.com/napa), which offers contemporary American fare along with sweeping vistas.

10 *New Age* Noon

Say farewell to Napa with a glass of cabernet or chardonnay at one of the valley's newer wineries. **Ashes & Diamonds** (4130 Howard Lane, Napa;

ashesdiamonds.com), owned by the former music executive Kashy Khaledi, has a retro-modern vibe. Khaledi works with top local grape growers to make wines the old-school way. **Odette Estate** (5998 Silverado Trail, Napa; odetteestate.com), in the Stags Leap District, occupies a futuristic recycled steel building that appears to be tucked inside a hill. This environmentally responsible winery specializes in the kind of full-bodied reds that can only come from Napa.

ABOVE Inside the wine cave at Odette Estate.

OPPOSITE Golden light envelops a Napa Valley vineyard.

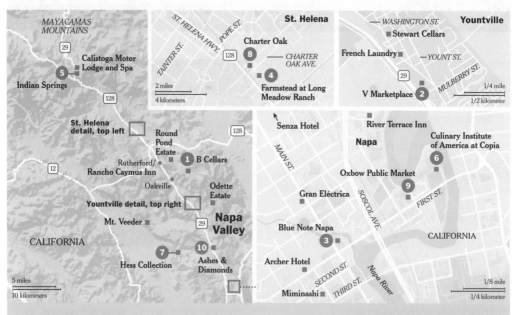

THE BASICS

The Napa Valley is about 50 miles north of San Francisco, just over an hour's drive. Make someone in your group the designated driver, or use ride-sharing.

Rancho Caymus Inn
1140 Rutherford Road, Rutherford
ranchocaymusinn.com

$$
Hacienda-style property, built in 1914 by a scion of the Morton Salt family. Original design elements include white oak beams in updated rooms and common areas.

Senza Hotel
4066 Howard Lane, Napa
senzahotel.com
$$$

Restored Victorian mansion from the 1870s. The heated pool is surrounded by gardens dotted with contemporary sculptures.

River Terrace Inn
1600 Soscol Avenue, Napa
riverterraceinn.com
$$$
Well-appointed rooms; close to riverside walks.

Oakland

Long overshadowed by its dolled-up big sister across San Francisco Bay, Oakland is its own town. Even as its status as one of the most diverse cities in the country is threatened by tech-boom-era gentrification, its thrilling cultural heterogeneity remains its greatest strength. The city's rather dull skyline belies its architectural splendor — from glamorous movie palaces to the Kevin Roche-designed midcentury-modern Oakland Museum of California to the 135-acre Mills College campus, where Beaux-Arts and Spanish Colonial Revival buildings are set among eucalyptus trees. The western terminus of the Transcontinental Railroad and a thriving port, Oakland remains a proud working-class town even as new developments remake its waterfront. — BY FREDA MOON AND EMILY BRADY

FRIDAY

1 *Putting It in Context* 3 p.m.

There's no better way to soak up some of Oakland's maritime history than with a drink at **Heinold's First and Last Chance Saloon** (48 Webster Street; 510-839-6761), a waterfront shack built from the wood from an old whaling ship. The place prides itself on looking much as it did when it first opened in 1883. Soon, it was a watering hole popular with seafarers, dockworkers, and a budding young writer named Jack London, who the proprietors say wrote notes for *The Call of the Wild* there. It's also a monument to the power of the San Andreas Fault: the Great Quake of 1906 settled the pylons underneath, which is why the floor slants and keeping your drink from sliding down the bar can be a challenge.

2 *Fired Up* 6 p.m.

For dinner, splurge at **Camino** (3917 Grand Avenue; caminorestaurant.com; $$$), where the food is cooked by wood fire, the seating is communal, and tips are not accepted — a practice favored by its husband-wife owners, Russell Moore and Allison Hopelain. As a direct descendant of Chez Panisse, where Moore, the chef, worked for two decades, it's emblematic

OPPOSITE Art Deco design glows in neon at the Grand Lake, one of Oakland's classic movie theaters.

RIGHT The city's jazz tradition lives on at the Sound Room.

of Northern California cooking in its purest, casual-yet-refined form. Each night's menu features three entrees: typically one meat (rib-eye steak and slow-cooked short ribs with grits, green beans, and fried sunchokes, for example), one fish (like local ling cod with green beans, tomato confit, cilantro, and saffron broth), and a vegetarian offering. Camino's cookbook, *This Is Camino*, makes a fine souvenir.

3 *Get Artsy* 8 p.m.

Once a month, a First Friday art walk (6 to 9 p.m.) takes over the Uptown neighborhood as dozens of galleries open for a street party that embodies the spirit of this changing city. After your stroll there (or on any Friday when the art walk is off), seek out live music. The **Sound Room** (2147 Broadway; soundroom. org) builds on a storied jazz tradition arising from Oakland's role as a landing place for generations of black migrants from the American South. It hosts local blues and soul singers, big band and West Coast Latin jazz groups, and international acts. **The Alley** (3325 Grand Avenue; thealleyoakland.com) is a well-worn piano bar with an eclectic crowd and decades of business cards papering the walls. **Cafe Van Kleef** (1621 Telegraph Avenue; cafevankleef.com), famed for its greyhound cocktails and politically connected clientele, has live music from folk to R&B.

SATURDAY

4 *Quiet Neighborhood* 10 a.m.

The Frederick Law Olmsted-designed **Mountain View Cemetery** (5000 Piedmont Avenue;

mountainviewcemetery.org) is a parklike landscape of California live oak, Italian cypress, Lebanese cedar, Italian stone pine, and palm trees in the Piedmont Hills. The cemetery dates to the 1860s and holds tombstones of some of the state's most influential residents, including Julia Morgan, who designed the nearby Chapel of the Chimes as well as Hearst Castle. On the second and fourth Saturdays of each month, there are free docent-led tours at 10 a.m.

5 *Shop Temescal* 11:30 a.m.

Tucked away in the Temescal neighborhood, two pedestrian alleys, Temescal Alley and Alley 49 (temescalalleys.com), are home to shops that feel as if they jumped off Etsy's home page. Browse the boutiques for objects like twee teapots and handmade coat racks, artfully produced books, and jewelry. Stop at the **Curbside Creamery** (482 49th Street; curbsideoakland.com), where the ice cream varieties include some that are vegan, made with cashew milk.

6 *Brunch View* 1 p.m.

The brunch at **Portal** (1611 Second Avenue; portaloakland.com; $$) is fabulous, so persevere if the line is long. The dishes are hearty and traditional: eggs Benedict, French toast, biscuits,

ABOVE A laid-back scene along Lake Merritt at sunset. At midday, the lake is active with rented boats and pedal boats. It's a favorite spot in Oakland at any time of day.

Mexican-inspired breakfast. There's also a California-centric selection of more than a dozen craft beers on tap. The backyard patio has a view of Lake Merritt, a placid patch of blue in the heart of the city.

7 *City Serenity* 3 p.m.

Walk north around **Lake Merritt** (lakemerritt. org), which fronts on Lakeside Park. To get out on the water, go to the **Lake Merritt Boating Center** (568 Bellevue Avenue) and rent a pedal boat, rowboat, canoe, kayak, or sailboat. Besides providing recreation, the lake functions as a wildlife refuge. Look for rare white pelicans and other waterbirds.

8 *Skillet-Fried* 6 p.m.

Swan's Market (swansmarket.com), a historic indoor market in Old Oakland, offers an exceptional selection of eating opportunities, from the Japanese set lunches at B-Dama to The Cook and Her Farmer's mind-blowing oyster po' boy. For a dinner that will carry you through to breakfast, try **Miss Ollie's** (901 Washington Street; realmissolliesoakland.com; $$), an Afro-Caribbean restaurant where the jerk shrimp are big and scorchingly spicy and the skillet-fried chicken is among the best in the Bay Area.

9 *At the Palace* 7:30 p.m.

Take in a film or performance at one of Oakland's preserved Art Deco movie palaces. At the **Grand Lake** (3200 Grand Avenue; renaissancerialto.com),

which features short Wurlitzer organ concerts before the movie showing, don't be surprised if you find left-leaning political views displayed up on the marquee, courtesy of the owner. The **Paramount** (2025 Broadway; paramounttheatre.com), a 1931 beauty, has transformed itself into a multipurpose venue for everything from classics like *The Wizard of Oz* to performances of the Oakland Interfaith Gospel Choir. The 1928 **Fox Theater** (1807 Telegraph Avenue; thefoxoakland.com) is now a concert venue with a varied schedule.

SUNDAY

10 *This Isn't Orange Juice!* 9 a.m.

Calling it brunch might be pushing it. Starting at 9 a.m., the **Fat Lady** (201 Washington Street; thefatladyrestaurant.com; $$) serves breakfast with booze. Dimly lit, with dripped-wax-draped candelabras, mismatched paintings and a long bar, this 1970s-era Jack London Square institution is housed in a former (circa 1880s) brothel and has a reputation built on myth and a mean corned beef hash.

11 *Harbor Views* 10 a.m.

Walk to the waterfront to the Sunday farmers' market. Stroll over to the 1934 USS *Potomac* (Foot of Clay Street; usspotomac.org), Franklin Delano Roosevelt's 165-foot "floating White House," for a docent-led dockside tour. Then drive through the industrial maze of shipping containers, idling trucks, and towering cranes to **Middle Harbor Shoreline Park** (530 Water Street; portofoakland.com), where the views of San Francisco's skyline are unbeatable.

ABOVE The patio at Portal provides views of Lake Merritt to enjoy along with brunch or dinner and craft beer.

THE BASICS

Fly to Oakland International Airport or San Francisco International. Take a BART train into town or rent a car.

Waterfront Hotel
10 Washington Street
jdvhotels.com
$$$
Nautically themed hotel in a prime location in Jack London Square, near the ferry to San Francisco.

Best Western Plus Bayside Hotel
1717 Embarcadero
bestwestern.com
$$$
Waterfront location, close to downtown and near the ferry.

Oakland Marriott City Center
1001 Broadway
marriott.com
$$$
High-rise with views of the bay.

Map labels:
1/2 mile
1 kilometer
EMERYVILLE
Temescal Alley and Alley 49/ **5**
Curbside Creamery
Mountain View Cemetery
4
580
123
24
TEMESCAL
Grand Lake Theatre
Oakland
980
9
80
BROADWAY
PIEDMONT AVE.
OAKLAND AVE.
Camino **2**
Grand Lake Theatre
The Alley
9
MANDELA PKWY.
The Sound Room **3**
LAKESIDE PARK
580
Paramount Theatre
Fox Theater
Cafe Van Kleef
7 Lake Merritt Boating Center
Lake Merritt
Middle Harbor Shoreline Park
980
Swan's Market/Miss Ollie's **8**
Oakland Marriott City Center
6 Portal
USS Potomac **11**
10 Fat Lady
1
Oakland Museum of California
Waterfront Hotel
Heinold's First and Last Chance Saloon
Mills College
880
San Francisco
Area of detail
San Francisco
580
San Francisco Bay
Oakland Inner Harbor
Best Western Plus Bayside Hotel
10 miles
20 kilometers
CALIFORNIA
ALAMEDA ISLAND

Palm Springs

Palm Springs was once the miles-from-Hollywood getaway that Malibu is now: a place for '60s movers and shakers to eat, drink, and sunbathe poolside while they awaited calls from studio execs. Today, after some hard-earned changes, this California desert town nestled in the Coachella Valley is becoming a destination for laid-back cool once again. The revival of modernism that inspired makeovers of its midcentury hotels, restaurants, and shops brought a revival of style, and the desert sun has never lost its appeal. Now Palm Springs attracts visitors who are just as happy climbing canyons as sipping cocktails on a lounge chair amid the design and architectural treasures of the past.
— BY ERICA CERULO

FRIDAY

1 *Cruising on Two Wheels* 3 p.m.

Because of its modest size, Palm Springs can easily become familiar over a couple of days, or even a few hours. Start your trip with a self-guided bike tour. **Big Wheel Tours** (760-779-1837; bwbtours.com) rents bicycles and can arrange bike and hiking tours. Free maps are available at the **Palm Springs Visitors Center** (2901 North Palm Canyon Drive; 760-778-8418; palm-springs.org). To scope out the dramatic terrain and local hot spots, pedal the Downtown Loop, which can be done in less than an hour, or the 10-mile Citywide Loop that takes you past the Moorten Botanical Gardens.

2 *Austria and Beyond* 7 p.m.

At **Johannes** (196 South Indian Canyon Drive; 760-778-0017; johannesrestaurants.com; $$$), the chef Johannes Bacher bills the food as modern Austrian, combining classic Central European specialties like spaetzle and sauerkraut with decidedly borrowed ingredients and flavors, ranging from polenta to wasabi. But one of the best dishes is also the most traditional: a heaping plate of Wiener schnitzel with parsley potatoes, cucumber salad, and cranberry compote.

3 *Partying Poolside* 9:30 p.m.

Back when Frank Sinatra held raucous shindigs at his Twin Palms home, Palm Springs was known for its party scene. These days, the best drinking establishments are in hotels. The white stucco exterior of the **Colony Palms Hotel** (572 North Indian Canyon Drive; 760-969-1800; colonypalmshotel.com) conceals a welcoming hideaway with stone walkways, towering palms, and, when needed, patio heaters. At the buzzing restaurant **Purple Palm**, ask to be seated by the pool and order a plate of Humboldt Fog chèvre, organic honey, and local dates with your drink to top off the night.

SATURDAY

4 *Modernist America* 9:30 a.m.

Along with the moneyed 20th-century tourists came eye-catching buildings: hotels, commercial spaces, and vacation homes in an architectural style eventually known as midcentury modern. These gems emphasize indoor-outdoor spaces, walls of glass, and minimal decoration. Leading a pilgrimage to these iconic structures is Trevor O'Donnell of **PS Architecture Tours** (323-578-6025; psarchitecturetours.com), who practices what he preaches: he owns a classic post-and-beam house (not on the tour) built in 1952 and once occupied by the architect Richard Harrison. On the three-hour excursion, design enthusiasts can catch glimpses

OPPOSITE Indian Canyons, a natural oasis on the Agua Caliente Indian Reservation just outside Palm Springs.

RIGHT The Kaufmann House, designed by Richard Neutra.

of the Albert Frey-designed Tramway Gas Station, Richard Neutra's 1946 Kaufmann Desert House, and the mass-produced but stunning Alexander homes. Your guide also points out architectural touchstones that you might otherwise miss, such as a concrete bell tower salvaged from the long-gone Oasis Hotel, which was designed by Lloyd Wright (son of Frank) in 1924.

5 *Chic Cheek* 1 p.m.

The wait for brunch at **Cheeky's** (622 North Palm Canyon Drive; 760-327-7595; cheekysps.com; $$) should be a tip-off: the bright, streamlined space, which feels airlifted from L.A. — in a good way — is popular. The standard eggs and waffles are spiced up with ingredients like beet relish, homemade herbed ricotta, and sour cherry compote.

6 *Used Goods* 3 p.m.

Stroll **Palm Canyon Drive**, a strip that's terrific for high-end vintage shopping, if a little dangerous for those who quickly reach for their credit cards. Among the many stores that focus on better-with-age décor, just a few have mastered the art of curating. At **a La MOD** (886 North Palm Canyon Drive; 760-327-0707; alamodps.com), nearly 70 percent of the merchandise, which is heavy on Lucite and lighting, is sourced locally, according to the shop's owners. **Modern Way** (2500 North Palm Canyon Drive; 760-320-5455; psmodernway.com) stocks an eclectic collection of larger pieces like an Arthur Elrod Lucite dining set, Bertoia diamond chairs, and Edward Wormley sofas. For something you can actually take home, shop **Bon Vivant** (766 North Palm Canyon Drive, No. 3; 760-534-3197; gmcb.com), where the charming proprietors make you feel like a genuine collector for purchasing an $18 engraved brass vase or a $5 tie clip.

7 *Stay Silly* 5 p.m.

At the **Palm Springs Yacht Club**, at the **Parker Palm Springs** hotel (4200 East Palm Canyon Drive;

760-770-5000; theparkerpalmsprings.com/spa), standard spa offerings like deep-tissue rubdowns and wrinkle-fighting facials come with a playful attitude of retro irony. The pampering is real. Expect to pay high-end prices (some treatment packages are well over $300) but go away feeling refreshed and maybe — is it possible? — a little younger.

8 *Friend of the House* 8 p.m.

Most of the favored area restaurants have an old-school vibe: tuxedoed waiters, a headwaiter who has worked there since opening day, and steak-and-lobster specialties. Though **Copley's** (621 North Palm Canyon Drive; 760-327-9555; copleyspalmsprings.com; $$$) might not have the culinary history of nearby Melvyn's Restaurant and Lounge, which opened as an inn in 1935, it has a different sort of storied past — it is housed in what was once Cary Grant's estate. It also has food that incorporates 21st-century flavors (one spring menu included dishes like a duck and artichoke salad with goat cheese, edamame, and litchi).

9 *Toasting Friends* 11 p.m.

The cocktail and microbrew crazes are still going strong in the desert, and the cavernous **Amigo Room** at the Ace Hotel (701 East Palm Canyon Drive; 760-325-9900; acehotel.com/palmsprings) remains at the front of the pack. In addition to pouring dozens of microbrews, the guys at the bar will measure, shake, and pour classic concoctions like the margarita and more offbeat options like the Figa (fig-infused vodka with Earl Grey and honey tangerine) that reek of late-night hipster cool. The mellow vibe, nightly entertainment (D.J.s, bands, bingo nights) and leather-banquette décor will keep you ordering.

SUNDAY

10 *Get Close with Cactus* 9 a.m.

Those looking for an early-morning calorie burn might prefer the uphill battles of Gastin or Araby Trail, but a hike through **Tahquitz Canyon** (500 West Mesquite Avenue; 760-416-7044; tahquitzcanyon.com), part of the natural oasis area called Indian Canyons, offers a leisurely alternative. A small entrance fee gets you access to a 1.8-mile loop and

the sights and smells that come with it: desert plants, lizards aplenty, and a stunning, 60-foot waterfall. Take a two-hour ranger-led tour or explore the trail at your own pace. You'll see arid desert and cool, palm-lined gorges.

11 *Pink Robots* Noon

For a one-of-a-kind experience that's both entertaining and eye-opening, drive out to the **Kenny Irwin Art and Light Show** (1077 East Granvia Valmonte; 760-774-0318; kennyirwinartist.com), a two-acre backyard sculpture park with massive, lighthearted, and very clever works that have to be seen to be believed. Metal and plastic junk from old vacuum cleaners to shopping carts is transformed with

welding and bright paint into giant robots, roller coasters, space vehicles, and even an intimidating version of Santa's sleigh. Visits are by appointment only, so be sure to call in advance.

OPPOSITE On tour in the Frey House II, which is built around a massive boulder. Designed by Albert Frey, it exemplifies the city's wealth of modernist architecture.

ABOVE Hiking at Tahquitz Canyon.

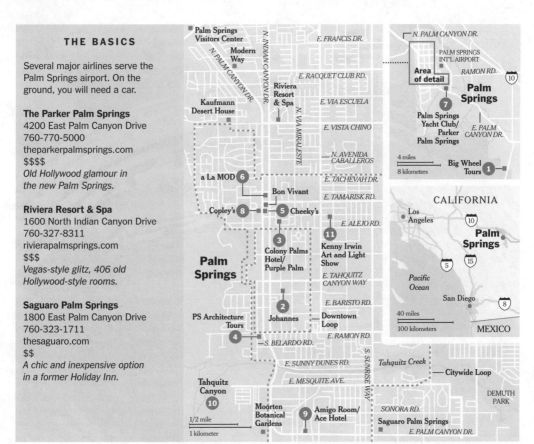

THE BASICS

Several major airlines serve the Palm Springs airport. On the ground, you will need a car.

The Parker Palm Springs
4200 East Palm Canyon Drive
760-770-5000
theparkerpalmsprings.com
$$$$
Old Hollywood glamour in the new Palm Springs.

Riviera Resort & Spa
1600 North Indian Canyon Drive
760-327-8311
rivierapalmsprings.com
$$$
Vegas-style glitz, 406 old Hollywood-style rooms.

Saguaro Palm Springs
1800 East Palm Canyon Drive
760-323-1711
thesaguaro.com
$$
A chic and inexpensive option in a former Holiday Inn.

Pasadena

Nestled in the San Gabriel Valley just 10 miles northeast of Los Angeles, Pasadena harbors a distinct, if at times chauvinistic, sense of individual self. Its old-money past continues to flourish in the form of grand mansions and a vast array of museums and gardens, many underwritten by prominent local families. And newer money has helped transform Old Pasadena, in decline for many years, into an energetic shopping and dining destination, with quirky shops and new restaurants. But it is the expansive outdoors, mountain views, and fine climate (except in August, when you could fry a hot dog at the Rose Bowl) that still make Pasadena, the famed City of Roses, a shining jewel of Southern California and an enduring object of jealousy. — BY JENNIFER STEINHAUER

FRIDAY

1 *Dream House* 3 p.m.

Real estate can go boom or bust, but either way envy is epidemic in Pasadena, and few homes are more desirable than the **Gamble House** (4 Westmoreland Place; 626-793-3334; gamblehouse.org). While the tour guides can reinforce a certain preciousness, there is no denying the allure of this Craftsman-style home, built in 1908 for David and Mary Gamble of the Procter & Gamble Company by the architects Charles Sumner Greene and Henry Mather Greene. To protect the floors, flat shoes are required for the hourlong tour. But they'll give you a pair of slippers if you're wearing your stilettos.

2 *Rose Bowl* 4:30 p.m.

Well, you're here, so why not see where it all happens each winter? You can tool around the Rose Bowl grounds, jog, enjoy the gardens, and imagine you are a rose queen—or one of the many whose efforts add up to the 80,000 hours needed to put together the **Tournament of Roses** (391 South Orange Grove Boulevard; 626-449-4100; tournamentofroses.com).

3 *Burritoville* 6:30 p.m.

There's a depressing number of fast-food restaurants in town, serving the same grub found in any American mall. But one standout is **El Toreo Cafe** (21 South Fair Oaks Avenue; 626-793-2577; $), a hole-in-the-wall that serves terrific and inexpensive Mexican food. Try the carnitas burritos and chile verde, with large helpings and authentic flair.

4 *Retail Hop* 8:30 p.m.

Many stores in Old Pasadena stay open late. Skip the chains-o-plenty and make your way down Colorado Boulevard, the central corridor, and its side streets. Among the finds: **Distant Lands Travel Bookstore and Outfitters** (20 South Raymond Avenue; 626-449-3220; distantlands.com), which sells travel paraphernalia like Africa maps and packing kits; **Elisa B.** (16 East Holly Street; 626-397-4770; elisab.com), where the sales staff will get you out of your mom jeans; and next to one of the city's well-loved dives, the Colorado, **Poo-Bah Records** (2636 East Colorado Boulevard; 626-449-3359; poobah.com), legendary among hip-hop heads, D.J.s, and anyone intimate with the underground and avant-garde music scenes in Los Angeles.

SATURDAY

5 *Morning Sweets* 9 a.m.

All good vacation days begin with hot chocolate, so follow the California Institute of Technology

OPPOSITE The Japanese garden at the Huntington Library, Art Collections, and Botanical Gardens.

BELOW Changing shoes outside the Rose Bowl.

students to **Euro Pane** (950 East Colorado Boulevard; 626-577-1828) and order a hot cup of the chocolaty goodness, along with fresh breads and flaky croissants, which are first-rate. A counter filled with children's books helps keep the young ones entertained.

6 *Fun Under the Sun* 10 a.m.

While children's museums often induce an instant throbbing in the temple — and an urge to reach for a hand sanitizer — a happy exception is **Kidspace Children's Museum** (480 North Arroyo Boulevard; 626-449-9144; kidspacemuseum.org), an active museum where adults can chill with a book under the sun while the kids ride tricycles, check out the dig site, and climb around the mini-model of the city's Arroyo Seco canyon, where it actually "rains" from time to time. The Splash Dance Fountain is a winner.

7 *Order the Obvious* 1 p.m.

No day in Pasadena should pass without a stop at **Pie 'n Burger** (913 East California Boulevard; 626-795-1123; pienburger.com; $), a local institution since 1963. Go ahead and have a chicken pot pie, which is beyond decent, or some pancakes if you're feeling all vegan about it, but honestly, the burger is the way to go. It is a juicy concoction served up in old-school paper liners, with the requisite Thousand Island dressing on the bun. Finish the whole thing

off with a sublime slice of Dutch apple or cherry pie. Just don't tarry — there are bound to be large groups of folks waiting to get their hands on burgers, too.

8 *Master Class* 3 p.m.

Even if you're feeling a bit tired, there is something oddly relaxing about the **Norton Simon Museum of Art** (411 West Colorado Boulevard; 626-449-6840; nortonsimon.org). There's Degas's *Little Dancer Aged 14*, Van Gogh's *Portrait of a Peasant*, Diego Rivera's *The Flower Vendor*. Natural light streams in from skylights, and a sensible layout makes this a pleasant place to while away the afternoon — not to mention examining the star collection of Western paintings and sculpture from the 14th to 20th centuries. Don't skip the South Asian art downstairs, especially the Buddha Shakyamuni, which sits majestically outdoors. The guided audio tours are quite good.

9 *Solid Italian* 7 p.m.

After a day of culture and sun soaking, nestle into **Gale's Restaurant** (452 South Fair Oaks Avenue; 626-432-6705; galesrestaurant.com; $$$). A totally local spot, it offers remarkably solid fare just down the road from all the hubbub. Couples, families, and friends who seem to have just finished a day outdoors snuggle amid the brick walls and small wooden tables, drinking wine from slightly cheesy Brighton goblets. Start it off with some warm roasted olives or a steamed artichoke and then move on to the country-style Tuscan steak or caprese salad. Desserts range from cakes and crumbles to peach crostata and poached pear with Gorgonzola and prosciutto.

SUNDAY

10 *Garden Party* 10:30 a.m.

An entire day barely covers a corner of the **Huntington Library, Art Collections, and Botanical Gardens** (1151 Oxford Road, San Marino; 626-405-2100; huntington.org). There are 120 acres of gardens, an enormous library of rare manuscripts and books,

and three permanent art galleries featuring British and French artists of the 18th and 19th centuries. Here is a good plan for a morning: Take a quick run through the exhibit of American silver. Ooh and ahh. Then pick one of the gardens to tour. The Desert Garden, with its bizarre-looking cactuses and lunarlike landscapes, is a winner, though the Japanese and Jungle Gardens are close rivals. Top it off at the Children's Garden, where interactive exhibits can get kids dirty, which pleases everyone but the one stuck changing all the wet shirts. Stay for tea; there's no dress code in the tea room.

OPPOSITE The Gamble House, designed by Charles Sumner Greene and Henry Mather Greene for members of a founding family of Procter & Gamble.

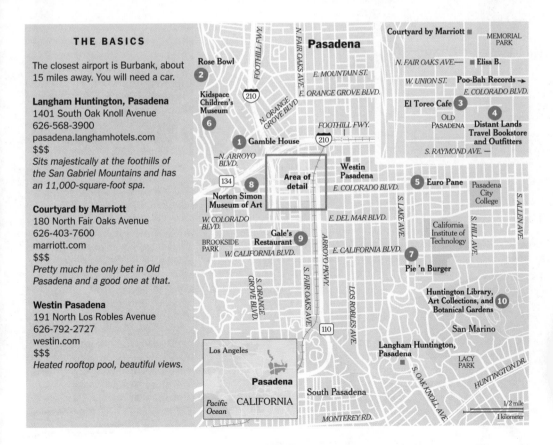

THE BASICS

The closest airport is Burbank, about 15 miles away. You will need a car.

Langham Huntington, Pasadena
1401 South Oak Knoll Avenue
626-568-3900
pasadena.langhamhotels.com
$$$
Sits majestically at the foothills of the San Gabriel Mountains and has an 11,000-square-foot spa.

Courtyard by Marriott
180 North Fair Oaks Avenue
626-403-7600
marriott.com
$$$
Pretty much the only bet in Old Pasadena and a good one at that.

Westin Pasadena
191 North Los Robles Avenue
626-792-2727
westin.com
$$$
Heated rooftop pool, beautiful views.

Sacramento

Despite its location at the confluence of two impressive rivers, its importance as the capital of the country's most populous state, and its thriving cultural scene, Sacramento gets no respect as a travel destination. Unlike California's glittering, glamorous coastal cities, it sits apart in the agricultural Central Valley, giving it an earnest, small-town feeling and a welcome lack of pretension. Yet it holds its own in youthful urbanity, and the first-time visitor is surprised to find a lush oasis with neighborhoods of midcentury modern homes, Craftsman bungalows, and ornate Victorians, all shaded by the sprawling trees that make much of the city feel like a leafy urban park.
— BY FREDA MOON

FRIDAY

1 *All About California* 2 p.m.

Make your first stop the **California Museum** (1020 O Street; californiamuseum.org), home to the California Hall of Fame, which, besides celebrating famous Californians, offers an overview of the state's history from the Spanish missions era to the internment of Japanese-Americans during World War II, from indigenous peoples to Hollywood's Red Scare. Afterward, take a walk through the 40-acre, Victorian-style **Capitol Park** (1300 L Street; capitolmuseum.ca.gov/the-museum/capitol-park), where there is a trout pond, a cactus garden, and a collection of native plants representing every county in this heterogenous state. If art is your passion, make time for the **Crocker Art Museum** (216 O Street; crockerart.org), a must-see institution.

2 *Hamburger Happiness* 6 p.m.

Contrary to restaurant lore and signage, **Broderick Roadhouse** (319 Sixth Street, West Sacramento; broderickroadhouse.com; $$) was not established in 1893. It actually started as a food truck in 2012 and,

on the strength of its hamburger game, quickly grew into a small and beloved local chain. This West Sacramento location, the original, retains the charm of a Western relic. If you come early for the 3 to 6 p.m. happy hour, the towering Old School burger and tap beer special is a steal.

3 *Showtime* 8 p.m.

Catch a show at the **Sofia Tsakopoulos Center for the Arts** (2700 Capitol Avenue; bstreettheatre.org), a performing arts complex close by the 30-year-old B Street Theatre. The two-theater venue includes both the 250-seat main stage and the 365-seat Sutter Theatre for Children. For serious post-theater cocktails, red velvet curtains, pressed tin ceilings, a horseshoe-shaped wooden bar, and live music — blues, jazz, big band and country — on weekend nights, **Shady Lady Saloon** (1409 R Street; shadyladybar.com) may be Sacramento's sexiest cocktail bar.

SATURDAY

4 *Get Outa Town* 8 a.m.

The paved 32-mile loop **Jedediah Smith Memorial Trail** (traillink.com) starts in Old Sacramento's Discovery Park and travels along the American River, a tubing hot spot during the scorching summer months. Stop at the **Nimbus Hatchery** (2001 Nimbus Road, Gold River; wildlife.ca.gov/Fishing/Hatcheries/Nimbus), which raises steelhead trout and Chinook salmon, and has a nature trail. If you're up for an ambitious ride (or a short drive), continue all the way to the town of Folsom — of Johnny Cash prison song

OPPOSITE Capitol Park, with the dome of the California State Capitol in the background. Like most of the rest of the city, the park is shaded by trees of many varieties.

RIGHT Customers line up for takeout at one of the locations of Chando's Tacos, a chain of taco stands ready to provide a quick, quintessentially California snack.

fame—which is loaded with Gold Country character. Before setting out on the trail, grab coffee at **Temple Coffee Roasters** (2200 K Street; templecoffee.com), a highfalutin caffeine palace with a floor hand-laid with 500,000 pennies, in an 1880s building in the trendy Midtown neighborhood.

5 *Tacos al Fresco* 1 p.m.

For a quick, quintessentially California snack, head to **Chando's Tacos** (863 Arden Way; chandostacos.com; $), a small local chain of taco stands where you can grab three flavorful street-food-style tacos and a fountain drink for less than ten dollars. Take your meal to the recently renovated pond at nearby **McKinley Park** (3330 McKinley Boulevard), where 1,200 rose bushes bloom from March through May. The garden was featured in Greta Gerwig's 2017 film *Lady Bird*—a love letter to her hometown—which has inspired walking and running tours of its film locations.

6 *Relax, Relieve* 2 p.m.

Work out the kinks from this morning's ride, and get relief from the midday sun, at **Asha Urban Baths** (2417 27th Street; ashaurbanbaths.com), an Old World-style, coed, swimming suit-required bathhouse with a soaking pool, sauna, steam room, and cold plunge. Drop-ins are welcome.

7 *California Crafted* 4:30 p.m.

Cruise down to the **R Street Corridor** (rstreetcorridor.com), a former railroad yard

ABOVE Davis, a small city dominated by the University of California, is a short train ride from Sacramento. This campus building is the new Shrem Museum of Art.

and industrial area, now home to intriguing shops and designers. For hyper-curated outdoor clothing and gear with a city streets-meets-Redwood forests sensibility, head to the **All Good** flagship store (808 R Street, No. 102; allgxxd.com), which also organizes hiking, surfing, and bouldering trips in California and beyond. Down the street, the **Warehouse Artist Lofts Public Market** (1108 R Street; rstreetwal.com) has a small but enticing food court and an exciting collection of shops.

8 *Beer Around Town* 6 p.m.

Sacramento is flush with beer, but you have time to try only a few spots. **New Helvetia** (1730 Broadway; newhelvetiabrew.com), which borrows the city's original name, has a neighborhood feel, complete with backyard picnic tables and a devoted running club. **Bike Dog** (915 Broadway; bikedogbrewing.com), in industrial West Sacramento, is popular with bicyclists, dogs, and serious beer geeks. And **Der Biergarten** (2332 K Street; beergardensacramento.com) is a funky outdoor beer garden with communal tables imported from Germany, a shipping-container kitchen, taps of mostly German beers, and a menu that includes classics like wurst and schnitzel.

9 *Playing With Fire* 8 p.m.

In the Southside Park neighborhood, **Binchoyaki** (2226 10th Street; binchoyaki.com) is a sassy little izakaya where perky 1960s-era oldies play and the open kitchen makes the compact dining room feel like a party. Specializing in Japanese-style charcoal-grilled skewers, the restaurant serves salty, umami-packed, and meaty morsels. A testament to the restaurant's mom-and-pop, handmade impulse, the bar is lined with planter trays sprouting mung beans

and pickling jars of beet-colored daikon and shochu liquor infused with plum. From 10 p.m. to midnight, there's an oyster happy hour on weekend nights.

SUNDAY

10 *The Three Bs* 8 a.m.

Bacon & Butter in the Tahoe Park neighborhood (5913 Broadway; baconandbuttersac.com; $$) is worth both the trek and the inevitable lines. The seasonal menu changes frequently, but has included creations like fried green tomato and ham hock with baby arugula, poached eggs, corn, and béarnaise sauce.

11 *All Aboard* 10 a.m.

Head to Amtrak's Sacramento Valley Station, a 1926 Renaissance Revival train station that has received a major facelift, and hop the Capitol

Corridor train for a ride 15 minutes west to the college town of Davis. From the 1913 Mission Revival Davis Station, it's a 20-minute walk to the **Jan Shrem and Maria Manetti Shrem Museum of Art** (254 Old Davis Road; manettishrem.org), which opened in 2016 at the University of California, Davis. The museum's porous, light-filled Grand Canopy design is itself a work of art.

ABOVE At the Shady Lady Saloon, cocktails shimmer in a setting of red-velvet curtains and glowing chandeliers. Live music might be blues, jazz, big band, or country.

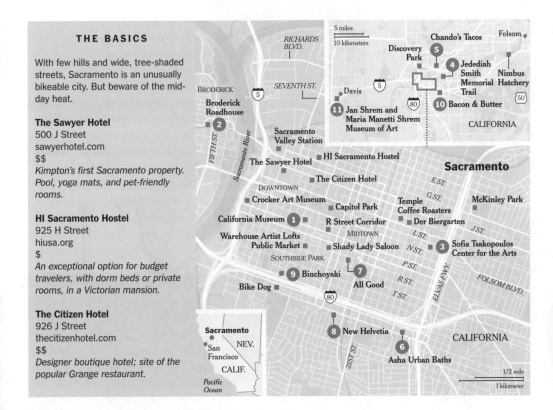

THE BASICS

With few hills and wide, tree-shaded streets, Sacramento is an unusually bikeable city. But beware of the midday heat.

The Sawyer Hotel
500 J Street
sawyerhotel.com
$$
Kimpton's first Sacramento property. Pool, yoga mats, and pet-friendly rooms.

HI Sacramento Hostel
925 H Street
hiusa.org
$
An exceptional option for budget travelers, with dorm beds or private rooms, in a Victorian mansion.

The Citizen Hotel
926 J Street
thecitizenhotel.com
$$
Designer boutique hotel; site of the popular Grange restaurant.

San Diego

San Diego has its own particular brand of laid-back cool. Its distinct neighborhoods, each announced with a retro-style, street-spanning sign, have their own personalities, but all share the breezy feeling of an oceanside city in seemingly perpetual sunshine. The Navy makes it a military town, Mexico is at the city limit, universities bring youthful energy, and the beach and Embarcadero draw surfers and strollers. With its easygoing vibe, San Diego is a vacation spot for low-stress California fun. — BY NELL MCSHANE WULFHART

FRIDAY

1 *Chill in the Sunshine* 3 p.m.

Take advantage of San Diego's perma-sunshine and relax at **Balboa Park** (balboapark.org). On weekends, its beautifully kept 1,200 acres are packed with people lawn bowling, visiting the 17 museums, and walking the trails. Wander through at your leisure, making sure to stop in the Botanical Building, a magnificent century-old lath structure filled with more than 2,000 plants. Pause for a drink at the open-air **Panama 66** (panama66.com), which has views of the May S. Marcy Sculpture Garden.

2 *Choose Your Sauce* 5:30 p.m.

The Little Italy neighborhood is booming, and one of the newer additions is the **Crack Shack** (2266 Kettner Boulevard; crackshack.com; $$), an open-air restaurant with concrete picnic tables, a bocce court, and a client base that seems to include every San Diegan under the age of 35. The fried chicken is made with locally raised, free-range chickens and accompanied by house-made dipping sauces. There's a good cocktail and beer list.

3 *Beer by the Flight* 6:30 p.m.

You could spend weeks testing out the offerings of San Diego's breweries (120 and counting), or you could just stop by the **Brew Project** (3683 Fifth Avenue; thebrewproject.com). This small bar in Hillcrest is a shortcut to getting to know one of the country's best craft beer scenes. With beer only from local

OPPOSITE *Unconditional Surrender, a waterfront landmark.*

RIGHT *Lucha Libre, a taco shop with a wrestling theme.*

breweries on tap, the Brew Project switches up the offerings daily. The beer flight is cleverly designed: Choose your beers from the menu, write their names on the five-glass holder, and the staff will fill it up with the four-ounce pours of your choice.

4 *Music and Mules* 8 p.m.

The **Observatory North Park** (2891 University Avenue; observatorysd.com), a historic theater, is one of the top places in the city for live music and stand-up comedy. The building dates from the 1920s and was once a movie theater, but these days it's often standing room only for acts as diverse as the California crooner Mayer Hawthorne and the British electronic group Hot Chip (the space hosts up-and-coming musicians, too). The concert hall is connected to the **West Coast Tavern** (westcoasttavern.com), a bar and restaurant that's open during shows and serves up nine variations on the Moscow Mule, including El Burro, made with tequila and orange bitters.

SATURDAY

5 *Stand and Paddle* 9 a.m.

Year-round aquatic sports are one of San Diego's big draws. If you don't have time to learn how to surf like a pro, try your hand at stand-up paddleboarding. Head to the calm waters of Mission Bay (it's easier to learn here than in the open ocean) and rent a paddleboard from **Aqua Adventures** (1548 Quivira Way; aqua-adventures.com). Launch off the dock, balancing yourself on the board, and paddle your way out into the water. If you're lucky, you may catch sight of a sea lion.

6 *Untraditional Taqueria* Noon

It's impossible to pinpoint the best tacos in a town with such a surfeit of options, but an interesting theme adds appeal. At **Lucha Libre** (3016 University Avenue; luchalibretacoshop.com; $) in North Park, that theme is masked and costumed Mexican wrestlers. The bright murals, gold seats, and walls decked with homages to the most famous luchadores make you feel as if you're eating inside Comic-Con, but the food — particularly the specialty taco with grilled crispy cheese and chipotle sauce, topped up with salsas from the extensive bar — is worth lingering over. Add a tamarind soda for the full Mexican experience.

7 *Pop Into a Shop* 1 p.m.

North Park is one of the hippest neighborhoods in San Diego, bursting with cool cafes, breweries, and shops. Stroll down 30th Street and explore at will. Shop, do some people watching, have a coffee, and take in an exhibit at the contemporary gallery/art supply store **Visual** (3776 30th Street; visualshopsd.com), which hosts group art shows and pop-up shops.

8 *Naval No More* 4 p.m.

Once a naval training station, **Liberty Public Market** (2820 Historic Decatur Road; libertypublicmarket.com) is a food hall in Point Loma that's jam-packed with stalls and outposts of the city's restaurants, cafes, and bakeries. Pick out an afternoon snack — maybe a lobster roll, some artisan cheese, or a creative cupcake — and buy a fantastically creamy nitro coffee from **WestBean Coffee Roasters**. Gather your goodies and grab one of the high stools at the back of the market to chow down. You might cruise some craft stalls, too, for a little more shopping.

9 *Pacific Sunset* 6:30 p.m.

Some of the most breathtaking scenery in the area is in Ocean Beach, a coastal neighborhood with a chilled-out vibe and a hippie bent. Head to Sunset Cliffs Boulevard and follow the trail along the cliffs, which drop off to the ocean below, in time for the sunset. You'll usually spot locals meditating or practicing yoga while looking out to sea, pelicans flying by in formation, and, down on the water, surfers waiting to catch the next wave. Once the sun has set (or before, depending on the time of year), take a stroll down Newport Avenue, the main street in what the residents call O.B. It's lined with breweries, kitschy secondhand stores, and restaurants advertising San Diego's famous fish tacos.

10 *Pre-Pizza Seitan* 9:30 p.m.

For a late dinner at one of San Diego's most popular restaurants, head to South Park, where the Italian staff at **Buona Forchetta** (3001 Beech Street; buonaforchettasd.com; $$) serves up pizza with chewy, heat-blackened crusts and toppings like

burrata cheese and house-made fennel sausage. There's almost always a long wait, so put your name on the list and head across the street to **Kindred** (1503 30th Street; barkindred.com), a buzzy vegan bar with a classed-up rock 'n' roll aesthetic and craft cocktails. Vegan snacks like seitan skewers with harissa and horseradish aioli will tide you over until your table at Buona Forchetta is ready.

SUNDAY

11 *Sunday in La Jolla* 11 a.m.

A 20-minute drive up the coast, La Jolla is a gorgeous small community with beautiful beaches and an upscale ambience, perfect for a Sunday stroll. Head down Prospect Street, the main drag, which is lined with high-end shops and restaurants, and then make a detour to the beach at Seal Rock,

where you'll often find dozens of the plump resident seals napping on the sand or bobbing in the water. Stop in at **El Pescador Fish Market** (634 Pearl Street; elpescadorfishmarket.com; $$), a La Jolla favorite for decades. Order lunch at the walk-up counter and grab a seat.

OPPOSITE ABOVE The Botanical Building, a must-stop for plant lovers and architecture buffs, in Balboa Park.

OPPOSITE BELOW Coffee break at Liberty Public Market.

ABOVE Stand-up paddleboarding in calm waters.

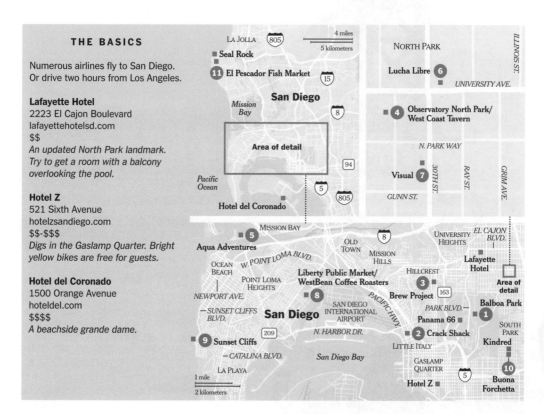

THE BASICS

Numerous airlines fly to San Diego. Or drive two hours from Los Angeles.

Lafayette Hotel
2223 El Cajon Boulevard
lafayettehotelsd.com
$$
An updated North Park landmark. Try to get a room with a balcony overlooking the pool.

Hotel Z
521 Sixth Avenue
hotelzsandiego.com
$$-$$$
Digs in the Gaslamp Quarter. Bright yellow bikes are free for guests.

Hotel del Coronado
1500 Orange Avenue
hoteldel.com
$$$$
A beachside grande dame.

San Francisco

San Francisco typically wows visitors with its heights. The hills sear themselves into memory after a few up-and-down-and-up-again cable car rides or punishing walks. Then there are the hilltop sights: the sweeping vistas and the picturesque Victorians. But surrounding all of that is coastline, miles of peninsula shore along the Pacific Ocean and the expansive natural harbor of San Francisco Bay. Once a working industrial area with pockets of outright blight, much of the city's waterfront has been polished into another of its pleasures. To sample what it offers, start exploring in the east, south of the Bay Bridge, and loop your way west to the Golden Gate and then south to Ocean Beach. In one weekend romp, you'll join San Franciscans in many of the places they love best—and see what remains of their city's maritime heart.

— BY JESSE MCKINLEY

FRIDAY

1 *A Ride Along the Water* 4 p.m.

China Basin, south of the Bay Bridge, is home to an entirely new neighborhood since big changes began around 2000. The University of California, San Francisco, has developed its **Mission Bay Campus**, adding handsome new buildings and public art including two soaring steel towers by Richard Serra, a San Francisco native. And the opening of **AT&T Park**, the baseball field that's home to the San Francisco Giants, brought new energy and new monuments, including tributes to greats like Willie Mays and Willie McCovey (the basin is often called McCovey Cove). Rent a bike at the **Bike Hut**, a nonprofit outlet at Pier 40 (415-543-4335; thebikehut.org), and pedal the wide promenade along the water.

2 *Embarcadero Imbibing* 5:30 p.m.

Once the home to a raised freeway—demolished after the 1989 Loma Prieta earthquake—and before that a busy wharf area receiving cargo from around

OPPOSITE Rocks and surf below the Golden Gate Bridge.

RIGHT Waterbar offers cool drinks, tasty oysters, and a sweeping view of San Francisco Bay and the San Francisco-Oakland Bay Bridge.

the world, the **Embarcadero** is now one of San Francisco's most inviting Friday night spots, filled with workweek-wearied downtown workers ready to relax. Two inviting spots for a drink and appetizers are **Waterbar** (399 Embarcadero; 415-284-9922; waterbarsf.com) and **Epic Steak** (369 Embarcadero; 415-369-9955; epicsteak.com). Views of the Bay Bridge are unbeatable at either, but oysters at Waterbar can really set the mood.

3 *Two Piers* 8 p.m.

The classic restaurants by Pier 39 and Fisherman's Wharf are fun to visit, or you can shift gears with **Hard Water** (Pier 3; 415-392-3021; hardwaterbar.com; $$), a tiny, New Orleans-inflected whiskey bar and restaurant. The kitchen turns out a mean fried chicken—the better to soak up the powerful cocktails. Whiskey flights are a gentle intro to a deep list. For a heartier meal, head a pier and a half over to the sophisticated Peruvian cebicheria **La Mar** (Pier 1$^{1}/_{2}$; 415-397-8880; lamarsf.com; $$$). Set in a former ferry landing, the restaurant's patio was the loading area; its bar, which serves an enticing array of pisco cocktails, was the ticketing area. Menu choices have included scallops with cevichera cream and the Peruvian specialty causa, a seasoned potato puree in small cylinders finished with tender grilled octopus and other toppings.

SATURDAY

4 *Flip, Flop, Fly* 9 a.m.

Yearning for a Saturday-morning workout? Go for a run at **Crissy Field**, once a waterfront airfield and now San Francisco's weekend outdoor gym, with masses of joggers, walkers, and cyclists cruising its paths. It's part of the **Presidio**, formerly a military complex guarding San Francisco Bay and the strategic strait at its entrance — the Golden Gate. Now it's all part of the Golden Gate National Recreation Area. Activities run from the quirky (crabbing classes at the Civil War-era Fort Point, under the Golden Gate Bridge) to the caffeinated (outdoor coffee at the **Warming Hut**; 983 Marine Drive; 415-561-3040). But the bounciest option is the **House of Air** (926 Mason Street; 415-345-9675; houseofair.com), a trampoline center in one of the repurposed buildings on the main Presidio post. Flanked by a kids' swimming school and an indoor climbing center, the House of Air also features training classes, a trampoline dodgeball court, and a bouncy castle for tots.

5 *Chow Time* Noon

Dining at the Presidio has come a long way since the days of reveille at dawn. Several restaurants now dot the northeastern corner, where much of the Presidio's development has occurred since it was transferred to the National Park Service in the mid-1990s. One spot that retains the old military feel is the **Presidio Social Club** (563 Ruger Street; 415-885-1888; presidiosocialclub.com; $$$). As unpretentious as an Army grunt, the club offers old-time drinks (the rye-heavy Sazerac, which dates to 1840) and a pleasantly affordable brunch. A dessert of beignets with hot cocoa can fuel you up for your next offensive.

6 *Inner Sunset Stroll* 2 p.m.

Detour off base to the Inner Sunset neighborhood and **Green Apple Books on the Park** (1231 Ninth Avenue; 415-742-5833; greenapplebooks.com). Don't be fooled by the narrow storefront; the shop reaches far into the interior space, and is big enough to be anchored by a dedicated children's area. Like its sister store — the venerable Green Apple Books, opened in 1967 — it also hosts events featuring an impressive lineup of writers. Afterward, stroll down the street and into **Local Take** (1371 Ninth Avenue; 415-664-4422; localtakesf.com) to browse quirky, locally made gifts.

7 *Nature and Art* 4 p.m.

Take a walk through the hills and woods on the Pacific coast side of the Presidio, where miles of hiking trails lead to scenic overlooks (presidio.gov). You may also find an artwork or two. The Presidio doesn't need much help being beautiful, but that hasn't stopped artists who have placed installations and sculpture on the grounds. One is Andy Goldsworthy, an environmental British sculptor whose ephemeral pieces in the park include *Spire* — a soaring wooden spike — and *Wood Line*, a serpentine forest-floor sculpture made of eucalyptus.

8 *Burning, Man* 6:30 p.m.

Few things say California more than beach bonfires, a proud tradition up and down the coast. In San Francisco, free spirits keep it going at **Ocean Beach**, the wide sand expanse south of Baker Beach (the spot where Burning Man, the now Nevada-based arts fest,

OPPOSITE At Crissy Field, a part of the Presidio, masses of joggers, walkers, and cyclists cruise the paths.

BELOW *Spire*, a sculpture by Andy Goldsworthy, at the Presidio. Miles of trails lead to ocean views.

was born). While the wind can be biting, the mood at the impromptu fires is usually warm as groups congregate with guitars, pipes, and good vibes. This is the only beach in the city that permits bonfires (March through October only), and under Golden Gate National Recreation Area rules, they must be extinguished by 9. So while bonfires go at any hour of the day, this is the classic time. Take a blanket and a pullover and watch the sunset, surf, and sparks collide.

9 *Dinner at the Edge* 8 p.m.

The **Cliff House** (1090 Point Lobos; 415-386-3330; cliffhouse.com) has been serving visitors at the end of the continent since the Civil War, and it is still perched on the same rocks, facing shark-fin-shaped Seal Rock and the crashing waves below. The **Bistro** ($$), upstairs, serves entrees and cocktails like the Ramos Fizz, a gin drink — and purported hangover cure — made with egg whites, half-and-half, and orange juice. Downstairs is the higher-end **Sutro's**

($$$), where the specialties include a two-crab sandwich and grilled scallops.

SUNDAY

10 *Other Side of the Park* 11 a.m.

The western edge of **Golden Gate Park**, facing Ocean Beach, has a Rodney Dangerfield feel, less known and appreciated than the park's cityside flanks. But its offerings are impressive, including a cheap and public nine-hole, par-3 golf course, a

lovely bison enclave, and serene fly-fishing ponds. A good place to convene for any park adventure is the **Park Chalet** (1000 Great Highway; 415-386-8439; parkchalet.com; $$$). In this somewhat hidden spot just off Ocean Beach, kids run free in the wilds of the park and parents enjoy a brunch buffet that advertises "bottomless champagne."

ABOVE The skyline, with San Francisco Bay in the background. A city of hills, valleys, and sea, San Francisco abounds in gorgeous views.

OPPOSITE A 21st-century addition, *Cupid's Span*, by Claes Oldenburg and Coosje van Bruggen, frames a view of the Ferry Building clock tower, a more traditional San Francisco landmark.

THE BASICS

Take the BART train from San Francisco International Airport to downtown. Get around the city using taxis and public transportation.

Hotel Vitale
8 Mission Street
415-278-3700
hotelvitale.com
$$$$
Style and luxury on the Embarcadero, across from the landmark Ferry Building.

Harbor Court Hotel
165 Steuart Street
415-882-1300
harborcourthotel.com
$$
Boutique hotel with bay views.

Union Street Inn
2229 Union Street
415-346-0424
unionstreetinn.com
$$$
Quiet and charming bed-and-breakfast.

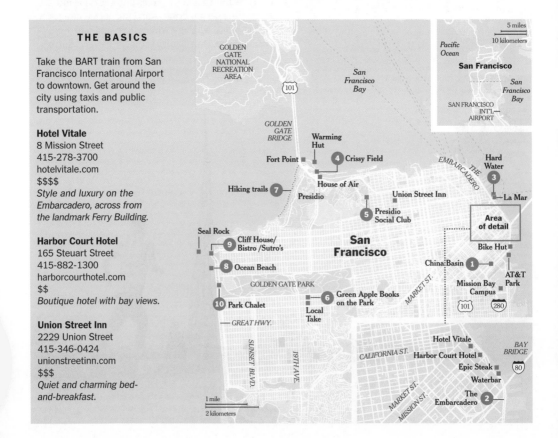

Santa Barbara

Santa Barbara may be tiny — its 90,000 residents could be seated in the Los Angeles Coliseum — but it packs Oprah-like cachet. Indeed, the billionaire media mogul and other A-listers have made this former outpost of Spain's American dominions their second home. Posh hotels, seven-figure mansions, and trendy boutiques have opened along the so-called American Riviera, catering to members of the Hollywood set who drive up every weekend to frolic among the languorous palms and suntanned celebrities. But don't let the crush of Ferraris and Prada fool you. With its perpetually blue skies and taco stands, Santa Barbara remains a laid-back town where the star attraction is still the beach.
— BY FINN-OLAF JONES

FRIDAY

1 *Lingering Glow* 5 p.m.

Santa Barbara's main beaches face southeast, but you can still catch the Pacific sunset by driving along Cliff Drive until it takes you to secluded **Hendry's Beach**. Hemmed by vertiginous cliffs that turn deep orange as the sun sets, the beach is popular with locals, surfers, and dolphins. Order a rum punch at the **Boathouse at Hendry's Beach** (2981 Cliff Drive; 805-898-2628; boathousesb.com), where you can still feel the warmth of the sun (or is it the fire pit?) long after it has set.

2 *Making Friends* 8 p.m.

Fresh California cuisine is the rule in this region of outstanding vineyards, luscious orchards, and right-off-the-boat seafood. Some of the freshest is at **Brophy Brothers Restaurant and Clam Bar** (119 Harbor Way; 805-966-4418; brophybros.com; $$$), which overlooks the harbor. Sit at the long communal table and strike up a conversation with your new friends. The night I was there, I was offered a job by a local developer. While I didn't take the job, I did sample the

OPPOSITE Sunset at Hendry's Beach. The main beaches in town face southeast, but at Hendry's the shore angles west, and the cliffs glow orange as the sun goes down.

RIGHT La Super Rica Taqueria, pronounced by Julia Child the best of several good places in Santa Barbara to get a fresh and authentic homemade taco.

clam chowder ("The best in town," I was told about five times), followed by a terrific grilled swordfish with artichoke sauce. Hmmm, what was that starting salary again?

SATURDAY

3 *Bike to Brunch* 10 a.m.

Rent a bike at **Wheel Fun Rentals** (633 East Cabrillo Boulevard; 805-966-2282; wheelfunrentals.com) and roll along the ocean to the **Shoreline Beach Cafe** (801 Shoreline Drive; 805-568-0064; shorelinebeachcafe.com), where you can eat blueberry pancakes laced with orange juice, or munch on a taco, while you feel the sand between your toes.

4 *Sacred Mission* 11:30 a.m.

It's hard not to feel awed when driving up the hill to **Old Mission Santa Barbara** (2201 Laguna Street; 805-682-4713; sbmission.org), a 1786 land-mark with ocher-colored columns that is known as the Queen of the 21 original Spanish missions built along the California coastline. Escape the crowds by wandering outside in the flower-scented Sacred Garden. If there's a docent around, ask if you can see the glazed terra-cotta sculpture of St. Barbara watching over Mary and Jesus. A masterpiece from 1522, it was discovered in a storage room that was

being cleaned out and is now installed in an alcove in the garden's private portico.

5 *Taco Heaven* 1 p.m.

Locals argue endlessly about the city's best taco joint. Julia Child threw her weight behind **La Super Rica Taqueria** (622 North Milpas Street; 805-963-4940; $), ensuring perpetual lines for its home-made tortillas filled with everything from pork and cheese to spicy ground beans. **Lilly's** (310 Chapala Street; 805-966-9180; lillystacos.com; $), a tiny spot in the center of town run by the ever-welcoming Sepulveda family, serves tacos filled with anything from pork to beef eye. And **Palapa** (4123 State Street; 805-683-3074; palaparestaurant.com; $) adds fresh

seafood to the equation in its cheery patio just north of downtown, where the grilled sole tacos are fresh and light. Try all three places and join the debate.

6 *Paper Chase* 3 p.m.

Walt Disney's original will. A letter by Galileo. Lincoln's second Emancipation Proclamation (the 13th Amendment). The **Karpeles Manuscript Library and Museum** (21 West Anapamu Street; 805-962-5322; rain.org/~karpeles) was started by David Karpeles, a local real estate tycoon, and has one of the world's largest private manuscript collections. If this whets your appetite for collecting, wander seven blocks to **Randall House Rare Books** (835 Laguna Street; 805-963-1909; randallhouserarebooks.com), where the aged tomes and rare documents have included a signed calling card from Robert E. Lee ($4,500) and the first official map of the State of California ($27,500).

ABOVE Sunset over the Pacific Ocean, viewed from the shore near the Santa Barbara Pier.

LEFT A guest room at San Ysidro Ranch, the longtime celebrity hangout where John F. Kennedy took his bride, Jacqueline, on their honeymoon.

OPPOSITE Two views of Mission Santa Barbara, known as the Queen of the original Spanish California missions.

7 *Shop Like the Stars* 5 p.m.

The main shopping drag, State Street, is filled with the usual chain stores like Abercrombie & Fitch. The consumerist cognoscenti head for the hills, to the Platinum Card district of **Montecito**, where you'll find local designers and one-off items along the eucalyptus-lined Coast Village Road. Highlights include **Antoinette** (No. 1046; 805-969-1515; antoinetteboutique.com), a mainstay for European designers working in the relaxed Santa Barbara style; **Angel** (No. 1221; 805-565-1599; wendyfoster.com), selling casual sportswear and accessories with a youthful vibe; and **Allora by Laura** (No. 1269; 805-563-2425; allorabylaura.com), a shiny, luxurious boutique featuring collections by Yigal Azrouël, Les Copains, and other designers.

8 *Celebrity Dining* 8 p.m.

J.F.K. and Jackie honeymooned there, Hollywood luminaries like Groucho Marx were regulars, and its 500 verdant acres have played host to guests ranging from Winston Churchill to Lucille Ball to Sinclair Lewis. The **San Ysidro Ranch** is one of the country's premier resorts, and its **Stonehouse** restaurant (900 San Ysidro Lane; 805-565-1700; sanysidroranch.com; $$$$) enjoys a similarly stellar reputation. Expect to see the T-shirt-with-blazer set sitting around an open fire while dining on dishes like warm mushroom salad, juniper-dusted venison loin,

and fresh pastries. Take a post-dinner stroll around the terraced gardens where many of the ingredients were grown.

9 *Glamorous State* 11 p.m.

State Street heats up after 11 o'clock as college students and moneyed folk from the glittering hills descend to its bars and nightclubs. **Wildcat Lounge** (15 West Ortega Street; 805-962-7970; wildcatlounge.com), a retro bar with red-vinyl banquettes, is a place to mingle with the university crowd and local bohos grooving to house music. Cater-corner is **Tonic** (634 State Street; 805-897-1800; tonicsb.com), an airy dance club that draws students and recent graduates to its cabanas. The

international set heads to **Eos Lounge** (500 Anacapa Street; 805-564-2410; eoslounge.com) to dance in a packed, tree-shaded patio that looks like Mykonos on the Pacific.

to Baja California through a five-mile gap among the Channel Islands, a cluster of rocky isles 20 or so miles off the coast. Catch a glimpse of the commute — and see breaching whales rise from the sea around you — from the decks of the *Condor Express*, a high-speed catamaran that makes daily whale-watching trips (301 West Cabrillo Boulevard; 805-882-0088; condorexpress.com). Porpoises, sea lions, and the occasional killer whale join in on the fun.

SUNDAY

10 *Paging Moby-Dick* 10 a.m.

From December to February, some 30,000 gray whales migrate down the Pacific Coast from Alaska

ABOVE A signature Santa Barbara view: beach, pier, and the mountains that rise outside of town.

OPPOSITE Mission Santa Barbara dates to 1786.

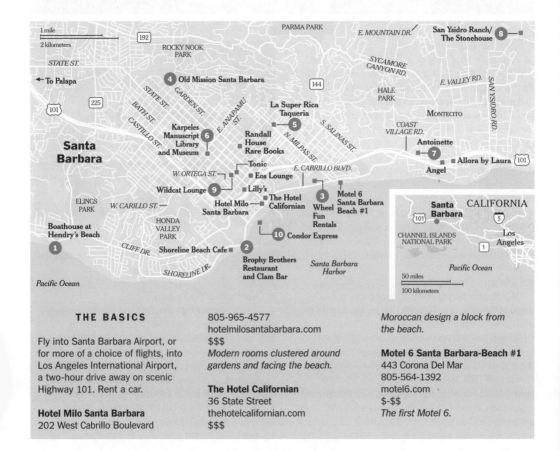

THE BASICS

Fly into Santa Barbara Airport, or for more of a choice of flights, into Los Angeles International Airport, a two-hour drive away on scenic Highway 101. Rent a car.

Hotel Milo Santa Barbara
202 West Cabrillo Boulevard

805-965-4577
hotelmilosantabarbara.com
$$$
Modern rooms clustered around gardens and facing the beach.

The Hotel Californian
36 State Street
thehotelcalifornian.com
$$$

Moroccan design a block from the beach.

Motel 6 Santa Barbara-Beach #1
443 Corona Del Mar
805-564-1392
motel6.com
$-$$
The first Motel 6.

Santa Monica

When Angelenos think of the perfect beach town, they think of Santa Monica. With its classic amusement pier, glittering bay, and surfers bobbing on swells, it certainly looks the part. But take a short walk inland, and there's a town asserting its unique identity: eight square miles and about 100,000 people surrounded by districts of the City of Los Angeles, but stubbornly remaining a separate city. A well-preserved Mission-style bungalow sits around the corner from a steel performance space by Frank Gehry. Shops sell goods ranging from vintage Parisian wedding gowns to a whimsical map made entirely of license plates. Enjoy the games and famed carousel of the Santa Monica Pier, and then step back from the beach to sample the city's variety the way Santa Monicans do.

— BY FRED A. BERNSTEIN AND LOUISE TUTELIAN

FRIDAY

1 *Landscape and Seascape* 4 p.m.

James Corner, an architect of the High Line park in Manhattan, has transformed a former parking lot into **Tongva Park** (tongvapark.smgov.net), a stunning 6.2-acre space with sculptural art, fountains, play areas, and winding walkways. Take a walk there, and then, for a sense of the setting that made Santa Monica, stroll in **Palisades Park** (Ocean Avenue at Santa Monica Boulevard; smgov.net/parks) and wander off on one of the sinuous paths overlooking the beach and Santa Monica Pier.

2 *Oyster Shack* 6 p.m.

The **Blue Plate Oysterette** (1355 Ocean Avenue; 310-576-3474; blueplatesantamonica.com; $$), one of the dozen or so Santa Monica restaurants that face the ocean, may be the most ocean-y, with its raw bar and daily specials like pan-seared rainbow trout. The casual blue-and-white restaurant, with a tin-pressed ceiling and blackboard menus, draws a chic, flip-flop-wearing crowd.

3 *The View That Moves* 8 p.m.

At sunset, the most thrilling view in town is at the beach, from the top of the solar-powered, 130-foot-high Pacific Wheel, the Ferris wheel at the **Santa Monica Pier**. Yes, it's touristy, and yes, it

might be crowded, but it is, after all, the city's iconic symbol. As you glide upward, watching the entire city of Santa Monica, and far beyond, slide into view, the whole scene will be bathed in the sunset-colored glow. If you prefer a view that's not mobile, head south into Venice to the rooftop lounge of the **Hotel Erwin** (1697 Pacific Avenue; 310-452-1111; hotelerwin.com), where the banquettes seem to hang over the beach. Gaze at a Santa Monica panorama while sipping a cocktail. You can reserve a table in advance through the hotel's website.

SATURDAY

4 *Duck for Breakfast* 8 a.m.

The lines spill out the door, so arrive early at **Huckleberry Bakery and Café** (1014 Wilshire Boulevard; 310-451-2311; huckleberrycafe.com; $$). Breakfast favorites include green eggs and ham, made with pesto and prosciutto, and the fried egg sandwich, with bacon, Gruyère, and arugula. The cheerful room, with wooden tables and colorful accents, feels like a large country bakery.

5 *Into the Mountains* 9 a.m.

The Backbone Trail, a 69-mile system, roughly follows the crest of the Santa Monica Mountains

OPPOSITE Palisades Park, overlooking the Pacific Ocean.

BELOW The Milbank House, designed by the firm that did Grauman's Chinese Theater, is one of the Craftsman-style houses on Adelaide Drive designated as city landmarks.

north from **Will Rogers State Historic Park** just north of Santa Monica (1501 Will Rogers State Park Road, off West Sunset Boulevard, Pacific Palisades; 310-454-8212; nps.gov/samo/planyour-visit/backbonetrail.htm). Hikers can take an easy, sage-scented, two-mile loop from the parking lot at Will Rogers up to Inspiration Point, a sensational overlook of Santa Monica Bay from the Palos Verdes Peninsula to Point Dume in Malibu. Do it on a clear day, and you'll see Catalina Island and the white dots of sails. Behind are the slopes of the Santa Monica Mountains, and in the distance, the high-rises of downtown Los Angeles. Up here, the muted chattering of birds and the hum of insects are the only sounds.

6 *Builders and Shoppers* Noon

Back in northern Santa Monica, natural sights give way to architectural ones. Two houses designated as city landmarks are the Craftsman-style **Milbank House** (236 Adelaide Drive) — designed by the same firm that did Grauman's Chinese Theater in Hollywood — and the stucco **Worrel "Zuni House"** (710 Adelaide Drive), which was built in the mid-1920s and has been described as a "Pueblo-Revival Maya fantasy." Some of the city's best shopping is nearby on Montana Avenue. **Brentwood General Store** (No. 1230; 310-394-9225; brentwoodgeneralstore.com), opened in 2001, is stocked with everything from jewelry and apothecary items to high-end home goods such as Simon Pearce vases, Cire Trudon candles, and Le Cadeaux salad bowls. **Rooms & Gardens** (No. 1311-A; 310-451-5154; roomsandgardens.com) sells furniture, antiques, accessories like pillows fashioned from antique Indian saris, and ikat dinnerware.

7 *Art Lovers, Art Buyers* 3 p.m.

For an art-filled afternoon, start at **Bergamot Station** (2525 Michigan Avenue; 310-453-7535; visitbergamot.com), built on the site of a former trolley-line stop, and dip into one or more of its collection of some 25 galleries with rotating exhibitions. Off the Third Street Promenade, find the unconventional **Adamm's Stained Glass Studio & Art Gallery** (1426 Fourth Street; 310-451-9390; adammsgallery.com), an interesting spot that even locals often overlook. The work of more than 175 glass artists is for sale, from gemlike paperweights to frilly perfume bottles and sculptural chandeliers.

8 *Bistro Evenings* 8 p.m.

There are lots of stylish hotels in Santa Monica, and some of them offer very good food. A case in point is **Fig** (101 Wilshire Boulevard; 310-319-3111; figsantamonica.com; $$$), a contemporary American bistro at the Fairmont Miramar Hotel. The menu features seasonal ingredients and dishes like a halibut "chop" or snap peas with mint. There is seating indoors, in an elegant room with starburst mirrors, as well as on the terrace with views of the ocean through the lush gardens. The huge Moreton Bay fig tree, from which the restaurant gets its name, will make you feel like climbing.

9 *Disco Nights* 11 p.m.

Santa Monica may be known for sunshine, but there's plenty to do after dark. For a taste of the local night life, head to **West End** (1301 Fifth Street; 310-451-2221; westendsm.com), formerly Zanzibar, a cavernous, dimly lit club with a sleek industrial design, large dance floor, work by local artists lining the walls (they are all for sale), and signature cocktails. There are both D.J.'s and bands that feature local and international artists playing a mix of hip-hop, salsa and bachata, reggae and more.

SUNDAY

10 *No Wet Suit Needed* 10 a.m.

Even in warm weather, the waters of Southern California can be frigid. For a more comfortable swim, duck into the **Annenberg Community Beach House** (415 Pacific Coast Highway; 310-458-4904; annenbergbeachhouse.com), a sleek public facility that opened in 2010. The pool is spectacular, and you can buy a day pass for a reasonable price. If you've

got to get in your laps after October, your best bet is the public **Santa Monica Swim Center** (2225 16th Street; 310-458-8700; santamonicaswimcenter.org), where the adult and children's pools are kept at 79 and 85 degrees, respectively.

11 *Sunday Retail* Noon

Amid the sneaker stores and used-book shops of artsy Main Street, in the Ocean Park neighborhood, look for the Frank Gehry-designed steel boxes of **Edgemar** (2415-2449 Main Street; edgemarcenter.org), which house retail tenants and a performance space around an open courtyard. Gehry's retail footprint in Santa Monica has shrunk since his **Santa Monica Place**, designed in 1980, was replaced by a new version (395 Santa Monica Place; santamonicaplace.com), a glassy open-air retail

complex that often has live music, HDTV displays, or seasonal events. If shopping makes you hungry, head for the top level and the **Curious Palate** market, which has a cafe with an artisanal, farm-to-table menu.

OPPOSITE Ocean-view dining at Santa Monica Place, a glassy open-air version of a California shopping mall.

ABOVE At sunset, the best view in town is at the beach, from the top of the solar-powered, 130-foot-high Pacific Wheel, the Ferris wheel at the Santa Monica Pier.

THE BASICS

Santa Monica is about a 20-minute drive from Los Angeles International Airport. There's a terrific bus system (bigbluebus.com), but most visitors find it more convenient to drive.

The Ambrose
1255 20th Street
310-315-1555
ambrosehotel.com
$$$
Feels like a Mission-style hideaway with stained-glass windows.

Hotel Shangri-La
1301 Ocean Avenue
855-649-4400
shangrila-hotel.com
$$$$
A storied, bright-white apparition on bluffs high above the Pacific.

Shore Hotel
1515 Ocean Avenue
310-458-1515
shorehotel.com
$$$$
Across Ocean Avenue from the pier.

Silicon Valley

Like the high-tech companies that give this hyper-prosperous region its name, Silicon Valley thrives on reinvention. Situated just south of San Francisco Bay, the valley was once home to orchards and vineyards. These days, of course, it bears fruit of a different sort, as the home of tech giants like Apple, Google, and Facebook. Buoyed by the resilience of tech companies, the valley's dozen or so cities, which include Mountain View and Palo Alto, continue to evolve from corporate strip malls to urban hubs. The valley now buzzes with cultural spaces, lively restaurants, and the energy of a hyper-educated workforce that has no problem keeping up. — BY ASHLEE VANCE

FRIDAY

1 *Small Town Downtown* 2 p.m.

San Jose may still call itself the capital of Silicon Valley, but picturesque **Los Gatos** is emerging as its trendier downtown, with historic cottages and upscale boutiques. The chains have begun an invasion, but dozens of independent shops remain, selling fashion, children's clothing, baby duds, shoes, accessories, home décor, and collectors' items. Start your prospecting on North Santa Cruz Avenue at West Main Street and follow your whims as you head north. The people cruising the streets in Los Gatos give off a vibe that matches the bright, charming town, which is full of surprises off the main drag.

2 *Inside Apple (Almost)* 4 p.m.

With the help of Foster + Partners, Apple is making a statement with its futuristic new headquarters — and not only with its spaceship-like circular design. Solar power, natural ventilation, drought-resistant landscaping: it checks all the boxes for tech-savvy adaptation to climate change. It's also a work site where 12,000 people apply similar savvy to making money. You can't tour inside, but at the **Apple Park Visitor Center** (10600 North Tantau Avenue, Cupertino; apple.com/retail/appleparkvisitorcenter), you can "see" inside a 3-D model with an iPad app. There's also a cafe and, of course, an Apple Store.

3 *American Fare* 8 p.m.

St. Michael's Alley (140 Homer Avenue, Palo Alto; 650-326-2530; stmikes.com; $$), a few blocks off crowded University Avenue in Palo Alto, has three elegant dining areas, including a bar anchored by an artful hunk of walnut. The business casual attire matches the informal cuisine, which leans toward Californian and American fare. One night's pan-roasted salmon filet, for instance, came with lentils, leeks, rainbow carrots, and mustard herb butter.

4 *Choose Your Libation* 10 p.m.

Shame on Stanford students for allowing such tame bars along their home turf, University Avenue. For a more energized crowd, head to nearby California Avenue. A favorite among Silicon Valley's young titans is **Antonio's Nut House** (321 California Avenue, Palo Alto; 650-321-2550), a low-key neighborhood place where patrons can chuck their peanut shells on the floor, scribble on the walls, and take a photo with a peanut-dispensing gorilla. Down the road is **La Bodeguita del Medio** (463 South California Avenue, Palo Alto; 650-326-7762; labodeguita.com), a small Cuban restaurant with a bar that serves sangria and rum, and a room for smoking hand-rolled cigars.

SATURDAY

5 *Engineers Under the Palms* 9 a.m.

The name Silicon Valley may have been coined in the early 1970s, but the tech timeline goes even further back here. For a sense of the computer lore of Palo

OPPOSITE Stanford University, still the Silicon Valley hub.

BELOW The first Apple, at the Computer History Museum.

Alto, drive to 367 Addison Avenue and take a look at the humble wood garage where Bill Hewlett and Dave Packard started their company in 1939. The contrast to today's high-tech complexes is glaring. Next swing by 844 East Charleston Road, an office building where Fairchild Semiconductor invented a commercial version of the integrated circuit in 1959. Then get to the intellectual center of it all, **Stanford University** (visitor center at Campus Drive and Galvez Street; 650-723-2560; stanford.edu), in time to do a little walking around before the 11:30 a.m. tour of the palm- and oak-shaded campus. While you're in the neighborhood, head up to **Facebook** (1 Hacker Way, Menlo Park) and take a selfie at the "like" sign out front. Everybody else does.

6 *Google Brunch* 1 p.m.

Some chefs parlay a reality show into a restaurant. Charlie Ayers used his stint as the top chef of the cafeteria at the Googleplex, Google's headquarters-cum-playground, to open **Calafia Café** (855 El Camino Real, Palo Alto; 650-322-9200; calafiapaloalto.com). It is split down the middle between a sit-down restaurant and to-go counter. The fare is a lunch-style version of Californian comfort food: tacos, salmon, lamb hash, turkey meatloaf, and, of course, a vegetarian menu. The **Googleplex** itself (1600 Amphitheatre Parkway, Mountain View) isn't open to the public, but you can get a glimpse from the public park next to the entrance that peeks inside the laid-back campus.

7 *Computers 101* 3 p.m.

Much of the history of Silicon Valley — and, by extension, the electronic revolution in our daily lives — is now lovingly captured at the **Computer History Museum** (1401 North Shoreline Boulevard,

Mountain View; 650-810-1010; computerhistory.org). It's well worth the trip to see some of the early tech devices that are now highly valued antiques, and you'll get a sense of how we got from room-filling mainframes to nanochips.

8 *Vietnamese Plates* 8 p.m.

Thanks to Google and its army of millionaires, Castro Street, the main drag in Mountain View, has undergone a culinary and night-life revival. Among the bubblier spots is **Xanh** (110 Castro Street, Mountain View; 650-964-1888; xanhrestaurant.com; $$), a sprawling Vietnamese fusion restaurant with a handsome patio and dining rooms bathed in green and blue lights. The playful names on the menu — Duck Duck Good, Mellow Yellow Noodles — fail to capture the elegance of the dishes, plated in delicate fashion with exotic sauces. On weekends, the bar/lounge turns into a quasi-nightclub, with D.J.'s and more cocktails.

9 *Geek Talk* 10 p.m.

Back in 2010, an Apple software engineer lost an iPhone 4 prototype at **Gourmet Haus Staudt** (2615 Broadway; 650-364-9232), a German beer garden in Redwood City. Images of the prototype were splattered on Gizmodo, foiling the company's well-known obsession with secrecy. The beer garden has since shaken off its notoriety and remains a low-key place for engineers to gab about the newest products of their wizardry.

SUNDAY

10 *Local Harvest* 9 a.m.

Farmers' markets dot the valley on Sundays. One of the most bountiful is the **Mountain View**

Farmers' Market, in the parking lot of the town's Caltrain Station (600 West Evelyn; 925-465-46906; cafarmersmkts.com), where flowers, fruits, and vegetables are sold along with locally raised meats and artisanal cheeses. Shoppers here can pick up prepared foods to munch on as well, including homemade ethnic cuisine specialties like pork dumplings and fresh samosas.

11 *Up to the Hills* 11 a.m.

It's called a valley for a reason. The Santa Cruz Mountains rise along the valley's western edge and provide a treasure hunt for people willing to explore. Wineries, including the **Thomas Fogarty Winery** (19501 Skyline Boulevard, Woodside; 650-851-6777; fogartywinery.com), sit atop the mountains, offering unrivaled views of the valley. Hikes abound. The

Windy Hill Open Space Preserve (650-691-1200; openspace.org), a 15-minute drive from Stanford in Portola Valley, has a range of trails that cut through 1,312 acres of grassland ridges and redwood forests. By the end of the hike, you'll be able to spot Stanford, the NASA Ames Research Center, and the mega-mansions like a valley pro.

OPPOSITE The garage where Hewlett-Packard began.

ABOVE The Computer History Museum surveys the history of computing from the abacus to the iPad.

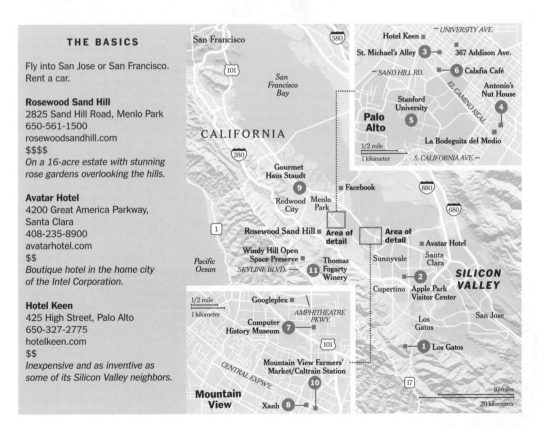

THE BASICS

Fly into San Jose or San Francisco. Rent a car.

Rosewood Sand Hill
2825 Sand Hill Road, Menlo Park
650-561-1500
rosewoodsandhill.com
$$$$
On a 16-acre estate with stunning rose gardens overlooking the hills.

Avatar Hotel
4200 Great America Parkway,
Santa Clara
408-235-8900
avatarhotel.com
$$
Boutique hotel in the home city of the Intel Corporation.

Hotel Keen
425 High Street, Palo Alto
650-327-2775
hotelkeen.com
$$
Inexpensive and as inventive as some of its Silicon Valley neighbors.

Honolulu

The name Honolulu can conjure up frenzied activity: exploring the sea with electric scooters, high-altitude extreme parasailing, close encounters with sharks, 40-miles-per-hour motorboat rides that guarantee you'll get wet. But Honolulu can also mean mellow: the fragrance of a custom-made orchid lei, the taste and texture of a perfect tuna sashimi slice, the elegance of a hula dancer, the deepening of the blues and greens of the sea as the sun sets. Even the steel-mesh netting to prevent falling rocks is partly hidden so as to blend with the landscape. Then there is the pace, the feeling that no one is ever too rushed to give you directions, take your dinner order, or explain the history of a 100-year-old banyan tree. — BY ELAINE SCIOLINO

FRIDAY

1 *Royalty Was Here* 2 p.m.

Who knew that **Iolani Palace** (364 South King Street; iolanipalace.org), the home of Hawaii's king and queen once upon a time, is the only official royal palace in the United States? In 1882 King Kalakaua and Queen Kapiolani moved into their newly built official residence, done in a unique "American Florentine" style. Fitted with telephones and electricity even before the White House, it was richly decorated with koa and other native woods. The king and queen were heads of state in their time, receiving foreign dignitaries and being received in places like Buckingham Palace.

2 *Leis and Papaya* 3:30 p.m.

Shopping for your weekend adventure starts with sensual self-indulgence. Head to Maunakea Street in Chinatown, where elderly women string flowers by hand to make leis. A lei of ginger wrapped inside orchids will perfume your room, and you, for days. Find a selection at **Pauahi Leis & Flowers** (1145 Maunakea Street; 808-521-6156). In Chinatown you can also find stands with luscious seasonal fruits and wander in and out of shops selling hundreds of different kinds of beads.

3 *The Perfect Hat* 5 p.m.

Everyone needs a good hat to protect against the unforgiving Hawaiian sun. You can pick up comfortable, broad-brimmed, straw gardening hats in just about any Honolulu hardware store. But why not indulge in luxury with a hand-woven one-of-a-kind Panama hat from **Newt at the Royal** (2259 Kalakaua Avenue; newtattheroyal.com)? Part of the Royal Hawaiian Hotel, Newt's sells Sombreros Montecristi, among the world's finest Panama hats, made not in Panama but in Ecuador. Napoleon, Theodore and Franklin Roosevelt, Truman Capote, and Cameron Diaz have all worn Sombreros Montecristi. The classic fedora is about $525; the finest, over $15,000.

4 *The Serenade That Delivers* 6 p.m.

It may seem corny, but a late afternoon mai tai at **House Without a Key** (2199 Kalia Road; halekulani.com), in the seafront garden at the Halekulani Hotel, is perfection. Even the most jaded travelers fall under the spell of the Hawaiian music and swaying hula dancer. But if it's trendiness you're after, try **L'Aperitif at La Mer**, in the same hotel, where the cocktails have been curated by Colin Field from the Ritz in Paris and the feel is classic and formal, with sumptuous floral arrangements, Art Deco wood carvings, and bartenders in white coats. A barefoot walk along Waikiki beach, with its pillowy white sand, follows naturally. Even locals who stay away from touristy Waikiki find it magical to jump into the water there to watch the sunset.

OPPOSITE Sandy Beach Park near Honolulu.

BELOW Waikiki, the gorgeous beach that made Honolulu a world-famous vacation spot, is flanked by high-rise hotels as it curves toward Diamond Head.

5 *Sushi Sublime* 8 p.m.

There are designer sushi restaurants in Honolulu where the waiters bark at you and order you not to linger too long over your raw fish. Then there's **Yanagi Sushi** (762 Kapiolani Boulevard; yanagisushi-hawaii. com; $$), comfortable and unpretentious. Start with a classic like the spicy tuna roll or try the divinely fresh and buttery toro (ahi belly) sushi, the price of which changes depending on season and availability. If you're feeling adventurous, try the broiled sea urchin, a local favorite.

SATURDAY

6 *Paradise by the Sea* 9 a.m.

Doris Duke, the American tobacco heiress, called **Shangri La** (shangrilahawaii.org), her home at the base of Diamond Head, "a Spanish-Moorish-Persian-Indian complex." She filled this 14,000-square-foot Islamic flight of fantasy with tiles from Iran, inlaid mother-of-pearl wooden chests from Syria, ceramics from Moorish Spain, marble mosaics from India, embroideries from Central Asia, and painted ceilings from Morocco. Guided tours must be reserved ahead, and they begin and end with a 20-minute shuttle ride from the **Honolulu Museum of Art** (900 South Beretania Street). Also included is a visit to the sumptuous and exotic Mughal Garden, styled after the royal gardens of India, which Duke visited during her 1935 honeymoon voyage.

7 *Asian Repast* Noon

Casual and spacious, **The Pig and the Lady** (83 North King Street; thepigandthelady.com; $$) in the Pacific Gateway Center in downtown Honolulu, is the place to go for an inventive, filling meal, espe-

cially if you like Vietnamese and Asian fare. Try the vegetarian pho, ginger beer, and one of the tempting desserts.

8 *The Magic of Wood* 2 p.m.

At **Nohea Gallery** (2424 Kalakaua Avenue; noheagallery.com), wood is celebrated in beautifully made items, including bowls, calabashes, and boxes by local master turners in woods like koa, mango, and macadamia. Koa, sometimes called Hawaiian mahogany, was used extensively in the Iolani Palace. Mark Twain wrote about the beauty of koa wood in his letters. A bowl can cost several hundred dollars, but you can also find affordable gifts here like green sea turtles in glazed ceramic and stone. They bring good luck, as the sea turtle swims forward, never backward.

9 *Down at the Cove* 3 p.m.

The hike down to hidden **Halona Beach Cove** (8450 Kalanianaole Highway, between Hanauma Bay and Sandy Beach), also known as Cockroach Cove, is

steep and rocky, so wear rubber-soled shoes. Expert divers will be tempted to plunge off the volcanic cliffs into the pure waters below. Less experienced swimmers can sunbathe and admire the view.

10 *Fit for a President* 7:30 p.m.

You too can dine like Barack and Michelle Obama, who were seen at **Alan Wong's** (1857 South King Street; alanwongs.com; $$$$) while President Obama was in office. Specialties of the evening may include the "Soup and Sandwich," a two-color Big Island tomato soup and grilled cheese sandwich with foie gras and kalua pig; ginger-crusted onaga; or the

OPPOSITE ABOVE Diamond Head, the unmissable landmark and symbol of Oahu, rises above Kapiolani Park.

OPPOSITE BELOW Shangri La, the home of the tobacco heiress Doris Duke, reflects her fascination with Islamic art.

president's favorite dish, twice-cooked soy-braised short ribs. Later, mellow out at small, dark, and crowded **Jazz Minds** (1661 Kapiolani Boulevard; honolulujazzclub.com).

SUNDAY

11 *A Spa Without Walls* 11 a.m.

Embrace Honolulu with vigor at **Kapiolani Park** (3840 Paki Avenue), unmissable at the foot of Diamond Head, the volcanic tuff cone and landmark the Hawaiians named Leahi. Work up a sweat with the joggers and rugby players while white terns soar above the ironwoods. Top that off with a swim across the road at the beach fronting the New Otani Kaimana Beach Hotel (2863 Kalakaua Avenue), and an open-air lunch at **Barefoot Beach Cafe** (2699 Kalakaua Avenue; barefootbeachcafe.com; $), a few minutes' walk away.

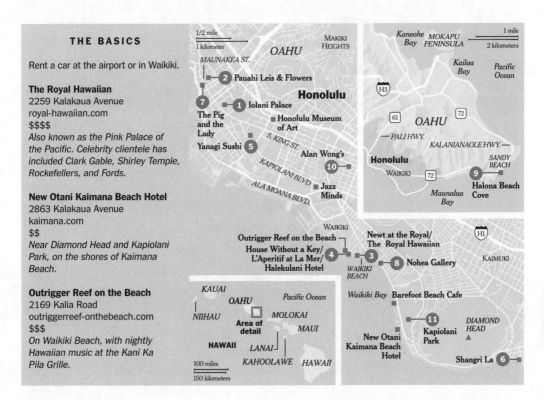

THE BASICS

Rent a car at the airport or in Waikiki.

The Royal Hawaiian
2259 Kalakaua Avenue
royal-hawaiian.com
$$$$
Also known as the Pink Palace of the Pacific. Celebrity clientele has included Clark Gable, Shirley Temple, Rockefellers, and Fords.

New Otani Kaimana Beach Hotel
2863 Kalakaua Avenue
kaimana.com
$$
Near Diamond Head and Kapiolani Park, on the shores of Kaimana Beach.

Outrigger Reef on the Beach
2169 Kalia Road
outriggerreef-onthebeach.com
$$$
On Waikiki Beach, with nightly Hawaiian music at the Kani Ka Pila Grille.

Kailua

The guidebooks say Kailua is basically a beach. But there's a town wrapped around the beach, and, around that, a whole other side of the 600-square-mile island of Oahu — the windward side, a world away from Waikiki. Kailua is barely half an hour from Honolulu, but separated from it by a soaring ribbon of razorback mountains, the Koolau Range. The green lava wall is pierced near its summit by two sets of highway tunnels, like airlocks in time and space. You will probably come from the Honolulu side, which is dry and sunny, its postcard loveliness folded among high-rises, offices, airport, and freeways. Emerge on the Kailua side — greener, quieter, lower, and slower, with marshes and palms and perfect Kailua Bay.
— BY LAWRENCE DOWNES

FRIDAY

1 *View to Windward* 3 p.m.

On your way in, leave the freeway at the Pali Highway (Route 61) exit and drive north, climbing steadily with the green, fluted mountain walls closing in — silvered with mist and plunging waterfalls when it rains. When highway builders, in the 1950s, reached the knife-edged Koolau summit, or pali, they punched tunnels through it and all but did away with the meandering mountain-goat path down the other side, with its treacherous winds and rock slides. After you go through the second tunnel, the windward side is before you: lush terrain of old fishponds, streams, marshes, soft volcanic cinder cones, and the blue, isle-dotted Kailua Bay. Stop at the **Nuuanu Pali State Wayside** (hawaiistateparks.org), a lookout well-marked by signs. You're looking down here from a thousand-foot precipice, a view that dazzled Mark Twain. And this is where, in 1795, King Kamehameha's army, invaders from the Big Island, pushed the army of Chief Kalanikupule to the pali's brink. The only way out was to plummet, and hundreds did. A plaque recounts the battle.

2 *Beach First* 4 p.m.

Once you're in Kailua, waste no time getting to **Kailua Beach Park** (Kailua Road and South Kalaheo Avenue). As you walk toward the bay, you'll see a field of impossible blue, sky down to water, and a broad crescent beach. The sand is cottony and

cool by the naupaka shrubs at the top of the beach, sloping down to firm wet velvet under the foam. Overhead, great frigatebirds, 'iwa in Hawaiian, hover in the whipping trade winds. Don't look for surfers here: the waves are gentle, good for swimming and body-surfing. This is also a good place to get out on the water on a paddle board or in a sea kayak. **Kailua Sailboards and Kayaks** (130 Kailua Road; 808-262-2555; kailuasailboards.com) provides rentals and lessons.

3 *Ice and Spice* 6 p.m.

A five-minute walk from the park is **Island Snow** (130 Kailua Road; 808-263-6339; islandsnow.com), where President Barack Obama and his daughters come for shave ice when they're on vacation in Kailua. His favorite flavors are supposedly lime, guava-orange, and cherry. You might like the coconut, with sweetened azuki beans. It won't spoil your dinner, which you might want to have at **Saeng's Thai Cuisine** (315 Hahani Street; 808-263-9727; restauranteur.com/saengs; $), an attractive place with cloths on the tables, pad Thai and spring rolls on the menu, and Thai iced tea (herbal teas with cream and sugar). There's also a full bar.

OPPOSITE The Lanikai Pillbox Trail, a mildly strenuous hike leading up to a panoramic view and the remains of concrete coastal lookouts built in World War II.

BELOW A team of paddlers in a racing canoe in Kailua Bay. Outrigger canoe racing is a part of the Hawaiian Islands' living Polynesian heritage.

4 *Sunrise Islands* 5:30 a.m.

Get up before dawn for Pacific sunrise watching. If you have jet lag operating in your favor, it will be easy. When the spectacle is over, enjoy a swim on the quiet, nearly deserted beach. Even at 6 a.m. the water is bathtub warm. Lie on your back and contemplate **Flat Island** off to the right, close-in, temptingly swimmable, and the Mokulua islets, **Moku Nui** and **Moku Iki**, a kayak trip away. Girding the bay to the left is a humpbacked volcanic crater, the Mokapu Peninsula, looking like the snake that swallowed an elephant in *The Little Prince*. It's a United States Marine base that has served as Obama's vacation gym.

5 *Early Risers* 7 a.m.

Kailua is a morning town, and by now runners are on the beach and ambling couples are walking dogs and clutching cups of coffee. Hit **Kalapawai Market** (306 South Kalaheo Avenue; 808-262-4359; kalapawaimarket.com), near the park entrance, for Kona coffee, bagels, and the morning paper. Or take the short walk to **Cinnamon's** (315 Uluniu Street; 808-261-8724; $$) for an omelet, steak and eggs, or French toast. Locals head to **Moke's Bread and Breakfast** (27 Hoolai Place; 808-261-5565; facebook.com/MokesBreadandBreakfast) for its lilikoi pancakes, served with a sweet, tangy sauce.

6 *An Older Oahu* 10 a.m.

Kailua was a thriving population center before European contact, a playground for chiefs, rich in farming and fish. For a plunge into antiquity, visit **Ulupo Heiau** (hawaiistateparks.org), a massive temple built of lava stone perhaps 400 years ago. Once it was terraced with wooden altars and statues and sacrifices. The surviving platform, 150 feet by 140 feet with walls up to 30 feet high, is a staggering work of ancient hand-to-hand rock laying. Get there from the parking lot of the YMCA (1200 Kailua Road). For another hint of the original Hawaii, drive to

Ho'omaluhia Botanical Garden (45-680 Luluku Road, Kaneohe; 808-233-7323; honolulu.gov/parks/hbg), which is replanted in native species.

7 *Island Retail* Noon

There's not a lot of shopping in Kailua, but it's worth poking around amid the shops and lunch spots downtown. **BookEnds** (600 Kailua Road; 808-261-1996), in the Kailua Shopping Center, has an excellent section on Hawaiian history and guidebooks for bird- and fish-spotting. **Global Village** (539 Kailua Road; 808-262-8183; globalvillagehawaii.com) is one of the shops with clothing and jewelry that fit the island vibe, and homegrown places sell art and antiques.

8 *Some Like Waves* 2 p.m.

Investigate another beach. **Kalama Beach Park** (248 North Kalaheo Avenue) is far quieter and more secluded than Kailua Beach, and if you like bigger waves, you'll be happier here. Or head out to the beach at **Waimanalo**, a short drive into a more Hawaiian state of mind. Oahu's windward side has local fishermen, dancers, musicians, artists — native Hawaiian families rooted for generations, with names like Mahoe, Aluli, and Pahinui. In Waimanalo, some houses fly the Hawaiian sovereignty flag, salving wounds unhealed since the overthrow of the native kingdom by the United States in 1893.

9 *Beach Shack Cuisine* 7 p.m.

Another Obama family favorite is **Buzz's Original Steak House** (413 Kawailoa Road; 808-261-4661; buzzsoriginalsteakhouse.com), by Kailua Beach Park. Open since 1962, this breezy, festive spot is celebrated as much for its cocktails as for its grilled meat and fish.

10 *Above the Bay* 9 a.m.

Get an overview on the **Lanikai Pillbox Trail**, a short, mildly strenuous hike to a ridgeline along a smooth-sloped cinder cone just above Lanikai Beach (kailuachamber.com/beaches). Trailhead signs are near the entrance to **Mid Pacific Country Club** (266 Kaelepulu Drive). The red-dirt trail starts out

crumbly and steep. It's a dry, hot hike, with cactus flowers and pili grass and butterflies. All the water is below you: Kaelepulu Stream, leading to the bay; Kawainui Marsh, the island's largest; the cobalt blue beyond the reef. At the summit are the hulks of two concrete pillboxes built in World War II as coastal lookouts. They're a good place to rest, drink, soak it all in.

11 *Beach Farewell* Noon

Revive back in town with brunch at **Crepes No Ka Oi** (143 Hekili Street; 808-263-4088; crepesnokaoi.com; $$). You can choose sweet, savory, or both; breakfast crepes include eggs, cheese, and meat. Afterward, stop at the beach

for a last gathering of those sensations of surf and warmth, of sun squinting and salt smell, to take home to the mainland with you.

OPPOSITE Kalapawai Market, a place to stop for coffee, bagels, and the morning paper on the way to a day of sun and ocean at Kailua Beach Park.

ABOVE Playing in the warm waves of Kailua Bay. Each in its own way, both ocean and sky here are an impossible blue.

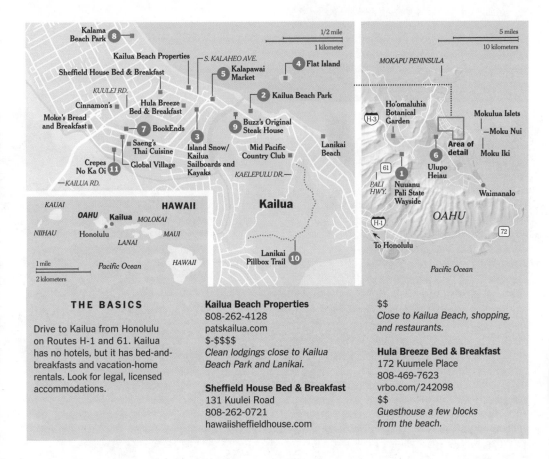

THE BASICS

Drive to Kailua from Honolulu on Routes H-1 and 61. Kailua has no hotels, but it has bed-and-breakfasts and vacation-home rentals. Look for legal, licensed accommodations.

Kailua Beach Properties
808-262-4128
patskailua.com
$-$$$$
Clean lodgings close to Kailua Beach Park and Lanikai.

Sheffield House Bed & Breakfast
131 Kuulei Road
808-262-0721
hawaiisheffieldhouse.com

$$
Close to Kailua Beach, shopping, and restaurants.

Hula Breeze Bed & Breakfast
172 Kuumele Place
808-469-7623
vrbo.com/242098
$$
Guesthouse a few blocks from the beach.

Kauai

Kauai is a hot spot, and its beautiful North Shore, where majestic mountains meet the surging sea, is hottest. Two or three decades ago, when Maui was the place, Kauaians grinned and thought, "Good, we've got ours and we're going to keep it that way." Now, residents make their livings catering to tourists and pampering the movie stars and magnates who are collecting North Shore trophy homes. But with 60,000 people, this is still the least populated of the four major Hawaiian islands, and its spacious white beaches ring a lush, untrammeled interior. Kauai roads may not be marked, and numbers are rarely posted, so it helps to memorize the two most important directional words — mauka, meaning toward the mountains, and makai, for toward the ocean. When you ask directions, be ready for an answer like this: "Go a mile to the big mango tree, take a left, and head makai."

— BY CHARLES E. ROESSLER

FRIDAY

1 *Big Stretch* 5 p.m.

Your drive from the airport, north and then west on the Kuhio Highway following the curves of the coast, will take you through small towns and lush tropical countryside, with the bonus of a few coastal views, all the way to Hanalei, the last town on the North Shore. (Don't be surprised if you also see a rooster or two — wild chickens, descendants of escapees from domesticated flocks, are abundant on Kauai.) But for the best reward, stay with the highway past Hanalei, all the way until it ends at Kauai's northwest tip. On the last stretch, the road narrows, shrinking to one-lane bridges over inlets and streams, against a misty backdrop of volcanic hills and cliffs. It ends at **Haena State Park** (hawaiistateparks.org), where reef-protected Kee Beach offers a serene spot to take in the remains of the day. If there's time and conditions are mellow, it's a short swim out to the reef for some quality snorkeling.

2 *Feast at Sunset* 6:30 p.m.

When you enter the **Princeville Resort** (5520 Ka Haku Road; 808-826-9644; princeville.com) make your way straight to the **Makana Terrace** ($$$) to take in the sweeping Hanalei Bay view. Settle in, order the signature cocktail, blending passion fruit and Champagne, and look out across the water. The mountains on the other side stood in for Bali Hai in the movie *South Pacific*. (Be sure to arrive before sunset.) You may also see some surfers if the waves are right — the North Shore is popular for surfing and all of its relatives — windsurfing, body-boarding, stand-up paddling. Stay for a buffet dinner ($$$), or move indoors in the hotel to the **Kauai Grill** ($$$), where the frequently changing menu includes entrees like soy-glazed short ribs with papaya-jalapeño purée. After dinner, walk down to the beach, spectacular under a full moon.

SATURDAY

3 *Morning by the Sea* 7:30 a.m.

Take a stroll on the Princeville walking path, paralleling the road leading into the planned community of **Princeville**, and look out over the Robert Trent Jones Jr. golf course. At this time of day there is a good chance of seeing double rainbows in the direction of the misty mountains.

OPPOSITE AND BELOW Hanalei Bay and the pier at Hanalei on a cloudy day in December. Magnates and movie stars have arrived, but Kauai is still the least populated of the four main Hawaiian islands.

4 *Botanicals* 9:30 a.m.

Limahuli Gardens in Haena (5-8291 Kuhio Highway; 808-826-1053; ntbg.org/gardens/limahuli), one of five National Tropical Botanical Gardens in

ABOVE Houses along the golf course in the North Shore planned community of Princeville.

BELOW Kauai is popular for surfing and all of its relatives —windsurfing, body-boarding, stand-up paddling.

OPPOSITE The cliffs of the Na Pali Coast, inaccessible by road. One way to see them is on a scenic helicopter ride.

the country, is in a valley where, 1,800 years ago, the first Hawaiians, with taro as their staple, developed a complex, hierarchical social system. On your self-guided tour, amid native plants like the ohia lehua tree and imports from Polynesia like breadfruit and banana trees, you can see the lava-rock terraces where taro was grown, fed by a series of fresh-water canals. You will also find exquisite vistas; the Polynesians chose a lovely spot. Guided tours are at 10 a.m.; reservations are required.

5 *Nene Spotting* 11 a.m.

Jutting out from the North Shore, the **Kilauea Lighthouse** (end of Kilauea Lighthouse Road; 808-828-0168; fws.gov/kilaueapoint) provided a life-saving beacon for the first trans-Pacific flight from the West Coast in 1927. Now it is part of the **Kilauea Point National Wildlife Refuge** and offers

both an unobstructed view of striking shoreline and a chance to spot dolphins, sea turtles, and whales. Birders who visit here check off species like the red-footed booby, the great frigatebird, and the nene, or Hawaiian goose.

6 *Saddle Up* Noon

Grab an ono (delicious) ahi wrap or other takeout lunch at **Kilauea Fish Market** (4270 Kilauea Lighthouse Road; 808-828-6244; $) to eat a few miles mauka as you listen to instructions for a two-hour horseback ride at the **Silver Falls Ranch** (2888 Kamookoa Road; 808-828-6718; silverfallsranch.com; call ahead to reserve in advance). Imagine what life must have been like for the cowboys who raised cattle for islanders in years past. As you meander through fern and eucalyptus toward Mount Namahana, the stately peak of an extinct volcano, listen for the small streams that trickle along, hidden by the ferns. This is the Kauai that most visitors miss and that most locals love.

7 *Kauaians' Favorite Beach* 4 p.m.

Another local favorite is **Kalihiwai Beach**, at the end of Kalihiwai Road, where a wide river empties into the ocean, and joggers, boogie boarders, and dog owners share a piece of the shore. There are no amenities but you can take a dip or body surf in the shore break. And this late in the afternoon, you shouldn't need sun block if you want to stretch out and catch a few Z's or watch the seabirds work the ocean.

8 *Laid-Back Fine Dining* 7 p.m.

Postcards (5-5075 Kuhio Highway; 808-826-1191; postcardscafe.com; $$-$$$) offers mostly organic food in the picturesque town of Hanalei. A recent meal started with taro fritters with pineapple ginger chutney, followed by grilled fish with peppered pineapple sage. The modest portions left room for a piece of banana and macadamia nut pie.

SUNDAY

9 *A Flyover* 9 a.m.

Get on board with **Sunshine Helicopters** (808-245-8881; sunshinehelicopters.com) at the tiny Princeville Airport on Highway 56 and soar into the heart of Kauai. The trip takes just 50 minutes, but you'll revisit it in dreams. You fly along the dark walls of Waialeale Crater, home to the Hawaiian gods and shoulder to the wettest spot on Earth (more than 450 inches of rain a year), Mount Waialeale (pronounced way-AH-lay-AH-lay). Among the waterfalls plunging around and below you as you sweep along the mountain faces is one that appeared in *Jurassic Park*. You soar over Waimea Canyon; knife into valleys once inhabited by the ancient Hawaiians, now home to wild pigs and goats; and glide along

the dramatic Na Pali Coast. Expect to pay in the neighborhood of $300 per person.

10 *Ship the Orchids Home* Noon

As you head to the Lihue Airport, stop in the town of Kapaa for high-end aloha shirts and skirts at **Hula Girl the Vintage Collection** (4-1340 Kuhio Highway; 808-822-1950; facebook.com/HulaGirlKauai); glass art at **Kela's** (4-1400 Kuhio Highway; 888-255-3527; glass-art.com); or works by Hawaii-based artists at

Aloha Images (4504 Kukui Street; 808-821-1382; alohaimages.com). At **Mermaids Cafe** (4-1384 Kuhio Highway; 808-821-2026; mermaidskauai.com; $$), order a focaccia sandwich or a tofu coconut curry plate. Make one last stop at **Orchid Alley** (4-1383 Kuhio Highway; 808-822-0486; orchidalleykauai.com) and have some tropical flowers shipped home to meet you on the mainland.

ABOVE Sunset at Kee Beach in Haena State Park, the last stop on the road west on the North Shore.

OPPOSITE The road to Kee narrows in the last stretch, shrinking to one-lane bridges over inlets and streams, against a misty backdrop of volcanic hills and cliffs.

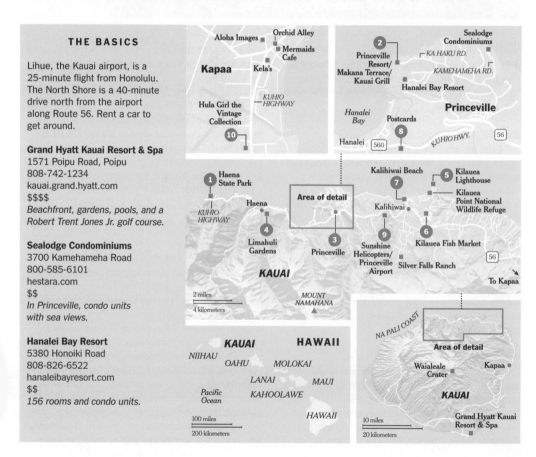

THE BASICS

Lihue, the Kauai airport, is a 25-minute flight from Honolulu. The North Shore is a 40-minute drive north from the airport along Route 56. Rent a car to get around.

Grand Hyatt Kauai Resort & Spa
1571 Poipu Road, Poipu
808-742-1234
kauai.grand.hyatt.com
$$$$
Beachfront, gardens, pools, and a Robert Trent Jones Jr. golf course.

Sealodge Condominiums
3700 Kamehameha Road
800-585-6101
hestara.com
$$
In Princeville, condo units with sea views.

Hanalei Bay Resort
5380 Honoiki Road
808-826-6522
hanaleibayresort.com
$$
156 rooms and condo units.

Aloha Images   Orchid Alley
■ Mermaids
Cafe
Kapaa   Kela's
KUHIO HIGHWAY
Hula Girl the Vintage Collection
10

2   Sealodge Condominiums
Princeville Resort/   KA HAKU RD.
Makana Terrace/   KAMEHAMEHA RD.
Kauai Grill
Hanalei Bay Resort
Hanalei Bay   Postcards   **Princeville**
8
Hanalei   560   KUHIO HWY.   56

1 Haena State Park   Kalihiwai Beach   **5** Kilauea Lighthouse
7   Kilauea Point National Wildlife Refuge
Haena   **Area of detail**
KUHIO HIGHWAY   Kalihiwai
4   **3**   **9**   **6**   Kilauea Fish Market
Limahuli Gardens   Princeville   Sunshine Helicopters/   Silver Falls Ranch   56
KAUAI   Princeville Airport
2 miles   MOUNT NAMAHANA   To Kapaa
4 kilometers   ▲

KAUAI   **HAWAII**
NIIHAU
OAHU   MOLOKAI
LANAI   MAUI
Pacific   KAHOOLAWE
Ocean
HAWAII
100 miles
200 kilometers

NA PALI COAST
Area of detail
Waialeale Crater   Kapaa
KAUAI
10 miles   Grand Hyatt Kauai Resort & Spa
20 kilometers

Maui

*"I went to Maui to stay a week and remained five,"
Mark Twain wrote in 1866. Whether lazing on a warm
sugary beach, gazing awestruck at a Haleakala sunrise,
or snorkeling to the song of humpback whales, visitors
to Maui today would likely feel the same. And while it
is known for its sparkling coastline and fertile green
interior, Hawaii's second-largest island appeals equally
to the urbane. Resorts hugging the south and west
shores claim some of the state's finest restaurants,
shops, and spas. A thriving arts community keeps
culture and creativity in high gear. In upcountry
Maui, on the slopes of the 10,000-foot Haleakala, you
can sample just-picked fruit or walk among fields of
lavender. Mark Twain had it right: it's not an easy
island to leave.* — BY JOCELYN FUJII

FRIDAY

1 *Beauty and the Beach* 2:30 p.m.

Tucked between the condo-studded town of Kihei
and the upscale resort of Wailea, the white-sand beach
of **Keawakapu** is south Maui's hidden jewel. Lined with
lavish Balinese- and plantation-style homes, this half-
mile playground has gentle waves, talcum-soft sands,
and free public parking along South Kihei Road. If it's
winter when you take a dip there, listen for the groans
and squeaks of the humpback whale, a haunting,
mystifying song.

2 *Drive-by Birding* 4 p.m.

For a glimpse of Maui's remarkable biodiversity,
take a stroll on the boardwalk at the **Kealia Pond
National Wildlife Refuge** (Milepost 6, Mokulele
Highway 311; 808-875-1582; fws.gov/kealiapond),
a 700-acre natural wetland and seabird sanctuary.
Among the birds that shelter here are endangered
Hawaiian stilts, black-crowned night herons, and
Hawaiian coots, as well as migrating birds like
ruddy turnstones.

3 *Fresh and Italian* 6 p.m.

The owners of a popular former Maui pizzeria
took their business upscale with **Matteo's Osteria**
(161 Wailea Ike Place, Wailea; 808-891-8466;
matteosmaui.com; $$), a wine bar and cafe offering
dozens of wines by the glass and a variety of Italian
dishes from spaghetti Bolognese (with beef from

Maui cattle) to local ahi with Calabrese tapenade.
The locals who loved the pizza can still find it
at lunch.

4 *Fine Arts* 7 p.m.

The stellar collection of contemporary art
(including Jun Kaneko, Toshiko Takaezu, and a bevy
of island superstars) at **Four Seasons Resort Maui
at Wailea** (3900 Wailea Alanui Drive; 808-874-8000;
fourseasons.com/maui) is reason enough to go there.
Add designer cocktails, live Hawaiian music, hula, and
jazz in the open-air Lobby Lounge, and it becomes a
seduction. Take the self-guided audio tour through
some of the resort's nearly 300-piece art collection,
then settle in for martinis and musical magic at the bar
by the grand piano. Live nightly entertainment covers
a gamut of musical tastes. (If you want a romantic
view, time your visit to catch the setting sun.)

SATURDAY

5 *Upcountry Adventures* 9 a.m.

Jump start your morning at **Grandma's Coffee
House** in the village of Keokea (9232 Highway 37, or
Kula Highway; 808-878-2140; grandmascoffee.com),
on the slopes of Haleakala volcano. On a wooden deck
with million-dollar views, sip Grandma's Original

OPPOSITE A windy beach on Maui, an island known for its
sparkling coastline and fertile green interior.

BELOW Kula Country Farm Stand sells just-picked fruit, like
pineapple and guavas, along with homemade mango bread.

Organic, an espresso roasted blend from the family's fifth-generation coffee farm. Then move on to the **Kula Country Farm Stand** (Highway 37, or Kula Highway, past Mile Marker 13, across from Rice Park; 808-878-8381; kulacountryfarmsmaui.com), a green-and-white produce stand selling just-picked fruit. Here's a chance to pick up fresh mangos (in season), rare pineapple guavas, and homemade mango bread before heading to lavender fields a few twists and turns away. With its view, acres of lavender, and fragrant jellies, scones, potions, and creams, **Ali'i Kula Lavender Farm** (1100 Waipoli Road; 808-878-3004; aklmaui.com) is a multisensory delight.

6 *Hot Art* Noon

Art is hot in **Makawao**, the cowboy town turned art colony that is about 1,600 feet above sea level on the slopes of Haleakala. Here you will find old wooden storefronts, mom-and-pop restaurants, chic boutiques, and hippie herb shops. At **Hot Island Glass** (3620 Baldwin Avenue; 808-572-4527; hotislandglass. com), the furnace burns hot and glass-blowing is performance art as molten glass evolves into jelly-fish, bowls, and oceanic shapes. Next door, Maui artists display their work in the airy plantation-style space of **Viewpoints Gallery** (3620 Baldwin Avenue; 808-572-5979; viewpointsgallerymaui.com).

7 *Put the Top Down* 3 p.m.

The hourlong drive from Maui's hilly upcountry to Lahaina, a popular resort town on the island's west coast, provides nonstop entertainment. With the shimmering Pacific on your left and the chiseled valleys of the West Maui Mountains to the right, you will be hard-pressed to keep your eyes on the road. Once you reach **Black Rock**, a lava outcropping north of Lahaina in the resort named Kaanapali, you'll find equally compelling underwater sights.

RIGHT Jumping off the cliffs of Black Rock, a lava outcropping just north of Lahaina.

Grab a snorkel and explore this Atlantis-like world of iridescent fish, spotted eagle rays, and giant green sea turtles.

8 *Farm to Fork* 7:30 p.m.

Peter Merriman of **Merriman's Kapalua** (One Bay Club Place; 808-669-6400; merrimanshawaii.com; $$$) is a pioneer in Hawaii regional cuisine, a culinary movement blending international flavors with local ingredients. The oceanfront restaurant features jaw-dropping views of Molokai island, and the menu highlights local ingredients, whether chèvre from upcountry goats, Maui lehua taro cakes, or line-caught fish from nearby waters. Look for kalua pig ravioli or wok-charred ahi so fresh that it tastes as if it were cooked on the beach. With the opening of his newer Monkeypod Kitchen in Wailea (monkeypodkitchen. com), featuring handcrafted beers and food (house-made hamburger buns, made-from-scratch pies and juices), Merriman has both coastlines covered.

9 *Tiki Torches* 9 p.m.

The old Hawaii—tikis and plumeria trees around buildings without marble and bronze—is elusive in today's Hawaii, but you'll find it at **Kaanapali Beach Hotel**'s oceanfront **Tiki Courtyard**, where the **Tiki Bar** (2525 Kaanapali Parkway; 808-667-0163; kbhmaui.com) offers authentic Hawaiian entertainment nightly. Hula by Maui children, lilting Hawaiian music by local entertainers, and the outdoor setting under the stars are a winning combination, especially when warmed by genuine aloha.

SUNDAY

10 *Make It to Mala* 9 a.m.

Brunch at **Mala Ocean Tavern** (1307 Front Street, Lahaina; 808-667-9394; malaoceantavern.com; $$) is like being on the ocean without leaving land. At this casual restaurant, you're practically sitting on the water, enjoying huevos rancheros with black beans or lamb sausage Benedict while dolphins frolic in the ocean and turtles nibble at the shore. Ask for a table outdoors.

11 *Fly Like an Eagle* 11 a.m.

For an adrenaline finish, head to the heights of West Maui, where **Kapalua Ziplines** (500 Office Road; 808-756-9147; kapaluaziplines.com) offers an unusually long zip-line course. Beginners need not

fear, as the two-and-a-half-hour zip (about $170) requires virtually no athleticism. The four-hour trip (about $190) is not for the weak-kneed. The zip line takes you over bamboo forests, gulches, and ridges, with the luscious coastline in the distance.

OPPOSITE ABOVE Find a touch of the old Hawaii — tikis and plumeria trees under the stars — at Kaanapali Beach Hotel's Tiki Bar. The lilting Hawaiian music is genuine.

ABOVE At Black Rock, grab a snorkel. Below the surface are iridescent fish, spotted eagle rays, and giant turtles.

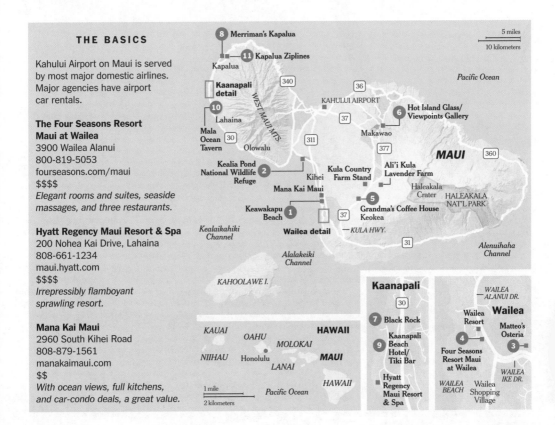

THE BASICS

Kahului Airport on Maui is served by most major domestic airlines. Major agencies have airport car rentals.

The Four Seasons Resort Maui at Wailea
3900 Wailea Alanui
800-819-5053
fourseasons.com/maui
$$$$
Elegant rooms and suites, seaside massages, and three restaurants.

Hyatt Regency Maui Resort & Spa
200 Nohea Kai Drive, Lahaina
808-661-1234
maui.hyatt.com
$$$$
Irrepressibly flamboyant sprawling resort.

Mana Kai Maui
2960 South Kihei Road
808-879-1561
manakaimaui.com
$$
With ocean views, full kitchens, and car-condo deals, a great value.

Molokai

You've got to really want to go to Molokai, a steppingstone Hawaiian island between Oahu and Maui. Its stunning beaches and rugged jungle interior invite exploration, and the tragic tale of its leper colony, where native Hawaiians used to be summarily exiled, inspire an unavoidable curiosity. But hotel rooms are few, tourist amenities scarce, and developers actively discouraged. Yet for those who remember an older Hawaii — magical, sensuous, isolated — or for those who want to find some sense of how things were on Maui, the Big Island, and Kauai before they were drawn into the hustle and flow of Oahu, Molokai is more than worth the trouble. Its lifestyle is more traditionally Polynesian, its people reserved yet, just beneath the surface, warm and full of an ancient joie de vivre. — BY CHARLES E. ROESSLER

FRIDAY

1 *The Moccasin* 1 p.m.

Pick up your rental car in the lava-rock terminal of tiny **Hoolehua Airport**, in the center of Molokai, and drive west on Highway 460 to **Maunaloa**, an old cattle ranching settlement. You won't encounter much traffic on this 10 miles of road, or anywhere on Molokai, which has 7,400 residents. The island is shaped roughly like a moccasin, 10 miles wide and 38 miles long from east to west. While eastern Molokai has a wet climate and junglelike foliage, the west end is arid with scrub vegetation. But it is rich in Hawaii's mythical history. Puu Nana, east of Maunaloa, is revered as the birthplace of the hula, which its practitioners consider to be a sacred dance, and every May dancers arrive to celebrate it. Molokai is also famous for its kahuna, powerful priests who could either provide life-giving herbal remedies or pray a healthy person to death.

2 *Clear Waters* 3 p.m.

Go for a swim at tiny **Dixie Maru Beach** at the end of a string of idyllic beaches lining the west coast. Ignore the temptation to swim at **Papohaku,**

OPPOSITE AND RIGHT Kaluapapa National Historic Park, the former leper colony that forms the core of Molokai's story of beauty and tragedy. A limited number of visitors are allowed; they arrive by mule ride or on foot.

two gorgeous miles of 100-yard-wide sandy beach; it harbors danger from sharp hidden coral reefs and treacherous rip currents. Dixie Maru, not much more than a protected cove, is enticing in its own way: clear, deep-blue water with a calming undulation. If you take a careful walk over the lava rocks framing the bay's left side, you may spot a honu (a sea turtle) bobbing and weaving along the shoreline. A sprawling resort called Molokai Ranch dominates the area. It closed in 2008 after Molokai residents rejected one proposal for its expansion, but there is another to reopen it as a renewable energy operation.

3 *Try the Opakapaka* 6 p.m.

A bare-bones place reminiscent of a '50s diner, with old Coca-Cola decals on the wall, the **Kualapuu Cookhouse** (102 Farrington Avenue, Highway 470, Kualapuu; 808-567-9655; $$-$$$) is a Molokai institution, serving fresh fish, beef, pork, and chicken dishes. Mahi-mahi and opakapaka (pink snapper) are local catches, subject to availability. The restaurant does not sell alcohol, but you can bring your own wine. Eat outdoors — you might share a picnic table with other customers who can tell you about life on the island. There may be live music — perhaps a ukelele and a one-string, gut-bucket bass — but be warned: the restaurant closes at 8 p.m.

SATURDAY

4 *Island Market* 10 a.m.

Saturday morning offers an opportunity to mix with the locals at the **Molokai Farmers Market** (Ala

Malama Street) in what passes for a downtown in tiny Kaunakakai, the island's largest town. On a short street lined with stands, browse in a convivial, relaxed atmosphere for papaya and poi, T-shirts, animal carvings, and shell jewelry. Molokai never surrendered to tourist-first faux aloha spirit: the people here are genuine. They call Molokai the Friendly Island, but it can turn into the surly island to the outsider who ignores local protocol. The outdoor market is an opportunity to take in the local color and meet the locals on neutral ground.

5 *Fishponds and Spears* Noon

Have lunch at **Molokai Pizza** (15 Kaunakakai Place, just off Highway 460, Kaunakakai; 808-553-3288), which boasts the best pan pizza on the island, along with deli sandwiches on its own bread. Then set out to explore the south shore, driving east from Kaunakakai on Route 450, the East Kamehameha V Highway. In the first 20 miles you'll see 19th-century churches and some of the 60 ancient fishponds that dominate the southern coast. The Hawaiians who built

ABOVE The verdant, isolated Halawa Valley.

OPPOSITE ABOVE An ancient Molokai fishpond.

OPPOSITE BELOW A fisherman casts his net on a school of fish in Honouli Wai Bay.

them seven or eight centuries ago used lava rocks to surround and trap fish attracted to underground streams. At Mile Marker 20, stop at **Murphey's Beach**, a popular snorkeling spot. Watch locals spearfishing for dinner while children frolic on the sand, shouting and laughing.

6 *Old Ways* 2 p.m.

The last seven miles of the trip to the east end rival Maui's famous Road to Hana in adventure and beauty. The pulse quickens as you drive inches away from the ocean on the one-lane road. Inland views are a window onto a traditional Hawaii. Foliage is dense, and families have their horses and goats tied close to the road. On many of their one-acre plots, gardens and fruit trees vie for space with chickens, dogs, rusted car skeletons, and modest homes. Fishing nets and hunting accouterments, including dog kennels, attest to the survival of old ways of finding food; wild pigs, goats, and deer are the hunters' prey.

7 *The Far East* 3 p.m.

The road ends at **Halawa Park** in the spectacular Halawa Valley, surrounded by mountains and ocean. The isolated beaches in the bay are good for a dip in summer and great for big-wave surfing in winter. In the verdant valley, an ancient complex of terraces and taro patches, built by the Polynesians who first settled this island, helped sustain life on Molokai

from about 650 A.D. to the mid-20th century, when other job opportunities lured residents away. What remained of the taro was destroyed by a tsunami in 1946 and floods in the 1960s. You can learn about attempts to restore it — and can hike to lovely Moalua Falls — if you have some extra time and arrange a private tour; book at **Hotel Molokai** in Kaunakakai. On your drive back, go a half-mile or so past Kaunakakai to **Kaiowea Park** to see the **Kapuaiwa Coconut Grove**, a cluster of tall coconut palms that remain from 1,000 of their kind planted here in the 1860s by King Kamehameha V.

8 *Night Life* 7 p.m.

Find Molokai's weekend social scene at the casual **Hiro's Ohana Grill** at the **Hotel Molokai** (1300 Kamehameha V Highway, Kaunakakai; 808-660-3400; hotelmolokai.com; $$). Ask about the fresh catch of the day or order a local dish like teriyaki chicken and listen to live music, likely to feature ukeleles. The adjoining bar, only yards away from the tranquil Pacific, conveys a feeling of timelessness as you sway in a hammock, catching the slight breeze. If you're still out and about at 10, join the line at **Kanemitsu Bakery** (79 Ala Malama Avenue; 808-553-5855) waiting for hot French bread. It's what's happening Saturday night in Kaunakakai.

SUNDAY

9 *The Colony* 10 a.m.

Drive up Highway 470 to the north shore. Much of it is impenetrable, with soaring cliffs pitched

straight down 2,000 feet. In the center is **Kalaupapa National Historic Park** (nps.gov/kala), a small peninsula where native Hawaiian victims of leprosy were dropped off by ship and isolated. It was also the home of Father Damien, now St. Damien of Molokai, the 19th-century priest and Hawaiian folk hero who worked with the lepers until he contracted their disease and died. The unique community that developed there has a small-town New England feel, with tidy churches and modest homes belying past horrors. It is open to small numbers of visitors by permit; they can hike a cliff trail down or go with **Molokai Mule Ride** (Kalae Highway, Kualapuu; 808-567-6088; muleride.com) Monday through Saturday. Get a good

view from the **Kalaupapa Overlook**, 1,700 feet above the peninsula in **Palaau State Park**. If you know the story, the sight of the village below sets the mind racing with searing images of lepers being tossed overboard offshore and ordered to sink or swim to the peninsula—never to leave again.

ABOVE Ignore the temptation to swim at Papohaku, two gorgeous miles of 100-yard-wide sandy beach. It harbors danger from sharp hidden coral reefs and rip currents.

OPPOSITE The grave of Father Damien, now St. Damien of Molokai, at Kalaupapa National Historic Park. He devoted his life to the people exiled to a leper colony there.

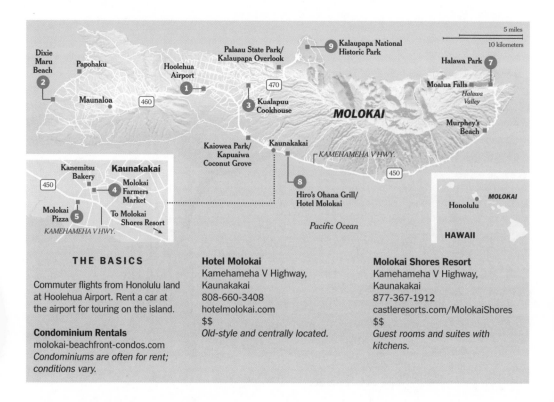

THE BASICS

Commuter flights from Honolulu land at Hoolehua Airport. Rent a car at the airport for touring on the island.

Condominium Rentals
molokai-beachfront-condos.com
Condominiums are often for rent; conditions vary.

Hotel Molokai
Kamehameha V Highway,
Kaunakakai
808-660-3408
hotelmolokai.com
$$
Old-style and centrally located.

Molokai Shores Resort
Kamehameha V Highway,
Kaunakakai
877-367-1912
castleresorts.com/MolokaiShores
$$
Guest rooms and suites with kitchens.

The Oregon Coast

You could drive down the southern third of the Oregon coast in a couple of hours, and you'd think, How beautiful! Highway 101, the Oregon Coast Highway, hugs the shoreline enough to give you views of the sand and windblown trees, rocks and crashing waves that give this stretch its fame. But to instill memories that will make these gorgeous seascapes your own, plan a leisurely weekend of detours and side trips with plenty of time to stop at the beaches and lighthouses, gulp the salt air, and kick back in the harbor towns.
— BY DAVID LASKIN

FRIDAY

1 *Park Land* 1 p.m.

In North Bend, leave Highway 101 to pick up Route 540 and head south as it leaves city streets behind to become the **Cape Arago Highway**. You'll descend quickly into Charleston, a tiny place with a working harbor, a fish-and-chips shack, and tidal shallows raked by whitecaps on windy days. The road—despite its "highway" designation, it's only a few miles long—leads from there to a series of three adjoining oceanside state parks (oregonstateparks.org). Stop at the first, **Sunset Bay**, for beachcombing and your first photo ops, but don't be tempted to stay too long. You'll need time at the next one, **Shore Acres**, to sniff the luxe ivory Elina roses in the well-kept garden of a former private estate perched atop a forbidding cliff.

2 *Cape Arago* 3 p.m.

The last stop on the road, before it loops around to point you back toward Charleston, is **Cape Arago State Park**, where you'll find the rocky headland, topped by a lighthouse, that all of this has been leading to. Hike on one of the cove trails down to the beach and look for seals and tidepools. When you've seen enough, drive back to Charleston and pick up Seven Devils Road, which will lead you to West Beaver Hill Road to complete the loop back to Highway 101.

OPPOSITE Highway 101 winds close to the water's edge along rocky coast south of Cape Sebastian State Park.

RIGHT Surf fishing in Port Orford, a town where every street seems to end in a view of the sea.

3 *Old Town Wine List* 4 p.m.

Find a little West Coast slice of Nantucket in **Bandon**, a town of 3,100 people with terrific beaches to the west and the silvery estuary of the Coquille River to the north and east. Check out the shops and galleries in the compact Old Town before heading to dinner at the **Alloro Wine Bar** (375 Second Street Southeast; 541-347-1850; allorowinebar.com; $$-$$$). It serves superb dishes like feather-light ravioli, sautéed local snapper, and fresh fava beans. Relax over a Walla Walla cabernet or another of the Northwest vintages on the wine list.

SATURDAY

4 *Sea Stacks* 10 a.m.

Take the lightly trafficked **Beach Loop Road** south of town. It parallels the coast for four and a half miles, and although there are a few too many cottages and motels, you forget all about them when you stop to wander on the beach amid fantastically carved sea stacks and watch colorful kites slashing against the sky. After the loop rejoins Highway 101, follow it as it leaves the coast for an inland stretch past ranches and cranberry bogs. When you come to Route 250, the Cape Blanco Road, turn right and drive through rolling sheep pastures reminiscent of Cornwall. It's not far to the sea.

5 *Blown Away* 11 a.m.

State parks are strung along this coast, and you can't hit them all. But **Cape Blanco** is a must-stop—the farthest west point on the Oregon coast, the state's oldest lighthouse, one of the windiest spots in the United States. Be prepared for that wind as you walk toward the stark circa-1870 lighthouse. The view at the headland is worth it, so stand and stare as long as you can withstand the blast.

6 *On the Edge* 1 p.m.

Imagine the shabby picturesque waterfront of an outer Maine island fused onto the topographic drama of Big Sur: that's **Port Orford**. Mountains covered with Douglas firs plunge toward the ocean, and you feel how truly you are at the continent's edge. The town itself has a salty, dreamy, small-town vibe; every street ends in blue sea framed by huge dark green humps of land. Look around and then find lunch. **Griff's on the Dock** (490 Dock Road; 541-332-8985; $$) and the **Crazy Norwegian's** (259 Sixth Street; 541-332-8601; $$) are good bets for fish and chips.

7 *End of the Rogue* 3 p.m.

The Rogue River, known for the whitewater along its 200-mile journey from the Cascades, looks wide, tame, and placid as it meets the sea in **Gold Beach**. The bridge that carries Highway 101 over it is a beauty, multiple-arched, elegant, and vaguely Deco. The city isn't particularly inviting—utilitarian motels hunkering along the strand, a drab dune obstructing views of the ocean. But don't miss the well-stocked **Gold Beach Books** (29707 Ellensburg Avenue; 541-247-2495; oregoncoastbooks.com), which in addition to covering every literary genre has an art gallery and coffee house. **Jerry's Rogue River Museum** (29985 Harbor

ABOVE The harbor in Crescent City, a town just south of the Oregon state line in California.

RIGHT Driftwood piled up by the surf at a beach along Beach Loop Drive in Bandon, Oregon.

Way; 541-247-4571; roguejets.com) is worth a look around and has an unusual feature—you can book a jetboat trip on the Rogue there. There's also good hiking just outside town at **Cape Sebastian State Park**, with miles of trails and views down the coast to California.

8 *Gold Beach Dining* 7 p.m.

If you can get a reservation, head out of town for dinner at the **Tu Tu' Tun Lodge** (96550 North Bank Rogue River Road; 541-247-6664; tututun.com; $$$), a fishing resort a few miles upstream on the Rogue. If you're staying in town, try **Spinner's Seafood Steak and Chop House** (29430 Ellensburg Avenue; 541-247-5160; spinnersrestaurant.com; $$$), which features hefty portions of entrees like grilled duck breast, wild salmon, and prime rib.

SUNDAY

9 *More and More Scenic* 9 a.m.

Have a filling breakfast at the **Indian Creek Café** (94682 Jerry's Flat Road; 541-247-0680) and get back on the road. From here on it just keeps getting better. About 14 miles south of Gold Beach you will enter **Samuel H. Boardman State Scenic Corridor**, a nine-mile section along Highway 101 with turnouts overlooking natural stone arches rising from the waves, trailheads accessing the Oregon Coast Trail, and paths winding down to hidden beaches and tide pools. The scenic summa may be **Whaleshead Beach**, a cove with the mystical beauty of a Japanese scroll—spray blowing off the crest of a wave,

massive sea rocks dazzled in the westering sun, and maybe a kid or two making tracks in the sand.

10 *Tsunami Zone* 11 a.m.

Glance around in **Brookings**, by far the toastiest town on the Oregon coast. Its curious microclimate — winter temperatures in the 80s are not unheard of — is a point of pride, as is its park devoted to preserving native wild azaleas. Then push on south into California to **Crescent City**, a place distinguished by its unfortunate history. In 1964 it was struck by a tsunami that destroyed 300 buildings and killed 11 residents. The vulnerability remains in this region of the Pacific coast. In 2011, the harbors in both Brookings and Crescent City

were severely damaged by the tsunami that swept away cities in coastal Japan. You're tantalizingly close to California's majestic redwoods here, so turn a few miles inland and make a final stop at **Jedediah Smith Redwoods State Park**, where you can wander among 200-foot-tall trees. Their majesty matches that of the rocky windswept coast you've just left behind.

ABOVE The Patterson Bridge in Gold Beach.

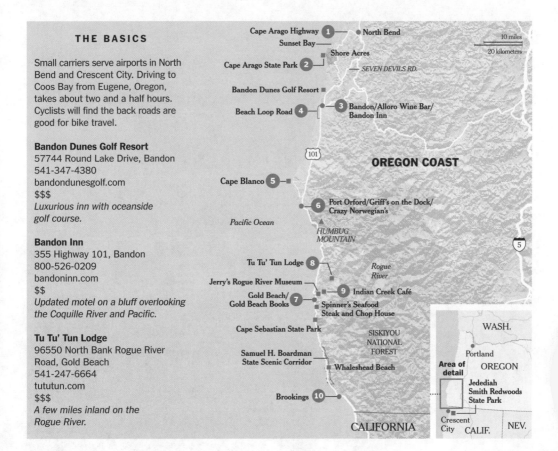

THE BASICS

Small carriers serve airports in North Bend and Crescent City. Driving to Coos Bay from Eugene, Oregon, takes about two and a half hours. Cyclists will find the back roads are good for bike travel.

Bandon Dunes Golf Resort
57744 Round Lake Drive, Bandon
541-347-4380
bandondunesgolf.com
$$$
Luxurious inn with oceanside golf course.

Bandon Inn
355 Highway 101, Bandon
800-526-0209
bandoninn.com
$$
Updated motel on a bluff overlooking the Coquille River and Pacific.

Tu Tu' Tun Lodge
96550 North Bank Rogue River Road, Gold Beach
541-247-6664
tututun.com
$$$
A few miles inland on the Rogue River.

Portland

"Nice" is an adjective that Portland can't seem to shake. But below the fleece-clad and Teva-wearing exterior lurks a cool and refreshingly unneurotic city that marches to its own cosmopolitan beat. Truth is, Portland doesn't want to be Seattle, its highly caffeinated neighbor to the north. With less traffic, better public transportation, and Mount Hood in its backyard, this self-styled City of Roses doesn't stand in anybody's shadow. Its vibrant downtown overflows with urban pleasures like chic restaurants, funky nightclubs, and sprightly neighborhoods crackling with youthful energy. But nobody's boasting. That's another nice thing about Portland. — BY DAVID LASKIN

FRIDAY

1 *Fresh Orientation* 6 p.m.

The pastel roses peak in the late spring at the **International Rose Test Garden** (850 SW Rose Garden Way; 503-227-7033; rosegardenstore.org), but the blooms last for months and the view from this terraced hillside garden is fantastic year-round. Even if clouds keep you from seeing Mount Hood, you still get a bird's-eye view of colorful wood-frame houses surrounding a tidy grove of skyscrapers. Breathe in the pine-scented air and stretch your legs on the hillside paths of this precipitous chunk of green, five minutes from downtown by car, or 15 minutes on the efficient MAX Light Rail.

2 *Bistro Bird* 7:30 p.m.

Little Bird (219 SW Sixth Avenue; 503-688-5952; littlebirdbistro.com; $$) is the second Portland restaurant from a favorite Portland chef, Gabriel Rucker, less formal and more affordable than his flagship **Le Pigeon** (738 East Burnside Street; 503-546-8796; lepigeon.com; $$). Little Bird's bright dining room has a pressed-tin ceiling and lace window curtains, and the dishes brought to its tables are "more accessible for the everyday diner," in Rucker's words. The cuisine in both restaurants is French; at Little Bird, that may mean cassoulet,

OPPOSITE The city and its guardian peak, Mount Hood.

RIGHT Sunset on the Willamette River.

hanger steak with frites, crispy veal sweetbreads, or leek and Gruyère crepes with duxelles cream sauce, mushroom salad, and hazelnuts.

3 *Downtown Jazz* 9:30 p.m.

Portland night life offers choices from torchy lounges to high-decibel indie hang-outs. Jazz is represented by the **Jack London Revue** (529 SW Fourth Avenue; 866-777-8932; jacklondonrevue.com), where you'll see national stars like Vernon Reid and local legends like the drummer Mel Brown, whose career stretches back to Motown and the Supremes.

SATURDAY

4 *Market to Teahouse* 10 a.m.

Even if you can't stand handcrafted soaps, dangly earrings, gauzy scarves, chunky ceramics, fancy pet bowls, messy street food, and the people who make them, the **Portland Saturday Market** is worth visiting (portlandsaturdaymarket.com). Tucked under the Burnside Bridge, the market is a perfect starting point for a leisurely walk amid the cast-iron buildings of Old Town and into Chinatown. Drop in at stores like **Floating World Comics** (400 NW Couch Street; 503-241-0227; floatingworldcomics.com), which treats comic books as an art form, or the nearly century-old **John Helmer Haberdasher** (969 SW Broadway; 503-223-4976; johnhelmer.com), for headwear from berets to straw hats. Wend your way to the serene **Lan Su Chinese Garden** (239 NW Everett Street; 503-228-8131; lansugarden.org), and refuel with tea in the ornate teahouse beside Zither Lake.

5 *Walk to Lunch* Noon

Downtown Portland has about five neighborhoods, each with its own mood and flavor, but it isn't very big. In 20 minutes, you can walk from Chinatown in the northwest to the cultural district in the southwest. Which brings you to lunch. At **Southpark Seafood Grill & Wine Bar** (901 SW Salmon Street; 503-326-1300; southparkseafood.com; $$), you can plunk down at the bar for a quick meal and ask for sightseeing suggestions from the young downtown crowd. Seafood holds center stage; check the menu for fisherman's stew or fried calamari with spicy aioli.

6 *The Precious and the Peculiar* 1 p.m.

A few steps take you to **Portland Art Museum** (1219 SW Park Avenue; 503-226-2811; portlandartmuseum.org), which has an impressive collection of photographs. They run the gamut from 19th-century daguerreotypes to contemporary landscapes. Another strong point in the permanent collection are the Japanese scrolls from the Edo period. If your tastes run in a less edifying direction, head north to the **Freakybuttrue Peculiarium** (2234 NW Thurman Street; 503-227-3164; peculiarium. com), an oddities museum, gallery, and ice cream parlor founded in 1967, where you'll find gag gifts, insect candies, macabre art, and more. It's creepy and strange, and kids will love it.

7 *Roll Out of Town* 3 p.m.

Stash your stuff, don your Spandex and rent a bike at **Waterfront Bicycles** (10 SW Ash Street No. 100; 503-227-1719; waterfrontbikes.com) for a ride along the Willamette River. If you're feeling mellow, ride the three-mile loop that goes north on the Waterfront Bike Trail in **Tom McCall Waterfront Park**, across the river via the Steel Bridge to the **Vera Katz East Bank Esplanade**, and back across on the Hawthorne Bridge. For a tougher workout, stay on the East Bank Esplanade and continue south on the **Springwater Corridor** for an 18-mile ride through the city's semirural outskirts. The trail terminates at the town of Boring (its slogan: "An Exciting Place to Live"). A newer trail, in different territory, is the **Banks-Vernonia State Trail** (oregonstateparks.org), which begins in the town of Banks and proceeds 20 miles on former railroad beds, crossing two 80-foot-high trestles along the way. (For that one, you can pick up a bike at **Banks Bicycles** at 14175 Northwest Sellers Road; 503-596-2433; banksbicycles.com.)

8 *Oregonian Bistro* 8 p.m.

Stow the bike shorts back in your suitcase and follow up your outdoorsy afternoon with a more urbane Portland experience, a dinner that venerates Paris. **Bistro Agnes** (527 Southwest 12th Avenue; 503-222-0979; bistroagnes.com; $$$) lives up to the promise of its name with the feel—and menu—of a real Parisian bistro. Mussels, cassoulet, coq au vin, steak frites—it's all pretty much here, and executed well.

9 *Hang Out, Rock On* 10:30 p.m.

Check out the latest indie bands at **Doug Fir Lounge**, connected to the trendy Jupiter Hotel (830 East Burnside Street; 503-231-9663; dougfirlounge. com). It's a primo spot to hang out, drink good local beer, rub shoulders with the young and pierced, and catch emerging groups from all over the country. The room is surprisingly modern and woodsy for a dance club, with gold-toned lighting, a fire pit, and walls clad in Douglas fir logs.

SUNDAY

10 *Petit Déjeuner* 10 a.m.

For another taste of Paris, pop over to **St. Honoré Boulangerie** (2335 NW Thurman Street; 503-445-4342; sainthonorebakery.com; $-$$), a French-style bakery where Dominique Geulin bakes almond croissants, apricot tarts, and Normandy apple toast, a mix of French toast, brioche, and custard. The cafe is airy, with huge windows and lots of wicker. Equally important, the coffee is among the city's finest.

11 *City of Books* 11 a.m.

It says a lot about Portland that **Powell's City of Books** (1005 West Burnside Street; 503-228-4651;

powells.com) is one of the city's prime attractions —a bookshop so big that it provides maps to help shoppers find their way around. The dusty, well-lighted store is larger than many libraries, with 68,000 square feet of new and used books. Plan to stay a while.

OPPOSITE The Portland Saturday Market in full swing. Portland's vibrant downtown overflows with youthful energy.

ABOVE Comb the shelves at Powell's City of Books.

THE BASICS

Bicycling is encouraged. Excellent public transportation includes light rail to the airport.

The Nines
525 Southwest Morrison Street
877-229-9995
thenines.com
$$$
Cool design, including an art collection, in a downtown building.

Sentinel
614 SW 11th Avenue
503-224-3400
sentinelhotel.com
$$$
New incarnation of a landmark hotel.

Kennedy School
5736 NE 33rd Avenue
503-249-3983
mcmenamins.com/kennedyschool
$$
Stay in an old elementary school, with a chalkboard in your room.

To Banks Bicycles/
Banks-Vernonia State Trail

1/2 mile
1 kilometer

NW THURMAN ST.
Freakybuttrue Peculiarium
10
St. Honoré Boulangerie
405

NW FRONT AVE.
Portland
5

NW 23D AVE.
NW TENTH AVE.
W. BURNSIDE ST.

Lan Su Chinese Garden
STEEL BRIDGE
Vera Katz East Bank Esplanade
84

Little Bird 2
Powell's City of Books 11
Floating World Comics
Le Pigeon

Bistro Agnes 8
Sentinel
The Nines
Portland Saturday Market
4

WASHINGTON PARK
Jack London Revue 3
7
9

1
Southpark Seafood Grill & Wine Bar 5
John Helmer Haberdasher
Waterfront Bicycles
Doug Fir Lounge/ Jupiter Hotel

International Rose Test Garden
26
Portland Art Museum 6
East Bank Esplanade

HAWTHORNE BRIDGE

Tom McCall Waterfront Park
Springwater Corridor

WASHINGTON
10 miles
20 kilometers

Kennedy School
Columbia River
Willamette River

Area of detail
Portland
CASCADE RANGE
MOUNT HOOD
5
26

OREGON
Willamette River

The San Juan Islands

You could spend years getting to know the more than 170 San Juan Islands of Washington, but in a single weekend, it's easy to become acquainted with three of the biggest. Lopez, Orcas, and San Juan are jewels of the Pacific Northwest, great for sailing, kayaking, hiking, biking, diving, or just relaxing. Visit, and you'll find out how a quarrel over the killing of a farm animal in the 19th century nearly led to war, spot wildlife in a way you've probably never done before, and find yourself drifting onto island time. — BY BOB MACKIN

FRIDAY

1 *You and the Island* 2 p.m.

Make the pleasant passage by car ferry (206-464-6400; wsdot.wa.gov/ferries) from Anacortes on the mainland to quiet Lopez Island. The eternal lure of the San Juans is their landscapes of forests, hills, and fjords. Thanks to an active land preservation effort, there is plenty of terrain open to the public to explore, and Lopez has its share of beautiful spots. Take a walk at **Lopez Hill** (lopezhill.org), where a web of public trails winds past mossy conifers and madrona trees with peeling cinnamon-red bark, or at the spectacular **Watmough Bay Preserve** (sjclandbank.org/watmough-bay-preserve-lopez-island), where a path leads to a strip of beach on a wooded inlet.

2 *A Table by the Bay* 7 p.m.

Drive to Lopez Village for dinner. You can't go wrong at wisteria-draped **Ursa Minor** (210 Lopez Road; 360-622-2730; ursaminorlopez.com; $$), where the ever-changing menu offers a "creative agrarian Northwest cuisine" reflecting the bounty of the island, with an emphasis on local lamb, fish, wild berries, and garden vegetables. Dishes are small plates designed to be shared.

SATURDAY

3 *Sea to Summit* 9 a.m.

Start today's explorations on Orcas Island, at **Moran State Park** (3572 Olga Road, Olga; 360-376-2326; parks.state.wa.us/547/Moran). In the park is Mount Constitution, which at 2,409 feet is the highest point in the San Juans. The 15-minute drive to the top is full of hairpin turns on a narrow road. But if the

weather cooperates, you'll be rewarded with breathtaking views as far as Vancouver, British Columbia; the Cascade and Olympic ranges; and the islands and ships in Puget Sound. The park was granted to Washington in 1921 by Robert Moran, a shipbuilding magnate and former mayor of Seattle. He also had a mansion on Orcas, which you can visit at the **Rosario Resort & Spa** (1400 Rosario Road, Eastsound; 360-376-2222; rosarioresort.com). Moran built the house when doctors told him to retire early, but he wound up living to 86—thanks, it is said, to the serene beauty of Orcas Island.

4 *Some Pig* 11 a.m.

Take the boat to San Juan Island, home of the strange tale of the Pig War. In 1859, an American settler killed a pig belonging to the Hudson's Bay Company, the powerful British corporation that once controlled much of North America. Within two months, more than 400 American troops, dispatched to protect the settler from arrest, faced off against some 2,000 British soldiers, sailors, and marines. But no shots were fired. Small detachments from both nations remained until 1872, when Kaiser Wilhelm I, acting as arbitrator, awarded the islands to the United States, not British Canada. Today, the British and American camps make up the **San Juan Island National Historical Park** (360-378-2902; nps.gov/sajh). During summer, it comes alive as local history buffs don period costumes for historical recreations.

5 *Whale Watch, Minus Boat* 2 p.m.

Pack a picnic, keep binoculars handy, be patient. That's the three-pronged strategy for enjoying your time at **Lime Kiln Point State Park** (1567 Westside Road, Friday Harbor; 360-378-2044; parks.state. wa.us/540/Lime-Kiln-Point). The 36-acre park has Douglas fir, arbutus, and even cactuses along its forest trails. But from late spring to early fall, it may be the world's best place to see orca whales from land. Park your car in the lot and hike the trail to the rocky outcrop in the shadow of the Lime Kiln Point lighthouse. Set up your picnic on the rocks and watch for the shiny black and white orcas. If you're lucky,

OPPOSITE Sunset and serenity in the San Juans.

they'll come close enough so that they can also see you. If you miss a pod on parade, you're still likely to see seals and eagles. The lighthouse, built in 1919, is now a whale behavior research center. In summer, park staff members are often available to provide information on the whales and also offer evening tours of the lighthouse; day tours can be arranged.

6 *Purple Pleasure* 4 p.m.

Lavender farming has made its way to the San Juans, so ask if there's lavender oil available when you choose hot stone massage, Swedish massage, reiki, or all three at **Lavendera Massage** (285 Spring Street, Friday Harbor; 360-378-3637; lavenderamassage.com), ideal after a spell of hiking and sitting on rocks. When you've achieved blissful relaxation, make a visit to the **Pelindaba Lavender Farm** (45 Hawthorne Lane, off Wold Road; 360-378-4248; pelindabalavender.com), where you're welcome to tour the rippling purple fields in flowering season.

7 *San Juan Island Locavore* 6 p.m.

This is Washington, and salmon should be on the menu. Expect it at **Coho Restaurant** (120 Nichols Street, Friday Harbor; 360-378-6330; cohorestaurant.com; $$$), along with shellfish from the Straits of Juan de Fuca, meat from a Lopez Island farm, and local produce from several island growers. The desserts are house-made, and the wine list is filled with vintages from Washington, Oregon, and California.

8 *Sculptured Trail* 8 p.m.

A visit to the **San Juan Islands Sculpture Park** (9083 Roche Harbor Road, Roche Harbor; 360-370-0035; sjisculpturepark.com) is a great way to spend the late, late afternoon. Scattered along the trails are more than 100 sculptures (by artists from the Pacific Northwest and beyond) looking magical in their open-air setting as the light fades.

SUNDAY

9 *Whale Talk* 10 a.m.

A modest two-story building, the former Odd Fellows Hall in Friday Harbor is the home of the **Whale Museum** (62 First Street; 360-378-4710; whale-museum.org), a remarkable collection of whale photographs, skeletons, and even some brains. Take a few minutes to listen to the library of whale vocalizations in a phone booth.

ABOVE A ferry system, carrying both passengers and their cars, runs a busy schedule and keeps the islands connected with one another and tied to the mainland.

OPPOSITE Boats docked near Eastsound on Orcas Island.

10 *A Drink of Lavender* Noon

The proprietors of the lavender farm you visited yesterday have cleverly opened the **Pelindaba Lavender shop** in downtown Friday Harbor near the ferry terminal (150 First Street; 866-819-1911; pelindabalavender.com). The lavender-infused lemonade is the perfect drink to quaff on a summer day's cruise among the San Juans as you make your way back toward the mainland.

11 *Foodie Quest* 4 p.m.

If you have a full free day and a yen for dining at talked-about restaurants, once back on the mainland drive north from Anacortes to Bellingham, where you can catch the ferry to **Lummi Island**. (Although it's only a couple of miles by water from Lopez, there's no direct ferry connection to Lummi from there or any of the other San Juans.) Be sure you have a reservation made weeks in advance for dinner at the celebrated **Willows Inn** (2579 West Shore Drive, Lummi Island; 360-758-2620; willows-inn.com; $$$$). Dinner is prix fixe, much of the food comes from the island, and the presiding cook is Blaine Wetzel, a former chef at the wildly acclaimed Copenhagen restaurant Noma.

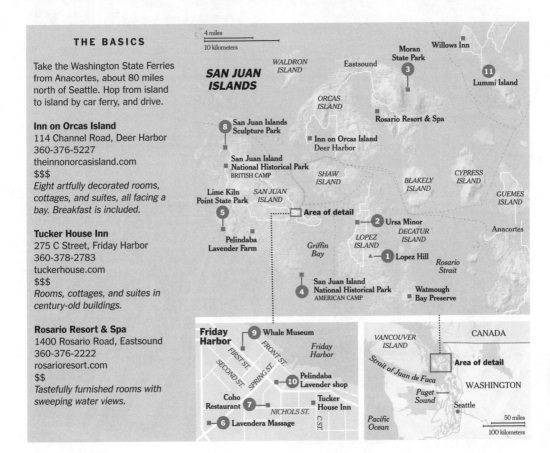

THE BASICS

Take the Washington State Ferries from Anacortes, about 80 miles north of Seattle. Hop from island to island by car ferry, and drive.

Inn on Orcas Island
114 Channel Road, Deer Harbor
360-376-5227
theinnonorcasisland.com
$$$
Eight artfully decorated rooms, cottages, and suites, all facing a bay. Breakfast is included.

Tucker House Inn
275 C Street, Friday Harbor
360-378-2783
tuckerhouse.com
$$$
Rooms, cottages, and suites in century-old buildings.

Rosario Resort & Spa
1400 Rosario Road, Eastsound
360-376-2222
rosarioresort.com
$$
Tastefully furnished rooms with sweeping water views.

SAN JUAN ISLANDS

4 miles
10 kilometers

WALDRON ISLAND
Eastsound
Moran State Park
Willows Inn
11
Lummi Island
ORCAS ISLAND
Rosario Resort & Spa
8 San Juan Islands Sculpture Park
Inn on Orcas Island Deer Harbor
San Juan Island National Historical Park BRITISH CAMP
SHAW ISLAND
BLAKELY ISLAND
CYPRESS ISLAND
GUEMES ISLAND
Lime Kiln Point State Park
SAN JUAN ISLAND
5
Pelindaba Lavender Farm
Griffin Bay
Area of detail
2 Ursa Minor
DECATUR ISLAND
Anacortes
LOPEZ ISLAND
1 Lopez Hill
Rosario Strait
4 San Juan Island National Historical Park AMERICAN CAMP
Watmough Bay Preserve

Friday Harbor
9 Whale Museum
Friday Harbor
FIRST ST.
FRONT ST.
SECOND ST.
SPRING ST.
10 Pelindaba Lavender shop
Coho Restaurant **7**
NICHOLS ST.
Tucker House Inn
C ST.
6 Lavendera Massage

VANCOUVER ISLAND
CANADA
Strait of Juan de Fuca
Area of detail
WASHINGTON
Puget Sound
Seattle
Pacific Ocean
50 miles
100 kilometers

Seattle

The sky is often gray, the residents tend to be muted (except when cheering their teams), calm waters lap the green cityscape; but beneath its mild exterior, Seattle has always careened wildly between boom and bust. For better or worse, boom is the mode of the day. Downtown is roaring with new construction and high-end repurposing of historic buildings. The food has never been better, and the traffic never worse. Some days can be wet, but as any photographer will tell you, the city is at its loveliest when slicked with rain. — BY DAVID LASKIN

FRIDAY

1 *Seattle in Overview* 3 p.m.

Volunteer Park (1247 15th Avenue East; 206-684-4075; seattle.gov/parks), a 10-minute cab or bus ride from downtown at the north end of Capitol Hill, has gardens designed a century ago by the Olmsted Brothers, a conservatory bursting with plants from regions around the world, and a squat brick water tower that you can ascend for terrific views of the city below and the mountains and sea beyond. If you prefer a moving orientation, take a spin on the **Seattle Great Wheel** (1301 Alaskan Way; 206-623-8607; seattlegreatwheel. com), a 175-foot-high Ferris wheel. It looks like a carnival ride that washed up at the end of a pier in Elliott Bay, but the view of water, city, and, if you're lucky, the Olympic Mountains more than compensates for the corniness. Gondolas are fully enclosed, so you can ride the wheel in comfort, rain or shine.

2 *Coolest Corridor* 5 p.m.

The Pike-Pine Corridor is Seattle's happiest urban makeover: from a warren of shabby flats and greasy spoons to an arty but not oppressively gentrified hamlet just across the freeway from downtown. When the locally revered **Elliott Bay Book Company** (1521 10th Avenue; 206-624-6600; elliottbaybook.com) abandoned Pioneer Square downtown to relocate here,

OPPOSITE The weekly regatta on Lake Union brings out the local sailors every Tuesday night in summer. The city surrounds the lake, making it a popular urban destination. Boats of several kinds are available for rent.

the literati gasped — but now it looks like a perfect neighborhood fit, what with the inviting communal tables at **Oddfellows** (1525 10th Avenue; 206-325-0807; oddfellowscafe.com; $$) two doors down, and a full spectrum of restaurants, vintage clothing shops, and home décor stores in the surrounding blocks. One good stop is **Standard Goods** (701 East Pike Street; 206-202-7610; thestandardgoods.com), for clothing, homeware, notions, and apothecary goods, emphasizing the American-made.

3 *Fresh and Local* 8 p.m.

One of the most talked-about restaurants in town, **Sitka & Spruce** (1531 Melrose Avenue East; 206-324-0662; sitkaandspruce.com; $$$), looks like a classy college dining room with a long refectory table surrounded by a few smaller tables, concrete floors, exposed brick, and duct work. But there's nothing sophomoric about the food. The chef and owner, Matt Dillon, follows his flawless intuition in transforming humble local ingredients (smelt, nettles, celery root, black trumpet mushrooms, turnips, pumpkin) into complexly layered, many-textured but never fussy creations. Examples have included beer-fried smelt with aioli, spiced pumpkin crepe with herbed labneh, and salmon with stinging nettles. Heed your server's advice that entrees are meant to be shared; you will have just enough room for dessert (like warm dates, pistachios, and rose-water ice cream; tahini ice cream with fruits; or a plate of local cheeses), and you may be pleasantly surprised by the bill.

SATURDAY

4 *Art and Water* 9 a.m.

There used to be two complaints about downtown Seattle: it offered no inspiring parks and no waterfront access worthy of the scenery. The **Olympic Sculpture Park** (2901 Western Avenue; 206-654-3100; seattleartmuseum.org), operated by the Seattle Art Museum, took care of both problems in one stroke. Masterpieces in steel, granite, fiberglass, and bronze by nationally renowned artists have wedded beautifully with maturing native trees, shrubs, ferns, and wildflowers. Wander the zigzagging paths and ramps past the massive weathered steel

hulls of Richard Serra's *Wake* and Alexander Calder's soaring painted-steel *Eagle* until you reach the harborside promenade. From there continue north to a pocket beach and into the adjoining grassy fields of waterfront **Myrtle Edwards Park**. It's all free.

5 *Urban Village* 11 a.m.

The development of South Lake Union into a thriving urban village, brainchild of the Microsoft tycoon Paul Allen, is alive and kicking. This former industrial no man's land now houses the city's best galleries, an ever increasing collection of dining spots, some nifty shops, and the Amazon campus. Use the South Lake Union Streetcar to hop from

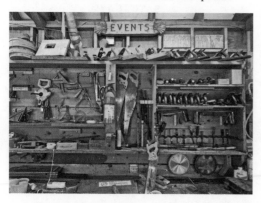

A/NT Gallery (2045 Westlake Avenue; 206-233-0680; antgallery.org), a nonprofit local artists' collective housed in a former bus terminal, to the **Center for Wooden Boats** (1010 Valley Street; 206-382-2628; cwb.org), where you can admire the old varnished beauties or rent a rowboat or sailboat for a spin around Seattle's in-city lake. Have brunch at **Assembly Hall** (2121 6th Avenue; 206-812-8413; assemblyhallseattle.com) or the adjoining **TanakaSan** (tanakasanseattle.com).

6 *Good-Looking Glass* 2 p.m.

Chihuly Garden and Glass (305 Harrison Street; 206-753-4940; chihulygardenandglass.com) show-cases the prodigious talent of the Northwest glass artist Dale Chihuly with a series of jaw-dropping indoor and open-air installations. Shimmering cones, spears, coils, discs, and snaky Medusa-heads of multicolored glass explode like frozen fireworks. There's another glass spectacle at the **Spheres** (2101 7th Avenue; seattlespheres.com), three con-joined, bulbous conservatories at the headquarters of Amazon. Conservatory tours are limited, but

ABOVE AND LEFT A dock and a tool shop at the Center for Wooden Boats, where you can admire classic boats or rent a rowboat or sailboat for a spin around Lake Union, Seattle's in-city lake. The center also offers boatbuilding workshops and other woodworking classes.

the building is a show in itself, viewable from the sidewalk day or night.

7 *Walk on Water* 4 p.m.

You don't have to leave the city limits to immerse yourself in the region's stunning natural beauty. Drive or take a bus 15 minutes from downtown to the **Washington Park Arboretum** (botanicgardens.uw. edu), and stroll through the flowering fruit trees. From there, pick up the milelong **Arboretum Waterfront Trail**. A network of well-maintained paths and boardwalks takes you through thickets of alder, willow, and elderberry into marshy islands alive with the trills of red-winged blackbirds and marsh wrens, and over shallows where kayakers prowl amid the rushes and the concrete pillars of the freeway overhead.

8 *La Dolce Vita* 8 p.m.

Maybe it's the stylish Italian vibe or the pretty people basking in the soft glow of dripping candles, or maybe it's the sumptuous, creatively classic food — whatever the secret ingredient, **Barolo Ristorante** (1940 Westlake Avenue; 206-770-9000; baroloseattle.com; $$$) always feels like a party. The pastas would do a Roman mother proud — gnocchi sauced with braised pheasant, leg of lamb ragù spooned over rigatoni. The rack of lamb with Amarone-infused cherries is sinfully rich, and the

seared branzino (sea bass) exhales the essence of the Mediterranean. Don't leave without at least a nibble of cannoli or tiramisù.

9 *Song and Dance* 10 p.m.

Capitol Hill, which on Saturday night seems to have more bars than parking spots, is night-life

TOP Lounging in front of the Spheres, a conservatory at Amazon's headquarters in Seattle.

ABOVE Sitka & Spruce looks like a classy college dining room, but there's nothing sophomoric about the food. Humble local ingredients like nettles and smelt are transformed here into sophisticated dishes.

central, and **Havana Social Club** (1010 East Pike Street; 206-323-2822; havanasocial.com) is at the throbbing epicenter. With its swaying palms and gold pressed-tin ceiling, the place feels like a quaint old tropical hotel, but instead of fox-trotting, linen-clad expats you'll find mostly young, pierced folks throwing back tequila and gyrating to soul, rap, and indie hits.

SUNDAY

10 *Bayou Brunch* 10:30 a.m.

Lake Pontchartrain meets Puget Sound for a New Orleans twist on breakfast at **Toulouse Petit**

(601 Queen Anne Avenue North; 206-432-9069; toulousepetit.com; $$), a funky bistro-style spot in Lower Queen Anne, near the Seattle Center. Grab a booth and settle in with a basket of hot, crispy beignets. Then indulge in something truly decadent, like pork cheeks confit hash topped with a couple of fried eggs, or eggs Benedict with crab and fines herbes. You can cleanse your system afterward with a brisk walk up the hill to **Kerry Park** (211 West Highland Drive) for a magnificent farewell view.

ABOVE TanakaSan, the sister restaurant of Assembly Hall. Both are good for brunch.

OPPOSITE A streetcar rolls along Westlake Avenue in South Lake Union, a thriving urban village within the city of Seattle. The streetcar line connects the neighborhood to downtown.

THE BASICS

The best and cheapest way to get from the airport to downtown is the Link Light Rail. Around town, drive or walk and take the bus.

Loews Hotel 1000
1000 First Avenue
206-957-1000
loewshotel.com/hotel-1000-seattle
$$$
Try out the golf simulator and a tub that fills from the ceiling.

Pan Pacific Hotel Seattle
2125 Terry Avenue
206-264-8111
panpacificseattle.com
$$$
Light and airy; a 15-minute walk to downtown.

Fairmont Olympic
411 University Street
206-621-1700
fairmont.com/seattle
$$$
The grande dame of Seattle hotels.

Northwest Seattle

Long ago the expanding city of Seattle swallowed up two of its neighbors, and neither of them has ever forgotten. Fremont and Ballard, once cities in their own right, are now Seattle neighborhoods of a particularly independent-minded kind. They're close together, though not contiguous, and still have unique character that resists complete assimilation — arty and free-spirited in Fremont; Nordic and proudly maritime in Ballard. Each is undergoing a kind of 21st-century renaissance, with shops and restaurants moving in, and a new, often young crowd arriving to live or just to play. But in either one, you can still lose yourself so thoroughly that you will barely even remember you're in the same town as the Space Needle. — BY DAN WHITE

FRIDAY

1 *Welcome to Fremont* 3 p.m.

As they cross the orange-and-blue Fremont Bridge on their way from downtown Seattle, drivers are met by a neon Rapunzel, a sign proclaiming Fremont the Center of the Universe, and instructions to set their watches back five minutes. From there on, it's a cross between a family-friendly bohemian enclave and a larger-than-life-size hipster sculpture garden. Don't be surprised if the cast-aluminum commuters standing near the bridge, waiting for a train that has not run for years, are wearing flamboyant clothes and headgear. Ever since *Waiting for the Interurban* was installed in 1979, whimsical Fremonters have clad them in continually changing costumes. (During the Abu Ghraib scandal someone put hoods over their heads, but it's not usually that political.) A block to the southeast, beneath the busy Aurora Bridge, the two-ton **Fremont Troll** crouches beneath a support wall, staring with his one eye and squashing a Volkswagen Bug in his left hand. Children sometimes crawl up his forearms and wedge their hands into his nostrils while parents take pictures.

2 *Scrap Art* 3:30 p.m.

You'll see a variety of outdoor art around Fremont — clown statues, dinosaur topiaries, a street sign pointing to Atlantis — but don't miss two more high spots. The seven-ton bronze **statue of Lenin** (Evanston Avenue North and North 36th Street), rescued from an Eastern European scrapyard after the Soviet collapse, loses some of its symbolic power when adorned with lights at Christmas or dressed in drag during Gay Pride Week. Another must-see is the **Fremont Rocket** (601 North 35th Street), a reborn piece of Cold War junk pointing 53 feet into the sky. Some Fremonters, still pining for their lost independence, claim that it is aimed at Seattle's City Hall.

3 *Retail Trail* 4 p.m.

Do some exploring on foot. Beneath the rocket, check out **Burnt Sugar** (601 North 35th Street; 206-545-0699; burntsugar.us), selling handbags, books, and more. Walk west on 35th Street to **Theo Chocolate** (3400 Phinney Avenue North; 206-632-5100; theochocolate.com), a chocolate factory that offers tours and has a retail shop. A bit farther south, find the entrance to the **Burke-Gilman Trail** near where Phinney Avenue intersects with North Canal Street and walk southeast along the Lake Washington Ship Canal amid the joggers and cyclists. Just before you reach the Fremont Bridge, head back north on Fremont Avenue to find shops like **Jive Time Records** (3506 Fremont Avenue North; 206-632-5483; jivetimerecords.com), **Ophelia's Books** (3504 Fremont Avenue North; 206-632-3759; opheliasbooks.com), and **Show Pony** (702 North

OPPOSITE Autumn shopping at the Sunday Farmers Market in Ballard, a Seattle neighborhood with an independent streak.

BELOW Cocoa beans at Theo Chocolate in Fremont, another part of town with its own quirky identity.

35th Street; 206-706-4188; showponyseattle.com), a clothing boutique.

4 *Japanese Modern* 7:30 p.m.

Plan ahead and reserve a table at **Kamonegi** (1054 North 39th Street; 206-632-0185; kamonegiseattle. com; $$), chef Mutsuko Soma's cozy 32-seat soba restaurant that opened in 2017. A satisfying meal there drawing from one night's menu included crisp sea-eel tempura, yakitori-style duck tsukune (meatballs), and bamboo baskets of hand-cut soba noodles with dipping sauce and wasabi.

SATURDAY

5 *Eggs of the Universe* 9 a.m.

Start the day at **Silence-Heart-Nest** (3508 Fremont Place North; 206-633-5169; silenceheartnest.com; $), a vegetarian cafe. It's a total-immersion experience in itself, with sari-clad wait staff asking diners to ponder business cards printed with inspirational verses while serving sesame waffles and Center of the Universe scrambled eggs. After breakfast, it's

ABOVE The bar at King's Hardware on Ballard Avenue.

OPPOSITE The Fremont Troll peers out from under the Aurora Bridge. His left hand is squashing a Volkswagen Bug.

time to leave Fremont. Drive northwest on Leary Way, which becomes Northwest 36th Street, and into Ballard, where neighborhood assertion goes in a different direction.

6 *Nordic Pride* 10:30 a.m.

Find the Vikings at the surprisingly beguiling **Nordic Museum** (2655 Northwest Market Street; nordicmuseum.org), which displays its collection and special exhibitions in a striking new zinc-cloaked structure. In spacious, light-filled galleries, trace the history and heritage of the hardy Nordic people in Europe and later as emigrants to America. Seafaring Scandinavians were the heart of old Ballard, and although ethnicities are mixed up now, the neighborhood still celebrates Norwegian Constitution Day every May 17 with a parade and much flag-waving. It was water, the kind without salt, that persuaded Ballardites to accept annexation to Seattle in 1907 despite their strong sense of community and identity. They needed access to Seattle's supply.

7 *Cohos on the Move* Noon

The nearly century-old **Hiram M. Chittenden Locks** (3015 Northwest 54th Street; 206-783-7059) help keep the salt water of Puget Sound from despoiling freshwater Lake Washington. They also lift boats from sea level to the lake's 26-foot elevation. Watch yachts and fishing boats steadily rise as the locks fill like a giant bathtub—a sight that can seem surreal. But the irresistible flourish is the glass-lined tunnel that, if you're here in salmon spawning season, lets you spy on cohos and chinooks as they make their way up the fish ladder, a series of ascending weirs. You can press your face a few millimeters away from the fat fish, which clunk into each other, form traffic jams, and sometimes turn their vacant expressions on the humans.

8 *The Sound of Lunch* 1:30 p.m.

Ballard's southern boundary is the Washington Lake Ship Canal, its western boundary is Puget Sound, and **Ray's Cafe**, at Ray's Boathouse Restaurant (6049 Seaview Avenue Northwest; 206-789-3770; rays.com) sits right about where they meet. Grab a table on the outdoor deck and order fish for lunch.

9 *Dunes in the City* 3 p.m.

The maritime spirit feels alive at **Golden Gardens Park** (8498 Seaview Place Northwest; 206-684-4075;

seattle.gov/parks/parkspaces/Golden.htm), arguably the loveliest picnic spot in all of Seattle, with sand dunes, a lagoon, secluded benches, occasional sightings of bald eagles, and heart-stopping views of the distant Olympic Mountains at sunset. Walk the paths, find a spot for relaxing, and chill.

10 *Dinner With Alice* 8 p.m.

Oysters from the cold Pacific waters off the coast of Washington are the specialty at the **Walrus and the Carpenter** (4743 Ballard Avenue Northwest; 206-395-9227; thewalrusbar.com; $$$), and the menu lists them by name, such as pickering passage, discovery bay, eld inlet. There's more seafood too, as well as meat dishes like steak tartare and duck prosciutto, and desserts like maple bread pudding and roasted dates. This is a festive place, with a convivial crowd enjoying the food, wine, and beer. Lovers of Lewis Carroll's Alice will recognize the source of the fanciful name: a poem in *Through the*

Looking Glass in which oysters are lured from their beds to suffer the same fate they are meeting here. You can finish out the night with Ballard's friendly mix of students, fishermen, professionals, and laborers over drinks at **King's Hardware** (5225 Ballard Avenue Northwest; 206-782-0027; kingsballard.com)

ABOVE Music at Ballard Sunday Farmers Market, which is open year-round.

OPPOSITE Golden Gardens Park in Ballard is one of the loveliest places for an afternoon escape in all of Seattle. The park has sand dunes and views of the Olympic Mountains.

or **Hattie's Hat** (5231 Ballard Avenue Northwest; 206-784-0175; hatties-hat.com).

SUNDAY

11 *Sunday Shoppers* 11 a.m.

Ballard's eastern edge feels more contemporary, with dining, shopping, and a lively social scene. Year-round, the **Ballard Sunday Farmers Market** (Ballard Avenue Northwest between Vernon Place and 22nd Avenue; sfmamarkets.com) brings out vendors and shoppers in a scene that some Ballardites insist surpasses Seattle's well-known Pike Place Market. Inspect the quintessentially Pacific Northwestern products: giant radishes, tiny potatoes called spud nuts, homemade cider, spiced blackberry wine. For vintage treasures and food trucks, check out the rival street market in Fremont (fremontmarket.com).

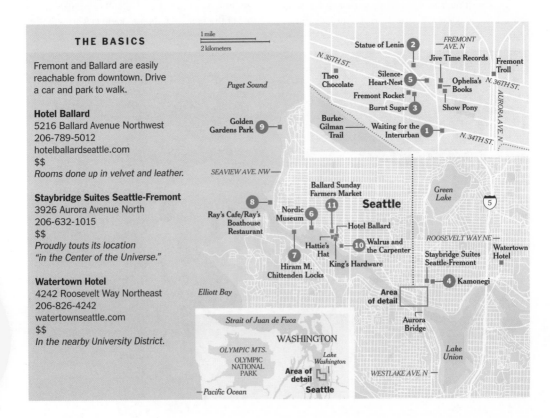

THE BASICS

Fremont and Ballard are easily reachable from downtown. Drive a car and park to walk.

Hotel Ballard
5216 Ballard Avenue Northwest
206-789-5012
hotelballardseattle.com
$$
Rooms done up in velvet and leather.

Staybridge Suites Seattle-Fremont
3926 Aurora Avenue North
206-632-1015
$$
Proudly touts its location "in the Center of the Universe."

Watertown Hotel
4242 Roosevelt Way Northeast
206-826-4242
watertownseattle.com
$$
In the nearby University District.

Index

Contributors

ADDITIONAL PHOTO CREDITS

Bewer, Tim/Lonely Planet Images/
  Getty Images 376
Bibiko, Walter/AWL Images RM/
  Getty Images 394
Cindy Karp/Getty Images 228 below
Clary, Timothy A./AFP/Getty Images
  117 below
Cory Aronec Photography/Getty
  Images 365
Cummins, Richard/Lonely Planet
  Images/Getty Images
  396 below
Daffey, Mark/Lonely Planet Images/
  Getty Images 18
Diamond, Mitch/Photodisc/Getty
  Images 504
Education Images/Universal Images
  Group/Getty Images 286
Felsen, Greg/Courtesy of Palm
  Springs Bureau of Tourism 659
Frei, Franz Marc/LOOK/Getty Images
  343
Geoffrey, George/Flickr RF/Getty
  Images 620
Heeb, Christian/AWL Images RM/
  Getty Images 126
Hoberman, Gerald/Getty Images
  214
Johnson, Dennis K./Lonely Planet
  Images/Getty Images 546
Karp, Cindy/Getty Images 227
Kenna, Caleb/Aurora Open/Getty
  Images 186
Klumpp, Don/Age Fotostock RM/
  Getty Images 294
Kuehl, Adam/VisitSavannah.com
  261
Li, Zubin/Getty Images 568
Louisville Tourism 272
Messerschmidt, A./WireImage/Getty
  Images 510
Michael N. Paras/Age Fotostock RM/
  Getty Images 130
Moran, Michael, Courtesy © Michael
  Moran/OTTO 485
Newman, Andy/Florida Keys News
  Bureau 218
Nowitz, Richard/Getty Images 10
Courtesy of the Omaha Convention
  and Visitor's Bureau 395
Reede, Dave/All Canada Photos/
  Getty Images 362
Richards, Paul J./AFP/Getty Images
  283

Rose, George/Getty Images 340
  above
Ruehle Design 364
Saks, Stephen/Lonely Planet
  Images/Getty Images 266
Sartore, Joel/National Geographic
  Creative/Getty Images 396 above
State of Tennessee 311 below
Tom Brewster Photography 658
Travel Portland 722, 723
VisitSavannah.com 260
Wells, Randy/The Image Bank/Getty
  Images 726
Woodhouse, Jeremy/Photographer's
  Choice RF/Getty Images 337

Acknowledgments

We would like to thank everyone at *The New York Times* and at TASCHEN who contributed to the creation of this book and to its revision for this third edition.

For the book project itself, special recognition must go to Nazire Ergün, Hanna Kirsch, and Nina Wiener at TASCHEN, the dedicated editors behind the scenes; to Natasha Perkel and Barbara Berasi, the *Times* artists whose clear and elegantly crafted maps make the itineraries comprehensible; to Phyllis Collazo of the *Times* staff, whose photo editing gave the book its arresting images; and to Olimpia Zagnoli, whose illustrations and illustrated maps enliven every article and each regional introduction.

Guiding the transformation of newspaper material to book form at TASCHEN were Marco Zivny and Aicha Becker, the book's designers; Josh Baker with Marco Zivny, art directors; David Knowles, layout designer; Philipp Sendner, production manager; Sean Monahan, who created the region maps; as well as Sean Monahan, Jonathan Newhall, Robert Noble, Mari Rustan, Anne Sauvadet, and Eric Schwartau who contributed to previous editions.

Florence and John Stickney copy-edited and fact-checked the manuscript. Heidi Giovine helped keep production on track at critical moments.

But the indebtedness goes much further back, and deeper into the *New York Times* staff and the list of the newspaper's many contributors. This book grew out of the work of all of the editors, writers, photographers, and others whose contributions and support for the weekly *36 Hours* column built a rich archive over many years.

For this legacy, credit must go first to Stuart Emmrich, who created the column in 2002 and then refined the concept over eight years. Without his vision, there would be no *36 Hours*. His successors in the role of Travel editor, Danielle Mattoon, Monica Drake, and Amy Virshup, have brought steady leadership to the column and support to the *36 Hours* books.

Suzanne MacNeille, the direct editor of *36 Hours* at *The Times*, and her predecessors, Denny Lee and Jeff Klein, have guided *36 Hours* superbly through the world by assigning and working with writers, choosing and assigning destinations, and assuring that the weekly column would entertain and inform readers while upholding *Times* journalistic standards. The former Escapes editor Mervyn Rothstein saw the column through some of its early years, assuring its consistent quality.

The talented *Times* photo editors who have overseen images and directed the work of photographers for *36 Hours* include Phaedra Brown, Jessica De Witt, Lonnie Schlein, Gina Privitere, Darcy Eveleigh, Laura O'Neill, Chris Jones, and the late John Forbes.

Among the many editors on the *Times* Travel and Escapes copy desks who have kept *36 Hours* at its best over the years, three who stand out are Florence Stickney, Steve Bailey, and Carl Sommers. Fact checkers and web editors have also added countless contributions to its success.

Finally, we must offer a special acknowledgment to Benedikt Taschen, whose longtime readership and interest in the *36 Hours* column led to the partnership of our two companies to produce this book.

— BARBARA IRELAND AND ALEX WARD

Copyright © 2019 *The New York Times*.
All Rights Reserved.

Editor Barbara Ireland
Project management Alex Ward
Photo editor Phyllis Collazo
Maps Natasha Perkel and Barbara Berasi
Spot illustrations Olimpia Zagnoli
Editorial coordination Nazire Ergün, Hanna Kirsch, and Nina Wiener
Art direction Marco Zivny and Josh Baker
Layout and design Marco Zivny and Aicha Becker
Production Philipp Sendner

EACH AND EVERY TASCHEN BOOK PLANTS A SEED!
TASCHEN is a carbon neutral publisher. Each year, we offset our annual carbon emissions with carbon credits at the Instituto Terra, a reforestation program in Minas Gerais, Brazil, founded by Lélia and Sebastião Salgado. To find out more about this ecological partnership, please check: www.taschen.com/zerocarbon
Inspiration: unlimited. Carbon footprint: zero.

© 2019 TASCHEN GmbH
Hohenzollernring 53, D–50672 Köln, **www.taschen.com**

ISBN 978-3-8365-7532-4   Printed in Latvia

YOU CAN FIND TASCHEN STORES IN

Berlin
Schlüterstr. 39

Beverly Hills
354 N. Beverly Drive

Brussels
Place du Grand Sablon /
Grote Zavel 35

Cologne
Neumarkt 3

Hollywood
Farmers Market,
6333 W. 3rd Street, CT-10

Hong Kong
Shop 01-G02 Tai Kwun
10 Hollywood Road
Central

London
12 Duke of York Square

London Claridge's
49 Brook Street

Miami
1111 Lincoln Rd.

Milan
Via Meravigli 17

Paris
2 rue de Buci

"If browsing is considered an art form, the TASCHEN store is a masterpiece."
— *Dwell*

PASSPORT TO THE WORLD

One volume, 150 cities from Abu Dhabi to Zurich

*"Gifts for travel types often verge on the novelty –
go practical instead with these truly comprehensive guides."*
— SUNDAY TIMES TRAVEL MAGAZINE, LONDON

GRAND TOUR
130 weekend wonders across Europe

"One of The Times' most brilliant and practical weekly features gets the TASCHEN treatment in this beautiful collection of weekend jaunts."
— FASHIONWEEKDAILY.COM, NEW YORK

EDITED BY BARBARA IRELAND

The New York Times

36

HOURS
EUROPE
3RD EDITION · 130 DESTINATIONS

TASCHEN

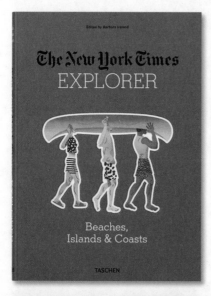

586

VANCOUVER

CANADA

730
Seattle

WEST
COAST
572-741

MIDW
& GREAT

492 Denver

WELCOME
TO
Fabulous

674

SAN FRANCISCO

504
LAS VEGAS

ALASKA

LOS ANGELES
620

SOUTHWEST
& ROCKY MOUNTAINS
446-571

HAWAII

MEXICO